Introduction to

ACCOUNTING

A User Perspective Volume II

Revised for 2009 by Katherene P. Terrell and Robert L. Terrell

Kumen H. Jones • Michael L. Werner • Katherene P. Terrell • Robert L. Terrell

Taken from:

Introduction to Accounting: A User Perspective
By Kumen H. Jones, Michael L. Werner, Katherene P. Terrell, and Robert L. Terrell

Custom Publishing

New York   Boston   San Francisco
London   Toronto   Sydney   Tokyo   Singapore   Madrid
Mexico City   Munich   Paris   Cape Town   Hong Kong   Montreal

**Pearson
Custom Publishing**
is a division of

www.pearsonhighered.com

ISBN 10: 0-558-09830-4
ISBN 13: 978-0-558-09830-8

To our sons Robert and Jonathon
. . . Katherene and Robert Terrell

Contents

CHAPTER 10 *The Balance Sheet and Income Statement: A Closer Look* *F-357*

INTRODUCTION TO MANAGEMENT ACCOUNTING: A USER PERSPECTIVE M-1

CHAPTER   4   *Cost Behavior*   *M-63*

CHAPTER   5   *Business Decisions Using Cost Behavior*   *M-97*

CHAPTER   8   *The Operating Budget*   *M-213*

Preface

As we enter the twenty-first century, we who are involved in accounting education at the collegiate level have reassessed the way we prepare our students for the business world. Technology changes more quickly than most of us can comprehend, complicating accounting education. Yet one constant remains: Business people must be prepared to perform tasks that only people can perform—in particular, communicating, thinking, and making decisions. Decision making is *the* critical skill in today's business world, and *Introduction to Accounting: A User Perspective,* helps students to better use accounting information and improve their decision-making skills.

This text provides an introduction to financial accounting and management accounting within the context of business and business decisions. Readers will explore accounting information's role in the decision-making process, and learn how to use accounting information found in various external and internal accounting reports. Seeing how accounting information can be used to make better business decisions will benefit all students, regardless of their major course of study or chosen career.

We agree with the recommendations made by the Accounting Education Change Commission in its *Position Statement No. Two: The First Course in Accounting.* We believe the course should be a broad introduction *to* accounting, rather than introductory accounting as it has traditionally been taught, and it should be taught from the perspective of the user, not the preparer. It should emphasize *what* accounting information is, *why* it is important, and *how* it is used by economic decision makers, both external and internal.

As you work with this text, you will find it focuses heavily on the uses of accounting information rather than the preparation of the information. This, however, is only one characteristic which distinguishes *Introduction to Accounting: A User Perspective,* from other texts you may have used in the past.

SUPPORT FOR THE INTERACTIVE CLASSROOM

We believe this text provides tools to actively involve students in their learning processes. The conversational tone of the text, its user perspective, and the logical presentation of topics all contribute to the ability of this text to meet that goal. However, several features are particularly important in developing a classroom atmosphere in which students share ideas, ask questions, and relate their learning to the world around them.

Throughout each chapter of the text, you will find Discussion Questions (DQs) that challenge students to reach beyond the surface of the written text to determine answers. Far from typical review questions, for which the students can scan a few pages of the text to locate an answer, many of the DQs provide relevant learning by relating students' personal experiences to the knowledge they gain through the text.

The DQs provide a variety of classroom experiences:

- Many DQs provide the basis for lively classroom discussions, requiring students to think about issues and formulate or defend their opinions.
- Some DQs are springboards for group assignments (in or out of the classroom) to put cooperative learning into practice.
- DQs may be assigned as individual writing assignments to allow students to practice and develop their writing skills.
- Combining individually written DQ responses with follow-up group discussions leading to group consensus can spark lively debate!
- Having students keep a journal of their responses to all DQs (regardless if they are used in another way) encourages solitary pondering of accounting concepts.

The DQs comprise a critically important part of the text's pedagogy designed to emphasize important points that students may skim across in their initial reading. Even if they are not formally part of the required work for your course, students will gain a greater understanding of the concepts discussed when they take time to consider each question as part of the text.

- Students get enthused about accounting when working with real companies. Chapter F1 and its appendix provide students with information to use library and Internet resources to research companies, and introduce students to annual reports and Form 10-K.
- We included the 2005 Family Dollar Stores, Inc. annual report with our text and use it to demonstrate financial analysis in Chapter F12. We added an annual report project to further involve students in the business world in Chapter F1.
- Financial Reporting Cases, at the end of Chapters F1 to F6 and Chapters F8 to F12, encourage students to use the Internet and the book website to link to real businesses and explore their financial statements. Three Accounting Cycle Cases are featured in Chapter F7.
- Including real-world situations presents a real challenge in presenting management accounting concepts because (a) many companies modify and tailor management accounting concepts to their individual needs, and (b) management accounting concepts often involve proprietary company policies and processes, so many companies guard their application of these concepts. When possible, however, we have tried to include as many real-world examples as possible in Chapters M1 through M8.

Adventures into *real* information about *real* companies always raises student interest! In addition to these features which help to foster an open, interactive environment in the classroom, a major distinction of this text is its total separation of the *use* of accounting information and its preparation.

SEPARATION OF ACCOUNTING AND BOOKKEEPING

With the exception of Chapter F7, the text approaches accounting totally from the user perspective. These chapters contain no bookkeeping. Is this an indication we believe that a knowledge of bookkeeping skills is unnecessary? On the contrary, bookkeeping is the nuts and bolts that holds our accounting systems together. What we have learned, though, is that bookkeeping procedures without a conceptual understanding of the uses of accounting information are meaningless. Beginning accounting students cannot digest the use of financial statements, the role of accounting information, the world of business, and the details of bookkeeping simultaneously. Once students have a basic knowledge of the other topics, however, learning details of the recording process becomes effective and efficient.

Separating accounting and bookkeeping makes both subjects easier to grasp and more enjoyable to learn. This approach also allows instructors and institutions to select an appropriate time and degree of bookkeeping coverage for their program. Some schools choose to have all students learn basic recording procedures; others may only require accounting majors to acquire these skills.

To facilitate the separation of accounting and bookkeeping, we introduce the accounting cycle in Chapter F7 and complete its coverage in appendices to Chapters F8, F9, F10, and M2. We placed the accounting cycle coverage in Chapter F7 because this is the point when students have enough basic knowledge of the use of accounting information to be ready for accounting procedures. Some schools leave this material until the end of the semester, some opt to cover the material at the beginning of the second semester, or in a separate course for accounting majors. For this reason, no references are made to Chapter F7 in the remaining chapters except in the appendices.

Chapter F7 and the appendices in Chapter F8 through F10 cover the complete accounting cycle from analyzing transactions through post-closing trial balance, including debits and credits, journals, general ledgers, worksheets, and financial statement preparation. Chapter F7 contains a number of long problems and three Accounting Cycle Cases that are condensed practice sets.

Management accounting, by its nature, has less bookkeeping procedure than financial accounting. In chapter M2, however, we have included appendices that cover the bookkeeping procedures required to record the topics presented.

In addition to the decision to focus on the uses of accounting information rather than the details of accounting procedures in this text, we have made several other deliberate and important choices about topical coverage many real-world examples as we could. In addition to these features which help to foster an open, interactive environment in the classroom, a major distinction of this text is its total separation of the use of accounting and its preparation.

TOPICS COVERED

We carefully considered the inclusion or exclusion of topics from this text consistent with our pedagogical goals of building foundations that support effective student learning. Because our focus introduces students to accounting information and its uses in decision making, we could not simply follow the traditional coverage of topics. As we considered individual topics, we continually explored whether their inclusion would enhance a student's ability to interpret and use accounting information throughout his or her personal and professional life. Based on our own experiences in industry and conversations we have had with both operations and accounting managers from many companies, we believe that *Introduction to Accounting: A User Perspective*, covers those financial accounting and management accounting topics that every accounting student should leave the course understanding well. In short, we sought quality of learning, not quantity of minutiae.

In the financial accounting portion of the text, for example, we cover the calculations of only two depreciation methods—straight line and double declining balance. By limiting the coverage of detailed depreciation calculations, we have the opportunity to focus on the concepts of cost allocation, expense recognition, financial statement differences between the two methods, and the distinction between gains and revenues, and losses and expenses. Students will not only know how to calculate depreciation expense, but also understand *why* they are calculating it and how to use those calculations in making business decisions. In the chapter, students learn how to properly interpret gains and losses. Most of them are surprised to find out that two companies buying identical assets for the same price can sell them later for the same amount and have different results—one company can have a gain and the other experience a loss.

Another example of building foundations to learning in the area of financial accounting is the introduction to the concept of the cost of borrowing. Instead of sending students straight to the present value tables, we take time to measure the cost of borrowing—an important foundation for intermediate accounting and learning how to account for interest costs in long-term liabilities.

In our coverage of the separation of a mixed cost into its variable and fixed components in the management accounting portion of the text, we discuss regression analysis, but do not include any calculations using this method. By limiting the coverage of detailed calculations, we have the opportunity to focus on the concept of cost separation without losing students in computations.

Another example in the management accounting portion is the introduction to the operating budget. Instead of sending students straight into the preparation of the budgets included in the operating budget, we present all the budgets conceptually first, and then walk them through budget preparation.

We also include some topics that traditional books omit. Chapter F1 includes discussions of each major type of business organization. As we discuss various topics, students learn to view the financial statements of each type of organization throughout the book. We pay particular attention to students' understanding of the difference between *reality* and the *measurement of reality* and the need to find both the *reality of cash* and the *reality of performance.*

Chapter M7 includes not only information on how to budget for capital expenditures, but where capital budgeting fits in a company's overall planning and control process. This chapter also discusses frankly some of the dysfunctional management behavior caused by inappropriate use of the capital budgeting process.

From our classroom experience with this text, we believe that the content is appropriate for college sophomores to embrace and take forward to additional courses. The carefully chosen sequence of topics helps to make them more understandable by establishing firm conceptual foundations.

SEQUENCE OF COVERAGE

To effectively present the user perspective, we developed a logical flow of topics so that each chapter builds on what the student has already learned. Students can easily understand how the topics fit together logically and how they are used together to make good decisions. Moreover, students can see that accounting and the information it provides is not merely something that exists unto itself, but rather it is something developed in response to the needs of economic decision makers.

If you could read the entire text before using it in your classroom, you would have a very clear picture of the experience awaiting your students. However, even a short tour through the material covered in each chapter will show you how we have structured our presentation of the topics to maximize student learning.

Chapter F1 provides a brief overview of business and the role of accounting in the business world, setting the stage for the introduction of accounting information. In the appendix, we provide students with information about public reporting of accounting information and research sources. Without the world of business, there would be no need for accounting information or the accounting profession.

Chapter F2 presents an introduction to economic decision making. Because the stated purpose of financial accounting information is to provide information to be used in making decisions, we believe an understanding of the decision-making process is not only appropriate, but essential. We explore the characteristics crucial to making accounting information useful in that process.

Chapter F3 introduces the balance sheet as the first of several financial tools developed to present accounting information in a useful form. In this chapter we focus on how equity financing affects businesses and how its results are reflected on balance sheets.

Chapter F4 continues the exploration of the balance sheet, this time examining the impact of debt financing. We present notes and bonds as financing options for businesses and introduce the cost of borrowing.

Chapter F5 presents the income statement and statement of owners' equity as additional financial tools. Now that students have been introduced to the first three financial statements used by economic decision makers, they can see how the statements relate to one another.

Chapter F6 compares the cash basis and accrual basis of accounting. Basic knowledge of the cash basis is important for two reasons. First, students should realize that accrual accounting is *one* basis of measurement and not *the* measurement basis. Second, understanding the weaknesses of cash basis accounting makes the logic of accrual accounting much easier to grasp. By the time students finish this chapter, they hunger to have a method of organizing and recording accounting data.

Chapter F7 introduces the eight steps of the accounting cycle using the teaching example in Chapter F6. We discuss the chronology of the accounting cycle and then walk students through each step. The end-of-chapter materials provide students with ample opportunity to practice the skills demonstrated in the chapter. This chapter can be bypassed and used at a later time.

Chapter F8 explores issues surrounding the acquisition, depreciation, and disposal of long-lived tangible assets under accrual accounting. As previously mentioned, this chapter examines effects of depreciation method choice, using straight line and double declining balance as examples. We also show students how to properly interpret gains and losses. The appendix demonstrates how to record the acquisition, depreciation, and disposal of assets.

Chapter F9 explores another challenging issue arising from the use of accrual basis accounting—merchandise inventory and inventory cost flow methods. Students learn how to calculate amounts under LIFO, FIFO, and average cost methods for both periodic and perpetual inventory systems. More important, they learn how the choice of method affects the accounting information provided on income statements and balance sheets. This chapter has two appendices. The first appendix involves inventory purchasing issues and presents a discussion of freight terms and cash discounts and how they alter the cost of purchasing. The second appendix presents the accounting cycle for periodic inventory systems and perpetual inventory systems including all recording, adjusting, and closing entries.

Chapter F10 returns to the balance sheet and income statement, taking a closer look at the way these two financial statements are organized. We explore the information provided in a classified balance sheet and an expanded multistep income statement in detail.

Chapter F11 introduces the statement of cash flows as another financial tool. After using the information provided by the other three financial statements, prepared under accrual accounting, students see the need to refocus their attention on cash. With an understanding of the purpose of the statement of cash flows in hand, students find its creation using both the direct and indirect methods easy to understand. More important, students learn how to read and interpret the information provided on the statement of cash flows.

Chapter F12 explains the importance of gathering various types of information to make the results of financial statement analysis most useful. Ratio analysis is the featured technique; information from the Family Dollar annual report illustrates the computations, comparisons, and analyses throughout the chapter.

Chapter M1 provides a brief overview of the environment and future of management accounting. We have included not only a description of how management accounting compares and contrasts with financial accounting, but also the historical forces that have led to the development of management accounting techniques. Further, we discuss the state of management accounting today and what kinds of management accounting information will be needed in the future.

Chapter M2 presents an introduction to various cost classifications used in management accounting situations. We cover the concepts of cost objects, direct and indirect costs, and product and period costs. Students are introduced to the differences in product cost for a merchandiser and a manufacturer and learn the components of the costs included in each of the three types of inventory in a manufacturing operation. Finally, we explore the calculation of cost of goods manufactured and cost of goods sold for a manufacturer and cost of services for a service type firm. The chapter appendix presents the journal entries associated with the information presented in the chapter.

Chapter M4 explores the subject of cost behavior. We explain the differences between fixed costs and variable costs, and how to classify costs by cost behavior. We also cover the concept of the relevant range and its effect on cost behavior information. We then present the characteristics of a mixed cost and discuss how to separate a mixed cost into its fixed and variable components using the engineering approach, the scatter graph, the high-low method, and regression analysis.

Chapter M5 extends the topic introduced in Chapter M4 by using cost behavior information to make business decisions. In this chapter we present the functional income statement and contribution income statement and the differences between them. We cover the calculation of per unit amounts for sales, variable cost, and contribution margin, as well as the contribution margin ratio and its importance as a management tool. We present the contribution margin income statement for a merchandiser and introduce the concept of cost-volume-profit analysis, which we use to determine the amount of sales required to break even or to earn a targeted profit in both single-product and multiple-product situations. Finally, we use CVP to perform sensitivity analysis to changes in selling price, variable cost, and fixed cost.

Chapter M6 presents the topic of isolating and using relevant cost information in decision making. Included is a discussion of the characteristics of relevant and irrelevant costs, and a consideration of qualitative factors that should be considered when making business decisions. The specific decision situations covered in the chapter are equipment replacement, whether to accept or reject a special order, and the effects of fixed costs and opportunity costs on a make or buy decision.

Chapter M7 provides an in-depth look at the capital budget. The overall business planning process is discussed and where the capital budget fits in that process. The four shared characteristics of all capital projects are presented, as well as the cost of capital and the concept of scarce resources. Students learn how to identify the information relevant to the capital budgeting decision. We present four techniques used to evaluate proposed capital projects including net present value, internal rate of return, payback, and accounting rate of return. There is an appendix to this chapter which presents the concept of the time value of money and all the calculations students need to compute net present values and internal rates of return.

Chapter M8 presents the operating budget, its benefits, preparation, and uses. First, we introduce and discuss all the budgets included in the operating budget from a conceptual standpoint. Then we present various approaches to budgeting, including perpetual, incremental, zero-based, top-down, bottom-up, imposed, and participative approaches. Next we discuss and stress the importance of the sales forecast in the budgeting process. Finally, we walk students through the preparation of all the budgets, and then discuss appropriate and inappropriate uses of the operating budget in the management process.

OTHER IMPORTANT FEATURES OF THIS TEXT

In addition to the Discussion Questions and the inclusion of the Family Dollar annual report, discussed in detail above, our text offers other features that will enhance the learning process.

- Learning Objectives—Previewing each chapter with these objectives allows students to see what direction the chapter is taking, which makes the journey through the material a bit easier.
- Marginal Glossary—Students often find the process of learning accounting terminology to be a challenge. As each new key word is introduced in the text, it is shown in bold and also defined in the margin. This feature offers students an easy way to review the key terms and locate their introduction in the text.
- Summary—This concise summary of each chapter provides an overview of the main points, but is in no way a substitute for reading the chapter.
- Review the Facts—Students can use these basic, definitional questions to review the key points of each chapter. The questions are in a sequence reflecting the coverage of topics in the chapter.
- Apply What You Have Learned—Our end-of-chapter assignment materials include a mix of traditional types of homework problems and innovative assignments requiring critical thinking and writing. Many of the requirements can be used as the basis for classroom discussions. You will find matching problems, short essay questions, and calculations. Assignments dealing directly with the use of financial statements are also included. Many of these applications also work well as group assignments.
- Glossary of Accounting Terms—An alphabetical listing of important accounting terms, including all of the key terms plus additional terms, defines the terms and lists the page on which the term first appears.

Katherene P. Terrell
Robert L. Terrell

Chapter 7

Accumulating Accounting Data

*Y*our mother recently retired, or tried to retire. The only problem was that her former clients continued to call her with small jobs. Because she could not say no, her retirement has turned into a new job as a consultant. Mom always worked for someone else and never kept records beyond weekly expense reports. At the end of the year she realized that she would soon need to prepare her tax return for the IRS and account to Social Security for the amount of her earnings. She is not sure what to report to either agency. You try to explain to her about expenses and net income but she is confused. When you ask to see her books, her response is, "What books?" Sounds like she could use your help.

Although financial statement users often do not care how the numbers got to the financial statements, the better a user understands the accounting process, the more he or she can understand the implications of those numbers. When we understand how the accounting system interprets the revenue recognition and the expense recognition principles, we understand the meaning of the income and expense numbers on the income statement. When we comprehend the checks and balances inherent in the accounting system, we can appreciate the need for internal control to protect those checks and balances. When we grasp the concept of financial statement articulation, we notice when something is not right with a set of financial statements. ■

So where do we begin? We will walk through each step of the accounting process, learning how to apply the accounting equation in each decision-making situation. We will apply the concepts discussed in Chapter 6 about revenue and expense recognition, accruals, and deferrals. We will exercise the financial statement concepts from Chapters 3, 4, and 5. In essence, we will utilize the decision-making skills we discussed in Chapter 2, applying accounting principles within an accounting system that transforms events and data into valuable accounting information.

LEARNING OBJECTIVES

After completing your work on this chapter, you should be able to do the following:

1. Identify the eight steps of the accounting cycle.
2. Distinguish between debits and credits and apply them to the accounting equation.
3. Describe accounts, journals, ledgers, and worksheets.
4. Record transactions in journals and post them to the general ledger.
5. Prepare trial balances and worksheets.
6. Prepare adjusting journal entries and reconcile a bank account.
7. Prepare financial statements from a worksheet.
8. Prepare closing journal entries.
9. Prepare a post-closing trial balance.

THE ACCOUNTING CYCLE

You may have found it frustrating to prepare financial statements from the transactions in Chapter 6 because you had no way of easily accumulating the number you needed for each item on the financial statements. Humans figured this out as early as ancient Roman times and developed a system to ease the frustration. We call this system the accounting cycle.

accounting cycle The sequence of steps repeated in each accounting period to enable the firm to analyze, record, classify, and summarize the transactions into financial statements.

The **accounting cycle** is the sequence of steps repeated in each accounting period to enable the firm to analyze, record, classify, and summarize the transactions into financial statements. The steps are:

Step 1: Analyzing Transactions

Step 2: Journalizing Transactions

Step 3: Posting Transactions to the General Ledger

Step 4: Preparing the Trial Balance (or Worksheet)

Step 5: Adjusting the Accounts and Reconciling the Bank Statement

Step 6: Preparing Financial Statements

Step 7: Preparing and Posting Closing Entries

Step 8: Preparing the Post-Closing Trial Balance

The accounting process is a cycle because some events occur daily, some monthly, and some annually (see Exhibit 7–1). At the end of the annual cycle, the process begins anew.

Exhibit 7–1
The Accounting Cycle:
A Dynamic System

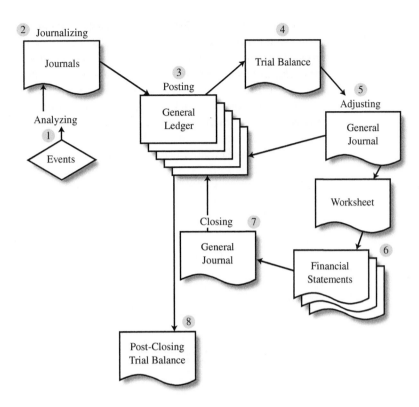

We will look at what happens in each step of the cycle and then learn how to apply each step of the cycle to the McCumber Company transactions we viewed in Chapter 6.

Step 1: Analyzing Transactions

Analyzing transactions, the most important step in the accounting cycle, consists of two parts (see Exhibit 7–2). The first is deciding when a transaction occurs. The simple answer is that a transaction occurs when an accounting element changes. For example, if a customer pays the company, cash increases and accounts receivable decreases. Assets both increase and decrease, and a transaction occurs. What if a company orders merchandise that the vendor will deliver in three weeks? Has

Exhibit 7–2
Analyzing Transactions

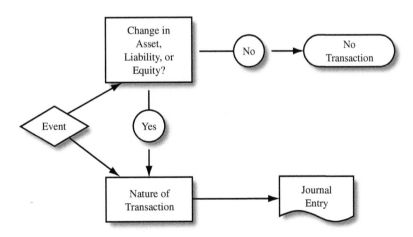

a transaction occurred? No. Neither assets, nor liabilities, nor equity has changed. When will this transaction occur? The transaction will occur when title to the merchandise passes from the vendor to the buyer during the shipping process. At that moment, the company will have new assets and a new liability.

The second part of analyzing transactions is identifying the nature of the transaction. If we correctly determine that a transaction occurs but misinterpret the transaction, we introduce an error into the accounting system. If we classify the merchandise purchase on credit as a long-term asset and reduce cash by the amount, we have created errors in four accounts—inventory, long-term assets, accounts payable, and cash are either overstated or understated. As you can see, knowing when to record a transaction and how to record the transaction are critical to maintaining the integrity of the accounting records. We make the decision about transactions as frequently as we journalize transactions.

Discussion Questions

7–1. With the many "accounting for dummies" software packages on the market, why do we need accountants?

7–2. What is the difference between a bookkeeper and an accountant?

Step 2: Journalizing Transactions

journal A book of original entry where a chronological record of an entity's transactions are listed.

Journalizing transactions is the act of recording accounting transactions into a journal. A **journal** is a book of original entry where we record a chronology of the business entity's transactions. In the days of pen and ink, the accountant or bookkeeper kept the journal in a book. Today, with computerization, a journal may be a listing of transactions on a computer printout or a file in the computer. Regardless of form, the journal lists transactions in order of occurrence. Employees, management, and auditors frequently use the journal's chronological listing of transactions to trace transactions and answer inquiries. For this reason, we record transactions formally into journals daily, weekly, or sometimes monthly for small businesses. Large companies use on-line, real-time processing techniques that create the journals as the transactions occur. Sophisticated cash register systems often create journals simultaneously as the cashier scans the items sold.

special journal A book of original entry designed to record a specific type of transaction.

general journal A book of original entry designed to record all transactions not otherwise recorded in a special journal.

Businesses use a number of journals to capture details. The most common forms are sales journals, cash receipt journals, cash payment journals, purchases journals, and the general journal. All except the general journal are called **special journals,** which record a specific type of transaction such as sales. The sales journal, for instance, contains a record of the firm's sales to its customers but no other type of transaction. We use the **general journal** to record all transactions that cannot be recorded in a special journal. If a firm has no special journals, it records all transactions in the general journal (see Exhibit 7–3). Why do we have special journals? Special journals save a great deal of time when a firm experiences many similar transactions during a period. The reason for this will become obvious when we discuss posting to the general ledger, the next step in the accounting cycle.

Journals have many uses in the business operation, but the long lists of data contained in them lack the quality of information. The next step in the cycle helps us to produce usable information.

Exhibit 7–3
Journalizing
Transactions

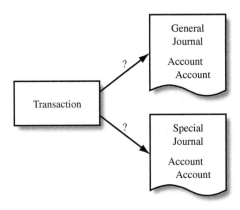

Step 3: Posting Transactions to the General Ledger

With the journals full of difficult to use data, we need a method of sorting or classifying the data into usable information. The information we desire is the amount of sales we made, the amount of cash or inventory we have, how much we owe for purchases, and so on. Each of the accounting elements provides us with information about the financial statements, so the elements become the classification system for accounting records.

account   A record that contains the history of all increases and decreases of an accounting element.

chart of accounts   A list of all the accounts used by a business entity. The list usually contains the name of the account and the account number.

general ledger   A book of final entry which includes a page for each account in the chart of accounts.

We sort transactions into the increases and decreases for each accounting element. Each accounting element has an **account,** which contains the history of all increases and decreases in the accounting element. A **chart of accounts** is a list of all the accounts used by a business entity. The chart of accounts lists each account with its account number (particularly important in computerized systems) in the order of assets, liabilities, equity, revenue, and expense accounts. To be systematic, charts of account normally appear in balance sheet and income statement order. The chart of accounts becomes a reference tool to accountants and expands as needed to record new types of transactions. Each business entity should tailor its chart of accounts to its business activities.

The entire group of accounts makes up the **general ledger.** Each account is a page or a file in the general ledger. At the end of a month or a week, the accounting system posts the journal transactions to the general ledger (see Exhibit 7–4). In a computerized system, the software actually re-sorts the transactions from a date order to an account number order and accumulates like account numbers in each account. Then we have a record of what happened to each account as a result of

Exhibit 7–4
Posting to the
General Ledger

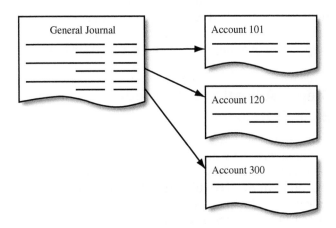

Exhibit 7–5
Preparing the Trial
Balance

General Ledger

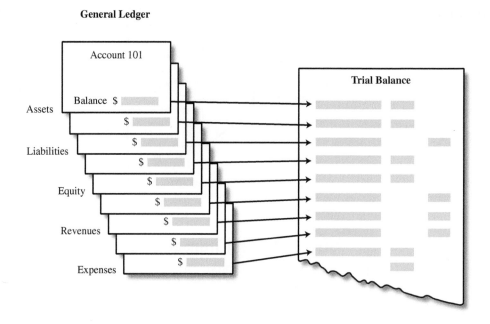

these transactions. We add all increases and subtract all decreases to the previous balance of the account to arrive at a new account balance. We use the general ledger account balances to prepare financial statements after two additional steps in the accounting cycle.

Step 4: Preparing the Trial Balance (or Worksheet)

Each time we post a month's or a week's transactions from the journals, we need to make sure that the accounting equation remains in balance. To accomplish this, we prepare a trial balance. A **trial balance** is a listing of each general ledger account balance to verify that the general ledger, and therefore the accounting equation, is in balance (see Exhibit 7–5). Accounting software packages often print a trial balance after each processing session. Others automatically check to be sure that the system is in balance and alert the operator if it is out of balance.

Frequently, accountants use a **worksheet** to aid in the preparation of the financial statements. Most firms prepare monthly financial statements and follow this step each time financial statements are prepared. (Some firms prepare financial statements weekly, quarterly, or semiannually.) The first two columns of the ten-column worksheet are the trial balance as of the balance sheet date. The worksheet allows the accountant to examine the accounts, adjust the accounts, and gather the data to prepare the financial statements. We will examine the details of worksheet preparation of a trial balance and a worksheet as we apply these concepts.

Step 5: Adjusting the Accounts and Reconciling the Bank Statement

At the end of an accounting period, prior to the preparation of financial statements, accountants review the accounts to properly match the expenses of the period with the revenues that they helped to produce and to make sure that the assets, liabilities, and equity accounts are properly stated (see Exhibit 7–6). The adjustment process may involve entries to defer or accrue revenues or expenses as we discussed in Chapter 6. The adjustment process requires the application of the following steps:

trial balance The listing of the general ledger account balances which proves that the general ledger and, therefore, the accounting equation are in balance.

worksheet A tool used by the accountant to accumulate the necessary information used to prepare the financial statements.

Exhibit 7-6
Adjusting the Accounts
and Reconciling the
Bank Statement

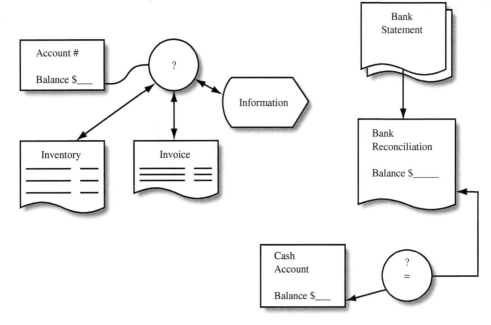

1. Identification of any accounts requiring adjustment
2. Determination of the correct balance in each account requiring adjustment
3. Preparation of the necessary adjusting entry or entries to bring the accounts into agreement with the balances determined in the previous step

Another major step in the adjusting process is reconciling the bank statement. Because most transactions ultimately result in the receipt or the payment of cash, it is important to reconcile the bank statement as part of the firm's internal control structure. Since cash represents the most liquid and easily transported of the firm's assets, the use of a checking account by a business entity requires the implementation of some important internal controls. For example, only designated persons should have the authority to sign checks, and the person designated to reconcile the bank account should have no other duties involving the receipt or disbursement of funds. We will prepare a bank reconciliation as we apply these concepts later in the chapter.

Step 6: Preparing Financial Statements

When the accountant is satisfied that the bank accounts are reconciled and the accounts listed on the worksheet represent fair amounts, he or she will prepare the financial statements (see Exhibit 7–7). The accountant should verify that the financial statements articulate. Specifically, the net income or net loss figure for the period must agree with the net income or net loss on the statement of owners' equity or the statement of retained earnings.

Discussion Question

7-3. How often should a company prepare its financial statements?

Exhibit 7-7
Preparation of the
Financial Statements

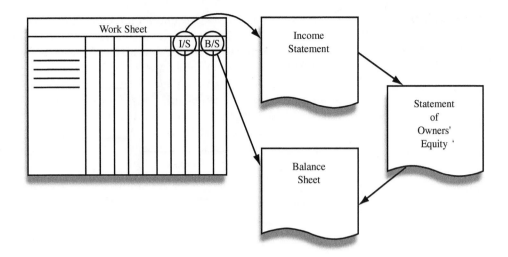

Step 7: Preparing and Posting Closing Entries

At the end of each fiscal year, after the accounting staff adjusts all the accounts and the auditors have finished the audit, we close the books. The closing process resets the temporary accounts to zero and moves the net income to the appropriate equity accounts (see Exhibit 7–8). **Temporary (or nominal) accounts** are all revenue,

Exhibit 7-8
Closing the
Temporary Accounts

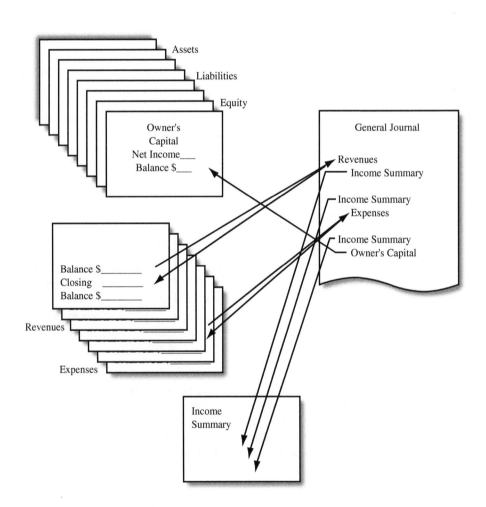

temporary (or nominal) accounts   The general ledger accounts that are closed to a zero balance at the end of the fiscal year in the closing process. Temporary accounts include revenues, expenses, gains, losses, owner withdrawals, and dividend accounts.

permanent (or real) accounts   The general ledger accounts that are never closed. The permanent accounts include assets, liabilities, and equity accounts except for owner withdrawals and dividends.

expense, gain, and loss accounts that are part of net income plus the owner withdrawals and dividend accounts. We do not close permanent accounts in this process. **Permanent (or real) accounts** include asset, liability, and equity accounts, except for owner withdrawals and dividend accounts. The closing entries zero the temporary accounts much like a trip switch on an automobile odometer. The odometer (like permanent accounts) continues to record miles, but we reset the trip switch (like temporary accounts) to zero before each event (like a new fiscal year). Each year we reset the temporary accounts to zero to accumulate the current year's net income. At the end of the year we close the net income into the equity accounts and start over again. We make four closing entries:

1. Close the revenue accounts to Income Summary.
2. Close the expense accounts to Income Summary.
3. Close the Withdrawals accounts to Owner's or Partner's Capital accounts or Dividends accounts to Retained Earnings.
4. Close Income Summary to Owner's or Partner's Capital accounts or Retained Earnings.

Step 8: Preparing the Post-Closing Trial Balance

post-closing trial balance
A trial balance prepared after all closing entries have been posted which proves that the only accounts remaining in the general ledger are the permanent accounts and that the accounting equation is still in balance.

After we prepare the closing entries and post them to the general ledger, only the balance sheet accounts should have a balance remaining. In addition, any owner withdrawal or dividend accounts should have a zero balance. We prepare a **post-closing trial balance** after the closing entries to prove that the closing entries zeroed the temporary accounts (see Exhibit 7–9). In a computerized system, this step is crucial to verify the integrity of the closing process and that the accounting equation remains in balance.

Before we apply the steps of the accounting cycle to the McCumber Company, we need to discuss several topics necessary to begin the data accumulation.

Exhibit 7–9
Post-Closing
Trial Balance

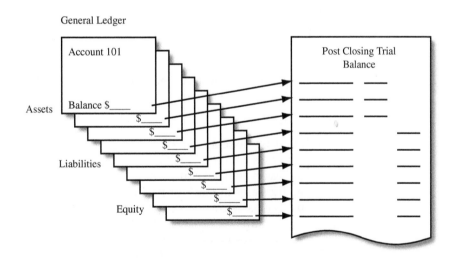

accounting system   The overall format used to gather data from source transactions to create the books and records which are used to prepare the financial statements of a business entity.

Debits and Credits

An **accounting system** gathers data from source transactions to create the books and records that transform the data into a manageable format that will eventually produce useful information in the form of financial statements. The accounting system bases its process on the basic accounting equation:

$$\text{Assets} = \text{Liabilities} + \text{Equity}$$

As we know from mathematics, a change in one side of the equation requires a change in the other side to keep the equation in balance. This concept is the origin of the term *double-entry bookkeeping*.

Over the past 7,000 years, accountants have developed the accounting system and an accounting language to describe the process. In the accounting system, debit means left and credit means right. Thus,

$$\text{Assets} = \text{Liabilities} + \text{Equity}$$
$$\text{Left} = \text{Right}$$
$$\text{Debit} = \text{Credit}$$

When our accounting system is in balance, the debits equal the credits; left equals right.

normal balance • The balance of the account derived from the type of entry (debit or credit) that increases the account.

We assign a normal balance to each account depending upon which side of the equation it normally resides. Therefore, assets have normal debit balances and liabilities and equity accounts have normal credit balances. An account's **normal balance** defines the type of entry that increases the account; debits increase debit balance accounts and credits decrease debit balance accounts.

$$\text{Assets} = \text{Liabilities} + \text{Equity}$$
$$\text{Normal Balance: Debit} = \text{Credit} + \text{Credit}$$

We also learned in Chapter 5 about the four components of equity. We can expand the accounting equation to include these components of equity as follows:

Assets = Liabilities + Owners' Contributions − Owners' Withdrawals + Revenues − Expenses
Debit = Credit   +   Credit   −   Debit   + Credit   − Debit

debit A term that means the left side of a general ledger account.

With the expanded equation we can identify the normal balances of revenues, expenses, and owners' withdrawals. Therefore, a **debit:**

1. Increases assets
2. Decreases liabilities
3. Decreases owners' equity
   a. Decreases owner's or partner's capital and capital stock accounts
   b. Increases owner's or partner's withdrawal accounts or the dividend account
   c. Decreases revenues or gains
   d. Increases expenses or losses

credit A term that means the right side of a general ledger account.

A **credit:**

1. Decreases assets
2. Increases liabilities
3. Increases owners' equity
   a. Increases owner's or partner's capital or capital stock accounts
   b. Decreases owner's or partner's withdrawal accounts or the dividend account
   c. Increases revenues or gains
   d. Decreases expenses or losses

The Account

Each account contains a summary of its activity during the year. It includes the following important information:

1. Account name and number
2. Date of each transaction
3. Beginning balance

Exhibit 7–10
The Account Form

Account Name	Cash in Bank				Account Number	101
2008		Post			Balance	
Date	Description	Ref.	Debit	Credit	Debit	Credit
Dec 1	Beginning Balance				34,589.26	
31		CR34	54,197.75		88,787.01	
31		CD57		56,110.68	32,676.33	

4. Each posting from journals including the date, reference, and amount
5. Ending balance

A typical account might look like that shown in Exhibit 7–10.

When you read the account, you learn that on December 1, 2008, this company began with $34,589.26 in the bank. It collected $54,197.75 recorded on page 34 of the Cash Receipts Journal and paid out $56,110.68 recorded on page 57 of the Cash Payments Journal. At month's end, the company had $32,676.33 in the bank. Notice that there are no dollar signs in the general ledger. Dollar signs appear in financial statements and reports, such as a trial balance, but not on journals, ledgers, or worksheets.

For discussion purposes, we often use an abbreviated account form called the T-account. The **T-account** represents the general ledger account with only two columns. The balance appears after a horizontal line. We use this form to save time when analyzing an account. Exhibit 7–11 contains the T-account version of the cash account illustrated in Exhibit 7–10.

T-account An account form that represents the general ledger account with only two columns.

Exhibit 7–11
T-Account

Cash in Bank 101

2008				
12-1	34,589.26			
12-31	54,197.75	56,110.68	12-31	
	32,676.33			

The Journal Entry

For simplicity, we will utilize only the General Journal in this chapter. Proper general journal entries contain the pertinent details of the transaction in an easy-to-read format. Exhibit 7–12 illustrates a general journal page that contains a journal entry.

Discussion Questions

7-4. From the entry made into the General Journal, describe what happened with this transaction.

7-5. Where will this entry be posted in the General Ledger?

7-6. Can each journal entry have only one debit and one credit?

Exhibit 7-12
The General Journal

General Journal			Page 423		
Date 2008		**Description**	**Post Ref.**	**Debit**	**Credit**
Jan	24	Account Receivable	110	23,425.00	
		Sales	401		23,425.00
		To record the sale of 1500 units to			
		John George, Inc. Terms 2/10, n 30			

The journal entry provides us with the following information:

1. The date of the transaction
2. The accounts affected by the transaction
3. A description of the transaction with any important details
4. The amounts of the debit or credit to each account

compound journal entry
Any entry recorded in the general journal that contains more than two accounts.

Notice that the debit equals the credit. Journal entries with more than two accounts are called **compound journal entries.** Regardless of the number of accounts involved, the total debits must equal the total credits for each transaction or the system will be out of balance. Now that we know what to do and how to do it, we can apply the accounting cycle to actual transactions.

ACCOUNTING CYCLE APPLICATION

To illustrate the accounting cycle, we will use the McCumber Company proprietorship accrual-basis transactions for January, 2008, that you examined in Chapter 6. We have reproduced those here for your convenience.

1. Gertie McCumber started the company on January 2 by investing $200,000.
2. McCumber Company borrowed $100,000 from the Friendly Bank on January 2 by signing a one-year, 12 percent note payable. Although the $100,000 does not have to be repaid until January 2, 2009, the interest charge must be paid each month, beginning on February 2, 2008.
3. The company purchased a vehicle on January 2 for $14,000 cash. Gertie estimates that the vehicle will fill the company's needs for four years, after which she estimates she can sell it for $2,000.
4. The company paid cash for $75,000 of merchandise inventory on January 8.
5. On January 15, the company sold merchandise that cost $42,000 for a total selling price of $78,000 and collected the cash the same day.
6. On January 22, the company sold merchandise that cost $15,000 for a total selling price of $32,000 on account (a credit sale). The terms of the sale were 30 days, meaning McCumber can expect to receive payment by February 21.
7. Cash payments for operating expenses in January totaled $22,500.

8. Besides the bank loan, the only amounts owed by the company at the end of the month were:
   a. $2,000 to company employees for work performed in January. They will be paid on February 3.
   b. A $700 utility bill that was received on January 26 and will be paid on February 15.

The first seven transactions should be recorded in the first two steps of the accounting cycle, analyzing and journalizing transactions. We analyzed these entries in Chapter 6 and now know how to properly record them in the general journal.

Steps 1 & 2–Analyzing and Journalizing Transactions

We would normally begin by examining the chart of accounts. McCumber's chart of accounts is as follows:

101	Cash in Bank
110	Accounts Receivable
120	Inventory
150	Automotive Equipment
155	Accumulated Depreciation
200	Accounts Payable
210	Wages Payable
220	Interest Payable
250	Notes Payable
300	Gertie McCumber, Capital
310	Gertie McCumber, Withdrawals
400	Sales
500	Cost of Goods Sold
600	Operating Expenses
620	Wages Expense
640	Utilities Expense
660	Interest Expense
680	Depreciation Expense

We have recorded each of transactions 1 through 7 on the general journal beginning with page 1.

After examining the general journal on the following page you might notice the following items:

1. Dates—We write the name of the month only at the top of each page, unless it changes in the middle of the page. All entries are in chronological order.
2. Account titles—We write all debits first in one journal entry and then the credits. Write debits on the margin and indent the credits five spaces.
3. Posting references—Nothing is written in this column. We write the account number in this column as we post to the general ledger in Step 3. This clues the bookkeeper as to whether the item is posted.
4. Debit and credit amounts—Since this problem is in whole dollars, we omitted the cents. There are no dollar signs because this is a journal.
5. Explanations—A complete explanation follows each journal entry so that the reader can understand the analysis of the transaction.
6. Compound entry—The January 22 journal entry is similar to the two entries on January 15. To save time writing two explanations, the January 22 entry combined the separate entries of January 15. Either way is acceptable in a general journal because the sale of merchandise involves all four accounts, but it may be thought of as two separate transactions or one complex transaction. A compound journal entry has more than one debit or credit.

General Journal — Page 1

Date 2008		Description	Post Ref.	Debit	Credit
Jan	1	Cash in Bank		200,000	
		McCumber, Capital			200,000
		To record the owner's capital			
		contribution.			
	2	Cash in Bank		100,000	
		Notes Payable			100,000
		To record loan from Friendly Bank			
		due January 2, 2001 with 12%			
		interest payable monthly.			
		Automotive Equipment		14,000	
		Cash in Bank			14,000
		To record the purchase of a vehicle, 4-			
		year useful life, $2,000 residual			
		value.			

General Journal — Page 2

Date 2008		Description	Post Ref.	Debit	Credit
Jan	8	Inventory		75,000	
		Cash in Bank			75,000
		To record the purchase of inventory.			
	15	Cash in Bank		78,000	
		Sales			78,000
		To record sales that cost $42,000.			
		Cost of Goods Sold		42,000	
		Inventory			42,000
		To record the cost of the previous sale.			
	22	Accounts Receivable		32,000	
		Cost of Goods Sold		15,000	
		Sales			32,000
		Inventory			15,000
		To record a sale terms net 30 that cost			
		$15,000.			
	31	Operating Expenses		22,500	
		Cash in Bank			22,500
		To record the payment of cash			
		operating expenses.			

Assuming that these transactions represent all transactions for the month of January, we can now post these to the general ledger in Step 3.

Step 3–Posting to the General Ledger

Although time consuming, the posting process presents no serious challenge. Posting requires attention to detail in the following procedures:

1. Post to the general ledger each entry in the order that it appears in the general journal.
2. Record the date as the same date as the entry in the general journal.
3. There is no need to write any description unless you wish to indicate a special notation.
4. For the posting reference on the general ledger, use the page number of the journal page, such as GJ1 or GJ2.
5. Record the amount of the entry in the correct debit or credit column.
6. Place the general ledger account number in the posting reference column of the general journal.

Exhibit 7–13 shows the postings of the first two general journal entries. Then Exhibit 7–14 presents the final appearance of the general journal pages 1 and 2 and the general ledger accounts for each account that has a balance after the monthly transactions.

Now that we have posted the general ledger, we can prepare the trial balance.

Step 4–Preparing the Trial Balance

To prepare the trial balance, simply list in order each general ledger account and its account balance. Put each debit balance in the debit column and each credit balance in the credit column. Total each column and verify that the debits equal the credits. The trial balance appears in Exhibit 7–15 on page F-227.

Because the debits equal the credits in the trial balance, our general ledger balances.

Discussion Questions

7-7. If the debits equal the credits, does this mean that the general ledger is correct? If not, what can be wrong?

7-8. If the debits do not equal the credits, what are the most likely causes of the imbalance?

When we want to prepare financial statements, we prepare a worksheet. The worksheet has five pairs of columns; each pair contains a debit and a credit column. To complete the worksheet, we use the following steps.

1. Place a heading on the worksheet that includes the company name, the title "Worksheet," and the period covered by the worksheet.

Exhibit 7-13
The Posting Process

General Journal				Page	1

Date 2008		Description	Post Ref.	Debit	Credit
Jan	1	Cash in Bank	101	200,000	
		McCumber, Capital	300		200,000
		To record the owner's capital			
		contribution.			
	2	Cash in Bank	101	100,000	
		Notes Payable	250		100,000
		To record loan from Friendly Bank			
		due January 2, 2001 with 12%			
		interest payable monthly.			

Account Name Cash in Bank   **Account Number** 101

2008		Post			Balance	
Date	Description	Ref.	Debit	Credit	Debit	Credit
Jan 1		GJ1	200,000		200,000	
2		GJ1	100,000		300,000	

Account Name Notes Payable   **Account Number** 250

2008		Post			Balance	
Date	Description	Ref.	Debit	Credit	Debit	Credit
Jan 2		GJ1		100,000		100,000

Account Name McCumber, Capital   **Account Number** 300

2008		Post			Balance	
Date	Description	Ref.	Debit	Credit	Debit	Credit
Jan 1		GJ1		200,000		200,000

Exhibit 7–14
After the Posting
Process

General Journal			Page 1		
Date 2008		Description	Post Ref.	Debit	Credit
Jan	1	Cash in Bank	101	200,000	
		McCumber, Capital	300		200,000
		To record the owner's capital			
		contribution.			
	2	Cash in Bank	101	100,000	
		Notes Payable	250		100,000
		To record loan from Friendly Bank			
		due January 2, 2001 with 12%			
		interest payable monthly.			
		Automotive Equipment	150	14,000	
		Cash in Bank	101		14,000
		To record the purchase of a vehicle, 4-			
		year useful life, $2,000 residual			
		value.			

General Journal			Page 2		
Date 2008		Description	Post Ref.	Debit	Credit
Jan	8	Inventory	120	75,000	
		Cash in Bank	101		75,000
		To record the purchase of inventory.			
	15	Cash in Bank	101	78,000	
		Sales	400		78,000
		To record sales that cost $42,000.			
		Cost of Goods Sold	500	42,000	
		Inventory	120		42,000
		To record the cost of the previous sale.			
	22	Accounts Receivable	110	32,000	
		Cost of Goods Sold	500	15,000	
		Sales	400		32,000
		Inventory	120		15,000
		To record a sale terms net 30 that cost			
		$15,000.			
	31	Operating Expenses	600	22,500	
		Cash in Bank	101		22,500
		To record the payment of cash			
		operating expenses.			

Exhibit 7-14
Continued

Account Name Cash in Bank — Account Number 101

2008 Date	Description	Post Ref.	Debit	Credit	Balance Debit	Balance Credit
Jan 1		GJ1	200,000		200,000	
2		GJ1	100,000		300,000	
		GJ1		14,000	286,000	
8		GJ2		75,000	211,000	
15		GJ2	78,000		289,000	
31		GJ2		22,500	266,500	

Account Name Accounts Receivable — Account Number 110

2008 Date	Description	Post Ref.	Debit	Credit	Balance Debit	Balance Credit
Jan 22		GJ2	32,000		32,000	

Account Name Inventory — Account Number 120

2008 Date	Description	Post Ref.	Debit	Credit	Balance Debit	Balance Credit
Jan 8		GJ2	75,000		75,000	
15		GJ2		42,000	33,000	
22		GJ2		15,000	18,000	

Account Name Automotive Equipment — Account Number 150

2008 Date	Description	Post Ref.	Debit	Credit	Balance Debit	Balance Credit
Jan 2		GJ1	14,000		14,000	

Account Name Notes Payable — Account Number 250

2008 Date	Description	Post Ref.	Debit	Credit	Balance Debit	Balance Credit
Jan 2		GJ1		100,000		100,000

Exhibit 7-14
Continued

Account Name *McCumber, Capital*   **Account Number** *300*

2008		Post			Balance	
Date	Description	Ref.	Debit	Credit	Debit	Credit
Jan 1		GJ1		200,000		200,000

Account Name *Sales*   **Account Number** *400*

2008		Post			Balance	
Date	Description	Ref.	Debit	Credit	Debit	Credit
Jan 15		GJ2		78,000		78,000
22		GJ2		32,000		110,000

Account Name *Cost of Goods Sold*   **Account Number** *500*

2008		Post			Balance	
Date	Description	Ref.	Debit	Credit	Debit	Credit
Jan 15		GJ2	42,000		42,000	
22		GJ2	15,000		57,000	

Account Name *Operating Expenses*   **Account Number** *600*

2008		Post			Balance	
Date	Description	Ref.	Debit	Credit	Debit	Credit
Jan 31		GJ2	22,500		22,500	

Exhibit 7-15
The Trial Balance

McCumber Company
Trial Balance
January 31, 2008

	Account	Debit	Credit
101	Cash in Bank	$266,500	
110	Accounts Receivable	32,000	
120	Inventory	18,000	
150	Automotive Equipment	14,000	
250	Notes Payable		$100,000
300	McCumber Capital		200,000
400	Sales		110,000
500	Cost of Goods Sold	57,000	
600	Operating Expenses	22,500	
	Totals	$410,000	$410,000

2. Head the columns with the titles:
   a. Account
   b. Trial Balance (followed by the date of the trial balance)
   c. Adjustments
   d. Adjusted Trial Balance
   e. Income Statement
   f. Balance Sheet
3. Place the trial balance amounts in the trial balance columns after the account name. It is easiest to list the accounts in the general ledger order and include accounts without balances that might be used in the worksheet. Verify that the trial balance balances.
4. Examine each account, using additional information you have available, to determine if any adjusting journal entries should be made (see Step 5). Write the adjustments in its columns, then add the two columns down to verify that the debits equal the credits.
5. After completing all adjustments, add the first four columns across to create an adjusted trial balance. Verify that the adjusted trial balance balances.
6. Place each amount listed on the adjusted trial balance in the appropriate income statement or balance sheet columns. Total the four columns. The amounts will not balance, but what you should find is that each set of columns is off by the same amount. That amount is net income. See Exhibit 7–16 for the completed worksheet.

Step 5–Adjusting the Accounts and Reconciling the Bank Statement

We examine each account to see whether the balance is reasonable and to determine whether any accrual, deferral, or correcting entry is needed. Cash normally appears first in the chart of accounts. The best way to examine the cash account is to reconcile the bank statement. Each month the bank sends a statement that lists the beginning and ending account balance according to the bank's records. It also lists each check that cleared and each deposit the bank received. Remember that the bank refers to debits and credits from the bank's perspective. The bank's debits and credits are the opposite of the company's debits and credits. How is this possible? Because our bank account has a debit balance, but our bank account is a liability to the bank and a liability has a credit balance. On February 5, 2008, McCumber received the following bank statement from Valley National Bank.

Exhibit 7–17 contains a standard bank reconciliation format. We will use it to reconcile McCumber's bank account and verify our cash balance.

Reconciling a bank statement uses the following process:

1. Record the bank statement's ending balance on the appropriate line.
2. Record any deposits recorded in the books that have not been included in the bank statement. These deposits should be at the end of the month. If you find other deposits missing, notify the bank at once. Most banks require that you notify them within 10 days of the bank statement date of any errors. Beyond that time, the bank assumes that the statement is correct.
3. Look at the list of checks that cleared the bank on the bank statement. List any checks that were written through the end of the month but did not appear on the bank statement. Those are outstanding checks.
4. Compute the corrected bank balance. Write the balance per the general ledger on the appropriate line. If that balance agrees with the book balance, the reconciliation is complete.

Exhibit 7-16
The Worksheet

McCumber Company
Worksheet
For the Month Ended January 31, 2008

#	Account Name	Trial Balance Debit	Trial Balance Credit	Adjustments Debit	Adjustments Credit	Adjusted Trial Balance Debit	Adjusted Trial Balance Credit	Income Statement Debit	Income Statement Credit	Balance Sheet Debit	Balance Sheet Credit
101	Cash in Bank	266,500				266,500				266,500	
110	Accounts Receivable	32,000				32,000				32,000	
120	Inventory	18,000				18,000				18,000	
150	Automotive Equipment	14,000				14,000				14,000	
155	Accumulated Depreciation				250		250				250
200	Accounts Payable				700		700				700
210	Wages Payable				2,000		2,000				2,000
220	Interest Payable				1,000		1,000				1,000
250	Notes Payable		100,000				100,000				100,000
300	McCumber Capital		200,000				200,000				200,000
400	Sales		110,000				110,000		110,000		
500	Cost of Goods Sold	57,000				57,000		57,000			
600	Operating Expense	22,500				22,500		22,500			
620	Wage Expenses			2,000		2,000		2,000			
640	Utilities Expense			700		700		700			
660	Interest Expense			1,000		1,000		1,000			
680	Depreciation Expense			250		250		250			
	Totals	410,000	410,000	3,950	3,950	413,950	413,950	83,450	110,000	330,500	303,950
	Net Income							26,550			26,550
								110,000	110,000	330,500	330,500

F–229

Valley National Bank

Account Name: McCumber Company
500 North Mulberry Street
Fargo, North Dakota

Account Number: 3489432
Date: January 31, 2008

Previous statement balance 12–31–07	$ 0.00
3 Deposits or other credits totaling	378,000.00
2 Checks or other debits totaling	89,000.00
Current balance as of statement date 01–31–08	$ 289,000.00

Account Transactions

Date	Debits	Credits	Description
01/02		200,000.00	Deposit
01/02		100,000.00	Deposit Loan Proceeds
01/17		78,000.00	Deposit

Checks

Date	Check #	Amount	Date	Check #	Amount
01/05	1001	14,000.00	01/19	1002	75,000.00

Exhibit 7–17
Standard Bank
Reconciliation Format

COMPANY NAME
Bank Reconciliation
Date

Balance per Bank Statement $_____
Add: Deposits in Transit

_____   _____
_____   _____
_____   _____   _____

Deduct: Checks Outstanding
#____ _____   #____ _____
#____ _____   #____ _____
#____ _____   #____ _____   _____

Corrected Bank Balance $_____

Balance per Books $_____
Add: _____
    _____
    _____   _____

Deduct: Service Charges $ _____
    _____
    _____   _____

Corrected Book Balance $_____

5. If the corrected bank balance and the book balance do not agree, you must look for the difference. This process can be simple or aggravating. Following are the most likely errors that occur and help with how to spot them:
   a. Bank service charges—Banks charge for many services and do not notify the firm of the charges except with the bank statement. These include check printing charges, monthly service fees, overdraft charges, and special service fees.
   b. Checks or deposits recorded incorrectly in the journals—Transposed check amounts, such as recording $275 as $257, will cause an error in the cash account. Transposition errors are always evenly divisible by nine. For example, if the check was recorded as $257 instead of $275 the difference is $18, evenly divisible by nine. When the difference between the corrected bank balance and the book balance is divisible by nine, look for a transposition error.
   c. Other deductions by the bank—Banks deduct checks returned from the firm's deposits and other items that may not be included in the bookkeeping records.
   d. If the balances still do not agree, the next step is to check the bank's encoding of the check or deposit amount against the amount of the deposit or check. The bank's encoding is in the bottom, right-hand corner of the check or deposit slip. Banks seldom make errors, but can on occasion.

McCumber's bank reconciliation has only one reconciling item. The bank statement includes all deposits for the month but omits the final check written on January 31. Because the account is so large, the bank did not deduct a service charge for the month.

McCUMBER COMPANY
Bank Reconciliation
January 31, 2008

Balance per Bank Statement	$289,000
Add: Deposits in Transit	-0-
Deduct: Checks Outstanding	
#1003 $22,500	22,500
Corrected Bank Balance	$266,500
Balance per Books	$266,500
Deduct: Service Charges $-0-	-0-
Corrected Book Balance	$266,500

Now that the Cash in Bank balance is verified, we can proceed down the list of accounts looking for possible adjustments.

1. Accounts Receivable traces to the last sale of the month and appears to be correct. With complicated activity, we would compare the A/R balance to a listing prepared by an accounts receivable clerk to verify accuracy.
2. Inventory consists of the unsold items that we purchased on January 8. Normally, we could compare this to a computer-generated inventory listing or to a physical count of the inventory.
3. The company still owns the vehicle listed in the Automotive Equipment account. However, since it was used this month, depreciation should be recorded in an adjusting journal entry. The depreciation expense equals $250 for the month computed as

$$\text{Cost } \$14{,}000 - \text{Residual Value } \$2{,}000 = \text{Depreciable Base } \$12{,}000$$
$$\$12{,}000 \ / \ 48 \text{ months} = \$250 \text{ per month}$$

The credit is recorded to Accumulated Depreciation, a contra asset account. A **contra asset** account is an asset account with a credit normal balance.

contra asset An asset with a credit normal balance.

4. Item 8 in McCumber's information tells us that McCumber owes employees $2,000 and a utility provider $700 at month end in addition to the bank loan. This information requires us to make three adjusting journal entries for the wages, the utilities, and the loan interest. To compute the loan interest

$$\text{Interest} = \text{Principal } \$100{,}000 \times \text{Rate } 12\% \times \text{Time } 1/12 = \$1{,}000$$

5. Notes Payable and McCumber's capital are correctly stated, as are Sales, Cost of Sales, and Operating Expenses. Sales can normally be verified from a sales journal or listing. We usually check the cost of goods sold percentage to determine whether the cost of sales amount seems reasonable.

We can prepare the four required journal entries in Exhibit 7–18.

The final step is to post these to the general ledger accounts. After posting the adjusting entries, the general ledger will agree with the worksheet in Exhibit 7–16.

Exhibit 7–18
Adjusting Journal
Entries

General Journal			Page 3		
Date 2008		**Description**	**Post Ref.**	**Debit**	**Credit**
Jan	31	Depreciation Expense	680	250	
		Accumulated Depreciation	155		250
		To record depreciation on vehicle.			
		($12,000 / 48 = $250)			
		Wage Expense	620	2,000	
		Wages Payable	210		2,000
		To accrue wages owed on 1-31-00.			
		Utilities Expense	640	700	
		Accounts Payable	200		700
		To accrue utility bill due 2-15-00.			
		Interest Expense	660	1,000	
		Interest Payable	220		1,000
		To accrue one month's interest.			
		($100,000 x 12% x 1/12 = $1,000)			

Step 6–Preparing Financial Statements

We have all the information we need from the worksheet to prepare the income statement, statement of owner's equity, and balance sheet. Exhibit 7–19 contains the completed financial statements.

Compare the financial statements in Exhibit 7–19 to the accrual-basis statements in Chapter 6 (page F-184), and you will see that they are identical.

Exhibit 7-19
McCumber Financial
Statements
January 31, 2008

McCumber Company
Income Statement
For the Month Ended January 31, 2008

Sales Revenue		$110,000
Cost of Goods Sold		57,000
Gross Margin		$ 53,000
Expenses:		
Cash Operating Expenses	$22,500	
Wages Expense	2,000	
Utilities Expense	700	
Interest Expense	1,000	
Depreciation Expense	250	
Total Operating Expenses		26,450
Net Income		$26,550

McCumber Company
Statement of Owner's Equity
For the Month Ended January 31, 2008

G. McCumber, Capital, January 1, 2008	$ 0
Investment by Owner	200,000
Net Income	26,550
G. McCumber, Capital, January 31, 2008	$226,550

McCumber Company
Balance Sheet
January 31, 2008

Assets:			Liabilities:		
Cash		$266,500	Accounts Payable		$ 700
Accounts Receivable		32,000	Wages Payable		2,000
Inventory		18,000	Interest Payable		1,000
Vehicle	$14,000		Note Payable		100,000
Less: Accumulated			Total Liabilities		$103,700
Depreciation	(250)				
Vehicle, Net		13,750	Owner's Equity:		
			G. McCumber, Capital		226,550
			Total Liabilities		
Total Assets		$330,250	and Owner's Equity		$330,250

Step 7–Closing the Accounts

For the sake of simplicity, assume that McCumber decided to have a January 31 year end. Many companies choose a fiscal year that differs from the calendar year but coincides with the end of the normal business cycle for the industry. This simplifies inventory taking and year-end accounting procedures. To close McCumber's books, we will attempt to zero the temporary or nominal accounts and close them to income summary. We can review the four normal closing entries for a sole proprietorship:

1. Close the revenue and gain accounts to Income Summary.
2. Close the expense and loss accounts to Income Summary.

3. Close the Withdrawals account to the owner's capital account.
4. Close the Income Summary account to the owner's capital account.

From the worksheet we can tell that there is one revenue account and seven expense accounts to close. The owner made no withdrawals during this period. Therefore, we must make only three closing entries as follows:

Date 2008		Description	Post Ref.	Debit	Credit
Jan	31	Sales	400	110,00	
		Income Summary	800		110,000
		To close the revenue account.			
		Income Summary	800	83,450	
		Cost of Goods Sold	500		57,000
		Operating Expenses	600		22,500
		Wage Expense	620		2,000
		Utilities Expense	640		700
		Interest Expense	660		1,000
		Depreciation Expense	680		250
		To close the expense accounts.			
		Income Summary	800	26,550	
		McCumber, Capital	300		26,550
		To close the Income Summary account.			

General Journal — Page 4

The posting process is the same as in Step 3. After posting the closing entries, the general ledger appears as follows:

Account Name Cash in Bank   **Account Number** 101

Date (2008)	Description	Post Ref.	Debit	Credit	Balance Debit	Balance Credit
Jan 1		GJ1	200,000		200,000	
2		GJ1	100,000		300,000	
		GJ1		14,000	286,000	
8		GJ2		75,000	211,000	
15		GJ2	78,000		289,000	
31		GJ2		22,500	266,500	

Account Name	Accounts Receivable			Account Number	110	

2008		Post			Balance	
Date	Description	Ref.	Debit	Credit	Debit	Credit
Jan 22		GJ2	32,000		32,000	

Account Name	Inventory			Account Number	120	

2008		Post			Balance	
Date	Description	Ref.	Debit	Credit	Debit	Credit
Jan 8		GJ2	75,000		75,000	
15		GJ2		42,000	33,000	
22		GJ2		15,000	18,000	

Account Name	Automotive Equipment			Account Number	150	

2008		Post			Balance	
Date	Description	Ref.	Debit	Credit	Debit	Credit
Jan 2		GJ1	14,000		14,000	

Account Name	Accumulated Depreciation			Account Number	155	

2008		Post			Balance	
Date	Description	Ref.	Debit	Credit	Debit	Credit
Jan 31		GJ3		250		250

Account Name	Accounts Payable			Account Number	200	

2008		Post			Balance	
Date	Description	Ref.	Debit	Credit	Debit	Credit
Jan 31		GJ3		700		700

Account Name	Wages Payable			Account Number	210	

2008		Post			Balance	
Date	Description	Ref.	Debit	Credit	Debit	Credit
Jan 31		GJ3		2,000		2,000

Account Name *Interest Payable*   **Account Number** *220*

2008		Post			Balance	
Date	Description	Ref.	Debit	Credit	Debit	Credit
Jan 31		GJ3		1,000		1,000

Account Name *Notes Payable*   **Account Number** *250*

2008		Post			Balance	
Date	Description	Ref.	Debit	Credit	Debit	Credit
Jan 2		GJ1		100,000		100,000

Account Name *McCumber, Capital*   **Account Number** *300*

2008		Post			Balance	
Date	Description	Ref.	Debit	Credit	Debit	Credit
Jan 1		GJ1		200,000		200,000
31	To close income summary	GJ4		26,550		226,550

Account Name *Sales*   **Account Number** *400*

2008		Post			Balance	
Date	Description	Ref.	Debit	Credit	Debit	Credit
Jan 15		GJ2		78,000		78,000
22		GJ2		32,000		110,000
31	To close	GJ4	110,000			0

Account Name *Cost of Goods Sold*   **Account Number** *500*

2008		Post			Balance	
Date	Description	Ref.	Debit	Credit	Debit	Credit
Jan 15		GJ2	42,000		42,000	
22		GJ2	15,000		57,000	
31	To close	GJ4		57,000	0	

Account Name *Operating Expenses*   **Account Number** *600*

2008		Post			Balance	
Date	Description	Ref.	Debit	Credit	Debit	Credit
Jan 31		GJ2	22,500		22,500	
31	To close	GJ4		22,500	0	

Account Name   Operating Expenses   Account Number   600

2008		Post			Balance	
Date	Description	Ref.	Debit	Credit	Debit	Credit
Jan 31		GJ2	22,500		22,500	
31	To close	GJ4		22,500	0	

Account Name   Wage Expense   Account Number   620

2008		Post			Balance	
Date	Description	Ref.	Debit	Credit	Debit	Credit
Jan 31		GJ3	2,000		2,000	
31	To close	GJ4		2,000	0	

Account Name   Utilities Expense   Account Number   640

2008		Post			Balance	
Date	Description	Ref.	Debit	Credit	Debit	Credit
Jan 31		GJ3	700		700	
31	To close	GJ4		700	0	

Account Name   Depreciation Expense   Account Number   680

2008		Post			Balance	
Date	Description	Ref.	Debit	Credit	Debit	Credit
Jan 31		GJ3	250		250	
31	To close	GJ4		250	0	

Account Name   Income Summary   Account Number   800

2008		Post			Balance	
Date	Description	Ref.	Debit	Credit	Debit	Credit
Jan 31	To close revenues	GJ4		110,000		110,000
	To close expenses	GJ4	83,450			26,550
	To close account	GJ4	26,550			0

Step 8–Preparing the Post-Closing Trial Balance

We have reached the final step in the process. By preparing the post-closing trial balance, we verify that each temporary account is closed and the general ledger remains in balance. The post-closing trial balance becomes the opening balances for the new fiscal year. Exhibit 7–20 contains McCumber's post-closing trial balance at January 31, 2008.

Exhibit 7–20
Post-Closing Trial
Balance

McCumber Company Post-Closing Trial Balance January 31, 2008			
	Account	Debit	Credit
101	Cash in Bank	$266,500	
110	Accounts Receivable	32,000	
120	Inventory	18,000	
150	Automotive Equipment	14,000	
155	Accumulated Depreciation		$ 250
200	Accounts Payable		700
210	Wages Payable		2,000
220	Interest Payable		1,000
250	Notes Payable		100,000
300	McCumber, Capital		226,550
	Total	$330,500	$330,500

So far we have examined how accountants measure reality and accumulate data to provide meaningful information to financial decision makers. Chapters 8 and 9 explore areas in which we allow flexibility in the recognition of revenues and expenses. These variations reduce the comparability of financial statement information between companies. Therefore, to be an informed user, you should understand the variations and their influence on the financial statements.

SUMMARY

The accounting cycle is an eight-step process of accumulating accounting data and transforming it into useful accounting information.

1. Analyzing transactions requires deciding when a transaction occurs and determining which accounts it affects. Analysis occurs at least daily.
2. Journalizing transactions records the transaction chronologically in a journal, a book of original entry. The proper journal for each entry depends on the unique accounting system the company employs. Some systems have only a general journal and others have special journals to record similar transactions. Journalizing occurs at least monthly.
3. Posting transactions transfers the journal information to the general ledger, sorted by account. Each account indicates the beginning and ending balance and all transactions recorded during the period for that account. Posting occurs at least monthly in most systems.
4. Preparing a trial balance proves that the general ledger (and the accounting equation) is in balance. We prepare a worksheet to aid in the preparation of financial statements. A trial balance should be prepared each time we post journals to the general ledger and worksheets are prepared as often as the firm prepares financial statements.
5. Adjusting the accounts records all accruals, deferrals, and corrections necessary to provide quality accounting information. We adjust accounts as often as we prepare financial statements.

6. Preparing the financial statements represents the final step in the transformation of data into information. Most firms prepare financial statements at least monthly for internal users and quarterly for external users.
7. Closing the temporary (nominal) accounts occurs one time each year after the final adjustments are made to the accounts. We close the temporary accounts to owner's equity, partner's equity, or to retained earnings.
8. Preparing the post-closing trial balance ensures that all temporary accounts were properly closed and that the permanent (real) accounts left in the general ledger are in balance. This occurs annually after the closing entries. The post-closing trial balance amounts become the opening balances for the new fiscal year.

The accounting system records transactions as either debits or credits. Debit means left and credit means right, referring to the sides of the accounting equation. Debits must always equal credits in each transaction, each journal, and the general ledger to keep the equation in balance. Debits increase assets and expenses, and decrease liabilities, equity, and revenue. Credits increase liabilities, equity, and revenues and decrease assets and expenses.

REVIEW THE FACTS

A. List the eight steps in the accounting cycle.
B. Distinguish between debits and credits and explain how they relate to the accounting equation.
C. Describe the differences between an account, a journal, a ledger, and a worksheet.
D. Explain the purposes of the general journal and special journals.
E. List the important elements of a general journal entry.
F. Describe how to post general journal entries to the general ledger.
G. Describe the purpose of the trial balance and the worksheet.
H. Describe at least four causes of a trial balance failing to balance.
I. Explain how a worksheet aids in the preparation of the financial statements. Include as part of your answer a description of the worksheet's five pairs of columns.
J. What is the purpose of the closing entries?
K. Describe the contents of the post-closing trial balance and explain its purpose.

APPLY WHAT YOU HAVE LEARNED

LO 1: Terminology

7-9. Presented below is a list of items relating to the concepts discussed in this chapter, followed by definitions of those items in scrambled order.

a. Accounting cycle
b. General Journal
c. General Ledger
d. Trial Balance
e. Debit

f. Credit
g. Account
h. Chart of Accounts
i. Posting
j. Journalizing

1. _____ A collection of all the accounts of a business entity
2. _____ The left side of an account

3. _____ The series of steps repeated each accounting period to enable a business entity to record, classify, and summarize financial information
4. _____ A book of original entry
5. _____ A device used to sort accounting data into similar groupings
6. _____ The process of recording into the general ledger from a journal
7. _____ The process of recording transactions into the book of original entry
8. _____ A listing to prove the equality of debits and credits
9. _____ The complete list of the account titles used by an entity
10. _____ The right side of an account

REQUIRED:

Match the letter next to each item on the list with the appropriate definition. Each letter will be used only once.

LO 1:   The Accounting Cycle

7–10. Identify and list in order of occurrence the steps of the accounting cycle.

LO 1:   The Accounting Cycle

7–11. Define the following terms.
- **a.** Journal
- **b.** Ledger
- **c.** Posting
- **d.** Trial balance
- **e.** Adjusting entries
- **f.** Closing entries

LO 2:   Normal Account Balances

7–12. Examine the following accounts.
1. _____ Cash
2. _____ Accounts Payable
3. _____ Smith, Capital Account
4. _____ Revenues
5. _____ Prepaid Insurance
6. _____ Merchandise Inventory
7. _____ Rent Expense
8. _____ Income Tax Expense
9. _____ Income Taxes Payable
10. _____ Common Stock

REQUIRED:

Indicate whether the normal balance of each account is a debit (DR) or credit (CR) in the space provided.

LO 2:   Permanent or Temporary Accounts

7–13. Examine the following accounts.
1. _____ Cash
2. _____ Accounts Payable
3. _____ Smith, Capital Account
4. _____ Revenues

5. _____ Prepaid Insurance
6. _____ Merchandise Inventory
7. _____ Rent Expense
8. _____ Income Tax Expense
9. _____ Income Taxes Payable
10. _____ Common Stock

REQUIRED:
Indicate whether the type of account is permanent (P) or temporary (T) in the space provided.

LO 2: Normal Account Balances

7–14. Examine the following accounts.

1. _____ Accounts Receivable
2. _____ Notes Payable
3. _____ Jones, Drawing Account
4. _____ Sales
5. _____ Prepaid Rent
6. _____ Supplies Inventory
7. _____ Insurance Expense
8. _____ Income Tax Expense
9. _____ Wages Payable
10. _____ Retained Earnings

REQUIRED:
Indicate whether the normal balance of each account is a debit (DR) or credit (CR) in the space provided.

LO 2: Permanent or Temporary Accounts

7–15. Examine the following accounts.

1. _____ Accounts Receivable
2. _____ Notes Payable
3. _____ Jones, Drawing Account
4. _____ Sales
5. _____ Prepaid Rent
6. _____ Supplies Inventory
7. _____ Insurance Expense
8. _____ Income Tax Expense
9. _____ Wages Payable
10. _____ Retained Earnings

REQUIRED:
Indicate whether the type of account is permanent (P) or temporary (T) in the space provided.

LO 2: Account Classification

7–16. Examine the following accounts.

1. _____ Prepaid Taxes
2. _____ Advertising Expense
3. _____ Retained Earnings
4. _____ Depreciation Expense
5. _____ Rent Revenue

6. _____ Automotive Equipment
7. _____ Allowance for Doubtful Accounts
8. _____ Truck Expense
9. _____ Gasoline Expense
10. _____ Common Stock

REQUIRED:
Indicate the classification of each of the accounts listed above.

a. Asset   d. Expense
b. Liability   e. Equity
c. Revenue   f. Contra Asset

LO 2: Account Classification

7–17. Examine the following accounts.

1. _____ Cash
2. _____ Accounts Payable
3. _____ Smith, Capital Account
4. _____ Revenues
5. _____ Prepaid Insurance
6. _____ Merchandise Inventory
7. _____ Rent Expense
8. _____ Income Tax Expense
9. _____ Income Taxes Payable
10. _____ Preferred Stock

REQUIRED:
Indicate the classification of each of the accounts listed above.

a. Asset   d. Expense
b. Liability   e. Equity
c. Revenue   f. Contra Asset

LO 2: Account Classification

7–18. You are presented with the following accounts.

1. _____ Accounts Receivable
2. _____ Notes Payable
3. _____ Jones, Drawing Account
4. _____ Sales
5. _____ Prepaid Rent
6. _____ Supplies Inventory
7. _____ Insurance Expense
8. _____ Income Tax Expense
9. _____ Wages Payable
10. _____ Additional Paid-in Capital

REQUIRED:
Indicate the classification of each of the accounts listed above.

a. Asset   d. Expense
b. Liability   e. Equity
c. Revenue   f. Contra Asset

LO 2 & 3: Normal Account Balances

7–19. Examine the following accounts.

1. _____ Prepaid Taxes
2. _____ Advertising Expense
3. _____ Retained Earnings
4. _____ Depreciation Expense
5. _____ Rent Revenue
6. _____ Automotive Equipment
7. _____ Allowance for Doubtful Accounts
8. _____ Truck Expense
9. _____ Gasoline Expense
10. _____ Common Stock

REQUIRED:
Indicate whether the normal balance of each account is a debit (DR) or credit (CR) in the space provided.

LO 2 & 3: Transaction Analysis

7–20. On May 1, Bill Simon started a computer repair business. Simon opened a bank account for the business by depositing $7,000. He paid two months' rent in advance totaling $400. On May 3, Simon purchased computer repair supplies for $700 and three computers at a total cost of $4,500. Simon hired a student helper, agreeing to pay the helper $1,000 per month of which he paid $500 on May 15 and May 31. On May 25, Simon paid $200 for a newspaper advertisement to announce the opening of the business. Bill earned $3,500 in July of which he collected $2,800 in cash.

REQUIRED:
Prepare journal entries to record these transactions.

LO 2 & 3: Transaction Analysis

7–21. On July 1, Katy Tener began the KT Travel Agency and deposited $10,000 in a company bank account. She paid $500 for one month's rent. On July 5 she purchased office supplies for $700 and three desks at a total cost of $1,500. Katy hired a travel consultant, agreeing to pay her $20 per hour. The consultant worked 100 hours in July which Katy will pay on August 1. Katy paid $100 on July 29 for a newspaper advertisement to announce the opening of the business. Katy booked a cruise for her first customer and received a check from the cruise line for $800 on July 22. On July 31, she borrowed $12,000 from the bank for two years at 9%.

REQUIRED:
Prepare journal entries to record these transactions.

LO 4: Transaction Analysis

7–22. On December 1, Jogina Sisemore, CPA, opened a practice. She contributed $5,000 to a company bank account and paid office rent for three months in advance, totaling $900. On December 2 she purchased a desk for cash of $500 and bought $1,200 worth of office supplies on account. Jogina also borrowed $1,500 from the First State Bank for three years at 6% to purchase computer equipment from a local dealer.

REQUIRED:
Prepare journal entries to record these transactions.

LO 4: Recording Transactions

7–23. The transactions for September, 2008, for Tom Miller's Two Mile High Flight School are as follows:

Sept. 1		Deposited $125,000 in a business bank account from personal funds.
	1	Purchased an airplane for $80,000.
	2	Purchased fuel for the airplane costing $1,500.
	2	Paid $260 for a newspaper advertisement.
	2	Paid rent on an airplane hangar for six months in advance totaling $3,000.
	5	Collected $100 for a new student's first lesson.
	5	Purchased a desk for $200.
	5	Borrowed $10,000 from the bank for two years at 8%.
	6	Purchased office supplies for $450.
	8	Collected $100 for the second lesson of our student.
	12	Withdrew $1,000 for personal living expenses.
	15	Paid the yellow pages advertising bill of $800.
	20	Ordered $1,000 of repair parts for the airplane.
	23	Received the parts ordered on the 20th, paying cash.
	29	Paid the utility bill received for $150.

REQUIRED:
Record each of the above transactions in a general journal.

LO 4: Recording Transactions

7–24. The Ace Termite Company transactions for October, 2008, are as follows:

Oct. 1		Proprietor Helen Laws deposited $35,000 in a business bank account from her personal savings account.
	1	Purchased a truck for $18,000.
	1	Borrowed $8,000 from the bank using the truck as collateral. Interest of 9% will be paid monthly on the first day of each month.
	2	Purchased spraying equipment for the truck costing $3,500 including $400 of chemicals.
	2	Paid $600 for a newspaper advertisement to run each week in October.
	2	Paid rent on an office for six months in advance totaling $6000.
	5	Collected $75 for spraying a new residence .
	5	Purchased a desk for $100 at a garage sale.
	5	Billed a customer $150 for spraying the lawn.
	6	Purchased office supplies for $200.
	8	Collected $100 for a termite inspection.
	9	Collected the $150 from the customer on the 5th.
	12	Withdrew $500 for personal living expenses.
	15	Paid the yellow pages advertising bill of $300.
	20	Ordered $1,000 of chemicals.
	23	Received the chemicals ordered on the 20th with payment due in 10 days.
	28	Collected $2,300 in termite inspections for a loan company and billed an apartment complex $1,200 for spraying 40 units.
	29	Paid the utility bill on the office for $135.

REQUIRED:
Record each of the above transactions in a general journal.

LO 4:   Recording Transactions

7–25. The transactions for December, 2007, for Brad Sanders Auto Repair Shop are as follows:

Dec. 1   Deposited $45,000 in a business bank account from his personal checking account.

1   Purchased a wrecker for $30,000.

1   Borrowed $25,000 at 8% interest from the bank to pay for the wrecker, using it as collateral. Interest is payable monthly on the first day of the month and a semiannual principal payment of $5,000 is due the first day of June and December each year.

2   Purchased shop equipment costing $12,500.

2   Paid $360 for a newspaper advertisement to announce the opening of his business.

2   Paid rent on garage and office for six months in advance totaling $8,100.

5   Signed a contract to perform maintenance service on all auto equipment for a car rental shop.

5   Purchased a desk and chair for $250.

5   Billed a customer $250 for auto repairs.

6   Purchased office supplies for $250.

8   Billed the rental agency $2,500 for work performed.

10   Collected the $250 from the customer on the 5th.

12   Withdrew $500 for personal living expenses.

15   Paid the telephone bill of $300.

21   Paid the local parts distributor $600 for parts used on jobs and ordered $1,300 of parts for inventory.

25   Received the parts ordered on the 21st and paid cash on delivery.

29   Paid the office and shop electric bill of $320.

31   Billed the rental agency $3,600 for services that used $680 of parts.

REQUIRED:
Record each of the above transactions in a general journal.

LO 4:   Posting Transactions

7–26. Refer to problem 7–21.

REQUIRED:
a. Prepare a chart of accounts for the KT Travel Agency.
b. Post the transactions in the general ledger.
c. Prepare a trial balance after completion of the posting process.

LO 4:   Posting Transactions

7–27. Refer to problem 7–22.

REQUIRED:
a. Prepare a chart of accounts for Jogina Sisemore, CPA.
b. Post the transactions to the general ledger.
c. Prepare a trial balance after completion of the posting process.

LO 4: Posting Transactions

7–28. Refer to problem 7–23.

REQUIRED:
a. Prepare a chart of accounts for the Two Mile High Flight School.
b. Post the transactions to the general ledger.
c. Prepare a trial balance after completion of the posting process.

LO 6: Adjusting Entries

7–29. The Arnold Ziffel Company had the following accrual information available at the end of the year 2008.

   a. Unpaid wages to employees were $2,500.
   b. Interest due on a loan to the bank was $1,000.
   c. Sales taxes collected during December and unpaid to the state were $3,000.
   d. A customer owed one year's interest on a note to Ziffel for $4,000.
   e. One of Ziffel's renters failed to pay the December rent of $5,000 because she was out of the country. She will pay this amount when she returns on January 10.

REQUIRED:
Prepare the appropriate general journal entries with explanations to record the above adjustments.

LO 6: Adjusting Entries

7–30. The Pat Haney Corporation had the following information available at the end of the year 2008.

   a. The accountant completed the 2008 depreciation schedule which showed the depreciation expense as $10,520. The Depreciation Expense account has a balance of $8,500.
   b. Commissions for December of $22,000 will be paid to Haney's sales staff on January 5. The Commissions Payable account has a zero balance.
   c. Haney's Accounts Receivable account shows $64,500. After the accountant completed an analysis, he discovered that it should be $68,400. The difference is a sale made on December 31 that was not recorded.
   d. A good customer borrowed $20,000 on July 1 for one year at 12% interest. The principal and interest will be paid on June 30, 2009.
   e. On July 1, Haney paid $14,000 in rent for one year on a temporary warehouse. The accountant recorded this payment as rent expense.

REQUIRED:
Prepare the appropriate general journal entries with explanations to record the above adjustments.

LO 6: Adjusting Entries

7–31. The Buttram Company has the following information available at year end.

a. Wages earned by employee but not paid at year end is $4,000.
b. A two-year insurance policy was paid for on October 1 for $2,000. The Insurance Expense account's balance is $2,000.
c. Service Fee Income earned but not collected at year end is $14,000. Accounts Receivable has a zero balance.
d. Real estate taxes unpaid at year end are $3,900.
e. Interest owed to the bank but not paid at year end is $2,200.

REQUIRED:
Prepare the appropriate general journal entries with explanations to record the above adjustments.

LO 6: Adjusting Entries—Prepaid Items

7–32. The Koch Company's trial balance at June 30, its year end, has the following balances before adjustments.

Unearned Rental Income	$7,200
Prepaid Rent Expense	3,600
Prepaid Insurance	4,200
Supplies Inventory	1,200

a. On May 1, the company paid the rent expense for one year in the amount of $3,600.
b. On April 1, the company collected rental income in advance for the following 24 months in the amount of $14,400.
c. On June 1, the company paid for its business umbrella insurance policy for the next two years in the amount of $4,200.
d. At year end, the physical count of the supplies inventory indicated that $295 of supplies were on hand.

REQUIRED:
Prepare the appropriate adjusting entries with explanations to record the above information.

LO 6: Adjusting Entries—Prepaid Items

7–33. The Earhart Company's trial balance at June 30, its year end, has the following balances before adjustments.

Unearned Rental Income	$14,400
Prepaid Rent	3,600
Insurance Expense	4,800
Supplies Inventory	200

a. On October 1, the company paid the rent expense of $3,600 for one year's rent in advance.
b. On March 1, the company collected rental income of $600 per month in advance, for the following 24 months.
c. On May 1, the company paid for a catastrophe insurance policy for the next two years at a rate of $2,400 per year. This was the only policy in force.
d. On June 30, the physical count of the supplies inventory on hand was $400.

REQUIRED:

Prepare the appropriate adjusting entries with explanations to record the above adjustments.

LO 6: Adjusting Entries—Prepaid Items

7–34. In 2007, the *Fare of the Hearty Cooking* magazine sold 1,000 annual subscriptions to its monthly magazine for $16 each. It also sold 500 two-year subscriptions for $25 each and 250 two-year subscriptions for $32 each.

REQUIRED:

a. Prepare the appropriate adjusting entries with explanations to record the adjustments necessary at the end of years 1 and 2 if the subscriptions were all sold at the beginning of 2007 and were originally recorded as income.

b. Prepare the appropriate adjusting entries with explanations to record the adjustments necessary at the end of years 1 and 2 if the subscriptions were all sold at the beginning of 2007 and were originally recorded as a liability.

LO 6: Adjusting Entries—Depreciation

7–35. At the beginning of the year the Smeltzer Company purchased a copy machine for $2,000. The firm believed the machine would have an estimated useful life of six years and a salvage value of $200. The firm also purchased a delivery van costing $28,000 with an estimated useful life of four years and a salvage value of $4,000. The company decided to use straight-line depreciation for both assets.

REQUIRED:

a. Prepare the appropriate adjusting entries with explanations to record the depreciation expense at the end of year 1.

b. Prepare the appropriate adjusting entries with explanations to record the depreciation adjustment at the end of year 1 if the Accumulated Depreciation account had a balance of $4,500 at the end of year 1 and these were the only depreciable assets the company owned.

LO 6: Adjusting Entries—Depreciation

7–36. At the beginning of the year the Walsh Company purchased a copy machine for $3,000. The firm believed the machine would have an estimated useful life of four years and a salvage value of $200. The firm also purchased a tractor costing $56,000 with an estimated useful life of six years and a salvage value of $2,000. The company decided to use straight-line depreciation for both assets.

REQUIRED:

a. Prepare the appropriate adjusting entries with explanations to record the depreciation adjustment at the end of year 1 assuming that the company recorded no depreciation in the first year.

b. Prepare the appropriate adjusting entries with explanations to record the depreciation adjustment at the end of year 1 if the Accumulated Depreciation account has a balance of $10,800 and these are the only depreciable assets the company owns.

LO 6: Adjusting Entries—Depreciation

7–37. At the start of the year the Marshall Corporation purchased a piece of equipment for $36,000. The firm believed the machine would have an estimated useful life of five years and a salvage value of $6,000. The firm also purchased a building costing $200,000 with an estimated useful life of 40 years and no residual value. The company uses straight-line depreciation.

REQUIRED:

a. Prepare the appropriate adjusting entries with explanations to record the depreciation adjustment at the end of year 1 if the company did not record any depreciation.

b. Prepare the appropriate adjusting entries with explanations to record the depreciation adjustment at the end of year 1 assuming that the Accumulated Depreciation account had a balance of $30,000 and these are the only depreciable assets the company owns.

LO 6: Adjusting Entries

7–38. At the beginning of the year the Lynn Hughes Company purchased a computer for $3,000. The firm believed the computer would last four years with a residual value of $200. The firm also purchased a truck costing $56,000 with an estimated useful life of four years and a salvage value of $6,000. The company uses straight-line depreciation for both assets. At year end, the general ledger contains the following accounts and balances:

Office Equipment	$ 2,800 Debit
Accumulated Depreciation	200 Debit
Automotive Equipment	56,000 Debit
Accumulated Depreciation	14,000 Credit
Depreciation Expense	14,000 Debit

REQUIRED:

Prepare the appropriate adjusting entries with explanations to record the depreciation adjustment at the end of year 1.

LO 6: Adjustments from Trial Balance Accounts with Supplemental Information

7–39. The following is a partial trial balance for the Denton Company as of December 31, 2008.

THE DENTON COMPANY
Partial Trial Balance
December 31, 2008

	Debit	Credit
Prepaid Insurance	$12,000	
Prepaid Rent Expense	18,000	
Interest Receivable	-0-	
Wages Payable		$10,000
Unearned Fee Income		36,000
Interest Income		12,000

Additional information includes the following:

    a. The insurance policy indicates that on December 31, 2008, seven months remain on the 24-month policy that originally cost $18,000.

    b. Denton has a note receivable with $2,500 of interest due and payable on January 1, 2009.

    c. The books show that two-thirds of the fees paid in advance by a customer on June 30 have now been earned.

    d. The company prepaid rent for nine months on July 1 at the rate of $2,000 per month.

    e. The wages payable on December 31 were $7,000. The amount in the Wages Payable account is from December 31, 2007.

REQUIRED:

Record in proper general journal form, the adjustments required by the above information.

LO 6: Adjustments from Trial Balance Accounts with Supplemental Information

    7–40. The following is a partial trial balance for the Reese Company as of December 31, 2008.

THE REESE COMPANY
Partial Trial Balance
December 31, 2008

	Debit	Credit
Prepaid Insurance	$ 6,000	
Prepaid Rent Expense	10,000	
Wages Expense	25,000	
Subscription Income		$72,000
Interest Expense	38,000	

Additional information includes the following:

    a. The company paid a $7,200 premium on a three-year business insurance policy on July 1, 2007.

    b. Reese borrowed $200,000 on January 2 and must pay 12% interest on January 2, 2009, for the entire year of 2008.

    c. The books show that $60,000 of subscriptions have now been earned and the balance is a liability.

    d. The company prepaid 10 months' rent in advance on November 1, 2008, to take advantage of a special discount that reduced the rent to $1,000 per month.

    e. Wages for December 31 of $3,000 will be paid to employees on January 6, 2009.

REQUIRED:

Record in proper general journal form, the adjustments required by the above information.

LO 6: Adjustments from Trial Balance Accounts with Supplemental Information

    7–41. The following is a partial trial balance for the Marr Company as of December 31, 2008.

THE MARR COMPANY
Partial Trial Balance
December 31, 2008

	Debit	Credit
Office Supply Expense	$ 36,000	
Merchandise Inventory	63,000	
Office Supply Inventory	400	
Wages Payable	41,500	
Wage Expense	4,000	

Additional information includes the following:

a. Office supplies on hand at year end were $1,230.
b. The ending merchandise inventory was $61,350.
c. The total payroll cost for the year 2008 was $50,000. At the end of last year, the company owed employees $4,000 for December wages and at December 31, 2008, the company owes employees $4,500 for December wages.

REQUIRED:

Record in proper general journal form, the adjustments required by the above information.

LO 6: Bank Reconciliation

7–42. The Fretz Company showed a cash balance of $2,517 on November 30, 2007. The company received the bank statement for November 2007 that showed a balance of $2,750. The other differences that appear between the company's book balance of cash and the bank statement include:

a. A deposit of $500 that was made on November 30 was not included in the bank statement.
b. Outstanding checks on November 30 were $1,280.
c. Bank service charges imposed by the bank were $35.
d. The bank included a debit memo for an NSF (nonsufficient funds) check totaling $512.

REQUIRED:

a. Prepare a bank reconciliation for the Fretz Company of November 30, 2007.
b. Prepare the general journal entries necessary to adjust the accounts.

LO 6: Bank Reconciliation

7–43. The Coyote Company received the bank statement for October 2007. The following information is available for the bank reconciliation of October 31, 2007:

Balance per general ledger	$7,500
Balance per bank statement	8,250
NSF check from customer returned by the bank	1,000
Outstanding checks total	2,365
Deposits in transit	1,800
Bank charges	60
Credit memo for collection from customer of amount owed on a note	1,245

REQUIRED:

a. Prepare a bank reconciliation for the Coyote Company of October 31, 2007.
b. Prepare the general journal entries necessary to adjust the accounts.

LO 6:   Bank Reconciliation

7–44. The Godfrey Company received the bank statement for December 2007. The company showed a cash balance of $1,838 on December 31, 2007, but the bank statement showed a balance of $3,500. The other differences that appear between the company's book balance of cash and the bank statement include:

1. A deposit of $300 that was made on December 31 was not included in the bank statement.
2. Outstanding checks on December 31 were $1,280.
3. Bank service charges imposed by the bank were $28.
4. The bank included a debit memo for credit card discounts totaling $690.
5. Included in the bank statement was a credit memo for $1,400 for the collection of an outstanding account owed by a customer.

REQUIRED:

a. Prepare a bank reconciliation for the Godfrey Company of December 31, 2007.
b. Prepare the general journal entries necessary to adjust the accounts.

LO 6 & 7:   Adjustments and the Impact on Financial Statements

7–45. The Wallberg Company has the following account balances at the end of the year:

Prepaid Insurance	$6,000
Rental Income	4,800
Wages Expense	7,660
Taxes Payable	4,398
Interest Income	2,325

The company also has the following information available at the end of the year:
1. $4,000 of the prepaid insurance has now expired.
2. $2,200 of the rental income has not yet been earned.
3. The company must accrue an additional $1,500 of wages expense.
4. The Taxes Payable account is overstated by $398.
5. The company has earned an additional $500 of interest income.

REQUIRED:

a. Prepare the journal entries necessary to adjust the accounts.
b. Use T-accounts to compute and present both the income statement and balance sheet account balances after the adjustments have been prepared.

LO 6 & 7:   Adjustments and the Impact on Financial Statements

7–46. The Mary McHaffie Company has the following account balances at the end of the year:

Insurance Expense	$4,000
Unearned Rental Income	3,800
Wages Payable	5,550
Taxes Expense	4,398
Depreciation Expense	7,625

The company also has the following information available at the end of the year:

1. $1,000 of the Insurance Expense has not yet expired.
2. $1,600 of the Unearned Rental Income has now been earned.
3. The company currently owes employees $1,200 of wages.
4. The company owes an additional $4,900 in real estate taxes.
5. Depreciation expense for the year is a total of $8,743.

REQUIRED:
a. Prepare the journal entries necessary to adjust the accounts.
b. Use T-accounts to compute and present both the income statement and balance sheet account balances after the adjustments have been prepared.

LO 6 & 7:   Adjustments and the Impact on Financial Statements

7–47. The Hale Company has the following account balances at the end of the year:

Insurance Expense	$5,400
Unearned Fee Income	3,525
Wages Payable	3,000
Advertising Expense	9,500
Depreciation Expense	3,850

The company also has the following information available at the end of the year:

1. $3,200 of the Insurance Expense has not yet expired.
2. $1,200 of the Unearned Fee Income was earned in the last month of the year.
3. The company must accrue an additional $1,800 of wages expense.
4. The company paid $1,900 for advertisements that will be shown next month.
5. Depreciation expense for the year is a total of $8,625.

REQUIRED:
a. Prepare the journal entries necessary to adjust the accounts.
b. Use T-accounts to compute and present both the income statement and balance sheet account balances after the adjustments have been prepared.

LO 6 & 7:   Adjustments and the Impact on Financial Statements

7–48. The Watson Company has the following account balances at the end of the year:

Supplies Expense	$2,000
Supplies on Hand	230
Unearned Subscription Income	3,758
Prepaid Rent Expense	4,950
Taxes Expense	1,259
Accumulated Depreciation	8,964

The company also has the following information available at the end of the year.

1. $500 of the supplies are still on hand.
2. $1,785 of the Unearned Subscription Income has now been earned.
3. Two months of rent at $850 per month is still prepaid.
4. The Taxes Expense account is overstated by $189.
5. Depreciation expense for the year is a total of $12,326.

REQUIRED:
a. Prepare the general journal entries necessary to adjust the accounts.
b. Use T-accounts to compute and present both the income statement and balance sheet account balances after the adjustments have been prepared.

Comprehensive

7–49. The Alco Home Improvement Center began operations on November 1, 2007. Transactions for the month of November are as follows:

Nov. 1   Herb Alco invested $45,000 in his new venture.
     5   Alco signed a lease on a store and paid six months' rent in advance of $9,450.
     6   Purchased $500 of office supplies from Mott's Office Supply on account.
     8   Purchased $25,000 merchandise for resale from Associated Supply on account.
    10   Paid $100 for the freight bill on the November 8 purchase.
    11   Paid $175 for a radio ad to announce the store opening.
    12   Borrowed $5,000 from First National Bank. Signed a 9%, 90-day note with interest payable on the last day of each month.
    14   Sold merchandise for cash of $4,000 that cost $2,400.
    15   Sold $2,500 merchandise that cost $1,750 on a 30-day account to J. Adams.
    16   Paid freight on sale to Adams of $75.
    17   Sold $3,000 merchandise that cost $1,950 on a 30-day account to A. Bear.
    19   Purchased $19,000 merchandise from the Rider Company on account.
    20   Made cash sales of $20,000 that cost $13,200.
    21   Paid Mott's Office Supply.
    23   Paid Associated Supply for the purchase on the 8th.
    24   Collected payment in full from A. Bear.
    25   Paid Rider Company for the purchase on the 19th.
    25   Received payment in full from J. Adams.
    26   Purchased a forklift to move merchandise for $5,000 cash.
    28   Paid utilities for the month of $800.
    29   Paid wages for the month of $4,000.
    30   Alco withdrew $1,000 for personal living expenses.

REQUIRED:
a. Journalize the transactions for the month of November in the general journal.
b. Open the necessary accounts in the general ledger and post the November transactions to the appropriate accounts in the general ledger.
c. Prepare a trial balance on November 30, 2007.
d. Prepare adjusting entries and complete a worksheet using the following information in addition to that listed in the transactions:

1. Alco depreciated the forklift for the entire month of November, assuming straight-line depreciation with no residual value and a five-year estimated life.
2. Alco accrued the interest on the bank loan for 18 days.
3. Alco incurred payroll tax expense of $900 for the month.

e. Prepare a balance sheet as of November 30, 2007, and a statement of income and a statement of owner's equity for the month ended November 30, 2007.

Comprehensive

7–50. The Baer Distributing Company began operations on December 1, 2007. Transactions for the month of December are as follows:

Dec. 1 Max Baer invested $75,000 in his new venture.
    2 Baer signed a lease on a warehouse and paid six months' rent in advance of $6,000.
    5 Purchased $1,500 of office supplies from Mardel Office Supply on account.
    7 Purchased $15,000 of merchandise for resale from Agape Supply on account.
    9 Paid $200 to the carrier for the freight bill on the December 7 purchase.
    11 Paid the Time Express newspaper $350 for an ad to announce the grand opening of the distribution center.
    11 Borrowed $10,000 from First National Bank. Signed a 10%, 180-day note.
    13 Sold merchandise for cash of $8,200 that cost $6,300.
    14 Sold $5,000 merchandise on account to J. Adair that cost $3,725.
    15 Paid freight on sale to Adair of $175.
    16 Sold $4,000 merchandise on account to J. Bronson that cost $3,050.
    17 Purchased $20,000 merchandise from the Lowe Company on account.
    19 Made cash sales of $10,000 that cost $7,950.
    21 Paid Mardel Office Supply.
    22 Paid Agape Supply for the purchase on the 5th.
    24 Collected payment in full from J. Adair.
    26 Paid Lowe Company for the purchase of the 17th.
    27 Received payment in full from Bronson.
    30 Purchased a used truck to deliver merchandise for $14,000 cash.
    30 Paid utilities for the month of $1,800.
    31 Paid wages for the month of $7,000.
    31 Baer withdrew $1,800 for personal living expenses.

REQUIRED:
a. Journalize the transactions for the month of December in the general journal.
b. Open the necessary accounts in the general ledger and post the December transactions to the appropriate accounts in the general ledger.
c. Prepare a trial balance at December 31, 2007.
d. Prepare adjusting entries and complete a worksheet using the following information in addition to that included in the transactions:

1. Baer depreciated the truck for the entire month of December, assuming straight-line depreciation with no residual value and a 3-year estimated life.
2. Baer accrued the interest on the bank loan for 18 days.
3. Baer incurred payroll tax expense of $1,900 for the month.

e. Prepare a balance sheet as of December 31, 2007, and a statement of income and a statement of owner's equity for the month ended December 31, 2007.

ACCOUNTING CYCLE CASES

These problems contain some concepts covered in Chapters 8, 9, and 10 and the appendices to those chapters.

Sole Proprietorship

7–51. John Robles began his retail clothing business, Fineries, on November 1, 2007, as a sole proprietor. The post-closing trial balance at November 30, 2007, appeared as follows:

FINERIES
Post-Closing Trial Balance
November 30, 2007

	Debits	Credits
Cash	$40,000	
Prepaid Rent	200	
Merchandise Inventory	24,000	
Fixtures	6,000	
Accumulated Depreciation		$ 1,000
Wages Payable		1,500
Robles, Capital		67,700
Totals	$70,200	$70,200

The following transactions occurred in the month of December, 2007.

Dec. 1 Robles invested an additional $100,000 cash in his venture.

    1 Bought store fixtures on account from the Acme Company for $13,600, terms n/30.

    1 Paid six months' rent in advance, $12,000.

    5 Purchased $8,000 of merchandise on account from Triad Company. The invoice date was December 5, terms 2/10, n/60.

    7 Paid for a 36-month contents policy for fire damage at a cost of $1,440.

    8 Purchased merchandise for resale for $25,000 cash.

    9 Returned damaged merchandise to Triad Company and received credit for $1,600.

    10 Sold merchandise to Jean Peoples on account for $12,600. The terms of the sale were 1/10, n/30.

    12 Paid the balance due to Triad Company.

    15 Cash sales for the first half of the month totaled $27,500.

    16 Sold merchandise to Janeal Foster on account for $10,000. The terms of the sale were 1/10, n/30.

    16 Paid wages for the first half of the month totaling $5,500, including the balance due from November.

    18 Purchased merchandise on account from Kerr Company for $9,500. The invoice date was December 20, and the terms were 2/10, n/30.

    20 Purchased office supplies totaling $250.

    22 Received merchandise returned by Janeal Foster. Issued a credit memo for $1,500.

    22 Received a check from Jean Peoples for her invoice less discount.

    25 Received a check from Janeal Foster for payment of invoice less discount.

    28 Sold merchandise on account to Paul Larsen, $8,600. The terms were 1/10, n/30.

    28 Paid utility bill of $300 for December.

28 Received telephone bill for $100 for the month of December.
28 Paid Kerr Company for the invoice of December 18, less discount.
31 Recorded cash sales for the second half of December totaling $44,900.
31 Paid wages for the second half of December, $4,500.
31 Received a bill for delivery services for December, $250.

REQUIRED:

a. Journalize the transactions for the month of December in the general journal.
b. Open the necessary accounts in the general ledger and post the December transactions to the general ledger.
c. Prepare a trial balance at December 31, 2007.
d. Prepare adjusting entries and complete a worksheet using the following information and that found in the transactions:

1. Robles accrued payroll tax expense of $1,200 for the month.
2. Store fixtures had a six-year life and no salvage value.
3. Ending inventory balance was $14,000.

e. Prepare a balance sheet as of December 31, 2007, a statement of income, and a statement of owner's equity for the month ended December 31, 2007.

Corporation

25pts. Feb. 26th *Due*

7–52. Jay Chambless started a retail hardware store, Chambless Home Haven, Inc., on December 1, 2008. The following transactions occurred in the month of December:

Dec. 1 Chambless invested $200,000 cash to purchase 100,000 shares of common stock of Chambless Home Haven, Inc. The stock had a par value of $1 per share, and there were 200,000 shares authorized.
1 Bought store fixtures on account from the Ace Company for $22,000, terms n/30.
1 Paid three months' rent in advance, $9,000.
5 Purchased merchandise on account from Taylor Company for $50,000. The invoice date was December 5, terms 2/10, n/30.
7 Paid for a 12-month contents policy for fire damage at a cost of $1,200.
8 Purchased merchandise for resale for $30,000 cash.
9 Returned damaged merchandise to Taylor Company and received credit for $16,000.
10 Sold merchandise to A.V. Hill on account, $24,000. The terms were 1/10, n/30.
12 Paid the balance due to Taylor Company.
15 Cash sales for the first half of the month totaled $30,000.
16 Sold merchandise to Mel Hays on account $5,000. The terms were 1/10, n/30.
16 Paid wages for the first half of the month totaling $7,000.
18 Purchased merchandise on account from McGee Company for $18,000. The invoice date was December 20, terms 2/10, n/30.
20 Purchased office supplies for cash of $400.
22 Received merchandise returned by Mel Hays. Issued a credit memo for $700.
22 Received a check from A.V. Hill for invoice less discount.
25 Received a check from Mel Hays for payment of invoice less discount.

28 Sold merchandise on account to Dennis Rhodes for $12,600, terms 1/10, n/30.

28 Paid utility bill of $600 for December.

28 Received telephone bill for $200 for the month of December due on January 12.

28 Paid McGee Company for the invoice of December 18, less discount.

31 Recorded cash sales for the second half of December totaling $35,200.

31 Paid wages for the second half of December, $7,500.

31 Received a bill for delivery services for December for $400 due January 10.

31 Chambless declared and paid a $.10 per share cash dividend.

REQUIRED:

a. Journalize the transactions for the month of December in the general journal.

b. Open the necessary accounts in the general ledger and post the December transactions to the appropriate accounts.

c. Prepare a trial balance at December 31, 2008.

d. Prepare adjusting entries and complete a worksheet using the following information:

1. Chambless accrued payroll tax expense of $2,000 for the month.
2. Fixtures are depreciated using the straight-line method over four years and no salvage value.
3. Ending inventory balance is $15,000.
4. The combined corporate tax rate is 40%.

e. Prepare a balance sheet as of December 31, 2008, a statement of income, and a statement of retained earnings for the month ended December 31, 2008.

f. Assume that Chambless selects a calendar year. Prepare the closing entries to close the year.

g. Prepare a post-closing trial balance at December 31, 2008.

Partnership

7-53. The Blues Brothers began a management consulting business on October 1, 2008, called Blues Brothers Consulting. The following transactions occurred in the month of October.

2008

Oct. 1 John Blue invested $6,000 in the partnership for a 60% interest in the business and his brother Art invested $4,000 for a 40% interest in the business.

1 Purchased a computer for $3,000 and a copy machine for $2,000. Each piece of equipment had an expected life of five years with no residual value. The computer was financed with a three-year, 10% interest bank loan that calls for monthly interest payments and annual principal payments on September 30 each year of $1,000.

1 Paid three months' rent in advance, $3,000.

5 Purchased office supplies on account from Spring Company for $700. The invoice date was October 5, terms 2/10, n/30.

6 Paid for a one-year contents policy for fire damage at a cost of $600.

7 Returned damaged merchandise to Spring Company and received credit for $100.

10 Performed consulting services and billed Sam Hall on account, $14,000. The terms were 1/10, n/30.

11 Received $4,000 for cash consulting services performed.

15 Paid for the office supplies purchased from Spring Company on the 5th.

15 Received $2,000 cash for consulting services performed.

15 Billed Gary Suter $5,000 for consulting fees, terms 2/10, n/30.

16 Paid secretary wages for the first half of the month totaling $1,000.

19 Purchased computer supplies on account from Dale Company, $400. The invoice date was October 19, terms 2/10, n/30.

20 Purchased office supplies for cash totaling $400.

20 Received payment from Sam Hall.

25 Received a check from Gary Suter for payment of invoice less discount.

28 Provided services on account to Dan Lee for $1,600. The terms were 1/10, n/30.

28 Paid utility bill of $300 for October.

28 Received telephone bill for $250 for the month of October.

28 Paid Dale Company for the invoice of October 19, less discount.

31 Paid wages for the second half of October, $1,500.

31 Received a bill for fax services for October, $100.

31 John withdrew $1,500 for personal expenses and Art withdrew $1,200.

REQUIRED:

a. Journalize the transactions for the month of October in the general journal.

b. Open the necessary accounts in the general ledger and post the October transactions to the appropriate accounts.

c. Prepare a trial balance at October 31, 2008.

d. Prepare adjusting entries and complete a worksheet using the following information and that listed in the transactions:

   1. Accrued payroll tax expense is $300 for the month.
   2. Office supplies of $100 were on hand at October 31.
   3. There were no computer supplies left at year end.
   4. The partnership agreement indicates that the partners share profits and losses equally.

e. Prepare a balance sheet as of October 31, 2008, a statement of income, and a statement of partners' capital for the month ended October 31, 2008.

f. Assume that the Blues Brothers selected October 31 as the year end. Prepare and post the closing entries to close the year.

g. Prepare a post-closing trial balance at October 31, 2008.

Chapter 8

Challenging Issues under Accrual Accounting: Long-Lived Depreciable Assets—A Closer Look

While working your way through college, you spent over two years in a campus copy shop. After learning the business from every angle, you have the opportunity to purchase the shop from Connie, the retiring owner. She recently replaced all the equipment and has maintained it well. Your accountant suggests that you use as rapid a depreciation method as possible. Not wanting to sound ignorant, you let the comment pass. Later, your friend Jon, an accounting major, explained some of the concepts to you but asks you to consider some additional issues. He wants to know how rapidly the technology changes in copiers, how many copies each machine can run economically before it begins to break down, and how many copies the shop runs each year. You vow to find the answers to these questions, but still do not understand all the implications of his issues. What do these issues have to do with the profitability of the copy shop?

Because accrual accounting recognizes revenues in the periods in which they were earned, and it tries to record expenses in the same periods as the revenues they helped earn, it requires more judgment and estimation than cash accounting. One of the best examples of the effects of estimates in accrual accounting is the depreciation of long-lived assets.

In this chapter, we extend our discussion of depreciation by considering several issues that further complicate the depreciation process. First, we consider the impacts of management's estimates of an asset's useful life and its residual value. Second, we examine the effects of management's selection of different depreciation methods. Third, we look at the effects of disposing of assets and how such transactions create a gain or loss. ■

After completing your work on this chapter, you should be able to do the following:

1. Explain the process of depreciating long-lived assets as it pertains to accrual accounting.
2. Determine depreciation expense amounts using both straight-line and double-declining-balance depreciation methods.
3. Describe in your own words the effects on the income statement and balance sheet of using different methods of depreciation.
4. Compare gains and losses to revenues and expenses.
5. Calculate a gain or loss on the disposal of a long-lived depreciable asset.
6. Explain the effects on a company's financial statements when management disposes of a depreciable asset.
7. Draw appropriate conclusions when presented with gains or losses on an income statement.
*8. Complete the recording process for long-lived assets and depreciation.

DEPRECIATION

As you recall from our discussion in Chapter 6, depreciation is defined as a systematic and reasoned allocation of the cost of a long-lived asset. Over time, the depreciation process transfers the historical cost of the asset from the balance sheet to depreciation expense on the income statement, to more closely match the expenses with the revenues they help produce. We measure **historical cost** as the total costs to bring an asset to a usable state. This includes the invoice price, applicable sales tax, installation costs, cost of insurance while in transit, shipping costs, and cost of training personnel to use the machine. It does not include repairs and maintenance or insurance once the asset becomes productive.

historical cost Total of all costs required to bring an asset to a productive state.

When a firm purchases **tangible property** to be used to produce revenues in more than one income statement period, it recognizes the item as a balance sheet asset that will produce future benefits to the company. Under the matching principle, the company allocates part of the cost of that asset to the period in which it produces revenues through depreciation expense on the income statement. Just how much it recognizes as expense in a given year depends on several factors, including the estimates of useful life and residual value made and the depreciation method used.

tangible property Property used in a business such as buildings, equipment, machinery, furniture, and fixtures.

The Effect of Estimates

Estimates of the length of the asset's useful life and the amount of its residual value directly affect the amount of depreciation expense recognized each year. For example, assume McMillan & Cox, a consulting firm, purchases a new computer network for $40,000. If management estimates that the computer system has a residual value of $4,000, the asset has a depreciable base of $36,000 (cost less residual value). The amount of depreciation expense recognized each year will be different

Exhibit 8–1
McMillan & Cox's New $40,000 Computer Network

Option	Details	Depreciable Base	Annual Expense
Decision 1	Residual value: $4,000 Useful life: 4 years	$36,000	$9,000
Decision 2	Residual value: $4,000 Useful life: 5 years	$36,000	$7,200
Decision 3	Residual value: $2,000 Useful life: 4 years	$38,000	$9,500
Decision 4	Residual value: $2,000 Useful life: 5 years	$38,000	$7,600

if the useful life is estimated to be four years rather than three or five years. By the same token, the depreciable base will be different if the residual value is estimated to be $2,000 rather than $4,000. Exhibit 8–1 shows how different depreciable bases result in different amounts of depreciation expense being recognized each year of the useful life of the machine.

Discussion Questions

8-1. What factors do you think a company should consider in determining the estimated useful life of a long-lived asset?

8-2. How do you think a company would go about determining the estimated residual value of a long-lived asset?

8-3. Consider a long-lived asset with a cost of $30,000. How would net income be affected by using an estimated useful life of six years and an estimated residual value of $6,000 rather than a four-year estimated useful life and a residual value of $5,000? Explain.

The Effect of Different Depreciation Methods

double-declining-balance method An accelerated depreciation method in which depreciation expense is twice the straight-line percentage multiplied by the book value of the asset.

accelerated depreciation methods Those methods that record more depreciation expense in the early years of an asset's life and less in the later years.

Most companies have more than one depreciable asset, and many firms use more than one depreciation method. As users of the financial accounting information provided by these companies, you should understand the impact of depreciation method choice on financial statements. To illustrate these effects, we will explore in detail the two most commonly used depreciation methods—straight-line depreciation and **double-declining-balance depreciation.**

Most companies use straight-line depreciation for financial statement reporting. Straight-line depreciation methods offer an equal amount of cost allocation every year over the life of the asset. Other methods, collectively called **accelerated depreciation methods,** record a large amount of depreciation expense in the early years of an asset's life and reduce that amount each year. In addition, the Internal Revenue Service requires that businesses use a prescribed depreciation method called the **Modified Accelerated Cost Recovery**

Exhibit 8-2
Straight-Line
Depreciation versus
Accelerated
Depreciation

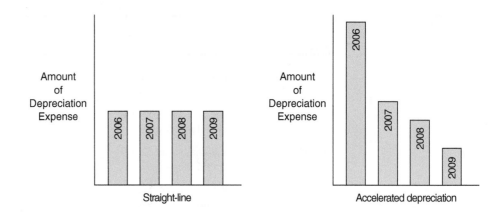

Modified Accelerated Cost Recovery System (MACRS) Depreciation method taxpayers use to calculate depreciation expense for tax purposes.

System (MACRS) for tax purposes. MACRS does not conform to GAAP, which therefore requires companies to use two different methods—one for tax purposes and another for financial statement purposes. As the name implies, MACRS is an accelerated depreciation method.

How do companies make the choice between using straight-line depreciation and an accelerated depreciation method? Recall that the matching principle requires us to match expenses with the revenues they help produce. Theoretically, we should use straight-line depreciation for an asset that produces the same amount of revenue in each period of its useful life, and, conversely, an accelerated depreciation method for an asset that produces more revenue in the early years and less as time goes by. However, the choice of depreciation method is more likely to be made on more practical grounds.

When considering the cost/benefit constraint, firms often select straight-line depreciation because it is easy to implement. Another reason is the anticipated effect on the financial statements during the asset's useful life. Exhibit 8-2 contrasts depreciation expense recorded under the straight-line method to the amount recorded if an accelerated method is used. As we explore the consequences of depreciation method choice, you can see the significant impact this decision can have on the accounting information offered to economic decision makers.

To illustrate that impact, we will contrast the results of straight-line depreciation with those of an accelerated depreciation method—the double-declining-balance method, which is the most widely used of the accelerated methods. We will explore the application of this method not simply so you can learn how to use it, but more importantly to demonstrate the impact of the choice of depreciation method on depreciation expense (and therefore on reported net income).

Straight-Line Depreciation

In Chapter 6, we introduced the concept of depreciation with an example of the straight-line method. To review how straight-line depreciation is calculated, assume Beavers Corporation purchased a milling machine on January 2, 2007, for a total price of $300,000. Beavers' management estimates the useful life of this machine to be five years, at the end of which the machine can be sold for an estimated $25,000. For simplicity, we will assume that Beavers owns only this machine.

We compute Beavers' yearly depreciation expense as $55,000:

Cost	$300,000
Less: Residual Value	25,000
Depreciable Base	$275,000
Divided by Useful Life	5
Annual Depreciation	$ 55,000

Exhibit 8–3
Book Value Using Production Method Straight-Line Depreciation

	Book Value Beginning of Year	Current Year's Production	Per Unit Depreciation	Current Year's Depreciation	Book Value End of Year
2007	$300,000	25,000	$2.75	$ 68,750	$231,250
2008	231,250	25,000	2.75	68,750	162,500
2009	162,500	20,000	2.75	55,000	107,500
2010	107,500	20,000	2.75	55,000	52,500
2011	52,500	10,000	2.75	27,500	25,000
Total		100,000		$275,000	

We could also decide that the life of this milling machine might be better measured by the number of units it could produce over its useful life. Instead of time as the straight-line measure, we could use units of production. If the milling machine can produce 100,000 units of hardware, we might measure its depreciation in units of product. This type of straight-line depreciation is called the **production depreciation method.** The production depreciation method is appropriate for many types of assets when the useful life is based not on time passing, but on the amount of usage. For these assets, the quantity used has more to do with length of life and residual value than the passage of time. In our example of the milling machine, if we measured depreciation in terms of units produced, we would calculate it in this manner:

production depreciation method A straight-line depreciation method that uses production activity as the base to assign depreciation expense.

Estimated units of production 100,000 units
Cost per thousand units = Depreciable base/Units
= $275,000/100,000 units
= $2.75 per unit printed

If Beavers produces 25,000 units the first year, we recognize $68,750 in depreciation expense. See Exhibit 8–3 for a breakdown of the depreciation over the life of the asset. Notice the difference in depreciation expense in each year is based upon the difference in production from one year to the next.

Discussion Questions

8-4. How would you set the units of production for the following types of assets?

  a. Long-distance truck
  b. Commercial airliner
  c. Milling machine
  d. Cruise ship

8-5. Name five assets that would best be depreciated by the passage of time.

Return to our regular straight-line example based on time. In each of the five years of the asset's useful life, we will transfer $55,000 of the original asset cost from the asset balance on the balance sheet to depreciation expense on the income statement. To see this point, locate Beavers Corporation's income statements and balance sheets for the years 2007 through 2011 in Exhibit 8–4. For ease of interpretation, we held constant most of the items not affected by the depreciation process applied to the machine.

Exhibit 8–4

Beavers Corporation's Financial Statements Using Straight-Line Depreciation

Income Statements

For the Years Ended December 31,	2007	2008	2009	2010	2011
Sales	$755,000	$755,000	$755,000	$755,000	$755,000
Cost of Goods Sold	422,000	422,000	422,000	422,000	422,000
Gross Margin	$333,000	$333,000	$333,000	$333,000	$333,000
Operating Expenses Other Than Depreciation	(236,000)	(236,000)	(236,000)	(236,000)	(236,000)
Depreciation Expense	(55,000)	(55,000)	(55,000)	(55,000)	(55,000)
Net Income	$ 42,000	$ 42,000	$ 42,000	$ 42,000	$ 42,000

Balance Sheets

December 31,	2007	2008	2009	2010	2011
ASSETS:					
Cash	$ 50,000	$ 96,000	$157,000	$213,000	$289,000
Accounts Receivable	206,000	257,000	293,000	334,000	355,000
Inventory	77,000	77,000	77,000	77,000	77,000
Machine	300,000	300,000	300,000	300,000	300,000
LESS: Accumulated Depreciation	(55,000)	(110,000)	(165,000)	(220,000)	(275,000)
Total Assets	$578,000	$620,000	$662,000	$704,000	$746,000
LIABILITIES AND STOCKHOLDERS' EQUITY:					
Accounts Payable	$206,000	$206,000	$206,000	$206,000	$206,000
Notes Payable	170,000	170,000	170,000	170,000	170,000
Common Stock	100,000	100,000	100,000	100,000	100,000
Additional Paid-in Capital	10,000	10,000	10,000	10,000	10,000
Retained Earnings	92,000	134,000	176,000	218,000	260,000
Total Liabilities and Stockholders' Equity	$578,000	$620,000	$662,000	$704,000	$746,000

Note that regardless of what else happened in Beavers' operations for the years 2007 through 2011, the amount of depreciation expense each year did not change. This constant depreciation expense is one of the main characteristics of straight-line depreciation. You should also note the direct correlation between the yearly depreciation expense shown on the income statements and the book value of the machine on the balance sheets. Recall from Chapter 6 that book value is the cost of a long-lived asset less all the depreciation expense recognized since the asset was placed in service (Exhibit 8–5). The total depreciation expense recognized since the asset was put in service is reflected in the balance of accumulated depreciation. Therefore,

$$\text{Book Value} = \text{Cost} - \text{Accumulated Depreciation}$$

Each year, as $55,000 of depreciation expense is recognized, the balance in accumulated depreciation increases by that amount, reducing the book value of the machine by that same $55,000. This example illustrates that straight-line depreciation causes the book value of assets to decline by the same amount each year. The book value at the end of 2011 is $25,000 ($300,000 – $275,000), which is equal to the

Exhibit 8–5
Book Value Using
Straight-Line
Depreciation

	Book Value Beginning of Year	Current Year's Depreciation	Book Value End of Year
2007	$300,000	$ 55,000	$245,000
2008	245,000	55,000	190,000
2009	190,000	55,000	135,000
2010	135,000	55,000	80,000
2011	80,000	55,000	25,000
Total Depreciation		$275,000	

estimated residual value. A total of $275,000 depreciation expense has been recorded, which is the amount of the depreciable base, and is therefore the maximum amount of allowable depreciation expense. At this point, the asset is considered to be fully depreciated.

Discussion Question

8-6. Refer back to Exhibit 8–1, which illustrates McMillan & Cox's four possible sets of estimates relating to its new copy machine. For each decision setting, determine the book value of the asset after three years of depreciation have been recorded.

Obviously, a different estimated useful life or a different estimated residual value would change the amount of yearly depreciation expense. So, too, would the selection of a different method of calculating yearly depreciation expense. To demonstrate how the choice of depreciation method can affect depreciation expense, we explore the most widely used accelerated depreciation method.

Double-Declining-Balance Depreciation

The double-declining-balance method received its name because it calculates depreciation expense at twice the straight-line rate, and it applies the doubled rate to its book value at the beginning of each period.

These are the simple steps to calculating double-declining-balance method each year:

1. Figure the straight-line rate in percentages.
   (100%/N, where N = number of years in the asset's useful life)
2. Double the straight-line percentage.
3. Multiply the doubled percentage by the asset's book value.

As an example, apply this method to Beavers' milling machine for the first year. These steps follow the previous directions:

1. Figure the straight-line percentage.   **100%/5 = 20% (per year)**
2. Double the straight-line percentage.   **20% × 2 = 40% (per year)**
3. Multiply the doubled percentage by the asset's book value.   **40% × $300,000 = $120,000**

Exhibit 8–6
Book Value Using
Double-Declining-
Balance Depreciation

	Book Value Beginning of Year		Double Rate	Current Year's Depreciation	Book Value End of Year
2007	$300,000	×	40%	$120,000	$180,000
2008	180,000	×	40%	72,000	108,000
2009	108,000	×	40%	43,200	64,800
2010	64,800	×	40%	25,920	38,880
2011	38,880			13,880	25,000
Total Depreciation				$275,000	

For 2007, Beavers Corporation would record $120,000 depreciation expense. Step 3 of this process uses the book value of the asset. Note that in the first year of the asset's useful life, before any depreciation has been recorded, the book value of the asset equals the cost of the asset. Though it may seem that the double-declining-balance method ignores the residual value, the maximum we can depreciate using the double-declining-balance method is the same depreciable base used in straight-line depreciation.

Exhibit 8–6 shows how we calculate the yearly depreciation expense for Beavers' $300,000 machine using double-declining-balance depreciation, a $25,000 residual value, and a five-year estimated useful life.

As you examine the calculations in the exhibit, you should note several points. First, the book value of the machine declines each year by the amount of depreciation expense recognized that year, just as with straight-line depreciation.

Second, the final year's depreciation does not equal 40 percent of the book value at the beginning of the year ($38,820 × 40% = $15,552). Because the asset cannot depreciate below its residual value, the amount of depreciation expense in 2011 has been limited to $13,880 ($38,880 – $25,000 = $13,880.) As shown in Exhibit 8–5, total depreciation over the five-year life of the asset is $275,000 for both straight-line and double-declining-balance methods.

Third, depreciation expenses start out high but quickly decrease. This rapid decrease is characteristic of all accelerated depreciation methods and has a profound effect on the financial statements of companies using accelerated depreciation methods. Beavers Corporation's income statements for the years 2007 through 2011 and its balance sheets at the end of each of those years using the double-declining-balance method of calculating depreciation illustrate this point in Exhibit 8–7. Again, many items not affected by the company's choice of depreciation method have been held constant from year to year.

Discussion Questions

8-7. Based on the financial statements of Beavers Corporation presented in Exhibit 8–7, and assuming no dividends were declared during 2007, what was the balance in retained earnings at the beginning of 2007?

8-8. Construct the 2007 statement of retained earnings if Beavers Corporation had not recorded any depreciation on its milling machine.

Exhibit 8-7
Beavers Corporation's Financial Statements Using Double-Declining-Balance Depreciation

Income Statements

For the Years Ended December 31,	2007	2008	2009	2010	2011
Sales	$755,000	$755,000	$755,000	$755,000	$755,000
Cost of Goods Sold	422,000	422,000	422,000	422,000	422,000
Gross Margin	$333,000	$333,000	$333,000	$333,000	$333,000
Operating Expenses Other Than Depreciation	(236,000)	(236,000)	(236,000)	(236,000)	(236,000)
Depreciation Expense	(120,000)	(72,000)	(43,200)	(25,920)	(13,880)
Net Income (Loss)	$(23,000)	$ 25,000	$ 53,800	$ 71,080	$ 83,120

Balance Sheets

December 31,	2007	2008	2009	2010	2011
ASSETS:					
Cash	$ 50,000	$ 96,000	$157,000	$213,000	$289,000
Accounts Receivable	206,000	257,000	293,000	334,000	355,000
Inventory	77,000	77,000	77,000	77,000	77,000
Machine	300,000	300,000	300,000	300,000	300,000
LESS: Accumulated Depreciation	(120,000)	(192,000)	(235,200)	(261,120)	(275,000)
Total Assets	$513,000	$538,000	$591,800	$662,880	$746,000
LIABILITIES AND STOCKHOLDERS' EQUITY:					
Accounts Payable	$206,000	$206,000	$206,000	$206,000	$206,000
Notes Payable	170,000	170,000	170,000	170,000	170,000
Common Stock	100,000	100,000	100,000	100,000	100,000
Additional Paid-in Capital	10,000	10,000	10,000	10,000	10,000
Retained Earnings	27,000	52,000	105,800	176,880	260,000
Total Liabilities and Stockholders' Equity	$513,000	$538,000	$591,800	$662,880	$746,000

Understanding the Impact of Depreciation Method Choice

When you compare Beavers Corporation's income statements and balance sheets prepared using straight-line depreciation (Exhibit 8–4) with those same statements prepared using double-declining-balance depreciation (Exhibit 8–7), you should notice several differences and similarities:

• There are significant differences in the reported depreciation expense in each of the five years.
• There are significant differences in the reported net income in each of the five years.
• *Total* depreciation expense and *total* net income over the five-year period are exactly the same regardless of which depreciation method is used. The differences occur in individual years, not over the total five-year period.
• There are significant differences in the amounts of accumulated depreciation on the balance sheets for years 2007 through 2010. The 2011 balance sheet, however, shows exactly the same amount of accumulated depreciation in both presentations. In fact, the 2011 balance sheets in the two presentations are identical.

Exhibit 8-8

Comparison of Depreciation Expense, Net Income, and Book Value of Beavers' Machine under the Two Depreciation Methods

	Straight-Line			Double-Declining-Balance		
Year	Depreciation Expense	Net Income	Book Value of Machine	Depreciation Expense	Net Income	Book Value of Machine
2007	$ 55,000	$ 42,000	$245,000	$120,000	($ 23,000)	$180,000
2008	$ 55,000	$ 42,000	$190,000	$ 72,000	$ 25,000	$108,000
2009	$ 55,000	$ 42,000	$135,000	$ 43,200	$ 53,800	$ 64,800
2010	$ 55,000	$ 42,000	$ 80,000	$ 25,920	$ 71,080	$ 38,880
2011	$ 55,000	$ 42,000	$ 25,000	$ 13,880	$ 83,120	$ 25,000
Total	$275,000	$210,000		$275,000	$210,000	

Neither the straight-line method nor the double-declining-balance method is better than the other. Exhibit 8–8 depicts how the depreciation method can have a substantial effect on reported net income and on portions of the balance sheet from year to year, but over the life of the asset, the method of depreciation is irrelevant.

Discussion Questions

8-9. Explain why the 2011 balance sheets for Beavers Corporation, using the two different depreciation methods, are identical, while all five income statements and the first four years' balance sheets are different.

8-10. Compare the amount of cash shown on the Beavers Corporation balance sheets using straight-line depreciation and double-declining-balance depreciation for each given year. Explain your findings.

8-11. Assume that Exhibit 8–8 depicts information from two different companies, and you are making an investment decision in 2008 with only the 2007 accounting information. How would you make a decision based on the given information?

DISPOSAL OF DEPRECIABLE ASSETS

Ideally, a firm would use a long-lived asset for exactly the time originally estimated, after which it would sell the asset for exactly the residual value originally estimated. In reality, this situation rarely occurs. The actual useful life of an asset normally differs from its estimated useful life, because a company may dispose of an asset at any time. A company holds an asset as long as it is productive, regardless of how long the company estimated it would hold it at the time of its purchase. Technological advances, competition, market changes, changes in business strategy, and many other factors affect the length of time an asset remains productive. A firm might sell an asset shortly after acquisition because it fails to be useful, or it may use an asset long after it is fully depreciated.

When a firm determines the estimated useful life of an asset, it needs to consider the possibility of both the technological obsolescence and the functional

technological obsolescence Occurs when an asset is no longer compatible with current technology.

functional obsolescence Occurs when an asset can no longer perform the function for which it was purchased.

obsolescence of the asset. **Technological obsolescence** occurs when technology exceeds the asset's current version. **Functional obsolescence** occurs when the firm can no longer use the asset to create revenue. Consider the case of computers. If you have a computer with workable software that fulfills all your needs, it does not matter to you whether it is the most current version of technology. It does not even matter that it may be technologically obsolete; it still is functional. If, however, your professor assigns an Internet assignment, and your computer cannot be connected to the Internet because it lacks the proper capacity to install and run the appropriate software, it has now become functionally obsolete. Functional obsolescence affects the asset's useful life. Both functional and technological obsolescence should be considered in determining the useful life of the asset.

A company has no guarantee that it will receive the estimated residual amount when it sells the asset. Technological obsolescence dramatically reduces the asset's residual value. Functional obsolescence may not reduce the asset's residual value if the asset has current technology. What is no longer functional to one company may still be functional to another company. The decision to keep or dispose of an asset should be based on the needs of the business, not on accounting considerations about depreciation.

As a general rule, disposing of depreciable assets is not an ongoing central activity in a company, it is incidental or peripheral to the major operation of the business. For this reason, we do not consider any increase or decrease in equity from the disposal of depreciable assets as a revenue or expense. Rather, equity changes from the disposition of assets represent the accounting elements reported on the income statement as gains (increases) and losses (decreases).

Gains and Losses—Important Accounting Elements

In *Statement of Financial Accounting Concepts #6*, the FASB defined gains and losses as follows:

gains Net inflows resulting from peripheral activities of a company. An example is the sale of an asset for more than its book value.

1. **Gains.** *Increases in equity from peripheral or incidental transactions of an entity and from all other transactions and other events and circumstances affecting the entity except those that result from revenues or investments by owners.*
2. **Losses.** *Decreases in equity from peripheral or incidental transactions of an entity and from all other transactions and other events and circumstances affecting the entity except those that result from expenses or distributions to owners.*

losses Net outflows resulting from peripheral activities of a company. An example is the sale of an asset for less than its book value.

With this knowledge of gains and losses, we can now expand the four components of capital from Chapter 5 to include them. The four components of capital are

1. Contributions by owners
2. Revenues and gains
3. Expenses and losses
4. Distributions to owners

Why do we distinguish between revenues and gains or between expenses and losses? Remember that an income statement provides information about the past performance of a company so that decision makers can better predict the company's future performance. Because gains and losses are incidental to a company's central operations and are usually one-time events, we cannot depend on them to predict the future success of a company's operations. Therefore, the income statement presents revenues and expenses as components of operating income and presents gains and losses separately. Decision makers can assign different predictive values to operating income (revenue minus expenses) and gains and losses. Gains and losses expand the net income equation from Chapter 5 as follows:

REVENUES + GAINS − EXPENSES − LOSSES = NET INCOME

Exhibit 8–9
Accounting Elements:
Gains and Losses

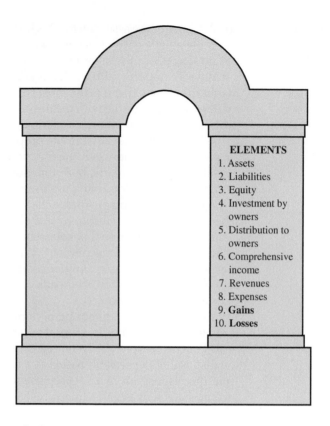

ELEMENTS
1. Assets
2. Liabilities
3. Equity
4. Investment by owners
5. Distribution to owners
6. Comprehensive income
7. Revenues
8. Expenses
9. **Gains**
10. **Losses**

Calculating Gains and Losses

We calculate gains and losses on the disposal of assets by comparing the value received and the value given. The value given consists of the book value of the asset on the date disposed. Depreciation should always be calculated and recorded up to date of disposal before we attempt to calculate any gain or loss.

Asset received − book value of asset given = gain (loss)

Return to the Beavers Corporation and its $300,000 milling machine. Assume Beavers depreciated this machine using the straight-line method over a five-year estimated useful life, with an estimated residual value of $25,000 (Exhibit 8–4).

On January 2, 2012, Beavers decides to sell the machine because it no longer benefits the company's operations. The machine has a $25,000 book value at the end of 2011 ($300,000 cost − $275,000 accumulated depreciation). Although the accounting records indicate a $25,000 book value, that seldom represents the market value. The book value is based on an estimate made five years ago and is irrelevant in the marketplace because buyers pay market value. Market value depends on the condition of the machine, the state of technology, and the selling price of comparable used machines. However, we use the book value to calculate accounting gains and losses.

Gain on Disposal Assume Beavers sells the machine for a cash price of $32,000. Because the company has received more than the book value of the machine, it recognizes a gain.

Asset received − book value of asset given = gain (loss)
$32,000 − $25,000 = $7,000

The $7,000 appears as a gain on the income statement for the year 2012. Exhibit 8–10 shows Beavers' income statements for the years 2011 and 2012 and its balance sheets at the end of each of those years, reflecting a $7,000 gain on the disposal of its machine.

Exhibit 8–10
Beavers Corporation's
Financial Statements
for 2011 and 2012
Reflecting a Gain on the
Sale of Its Machine

BEAVERS CORPORATION

Income Statements

For the Years Ended December 31,	2011	2012
Sales	$755,000	$941,000
Cost of Goods Sold	422,000	525,000
Gross Margin	$333,000	$416,000
Operating Expenses		
Other Than Depreciation	(236,000)	(319,000)
Depreciation Expense	(55,000)	-0-
Operating Income	$ 42,000	$ 97,000
Gain on Sale of Machine	-0-	7,000
Net Income	$ 42,000	$104,000

Balance Sheets

December 31,	2011	2012
ASSETS:		
Cash	$289,000	$225,000
Accounts Receivable	355,000	313,000
Inventory	77,000	172,000
Machine	300,000	-0-
LESS: Accumulated Depreciation	(275,000)	-0-
Total Assets	$746,000	$710,000
LIABILITIES AND STOCKHOLDERS' EQUITY:		
Accounts Payable	$206,000	$216,000
Notes Payable	170,000	20,000
Common Stock	100,000	100,000
Additional Paid-in Capital	10,000	10,000
Retained Earnings	260,000	364,000
Total Liabilities and Stockholders' Equity	$746,000	$710,000

As you examine these financial statements, consider the following points:

- On the income statement for the year 2012, the $7,000 gain is shown in a different place than revenues from Beavers' ongoing major operations.
- The $7,000 gain has exactly the same effect on net income as the revenues from Beavers' ongoing major operations on the income statement for the year 2012.
- Both the cost of the machine ($300,000) and the accumulated depreciation ($275,000) have been removed from the balance sheet at the end of the year 2012.

Discussion Question

8-12. Note that Beavers Corporation's income statements are presented in a multistep format in Exhibit 8–10. What specific items on the income statements are unique to this format and would not appear on a single-step statement?

Loss on Disposal   Assume Beavers sells the machine for a cash price of only $19,000. Because the company received less than the book value of the machine, it recognizes a loss.

$$\text{Asset received} - \text{book value of asset given} = \text{gain (loss)}$$
$$\$19,000 - \$25,000 = \$(6,000)$$

The $6,000 will be reported as a loss on the income statement for the year 2012. Exhibit 8–11 shows Beavers' income statements for the years 2011 and 2012 and its balance sheets at the end of each of those years, reflecting a $6,000 loss on the disposal of its machine.

As you study these financial statements, consider the following points:

- On the income statement for the year 2012 the $6,000 loss is shown in a different place than expenses required to support Beavers' ongoing major operations.
- The $6,000 loss has exactly the same effect on net income as the expenses required to support Beavers' ongoing major operations on the income statement for the year 2012.

Exhibit 8–11
Beavers Corporation's Financial Statements for 2011 and 2012 Reflecting a Loss on the Sale of Its Machine

BEAVERS CORPORATION

Income Statements

For the Years Ended December 31,	2011	2012
Sales	$755,000	$941,000
Cost of Goods Sold	422,000	525,000
Gross Margin	$333,000	$416,000
Operating Expenses		
Other Than Depreciation	(236,000)	(319,000)
Depreciation Expense	(55,000)	-0-
Operating Income	$ 42,000	$ 97,000
Loss on Sale of Machine	-0-	(6,000)
Net Income	$ 42,000	$ 91,000

Balance Sheets

December 31,	2011	2012
ASSETS:		
Cash	$289,000	$212,000
Accounts Receivable	355,000	313,000
Inventory	77,000	172,000
Machine	300,000	-0-
LESS: Accumulated Depreciation	(275,000)	-0-
Total Assets	$746,000	$697,000
LIABILITIES AND STOCKHOLDERS' EQUITY:		
Accounts Payable	$206,000	$216,000
Notes Payable	170,000	20,000
Common Stock	100,000	100,000
Additional Paid-in Capital	10,000	10,000
Retained Earnings	260,000	351,000
Total Liabilities and Stockholders' Equity	$746,000	$697,000

- Both the cost of the machine ($300,000) and the accumulated depreciation ($275,000) have been removed from the balance sheet at the end of the year 2012.

In our examples of both a gain and a loss, we have assumed that Beavers was able to sell its machine for some amount of cash. However, there are times when an asset has no market value and must simply be abandoned. If this were the case with the Beavers machine, it would result in a loss of $25,000 ($0 cash received − $25,000 book value = a $25,000 loss).

Discussion Question

8-13. Look again at Beavers Corporation's income statements and balance sheets in Exhibit 8-11. What items on the financial statements for the year 2012 would be different (and by how much) if Beavers had simply abandoned the machine?

Disposal with No Gain or Loss   Assume now that Beavers sells the machine for a cash price of $25,000. Because the company received exactly the book value of the machine, there is neither a gain nor a loss.

Asset received − book value of asset given = gain (loss)
$25,000 − $25,000 = $0

As Exhibit 8–12 shows, the sale of the machine will not directly affect the income statement for the year 2012, but it will affect the balance sheet.

As you examine these statements, there are two points you should note:

- There is no gain or loss from the disposal of the machine on the income statement for the year 2012.
- Both the cost of the machine ($300,000) and the accumulated depreciation ($275,000) have been removed from the balance sheet at the end of the year 2012.

Thus far you have seen how to calculate gains and losses, and how these elements affect a company's financial statements. We now are ready to see how to properly interpret gains and losses when they are a part of the accounting information made available during the decision-making process.

UNDERSTANDING THE TRUE MEANING OF GAINS AND LOSSES

Assume that two companies have business activities that are identical in almost all respects. The companies have the exact same sales for the year, and all their operating expenses (except depreciation) are the same.

The two companies in this example are Straight Arrow Automotive and Accelerated Automotive. Both companies purchased a fleet of trucks for $228,000 on January 2, 2008. In addition, both companies estimated a useful life of four years and a residual value of $92,000 for the trucks. Because Straight Arrow Automotive uses straight-line depreciation and Accelerated Automotive uses the double-declining-balance method, we expect to see differences in their financial statements. Exhibit 8–13 contains the 2008 income statement and balance sheet for each company.

Exhibit 8-12

Beavers Corporation's Financial Statements for 2011 and 2012 Reflecting the Sale of Its Machine for Book Value

BEAVERS CORPORATION

Income Statements

For the Years Ended December 31,	2011	2012
Sales	$755,000	$941,000
Cost of Goods Sold	422,000	525,000
Gross Margin	$333,000	$416,000
Operating Expenses		
Other Than Depreciation	(236,000)	(319,000)
Depreciation Expense	(55,000)	-0-
Operating Income	$ 42,000	$ 97,000
Gain (Loss) on Sale of Machine	-0-	-0-
Net Income	$ 42,000	$ 97,000

Balance Sheets

December 31,	2011	2012
ASSETS:		
Cash	$289,000	$218,000
Accounts Receivable	355,000	313,000
Inventory	77,000	172,000
Machine	300,000	-0-
LESS: Accumulated Depreciation	(275,000)	-0-
Total Assets	$746,000	$703,000
LIABILITIES AND STOCKHOLDERS' EQUITY:		
Accounts Payable	$206,000	$216,000
Notes Payable	170,000	20,000
Common Stock	100,000	100,000
Additional Paid-in Capital	10,000	10,000
Retained Earnings	260,000	357,000
Total Liabilities and Stockholders' Equity	$746,000	$703,000

Discussion Questions

Refer to Exhibit 8–13 to answer the following questions.

8-14. The amount of depreciation expense recorded by each company is given. Provide computations to explain how these amounts were determined.

8-15. The financial statements indicate four items on the income statements that differ between the companies. Six items on the balance sheets differ between the companies. Identify each item and explain the cause of the difference.

8-16. Assuming that no dividends were paid by either company, what was the balance in retained earnings on January 1, 2007, for each company?

Exhibit 8-13
2008 Financial Statements of Straight Arrow Automotive and Accelerated Automotive

Income Statements
For the Year Ending December 31, 2008

	Straight Arrow Automotive		Accelerated Automotive	
Sales	$769,000		$769,000	
LESS: Cost of Goods Sold	295,500		295,500	
Gross Margin		$473,500		$473,500
Wages Expense	$ 67,500		$ 67,500	
Utilities Expense	31,000		31,000	
Depreciation Expense	34,000		114,000	
Total Operating Expenses		(132,500)		(212,500)
Operating Income		$341,000		$261,000
Other Revenues and Expenses:				
Interest Expense		(120,000)		(120,000)
Net Income		$221,000		$141,000

Balance Sheets
December 31, 2008

	Straight Arrow Automotive		Accelerated Automotive	
ASSETS:				
Cash		$226,000		$226,000
Accounts Receivable		198,000		198,000
Inventory		223,000		223,000
Trucks	$228,000		$228,000	
Accumulated Depreciation	(34,000)		(114,000)	
Trucks, Net		194,000		114,000
Total Assests		$841,000		$761,000
LIABILITIES:				
Accounts Payable	$ 22,000		$ 22,000	
Notes Payable	61,000		61,000	
Total Liabilities		$ 83,000		$ 83,000
Owners' Equity:				
Common Stock	$200,000		$200,000	
Additional Paid-in Capital	194,000		194,000	
Contributed Capital	394,000		394,000	
Retained Earnings	364,000		284,000	
Total Shareholders' Equity		758,000		678,000
Total Liabilities				
and Owners' Equity		$841,000		$761,000

8-17. What are the depreciation expense and accumulated depreciation for each company? Are these two items always the same?

8-18. What are the accumulated depreciation and book value of the trucks for each company? Why are Accelerated Automotive's figures the same, but Straight Arrow's figures different?

Income Statements
For the Year Ending December 31, 2009

	Straight Arrow Automotive		Accelerated Automotive	
Sales	$769,000		$769,000	
LESS: Cost of Goods Sold	295,500		295,500	
Gross Margin		$473,500		$473,500
Wages Expense	$ 67,500		$ 67,500	
Utilities Expense	31,000		31,000	
Depreciation Expense	34,000		22,000	
Total Operating Expenses		(132,500)		(120,500)
Operating Income		$341,000		$353,000
Other Revenues and Expenses:				
Interest Expense		(120,000)		(120,000)
Net Income		$221,000		$233,000

Balance Sheets
December 31, 2009

	Straight Arrow Automotive		Accelerated Automotive	
ASSETS:				
Cash		$ 426,000		$426,000
Accounts Receivable		253,000		253,000
Inventory		223,000		223,000
Trucks	$228,000		$228,000	
Accumulated Depreciation	(68,000)		(136,000)	
Trucks, Net		160,000		92,000
Total Assets		$1,062,000		$994,000
LIABILITIES:				
Accounts Payable	$ 22,000		$ 22,000	
Notes Payable	61,000		61,000	
Total Liabilities		$ 83,000		$ 83,000
Owners' Equity:				
Common Stock	$200,000		$200,000	
Additional Paid-in Capital	194,000		194,000	
Contributed Capital	$394,000		$394,000	
Retained Earnings	585,000		517,000	
Total Shareholders' Equity		979,000		911,000
Total Liabilities				
and Owners' Equity		$1,062,000		$994,000

The impact of the choice of depreciation method becomes even more evident over time. Exhibit 8–14 shows the income statements and balance sheets of Straight Arrow Automotive and Accelerated Automotive at the end of 2009. Again, we have held constant the items that are not affected by the use of different depreciation methods.

Discussion Question

8-19. Provide computations and an explanation to show how Accelerated Automotive's depreciation expense amount of $22,000 was determined (Exhibit 8–14).

Even more profound than the differences occurring on the financial statements as the companies record depreciation, is the effect of an early disposal. Suppose that Straight Arrow Automotive and Accelerated Automotive both decide to sell their trucks on December 31, 2009. All trucks have the identical age, condition, and market value. In exchange for its truck fleet, each company receives $150,000 cash—the market value of the truck fleet on the day of the sale. Because the sale occurs on the last day of the year, both companies must record depreciation for the full year, as reflected in the previous statements.

Discussion Question

8-20. Were the companies wise to sell the fleet? Did they get "a good deal"? What information would help you decide whether the companies made a smart move?

Even though Straight Arrow Automotive and Accelerated Automotive incurred the identical transactions, the financial statement presentation of the results of the sale appears quite different, as shown in Exhibit 8–15.

When both companies made exactly the same transaction, why do the financial statements show different results of the sale? Straight Arrow Automotive recorded a $10,000 loss, but the same activity resulted in a $58,000 gain for Accelerated Automotive. However, both companies paid cash of $228,000 for the trucks and sold them for $150,000 after using the fleet for two years. The moral of the story? Smart financial statement users understand the true meaning of gains or losses on productive, depreciable assets. Remember, gains and losses on depreciable assets represent only the difference between the book value and the market value of assets sold. Do not assume that a gain indicates the sale was "good for business," or that a loss signifies that management made a bad move. In our example, we do not have enough information to determine whether the sale of the trucks for $150,000 was a wise business decision or a poor one. Clearly, though, the sale was no wiser for one company than for the other.

Also note that the retained earnings balance shown by Straight Arrow Automotive and Accelerated Automotive in Exhibit 8–15 is the same—$575,000. If Straight Arrow shows a loss on the sale and Accelerated shows a gain on the sale, how can both show the same retained earnings balance? The answer lies in the fact that both companies transferred the same amount of cost to the income statement over the life of the assets. See Exhibit 8–16 to verify that the same cost of $78,000 was transferred to each income statement—the same amount as the difference between the purchase price of $228,000 and the sale price of $150,000.

Because accelerated depreciation methods transfer costs more rapidly than straight-line methods, firms that employ accelerated depreciation methods have a greater chance of showing gains on the disposal of an asset before the end of its useful life. The earlier the disposition, the more likely the firm is to record a gain.

Exhibit 8-15

Impact of the Sale of Trucks at the End of 2009 on the Financial Statements of Straight Arrow Automotive and Accelerated Automotive

Income Statements
For the Year Ending December 31, 2009

	Straight Arrow Automotive		Accelerated Automotive	
Sales	$769,000		$769,000	
LESS: Cost of Goods Sold	295,500		295,500	
Gross Margin		$473,500		$473,500
Wages Expense	$ 67,500		$ 67,500	
Utilities Expense	31,000		31,000	
Depreciation Expense	34,000		22,000	
Total Operating Expenses		(132,500)		(120,500)
Operating Income		$341,000		$353,000
Other Revenues and Expenses:				
Gain on Sale of Trucks				58,000
Loss on Sale of Trucks		(10,000)		
Interest Expense		(120,000)		(120,000)
Net Income		$211,000		$291,000

Balance Sheets
December 31, 2009

	Straight Arrow Automotive		Accelerated Automotive	
ASSETS:				
Cash	$576,000		$576,000	
Accounts Receivable	253,000		253,000	
Inventory	223,000		223,000	
Totals Assets		$1,052,000		$1,052,000
LIABILITIES:				
Accounts Payable	$ 22,000		$ 22,000	
Notes Payable	61,000		61,000	
Total Liabilities		$ 83,000		$ 83,000
Owners' Equity:				
Common Stock	$200,000		$200,000	
Additional Paid-in Capital	194,000		194,000	
Contributed Capital	$394,000		$394,000	
Retained Earnings	575,000		575,000	
Total Shareholders' Equity		969,000		969,000
Total Liabilities and Owners' Equity		$1,052,000		$1,052,000

Exhibit 8-16

Total Costs Transferred to Expense by Straight Arrow Automotive and Accelerated Automotive

		Straight Arrow Automotive	Accelerated Automotive
2008	Depreciation Expense	$34,000	$114,000
2009	Depreciation Expense	34,000	22,000
2009	Result of Sale (Gain) or Loss	10,000	(58,000)
TOTAL COST TRANSFERRED		$78,000	$ 78,000

As you can see from our discussion of the items presented in this chapter, the depreciation and disposal of long-lived depreciable assets can have a significant impact on a company's reported net income for a given year during the useful life of an asset. The issues surrounding depreciation are complex, and users of financial statements must have some understanding of them if they hope to be able to use financial statements for predicting a company's future or assessing its past performance.

Many issues besides depreciation have complicating effects under the accrual basis of accounting. We will continue our discussion of these complications in Chapter 9, where we consider issues surrounding the sale of merchandise inventory.

SUMMARY

Depreciation is the process of allocating the cost of long-lived assets to the periods in which they help to earn revenues. When a firm purchases an asset, its historical cost is recorded on the balance sheet. As time passes, the company transfers the cost from an asset on the balance sheet to an expense on the income statement. The recording of depreciation expense accomplishes this transfer. The amount of accumulated depreciation for an asset represents all the depreciation expense related to that asset that has been recognized thus far. We report accumulated depreciation on the balance sheet as a reduction of the asset cost.

GAAP allows several depreciation methods. Straight-line methods allocate cost evenly over the asset life measured either in time or productivity. Accelerated depreciation methods, such as the double-declining-balance method, recognize a greater amount of depreciation expense in the early years of an asset's life and a smaller amount in the later years.

The choice of depreciation methods affects companies' financial statements. In total, over the useful life of an asset, straight-line and double-declining-balance depreciation methods record the same amount of depreciation expense. In any particular period, however, different depreciation methods usually result in different amounts of depreciation expense, which causes a difference in reported net income. Because the amount of depreciation expense affects accumulated depreciation, the balance sheets of companies using different depreciation methods will also be different during most of the asset's life.

Eventually, a company disposes of its depreciable assets, and these transactions usually result in a gain or a loss. Gains increase and losses decrease net income in a manner similar to that of revenues and expenses, but gains and losses do not appear in operating income. Gains and losses result from activities peripheral to the major activity of the company; revenues and expenses are direct results of the company's primary business activity.

An asset's book value is its original cost less the amount of its accumulated depreciation. If an asset sells for more than its book value, the transaction results in a gain. Conversely, selling an asset for less than its book value results in a loss.

If the disposal of an asset results in a gain or loss, that outcome is reported on the income statement. If, however, an asset is sold for exactly its book value, the transaction results in no gain or loss. In any case, when a company disposes of an asset, both the asset and its corresponding accumulated depreciation account are removed from the balance sheet.

Gains and losses on the sale of productive depreciable assets does not indicate that the company has won or lost anything. The cost of using an asset over its life is the difference between its original cost and its final sales price. Gains and losses simply adjust the total depreciation charged to the income statement to total cost of using the asset. Accelerated methods tend to show more gains if an asset is sold in the early years of its life.

APPENDIX—RECORDING LONG-LIVED ASSETS AND DEPRECIATION

After completing Chapter 7, you can look at the journal entries for long-lived assets and depreciation. The recording process for long-lived assets involves three types of entries:

1. Purchase of an asset
2. Annual depreciation
3. Disposal of an asset

To record these types of entries, we need to have four accounts available for use:

1. Long-lived asset
2. Accumulated depreciation (a contra asset account)
3. Depreciation expense
4. Gain (Loss) on the disposal of assets

Remember that debits increase assets, expenses, and losses, and credits increase liabilities, equity, revenues, and gains. All journal entries must contain equal dollar amounts of debits and of credits.

We can examine the journal entries that the Beavers Corporation made to record the transactions for its milling machine. The following illustrates the straight-line example when Beavers sells the asset for $32,000.

Straight-Line Depreciation

1. Purchase of an asset:

2007		Debit	Credit
January 2	Milling Machine	300,000	
	Cash		300,000
	To record the purchase of a milling machine.		

2. Annual Depreciation:

2007		Debit	Credit
December 31	Depreciation Expense	55,000	
	Accumulated Depreciation		55,000
	To record annual depreciation expense.		

This same entry is made each year on December 31 for the years 2008, 2009, 2010, and 2011.

3. Disposal of an asset:

2012		Debit	Credit
January 2	Cash	32,000	
	Accumulated Depreciation	275,000	
	Milling Machine		300,000
	Gain on Sale of Asset		7,000
	To record the sale of the milling machine.		

Before we make the final entry to record the disposal, we must record any expired and unrecorded depreciation. Because the milling machine was last depreciated on December 31, 2011, and is now fully depreciated, no entry is required. The final entry removes the asset and accumulated depreciation accounts from the asset accounts. Because a gain increases equity, a gain creates a credit to balance the journal entry. Look at the following T-accounts to see how the entries affect each account.

	Milling Machine			Accumulated Depreciation		
1-2-07	300,000					
12-31-07					55,000	12-31-07
12-31-08					55,000	12-31-08
12-31-09					55,000	12-31-09
12-31-10					55,000	12-31-10
12-31-11					55,000	12-31-11
	300,000				275,000	
1-2-12		300,000	275,000			
	-0-				-0-	

Notice that the accounts show the history of what happened to this asset. See now how the entries change when Beavers selects the double-declining-balance method of depreciation.

Double-Declining-Balance Depreciation

1. Purchase of an asset:

2007		Debit	Credit
January 2	Milling Machine	300,000	
	Cash		300,000
	To record the purchase of a milling machine.		

2. Annual Depreciation:

2007		Debit	Credit
December 31	Depreciation Expense	120,000	
	Accumulated Depreciation		120,000
	To record annual depreciation expense for 2007.		

2008		Debit	Credit
December 31	Depreciation Expense	72,000	
	Accumulated Depreciation		72,000
	To record annual depreciation expense for 2008.		

2009		Debit	Credit
December 31	Depreciation Expense	43,200	
	Accumulated Depreciation		43,200
	To record annual depreciation expense for 2009.		

2010		Debit	Credit
December 31	Depreciation Expense	25,920	
	Accumulated Depreciation		25,920
	To record annual depreciation expense for 2010.		

2011		Debit	Credit
December 31	Depreciation Expense	13,880	
	Accumulated Depreciation		13,880
	To record annual depreciation expense for 2011.		

A different entry is made each year on December 31 for the years 2008, 2009, 2010, and 2011.

3. Disposal of an asset:

2012		Debit	Credit
January 2	Cash	32,000	
	Accumulated Depreciation	275,000	
	Milling Machine		300,000
	Gain on Sale of Asset		7,000
	To record the sale of the milling machine.		

Notice that the purchase entry is the same regardless of the depreciation method. When the asset has been fully depreciated, the sale entry is also the same. See how these entries affect the individual accounts.

	Milling Machine			Accumulated Depreciation	
1-2-07	300,000				
12-31-07				120,000	12-31-07
12-31-08				72,000	12-31-08
12-31-09				43,200	12-31-09
12-31-10				25,920	12-31-10
12-31-11				13,880	12-31-11
	300,000			275,000	
1-2-12		300,000	275,000		
	-0-			-0-	

Recording a Loss

When the asset is fully depreciated, the method of depreciation makes no difference when the asset is sold. How would the final entry change if Beavers received only $19,000 for the machine on January 2, 2012?

2012		Debit	Credit
January 2	Cash	19,000	
	Accumulated Depreciation	275,000	
	Loss on Sale of Asset	6,000	
	Milling Machine		300,000
	To record the sale of the milling machine.		

Because a loss reduces equity, the loss creates a debit entry to the loss account to balance the journal entry.

Sale at Book Value

When a sale occurs for book value, no gain or loss is recognized. Look at the journal entry to record the sale for $25,000.

2012		Debit	Credit
January 2	Cash	25,000	
	Accumulated Depreciation	275,000	
	Milling Machine		300,000
	To record the sale of the milling machine.		

Sale before the End of Asset Life

If we look at the sale of Accelerated Automotive's fleet in the second year of life, we see how the journal entries unfold for an asset that has not been fully depreciated. The entries are the same as for a fully depreciated asset, except that we must be careful to record any unrecognized depreciation from the last time depreciation was recorded to the date of disposal.

1. Purchase of an asset:

2007		Debit	Credit
January 2	Truck Fleet	228,000	
	Cash		228,000
	To record the purchase of a truck fleet.		

2. Annual Depreciation:

2007		Debit	Credit
December 31	Depreciation Expense	114,000	
	Accumulated Depreciation		114,000
	To record the first year's depreciation expense.		

3. Disposal of an asset:
   a. First, bring the asset's depreciation up to date. The fleet was last depreciated on December 31, 2007, one year ago. A full year's depreciation expired since that time, but has not been recorded.

2008		Debit	Credit
December 31	Depreciation Expense	22,000	
	Accumulated Depreciation		22,000
	To record the second year's depreciation expense.		

   b. Second, record the asset disposal in accordance with the terms of the sale.

		Debit	Credit
December 31	Cash	150,000	
	Accumulated Depreciation	136,000	
	Truck Fleet		228,000
	Gain on Sale of Asset		58,000
	To record the sale of the truck fleet.		

SUMMARY TO APPENDIX

Recording transactions for long-lived assets involves four accounts: a long-lived asset, accumulated depreciation, depreciation expense, and a gain or loss on the disposal of the asset. We record the original purchase of the asset as a debit to the asset account. Annual depreciation results in a debit to depreciation expense and a credit to the accumulated depreciation, a contra asset account. When the owner sells an asset, we must first recognize all depreciation up to the date of disposal. When depreciation is current, we debit the asset received (usually cash), debit the accumulated depreciation, credit the asset, and credit gain on sale or debit loss on sale as the balancing item in the journal entry.

REVIEW THE FACTS

A. Provide three examples of long-lived depreciable assets.

B. In your own words, describe the depreciation process.

C. What two estimates made by management will affect the amount of depreciation recorded each period?

D. What is the depreciable base of an asset?

E. Explain the two bases we can use for straight-line allocation of the cost of fixed assets.

F. Explain what is meant by an accelerated depreciation method. Theoretically, in what situation is an accelerated depreciation method the appropriate choice?

G. Explain how the amount of depreciation expense is calculated using straight-line depreciation.

H. What is meant by an asset's book value?

I. What does the amount of accumulated depreciation represent?

J. In your own words, describe the process of determining depreciation expense using the double-declining-balance method.

K. Compared to straight-line depreciation, what is the effect of an accelerated depreciation method on the balance sheet? On the income statement?

L. Regardless of what depreciation method is used, at what point is an asset considered "fully depreciated"?

M. On what financial statement do gains and losses appear?

N. What is the difference between a revenue and a gain? A loss and an expense?

O. How is a gain or loss calculated?

P. What effect does the disposal of an asset that results in no gain or loss have on the income statement? On the balance sheet?

APPLY WHAT YOU HAVE LEARNED

LO 1: Terminology

8–21. Presented below is a list of items relating to the concepts discussed in this chapter, followed by definitions of those items in scrambled order.

a. Accelerated depreciation	**f.** Straight-line depreciation
b. Book value	**g.** Gains
c. Gain on sale of asset	**h.** Loss on sale of asset
d. Losses	**i.** Depreciable base
e. Estimated useful life	**j.** Production method

1. _____ A factor determining how much of an asset's cost will be allocated to the periods supposedly benefited.

2. _____ A depreciation method that uses activity instead of time as the basis of allocation.

3. _____ More of the cost of a long-lived asset is converted to expense in the early years of its life than in later years.

4. _____ The cost of a long-lived asset less the estimated residual value.

5. _____ Results when a depreciable asset is sold for more than its book value.

6. _____ An equal amount of a long-lived asset's cost is converted to expense in each year of its useful life.

7. _____ Net inflows resulting from peripheral activities.

8. _____ The cost of a long-lived depreciable asset less its accumulated depreciation.

9. _____ Results when a depreciable asset is sold for less than its book value.

10. _____ Net outflows resulting from peripheral activities.

REQUIRED:

Match the letter next to each item on the list with the appropriate definition. Each letter will be used only once.

LO 1: Depreciation Process

8–22. Evaluate the following: "The depreciation process is a process designed to value fixed assets on the balance sheet."

LO 2: Computation of Depreciation Expense— Straight-Line Method

8–23. Jerry Garcia and Company purchased a lathe for use in its manufacturing operation. The machine cost $150,000, has a five-year estimated useful life, and will be depreciated using the straight-line method. The only thing remaining to be determined before yearly depreciation expense can be calculated is the estimated residual value. The alternatives are

1. $10,000 estimated residual value
2. $20,000 estimated residual value
3. $30,000 estimated residual value

REQUIRED:

a. Calculate the yearly depreciation expense for the new lathe under each of the alternatives given.
b. Which of the three alternatives will result in the highest net income?
c. How long will the new lathe be useful to Garcia and Company?

LO 2: Computation of Depreciation Expense— Straight-Line Method

8–24. Lottinvilles has just purchased a minicomputer for use in its manufacturing operation. The machine cost $75,000, has a four-year estimated useful life, and will be depreciated using the straight-line method. The only thing remaining to be determined before yearly depreciation expense can be calculated is the estimated residual value. The alternatives are

1. $7,500 estimated residual value
2. $12,500 estimated residual value
3. $17,500 estimated residual value

REQUIRED:

a. Calculate the yearly depreciation expense for the new minicomputer under each of the alternatives given.
b. Which of the three alternatives will result in the highest net income? Which of the three alternatives will result in the lowest net income?
c. How long will the new minicomputer be useful to Lottinvilles?

LO 2: Computation of Depreciation Expense— Straight-Line Method

8–25. Nathan Verner Publishing Company purchased a new printing press for a total installed cost of $700,000. The printing press will be depreciated using the straight-line method, in accordance with corporate policy. Robert Sheets, the corporate controller, is trying to decide on an estimated useful life and an estimated residual value for the asset. The alternatives are

1. A six-year estimated useful life with a $40,000 estimated residual value
2. A five-year estimated useful life with a $100,000 estimated residual value
3. A four-year estimated useful life with a $140,000 estimated residual value

REQUIRED:

a. Calculate the yearly depreciation expense for the new printing press under each of the alternatives given.
b. Which of the three alternatives will result in the lowest yearly net income? Which of the three alternatives will result in the highest yearly net income?
c. What should be the deciding factor in selecting among the three alternatives?

LO 2: Computation of Depreciation Expense— Straight-Line Method

8–26. The Pizzeria Restaurant Company purchased a new walk-in freezer for a total installed cost of $250,000. The walk-in freezer will be depreciated using the straight-line method, in accordance with corporate policy. David Noel the corporate controller, is trying to determine an estimated useful life and residual value for the asset. His alternatives are

1. A five-year estimated useful life with a $10,000 estimated residual value
2. A four-year estimated useful life with a $25,000 estimated residual value
3. A three-year estimated useful life with a $50,000 estimated residual value

REQUIRED:

a. Calculate the yearly depreciation expense for the new printing press under each of the alternatives given.
b. Which of the three alternatives will result in the lowest yearly net income? Which of the three alternatives will result in the highest yearly net income?
c. What should be the deciding factor in selecting among the three alternatives?

LO 2: Computation of Double-Declining-Balance Depreciation Expense and Book Value

8–27. Wede Company purchased a high-tech assembler on January 2, 2008, for a total cost of $600,000. The assembler has an estimated useful life to the company of five years. Wede thinks it can sell the used assembler for $40,000 after five years. The company chose to depreciate the new assembler using the double-declining-balance method.

REQUIRED:

a. Prepare a schedule showing the amount of depreciation expense for each of the five years of the estimated useful life.

b. What will be the book value of the assembler at the end of the five-year estimated useful life?

c. What does book value represent?

LO 2: Computation of Double-Declining-Balance Depreciation Expense and Book Value

8-28. Bronson Company purchased an earthmoving machine on January 2 for a total cost of $900,000. The earthmover has an estimated useful life to the company of four years. Bronson believes it can sell the used earthmover for $80,000 after four years. The company selected the double-declining-balance method of depreciation.

REQUIRED:

a. Prepare a schedule showing the amount of depreciation expense for each of the four years of the estimated useful life.

b. What will be the book value of the earthmover at the end of the four-year estimated useful life?

c. What does book value represent?

LO 2: Computation of Depreciation Expense— Straight-Line and Double-Declining Balance

8-29. Resler Company purchased a sophisticated stamping machine on January 2 for $480,000. The estimated useful life of the stamping machine is six years. Resler estimates the machine's residual value is $40,000.

REQUIRED:

a. Calculate the yearly depreciation expense for the stamping machine assuming the company uses the straight-line depreciation method.

b. Prepare a schedule showing the amount of depreciation expense for each of the six years of the estimated useful life assuming the company uses the double-declining-balance depreciation method.

LO 2: Computation of Depreciation Expense— Straight-Line and Double-Declining Balance

8-30. WebCo, Inc. purchased a pasteurizing machine on January 2 for $375,000. The estimated useful life of the machine is four years with a residual value of $45,000.

REQUIRED:

a. Calculate the yearly depreciation expense for the machine assuming the company uses the straight-line depreciation method.

b. Prepare a schedule showing the amount of depreciation expense for each of the four years of the estimated useful life assuming the company uses the double-declining-balance depreciation method.

LO 2 & 5: Computation of Depreciation Expense and Gains or Losses—Production Method

8–31. Knoorfleet Inc. purchased a delivery truck on January 2, 2007, for $70,000. Knoorfleet estimates the estimated useful life of the vehicle is 1,000,000 miles, and the residual value at $10,000. The truck is driven 200,000 miles in 2007; 225,000 miles in 2008; 300,000 miles in 2009; and 275,000 miles in 2010.

REQUIRED:

a. Calculate the yearly depreciation expense for the vehicle assuming the company uses the production depreciation method.

b. Calculate the gain or loss on the sale if Knoorfleet sells the truck at the end of 2010 for $15,000.

c. Calculate the gain or loss on the sale if Knoorfleet sells the truck at the end of 2010 for $5,000.

d. Calculate the gain or loss on the sale if Knoorfleet sells the truck at the end of 2010 for $1,000.

LO 2 & 5: Computation of Depreciation Expense and Gains or Losses—Production Method

8–32. Janek Inc. purchased a printing press on January 2, 2007, for $95,000. Janek estimates the useful life of the press is 2,000,000 pages or five years, after which he can sell the press for $5,000. The press produces 500,000 pages in 2007; 400,000 pages in 2008; 430,000 pages in 2009; 600,000 pages in 2010; and 350,000 pages in 2011.

REQUIRED:

a. Calculate the yearly depreciation expense for the press assuming the company uses the production depreciation method.

b. Calculate the gain or loss on the sale if Janek sells the press at the end of 2011 for $15,000.

c. Calculate the gain or loss on the sale if Janek sells the press at the end of 2011 for $5,000.

d. Calculate the gain or loss on the sale if Janek sells the press at the end of 2011 for $2,000.

LO 2 & 5: Computation of Depreciation Expense and Gains or Losses—Production Method

8–33. Runnels, Inc. purchased a lathe on January 2, 2008, for $200,000. Runnels estimates its useful life as 1,600,000 hours or four years, and its residual value at $4,000. He uses the lathe for 500,000 hours in 2008; 430,000 hours in 2009; 300,000 hours in 2010; and 300,000 hours in 2011.

REQUIRED:

a. Calculate the yearly depreciation expense for the machine assuming the company uses the production depreciation method.

b. Calculate the gain or loss on the sale if Runnels sells the lathe after four years for $12,000.

c. Calculate the gain or loss on the sale if Runnels sells the lathe after four years for $3,000.

d. Calculate the gain or loss on the sale if Runnels sells the lathe after four years for $10,000.

LO 2 & 3: Computation of Depreciation Expense—
Straight-Line and Double-Declining Balance

8–34. Pepco Inc. purchased a fleet of delivery trucks on January 2, 2007, for $700,000. The estimated useful life of the fleet is four years, after which Pepco estimates it can sell the entire fleet for $50,000.

REQUIRED:

a. Calculate the yearly depreciation expense for the fleet of vehicles assuming the company uses the straight-line depreciation method.

b. Prepare a schedule showing the amount of depreciation expense for each of the four years of the estimated useful life assuming the company uses the double-declining-balance depreciation method.

c. Address the following questions:

   (1) Double-declining-balance calculates depreciation at twice the straight-line rate. Why is the amount of depreciation expense in 2007 under double-declining-balance not exactly twice the amount under straight-line for 2007?

   (2) Over the four-year estimated useful life of the vehicles, how much depreciation expense will be charged against income using the straight-line method? How much will be charged against income using the double-declining-balance method?

   (3) Discuss the impact on the net income of each method of depreciation in the first two years of life of the asset.

LO 2 & 3: Computation of Depreciation Expense—
Straight-Line and Double-Declining-Balance Methods

8–35. Lisa and Mark, Inc. purchased a fleet of taxis on January 2, 2007, for $600,000. The corporation estimates the useful life of the vehicles is three years, after which it can sell the entire fleet for $50,000.

REQUIRED:

a. Calculate the yearly depreciation expense for the fleet of vehicles assuming the company uses the straight-line depreciation method.

b. Prepare a schedule showing the amount of depreciation expense for each of the three years of the estimated useful life assuming the company uses the double-declining-balance depreciation method.

c. Address the following questions:

   (1) Double-declining-balance calculates depreciation at twice the straight-line rate. Why is the amount of depreciation expense in 2007 under double-declining-balance not exactly twice the amount under straight-line for 2007?

   (2) Over the three-year estimated useful life of the vehicles, how much depreciation expense will be charged against income using the straight-line method? How much will be charged against income using the double-declining-balance method?

   (3) Discuss the impact on the net income of each method of depreciation in the first two years of life of the asset.

LO 4 & 5: Computation of Gain or Loss

8–36. Cruse Company purchased a machine on January 2, 2008 for $200,000. When originally purchased, the machine had an estimated useful life of five years and an estimated residual value of $25,000. The company uses straight-line depreciation. It is now June 30, 2011, and the company has decided to dispose of the machine.

REQUIRED:
a. Calculate the book value of the machine as of June 30, 2011.
b. Calculate the gain or loss on the sale of the machine assuming Cruse sells it for $102,000.
c. Calculate the gain or loss on the sale of the machine assuming Cruse sells it for $25,000.

LO 4 & 5:   Computation of Gain or Loss

8–37. Farr Company purchased a machine on January 2, 2007 and paid $150,000 for it. When originally purchased, the machine had an estimated useful life of four years and an estimated residual value of $10,000. The company uses straight-line depreciation. It is now September 30, 2009, and the company has decided to dispose of the machine.

REQUIRED:
a. Calculate the book value of the machine as of September 30, 2009.
b. Calculate the gain or loss on the sale of the machine assuming Farr sells it for $172,000.
c. Calculate the gain or loss on the sale of the machine assuming Farr sells it for $25,000.

LO 4 & 5:   Computation of Gain or Loss

8–38. Simpson Company purchased a machine in January 2001 for $450,000. When originally purchased, the machine had an estimated useful life of 10 years and an estimated residual value of $50,000. The company uses straight-line depreciation. It is now January 2, 2008, and the company has decided to dispose of the machine.

REQUIRED:
a. Calculate the book value of the machine as of December 31, 2007.
b. Calculate the gain or loss on the sale of the machine assuming Simpson sells it for $130,000.
c. Calculate the gain or loss on the sale of the machine assuming Simpson sells it for $30,000.

LO 4, 5, & 6:   Impact of Depreciation Methods on Gains and Losses

8–39. Millie and Maude are twins. Each has her own company. Three years ago, on the same day, they each purchased copiers for use by their companies. The machines were identical in every way and cost exactly the same amount ($28,000). The machines had the same estimated useful life (five years) and the same estimated residual value ($3,000). The only difference was the depreciation method chosen. Millie chose to depreciate her copier using straight-line based on time, while Maude selected an accelerated depreciation method.

Owing to rapid technological developments in the machines, Millie decided at the end of two years to sell her old machine and buy a new one. Maude decided to do the same thing. In fact, they each received exactly the same amount when they sold their machines ($16,500). Later, while they were having lunch together, Maude mentioned that when she sold her copier, she had a gain of more than $6,000 on the sale. Millie kept quiet, but was confused because she knew she had sold her copier for exactly the same amount as Maude, yet the sale of her copier had resulted in a loss of $1,500.

REQUIRED:

Explain how Millie could have had a loss of $1,500 on the sale of her copier, while Maude had a sizable gain.

LO 4, 5, & 6:   Impact of Depreciation Methods on Gains and Losses

8–40. Redd and Fred each ran their own automotive repair shop. Each bought a new piece of equipment costing $10,000 on January 2. The equipment is expected to have a five-year life and no salvage value. Redd used straight-line depreciation and Fred used double-declining-balance depreciation. At the end of three years, each of them sold their machines for $5,500.

REQUIRED:
a. Compute the depreciation for both Redd and Fred through the third year.
b. Compute the gain or loss that each would recognize on the sale of the machine.
c. If the gain or loss is different for each of them, explain why.

LO 4, 5, & 6:   Impact of Depreciation Methods on Gains and Losses

8–41. Ethel and Lucy each ran their own cooking school. Each bought a new piece of equipment costing $20,000 on January 2. The equipment is expected to have a five-year life and no salvage value. Ethel used straight-line depreciation and Lucy used double-declining-balance depreciation. At the end of three years, each of them sold their machines for $11,000.

REQUIRED:
a. Compute the depreciation for both Ethel and Lucy through the third year.
b. Compute the gain or loss that each would recognize on the sale of the machine.
c. If the gain or loss is different for each of them, explain why.

LO 4, 5, & 6:   Impact of Depreciation Methods on Gains and Losses

8–42. Ricky and Fred each ran their own construction business. Each bought a new piece of equipment costing $40,000 on January 2. The equipment is expected to have a five-year life and no salvage value. Ricky used straight-line depreciation and Fred used double-declining-balance depreciation. At the end of three years, each of them sold their machines for $22,000.

REQUIRED:
a. Compute the depreciation for both Ricky and Fred through the third year.
b. Compute the gain or loss that each would recognize on the sale of the machine.
c. If the gain or loss is different for each of them, explain why.

LO 7: Meaning of Gains and Losses

8–43. Explain in your own words what a gain or loss on the sale of a piece of equipment means and how the gain or loss relates to depreciation expense.

LO 7: Comprehensive

8–44. Exhibit 8–7 in the text illustrates Beavers Corporation's financial statements, based on double-declining-balance depreciation. Use the income statements and balance sheets presented in the exhibit as a basis for completing the following requirements.

REQUIRED:
a. Prepare statements of retained earnings for Beavers Corporation as of the end of 2007, 2008, 2009, and 2010.
b. What can you conclude about the dividend policy of Beaver Corporation from the information provided and your response to Requirement a?
c. If no depreciation had been recorded, how would the statements of retained earnings have been different?

LO 7: Comprehensive

8–45. Barker Company opened for business on January 2, 2008. During its first month of operation, the company had the following transactions.

Jan 2: Purchased a truck for $10,000 and paid cash. The truck has an estimated useful life of three years. The company estimates the truck's residual value to be $1,000, and uses straight-line depreciation.

Jan 2: Purchased $40,000 of merchandise inventory on account. Payment in full is due February 2.

Jan 3: Paid January office rent of $2,500.

Jan 5: Purchased $15,000 of merchandise inventory and paid cash on that date.

Jan 10: Sold $12,000 of merchandise inventory for $25,000 to a customer and received the cash on that date.

Jan 20: Sold $7,000 of merchandise inventory for $11,000. The sale was on account and the customer has until February 20 to pay.

Jan 24: Paid miscellaneous January operating expenses totaling $8,000.

Jan 31: Received bills for utilities, advertising, and phone service totaling $1,200. All these bills were for services performed in January. They will all be paid the first week in February.

Use the January 2008 income statements for Barker Company prepared under the cash and accrual bases of accounting to complete the following requirements.

REQUIRED:
a. Explain why the Cost of Goods Sold amounts on the two income statements differ?
b. Barker purchased $55,000 of merchandise inventory during January 2008. However, under the accrual basis of accounting, the company properly expensed $19,000 as cost of goods sold for the month. Explain where (if anywhere) the company shows the remaining $36,000 of merchandise inventory?
c. Barker purchased $55,000 of merchandise inventory during January 2008. Under the cash basis of accounting, the company properly expensed $15,000 as cost of goods sold for the month. Explain where (if anywhere) the company shows the remaining $40,000 of merchandise inventory?

d. Both income statements show an expense related to the truck purchased on January 2, 2008. How were the amounts on each income statement determined? Include in your answer what the amounts represent and why the cost of the truck is treated as it is.

e. What will be the book value of the truck on the December 31, 2008, balance sheet under
   (1) cash basis accounting?
   (2) accrual basis accounting?

f. What will be the book value of the truck on the December 31, 2010, balance sheet under
   (1) cash basis accounting?
   (2) accrual basis accounting?

g. Comment generally on why the net income (loss) amounts on the two income statements are so different.

BARKER COMPANY
Income Statement
For the Month Ending January 31, 2008

Cash Basis

Sales	$25,000	
LESS: Cost of Goods Sold	15,000	
Gross Margin		$10,000
Operating Expenses:		
Truck	$10,000	
Rent	2,500	
Miscellaneous Expenses	8,000	
Total Operating Expenses		(20,500)
Net Income (Loss)		$(10,500)

BARKER COMPANY
Income Statement
For the Month Ending January 31, 2008

Accrual Basis

Sales	$36,000	
LESS: Cost of Goods Sold	19,000	
Gross Margin		$17,000
Operating Expenses:		
Rent	$2,500	
Depreciation—Truck	250	
Miscellaneous Expenses	8,000	
Accrued Expenses	1,200	
Total Operating Expenses		(11,950)
Net Income (Loss)		$ 5,050

LO 8: Recording Assets and Depreciation

*8–46. Cunningham Corporation purchased a new piece of equipment for $60,000 cash. Cunningham estimates the useful life of the equipment at five years with a salvage value of $10,000.

REQUIRED:

a. Prepare the journal entry to record the purchase of the asset.

b. Prepare the journal entries to record the depreciation for the first year of life of the asset.

LO 8:   Recording Assets and Depreciation

*8–47. Buffington, Inc. purchased a new piece of equipment for $560,000. The company paid $125,000 in cash and borrowed the remainder from the bank. Buffington estimates the useful life of the equipment at six years with a salvage value of $60,000.

REQUIRED:
  a. Prepare the journal entry to record the purchase of the asset.
  b. Prepare the journal entry to record the depreciation for the first year of life of the asset.

LO 8:   Recording Assets and Depreciation

*8–48. Buffington, Inc. purchased a new piece of equipment for $560,000. The company paid $125,000 in cash and borrowed the remainder from the bank. Buffington estimates the useful life of the equipment at six years with a salvage value of $60,000.

REQUIRED:
  a. Compute the gain or loss if the company sells the equipment for $86,000 at the end of the fourth year using straight-line depreciation.
  b. Prepare the journal entry to record the sale of the equipment.

LO 8:   Recording Assets and Depreciation

*8–49. Ralph Corporation purchased a new piece of equipment for $75,000 cash. Ralph estimates the useful life of the equipment at seven years with a salvage value of $5,000.

REQUIRED:
  a. Prepare the journal entry to record the purchase of the asset.
  b. Prepare the journal entry to record the depreciation for the first year of life of the asset.

LO 8:   Recording Assets and Depreciation

*8–50. Dustin Corporation purchased a new piece of equipment for $75,000. The company paid $5,000 in cash and borrowed the remainder from the bank. Dustin estimates the useful life of the equipment at seven years with a salvage value of $12,000.

REQUIRED:
  a. Prepare the journal entry to record the purchase of the asset.
  b. Prepare the journal entry to record the depreciation for the first year of life of the asset.

LO 8:   Recording Assets and Depreciation

*8–51. Dustin Corporation purchased a new piece of equipment for $75,000. The company paid $5,000 in cash and borrowed the remainder from the bank. Dustin estimates the useful life of the equipment at seven years with a salvage value of $12,000.

REQUIRED:
  a. Compute the gain or loss if the company sells the equipment for $8,000 at the end of the fourth year using double-declining-balance depreciation.
  b. Prepare the journal entry to record the sale of the equipment.

LO 8: Recording Assets and Depreciation

*8–52. Randall Company purchased a stamping machine on January 2, 2007, for $480,000. The estimated useful life of the stamping machine is five years. The machine has an estimated residual value of $40,000.

REQUIRED:
a. Calculate the yearly depreciation expense for the stamping machine assuming the company uses the straight-line depreciation method.
b. Record the journal entries for the depreciation that would be required each year.
c. Prepare the required journal entries to record the sale of the machine at the end of two years for $200,000.

LO 8: Recording Assets and Depreciation

*8–53. Wooten Company purchased a pasteurizing machine on January 2, 2007, for $375,000. The estimated useful life of the machine is five years. The machine has an estimated residual value of $40,000.

REQUIRED:
a. Calculate the yearly depreciation expense for the machine assuming the company uses the double-declining-balance depreciation method and prepare the journal entries to record depreciation each year.
b. Assuming the machine is sold at the end of 2009 for $50,000, prepare the required entries to record the sale.
c. Assuming the machine is sold at the end of April 2009 for $50,000, prepare the required entries to record the sale.

LO 8: Recording Assets and Depreciation

*8–54. Chesley, Inc. purchased a fleet of delivery trucks on January 2, 2007, for $700,000. The estimated useful life of the vehicles is four years, after which Chesley thinks it will be able to sell the entire fleet for $50,000.

REQUIRED:
a. Calculate the yearly depreciation expense for the fleet of vehicles assuming the company uses the straight-line depreciation method and prepare the journal entries to record the depreciation.
b. Assume the fleet is sold at the end of the life for $70,000. Prepare the journal entries to record the transaction.
c. Assume the fleet is sold on March 31, 2010, for $30,000. Prepare the journal entries to record the transaction.

LO 8: Recording Assets and Depreciation

*8–55. Ricky and Fred each run their own construction business. Each bought a new piece of equipment costing $40,000 on January 2, 2007. The equipment is expected to have a five-year life and no salvage value. Ricky uses straight-line depreciation and Fred uses double-declining-balance depreciation. On June 30, 2010, each of them sold their machines for $22,000.

REQUIRED:
a. Compute the depreciation for both Ricky and Fred through the date of sale.

b. Compute the gain or loss that each would recognize on the sale of the equipment.

c. Prepare the journal entries necessary to record the purchase, annual depreciation, and sale of Ricky's and Fred's equipment.

FINANCIAL REPORTING CASES

Comprehensive

8–56. Visit the website for Sonic Corporation at www.sonicdriveins.com. Locate the current copy of the annual report and find the Notes to Financial Statements.

REQUIRED:

a. Read Note 1 and summarize the information presented about Property, Plant and Equipment. Include in your summary the method or methods used for depreciation and the methods used to record Property, Plant, and Equipment.

b. Go to the website for this text, www.pearsoncustom.com/terrell, and visit the Research Navigator. Find a recent article or press release about Sonic Corporation's acquisition of new locations or assets and print it. Write a one-page reaction paper to the article.

Comprehensive

8–57. Visit the website for Darden Restaurants at www.Darden.com. Locate the current copy of the annual report and find the Notes to Financial Statements. Read Note 1 about Property, Plant and Equipment and the Note on long-lived assets.

REQUIRED:

a. What type of depreciation method(s) does Darden employ?

b. What are the useful lives assigned to the different types of assets by Darden?

c. How much depreciation expense did Darden recognize in the last year? How can you determine this amount?

d. Go to the website for this text, www.pearsoncustom.com/terrell, and visit the Research Navigator. Find a recent article or press release about Darden's acquisition of new locations or assets and print it. Write a one-page reaction paper to the article.

Comprehensive

8–58. Visit the A T & T website at www.att.com. Locate the current copy of the annual report and find the Notes to Financial Statements. Read Note 1 about Property, Plant and Equipment and the Note on long-lived assets.

REQUIRED:

a. Determine the type of depreciation methods used for different types of long-lived assets.

b. How much depreciation expense did AT&T recognize for the current year? List the number of places you found the depreciation amount.

c. Go to the website for this text, www.pearsoncustom.com/terrell, and visit the Research Navigator. Find a recent article or press release about AT&T's acquisition of long-lived assets and print it. Write a one-page reaction paper to the article.

Chapter 9

Challenging Issues under Accrual Accounting: Merchandise Inventory and Cost of Goods Sold

*Y*our boss has offered you a promotion to manage the inventory in a new division the company is opening in Denver. You want this opportunity because you love to ski, and you enjoy working with inventory. You will be part of the team that selects the inventory software package and designs the inventory protection system. Part of your compensation package includes a bonus at the end of the year based upon both the gross profit percentage and the net income. How does inventory management relate to gross profit and net income? Your secretary reminds you to be careful about LIFO and FIFO. What is she talking about and how does that tie into profits? Time to find an accounting textbook.

In Chapter 8, we explored one source of variation across companies' financial statements—choice of depreciation method. Remember that GAAP allow companies a choice, among generally accepted accounting principles, because different industries have different operating characteristics. Accounting principles do not specify just one practice that fits all.

To gauge the cost of goods a firm sells, GAAP allow several alternative methods that measure the cost flow of inventory. The way a company accounts for its merchandise inventory purchases and sales can have a direct and significant impact on the firm's reported net income. ■

After completing your work on this chapter, you should be able to do the following:

1. Explain goods available for sale (GAFS) and name its components.
2. Describe the relationship between ending inventory and cost of goods sold.
3. Differentiate between the physical flow of merchandise and the cost flow of merchandise.
4. Explain the differences between periodic and perpetual inventory systems.
5. List different inventory cost flow assumptions and contrast how the use of each affects reported net income on the income statement.
6. Calculate cost of goods sold and ending inventory using FIFO, LIFO, and average cost inventory cost flow assumptions.
*7. Calculate cash discounts and invoice due dates, and determine who bears the freight expense from the freight terms.
*8. Complete the recording process for inventory purchases and sales.

TRACKING INVENTORY COSTS

Merchandising Companies

merchandise inventory
The physical units (goods) a company buys to resell as part of its business operation. Also called inventory.

beginning inventory The amount of merchandise inventory (units or dollars) on hand at the beginning of the income statement period.

purchases The amount of merchandise inventory bought during the income statement period.

goods available for sale (GAFS) The total amount of merchandise inventory a company has available to sell in a given income statement period.

cost of goods sold (COGS) The cost of the merchandise inventory no longer on hand, and assumed sold during the period. Also called cost of sales.

ending inventory The amount of inventory (in units or dollars) still on hand at the end of an accounting period.

The tangible products that merchandisers sell are called **merchandise inventory,** or **inventory.** For example, Office Depot sells office equipment, Lazy Boy sells desks and chairs, and Chrysler sells cars and trucks. The product each firm sells is called inventory. However, to customers, these products may be long-lived assets.

When we discuss inventory, we must consider two aspects: the number of units of inventory and the cost of each of those units. To apply the matching principle, we must determine the quantity of units sold and how much expense matches the sales of the period. A mathematical relationship exists between the beginning inventory, the purchases during the period, the cost of goods sold, and the ending inventory.

At the beginning of an income statement period, a firm has an amount of merchandise inventory on hand called **beginning inventory.** During the period, the firm buys additional inventory we call **purchases.** The cost of purchases includes all the costs to bring the item to a saleable state, including freight, packaging, and make-ready costs. A firm can sell only the goods it has on hand during a period, represented by the total of the beginning inventory plus the amount it bought (purchases). We call this total the **goods available for sale (GAFS).** Whether we are referring to the physical count of inventory units or its cost, the following relationship between beginning inventory (BI), purchases (Purch), and goods available for sale (GAFS) holds true:

$$\text{Beginning Inventory} + \text{Purchases} = \text{Goods Available for Sale}$$
$$\text{BI} \qquad + \quad \text{Purch} \quad = \qquad \text{GAFS}$$

Once a firm has goods to sell, reality dictates that at the end of the period, the merchandise is either gone or still on hand. We recognize the inventory that is gone as an income statement expense of the period called **cost of goods sold (COGS)** or **cost of sales.** The inventory still on hand is the **ending inventory,** a balance sheet asset, because it has probable future economic benefit since it can generate future sales. We can calculate the cost of goods sold (COGS) by subtracting the ending inventory from goods available for sale. Thus, the total amount that we could have sold (GAFS) minus the amount we still had at the end of the period (EI) equals the amount that we sold (COGS):

$$GAFS - EI = COGS$$

Conversely, if we know cost of goods sold, we can determine a company's ending merchandise inventory for a given period. The total amount we could have sold (GAFS) less the amount we did sell (COGS) is the amount we should have left at the end of the period (EI):

$$GAFS - COGS = EI$$

These relationships hold true whether we are considering the quantity of inventory (physical units) or the cost of that inventory.

Discussion Question

9-1. If inventory is gone at the end of a period but was not sold, what might have happened to it?

Exhibit 9–1 shows examples of these relationships in terms of both units and dollar amounts for the Strawn Book Company for one month's operations. The month starts with 200 books on hand; Strawn buys 600 new books, sells 650 books, and has 150 books on hand at the end of the month. This information contains four different data items. We need only three of these items to compute any fourth item. In the first table in the exhibit, we use ending inventory to calculate cost of goods sold, and in the second table, we use cost of goods sold to calculate ending inventory. It is important to learn from these two calculations that the total of ending inventory and cost of goods sold will always equal goods available for sale (in units and in dollars).

Exhibit 9–1
Relationships among BI, Purch, GAFS, EI, and COGS for Strawn Book Company

	Units	Cost	
Beginning Inventory	200	$2,000	BI
+ Purchases	600	6,000	+ Purch
= Goods Available for Sale	800	$8,000	= GAFS
− Ending Inventory	150	1,500	− EI
= Cost of Goods Sold	650	$6,500	= COGS

OR

	Units	Cost	
Beginning Inventory	200	$2,000	BI
+ Purchases	600	6,000	+ Purch
= Goods Available for Sale	800	$8,000	= GAFS
− Cost of Goods Sold	650	6,500	− COGS
= Ending Inventory	150	$1,500	= EI

Discussion Question

9-2. You invite your friends to a party. You check your supplies and find hot dogs, dip, and pretzels. You go to the store to buy soda, chips, hot dog buns, peanuts, and ice cream. Following an enjoyable party, you survey the aftermath and find the pantry and refrigerator bare. The freezer is full of ice cream because everyone forgot to eat it. To figure out how much the party cost you, describe the following:

a. beginning inventory
b. purchases
c. goods available
d. ending inventory
e. "cost" of the party

raw materials inventory
The inventory of raw materials to be transferred into production in a manufacturing company.

work-in-process inventory
The cost of raw materials, labor, and other expenses associated with unfinished units during the process of converting raw materials into finished goods for a manufacturing company.

finished goods inventory
The inventory ready to sell in a manufacturing company. Also called finished goods.

cost of goods manufactured
The cost of converting raw materials into finished goods in a manufacturing firm. The cost is equivalent to purchases in a merchandising firm.

Manufacturing Companies

The inventory that manufacturing companies sell can have different forms—goods ready for retail sale or component parts for other manufacturers. Manufacturers convert raw materials to another form for customers. In the manufacturing process, a manufacturer has three inventories. A manufacturer buys raw materials and keeps these costs in its **raw materials inventory.** While the workers convert the raw materials into the finished product, the material costs and other costs accumulate in the **work-in-process inventory.** The manufacturer calls its final products *finished goods* and records the cost in the **finished goods inventory.** When the manufacturer sells the inventory, the cost of goods sold formula is exactly the same for a manufacturer and a merchandiser except the manufacturer has **cost of goods manufactured** instead of purchases. As you can see, although the same concepts for tracking costs presented for merchandising firms apply to manufacturing firms, manufacturing accounting is complicated. Therefore, we will present manufacturing costs beginning with Chapter 1 of management accounting.

INVENTORY SYSTEMS

A firm selects the type of inventory system it uses to determine the reality of the inventory quantity it has and the measurement of that reality. Over time, businesses have developed two major inventory systems—the periodic and the perpetual methods. Each has advantages and disadvantages in comparison.

Periodic Inventory System

periodic inventory system
An inventory system in which all inventory and cost of goods sold calculations are done at the end of the income statement period.

Under a **periodic inventory system,** the purchases of new inventory are treated as an expense until the end of the period. Unsold goods (ending inventory) become an asset on the balance sheet. We make the cost of goods sold calculations at the end of the income statement period similar to the calculations in Exhibit 9–1. Detailed inventory records are not updated during the period. Companies using this system do not track which products have been sold until the end of period, when the company prepares its financial statements.

The strength of the periodic inventory system is that it involves relatively little additional record keeping. This fact may be important to a firm with 10,000 different inventory items. Its greatest weakness is that it does not provide the company with any day-to-day information about the status of its inventory.

Prior to the computer age, most companies with a moderate volume of inventory employed the periodic inventory system, because keeping detailed inventory records manually was too time consuming. The costs of keeping timely inventory information far outweighed the benefits of the knowledge. However, current computer technology has made the task of keeping daily records of inventory transactions a low-cost and reasonably efficient process. Today's software includes features that automatically reorder inventory when it reaches a preselected level. Scanning devices even automate the record-keeping process. Consequently, the perpetual inventory system has grown in popularity.

Inventory data consists of two components: units and dollar costs. Although many companies now keep detailed information about the quantity of the inventory units, it is not certain that all companies keep perpetual cost information. Keeping cost information requires much more time, expense, and computer storage space. Some companies may keep both the units and dollar costs on the periodic system, and others may keep only the dollar costs on the periodic basis. Therefore, we will consider the accounting treatment of the periodic system to determine cost of goods sold and ending inventory.

Perpetual Inventory System

perpetual inventory system
An inventory system in which both the physical count of inventory units and the cost classification (asset or expense) are updated when a transaction involves inventory.

Under a complete **perpetual inventory system,** both the physical count of inventory units and the cost classification (asset or expense) are updated whenever the transaction involves inventory. A perpetual inventory system considers inventory an asset until it is sold, when it is transferred to the expense cost of goods sold. Each inventory item has its own control report that the system updates daily, weekly, or monthly depending upon the needs of the business. So a business that sells 1,000 different items will have 1,000 control reports, one for each item. If all the units in Exhibit 9–1 were the same inventory item, the control report for the month of June might look like Exhibit 9–2.

This report shows four important facts for this inventory:

1. the beginning balance of 200 units that cost $2,000
2. the total purchases during the month of 600 units that cost $6,000
3. the total sales during the month of 650 units that cost $6,500
4. the ending balance of inventory of 150 units that cost $1,500

Exhibit 9–2
Inventory Control Report under Perpetual Inventory System

Date	Explanation	Purchases Units	Purchases Unit Cost	Purchases Total Cost	Cost of Goods Sold Units	Cost of Goods Sold Unit Cost	Cost of Goods Sold Total Cost	Inventory Balance Units	Inventory Balance Unit Cost	Inventory Balance Total Cost
6-1	Beg. Balance							200	$10	$2,000
6-10	Purchase	400	$10	$4,000				600	$10	$6,000
6-15	Sale				300	$10	$3,000	300	$10	$3,000
6-20	Purchase	200	$10	$2,000				500	$10	$5,000
6-30	Sale				350	$10	$3,500	150	$10	$1,500
	Total	600		$6,000	650		$6,500			

We expect to find the cost of goods sold of $6,500 on the income statement for the period and the ending balance of inventory of $1,500 on the balance sheet for the last day of the period. In addition, we see the history of the purchases and sales for the inventory item. This detail provides marketing managers, purchasing agents, and other company employees valuable information. In this way, accounting data contribute to the efficient operation of the entire business.

Strawn uses a computerized accounting system to generate its inventory control reports automatically. Computerized systems capture purchases and sales data either by keyboard entries or by a scanning device. Retailers use scanners to read bar codes—formally known as Universal Product Codes (UPCs)—printed on the inventory labels. The computer can be programmed to assign a given cost to a given inventory item and thus can perform the necessary calculations to update inventory records. In addition to ringing up the sales price of a book, the computer software simultaneously updates the inventory records by changing the number of physical units on hand and transferring the cost of the book sold from merchandise inventory to cost of goods sold. This technology gives Strawn's employees a timely report to help them determine the number of books sold and the number of books remaining on the shelf without physically counting them.

Discussion Questions

9-3. Assume that a book's inventory control report shows 25 books remaining on the shelf. Just to make sure, the bookstore manager goes over to the shelf, counts the remaining books, and finds there are only 22. What might explain the discrepancy?

9-4. If you were the manager responsible for inventory, how often would you count the items to verify the inventory control records? Are there any events that might encourage you to perform a physical count?

The Necessity of a Physical Inventory Count

Regardless of whether a firm chooses a periodic or perpetual inventory system, it must conduct physical counts of its inventory at least annually to satisfy Internal Revenue Service regulations and auditors' requirements. The nature of the inventory determines the most cost-effective frequency for physical inventory counts. Normally, the higher the number of different items and the lower the cost per unit, the less frequently the company physically counts. Consider the case of a grocery store or variety store that contains thousands of different items with relatively low cost per item. Contrast this with a car dealership. A cost-benefit analysis would tell you that one person could count the cars on the lot in an hour, and if there were a discrepancy of one vehicle, the dollar value would be substantial. A whole team of employees would have to work eight or 10 hours to count the items in a grocery store, and the dollar value of missing items might be less than the dollar cost of the employees' wages to count.

Beyond the need to satisfy external parties' requirements, why would a company conduct a physical count? If the company maintains a periodic inventory system, the physical count is mandatory to determine the amount of both the ending inventory and, consequently, the cost of goods sold. Does this mean that a firm with a perpetual inventory system can omit the physical count? The accounting system generates the amount of ending inventory, called **book inventory**. Book inventory may or may not coincide with the merchandise inventory actually on hand

book inventory The amount of ending inventory (units and dollars) resulting from transactions recorded by a perpetual inventory system.

Exhibit 9–3
Adjusted Record of
Ending Inventory after
Physical Count

	Per Books		Per Physical Count	
	Units	Cost	Units	Cost
Beginning Inventory, January 1	200	$2,000	200	$2,000
+ Purchases	600	6,000	600	6,000
= Goods Available for Sale	800	$8,000	800	$8,000
− Ending Inventory, January 31	150	1,500	130	1,300
= Cost of Goods Sold	650	$6,500	670	$6,700

at the end of the period. Errors in the recording process, shoplifting, and employee theft can occur to cause the book inventory to differ from the actual inventory. In addition, inventory can be intentionally or accidentally damaged, discarded, or spoiled. Some inventory actually evaporates over time. The results of a physical inventory help management to pinpoint possible problems to improve the internal control procedures, and physical control of the inventory. Remember that for most merchandising firms, inventory may represent the largest investment in assets. Safeguarding a large asset is critical to the success of the firm.

Results of the physical inventory count take precedence over the book inventory generated by the inventory records. We adjust both the inventory asset and the cost of goods sold for the period for any differences between the physical count and the book inventory so that the periodic count is reflected in the financial statements. To illustrate, assume that Strawn Book Company takes a physical count of books and finds only 130 books on hand instead of 150 that the inventory record shows. Exhibit 9–3 shows the calculation of cost of goods sold and ending inventory based on the physical records and the amounts adjusted for the ending physical count.

In this case, an adjustment of the records is necessary to reflect reality: The amount shown on the balance sheet as ending inventory must be the amount actually on hand. Because we know that cost of goods available for sale ($8,000) will end up as either cost of goods sold or ending inventory, a change in the amount shown as ending inventory will cause a change in the amount shown as cost of goods sold. The cost of goods sold reported as an expense on the income statement for the period is $6,700. The merchandise inventory reported as an asset on the balance sheet is $1,300, which reflects the reality of the number of units actually on hand at the end of the period. With this adjustment of the records, Strawn Book Company's financial statement amounts will more accurately reflect reality.

Discussion Questions

9–5. If careless employees break inventory items and discard them, or dishonest employees steal inventory items, how is a company's income statement affected?

9–6. Which causes companies more losses each year in the United States, employee theft or shoplifting? (Hint: Visit the website of the Association of Certified Fraud Examiners at www.acfe.com.)

9–7. How can companies guard against shoplifting and employee theft?

The Physical Movement of Inventory (Reality)

A merchandising company purchases goods from a manufacturer or wholesale distributor that delivers the goods to the company's warehouse. A firm's warehouse may not always be a building with four walls and a roof. The natural differences among products causes the warehousing function to differ. Consider the following examples:

1. Corn delivered to a silo
2. Gravel stored in a pit
3. Oil placed in an underground storage tank
4. Cars, trucks, and vans parked on a lot

first in, first out (FIFO) The inventory flow concept based on the assumption that the first units of inventory purchased are the first ones sold.

When a farmer delivers corn to a silo, he deposits the corn in the top of the silo and receives payment from the grain dealer. When the grain dealer sells the corn to a customer, the customer extracts the corn from the bottom of the silo. Silos function because of the law of gravity, so the oldest corn is in the bottom of the silo and the newest corn is in the top of the silo. Therefore, the physical movement of the corn is on a **first-in, first-out (FIFO)** basis. The first corn deposited into the silo is the first corn removed from the silo.

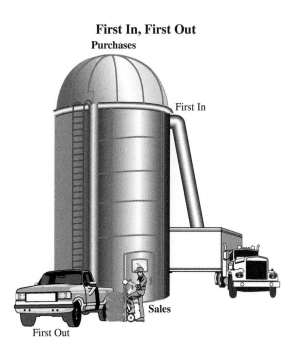

First In, First Out

Purchases

First In

Sales

First Out

last in, first out (LIFO) The inventory flow concept based on the assumption that the last units of inventory purchased are the first ones sold.

Gravel dealers frequently keep the gravel inventory in a pit. When new gravel arrives at the dealer's location, the truck driver dumps the gravel into the pit. When the gravel dealer makes a sale, she removes the gravel from the top of the pit because she cannot access the bottom. The physical movement of the gravel is on a **last-in, first-out (LIFO)** basis. The last gravel deposited into the pit is the first gravel to be removed.

Last In, First Out

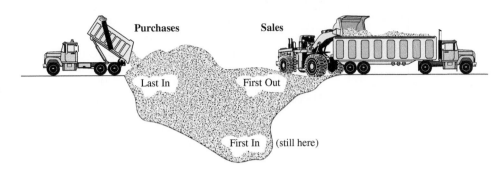

When an oil producer delivers oil to a customer, it frequently delivers the oil to an aboveground storage tank. Because of the physical properties of oil, it blends with other oil when added into a container. So when oil enters a storage tank, it mixes with other oil and loses its unit identity. Therefore, any oil extracted from the tank is a mixture of all oil added to the tank. We might say that extracted oil represents an average of the oil inventory.

Average Cost

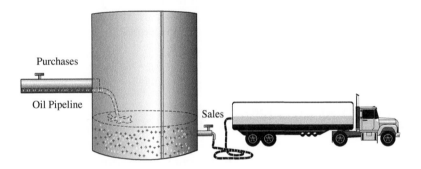

Finally, look at a dealer's lot of cars, trucks, and vans. Each vehicle has unique characteristics and a serial number. The dealer places the vehicles wherever there is room and frequently moves the vehicles around the lot. Customers purchase their choice of vehicle, based not on its location, but on its ability to suit their needs. Each customer specifically identifies the vehicle he or she wants. The physical movement of the vehicles is based upon the specific identification of the desired unit.

Discussion Questions

9-8. For what products would it be important that the first units purchased be the first ones sold? Explain.

9-9. Describe five different categories of products for sale in a grocery store. How do stock personnel typically restock the shelves for each of these products? Why?

9-10. If you owned a retail computer store, what reasons would you have for insisting that your employees sell the first computer received before the ones that arrived at the store later?

The Flow of Inventory Cost (Measurement of Reality)

We have discussed the physical flow of units in and out of inventory. But what about the cost of these units? As a firm purchases inventory, we add its cost to inventory in the accounting records. Likewise, as the firm sells the merchandise, we remove its cost from inventory and transfer it to cost of goods sold. You might suppose that accounting rules require the flow of costs through a company's accounting records to reflect the reality of the way the physical units flow through the company's inventory. However, accounting rules do not require that the cost flow for inventory mirror the flow of physical units. Regardless of how physical units flow through inventory, a company may select any cost flow assumption it chooses. Thus we see another example of how reality and the measurement of reality may differ.

COST FLOW ASSUMPTIONS

When a company purchases one product and sells it before it buys another product, the physical flow of product equals the cost flow of the product. However, when a firm buys many products at different times for different amounts, the physical inventory flow (reality) and the cost flow (measurement of reality) seldom coincide. As you might guess from our discussion of the physical flow of goods, accounting has four basic cost flow assumptions:

1. First in, first out (FIFO)
2. Last in, first out (LIFO)
3. Average cost
4. Specific identification

The most common physical flow of goods is first in, first out (FIFO); however, GAAP do not require that the inventory cost method match the physical flow of inventory. Many firms use more than one cost flow assumption by using different assumptions for different types of inventory.

A firm may select any of the inventory costing methods regardless of the way the physical units of merchandise inventory flow through the warehouse. This results in another situation in which the difference between reality and the measurement of reality leads to some complexities in accrual accounting. Due to current U.S. tax laws, many firms select the LIFO costing method to reduce taxes, even though it does not match the physical flow of goods. Financial statement users should understand the way in which companies track inventory costs and arrive at the amounts presented on their financial statements, because as you will see, the inventory costing method selected changes the net income and balance sheet assets. To understand these differences, we will explore different cost flow assumptions that take different approaches to measuring the flow of inventory costs through both a periodic and a perpetual inventory system. Because the specific identification method is unique and results in the same valuation regardless of periodic or perpetual system, we will look at this method first.

Specific Identification Cost Flow Assumption

specific identification The method of inventory cost flow that identifies each item sold by a company.

Dobbs Motor Company sells antique automobiles to an exclusive clientele and appropriately uses the **specific identification** method to cost its vehicles. Exhibit 9–4 details the cars in the inventory at the beginning of March, those purchased during the month, and those sold during March.

Exhibit 9–4
Dobbs Motor Company Inventory Transactions for March 2007

Date of Purchase	Description	Cost	Date Sold	Selling Price
10-15-2007	1926 Bentley	$35,000	3-5-2008	$45,000
12-25-2007	1935 Mercedes	42,000		
1-25-2008	1955 Thunderbird	25,000	3-9-2008	38,000
2-10-2008	1935 Model T Ford	24,000	3-18-2008	36,000
3-10-2008	1940 Cadillac	38,000		
3-25-2008	1932 Silver Cloud	80,000		

We can analyze this information to determine Dobbs' sales, cost of goods sold, and gross profit for the month of March as follows:

1. Sales total $119,000. ($45,000 + $38,000 + $36,000)
2. The beginning inventory consisted of the first four cars listed:

1926 Bentley	$ 35,000
1935 Mercedes	42,000
1955 Thunderbird	25,000
1935 Model T Ford	24,000
Total Cost	$126,000

3. Dobbs purchased two cars during March:

1940 Cadillac	$ 38,000
1932 Silver Cloud	80,000
Total Cost	$118,000

4. The cost of goods sold included three cars:

1926 Bentley	$35,000
1955 Thunderbird	25,000
1935 Model T Ford	24,000
Total Cost	$84,000

5. The ending inventory includes three cars:

1935 Mercedes	$ 42,000
1940 Cadillac	38,000
1932 Silver Cloud	80,000
Total Cost	$160,000

6. Summary of information in the format of the income statement:

Sales		$119,000
Cost of Goods Sold:		
Beginning Inventory	$126,000	
Purchases	118,000	
Goods Available for Sale	$244,000	
Ending Inventory	160,000	
Cost of Goods Sold		84,000
Gross Profit		$ 35,000

Because each inventory item is unique, there is no cost determination difference between a periodic system and a perpetual system with a specific identification method. The same is true if each product included in beginning inventory and each item purchased (or made) during the period cost exactly the same amount per unit. LIFO, FIFO, and average cost methods would result in identical measurements of reality. However, the cost of products rarely remains constant because of technological advances, economic conditions, and competition. We will look at the effect on inventory and cost of goods sold caused by changing prices using the periodic and perpetual inventory systems.

COST FLOW ASSUMPTIONS UNDER A PERIODIC SYSTEM

Changes in the cost of inventory items over time cause different cost flow assumptions to result in different amounts for cost of goods sold and ending inventory. To illustrate this in a periodic system, we examine the effect of three different cost flow assumptions on one product sold by the Harwood Equipment Company. Exhibit 9–5 contains the inventory activity for Harwood during September. We can analyze the information based on our knowledge of inventory cost, cost of goods sold, and gross profit.

1. Harwood sold three units at $1,500 for a total of $4,500.
2. Harwood had a beginning inventory of one unit that cost $800.

Exhibit 9–5
Harwood Equipment
Company Inventory
Transactions

Date	Transaction	Units	Unit Cost	Unit Selling Price
9-1	Beginning Inventory	1	$ 800	
9-3	Purchase	2	1,025	
9-17	Sale	1		$1,500
9-22	Purchase	1	1,100	
9-26	Purchase	1	1,200	
9-29	Purchase	1	1,450	
9-30	Sale	2		1,500

3. Harwood purchased the following items:

9-3	2 @ $1,025	$2,050
9-22	1 @ $1,100	1,100
9-26	1 @ $1,200	1,200
9-29	1 @ $1,450	1,450
Total purchases		$5,800

4. The goods available for sale is $6,600: Beginning inventory of $800 plus purchases of $5,800.

The goods available for sale will be $6,600 no matter which method we use to determine the cost of goods sold and the ending inventory. In the periodic system, we determine the cost of the units sold and the cost of the ending inventory for the whole period of time.

First-In, First-Out Method (FIFO)

Using the first-in, first-out (FIFO) cost method under a periodic system, we assume that the first units owned were sold, and the last units purchased make up the ending inventory. Harwood had six units to sell during September, sold three, and had three remaining at the end of the month. Using FIFO, we assume that the first three units owned were sold:

Beginning inventory	1 @ $800	$ 800
September 3 purchase	2 @ $1,025	2,050
Cost of units sold		$2,850

Likewise, the ending inventory comes from the last purchases:

September 29	1 @ $1,450	$1,450
September 26	1 @ $1,200	1,200
September 22	1 @ $1,100	1,100
Cost of ending inventory		$3,750

FIFO METHOD (PERIODIC)

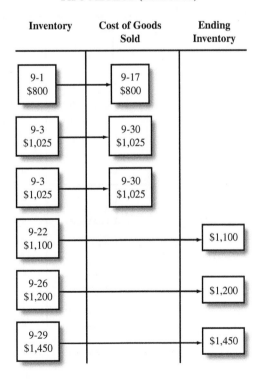

By using the cost of sales calculation, we can determine from an accounting viewpoint which units were sold and which units remain.

	Units	Cost
Beginning inventory	1	$ 800
Purchases	5	5,800
Goods available for sale	6	$6,600
Ending inventory	3	3,750
Cost of goods sold	3	$2,850

Last-In, First-Out Method (LIFO)

Using the last-in, first-out (LIFO) cost method under a periodic system, we assume that the last units owned were sold, and the first units purchased comprise the ending inventory—exactly the opposite of the FIFO method. Harwood had six units to sell during September, sold three, and had three remaining at the end of the month. Under LIFO, we assume that the last three units purchased were sold:

September 29	1 @ $1,450	$1,450
September 26	1 @ $1,200	1,200
September 22	1 @ $1,100	1,100
Cost of units sold		$3,750

Likewise, the ending inventory comes from the first units owned:

Beginning inventory	1 @ $800	$ 800
September 3 purchase	2 @ $1,025	2,050
Cost of ending inventory		$2,850

LIFO METHOD (PERIODIC)

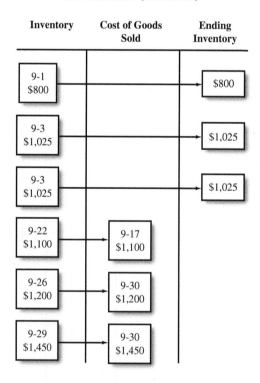

By using the cost of sales calculation we can determine from an accounting view-point, which units were sold and which units remain.

	Units	Cost
Beginning inventory	1	$ 800
Purchases	5	5,800
Goods available for sale	6	$6,600
Ending inventory	3	2,850
Cost of goods sold	3	$3,750

Average Cost Method

average cost method The inventory cost flow method that assigns an average cost to the units of inventory on hand at the time of each sale.

Instead of separating the inventory cost into two groups, the **average cost method** assigns the same cost to each inventory unit. Harwood owned six units of inventory that cost $6,600. The average cost method is simple to apply. Divide the cost of goods available for sale by the number of units available to determine the average unit cost.

$$\text{Average cost} = \frac{\text{Total cost of goods available for sale}}{\text{Number of units available for sale}} = \frac{\$6,600}{6} = \$1,100 \text{ per unit}$$

Use the cost of sales calculation to measure the cost of the units sold and the cost of the units remaining from an accounting viewpoint.

AVERAGE COST METHOD (PERIODIC)

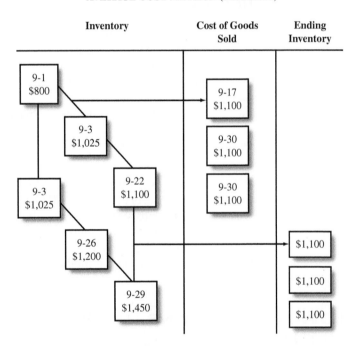

	Units	Cost
Beginning inventory	1	$ 800
Purchases	5	5,800
Goods available for sale	6	$6,600
Ending inventory	3	3,300
Cost of goods sold	3	$3,300

HARWOOD EQUIPMENT COMPANY
Schedule of Gross Profit
For the Month of September, 2007

	FIFO	LIFO	Average Cost
Sales	$4,500	$4,500	$4,500
Cost of Goods Sold:			
Beginning Inventory	$ 800	$ 800	$ 800
Purchases	5,800	5,800	5,800
Goods Available for Sale	$6,600	$6,600	$6,600
Ending Inventory	3,750	2,850	3,300
Cost of Goods Sold	$2,850	$3,750	$3,300
Gross Profit	$1,650	$ 750	$1,200

Comparison of Methods

We stated earlier that the three assumptions produced different results. Exhibit 9–6 indicates these differences in cost of goods sold, ending inventory, and gross profit.

Discussion Questions

9-11. What accounts for the difference in cost of goods sold, ending inventory, and gross profit among the three methods?

9-12. Which units actually were sold in each scenario?

9-13. What would happen to gross profit for each method if the costs were decreasing with each purchase instead of increasing?

As you may have concluded, the differences among methods occur because of the changing prices. As prices rise, LIFO produces the highest cost of sales and the lowest ending inventory. As prices fall, the opposite occurs and FIFO produces the highest cost of sales and the lowest ending inventory. Normally, the average cost method will produce costs in between LIFO and FIFO. Now consider what results when we apply the perpetual method to these three cost methods.

COST FLOW ASSUMPTIONS UNDER A PERPETUAL INVENTORY SYSTEM

Under the periodic system, we applied the cost methods to the entire period. When we utilize a perpetual system, we determine the cost of inventory items sold at the time of each sale. This complicates the decision-making process and produces different results for LIFO and average cost methods. We will use the same information for Harwood Equipment Company for our study of the perpetual system. As we analyzed the information under the periodic system, we were not concerned about the dates of the sales. Under the perpetual system, the sale date controls the application of the cost flow method.

Consider the Harwood transactions. Which items were sold on September 17 and 30? In reality, the items sold were probably the ones conveniently located in the warehouse. About the only thing you can determine, however, is that the unit sold on September 22 was purchased before September 22. Because the purchase prices of the units varied, we cannot determine the cost of goods sold unless we know which units were sold. The cost allocation methods define the accounting measurement of which items were sold, regardless of which specific products left the warehouse. Our goal remains to separate the $6,600 into cost of goods sold and the ending inventory.

First-In, First-Out Method

The first-in, first-out (FIFO) method in a perpetual system assumes that the first items purchased are the first to be sold, exactly as in the periodic system. The first sale took place on September 17. At that time, Harwood held three units, and the earliest of those was from the beginning inventory, which cost $800. The second sale took place on September 30 when Harwood held five units. The first units acquired were purchased on September 3 for $1,025 each. Therefore, we can separate the cost of sales and ending inventory as follows:

Units sold:

Beginning inventory	1 @ $800	$ 800
September 3 purchase	2 @ $1,025	2,050
Cost of units sold		$2,850

Ending inventory:

September 29	1 @ $1,450	$1,450
September 26	1 @ $1,200	1,200
September 22	1 @ $1,100	1,100
Cost of ending inventory		$3,750

FIFO METHOD (PERPETUAL)

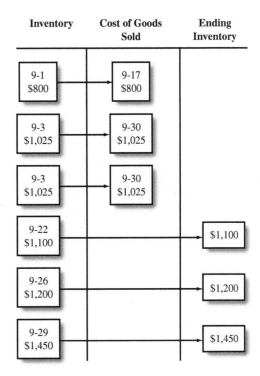

The cost of goods sold calculation will appear as follows:

	Units	Cost
Beginning inventory	1	$ 800
Purchases	5	5,800
Goods available for sale	6	$6,600
Ending inventory	3	3,750
Cost of goods sold	3	$2,850

Discussion Questions

9-14. Compare the cost of goods sold and ending inventory amounts with the FIFO example under the periodic system on page F-314. Is the result of your comparison a coincidence?

9-15. When Harwood makes its next sale of two items, which two will the FIFO method in a perpetual system assume are sold?

We will now turn our attention to the LIFO method in a perpetual system.

Last-In, First-Out Method

The last-in, first-out (LIFO) method under the perpetual system assumes that the last units placed in inventory are the first units sold. In applying this assumption, we assume that the very last item purchased is the one sold. On September 17, Harwood held three units, the most recently purchased on September 3 for $1,025. Under LIFO, we designate the $1,025 unit as sold on September 17. On September 30, Harwood held five units, the last two of which were purchased on September 29 and 26, costing $1,450 and $1,200 respectively. We can separate the cost of goods sold and the ending inventory as follows:

Units sold:

September 29	1 @ $1,450	$1,450
September 26	1 @ $1,200	1,200
September 3	1 @ $1,025	1,025
Cost of units sold		$3,675

Likewise, the ending inventory comes from the first units owned:

Beginning inventory	1 @ $800	$ 800
September 3 purchase	1 @ $1,025	1,025
September 22 purchase	1 @ $1,100	1,100
Cost of ending inventory		$2,925

By using the cost of sales calculation, we can determine from an accounting viewpoint which costs transfer to cost of goods sold on the income statement and which costs remain on the balance sheet in ending inventory.

	Units	Cost
Beginning inventory	1	$ 800
Purchases	5	5,800
Goods available for sale	6	$6,600
Ending inventory	3	2,925
Cost of goods sold	3	$3,675

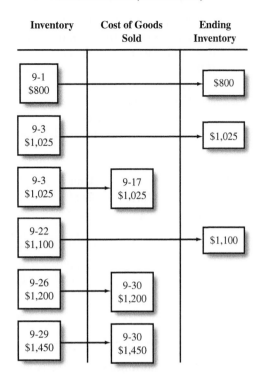

Discussion Questions

9-16. Compare the cost of goods sold and ending inventory amounts with the LIFO example under the periodic system on page F-314. Can you draw a conclusion about LIFO costs under the different inventory systems?

9-17. If Harwood sells two more units in October before purchasing any more of the item, which two will be assumed sold under LIFO in a perpetual system?

Although the results for LIFO differ for the periodic and the perpetual systems, the methods of determining the costs are relatively simple. This is not as true when we look at the moving average method of costing inventory under the perpetual system.

Moving Average Cost Method

moving average cost method The inventory cost flow method that assigns an average cost to the units of inventory on hand at the time of each sale in a perpetual inventory system.

The **moving average cost method** derives its name from the process that computes a new weighted average cost of all units of inventory on hand each time a new purchase is made. We will carefully build a table in which we can make the calculations for the moving average. Applying average cost logic, we assign all units on hand an average cost and assume that one of the units at that cost was sold. Remember that each time Harwood purchases new units, the average cost changes. The formula to determine the average at any time is:

$$\text{Weighted average cost} = \frac{\text{Total cost of inventory on hand}}{\text{Number of units on hand}}$$

We construct the weighted average table with the following columns:

(A) Number of units for the current transaction
(B) Unit cost for the current transaction
(C) Total cost of the transaction (A × B)
(D) Cumulative cost equals column D from the prior transaction plus C from the current transaction
(E) Cumulative units equal column E from the prior transaction plus A from the current transaction
(F) Average cost equals D divided by E

	Date	Description	(A) #of Units	(B) Unit Cost	(C) Total Cost	(D) Cumulative Cost	(E) Cumulative Units	(F) Average Cost
(1)	9-1	Beginning Inventory	1	$800	$800	$800	1	$800
(2)	9-3	Purchase	2	1,025	2,050	2,850	3	950
(3)	9-17	Sale	<1>	<950>	<950>	1,900	2	950
(4)	9-22	Purchase	1	1,100	1,100	3,000	3	1,000
(5)	9-26	Purchase	1	1,200	1,200	4,200	4	1,050
(6)	9-29	Purchase	1	1,450	1,450	5,650	5	1,130
(7)	9-30	Sale	<2>	<1,130>	<2,260>	3,390	3	1,130

We can examine each line to verify the calculations:

(1) The beginning inventory is one unit at a cost of $800.
(2) After the first purchase of two units for $2,050, apply the formula:

$$\text{Weighted average cost} = \frac{\text{Total cost of inventory on hand}}{\text{Number of units on hand}} \text{ or } \frac{D}{E} = \frac{\$2,850}{3} = \$950$$

(3) Cumulative cost is $800 + $2,050 − $950 = $1,900. Cumulative units are 1 + 2 − 1 = 2. Apply the formula and the average remains $950 ($1,900 / 2 = $950). Notice that sales do not change the average cost; only purchases change the average cost.
(4) After an additional purchase of one unit for $1,100, apply the formula:

$$\text{Weighted average cost} = \frac{D}{E} = \frac{\$1,900 + \$1,100}{3} = \$1,000$$

(5) After an additional purchase of one unit for $1,200, apply the formula:

$$\text{Weighted average cost} = \frac{D}{E} = \frac{\$3,000 + \$1,200}{4} = \$1,050$$

(6) After an additional purchase of one unit for $1,450, apply the formula:

$$\text{Weighted average cost} = \frac{D}{E} = \frac{\$4,200 + \$1,450}{5} = \$1,130$$

(7) After the sale of two units, the ending inventory results in three units at a total cost of $3,390.

The cost of goods sold calculation will appear as follows:

	Units	Cost
Beginning inventory	1	$ 800
Purchases	5	5,800
Goods available for sale	6	$6,600
Ending inventory	3	3,390
Cost of goods sold	3	$3,210

Exhibit 9-7
Comparison of
Inventory Cost
Assumptions under a
Perpetual System

HARWOOD EQUIPMENT COMPANY
Schedule of Gross Profit
For the Month of September, 2007

	FIFO	LIFO	Average Cost
Sales	$4,500	$4,500	$4,500
Cost of Goods Sold:			
Beginning Inventory	$ 800	$ 800	$ 800
Purchases	5,800	5,800	5,800
Goods Available for Sale	$6,600	$6,600	$6,600
Ending Inventory	3,750	2,925	3,390
Cost of Goods Sold	$2,850	$3,675	$3,210
Gross Profit	$1,650	$825	$1,290

Comparison of Methods

Similar to the periodic system, the three assumptions produced different results. Exhibit 9–7 indicates the differences in cost of goods sold, ending inventory, and gross profit under the perpetual method.

Discussion Questions

9-18. What accounts for the difference in the cost of goods sold, ending inventory, and gross profit among the three methods?

9-19. Which units actually were sold in each scenario?

9-20. What would happen to gross profit for each method if the costs decreased with each purchase instead of increasing?

    The comparison of the three methods in a perpetual system produces similar results to the periodic method because FIFO produces the highest gross profit, LIFO the lowest, and the moving average is in between FIFO and LIFO. The opposite is generally true when prices decrease during a period, depending on the timing of the purchases and sales during the period. Remember that FIFO produces the same results in a periodic or perpetual system, which seldom happens with LIFO or average cost methods.

    We examined the effects of each method for both periodic and perpetual systems. Now we will look at the effect that inventory assumptions and the inventory system have on financial statements.

The Effects of Inventory Cost Flow Assumption Choice

Assume that Harwood Equipment Company had no other transactions during September except those related to this product and the payment of $200 in warehouse rent. Exhibit 9–8 portrays the August 31, 2007, balance sheet representing the beginning balances, the September income statement, and the resulting balance sheet for September 30, 2007, under all three cost flow assumptions for a periodic inventory system.

Exhibit 9–8
Comparative Financial Statements Using a Periodic System for FIFO, LIFO, and Average Cost Methods

HARWOOD EQUIPMENT COMPANY
Income Statement
For the Month Ended September 30, 2007

	FIFO	LIFO	Average Cost
Sales	$4,500	$4,500	$4,500
Cost of Goods Sold	2,850	3,750	3,300
Gross Margin	$1,650	$ 750	$1,200
Operating Expenses:			
Warehouse Rent	200	200	200
Net Income	$1,450	$ 550	$1,000

HARWOOD EQUIPMENT COMPANY
Balance Sheet
August 31, 2007, and September 30, 2007

		FIFO	LIFO	Average Cost
ASSETS:	**August 31**		**September 30**	
Cash	$21,000	$22,300	$22,300	$22,300
Accounts Receivable	1,500	4,500	4,500	4,500
Merchandise Inventory	800	3,750	2,850	3,300
Total Assets	$23,300	$30,550	$29,650	$30,100
LIABILITIES AND STOCKHOLDERS' EQUITY:				
Accounts Payable	$ -0-	$ 5,800	$ 5,800	$ 5,800
Common Stock	15,000	15,000	15,000	15,000
Additional Paid-in Capital	8,000	8,000	8,000	8,000
Retained Earnings	300	1,750	800	1,300
Total Liabilities and Stockholders' Equity	$23,300	$30,550	$29,650	$30,100

Exhibit 9–9 portrays the August 31, 2007, balance sheet representing the beginning balances, the September income statement, and the resulting balance sheet for September 30, 2007, under all three cost flow assumptions for a perpetual inventory system. As you examine Exhibit 9–9, compare it with the results in Exhibit 9–8 for a periodic system.

Discussion Questions

9–21. The financial statements prepared using FIFO in Exhibits 9–8 and 9–9 show Harwood to be more profitable than the financial statements for LIFO or average cost regardless of the inventory system used. Is the company more profitable if it used FIFO instead of LIFO or average cost?

9–22. Did Harwood pay for the purchases of inventory during September? How can you determine this?

Exhibit 9-9

Comparative Financial Statements Using a Perpetual System for FIFO, LIFO, and Average Cost Methods

HARWOOD EQUIPMENT COMPANY
Income Statement
For the Month Ended September 30, 2007

	FIFO	LIFO	Average Cost
Sales	$4,500	$4,500	$4,500
Cost of Goods Sold	2,850	3,675	3,210
Gross Margin	$1,650	$ 825	$1,290
Operating Expenses:			
Warehouse Rent	200	200	200
Net Income	$1,450	$ 625	$1,090

HARWOOD EQUIPMENT COMPANY
Balance Sheet
August 31, 2007, and September 30, 2007

		FIFO	LIFO	Average Cost
ASSETS:	**August 31**		**September 30**	
Cash	$21,000	$22,300	$22,300	$22,300
Accounts Receivable	1,500	4,500	4,500	4,500
Merchandise Inventory	800	3,750	2,925	3,390
Total Assets	$23,300	$30,550	$29,725	$30,190
LIABILITIES AND STOCKHOLDERS' EQUITY:				
Accounts Payable	$ -0-	$ 5,800	$ 5,800	$ 5,800
Common Stock	15,000	15,000	15,000	15,000
Additional Paid-in Capital	8,000	8,000	8,000	8,000
Retained Earnings	300	1,750	925	1,390
Total Liabilities and Stockholders' Equity	$23,300	$30,550	$29,725	$30,190

9-23. Did Harwood's customers pay for their purchases during September? How can you determine this?

9-24. How do you explain the increase in cash from $21,000 to $22,300 from August to September?

Companies may choose from a variety of inventory cost flow assumptions. We have explored three approaches most commonly used in periodic and perpetual inventory systems and have seen how these different cost flow assumptions result in different net profits on the income statements and inventory amounts on the balance sheets. The reality of the sales and delivery of inventory to the customer is the same. What differs is the measurement of that reality. However, the choice of inventory method does not change the ultimate profitability of a company. To illustrate, we will extend our example to October.

Assume that Harwood purchased no additional units in October but sold the remaining three units in October. Further assume that the only expense in October was the warehouse rent of $200.

The cost of goods sold calculation for the *periodic* system is as follows:

	Units	FIFO	LIFO	Average Cost
Beginning inventory	3	$3,750	$2,850	$3,300
Purchases	0	-0-	-0-	-0-
Goods available for sale	3	$3,750	$2,850	$3,300
Ending inventory	0	-0-	-0-	-0-
Cost of goods sold	3	$3,750	$2,850	$3,300

The cost of goods sold calculation for the *perpetual* system is as follows:

	Units	FIFO	LIFO	Average Cost
Beginning inventory	3	$3,750	$2,925	$3,390
Purchases	0	-0-	-0-	-0-
Goods available for sale	3	$3,750	$2,925	$3,390
Ending inventory	0	-0-	-0-	-0-
Cost of goods sold	3	$3,750	$2,925	$3,390

Now we can see the effect that October's activity has on the balance sheet and income statement. Exhibit 9–10 contains the October balance sheets and income statements for all three cost methods under a periodic inventory system.

Exhibit 9–10
Comparative Financial Statements Using a Periodic System for FIFO, LIFO, and Average Cost Methods

HARWOOD EQUIPMENT COMPANY
Income Statement
For the Month Ended October 31, 2007

	FIFO	LIFO	Average Cost
Sales	$4,500	$4,500	$4,500
Cost of Goods Sold	3,750	2,850	3,300
Gross Margin	$ 750	$1,650	$1,200
Operating Expenses:			
Warehouse Rent	200	200	200
Net Income	$ 550	$1,450	$1,000

HARWOOD EQUIPMENT COMPANY
Balance Sheet
October 31, 2007

	FIFO	LIFO	Average Cost
ASSETS:			
Cash	$20,800	$20,800	$20,800
Accounts Receivable	4,500	4,500	4,500
Merchandise Inventory	-0-	-0-	-0-
Total Assets	$25,300	$25,300	$25,300
LIABILITIES AND STOCKHOLDERS' EQUITY:			
Accounts Payable	$ -0-	$ -0-	$ -0-
Common Stock	15,000	15,000	15,000
Additional Paid-in Capital	8,000	8,000	8,000
Retained Earnings	2,300	2,300	2,300
Total Liabilities and Stockholders' Equity	$25,300	$25,300	$25,300

Exhibit 9-11
Comparative Financial Statements Using a Perpetual System for FIFO, LIFO, and Average Cost Methods

HARWOOD EQUIPMENT COMPANY
Income Statement
For the Month Ended October 31, 2007

	FIFO	LIFO	Average Cost
Sales	$4,500	$4,500	$4,500
Cost of Goods Sold	3,750	2,925	3,390
Gross Margin	$ 750	$1,575	$1,110
Operating Expenses:			
Warehouse Rent	200	200	200
Net Income	$ 550	$1,375	$ 910

HARWOOD EQUIPMENT COMPANY
Balance Sheet
October 31, 2007

	FIFO	LIFO	Average Cost
ASSETS:			
Cash	$20,800	$20,800	$20,800
Accounts Receivable	4,500	4,500	4,500
Merchandise Inventory	-0-	-0-	-0-
Total Assets	$25,300	$25,300	$25,300
LIABILITIES AND STOCKHOLDERS' EQUITY:			
Accounts Payable	$ -0-	$ -0-	$ -0-
Common Stock	15,000	15,000	15,000
Additional Paid-in Capital	8,000	8,000	8,000
Retained Earnings	2,300	2,300	2,300
Total Liabilities and Stockholders' Equity	$25,300	$25,300	$25,300

Exhibit 9–11 contains the October 31, 2007, balance sheets and income statements under all three cost assumptions in a perpetual system. Note the similarities and differences between the October 31, 2007, financial statements for the periodic and perpetual systems and each of the cost flow assumptions.

Discussion Questions

9-25. Because the balance sheet is affected by the income statement, how can the ending balance sheets at the end of October be identical under all three inventory cost flow methods for both periodic and perpetual systems when the income statements for October were different?

9-26. Compute the total gross profit for September and October for each inventory cost method for both the periodic and perpetual systems? How do they compare?

9-27. Which method (FIFO, LIFO, or average cost) matches the most recent cost to current revenues?

9-28. Which inventory cost method is the best to use? Which inventory system is the best to use?

After examining Harwood Equipment Company's financial statements for two months, you might rightly come to the conclusion that no one method of determining inventory cost flow is better than another. Likewise, the type of inventory system does not change the profit reality over time. From the time a firm buys its first item of inventory to the time it sells its last item of inventory, its total gross profit over time will be equal, regardless of inventory method or system. For one firm, we may conclude that the choice of inventory costing method is relevant in the short term and irrelevant in the long term. It becomes important, however, when comparing the profitability of two firms that use different costing methods.

As was the case with accounting for depreciation of long-lived assets, accounting for the cost of merchandise inventory has a significant impact on a company's reported net income for a given income statement period and for the reported inventory on the balance sheet. Informed financial statement users must have an understanding of the impact of inventory cost flow method choice to utilize the information to the fullest extent possible.

Now that you have an understanding of some of the issues and situations that impact financial statements, we will explore in more detail the construction of the balance sheet and income statement in Chapter 10.

SUMMARY

Merchandise inventory represents the physical units of goods that a company plans to sell. Inventory on hand at the beginning of a given income statement period (beginning inventory) and the inventory bought during the period (purchases) constitute the total amount of goods the company could sell (goods available for sale). Goods available for sale will either remain on hand at the end of the period or be assumed sold.

Accountants developed two types of systems to track inventory costs. The periodic system counts inventory and traces costs only at the end of each income statement period, whereas the perpetual system updates inventory counts and costs each time a sale or purchase is made. Perpetual inventory systems usually make use of computer technology and scanners that read UPC. Even though inventory records are updated continuously when a perpetual system is in place, physical inventory counts are still necessary. Determining the actual amount of inventory on hand may uncover theft, damage, or spoilage of inventory. Some businesses use a perpetual system to track the number of units in inventory and integrate the counts into automatic purchasing reorder systems, but they may cost the inventory under a periodic system.

In a periodic system using accrual-basis accounting, we use the computation of cost of goods sold to determine the amount of expense on the income statement. The ending inventory is reported on the balance sheet as an asset. Under accrual accounting in a perpetual inventory system, when a company purchases inventory, its cost is considered an asset to the company and is listed as such on the balance sheet. As inventory is sold, its cost is converted from an asset to an expense, which is listed on the income statement as cost of goods sold. It follows, then, that the total cost of goods available for sale will end up either as ending inventory (an asset on the balance sheet) or as cost of goods sold (an expense on the income statement).

The physical flow of inventory may differ from the flow of inventory costs. Several methods have been developed to trace inventory costs as they move from the balance sheet to the income statement. All these methods are cost flow assumptions that prescribe which inventory items are assumed to be the ones sold.

Specific identification relates the exact cost of each unit of inventory to cost of goods sold when the item is sold. Firms that deal in expensive and unique items (such as cars, boats, and luxury items) utilize the specific identification method. The first-in, first-out (FIFO) method assumes that the first units of inventory purchased are the first ones sold. Conversely, the last-in, first-out (LIFO) method assumes that the last units of inventory purchased are the first sold. The average cost method assigns a weighted average cost to the units of inventory.

In a periodic system, we apply the cost assumptions for the entire period. In a perpetual system, we apply FIFO, LIFO, and moving average cost assumptions at the time of each sale, which produces different results than when we apply the assumptions for the entire period. Average cost method under a periodic system calculates one inventory cost for all goods sold and remaining in inventory while the moving average method under a perpetual system recalculates the average each time a new purchase is made.

Companies may choose to use any of these cost flow assumptions. If the price they pay for inventory items varies during the period, the choice will impact both net income and asset values reported on the company's financial statements each year. In the long run, however, choice of inventory cost method makes no difference to one firm. Financial statement users must be aware of the differences that inventory methods make when comparing companies that use different inventory cost methods.

APPENDIX—INVENTORY PURCHASING ISSUES

Two issues arise for firms that purchase merchandise inventory—freight costs and cash discounts. When negotiating purchase terms, buying agents pay particular attention to the freight and payment terms. Careful negotiations can decrease the cost of purchasing merchandise.

Cash Discounts

A firm frequently encourages its customer to pay invoices quickly by offering a cash discount, which improves the firm's cash flow. A company may devise its own credit terms that appeal to its customers; the following represent frequently used payment terms and their meaning.

1. *2/10, net 30 days*—A two percent discount is allowed if paid within 10 days from the invoice date; otherwise payment is due 30 days after the invoice date.
2. *net 30 days*—The net amount is due 30 days after the invoice date with no cash discount.
3. *1/10, EOM, net 60 days*—A one percent discount is allowed if paid within 10 days after the end of the month; otherwise payment is due 60 days from the invoice date.

Return to our example of Harwood Equipment Company. If the purchase on September 3 had terms of 2/10, net 30, Harwood would pay the invoice by September 13 to receive a two percent discount. Payment required by September 13 would be 98 percent of $2,050, or $2,009. The discount of $41 (2% x $2,050) reduces the cost of the purchase to Harwood. Good cash managers take advantage of cash discounts.

Discussion Questions

9–29. When would payment be due by Harwood if the terms were net 30 days? 1/10 EOM, net 60 days?

9–30. What is the annual percentage rate of a two percent discount for payment in 10 days instead of 30 days? One percent discount for 15 days instead of 30 days?

Freight Terms

Freight terms define the point at which title passes between the seller and the purchaser. FOB (free on board) shipping point indicates that the title passes when the merchandise leaves the seller's shipping dock. FOB destination indicates that the title passes when the merchandise arrives at the purchaser's loading dock. Transportation costs transfer to the buyer at the FOB point when the title passes. Therefore, if the terms are FOB shipping point, title passes at the sellers dock and the buyer bears the freight expense. If the terms are FOB destination, the seller owns the goods until delivery and bears the freight expense.

Payment of the freight adds another complication. When the seller arranges for transportation, it contracts either for freight prepaid or freight collect. Shippers such as United Parcel Service contract mostly for prepaid freight, while other common carriers can accommodate either payment method. When the terms are FOB destination and the seller pays the shipper directly, or when the terms are FOB shipping point and the seller sends the goods freight collect, the correct entity pays the expense. However, when the seller ships freight prepaid for FOB shipping point, the seller must bill the buyer for the freight cost. If the seller ships freight collect for FOB destination, the buyer must deduct the freight costs from its accounts payable when it pays the seller.

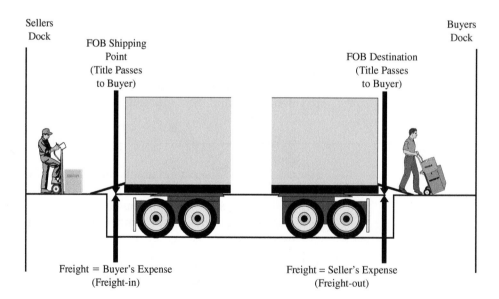

If Harwood buys two units from Taylor Equipment, Inc. on September 3 terms FOB shipping point, freight collect, Harwood will pay the $125 shipping costs directly to the common carrier. If Harwood buys the goods freight collect with terms FOB destination, Harwood will pay the carrier direct and pay its vendor only $1,925 in full payment of the $2,050 invoice amount.

Discussion Question

9-31. If Harwood buys two units from Taylor Equipment on September 3 with terms of 2/10, net 30, FOB shipping point, freight prepaid and the shipping charges are $210, how much will Harwood pay Taylor if it pays on September 3? October 3?

APPENDIX—RECORDING INVENTORY

After completing Chapter 7, you can look at the journal entries required to account for inventory. The recording process differs for periodic and perpetual inventory systems. We will look at the periodic system first.

Periodic Inventory Systems

The recording process for periodic inventory systems involves eight types of entries:

1. Purchase of the inventory
2. Return of defective merchandise
3. Payment of freight charges on purchases
4. Payment of the vendor
5. Recording ending inventory in closing entries
6. Sale of inventory
7. Payment of freight charges on sales
8. Receipt of cash from customer

To record these entries, we will utilize several new accounts:

Asset account:	Inventory or Merchandise Inventory
Expense accounts:	Purchases
	Purchase Discounts
	Purchase Returns and Allowances
	Freight-in (a cost of goods sold expense)
	Freight-out (a selling expense)
Revenue accounts:	Sales
	Sales Returns and Allowances
	Sales Discounts

To apply these concepts, we use the transactions during September 2007 for Harwood Equipment Company with the addition of a few items. In a periodic system, the costs of purchasing merchandise are charged to the previously listed expense accounts for Purchases, Purchase Returns and Allowances, Freight-in, and Purchase Discounts. We ignore the asset account for Inventory until the closing entries for the year.

To record the purchase of two units from Taylor on September 3, terms 2/10, net 30, FOB destination, freight collect:

2007		Debit	Credit
September 3	Purchases	2,050	
	Accounts Payable—Taylor		2,050
	To record purchase of two units,		
	terms 2/10, net 30, FOB destination.		

To record the receipt and payment of a freight bill to Mistletoe Express for $125:
Because this freight is not the expense of Harwood, it will reduce the amount that Harwood must pay to Taylor for the invoice.

		Debit	Credit
September 4	Accounts Payable—Taylor	125	
	Cash		125
	To record the payment of freight collect on FOB destination.		

To record payment of the invoice within the discount period:

		Debit	Credit
September 12	Accounts Payable—Taylor	1,925	
	Purchase Discounts		41
	Cash		1,884
	To record the payment of Taylor's 9-3-2007 invoice.		

The payment to Taylor was for a $2,050 invoice less a two percent discount and freight charges of $125 leaving an amount due of $1,884 ($2,050 − $41 − $125).

To record the sale on September 17 of one unit to Earhart Industries for $1,500, terms 2/10, net 30, FOB shipping point, freight collect:

		Debit	Credit
September 17	Accounts Receivable—Earhart	1,500	
	Sales		1,500
	To record sale to Earhart, 2/10, net 30, FOB shipping point.		

Because Harwood shipped the goods freight collect, the buyer will pay its freight costs. In the periodic system, no recognition occurs for the cost of each sale because the purchases are being recorded as an expense and the income statement computes the cost of goods sold with the cost of sales calculation.

To record the purchase of one unit from Allen Corp., terms 1/15, net 30, FOB shipping point, freight collect (shipping charges were $93):

		Debit	Credit
September 22	Purchases	1,100	
	Accounts Payable—Allen		1,100
	To record purchase from Allen, 1/15, net 30, FOB shipping point.		

To record the payment of the freight to Mistletoe Express:

		Debit	Credit
September 24	Freight-in	93	
	Cash		93
	To record the freight charges on the Allen purchase.		

Because the terms of the purchase were FOB shipping point, Harwood records the freight bill as an expense.

To record the purchase of one unit from the Bostwick Exchange, terms 2/10, net 30, FOB destination, freight prepaid (shipping charges $85):

		Debit	Credit
September 26	Purchases	1,200	
	Accounts Payable—Bostwick		1,200
	To record purchase from Bostwick 2/10, net 30, FOB destination.		

After Harwood received the Bostwick purchase, the inventory control specialist realized that the equipment item was defective. Harwood notified Bostwick and on

September 28, Bostwick issued a credit memorandum to Harwood. Harwood returned the merchandise to Bostwick freight collect.

To record the return of the Bostwick purchase:

		Debit	Credit
September 28	Accounts Payable—Bostwick	1,200	
	Purchases returns and allowances		1,200
	To record the return of defective		
	merchandise to Bostwick.		

To record the purchase of one unit from Allen Corp., terms 1/15, net 30, FOB shipping point, freight collect (shipping costs $115):

		Debit	Credit
September 29	Purchases	1,450	
	Accounts Payable—Allen		1,450
	To record the purchase from Allen,		
	1/15, net 30, FOB shipping point.		

To record the freight expense on the Allen purchase:

		Debit	Credit
September 30	Freight-in	115	
	Cash		115
	To record payment of freight expense		
	on Allen purchase.		

To record the sale of two units to Kiamichi, Inc., terms 1/10, net 30, FOB destination, freight prepaid:

		Debit	Credit
September 30	Accounts Receivable—Kiamichi	3,000	
	Sales		3,000
	To record the sale to Kiamichi, 1/10,		
	net 30, FOB destination.		

To record payment of freight on Kiamichi sale for $146 on September 30:

		Debit	Credit
September 30	Freight-out	146	
	Cash		146
	To record payment of freight on		
	Kiamichi sale.		

Periodic Inventory Closing Entries

We close all revenue and expense accounts (temporary accounts) at the close of each year. Assume that the following revenue and expense accounts appeared on the adjusted trial balance of Harwood Equipment Company at its year end of December 31, 2007:

	Debit	Credit
Sales		75,000
Sales Returns and Allowances	1,500	
Sales Discounts	940	
Purchases	48,000	
Purchases Returns and Allowances		2,400
Purchase Discounts		800
Freight-in	2,300	
Warehouse Rent	2,400	
Freight-out	1,950	

In addition, the Inventory account shows a balance of $2,300, which represents the beginning balance on January 1, 2007. In a periodic inventory system, only two closing entries are made to the Inventory account each year. Therefore, the Inventory asset account always carries the beginning inventory amount except for the last day of the fiscal year. The physical count of the inventory on December 31 indicated a $4,550 inventory using the FIFO costing assumption.

The following are the closing entries for Harwood for 2007:

		Debit	Credit
December 31	Sales	75,000	
	Purchase Returns and Allowances	2,400	
	Purchase Discounts	800	
	Income Summary		78,200
	To close the accounts with credit balances.		
December 31	Income Summary	57,090	
	Sales Returns and Allowances		1,500
	Sales Discounts		940
	Purchases		48,000
	Freight-in		2,300
	Warehouse Rent		2,400
	Freight-out		1,950
	To close accounts with debit balances.		
December 31	Income Summary	2,300	
	Inventory		2,300
	To close the beginning inventory amount.		
December 31	Inventory	4,550	
	Income Summary		4,550
	To record the ending inventory amount.		

The periodic system income statement for Harwood Equipment Company for the year 2007 is as follows:

HARWOOD EQUIPMENT COMPANY
Income Statement
For the Year Ended December 31, 2007

Sales			$75,000
Less: Sales Returns & Allowances		$ 1,500	
Sales Discounts		940	2,440
Net Sales			$72,560
Cost of Goods Sold:			
Beginning Inventory		$ 2,300	
Purchases	$48,000		
Less: Returns & Allowances	$2,400		
Discounts	800	(3,200)	
Add: Freight-in		2,300	
Net Purchases		47,100	
Goods Available for Sale		$49,400	
Less: Ending Inventory		4,550	
Cost of Goods Sold			44,850
Gross Profit			$27,710
Operating Expenses:			
Warehouse Rent		$ 2,400	
Freight-out Expense		1,950	4,350
Net Income			$23,360

We now turn our attention to the recording process for the perpetual inventory system.

Perpetual Inventory Systems

The recording process for perpetual inventory systems involves nine types of entries:

1. Purchase of the inventory
2. Return of defective merchandise
3. Payment of freight charges on purchases
4. Payment of the vendor
5. Recording ending inventory in closing entries
6. Sale of inventory
7. Recording of cost of goods sold
8. Payment of freight charges on sales
9. Receipt of cash from customer

To record the entries we will use the following accounts:

Asset account:	Inventory or Merchandise Inventory
Expense accounts:	Cost of Goods Sold
	Freight-out (a selling expense)
Revenue accounts:	Sales
	Sales Returns and Allowances
	Sales Discounts

To introduce these procedures for the perpetual system, we will use the same transactions as we used for the periodic system. In a perpetual system, all inventory costs are debited directly to the asset account, and reductions for returns or discounts are likewise credited directly to the asset account. Each time a unit is sold, we credit the Inventory account for its cost and debit the Cost of Goods Sold expense account.

To record the purchase of two units from Taylor on September 3, terms 2/10, net 30, FOB destination, freight collect:

2007		Debit	Credit
September 3	Inventory	2,050	
	Accounts Payable—Taylor		2,050
	To record purchase of two units,		
	terms 2/10, net 30, FOB destination.		

To record the receipt and payment of a freight bill to Mistletoe Express for $125: Because this freight is not the expense of Harwood, it will reduce the amount that Harwood must pay to Taylor for the invoice.

		Debit	Credit
September 4	Accounts Payable—Taylor	125	
	Cash		125
	To record the payment of freight		
	collect on FOB destination.		

To record payment of the invoice within the discount period:

		Debit	Credit
September 12	Accounts Payable—Taylor	1,925	
	Inventory		41
	Cash		1,884
	To record the payment of Taylor's		
	9-3-2007 invoice.		

The payment to Taylor was for a $2,050 invoice less a two percent discount and freight charges of $125 leaving an amount due of $1,884 ($2,050 − $41 − $125). Because we debited the Inventory account for the whole amount before the discount on the invoice date, we reduce the Inventory account for the discount to lower the cost of the purchase to $2,009.

To record the sale on September 17 of one unit to Earhart Industries for $1,500, terms 2/10, net 30, FOB shipping point, freight collect:

		Debit	Credit
September 17	Accounts Receivable—Earhart	1,500	
	Sales		1,500
	To record sale to Earhart, 2/10,		
	net 30, FOB shipping point.		

Because Harwood shipped the goods freight collect, the buyer will pay its freight costs. In the perpetual system, we must recognize the cost of each sale, we also make the following entry:

		Debit	Credit
September 17	Cost of Goods Sold	800	
	Inventory		800
	To record the cost of the sale under		
	the FIFO cost assumption.		

To record the purchase of one unit from Allen Corp., terms 1/15, net 30, FOB shipping point, freight collect (shipping charges were $93):

		Debit	Credit
September 22	Inventory	1,100	
	Accounts Payable—Allen		1,100
	To record purchase from Allen, 1/15,		
	net 30, FOB shipping point.		

To record the payment of the freight to Mistletoe Express:

		Debit	Credit
September 24	Inventory	93	
	Cash		93
	To record the freight charges on the		
	Allen purchase.		

Because the terms of the purchase were FOB shipping point, Harwood records the freight bill as a cost of the inventory.

To record the purchase of one unit from the Bostwick Exchange, terms 2/10, net 30, FOB destination, freight prepaid (shipping charges $85):

		Debit	Credit
September 26	Inventory	1,200	
	Accounts Payable—Bostwick		1,200
	To record purchase from Bostwick		
	2/10, net 30, FOB destination.		

After Harwood received the Bostwick purchase, the inventory control specialist realized that the equipment item was defective. Harwood notified Bostwick and on September 28, Bostwick issued a credit memorandum to Harwood. Harwood returned the merchandise to Bostwick freight collect.

To record the return of the Bostwick purchase:

		Debit	Credit
September 28	Accounts Payable—Bostwick	1,200	
	Inventory		1,200
	To record the return of defective		
	merchandise to Bostwick.		

To record the purchase of one unit from Allen Corp., terms 1/15, net 30, FOB shipping point, freight collect (shipping costs $115):

		Debit	Credit
September 29	Inventory	1,450	
	Accounts Payable—Allen		1,450
	To record the purchase from Allen,		
	1/15, net 30, FOB shipping point.		

To record the freight expense on the Allen purchase:

		Debit	Credit
September 30	Inventory	115	
	Cash		115
	To record payment of freight expense		
	on Allen purchase.		

To record the sale of two units to Kiamichi, Inc., terms 1/10, net 30, FOB destination, freight prepaid:

		Debit	Credit
September 30	Accounts Receivable—Kiamichi	3,000	
	Sales		3,000
	To record the sale to Kiamichi, 1/10,		
	net 30, FOB destination.		

		Debit	Credit
September 30	Cost of Goods Sold	2,009	
	Inventory		2,009
	To record the cost of the sale made		
	to Kiamichi at $2,009.		

To record payment of freight on Kiamichi sale for $146 on September 30:

		Debit	Credit
September 30	Freight-out	146	
	Cash		146
	To record payment of freight on		
	Kiamichi sale.		

Perpetual Inventory Closing Entries

We close all revenue and expense accounts (temporary accounts) at the close of each year. Assume that the following revenue and expense accounts appeared on the adjusted trial balance of Harwood Equipment Company at its year end of December 31, 2007:

	Debit	**Credit**
Sales		75,000
Sales Returns and Allowances	1,500	
Sales Discounts	940	
Cost of Goods Sold	44,440	
Warehouse Rent	2,400	
Freight-out	1,950	

In addition, the Inventory account shows a balance of $4,960 which represents the ending balance on December 31, 2007. The physical count of the inventory on December 31 indicated a $4,550 inventory using the FIFO costing assumption.

The following are the closing entries for Harwood for 2007:

		Debit	Credit
December 31	Sales	75,000	
	Income Summary		75,000
	To close the accounts with credit balances.		

		Debit	Credit
December 31	Income Summary	48,790	
	Cost of Goods Sold		44,440
	Warehouse Rent		2,400
	Freight-out		1,950
	To close accounts with debit balances.		

		Debit	Credit
December 31	Income Summary	410	
	Inventory		410
	To adjust the ending inventory amount to the physical count.		

The perpetual system income statement for Harwood Equipment Company for the year 2007 is as follows:

HARWOOD EQUIPMENT COMPANY
Income Statement
For the Year Ended December 31, 2007

Sales		$75,000
Less: Sales Returns & Allowances	$1,500	
Sales Discounts	940	2,440
Net Sales		$72,560
Cost of Goods Sold		44,850
Gross Profit		$27,710
Operating Expenses:		
Warehouse Rent	$2,400	
Freight-out Expense	1,950	4,350
Net Income		$23,360

Remember that the FIFO method produces the same results in a periodic or perpetual system. Therefore, both income statements show the same final results in net income—only the presentation of the cost of goods sold section differs.

SUMMARY OF THE APPENDICES

Cash discounts encourage customers to pay invoices ahead of normal credit terms by reducing the amount paid for the invoice. The terms quoted on the invoice indicate the discount period length and the percentage of the discount.

Freight terms define the point that title passes from seller to buyer. When terms are FOB shipping point, title passes when goods leave the sellers shipping dock and the buyer bears the freight expense. When terms are FOB destination, title passes when the goods arrive at the buyers loading dock and the seller bears the freight expense.

Periodic inventory systems record purchases in detailed expense accounts. The inventory asset account carries the beginning inventory all year and closing entries adjust the balance to the ending inventory balance at year end. The Cost of Goods Sold section of the income statement computes the cost of goods sold using the balances of the Purchases, Purchase Returns and Allowances, Purchase Discounts, and Freight-in accounts. The Freight-out account accumulates freight paid for customers and is considered a selling expense.

Perpetual inventory systems accumulate all inventory costs, including Freight-in reduced by cash discounts and returns or allowances, in the asset Inventory account. As each sale is made, the cost of the sale is transferred to the Cost of Goods Sold account by debiting it and crediting the Inventory account. The only year-end adjustment to inventory reconciles the balance to the physical inventory count.

REVIEW THE FACTS

A. Define the terms *inventory* and *merchandise inventory.*
B. What two amounts are added to determine goods available for sale (GAFS)?
C. GAFS is allocated to two places in financial statements. Name them.
D. Under accrual accounting, the cost of inventory still on hand at the end of the period is shown on which financial statement?
E. Under accrual accounting, the cost of inventory no longer on hand at the end of the period is shown on which financial statement?
F. Explain the difference between the physical flow of merchandise and the cost flow of merchandise.
G. What are the two types of inventory systems? Explain the differences between them.
H. List three causes of differences between book inventory and the results of a physical inventory count.
I. Why are FIFO, LIFO, and average cost referred to as "assumptions"?
J. Describe in your own words the differences among the FIFO, LIFO, and average cost methods.

APPLY WHAT YOU HAVE LEARNED

LO 1: Terminology

9–32. Presented below is a list of items relating to the concepts presented in this chapter, followed by definitions of those items in scrambled order:

a. Periodic inventory system   e. Merchandise inventory
b. Perpetual inventory system   f. First-in, first-out method
c. Goods available for sale   g. Last-in, first-out method
d. Cost of goods sold   h. Average cost method

1. _____ The total amount of merchandise inventory a company can sell during a particular income statement period.
2. _____ All inventory and cost of goods sold calculations are done at the end of the period.
3. _____ Cost of goods sold is determined based on the assumption that the first units acquired are the first ones sold.
4. _____ Updates both the physical count of inventory units and the cost classification of those units when a transaction involves inventory.
5. _____ The physical units of product a company buys and then resells as part of its business operation.

6. _____ Cost of goods sold is based on the assumption that the last units acquired are the first ones sold.
7. _____ Cost of goods sold is determined based on the total cost of inventory units divided by the number of units.
8. _____ The cost of merchandise inventory that has been converted from an asset on the balance sheet to an expense on the income statement.

REQUIRED:
Match the letter next to each item on the list with the appropriate definition. Each letter will be used only once.

LO 1: Elements of Cost of Goods Sold

9–33. Ned Flanders Company began the month of March with 304 units of product on hand at a total cost of $3,648. During the month, the company purchased an additional 818 units at $30 per unit. Sales for March were 732 units at a total cost of $10,068.

REQUIRED:
From the information provided, complete the following schedule:

		Units	Cost
	Beginning Inventory	_____	$_____
+	Purchases	_____	_____
=	Goods Available for Sale	_____	_____
−	Cost of Goods Sold	_____	_____
=	Ending Inventory	_____	_____

LO 1: Elements of Goods Available for Sale

9–34. Identify the various components of goods available for sale and define each component.

LO 1: Elements of Cost of Goods Sold

9–35. Kenny G. Company began the month of June with 150 units of product on hand at a total cost of $3,000. During the month, the company purchased an additional 460 units at $40 per unit. Sales for June were 510 units at a total cost of $17,400.

REQUIRED:
From the information provided, complete the following schedule:

		Units	Cost
	Beginning Inventory	_____	$_____
+	Purchases	_____	_____
=	Goods Available for Sale	_____	_____
−	Ending Inventory	_____	_____
=	Cost of Goods Sold	_____	_____

LO 1: Elements of Cost of Goods Sold

9–36. Edward Murdoch Company began the month of April with 452 units of product on hand at a cost of $54 per unit. During the month, the company purchased an additional 1,500 units at a total cost of $40,500. At the end of April, 616 units were still on hand at a cost of $16,632.

REQUIRED:

From the information provided, complete the following schedule:

		Units	Cost
	Beginning Inventory	___	$___
+	Purchases	___	___
=	Goods Available for Sale	___	___
−	Ending Inventory	___	___
=	Cost of Goods Sold	___	___

LO 1: Elements of Cost of Goods Sold

9–37. Vaughan and Miles Company began the month of July with 412 units of product on hand at a cost of $34 per unit. During the month, the company purchased an additional 1,300 units at a total cost of $22,100. At the end of July, 712 units were still on hand at a cost of $12,104.

REQUIRED:

From the information provided, complete the following schedule:

		Units	Cost
	Beginning Inventory	___	$___
+	Purchases	___	___
=	Goods Available for Sale	___	___
−	Ending Inventory	___	___
=	Cost of Goods Sold	___	___

LO 1: Elements of Cost of Goods Sold

9–38. Paula Cole and Company began the month of February 2007 with 650 units of product on hand at a total cost of $11,050. During the month, the company purchased an additional 1,884 units at $36 per unit. Sales for February were 1,734 units at $64 per unit. The total cost of the units sold was $30,812 and operating expenses totaled $18,900.

REQUIRED:

a. From the information provided, complete the following schedule:

		Units	Cost
	Beginning Inventory	___	$___
+	Purchases	___	___
=	Goods Available for Sale	___	___
−	Ending Inventory	___	___
=	Cost of Goods Sold	___	___

b. Prepare Paula Cole and Company's income statement for the month ended February 28, 2007.

LO 1: Elements of Cost of Goods Sold

9–39. Bill Mathes and Company began the month of October 2008 with 470 units of product on hand at a total cost of $7,520. During the month, the company purchased an additional 1,244 units at $34 per unit. Sales for October were 1,280 units at $60 per unit. The total cost of the units sold was $21,290 and operating expenses totaled $11,300.

REQUIRED:

a. From the information provided, complete the following schedule:

		Units	Cost
	Beginning Inventory	____	$____
+	Purchases	____	____
=	Goods Available for Sale	____	____
−	Ending Inventory	____	____
=	Cost of Goods Sold	____	____

b. Prepare Bill Mathes and Company's income statement for the month ended October 31, 2008.

LO 2: Relationship between Cost of Goods Sold and Ending Inventory

9–40. How do changes in the ending inventory affect the cost of goods sold?

LO 3 & 4: Cost Flow vs. Physical Flow of Goods

9–41. Joan Stone TV Sales and Service began the month of March with two identical TV sets in inventory. During the month, six additional TV sets (identical to the two in beginning inventory) were purchased as follows:

2 on March 9
1 on March 13
3 on March 24

The company sold two of the TV sets on March 12, another one on March 17, and two more on March 28.

REQUIRED:

a. Assuming the company uses a perpetual inventory system and the first-in, first-out cost flow method:
   (1) Which two TV sets were sold on March 12?
   (2) Which one was sold on March 17?
   (3) Which two TV sets were sold on March 28?
   (4) The cost of which three TV sets will be included in Stone's inventory at the end of March?
b. If the company uses a perpetual inventory system and the last-in, first-out cost flow method, the cost of which three TV sets will be included in Stone's inventory at the end of March?

LO 3 & 4: Cost Flow vs. Physical Flow of Goods

9–42. Pfeiffer's Piano Sales & Service began the month of February with two identical pianos in inventory. During the month, six additional pianos (identical to the two in beginning inventory) were purchased as follows:

2 on February 10
1 on February 20
3 on February 26

The company sold two of the pianos on February 12, another one on February 17, and two more on February 28.

REQUIRED:

a. Assuming the company uses a perpetual inventory system and the first-in, first-out cost flow method:
   (1) Which two pianos were sold on February 12?
   (2) Which one was sold on February 17?
   (3) Which two pianos were sold on February 28?
   (4) The cost of which three pianos will be included in Pfeiffer's inventory at the end of February?

b. If the company uses a perpetual inventory system and the last-in, first-out cost flow method, the cost of which three pianos will be included in Pfeiffer's inventory at the end of February?

LO 4:   Inventory Cost

9–43. The Springer Company purchased 500 drill presses from the Falcon Machinery Company. Each drill press cost $350. The presses are to be sold for $700 each. Springer paid $1,850 for freight and $260 for insurance while the presses were in transit. Springer Company hired two more salespeople for a cost of $4,000 per month.

REQUIRED:
Calculate the cost of the inventory of drill presses to be recorded in the books and records.

LO 4:   Inventory Cost

9–44. The Baker Company acquired 4,000 hand saws from the Snaggletooth Saw Company. Each saw cost $10. The saws are to be sold for $25 each. Baker paid $750 for freight and $250 for insurance while the saws were in transit. Baker Company ran a special newspaper ad costing $800 to advertise the saws.

REQUIRED:
Calculate the cost of the inventory of saws to be recorded in the books and records.

LO 4:   Inventory Cost

9–45. The Winter Company acquired 10,000 cases of wine from the Sonoma Wine Company. Each case of wine cost $130 and contains 12 bottles. The wine will sell for $20 per bottle. Sonoma paid $1,200 for freight and $550 for insurance while the cases were in transit. Winter Company ran a special newspaper ad costing $1,800 to advertise the wine.

REQUIRED:
Calculate the cost of the inventory of wine to be recorded in the books and records.

LO 4: Inventory Cost

9–46. The Zeus Grocery Store began operations on July 1. The following transactions took place in the month of July.

    a. Cash purchases of merchandise during July were $500,000.
    b. Purchases of merchandise on account during July were $400,000.
    c. The cost of freight to deliver the merchandise was $25,000.
    d. Warehouse costs including taxes, depreciation, and utilities totaled $19,000 for the month.
    e. Zeus returned $22,000 of merchandise purchased in part b to the supplier.
    f. The grocery store manager's salary is $3,000 for the month.

REQUIRED:
Calculate the amount that the Zeus should include in the valuation of its merchandise inventory.

LO 4: Inventory Cost

9–47. The Michaelangelo Gift Shop began operations on September 1. The following transactions took place in the month of September.

    a. Cash purchases of merchandise during September were $175,000.
    b. Purchases of merchandise on account during September were $225,000.
    c. The cost of freight to deliver the merchandise was $5,000.
    d. Rental expenses including utilities totaled $6,000 for the month.
    e. Michaelangelo returned $13,000 of merchandise purchased in part b to the supplier.
    f. The store manager's salary is $3,000 for the month.
    g. Advertising for the month of September totaled $4,000.

REQUIRED:
Calculate the amount that the Michaelangelo should include in the valuation of its merchandise inventory.

LO 4, 5, & 6: Periodic Inventory Systems

9–48. The University Bookstore reported the following information for the year regarding sweatshirts with the school logo.

Date	Units	Unit Cost	Total Cost
Inventory @ January 2	1,000	$10	$10,000
Purchases:			
January 15	1,500	11	16,500
March 23	1,200	12	14,400
June 10	1,000	13	13,000
August 18	1,100	10	11,000
December 1	1,400	11	15,400
Total Goods Available for Sale	7,200		$80,300

At the end of the year a physical count is taken and there are 1,800 sweatshirts left on December 31.

REQUIRED:

Use the periodic inventory system and determine the ending inventory and the cost of goods sold using the following cost flow assumptions:

a. LIFO
b. FIFO
c. Weighted average

LO 4, 5, & 6: Periodic Inventory Systems

9–49. The University Bookstore reported the following information for the year regarding ball caps with the school logo.

Date	Units	Unit Cost	Total Cost
Inventory @ January 2	500	$10	$ 5,000
Purchases:			
January 23	800	11	8,800
March 14	600	12	7,200
July 5	500	12	6,000
August 10	1,100	10	11,000
December 15	1,200	9	10,800
Total Goods Available for Sale	4,700		$48,800

At the end of the year a physical count is taken and there are 600 ball caps left on December 31.

REQUIRED:

Use the periodic inventory system and determine the ending inventory and the cost of goods sold using the following cost flow assumptions:

a. LIFO
b. FIFO
c. Weighted average

LO 4, 5, & 6: Periodic Inventory Systems

9–50. The Widget Manufacturing Company reported the following information for the year regarding widgets :

Date	Units	Unit Cost	Total Cost
Inventory @ January 2	5,000	$10	$ 50,000
Purchases:			
January 23	8,000	12	96,000
March 14	7,000	13	91,000
July 5	6,000	12	72,000
August 10	11,000	10	110,000
December 15	12,000	9	108,000
Total Goods Available for Sale	49,000		$527,000

At the end of the year a physical count is taken and there are 8,350 widgets left on December 31.

REQUIRED:

Use the periodic inventory system and determine the ending inventory and the cost of goods sold using the following cost flow assumptions:

a. LIFO
b. FIFO
c. Weighted average

LO 4, 5, & 6:   Periodic Inventory Systems

9–51. The Powell Jewelry Manufacturing Company purchases silver by the ounce to manufacture fine jewelry. During the month of August, its first month of operations, Powell acquired the following:

	Quantity	Cost per Ounce	Total Cost
August 1	50 ounces	$35.00	$1,750
August 8	25 ounces	40.00	1,000
August 19	30 ounces	42.00	1,260
August 22	10 ounces	43.00	430
August 30	20 ounces	45.00	900
Total Goods Available for Sale	135 ounces		$5,340

Powell's inventory at the end of August is 27 ounces of silver. Assume a periodic system of inventory.

REQUIRED:

Compute the cost of the inventory at August 31, and the cost of goods sold for the month of August, under each of the following cost flow assumptions:

a. FIFO
b. LIFO
c. Weighted average

LO 4, 5, & 6:   Periodic Inventory Systems

9–52. The Reo Rock Company purchases rock by the ton to sell to homebuilders. During the month of June, its first month of operations, Reo purchased the following:

	Quantity (tons)	Cost per Ton	Total Costs
June 1	700	$100	$ 70,000
June 6	250	140	35,000
June 17	300	125	37,500
June 24	150	130	19,500
June 30	200	145	29,000
Total Goods Available for Sale	1,600		$191,000

Reo's inventory at the end of June is 230 tons of rock. Assume a periodic system of inventory.

REQUIRED:

Compute the cost of the inventory at June 30, and the cost of goods sold for the month of August, under each of the following cost flow assumptions:

a. FIFO
b. LIFO
c. Weighted average

LO 4, 5, & 6: Perpetual Inventory Systems

9-53. The Widget Manufacturing Company reported the following information for the year regarding widgets:

Date	Units	Unit Cost	Total Cost
Inventory @ January 2	5,000	$10	$ 50,000
Purchases:			
January 23	8,000	12	96,000
March 14	7,000	13	91,000
July 5	6,000	12	72,000
August 10	11,000	10	110,000
December 15	12,000	9	108,000
Total Goods Available for Sale	49,000		$527,000

Sales of widgets occurred in the following manner:

January 28	6,000 units
February 15	3,000 units
July 6	15,000 units
August 12	10,000 units
December 24	6,650 units

At the end of the year a physical count is taken and there are 8,350 widgets left on December 31.

REQUIRED:

Use the perpetual inventory system and determine the ending inventory and the cost of goods sold using the following cost flow assumptions:

a. LIFO
b. FIFO
c. Moving average

LO 4, 5, & 6: Perpetual Inventory Systems

9-54. The Powell Gold Mine Company mines silver by the ounce to sell to manufacturers of fine jewelry. During the month of August, its first month of operations, Powell had the following transactions:

		Purchases (ounces)	Cost per Ounce	Total Costs
August 1		50	$35	$1,750
August 3	Sold 40 ounces			
August 8		25	40	1,000
August 11	Sold 20 ounces			
August 19		30	42	1,260
August 20	Sold 18 ounces			
August 22		10	43	430
August 29	Sold 30 ounces			
August 30		20	45	900
Total Goods Available for Sale		135		$5,340

Powell's inventory at the end of August is 27 ounces of silver. Assume a perpetual system of inventory.

REQUIRED:

Compute the cost of the inventory at August 31, and the cost of goods sold for the month of August, under each of the following cost flow assumptions:

a. FIFO
b. LIFO
c. Moving average

LO 4, 5, & 6: Periodic Inventory Systems

9–55. The Reo Rock Company purchases rock by the ton to sell to homebuilders. During the month of June, its first month of operations, Reo engaged in the following transactions:

		Purchases (tons)	Cost per Ton	Total Costs
June 1		700	$100	$70,000
June 3	Sold 400 tons			
June 6		250	140	35,000
June 17		300	125	37,500
June 20	Sold 400 tons			
June 24		150	130	19,500
June 26	Sold 570 tons			
June 30		200	145	29,000
Total Goods Available for Sale		1,600		$191,000

Reo's inventory at the end of June is 230 tons of rock. Assume a perpetual system of inventory.

REQUIRED:

Compute the cost of the inventory at June 30, and the cost of goods sold for the month of June, under each of the following cost flow assumptions:

a. FIFO
b. LIFO
c. Moving average

LO 5 & 6: Comparison of Cost Flow Assumptions

9–56. Cox Company buys and then resells a single product as its primary business activity. This product is called the Whatzit and is subject to rather severe cost fluctuations. Following is information concerning Cox's inventory activity for the Whatzit product during the month of July:

July 1	431 units on hand, $3,017
July 2	Sold 220 units
July 9	Purchased 500 units @ $11 per unit
July 12	Purchased 200 units @ $9 per unit
July 16	Sold 300 units
July 21	Purchased 150 units @ $6 per unit
July 24	Purchased 50 units @ $8 per unit
July 29	Sold 500 units

REQUIRED:

Assuming Cox employs a perpetual inventory system, calculate cost of goods sold (units and cost) for the month of July and ending inventory (units and cost) at July 31 using the following cost flow assumptions:

a. FIFO
b. LIFO

c. Moving average (round all unit cost calculations to the nearest penny)
d. Which of the three methods resulted in the highest cost of goods sold for July? Which one will provide the highest ending inventory value for Cox's balance sheet?
e. How would the differences among the three methods affect Cox's income statement and balance sheet for the month?

LO 5 & 6:   Comparison of Cost Flow Assumptions

9–57. Frank Naifeh Company buys and then resells a single product as its primary business activity. Following is information concerning Naifeh's inventory activity for the product during October:

October 1	216 units on hand @ $4 per unit
October 5	Sold 80 units
October 7	Purchased 150 units @ $7 per unit
October 11	Purchased 100 units @ $11 per unit
October 15	Sold 200 units
October 21	Purchased 300 units @ $13 per unit
October 25	Purchased 50 units @ $18 per unit
October 29	Sold 350 units

REQUIRED:
a. Assuming Naifeh employs a perpetual inventory system, calculate cost of goods sold (units and cost) for the month of October, using the following cost flow assumptions:
   (1) FIFO
   (2) LIFO
   (3) Moving average (round all unit cost calculations to the nearest penny)
b. Which of the three methods resulted in the highest cost of goods sold for October? Which one will provide the highest ending inventory value for Naifeh's balance sheet?
c. How would the differences among the three methods affect Naifeh's income statement and balance sheet for the month?

LO 5 & 6:   Comparison of Cost Flow Assumptions

9–58. David Harris Company buys and then resells a single product as its primary business activity. Following is information concerning the David Harris Company's inventory activity for the product during August:

August 1	216 units on hand @ $18 per unit
August 5	Sold 80 units
August 7	Purchased 150 units @ $13 per unit
August 11	Purchased 100 units @ $11 per unit
August 15	Sold 200 units
August 21	Purchased 300 units @ $7 per unit
August 25	Purchased 50 units @ $4 per unit
August 29	Sold 350 units

REQUIRED:
a. Assuming Harris employs a perpetual inventory system, calculate cost of goods sold (units and cost) for the month of August, using the following cost flow assumptions:
   (1) FIFO
   (2) LIFO

(3) Moving average (round all unit cost calculations to the nearest penny)
b. Which of the three methods resulted in the highest inventory amount for Harris' August 31 balance sheet?
c. How would the differences among the three methods affect Harris' income statement and balance sheet for the month?

LO 5 & 6:   Comparison of Cost Flow Assumptions

9–59. Dennis Lee Company buys and then resells a single product as its primary business activity. Following is information concerning Lee's inventory activity for the product during the month of July:

July 1	216 units on hand @ $4 per unit
July 5	Sold 80 units
July 7	Purchased 150 units @ $4 per unit
July 11	Purchased 100 units @ $4 per unit
July 15	Sold 200 units
July 21	Purchased 300 units @ $4 per unit
July 25	Purchased 50 units @ $4 per unit
July 29	Sold 350 units

REQUIRED:
a. Assuming Lee employs a perpetual inventory system, calculate cost of goods sold (units and cost) for the month of July, using the following cost flow assumptions:
(1) FIFO
(2) LIFO
(3) Moving average (round all unit cost calculations to the nearest penny)
b. Which of the three methods resulted in the highest cost of goods sold for July?
c. Describe the differences among income statements and balance sheets prepared under the three cost flow assumptions.

LO 5 & 6:   Impact of Errors on Financial Statements

9–60. The Rugby Company's records reported the following at the end of the fiscal year:

Beginning Inventory	$ 25,000
Ending Inventory	35,000
Cost of Goods Sold	128,000

The staff completed a physical inventory and found that the inventory was actually $39,500.

REQUIRED:
Determine the effect of the inventory error on each of the financial statements.

LO 5 & 6:   Impact of Errors on Financial Statements

9–61. The Owens Company's records reported the following at the end of the fiscal year:

Beginning Inventory	$ 80,000
Ending Inventory	75,000
Cost of Goods Sold	280,000

The staff completed a physical inventory and found that the inventory was actually $68,000.

REQUIRED:

Determine the effect of the inventory error on each of the financial statements.

LO 5 & 6: Impact of Errors on Financial Statements

9–62. The Corning Company's records reported the following at the end of the fiscal year:

Beginning Inventory	$190,000
Ending Inventory	160,000
Cost of Goods Sold	495,000

The staff completed a physical inventory and found that the inventory was actually $168,000.

REQUIRED:

Determine the effect of the inventory error on each of the financial statements.

Comprehensive

9–63. Benny Blades Company and Emeril Behar Company both began their operations on January 2, 2008. Both companies experienced exactly the same reality during 2008: They purchased exactly the same number of units of merchandise inventory during the year at exactly the same cost, and they sold exactly the same number of inventory units at exactly the same selling price during the year. They also purchased exactly the same type and amount of property, plant, and equipment and paid exactly the same amount for those purchases.

At the end of 2008, the two companies prepared income statements for the year. Blades reported net income of $92,000 and Behar reported net income of $55,000.

REQUIRED:

List and discuss all items you can think of that might have caused the reported net income for the two companies to be different. (Note: Do not restrict yourself to items covered in Chapter 9.)

Comprehensive

9–64. Pete Rush and Company is a merchandiser. The company uses a perpetual inventory system, so both the physical count of inventory units and the cost classification (asset or expense) are updated when a transaction involves inventory. The company's accounting records yielded the following schedule for October:

		Units	Cost
	Beginning Inventory, October 1	200	$ 600
+	Purchases during October	1,700	5,100
=	Goods Available for Sale	1,900	$5,700
−	Cost of Goods Sold	1,500	4,500
=	Ending Inventory, October 31	400	$1,200

On October 31, Rush conducted a physical count of its inventory and discovered there were only 375 units of inventory actually on hand.

REQUIRED:

a. Show Rush's schedule of cost of goods sold and ending inventory as it should be, to reflect the results of the physical inventory count on October 31.

b. Explain in your own words how the company's income statement and balance sheet will be affected by the results of the physical inventory count on October 31.
c. What are some possible causes of the difference between the inventory amounts in Rush's accounting records and the inventory amounts from the physical count?

LO 7:   Freight Terms and Cash Discounts

*9–65. The Fallwell Company made the following purchases from the Grode Company in August of the current year:

Aug. 2   Purchased $5,000 of merchandise, terms 1/10, n/30, FOB shipping point. The goods were received on August 8.
Aug. 5   Purchased $2,000 of merchandise, terms 2/10, n/45, FOB shipping point. The goods were received on August 15.
Aug. 10   Purchased $4,000 of merchandise, terms 3/10, n/15, FOB destination. The goods were received on August 18.

REQUIRED:
For each of the listed purchases, answer the following questions.
a. When is the payment due assuming the company takes advantage of the discount?
b. When is the payment due if the company does not take advantage of the discount?
c. What is the amount of the cash discount allowed?
d. Assume the freight charges are $250 on each purchase. Which company is responsible for the freight charges?
e. What is the total amount of inventory costs for the month of August assuming that all discounts were taken?

LO 7:   Freight Terms and Cash Discounts

*9–66. The Gruber Company made the following purchases from the Belte Company in May of the current year:

May 2   Purchased $3,000 of merchandise, terms 2/10, n/30, FOB destination point. The goods were received on May 10.
May 10   Purchased $2,800 of merchandise, terms 2/10, n/60, FOB shipping point. The goods were received on May 19.
May 20   Purchased $6,000 of merchandise, terms 3/10, n/20, FOB destination. The goods were received on May 23.

REQUIRED:
For each of the listed purchases, answer the following questions.
a. When is the payment due assuming the company takes advantage of the discount?
b. When is the payment due if the company does not take advantage of the discount?
c. What is the amount of the cash discount allowed?
d. Assume the freight charges are $400 on each purchase. Which company is responsible for the freight charges?
e. What is the total amount of inventory costs for the month of May assuming that all discounts were taken?

LO 7: Freight Terms and Cash Discounts

*9–67. The Payne Company made the following purchases from the Ritz Company in July of the current year:

July 3   Purchased $7,000 of merchandise, terms 2/10, n/15, FOB shipping point. The goods were received on July 9.

July 7   Purchased $1,700 of merchandise, terms 1/10, n/60, FOB shipping point. The goods were received on July 17.

July 20   Purchased $9,000 of merchandise, terms 4/10, n/10, FOB destination. The goods were received on July 23.

REQUIRED:
For each of the listed purchases, answer the following questions.
  a. When is the payment due assuming the company takes advantage of the discount?
  b. When is the payment due if the company does not take advantage of the discount?
  c. What is the amount of the cash discount allowed?
  d. Assume the freight charges are $400 on each purchase. Which company is responsible for the freight charges?
  e. What is the total amount of inventory costs for the month of July assuming that all discounts were taken?

LO 7: Recording Purchase, Purchase Discounts, and Freight Costs for a Periodic Inventory System

*9–68. The Fallwell Company made the following purchases from the Grode Company in August of the current year:

Aug. 2   Purchased $5,000 of merchandise, terms 1/10, n/30, FOB shipping point. The goods were received on August 8.

Aug. 5   Purchased $2,000 of merchandise, terms 2/10, n/45, FOB shipping point. The goods were received on August 15.

Aug. 10   Purchased $4,000 of merchandise, terms 3/10, n/15, FOB destination. The goods were received on August 18.

REQUIRED:
  a. For each of the listed purchases, prepare the journal entries to record the purchase assuming the discount is taken.
  b. For each of the listed purchases, prepare the journal entries to record the purchase and the freight charge assuming the discount is not taken.

LO 7: Recording Purchase, Purchase Discounts, and Freight Costs for a Periodic Inventory System

*9–69. The Gruber Company made the following purchases from the Belte Company in May of the current year:

May 2   Purchased $3,000 of merchandise, terms 2/10, n/30, FOB destination point. The goods were received on May 10. Paid freight charges of $200 when the goods were received.

May 10   Purchased $2,800 of merchandise, terms 2/10, n/60, FOB shipping point. The goods were received on May 19.

May 20   Purchased $6,000 of merchandise, terms 3/10, n/20, FOB destination. The goods were received on May 23. Paid freight charges of $100 upon receipt of the goods.

REQUIRED:

  a. For each of the listed purchases, prepare the journal entries to record the purchase and the freight charge assuming the discount is taken.
  b. For each of the listed purchases, prepare the journal entries to record the purchase and the freight charge assuming the discount is not taken.

LO 7:   Recording Purchase, Purchase Discounts, and Freight Costs for a Perpetual Inventory System

*9–70. The Payne Company made the following purchases from the Ritz Company in July of the current year:

July 3	Purchased $7,000 of merchandise, terms 2/10, n/15, FOB shipping point. The goods were received on July 9.
July 7	Purchased $1,700 of merchandise, terms 1/10, n/60, FOB shipping point. The goods were received on July 17.
July 20	Purchased $9,000 of merchandise, terms 4/10, n/10, FOB destination. The goods were received on July 23. Paid freight charges of $50 upon receipt of the goods.

REQUIRED:

  a. For each of the listed purchases, prepare the journal entries to record the purchase and the freight charge assuming the discount is taken.
  b. For each of the listed purchases, prepare the journal entries to record the purchase and the freight charge assuming the discount is not taken.

LO 8:   Preparation of Journal Entries for a Perpetual Inventory System

*9–71. The Edwards Company has a beginning inventory of $50,000 and completes the following transactions during the month.

June 1	Purchased 1,000 radios for cash from the Barrow Company at a cost of $20 per unit, terms 2/10, n/30.
June 3	Purchased 2,500 clocks on account from the Adams Company at a cost of $10 per unit, terms 1/10, n/30.
June 6	Purchased 3,000 clocks on account from the Adams Company at a cost of $10 per unit, terms 1/10, n/30.
June 12	Paid for the units purchased in the June 3 transaction.
June 17	Paid for the units purchased in the June 6 transaction.
June 25	Paid cash for office supplies costing $2,000.
June 26	Purchased on account a piece of office furniture costing $800.

REQUIRED:

Prepare the general journal entries to record the transactions using the perpetual inventory method.

LO 8:   Preparation of Journal Entries for a Periodic Inventory System

*9–72. The Edwards Company has a beginning inventory of $50,000 and completes the following transactions during the month.

June 1	Purchased 1,000 radios for cash from the Barrow Company at a cost of $20 per unit, terms 2/10, n/30.
June 3	Purchased 2,500 clocks on account from the Adams Company at a cost of $10 per unit, terms 1/10, n/30.
June 6	Purchased 3,000 clocks on account from the Adams Company at a cost of $10 per unit, terms 1/10, n/30.
June 12	Paid for the units purchased in the June 3 transaction.
June 17	Paid for the units purchased in the June 6 transaction.
June 25	Paid cash for office supplies costing $2,000.
June 26	Purchased on account a piece of office furniture costing $800.

REQUIRED:
Prepare the general journal entries to record the transactions using the periodic inventory method.

LO 8: Entries to Record Ending Inventory—Perpetual Method

*9–73. Refer to Problem 9–61. Assume that at the end of the period the inventory is $45,000.

REQUIRED:
Prepare the entry necessary to adjust the ending inventory to the proper balance.

LO 8: Entries to Record Ending Inventory—Periodic Method

*9–74. Refer to Problem 9–62. Assume that at the end of the period the inventory is $45,000.

REQUIRED:
Prepare the entries necessary to close the beginning inventory and to create the ending inventory.

LO 8: Entries to Record a Perpetual Inventory System

*9–75. The Sosa Company maintains a perpetual inventory system. It accepts all purchases FOB destination and returns merchandise at the supplier's expense. The following items represent a summary of the data from the records for April, the first month of operation.

Purchases on account	$490,000
Purchases for cash	160,000
Purchase returns of merchandise for credit	50,000
Cash operating expenses	100,000
Sales on account	850,000
Cash sales	200,000
Cost of goods sold per inventory records	525,000

REQUIRED:
a. Prepare journal entries dated April 30, to record the purchase, purchase returns, sales, and operating expenses.
b. Prepare the appropriate closing entries.

LO 8: Entries to Record a Periodic Inventory System

*9–76. The Sosa Company maintains a periodic inventory system. It accepts all purchases FOB destination and returns merchandise at the supplier's expense. The following items represent a summary of the data from the records for April, the first month of operation.

Purchases on account	$490,000
Purchases for cash	160,000
Purchase returns of merchandise for credit	50,000
Cash operating expenses	100,000
Sales on account	850,000
Cash sales	200,000
Inventory per physical count on April 30	75,000

REQUIRED:

a. Prepare journal entries dated April 30, to record the purchase, purchase returns, sales, and operating expenses.

b. Prepare the appropriate closing entries.

LO 8: Entries to Record a Perpetual Inventory System

*9–77. The Alou Company maintains a perpetual inventory system. It accepts all purchases FOB destination and returns merchandise at the supplier's expense. The following items represent a summary of the data from the records for July.

Beginning inventory	$ 85,000
Purchases on account	355,000
Purchases for cash	280,000
Purchase returns of merchandise for credit	80,000
Cash operating expenses	125,000
Sales on account	642,000
Cash sales	258,000
Cost of goods sold per inventory records	475,000

REQUIRED:

a. Prepare journal entries dated July 31, to record the purchase, purchase returns, sales, and operating expenses.

b. Prepare the appropriate closing entries.

LO 8: Entries to Record a Periodic Inventory System

*9–78. The Alou Company maintains a periodic inventory system. It accepts all purchases FOB destination and returns merchandise at the supplier's expense. The following items represent a summary of the data from the records for July.

Beginning inventory	$ 85,000
Purchases on account	355,000
Purchases for cash	280,000
Purchase returns of merchandise for credit	80,000
Cash operating expenses	125,000
Sales on account	642,000
Cash sales	258,000
Inventory per physical count on July 31	165,000

REQUIRED:

a. Prepare journal entries dated July 31, to record the purchase, purchase returns, sales, and operating expenses.

b. Prepare the appropriate closing entries.

LO 8: Entries to Record a Perpetual Inventory System

*9–79. The Rose Company maintains a perpetual inventory system. It accepts all purchases FOB destination and returns merchandise at the supplier's expense. The following items represent a summary of the data from the records for August.

Beginning inventory	$ 37,000
Purchases on account	126,000
Purchases for cash	138,000
Purchase returns of merchandise for credit	30,000
Cash operating expenses	103,000
Sales on account	321,000
Cash sales	258,000
Cost of goods sold per inventory records	129,000

REQUIRED:

a. Prepare journal entries dated August 31, to record the purchase, purchase returns, sales, and operating expenses.

b. Prepare the appropriate closing entries.

LO 8: Entries to Record a Periodic Inventory System

*9–80. The Morgan Company maintains a periodic inventory system. It accepts all purchases FOB destination and returns merchandise at the supplier's expense. The following items represent a summary of the data from the records for September.

Beginning inventory	$ 25,000
Purchases on account	133,000
Purchases for cash	120,000
Purchase returns of merchandise for credit	20,000
Cash operating expenses	195,000
Cash sales	236,000
Inventory per physical count on September 30	75,000

REQUIRED:

a. Prepare journal entries dated September 30, to record the purchase, purchase returns, sales, and operating expenses.

b. Prepare the appropriate closing entries.

LO 8: Adjusting Entries for Errors in Inventory Systems

*9–81. The Sweiss Company manufactures a product for the computer industry. At the end of the first year of operations the company reported the following information under the perpetual inventory method.

Beginning Inventory	$ -0-
Cost of Goods Sold	295,000
Ending Inventory	88,000

The company determined that the ending inventory was in error and was actually $95,000.

REQUIRED:
a. Prepare the journal entry or entries necessary to correct this discovery.
b. Assume the company uses a periodic system of inventory and prepare the necessary journal entry or entries to correct this discovery.

LO 8: Adjusting Entries for Errors in Inventory Systems

*9–82. The Pippen Company manufactures a product for the automotive industry. At the end of the first year of operations the company reported the following information under the perpetual inventory method.

Beginning Inventory	$ -0-
Cost of Goods Sold	880,000
Ending Inventory	165,000

The company determined that the ending inventory was in error and was actually $148,000.

REQUIRED:
a. Prepare the journal entry or entries necessary to correct this discovery.
b. Assume the company uses a periodic system of inventory and prepare the necessary journal entry or entries to correct this discovery.

LO 8: Adjusting Entries for Errors in Inventory Systems

*9–83. The Dowers Company manufactures seats for the aircraft industry. At the end of the first year of operations the company reported the following information under the perpetual inventory method.

Beginning Inventory	$ -0-
Cost of Goods Sold	996,000
Ending Inventory	287,000

The company determined that the ending inventory was in error and was actually $298,000.

REQUIRED:
a. Prepare the journal entry or entries necessary to correct this discovery.
b. Assume the company uses a periodic system of inventory and prepare the necessary journal entry or entries to correct this discovery.

FINANCIAL REPORTING CASES

Comprehensive

9–84. Visit the website for The Pep Boys Corporation at www.pepboys.com. Locate the current copy of the annual report and find the Notes to Financial Statements. Read Note 1 and review the section on inventories plus the Note on inventories.

REQUIRED:
Answer the following questions referring to the Notes to the Financial Statements and the financial statements.

a. How are the inventories stated on the balance sheet?
b. What is the gross profit for the year?
c. What is the total cost of goods sold for the year?
d. What is the percentage of gross profit and cost of good sold in relation to sales for the year?
e. Under what assumption does The Pep Boys compute its inventories?
f. Go to the website for this text, www.pearsoncustom.com/terrell, and visit the Research Navigator. Find a recent article or press release about The Pep Boys' inventories, gross profit, or cost of goods sold and print it. Write a one-page reaction paper to the article.

Comprehensive

9–85. Visit the Darden Restaurants' website for at www.Darden.com. Locate the current copy of the annual report and find the Notes to Financial Statements. Read Note 1 and review the section on inventories plus the Note on inventories.

REQUIRED:
Answer the following questions referring to the Notes to the Financial Statements and the financial statements.
a. How are the inventories stated on the balance sheet?
b. What is the gross profit for the year?
c. What is the total cost of goods sold for the year?
d. What is the percentage of gross profit and cost of good sold in relation to sales for the year?
e. Under what assumption does Darden compute its inventories?
f. Go to the website for this text, www.pearsoncustom.com/terrell, and visit the Research Navigator. Find a recent article or press release about Darden Restaurants' inventories, gross profit, or cost of goods sold and print it. Write a one-page reaction paper to the article.

Comprehensive

9–86. Visit the Brown-Forman Corporation website for at www.Brown-Forman.com. Locate the current copy of the annual report and find the Notes to Financial Statements. Read Note 1 and review the section on inventories plus the Note on inventories.

REQUIRED:
Answer the following questions referring to the Notes to the Financial Statements and the financial statements.
a. How are the inventories stated on the balance sheet?
b. What is the gross profit for the year?
c. What is the total cost of goods sold for the year?
d. What is the percentage of gross profit and cost of good sold in relation to sales for the year?
e. Under what assumption does Brown-Forman compute its inventories?
f. Go to the website for this text, www.pearsoncustom.com/terrell, and visit the Research Navigator. Find a recent article or press release about Brown-Forman's inventories, gross profit, or cost of goods sold and print it. Write a one-page reaction paper to the article.

Chapter 10

The Balance Sheet and Income Statement: A Closer Look

Your brother-in-law, the one you like, just sent you an annual report of a company that he believes will be the next Microsoft in terms of growth and market domination. He wants you to consider getting in on the ground floor and knows that you have a little money set aside that you might want to invest. Although you have only seen a few annual reports, none seemed this complex. The balance sheet contains a lot of "intangible" assets. If these assets are not tangible, what are they, thin air? The income statement has numerous items after operating income. Should you really care about those figures? To top it off, the earnings per share has six different amounts. Which one of them is the right one to use to compute a basic market price? The highest is only $0.45 a share, and your brother-in-law wants you to pay $12 per share for this stock! That is almost 27 times the annual income per share, if you are looking at the right one. Maybe this brother-in-law is a real turkey, just like the other three.

Balance sheets and income statements are generally more complex than the ones we have explored so far. An understanding of the organization of these two financial statements is crucial, particularly when very detailed information is included. Even complex balance sheets and income statements are organized in a manner that serves to clarify rather than complicate the information provided.

In this chapter, to help you to better comprehend the information provided by them, we will explore in further detail the organization of the balance sheet and income statement. After all, the primary purpose of these and other financial statements is to provide information useful to economic decision makers. In addition, understanding the construction of the income statement and balance sheet is necessary to do financial statement analysis, which we will discuss in Chapter 12. ∎

LEARNING OBJECTIVES

After completing your work on this chapter, you should be able to do the following:

1. Describe how the balance sheet and income statement were developed as financial statements.
2. Explain the organization and purpose of the classified balance sheet.
3. Explain why recurring and nonrecurring items are presented separately on the income statement.
4. Interpret the net of tax disclosure of extraordinary items and discontinued operations.
5. Calculate earnings per share and properly disclose it on the income statement.
6. Describe the additional information provided by comparative financial statements.
*7. Complete the recording process for income taxes.

HISTORY AND DEVELOPMENT OF THE BALANCE SHEET AND INCOME STATEMENT

Ever since human beings began living in organized societies, they have kept track of their business affairs by accounting for economic events and transactions, recording them on stone or clay tablets, papyrus, paper, or whatever writing material was available.

Originally, accounting records were kept to assist in conducting a company's operation rather than to report on the operation of a company. Amounts owed to suppliers, for example, were recorded primarily so a company could keep track of what had and had not been paid, without regard for balance sheet presentation. Eventually, however, recordkeeping began for the specific purpose of preparing financial statements. In *A History of Accounting Thought,* Michael Chatfield describes this transition as follows:

> More than most accounting tools, financial statements are the result of cumulative historical influences. Before the Industrial Revolution they were usually prepared as arithmetic checks of ledger balances. Afterward the roles were reversed and it was account books which were reorganized to facilitate statement preparation. As statements became communication devices rather than simple bookkeeping summaries, the journal and ledger evolved from narratives to tabulations of figures from which balances could easily be taken.[1]

Financial statements as we know them are a relatively recent phenomenon. While accounting has been with us since about 5000 B.C., the balance sheet's function as a financial statement only emerged during the Renaissance, around A.D. 1600. For the next several hundred years the balance sheet was the primary output of the accounting process. Accountants developed the income statement in the late

---

[1]Michael Chatfield, *A History of Accounting Thought* (Huntington, NY: R. E. Kriger Publishing Co., 1974), 164.

1800s, but did not consider the information nearly as important as the balance sheet figures. In his landmark work, *Accounting Evolution to 1900*, A. C. Littleton makes the following observation:

> . . . it seems that the primary motive for separate financial statements was to obtain information regarding capital; this was the center of the interest of partners, shareholders, lenders, and the basis of the calculation of early property taxes. Thus balance-sheet data were stressed and refined in various ways, while expense and income data were incidental—in fact, the latter in the seventeenth century were presented merely as a "proof of estate"—to demonstrate by another route the correctness of the balance sheet.[2]

At the beginning of the 20th century, banks served as the chief form of external financing to U.S. companies. For this reason, creditors were the primary audience for whom financial statements were prepared. Creditors looked at a company's ability to repay its debts and at the balance sheet—which focuses on the relationships among assets, liabilities, and owners' equity—to assure themselves.

During the first two decades of the 20th century, U.S. companies changed the methods of financing expansion. Relying less on debt financing and more on equity financing, companies began to borrow less from banks and issue more capital stock. When selling stock became the major source of external financing, stockholders became the primary users of financial statements. Stockholders were interested in the performance of the company and its impact on dividend payments and the value of the company's stock. Stockholders focused on net income, so the income statement came to be considered more important than the balance sheet. Over time even long-term creditors realized that earning power was crucial to debt repayment, so they also began to rely more on the income statement than on the balance sheet.

By the 1930s, it became apparent that the balance sheet and the income statement are best used together. Neither is more important than the other because each provides valuable information for economic decision makers. By learning more about the detailed structure of the balance sheet and income statement, you can make the best use of the information provided by each statement.

ORGANIZATION OF THE BALANCE SHEET

In introducing the balance sheet in Chapter 3, we used this simple equation:

Assets = Liabilities + Owners' Equity

The equation does not distinguish one asset from another or one liability from another. A balance sheet prepared for Eliason and Company at December 31, 2007, using the basic format would look like Exhibit 10–1.

This balance sheet gives economic decision makers little useful information about the financial position of Eliason and Company at December 31, 2007. Even if the company uses the cash basis of accounting (meaning the $1,516,800 of assets is cash), we see no indication of how soon the $851,000 of liabilities must be paid or how much of the $665,800 of stockholders' equity represents contributed capital and how much represents retained earnings.

Why does any of this matter and what difference does it make to those who use the balance sheet? The answer is obvious if you remember that economic decision

---

[2]A. C. Littleton, *Accounting Evolution to 1900* (New York: Russell & Russell, 1966), 153.

Exhibit 10–1
Basic Format
Balance Sheet

ELIASON AND COMPANY
Balance Sheet
December 31, 2007

Total Assets	$1,516,800
Liabilities	$851,000
Stockholders' Equity	665,800
Total Liabilities and Stockholders' Equity	$1,516,800

makers are attempting to predict the future and timing of cash flows by looking at the balance sheet. Accountants developed a more detailed balance sheet in response to users need for additional information.

The Classified Balance Sheet

classified balance sheet
A balance sheet showing assets and liabilities categorized into current and long-term items.

A **classified balance sheet** prepared from the same accounting data as Exhibit 10–1 for Eliason and Company at December 31, 2007, would look like Exhibit 10–2. Notice that the assets still total $1,516,800; total liabilities are still $851,000; and stockholders' equity is still $665,800. The only difference in the two balance sheet presentations is the amount of detail disclosed.

As we explain why the classified balance sheet is organized as it is, we will make reference to the Eliason and Company classified balance sheet in Exhibit 10–2.

Discussion Question

10–1. Which of the two balance sheet presentations for Eliason and Company do you think would be more useful in predicting the future and timing of the company's cash flow? Provide three specific examples to support your position.

current assets Assets that are either cash or will become cash within one year.

operating cycle The length of time it takes for an entity to complete one revenue producing cycle from purchase of goods to collection of cash.

The accrual accounting basis of measurement creates a need to segregate, or classify, assets on the balance sheet because, under this basis, items besides cash are considered assets. Two classifications of assets are identified on Eliason's balance sheet: current and long-term. **Current assets** are assets that either are cash already or are expected to become cash within one year or one operating cycle, whichever is longer. An **operating cycle** is the length of time it takes for an entity to complete one revenue producing cycle. For a manufacturer, a revenue cycle is the length of time from receiving raw materials, including producing and selling the final product, to collecting cash from its customers. For a merchandiser, the operating cycle is the time it takes from receiving merchandise to collecting the cash from its customers. Most businesses have several operating cycles in one year. Some businesses, such as wineries, timber operations, or long-term construction companies have operating cycles that last as long as five years or more. As you can see from Exhibit 10–2, accounts receivable and inventory are examples of current assets.

long-term assets Assets that are expected to benefit the company for longer than one year.

Long-term assets are those assets that are expected to benefit the organization more than one year or that are not anticipated to become cash within one year. Depreciable assets such as buildings, equipment, and vehicles are examples of long-term assets. Because of the way the classified balance sheet is organized, users

Exhibit 10-2
Classified Balance
Sheet

ELIASON AND COMPANY
Balance Sheet
December 31, 2007

ASSETS:

Current Assets:

Cash		$ 100
Accounts Receivable		251,000
Inventory		298,900
Prepaid Expenses		50,000
Total Current Assets		$ 600,000

Long-Term Assets:

Land		$125,000
Plant and Equipment	$1,075,000	
Less: Accumulated Depreciation	(283,200)	
Plant and Equipment, Net		791,800
Total Long-Term Assets		916,800
Total Assets		$1,516,800

LIABILITIES:

Current Liabilities:

Accounts Payable		$ 501,000
Short-Term Note Payable		50,000
Total Current Liabilities		$ 551,000

Long-Term Liabilities:

Bonds Payable		300,000
Total Liabilities		$ 851,000

STOCKHOLDERS' EQUITY:

Common Stock, No Par Value,

10,000 Shares Issued and Outstanding		$400,000
Retained Earnings		265,800
Total Stockholders' Equity		665,800
Total Liabilities and Stockholders' Equity		$1,516,800

can tell in a quick glance just which assets (and their dollar amount) the company thinks will be turned into cash within the next year (current assets) and which ones are not expected to be converted into cash (long-term assets).

Assets are listed on a classified balance sheet in order of decreasing liquidity. **Liquidity** means nearness to cash. Notice that we always list cash first on the balance sheet because by definition it is the most liquid asset. The farther down you read the asset section of a classified balance sheet, the less likelihood there is that an item will be converted to cash in the near future. In the case of Eliason and Company, current assets total $600,000 and long-term assets total $916,800.

liquidity An item's nearness to cash.

Discussion Questions

10-2. Are there any items listed as current assets on Eliason's December 31, 2007, classified balance sheet (Exhibit 10–2) that you think will never be converted into cash? If there are, why do you think they are classified as current assets?

10-3. Eliason has classified plant and equipment as long-term assets in 2007. Does this mean the company cannot sell one of its buildings in 2008? Explain your reasoning.

investments Assets that represent long-term ownership in subsidiaries, or funds set aside for specific purposes, bond sinking funds, or bonds of other companies.

intangible assets Assets consisting of contractual rights such as patents, copyrights, and trademarks.

amortization The systematic allocation of the cost of intangible assets with finite lives over their economic lives.

Some firms possess two other classifications of assets—investments and intangibles. **Investments** represent long-term commitments to ownership of other entities (called subsidiaries) or investments in trust funds set aside for a specific purpose, bond sinking funds (money set aside to repay the firm's own bonds payable), or bonds of other corporations. The firm does not intend to utilize these assets within the next year. Their location in the balance sheet indicates how soon the company might convert these investments to cash.

Intangible assets denote company investments in contractual arrangements such as patents, copyrights, trademarks, trade names, and purchased goodwill. These investments provide the firm with future economic benefits. Similar to the way we depreciate long-term assets, we amortize the cost of intangible assets with finite lives over their economic lives. The **amortization** of intangible assets tries to match the cost of the asset with the periods of time benefited or with the revenue it helps to create.

Discussion Questions

10–4. For what reasons would a company set aside special funds in a long-term account?

10–5. Do intangibles such as copyrights, patents, and trademarks have value? Do companies try to protect the value of such intangibles?

10–6. How would you determine the economic life of an intangible?

When we classify liabilities in liquidity order, we look at how quickly they must be settled. If settlement involves cash, liquidity represents the order of payment. If settlement requires performance, such as delivery of goods or services, liquidity refers to how soon performance is required. Liquidity and priority of claims require that liabilities be listed on the balance sheet before stockholders' equity: If a company goes out of business, obligations to creditors must be paid before funds can be distributed to the owners.

current liabilities Liabilities that must be settled within one year.

long-term liabilities Debts that are not due for settlement until at least one year from now.

Current liabilities require settlement within one year. Certainly, the suppliers to whom Eliason and Company owes a total of $501,000 (accounts payable) expect repayment within the year, usually within 30 to 60 days. Eliason classifies debts not requiring settlement within the next year as **long-term liabilities.** Because of the way the balance sheet is organized, users know at a quick glance which liabilities are expected to be retired within the next year (current liabilities) and which ones are not (long-term liabilities). This enables them to assess future cash flows. Eliason's current liabilities total $551,000 and long-term liabilities total $300,000.

Exhibit 10–3 illustrates the current and long-term classifications of assets and liabilities.

Exhibit 10–3
Examples of Current and Long-Term Assets and Liabilities

Assets		Liabilities	
Current	**Long-Term**	**Current**	**Long-Term**
• Cash	• Land	• Accounts	• Notes Payable
• Inventory	• Plant	Payable	• Bonds Payable
• Accounts	• Equipment	• Short-Term	• Mortgages
Receivable		Notes Payable	Payable

Discussion Questions

10-7. Provide three examples of current liabilities and three examples of long-term liabilities not shown on the Eliason and Company balance sheet in Exhibit 10-2.

10-8. Eliason shows $600,000 of current assets and $551,000 of current liabilities. Who might be interested in these amounts, and why?

The stockholders' equity section of a classified balance sheet is also separated into two classifications. Because all equity is either contributed by owners or earned, we classify equity into contributed and earned. Preferred stockholders have first priority in paying out dividends and in liquidation. Therefore, the contributed or paid-in section of equity begins with preferred stock, second is common stock, then the remaining paid-in capital accounts. In the case of Eliason and Company, we first list the $400,000 classified as no-par common stock. Because there are no other contributed equity accounts, we list retained earnings next. At December 31, 2007, Eliason and Company had a retained earnings balance of $265,800.

Discussion Questions

10-9. Explain the exact meaning of the $265,800 of retained earnings on Eliason and Company's balance sheet.

10-10. On average, how much did Eliason and Company receive for each share of stock sold?

10-11. What is the total current market value of the Eliason and Company stock?

ORGANIZATION OF THE INCOME STATEMENT

When we introduced the income statement in Chapter 5, we used the following simple equation:

Revenues − Expenses = Net Income

An income statement prepared for Eliason and Company for the year ended December 31, 2007, using this simple format, would look like Exhibit 10-4.

Exhibit 10-4
Basic Format
Income Statement

ELIASON AND COMPANY	
Income Statement	
For the Year Ended December 31, 2007	
Revenue	$752,500
Less: Expenses	840,400
Net Loss	$ (87,900)

Exhibit 10–5
Expanded Format
Income Statement

ELIASON AND COMPANY
Income Statement
For the Year Ended December 31, 2007

Sales Revenue		$752,500
Less: Cost of Goods Sold		352,800
Gross Profit on Sales		$399,700
Less: Operating Expenses:		
Selling	$60,250	
General and Administrative	96,250	
Total Operating Expenses		156,500
Operating Income		$243,200
Less: Interest Expense		30,650
Income Before Taxes		$212,550
Less: Income Taxes		64,660
Income Before Extraordinary Item		$147,890
Extraordinary Loss (Less: Income Taxes of $87,420)		(235,790)
Net Loss		$(87,900)

Net income or net loss discloses whether or not a company has been profitable for a given period. Although net income or loss is very important, the net loss for 2007 does not tell Eliason's performance story very well.

Accountants have developed income statement presentation guidelines to furnish a more complete picture of what happened to a business during a particular income statement period. Income statements prepared following these guidelines provide more detail than given in the basic format shown in Exhibit 10–4, as well as important information about the characteristics of the revenues and expenses. Exhibit 10–5 presents an income statement for Eliason and Company for the year ended December 31, 2007, prepared using the expanded format.

Although this income statement bears little resemblance to the one presented earlier in our discussion, revenues still total $752,500; total deductions from revenues still total $840,400; and the net loss is still $87,900. You should be familiar with the beginning of the format because only the last few lines are new.

Discussion Questions

10–12. Is Exhibit 10–5 a single-step or multistep income statement? How can you tell?

10–13. If you were considering some kind of economic involvement with Eliason and Company, which number on the expanded income statement would you consider most reliable in predicting the company's future profitability? Explain.

Recurring and Nonrecurring Items

Besides presenting more detail concerning Eliason and Company's regular revenues and expenses for 2007, the income statement in Exhibit 10–5 shows an ex-

nonrecurring item Results of activities that cannot be expected to occur again, and therefore should not be used to predict future performance.

traordinary loss of $235,790, which is separated from the company's regular, recurring revenues and expenses. An extraordinary loss (or gain) is one of the items the accounting profession has determined should be shown separately as a nonrecurring item on the income statement.

A **nonrecurring item** can be broadly defined as any item (either positive or negative) that should not be considered a normal part of continuing operations because it is not expected to recur. We will explore the logic of separating recurring and nonrecurring items on the income statement.

Suppose an event happened to a company during the income statement period that was not expected to recur. Whether the event was good or bad, the company must report its occurrence, even though it is not likely to happen again. If you were attempting to predict the company's ability to generate future profits and cash flows, and the company included this one-time event with revenues and expenses that happen each year, your prediction would not be realistic. Therefore, if nonrecurring items do not represent the ongoing results of a company's operations, we should report them separately from recurring items to protect the integrity of reported earnings.

If the extraordinary loss is truly a nonrecurring item for Eliason, then the net loss of $87,900 for 2007 is not a good predictor of future profitability and cash flow. In fact, the best predictive number on this income statement is probably $147,890 listed as the income before extraordinary item.

In this section, we will more fully explain the presentation and interpretation of information about nonrecurring items on the income statement. Throughout our discussion, we will use the Pursifull, Inc. income statement for the year ended December 31, 2007, presented in Exhibit 10–6.

Exhibit 10–6
Income Statement for Pursifull, Inc. for the Year Ended December 31, 2007

PURSIFULL, INC. Income Statement For the Year Ended December 31, 2007		
Sales		$858,600
Less: Cost of Goods Sold		456,800
Gross Profit on Sales		$401,800
Less: Operating Expenses:		
Selling	$ 94,450	
General and Administrative	116,050	
Total Operating Expenses		210,500
Operating Income		$191,300
Less: Interest Expense		30,650
Income from Continuing Operations Before Taxes		$160,650
Less: Income Taxes		64,260
Income from Continuing Operations		$ 96,390
Loss on Discontinued Operations		
Income from Discontinued Operations		
(Less: Income Taxes of $11,520)	$ (17,280)	
Income Before Extraordinary Item		$ 79,110
Extraordinary Gain (Less: Income Taxes of $88,000)		132,000
Net Income		$211,110

The first half of Pursifull's income statement reflects results of activities that will probably continue in the future. The income tax amount shown ($64,260) relates only to the ongoing activities of the company and is calculated as:

Income Tax Expense = Income from Continuing Operations Before Tax × Tax Rate
$64,260 = $160,650 × 40%

Notice the item identified as Income from Continuing Operations. The $96,390 represents the net results of Pursifull's ongoing operations, which we assume have a predictive value for future earnings. Information provided on the income statement below this point relates to nonrecurring items. The income from Continuing Operations separates the recurring from nonrecurring activities. Some income statements show the title as Income Before Extraordinary Items. Regardless of the title, nonrecurring items always come after the income tax expense.

There are two general types of nonrecurring items, listed in their order of presentation on the income statement:

1. Discontinued operations
2. Extraordinary items

Proper classification of items as recurring or nonrecurring is critical to the usefulness of the accounting information. A company might be tempted to treat an item as nonrecurring because it reduces net income or to include an item with recurring revenues when it increases net income. To prevent companies from confusing the users of financial statements this way, the accounting profession restricts the items that may be considered nonrecurring. We will consider the criteria for each of these items after we discuss the income tax effects of these nonrecurring items.

Income Tax Disclosure

On Pursifull's income statement the income tax amount shown in the income from continuing operations section of $64,260 is the amount of tax expense associated with the ongoing, recurring operation of the business. But how should the company disclose the income tax effect of the nonrecurring items shown on the income statement? The nonrecurring events cannot escape income tax consequences, and those consequences must be disclosed.

Since we present nonrecurring items separately from continuing operations, lumping their tax effect with the tax expense shown for continuing operations would distort the information. For example, the net tax effect on Pursifull's income statement is $140,740 ($64,260 + $11,520 + $88,000). If we showed this on the income statement, it would appear as follows:

Income from Continuing Operations Before Taxes	$160,650
Less: Income Taxes	140,740
Income from Continuing Operations	$ 19,910

This example makes it appear that Pursifull, Inc. pays 87.6 percent income tax. On the contrary, we could show two different amounts of income taxes as follows:

Income from Continuing Operations Before Taxes		$160,650
Less: Income Taxes from Continuing Operations	$64,260	
Income Taxes from Nonrecurring Events	76,480	140,740
Income from Continuing Operations		$ 19,910

This financial statement leaves readers to ponder the difference and still distorts the income from continuing operations. To eliminate the distortion and confusion, members of the accounting profession decided that the only tax expense shown on the income statement as a separate line item will be the amount associated with continuing operations. Therefore, the two major types of nonrecurring items included on the income statement are shown "less income tax," or "net of tax."

net of tax The proper presentation format for nonrecurring items shown below income from continuing operations on the income statement.

Net of tax means the amount shown for an item has been adjusted for any income tax effect. To calculate the tax expense, simply multiply the effective tax rate by the amount of the nonrecurring gain or loss. In Pursifull's example, we calculate the amounts as:

Income from Discontinued Operations $28,800 \times 40\% = \$11,520$
Extraordinary Gain $220,000 \times 40\% = \$88,000$

How did we determine the full amount of the nonrecurring item? There are two accurate ways. The first is to simply add the tax to the gain or loss amount. The second is to divide the net of tax amount of gain or loss by the reciprocal of the tax amount or (1 − Tax Rate), in this case 60 percent.

Income from Discontinued Operations = \$17,280 + \$11,520 = \$28,800
or = \$17,280/.60   = \$28,800

When a business experiences a gain, the total income of the business increases and the Internal Revenue Service will require more taxes. The gain increases the amount of taxes owed, which in turn reduces the amount of the gain (see Exhibit 10–7). When a business experiences a loss, the total income of the business decreases and the Internal Revenue Service will require less taxes. The loss decreases the amount of taxes owed, which in turn reduces the amount of the loss.

Current accounting rules require that on the face of the income statement the tax effect on each of these nonrecurring items, and the amount of that item after the tax effect, be shown. With this information, financial statement users can determine the actual amount of the item before any tax effect.

Now look again at the income statement for Pursifull, Inc. (Exhibit 10–6 on page F-365). Notice that the statement includes examples of both major types of nonrecurring items, and all receive the same general presentation: Each is shown below the Income from Continuing Operations line, and each is shown "net of tax."

We now explore the criteria for and specific presentation of each of these types of nonrecurring items.

Exhibit 10–7
Effect of Tax on
Gains and Losses

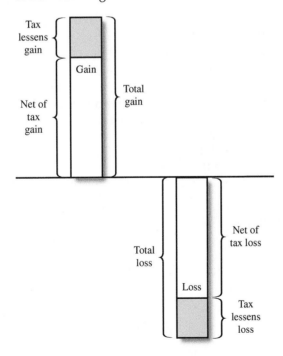

Discontinued Operations

business component A portion of an entity for which assets, results of operations, and activities can be separately identified.

discontinued operations The disposal of a business component. One of the nonrecurring items, shown net of taxes, after income from continuing operations on the income statement.

If a company disposes of a major component of its business, the results of operations for the component of the company sold and any gain or loss from the actual disposal of the business component are reported as nonrecurring items on the income statement. A **business component** is a portion of an entity for which assets, results of operations, and activities can be separately identified. When a company disposes of a business component, the **discontinued operations** gain or loss is considered a nonrecurring item, shown net of taxes, after income from continuing operations on the income statement.

Once a judgment has been made that the discontinued operations should be considered the disposal of a business component, GAAP require specific disclosures on the income statement. To illustrate, recall Exhibit 10–6, the income statement for Pursifull, Inc. for the year ended December 31, 2007.

Pursifull, Inc. buys and resells toys. Many years ago, Pursifull purchased a company that manufactured hats. Although this portion of the business has always been profitable, current management did not believe that the hat business fit into the corporation's strategic plans and sold it during 2007.

To compute the amount of the gain or loss from discontinued operations, we must review the facts. In 2007, prior to being sold, the hat operation had revenues of $162,500 and expenses of $101,300. When the company sold the hat operation, it incurred a $90,000 pretax loss on the sale. We can calculate the final gain or loss for the discontinued operation as follows:

Revenues	$162,500
Expenses	101,300
Loss on Sale	(90,000)
Pretax Loss	$ 28,800
Less: Income Tax	11,520
Net Loss Reported	$ (17,280)

After applying the sax savings, the total loss of $(17,280) under discontinued operations is properly reported on Pursifull's 2007 income statement.

Extraordinary Items

extraordinary item A gain or loss that is both unusual in nature and infrequent in occurrence. One of the nonrecurring items shown net of tax on the income statement.

For an event to result in an **extraordinary item** under GAAP, the event must be **both** unusual in nature and infrequent in occurrence. If an event is either unusual in nature or infrequent in occurrence, it qualifies as a special expense reported in the operating expenses or special revenue reported in other revenues and gains segment of the income statement. The statement preparer must exercise judgment in deciding whether to classify the result of an event as an extraordinary item or a special item in continuing operations.

When applying the criterion of "unusual in nature," the accountant must consider the operating environment of the business entity.

> The environment of an entity includes such factors as the characteristics of the industry or industries in which it operates, the geographical location of its operations, and the nature and extent of government regulation. Thus, an event or transaction may be unusual in nature for one entity but not for another because of differences in their respective environments.
>
> —(*APB Opinion No. 30*, paragraph 21)

So, a gain or loss that would be considered unusual for one company might be considered an ordinary event for another company.

Accountants must also consider the operating environment of the entity when applying the criterion of "infrequent in occurrence." To be considered infrequent, an event must not be expected to recur in the foreseeable future.

As you use financial statement information, a basic appreciation of how these criteria are applied will enhance your ability to interpret the impact of extraordinary items. The following events or transactions meet the criteria of both unusual and infrequent and should therefore be presented as extraordinary items on the income statement.

1. A hailstorm destroys a large portion of a tobacco manufacturer's crops in an area where hailstorms are rare.
2. A steel fabricating company sells the only land it owns. The company acquired the land 10 years ago for future expansion but shortly thereafter abandoned all plans for expansion and held the land for appreciation in value instead.
3. A company sells a block of common stock of a publicly traded company. The block of shares, which represents less than 10 percent of the publicly held company, is the only security investment the company has ever made.
4. An earthquake in Texas destroys one of the oil refineries owned by a large multinational oil company.

Discussion Question

10–14. The following examples do not qualify as extraordinary items. For each one, explain specifically what criterion/criteria have not been met.

    a. A citrus grower's Florida crop is damaged by frost. . . .
    b. A company which operates a chain of warehouses sells excess land around one of its warehouses. Normally, when the company buys land for a new warehouse, it buys more land than it needs for the warehouse expecting that the land will appreciate in value. . . .
    c. A large diversified company sells from its portfolio a block of shares which it has acquired for investment purposes. This is the first sale from its portfolio of securities. . . .
    d. A textile manufacturer with only one plant moves to another location. It has not relocated a plant in twenty years and has no plans to do so in the foreseeable future. . . .

—(*AICPA Accounting Interpretations,*
AIN-APB30, #1)

Because extraordinary items enter the income statement after income from continuing operations, we present them net of tax. Return to the income statement for Pursifull, Inc. (Exhibit 10–6). Pursifull reported an extraordinary gain of $132,000 ($220,000 less income taxes of $88,000). This gain resulted from the city government's purchase of Pursifull's land adjacent to the municipal airport. The government expropriated the land to complete an airport expansion, and Pursifull had no choice but to sell the property to the government. Normally forced sales to government agencies do not create a taxable gain if the citizen or business entity replaces the property with property that costs as much as the proceeds of the sales. Because Pursifull decided not to replace the land, the transaction was taxable.

Exhibit 10–8

Pursifull's Stockholders' Equity Section of the Balance Sheet for December 31, 2007 and 2006

		2007	2006
PURSIFULL, INC. Stockholders' Equity Section December 31			
Contributed Capital:			
9% Preferred Stock, $100 Par Value			
5,000 authorized, issued and outstanding		$ 500,000	$ 500,000
Common Stock, $10 Par Value, authorized 100,000			
shares, issued and outstanding 90,000 and 85,000		900,000	850,000
Additional Paid-in Capital		450,000	390,000
Total Contributed Capital		$1,850,000	$1,740,000
Retained Earnings		796,690	675,580
Total Stockholders' Equity		$2,646,690	$2,415,580

This type of transaction is both unusual in nature and infrequent in occurrence for Pursifull. Therefore we should report it as an extraordinary item.

The FASB continues to change its requirements. In 1997, FASB released *SFAS No. 130* that requires companies to report comprehensive income. **Comprehensive income** measures all changes in equity from nonowner sources. (Owner sources include contributions made by owners and distributions to owners.) In many instances, especially for small companies, comprehensive income may be equal to the income on the income statement. Pursifull's stockholders' equity section appears in Exhibit 10–8.

comprehensive income
The change in equity during a period from nonowner sources.

Discussion Questions

10–15. How much did Pursifull receive from the sale of the stock? How much per share did Pursifull receive on average for the stock sold before 2007? During 2007?

10–16. How much did Pursifull pay in dividends during 2007? If dividends were paid after the sale of the common stock, how much did Pursifull pay per preferred share and per common share?

We can calculate Pursifull's comprehensive income by the following formula:

Comprehensive Income = Ending Equity − Beginning Equity − Owners' Contributions + Owners' Distributions

$211,110 = $2,646,690 − 2, 415,580 − 110,000 + 90,000

This figure is equal to net income on the income statement plus several items of unrecognized and/or unrealized income currently included in stockholders' equity. FASB gave firms until 1998 to implement this requirement and a choice of one of three methods to comply with its provisions:

1. A separate statement of comprehensive income
2. A combined statement of income and comprehensive income
3. Special presentation in the statement of stockholders' equity

Most firms select the third option. This issue is beyond the scope of this course, but we include the information because most of the annual reports you may examine will include comprehensive income in one of these places in the financial statements.

Comprehensive Income is an Accounting Element.

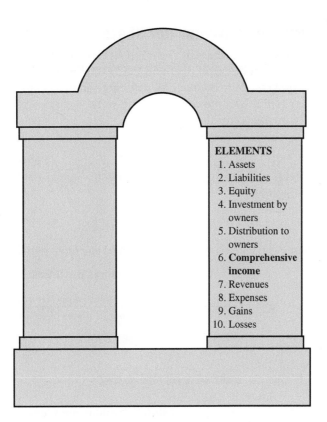

ELEMENTS
1. Assets
2. Liabilities
3. Equity
4. Investment by owners
5. Distribution to owners
6. **Comprehensive income**
7. Revenues
8. Expenses
9. Gains
10. Losses

EARNINGS PER SHARE

earnings per share (EPS)
A calculation indicating how much of a company's total earnings is attributable to each share of common stock.

Many investors and other financial statement users rely on one statistic more than any other to measure a company's performance—earnings per share. To comply with GAAP, income statements must disclose the firm's **earnings per share (EPS),** which reveals how much of a company's total earnings is attributable to each share of common stock. We calculate basic earnings per share with the following formula:

$$\text{Earnings per share} = \frac{\text{Net income} - \text{Preferred dividend requirement}}{\text{Weighted average number of shares of common stock oustanding}}$$

basic earnings per share
A simple calculation of earnings per share based on shares outstanding on the balance sheet date.

convertible securities
Debt or equity securities that can be converted into shares of the company's common stock.

diluted earnings per share
A calculation of earnings per share including all potentially dilutive securities.

GAAP require that two measures of EPS be calculated—basic and diluted. **Basic earnings per share** computes EPS based on the reality of the status of the company on the balance sheet date. If a company has convertible securities on its balance sheet, the current status of the company may change in the future. **Convertible securities** are debt or equity securities that owners may, at their option, convert to common stock. Examples are convertible bonds and convertible preferred stocks. Because these pose a possible dilutive threat to the current and future common stockholders, we must disclose the consequences of having such securities. The dilutive threat arises because the owners of the bonds or preferred stocks may convert these to common stock. The earnings must then be shared among more stockholders and the earnings per share will decrease. **Diluted earnings per share** includes the potential impact of any issued dilutive securities. When we calculate the diluted earnings per share, we modify the formula as if the conversion took place in the beginning of the year. We can illustrate the appropriate changes in the example.

Calculating Earnings per Share

Assume that each share of preferred stock is convertible into six shares of common stock and that Pursifull, Inc. sold the 5,000 shares of new stock on April 1, 2007. We must first compute the weighted average shares of stock outstanding for the year, similar to the way we computed the weighted average cost of inventory. Look at the following computational chart:

Date	(A) Number of Shares Outstanding	(B) Period of Time	(A) × (B)
January 1	85,000	3/12	21,250
April 1	90,000	9/12	67,500
	Weighted average shares		88,750

Now we can calculate basic and diluted earnings per share for Pursifull:

Basic Earnings per Share:

$$EPS = \frac{\text{Net income} - \text{Preferred dividend requirement}}{\text{Weighted average number of shares of common stock outstanding}}$$

$$= \frac{\$211,110 - \left(9\% \times \$500,000\right)}{88,750} = \frac{\$211,110 - \$45,000}{88,750}$$

$$= \$1.87 \text{ per share (rounded)}$$

Diluted Earnings per Share:

$$EPS = \frac{\text{Net income} - \text{Preferred dividend requirement}}{\text{Weighted average number of shares of common stock outstanding}}$$

$$= \frac{\$211,110 \quad 0}{88,750 + \left(6 \quad 5,000\right)} = \frac{\$211,110}{118,750} = \$1.78 \text{ per share (rounded)}$$

To understand the calculation of diluted EPS, look first to the numerator of the equation. If the preferred stock is converted at the beginning of the year, there is no requirement to pay dividends for the year. The denominator changes because, if the preferred stock is converted, there will be an additional 30,000 shares outstanding all year. The result lowers the EPS by $0.09 per share and warns prospective investors that this is the worst-case scenario for the current earnings attributed to one share of stock.

Income Statement Presentation

GAAP require that basic and fully diluted earnings per share be prominently displayed on the income statement for each item on the income statement below income tax expense. Exhibit 10–9 illustrates the proper statement presentation for Pursifull, Inc.

We can look at the calculations of (a) through (d):

Basic EPS

(a) $\dfrac{\$96,390 - \$45,000}{88,750} = \$0.58$

(b) $\dfrac{\$(17,280)}{88,750} = \$(0.20)$

(c) $\dfrac{\$79,110 - \$45,000}{88,750} = \$0.38$

(d) $\dfrac{\$132,000}{88,750} = \$1.49$

Diluted EPS

(a) $\dfrac{\$96,390}{118,750} = \$0.81$

(b) $\dfrac{\$(17,280)}{118,750} = \$(.014)$

(c) $\dfrac{\$79,110}{118,750} = \$0.67$

(d) $\dfrac{\$132,000}{118,750} = \$1.11$

Exhibit 10-9
Income Statement for Pursifull, Inc. for the Year Ended December 31, 2007

PURSIFULL, INC.
Income Statement
For the Year Ended December 31, 2007

			Basic	Diluted	
Sales		$858,600			
Less: Cost of Goods Sold		456,800			
Gross Profit on Sales		$401,800			
Less: Operating Expenses:					
Selling	$ 94,450				
General and Administrative	116,050				
Total Operating Expenses		210,500			
Operating Income		$191,300			
Less: Interest Expense		30,650			
Income from Continuing Operations Before Taxes		$160,650	Basic	Diluted	
Less: Income Taxes		64,260	EPS	EPS	
Income from Continuing Operations		$96,390	$.58	$.81	(a)
Loss on Discontinued Operations					
(Less: Income Taxes of $11,520)		(17,280)	(.20)	(.14)	
Income Before Extraordinary Item		$79,110	$.38	$.67	
Extraordinary Gain					
(Less: Income Taxes of $88,000)		132,000	1.49	1.11	
Net Income		$211,110	$1.87	$1.78	

We have applied the EPS formula to each income item, treating that item as the numerator in place of net income. Notice that only the net income from continuing operations, net income before extraordinary items and accounting principle change, and net income subtract the preferred dividends from the numerator in computing basic earnings per share. Mathematically, you should ignore the preferred dividends in all other EPS calculations.

The income statement provides users with a great deal of information with which to predict the future amount and timing of a company's cash flows. Understanding the details of the information provided in an income statement will make you a wiser financial statement user. But one year's information is for a relatively short period of time—too short to be used in making many long-term economic decisions. For this reason, serious analysis of income statement and balance sheet information requires financial statements for more than one accounting period.

COMPARATIVE FINANCIAL STATEMENTS

comparative financial statements Financial statements showing results from two or more consecutive periods.

Comparative financial statements show results for two or more consecutive periods—usually years or quarters. Financial statement analysts use comparative statements to develop a sense of the big picture of the company's performance over time. Comparative statements help the statement user to find trends in the information that improve future income and cash flow predictions. Companies registered with the SEC are required to present at least two years' balance sheets and three years' income statements and cash flow statements plus selected financial information for at least five consecutive years. The Committee on Accounting Procedure described the importance of comparative financial statements this way:

Such presentation emphasizes the fact that statements for a series of periods are far more significant than those for a single period and that the accounts for one period are but an installment of what is essentially a continuous history.

—(ARB 43, Chapter 2, paragraph 1)

To illustrate the presentation of comparative financial statements, we provide the 2007 and 2008 income statements and balance sheets for Norton, Inc. in Exhibit 10–10.

Discussion Questions

10–17. Using the comparative income statements and balance sheets of Norton, Inc. presented in Exhibit 10–10, prepare the company's 2008 statement of retained earnings.

10–18. What specific information that was not apparent from Norton's income statements or balance sheets did the statement of retained earnings you developed for Discussion Question 10–17 provide?

Comparative financial statements enhance the user's ability to analyze a company's past performance and present condition. They also make it possible to perform several analytical techniques, which we will explore in later chapters. Financial statement analysis, in fact, begins with the use of the statement of cash flows—the fourth financial statement, which we introduce in the next chapter.

SUMMARY

Both the balance sheet and income statement are useful tools. By learning more about the construction and organization of these statements, users of balance sheet and income statement information are able to use the information contained in the statements more effectively.

The classified balance sheet separates assets into four major categories: current, long-term, investments, and intangibles. Liabilities on a classified balance sheet are separated into current and long-term. These classifications provide additional information to decision makers.

Income statements often include items that are not part of the company's normal operations and are not expected to recur. Inflows or outflows of this type must be separated from results of activities that are expected to recur as part of the company's normal, ongoing operations. Reporting recurring items and nonrecurring items separately offers financial statement users additional useful information. Two major types of nonrecurring items (discontinued operations and extraordinary items) are presented below income from continuing operations and are shown net of tax. The other most common type of nonrecurring item, one that is unusual or infrequent but not both, is shown within the section of the income statement related to continuing operations, but is identified as a special item.

Comprehensive income represents the change in equity from nonowner sources. GAAP now require that comprehensive income be prominently displayed in the financial statements. GAAP also require that basic and diluted earnings per

Exhibit 10–10
2008 and 2007 Financial Statements for Norton, Inc.

NORTON, INC.
Income Statements
For the Years Ended December 31, 2008 and 2007
(in thousands)

		2008		2007
Sales		$14,745		$12,908
Less: Cost of Goods Sold		10,213		8,761
Gross Profit on Sales		$ 4,532		$ 4,147
Less: Operating Expenses				
Selling	$1,022		$ 546	
General and Administrative	2,721		2,451	
Total Operating Expenses		3,743		2,997
Operating Income		$ 789		$ 1,150
Less: Interest Expense		172		137
Income Before Taxes		$ 617		$ 1,013
Less: Income Taxes		123		355
Net Income		$ 494		$ 658

NORTON, INC.
Balance Sheets
December 31, 2008 and December 31, 2007
(in thousands)

Assets:		2008		2007
Current Assets:				
Cash		$ 2,240		$1,936
Accounts Receivable		2,340		2,490
Merchandise Inventory		776		693
Prepaid Expenses		200		160
Total Current Assets		$ 5,556		$5,279
Plant and Equipment:				
Buildings	$7,723		$6,423	
Less: Accumulated Depreciation	3,677		3,534	
Buildings, Net		$ 4,046		$2,889
Equipment	$2,687		$2,387	
Less: Accumulated Depreciation	1,564		1,523	
Equipment, Net		1,123		864
Total Plant and Equipment		$ 5,169		$3,753
Total Assets		$10,725		$9,032
Liabilities:				
Current Liabilities:				
Accounts Payable		$ 1,616		$1,080
Notes Payable		2,720		2,920
Total Current Liabilities		$ 4,336		$4,000
Long-Term Liabilities		2,000		1,600
Total Liabilities		$ 6,336		$5,600
Stockholders' Equity:				
Common Stock, No Par Value		$ 3,000		$2,400
Retained Earnings		1,389		1,032
Total Stockholders' Equity		$ 4,389		$3,432
Total Liabilities and Stockholders' Equity		$10,725		$9,032

share be disclosed on the income statement for each item of income from *income from continuing operations* through *net income*. Comparative financial statements, providing information for two or more consecutive periods, offer a clearer view of a company's performance and financial position.

APPENDIX— RECORDING INCOME TAX EXPENSE

In previous chapters we ignored the effect of income taxes on income statements. Because proprietorships and partnerships have no income taxes, this treatment is proper for them. However, a corporation pays corporate income taxes because it has the legal status of a person. Accounting for income taxes requires two basic entries and requires three new accounts. We will make entries to:

1. Accrue the income tax expense as computed for the income statement.
2. Record the payment of accrued taxes.
3. Record the payment of prepaid or estimated taxes.

To make these entries we will need the following accounts:

1. Expense account—Income Tax Expense
2. Current liability account—Income Taxes Payable
3. Prepaid asset account—Prepaid Income Taxes

We can look at the Pursifull, Inc. example in Exhibit 10–6 on page F-381 and prepare the journal entries to record the expense and the liability. We make the entries to record the expense and liability for the income taxes without regard to the character of the income tax. Remember that the aim of recording and reporting differ. Recording accumulates the reality of measurement of transactions and events (data) while reporting provides information (organized data) to users. In the recording process, we record Pursifull's total income tax expense and liability.

To record income tax expense and liability:

2007		Debit	Credit
December 31	Income Tax Expense	140,740	
	Income Taxes Payable		140,740
	To record the 2007 expense per the income statement.		

($64,260 − 11,520 + $88,000)

Assume that Pursifull paid the resulting liability on March 15, 2008, when the CFO filed the corporate tax return.

To record payment of tax liability:

2008		Debit	Credit
January 15	Income Taxes Payable	140,740	
	Cash		140,740
	To record payment of 2007 income taxes.		

The Internal Revenue Service has requirements for corporations to pay estimated income taxes four times each year, a concept similar to individuals allowing withholding taxes to be taken from each paycheck. This transfers money to the government during the year and prevents the corporations from using the cash for other purposes and being unable to pay the taxes at year end. Assume that on April

15, June 15, September 15, and December 15 Pursifull paid the IRS estimated taxes of $30,000 in anticipation of the 2007 expense and made a final payment on March 15, 2008, when the tax return was filed. Look how the entries would be made:

To record estimated tax payments:

2007		Debit	Credit
April 15	Prepaid Income Taxes	30,000	
	Cash		30,000
	To record estimated income tax payments for 2007.		

The entries for June 15, September 15, and December 15 would be exactly the same.

To record accrual of income tax expense:

December 31	Income Tax Expense	140,740	
	Prepaid Income Taxes		120,000
	Income Taxes Payable		20,740
	To record income tax expense for 2007.		

To record final payment of taxes:

2008			
March 15	Income Taxes Payable	20,740	
	Cash		20,740
	To record payment of the final tax liability for 2007.		

SUMMARY OF APPENDIX

We record income tax expense in the same manner as other expenses. The cash outflow may precede the expense accrual and be recorded as a prepaid expense. The cash outflow may follow the accrual and extinguish the liability. In the recording process, we ignore income statement separation of the income tax expense into recurring and nonrecurring activities and add all the amounts together into one amount.

REVIEW THE FACTS

A. What was the original purpose of accounting records?
B. What caused the shift in attention from the balance sheet to the income statement?
C. Explain why a decision maker may prefer a classified balance sheet to one using the simplest possible format.
D. What is the difference between current and long-term assets? Offer two examples of each.
E. In what order are assets presented on a classified balance sheet?
F. Describe investment and intangible assets and provide two examples of each that are not listed in the chapter.
G. Describe the difference between current and long-term liabilities and provide two examples of each.
H. Explain the difference between recurring and nonrecurring items on an income statement. Why are these items reported separately?
I. Identify the two major types of nonrecurring items that are shown net of tax on the income statement.

J. Explain the effect of taxes on both gains and losses.
K. What is a business component?
L. What criteria must be met for an item to be considered extraordinary?
M. What does income from discontinued operations represent?
N. Define comprehensive income.
O. Define earnings per share and distinguish between basic and diluted earnings per share.
P. Describe comparative financial statements and explain their benefits to economic decision makers.

APPLY WHAT YOU HAVE LEARNED

LO 2: Balance Sheet Terminology

10–19. Presented below are items related to the organization of the classified balance sheet, followed by the definitions of those items in scrambled order.

a. Liquidity
b. Current assets
c. Long-term assets
d. Current liabilities
e. Intangible asset
f. Long-term liabilities
g. Stockholders' equity
h. Total liabilities and stockholders' equity
i. Plant and equipment, net
j. Investments

1. _____ Obligations not requiring payment within the next year
2. _____ Items controlled by a company that are not expected to become cash within the next year
3. _____ Describes an item's nearness to cash
4. _____ The owners' residual interest in a corporation
5. _____ Long-lived tangible assets less all the depreciation expense ever recognized on those assets
6. _____ Obligations that must be retired within the next year
7. _____ Equal to total assets
8. _____ Items controlled by a company that are expected to become cash within the next year
9. _____ An investment in a contractual arrangement such as a patent
10. _____ A long-term commitment to ownership of other entities

REQUIRED:
Match the letter next to each item with the appropriate definition. Each letter will be used only once.

LO 2: Balance Sheet Accounts

10–20. a. What are investments on a balance sheet and how are they classified?
b. Provide three examples of investments and discuss how they would be classified on the balance sheet.

LO 2: Balance Sheet Accounts

10–21. a. Define intangible assets in your own words.
b. Provide three examples of intangible assets and discuss how they would be classified on the balance sheet.
c. What is the term applied to the process of matching the cost of an intangible with the periods of time benefited or with the revenues they help to create?

LO 2: Balance Sheet Accounts

10–22. Presented below are the major sections of the classified balance sheet, followed by a list of items normally shown on the balance sheet.

a. Current assets   e. Long-term liabilities
b. Long-term assets   f. Contributed capital
c. Current liabilities   g. Retained earnings
d. Intangible asset   h. Investments

1. _____ Accounts payable
2. _____ Common stock
3. _____ Franchise
4. _____ Accounts receivable
5. _____ Note payable due within one year
6. _____ Prepaid expenses
7. _____ Preferred stock
8. _____ Note payable due in two years
9. _____ Amounts earned by the company but not yet distributed to the owners of the business
10. _____ Amounts received in excess of par value on the sale of stock
11. _____ Bonds held for the interest to be earned
12. _____ Land
13. _____ Stock of a subsidiary
14. _____ Wages payable
15. _____ Vehicles
16. _____ Copyright
17. _____ Cash
18. _____ Buildings
19. _____ Bonds payable
20. _____ Trade mark

REQUIRED:
Indicate where each item on the list should be shown on the classified balance sheet by placing the letter of the appropriate balance sheet section in the space provided. The letters may be used more than once.

LO 2: Preparation of Balance Sheet

10–23. The following items relate to the Dana Corporation at December 31, 2007:

Land	$210,000
Cash	14,600
Accounts Receivable	92,300
Accounts Payable	74,000
Common Stock (75,000 Shares Outstanding)	300,000
Bonds Payable	100,000
Additional Paid-in Capital—Common Stock	10,000
Inventory	118,000
Prepaid Expenses	11,200
Taxes Payable	17,000
Short-Term Note Payable	50,000
Buildings and Equipment	400,000
Retained Earnings	?
Wages Payable	35,800

Accumulated Depreciation (which is not reflected in the previous totals) is $142,000 on the Buildings and Equipment.

REQUIRED:

a. What is the par value of Dana Corporation's common stock? Explain how you determined your answer.

b. How much cash did Dana Corporation receive from the sale of its common stock? Explain how you determined your answer.

c. Prepare a classified balance sheet for Dana Corporation at December 31, 2007.

LO 2: Preparation of Balance Sheet

10–24. The following items relate to Wesnidge and Company at December 31, 2008:

Accounts Payable	$172,000
Common Stock ($2 Par Value)	400,000
Bonds Payable	307,700
Prepaid Expenses	9,800
Taxes Payable	47,000
Short-Term Note Payable	70,000
Buildings and Equipment	875,000
Additional Paid-in Capital—Common Stock	240,000
Land	490,000
Cash	124,200
Accounts Receivable	212,000
Inventory	338,000
Retained Earnings	?
Wages Payable	77,600

Accumulated Depreciation (which is not reflected in the previous totals) is $271,000 on the Buildings and Equipment.

REQUIRED:

a. How many shares of Wesnidge and Company's common stock are outstanding at December 31, 2008? Explain how you determined your answer.

b. How much cash did Wesnidge and Company receive from the sale of its common stock? Explain how you determined your answer.

c. Prepare a classified balance sheet for Wesnidge and Company at December 31, 2008.

LO 2: Preparation of Balance Sheet

10–25. The following items relate to the Janis Marple Company at December 31, 2007:

Accounts Payable	$516,000
Common Stock ($2 Par Value)	800,000
Bonds Payable	923,100
Prepaid Expenses	29,400
Taxes Payable	141,000
Short-Term Note Payable	210,000
Buildings and Equipment	985,000
Additional Paid-in Capital—Common Stock	240,000
Land	690,000

Cash	124,200
Accounts Receivable	212,000
Inventory	338,000
Retained Earnings	?
Wages Payable	132,800

Accumulated Depreciation (which is not reflected in the previous totals) is $385,000 on the Buildings and Equipment.

REQUIRED:

a. How many shares of Marple Company's common stock are outstanding at December 31, 2007? Explain how you determined your answer.
b. How much cash did Marple Company receive from the sale of its common stock? Explain how you determined your answer.
c. Prepare a classified balance sheet for Marple Company at December 31, 2007.

LO 2: Classified Balance Sheet

10–26. Assets on the classified balance sheet are identified as either current or long-term. Liabilities on the classified balance sheet are also identified as either current or long-term.

REQUIRED:

a. What criterion is used to determine whether an asset or liability is classified as current or long-term?
b. Explain in your own words why the following parties would be interested in the separation of current and long-term assets and liabilities on a company's balance sheet:
   (1) Short-term creditors (other businesses from whom the company buys inventory, supplies, etc.)
   (2) Long-term creditors (banks and others from whom the company borrows money on a long-term basis)
   (3) The company's stockholders
   (4) The company's management

LO 2: Classified Balance Sheet

10–27. Stockholders' equity on the classified balance sheet of a corporation is divided into two major categories: contributed capital and retained earnings.

REQUIRED:

a. Explain in your own words what each of the two major categories under stockholders' equity represents.
b. Explain in your own words why the following parties would be interested in the relative amounts of contributed capital and retained earnings in the stockholders' equity section of a company's balance sheet:
   (1) Short-term creditors (other businesses from whom the company buys inventory, supplies, etc.)
   (2) Long-term creditors (banks and others from whom the company borrows money on a long-term basis)
   (3) The company's stockholders
   (4) The company's management

LO 3: Income Statement Terminology

10–28. Presented below are several sections of the multistep income statement, followed by several independent situations or transactions.

    a. Sales   **d.** Discontinued operation
    b. Cost of goods sold   **e.** Extraordinary item
    c. Income from continuing operations

    1. _____ A manufacturing company sells a warehouse with a book value of $20,000 for $20,000.

    2. _____ A company located on the American Gulf Coast experiences damage from a hurricane.

    3. _____ A company sells units of inventory in the normal course of its business operation.

    4. _____ A company located in San Francisco, California, experiences a loss from earthquake damage. This loss is determined to be a "special" item.

    5. _____ A company disposes of a major component of its business.

    6. _____ A company pays wages, rent, utilities, and so forth.

    7. _____ A company located in Columbia, South Carolina, experiences a loss from earthquake damage. This loss is determined to be both unusual in nature and infrequent in occurrence.

REQUIRED:

Indicate where the result of each situation or transaction should be shown on the multistep income statement by placing the letter of the appropriate income statement section in the space provided. The letters may be used more than once. Note: The results of some situations or transactions may not be shown on the income statement. If so, place the letter *n* in the space provided.

LO 3: Income Statement Terminology

10–29. Presented below are items related to the multistep income statement as discussed in this chapter, followed by the definitions of those items in scrambled order.

    a. Gross profit on sales   **d.** Discontinued operation
    b. Operating expenses   **e.** Extraordinary item
    c. Income from continuing   **f.** Recurring item
        operations   **g.** Nonrecurring item

    1. _____ A material gain or loss that is both unusual in nature and infrequent in occurrence

    2. _____ Generally, the difference between normal ongoing revenues and normal ongoing expenses

    3. _____ The difference between sales and cost of goods sold

    4. _____ Any item that should not be considered a normal part of continuing operations because it is not expected to happen again

    5. _____ Sacrifices incurred in the normal day-to-day running of a business

    6. _____ Any item considered a normal part of continuing operations because it is expected to happen on an ongoing basis

    7. _____ The disposal of a business component

REQUIRED:

Match the letter next to each item with the appropriate definition. Each letter will be used only once.

LO 3: Income Tax Disclosure

10–30. a. What is the purpose of reporting discontinued items and extraordinary gains and losses of net income taxes?

b. Discuss the meaning of the phrase "net of tax" and how this is reported on the income statement.

LO 3: Discontinued Operations

10–31. On March 1, 2007, the board of directors of the Tabitha Company approved the disposal of a component of its business. For the period of January 1 through February 28, 2007, the component had revenues of $200,000 and expenses of $350,000. The company sold the assets of the component at a loss of $100,000 on March 15, 2007.

REQUIRED:
Describe how the corporation should report the previous information on the financial statements. Be as specific as possible.

LO 3: Discontinued Operations

10–32. On July 1, 2008, the board of directors of Elwood Company approved the sale of a component of its business. For the period of January 1 through June 30, 2008, the component had revenues of $1,100,000 and expenses of $1,500,000. The company sold the assets of the component at a gain of $200,000 on July 31, 2008.

REQUIRED:
Describe how the corporation should report the previous information on the financial statements. Be as specific as possible.

LO 3: Discontinued Operations

10–33. On October 1, 2008, the board of directors of Dodd Company approved the disposal of a component of its business. For the period of January 1 through September 30, 2008, the component had revenues of $1,500,000 and expenses of $2,500,000. The company sold the assets of the component at a gain of $300,000.

REQUIRED:
Describe how the corporation should report the previous information on the financial statements. Be as specific as possible.

LO 4: Multistep Income Statement

10–34. The following items relate to Kim Cook, Inc., for the year ended December 31, 2007:
- Sales for the year totaled $665,000.
- Cost of goods sold for the year totaled $271,000.
- Regular operating expenses for the year were $145,000.
- Interest expense for the year was $27,000.
- On February 18, 2007, one of Cook's warehouses burned to the ground. The company's loss (after the insurance settlement) was $106,000 before any tax effect. This loss was determined to be both unusual in nature and infrequent in occurrence.
- Cook's income tax rate is 40% on all items.

REQUIRED:
Prepare Cook's income statement for the year ended December 31, 2007, using the expanded multistep format presented in this chapter.

LO 4: Multistep Income Statement

10–35. The following items relate to Linda Doyle and Company for the year ended December 31, 2008:
- Sales for the year totaled $575,000.
- Cost of goods sold for the year totaled $372,500.
- Regular operating expenses for the year were $121,500.
- Interest expense for the year was $16,000.
- On September 5, 2008, Doyle sold the only land it owned at a pretax gain of $50,000. The land was acquired in 1996 for future expansion, but shortly thereafter the company abandoned all plans for expansion and held the land for appreciation.
- Doyle's income tax rate is 30% on all items.

REQUIRED:
Prepare Doyle's income statement for the year ended December 31, 2008, using the expanded multistep format presented in this chapter.

LO 4: Multistep Income Statement

10–36. The following items relate to Fred Cole Company for the year ended December 31, 2008:
- Sales for the year totaled $1,075,000.
- Cost of goods sold for the year totaled $667,000.
- Operating expenses for the year were $102,500.
- Interest expense for the year was $43,000.
- On June 30, 2008, Cole sold a major component of its business at a loss of $95,000 before any tax effects. This component of the company represented a major line of business that was totally separate from the rest of Cole's operation.
- Prior to being sold, the business component had sales during 2008 of $150,000, cost of goods sold of $90,000, and operating expenses of $45,000. These amounts are not included in the previous information provided.
- Cole's income tax rate is 40% on all items.

REQUIRED:
Prepare Cole's income statement for the year ended December 31, 2008, using the expanded multistep format presented in this chapter.

LO 4: Multistep Income Statement

10–37. The following items relate to Toni Bradshaw, Inc. for the year ended December 31, 2008:
- Sales for the year totaled $465,000.
- Cost of goods sold for the year totaled $239,000.
- Operating expenses for the year were $113,200.
- Interest expense for the year was $11,000.
- On July 16, 2008, Bradshaw sold a major component of its business at a gain of $50,000 before any tax effects. This component of the company represented a major line of business that was totally separate from the rest of Bradshaw's operation.

- Prior to being sold, the business segment had sales during 2008 of $60,000, cost of goods sold of $40,000, and operating expenses of $35,000. These amounts are not included in the previous information provided.
- Bradshaw's income tax rate is 30% on all items.

REQUIRED:

Prepare Bradshaw's income statement for the year ended December 31, 2008, using the expanded multistep format presented in this chapter.

LO 4:   Discussion of Income Statement

10–38. The multistep income statement as presented in this chapter separates recurring items from nonrecurring items. Further, two major types of nonrecurring items are shown on the income statement net of tax.

REQUIRED:

a. Explain in your own words the rationale behind showing recurring and nonrecurring items separately on the multistep income statement.
b. Explain in your own words what the phrase "net of tax" means and why two major types of nonrecurring items are shown in this manner on the income statement.

LO 5:   Earnings Per Share—Simple Capital Structure

10–39. The Jacobs Company reported income after taxes for the year ended December 31, 2008, of $337,600. At the end of the year 2008, the Jacobs Company had the following shares of capital stock outstanding:
Preferred Stock, 5%, $200 par value, nonconvertible, 10,000 issued and outstanding.
Common Stock, $2 par value, 40,000 shares issued and outstanding.

REQUIRED:

Calculate basic earnings per share for 2008.

LO 5:   Earnings Per Share—Simple Capital Structure

10–40. The Schweizer Company reported income after taxes for the year ended December 31, 2007, of $337,600. During the year 2007, the Schweizer Company had the following shares of capital stock outstanding:
Preferred Stock, 5%, $200 par value, nonconvertible, 10,000 issued and outstanding.
Common Stock, $2 par value, 40,000 shares issued and outstanding on January 1, 2007.
Additional 5,000 shares issued April 1, 2007.

REQUIRED:

Calculate basic earnings per share for 2007.

LO 5:   Earnings Per Share—Simple Capital Structure

10–41. The Ward Company reported income after taxes for the year ended December 31, 2008, of $775,200. During the year 2008, the Ward Company had the following shares of capital stock outstanding:
Preferred Stock, 5%, $100 par value, nonconvertible, 20,000 issued and outstanding.

Common Stock, $3 par value, 80,000 shares issued and outstanding on January 1, 2008.
 Additional 10,000 shares issued July 1, 2008.

REQUIRED:
Calculate basic earnings per share for 2008.

LO 5: Earnings per Share—Complex Capital Structure

10–42. The Schweizer Company reported income after taxes for the year ended December 31, 2008, of $337,600. During the year 2008, the Schweizer Company had the following shares of capital stock outstanding:
 Preferred Stock, 5%, $200 par value, 10,000 issued and outstanding, each share convertible into three shares of common stock.
 Common Stock, $2 par value, 40,000 shares issued and outstanding on January 1, 2008.
 Additional 5,000 shares issued October 1, 2008.

REQUIRED:
 a. Calculate basic earnings per share.
 b. Calculate diluted earnings per share.

LO 5: Earnings per Share—Complex Capital Structure

10–43. The Ward Company reported income after taxes for the year ended December 31, 2007, of $775,200. During the year 2007, the Ward Company had the following shares of capital stock outstanding:
 Preferred Stock, 5%, $100 par value, convertible, 20,000 issued and outstanding. Each share of preferred stock is convertible into five shares of common stock.
 Common Stock, $3 par value, 80,000 shares issued and outstanding on January 1, 2007.
 Additional 10,000 shares issued July 1, 2007.

REQUIRED:
 a. Calculate basic earnings per share.
 b. Calculate diluted earnings per share.

LO 5: Earnings per Share—Complex Capital Structure

10–44. The Ward Company reported income after taxes for the year ended December 31, 2007, of $775,200. During the year 2007, the Ward Company had the following shares of capital stock outstanding:
 Preferred Stock, 5%, $100 par value, convertible, 20,000 issued and outstanding. Each share of preferred stock is convertible into five shares of common stock.
 Common Stock, $3 par value, 80,000 shares issued and outstanding on January 1, 2007.
 Additional 10,000 shares issued April 1, 2007.
 Additional 5,000 shares issued October 1, 2007.

REQUIRED:
 a. Calculate basic earnings per share.
 b. Calculate diluted earnings per share.

LO 7: Income Tax Entries

*10–45. The Hassenfuss Company reports $385,000 of net income subject to a 40% tax rate. The company has paid timely estimated tax payments of $87,000.

REQUIRED:
Prepare the journal entry to record the income tax expense and the remaining liability for the year.

LO 7: Income Tax Entries

*10–46. The Warren Company reports $160,000 of net income before taxes and an extraordinary gain of $10,000. The company is subject to a 30% tax rate. The company has paid timely estimated tax payments of $25,000.

REQUIRED:
Prepare the journal entry or entries to record the income tax expense and the remaining liability for the year.

LO 7: Income Tax Entries

*10–47. The Xena Corporation reports $200,000 of net operating income before taxes and an extraordinary loss of $25,000. The company is also reporting a loss from discontinued operations of $70,000. The company is subject to a 35% tax rate. The company has paid timely estimated tax payments of $10,000.

REQUIRED:
Prepare the journal entry or entries to record the income tax expense and the remaining liability for the year.

FINANCIAL REPORTING CASES

Comprehensive

10–48. Visit the Target Corporation website at www.Target.com. Locate the current copy of the annual report, find the financial statements, and answer the following questions for all years presented.

REQUIRED:
a. Determine the amount of extraordinary gain or loss incurred by the company. What event(s) caused the extraordinary gain or loss?
b. Does the company report any disposals of components? If so, how much did it report and what component(s) were disposed?
c. What is the amount of earnings per share? Does the company report both basic and diluted earnings per share? If so, how much of each?
d. What is the amount of current assets and current liabilities reported by the company? Explain the meaning of these amounts.
e. Does the company report comprehensive income on the financial statements? If so, where and how is it reported?
f. Go to the website for this text, www.pearsoncustom.com/terrell, and visit the Research Navigator. Find a recent article or press release about Target's financial status and print it. Write a one-page reaction paper to the article.

Comprehensive

10–49. Visit the Darden Restaurant Corporation website at <u>www.Darden.com</u>. Locate the current copy of the annual report, find the financial statements, and answer the following questions for all years presented.

REQUIRED:
  a. Determine the amount of extraordinary gain or loss incurred by the company. What event(s) caused the extraordinary gain or loss?
  b. Does the company report any disposals of components? If so, how much did it report and what component(s) were disposed?
  c. What is the amount of earnings per share? Does the company report both basic and diluted earnings per share? If so, how much of each?
  d. What is the amount of current assets and current liabilities reported by the company? Explain the meaning of these amounts.
  e. Does the company report comprehensive income on the financial statements? If so, where and how is it reported?
  f. Go to the website for this text, <u>www.pearsoncustom.com/terrell</u>, and visit the Research Navigator. Find a recent article or press release about Darden's financial status and print it. Write a one-page reaction paper to the article.

Comprehensive

10–50. Visit the Ford Motor Company website at <u>www.Ford.com</u>. Locate the current copy of the annual report, find the financial statements, and answer the following questions for all years presented.

REQUIRED:
  a. Determine the amount of extraordinary gain or loss incurred by the company. What event(s) caused the extraordinary gain or loss?
  b. Does the company report any disposals of components? If so, how much did it report and what component(s) were disposed?
  c. What is the amount of earnings per share? Does the company report both basic and diluted earnings per share? If so, how much of each?
  d. What is the amount of retained earnings reported by the company? Explain the meaning of these amounts.
  e. Does the company report comprehensive income on the financial statements? If so, where and how is it reported?
  f. Go to the website for this text, <u>www.pearsoncustom.com/terrell</u>, and visit the Research Navigator. Find a recent article or press release about Ford's financial status and print it. Write a one-page reaction paper to the article.

Introduction to Management Accounting
A User Perspective

Chapter 1

Management Accounting: Its Environment and Future

*T*imes have changed! During the 1970s and 1980s the United States saw a serious erosion in its position as the world's business leader. Industry after industry in the United States began to suffer from the effects of significant foreign competition. At the time, experts offered any number of reasons to explain what was happening. Low labor costs in foreign countries, excessively high labor costs at home, too much government regulation of U.S. industries, and too little government regulation of U.S. industries were just a few of the explanations offered.

Because the "reasons" given were simplistic, the "solutions" were simplistic. U.S. industries lobbied Congress for tariffs on imported products (essentially a form of tax) to offset the low labor costs in foreign countries. The issue of excessively high labor rates was used by U.S. companies in negotiating labor costs with their employees, either to hold the line on wage increases, or in some instances to actually negotiate lower wage rates. Throughout the 1970s and 1980s, the U.S. government alternatively deregulated and then reregulated some American industries to try and increase U.S. companies' competitiveness globally.

Eventually, as the quick fix, simplistic approaches did not solve the competitiveness problem, managers in the United States began to see that the problem arose from differences in organizational structure and worker productivity between U.S. businesses and their foreign competitors. Consider the following comparison of U.S. and Japanese auto manufacturers in the mid-1980s.[1]

---

[1]John Lee, *Managerial Accounting Changes for the 1990s (Addison Wesley, 1987)*, 14.

Ford
- Produced an average of two engines a day per employee
- Daily production required 777 square feet of plant space

Toyota
- Produced an average of nine engines a day per employee
- Daily production required 454 square feet of plant space

Chrysler
- Had about 500 in-plant job classifications

Toyota
- Had 7 in-plant job classifications

A Typical U.S. Auto Plant
- A change from metal-stamping one model to another required 6 hours

Toyota
- The same change required 3–5 minutes

Because of more efficient production techniques and differences in pay scales for workers, Toyota's net income in 2005 was 5.4 times Ford's with slightly less net revenues than Ford's. The erosion of profits over the past three decades leaves Ford with only 4.8% equity in its assets (95.2% debt) while Toyota has 37.2% equity in its assets (62.8% debt).

The automobile industry was by no means alone. By the mid-1980s, U.S. companies in many different industries had realized the need to change business operations to remain competitive. Beginning in the last half of the 1980s and continuing through today, many of those businesses began to take significant steps to increase their competitiveness.

Our focus will be not on the specific changes that managers made but rather on the way these changes have affected their accounting needs and how accounting information has responded. ∎

LEARNING OBJECTIVES

After completing your work on this chapter, you should be able to do the following:

1. Describe management accounting and contrast it with financial accounting.
2. Explain major historical developments that have affected management accounting.
3. Describe how changes in management accounting affect today's businesses.
4. Explain how businesspeople use management accounting information and skills.

WHAT IS MANAGEMENT ACCOUNTING?

management accounting
The branch of accounting designed to provide information to internal economic decision makers (managers).

managerial accounting
Another name for management accounting.

cost accounting A narrow application of management accounting dealing specifically with procedures designed to determine how much a particular item (usually a unit of manufactured product) costs.

Management accounting is the branch of accounting designed to provide information to the firm's internal economic decision makers, or managers. It is also sometimes called **managerial accounting** or **cost accounting.** Because these three terms are often used interchangeably in accounting literature, confusion can result. Management accounting is

> . . . the process of identification, measurement, accumulation, analysis, preparation, interpretation, and communication of financial information used by management to plan, evaluate, and control . . . an organization . . .
>
> Statement on Management Accounting (No.1A. IMA, 1981)

Management accounting and managerial accounting mean exactly the same thing. We will use the term *management accounting* throughout our discussions of the subject. However, in references to other writings you may see the term *managerial accounting.*

The third term, *cost accounting,* is a narrow application of management accounting. Cost accounting deals specifically with procedures designed to determine how much a particular item (usually a unit of manufactured product) costs.

CONTRASTING FINANCIAL AND MANAGEMENT ACCOUNTING

Financial accounting provides information to external decision makers—to people outside the company. Management accounting, in contrast, provides information to internal decision makers. Exhibit 1–1 lists only some of the many external and internal users of a company's accounting information.

Exhibit 1–1
External and Internal Decision Makers

External	Internal
• Stockholders (present and potential)	• Marketing managers
• Bankers and other lending institutions	• Salespersons
• Bondholders (present and potential)	• Production managers
• Suppliers	• Production supervisors
• Customers	• Strategic planners
• Competitors	• Company president
	• Engineers

Discussion Questions

1–1. For each of the external parties listed in Exhibit 1–1, suggest one economic decision they might make regarding a company.

1–2. Name two external parties in addition to those listed in Exhibit 1–1, and provide an example of an economic decision each might make regarding a company.

1–3. For each of the internal parties listed in Exhibit 1–1, describe one economic decision they might make regarding their company.

1–4. Name two more internal parties in addition to those listed in Exhibit 1–1, and give an example of an economic decision each might make regarding the company.

Discussion Questions 1–1 through 1–4 highlight the different nature of the decisions made by external and internal parties. If you review your answers to these questions, you will discover that the decisions external parties make focus on the company as a whole, whereas the decisions internal parties make usually center on some *part* of the company. Because people use financial accounting information and management accounting information differently, the nature of the two differs.

Accounting Rules

Financial accounting information must be prepared in accordance with rules known as Generally Accepted Accounting Principles (GAAP). No such rules apply to management accounting. Because management accounting information is prepared for use by those working within the company, its users can question the content, meaning, level of detail, and validity of the accounting information they receive. They can also determine the format of the information. As discussed later, in addition to accountants, managers may also gather and prepare management accounting information. In sum, internal decision makers can generally make certain the information they receive is exactly what they want. External decision makers must accept the financial accounting information they receive, like it or not.

Level of Detail

In contrast to the general-purpose nature of financial accounting information, firms prepare management accounting information to address specific company issues. Therefore, it is often much more detailed than financial accounting information. For example, it may be fine for a potential investor to know that IBM's sales were $82 billion last year, but this information would be nearly useless to the national sales manager for IBM ThinkPads™, the company's line of notebook computers, who needs to know that product's sales numbers for last year.

Discussion Question

1–5. In addition to sales information, what other accounting information would you want if you were the national sales manager for IBM ThinkPads™?

In addition to preparing general-purpose financial statements for the public, a company's accountants also prepare management accounting information for the managers or employees who need it. For a given internal decision, a user may need specific information from a division, product line, product, or department. The company's accountants should be able to customize information to fit the needs of the user.

For example, Sara Lee Corporation has production facilities in key locations. Each facility requires various types of maintenance, including mowing the lawn and weeding the flower beds outside the buildings. This maintenance costs money. The amount spent for grounds maintenance at any one facility is totally irrelevant to external parties. The maintenance supervisor at that facility, however, would find that amount quite relevant. Sara Lee's accountants should be able to customize a report providing the supervisor with pertinent cost information.

Timeliness

Timeliness is important to both financial and management accounting information users. Regardless of whether the user is external or internal, accounting information is useful only if it is available in time to help the decision maker.

Because it has become customary, users of financial accounting information expect that financial results will be available quarterly. However, managers making frequent decisions need information much more often. They need information monthly, weekly, or even daily, so they can make informed decisions. Because of the fast pace of business decision making, sometimes it is better to forfeit precision in favor of speed. Management accountants must strike a balance between information accuracy and timeliness to provide managers with information that is accurate enough to make good decisions, and yet timely enough to make a difference.

Future Orientation

Although financial accounting information should have predictive value, it primarily depicts historical results. In contrast, management accounting has a forward-looking orientation. Management accounting focuses on estimating future revenues, costs, and other measures to forecast future activities and their results. Firms use these forecasts to plan their course of action toward future goals.

As you can see, because of the fundamental differences between the information needs of external and internal parties, financial and management accounting differ. Exhibit 1–2 summarizes the differences we have discussed.

Exhibit 1–2
Contrast of Financial and Management Accounting

Feature	Financial Accounting	Management Accounting
• Principal users	External parties	Internal parties
• Rules and regulations	Governed by GAAP	No rules
• Level of detail	Deals with the company as a whole	Deals with various parts of the company
• Timeliness	Quarterly and annually	As users need
• Orientation	The past	The future

WHERE ACCOUNTING FITS IN A COMPANY

treasurer The corporate officer who is responsible for cash and credit management and for planning activities, such as investment in long-lived property, plant, and equipment.

Exhibit 1–3 presents a typical corporate organizational structure. Note where financial and management accounting fit within a company.

The accounting function centers around the treasurer and the controller. Generally, the **treasurer** is responsible for managing cash and credit and for planning activities, such as investment in long-lived property, plant, and equipment. The **controller** is a company's chief accountant. This person is responsible for preparing accounting reports for both external and internal decision makers.

Exhibit 1-3
Corporate Organization

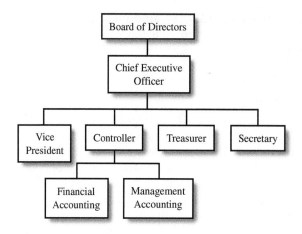

Board of Directors

Chief Executive Officer

Vice President

Controller

Treasurer

Secretary

Financial Accounting

Management Accounting

controller A company's chief accountant, who is responsible for the preparation of accounting reports for both external and internal decision makers.

In a large company, such as Sara Lee or Rockwell, the treasurer and controller are both likely to have large staffs reporting to them. At a midsized company, one or two people may perform all the duties of the treasurer and controller. In small firms, one person may perform all the functions.

Discussion Question

1-6. What possible problems may arise when the same accountants prepare reports for both external parties and internal parties?

THE EVOLUTION OF MANAGEMENT ACCOUNTING

Accounting and accounting records have existed since the dawn of civilization. Indeed, formal accounting systems have been in use for thousands of years. The need for accounting information for management decision-making purposes, however, did not exist until the early 19th century. Before that time almost all businesses were proprietorships or small partnerships. Businesses had no permanent employees to speak of and no management as we know it today. Management usually consisted of the proprietor or partners and immediate family members. Because businesses had no management, they had no need for management accounting information. Virtually all transactions were between the company and parties outside the company. Transactions with external parties such as suppliers, contract labor, and customers were easy to measure and evaluate: A company was successful if it collected more cash from its customers than it paid to suppliers and contract laborers.

In the hundred years between 1825 and 1925, however, four significant changes took place in business operation and organization: the emergence of permanent employees, the Industrial Revolution, the rise of scientific management, and diversification. These changes altered the nature of management accounting.

Emergence of Permanent Employees

For the most part, businesses had no employees before the 1880s. Businesses purchased labor with a piece rate contract and hired independent contractors to complete all their production functions. A chair manufacturer, for example, purchased wood at a certain price per board foot. Then the company contracted someone to turn the wood into legs, arms, seats, and backs at some specified rate per item. When the pieces were produced and paid for, the company contracted someone else to assemble the chairs, and paid that person some specified amount per chair assembled. Determining the cost of a chair produced was very simple—the sum of the wood cost, the amount paid per component piece (arm, leg, and so on), and the cost of assembling it. The company was not terribly interested in how long it took any of these contractors to complete their tasks, so long as they met the needs of the company.

Then companies began hiring permanent employees to fill the role of the independent contractors. Why the switch to permanent employees happened and whether it was positive or negative has been hotly debated by scholars for over 100 years. From the company's standpoint, moving from a contract system to a wage system gave the firm greater control of the production process and, in fact, created what we now know as the factory. From the laborer's standpoint, the change was likely an exchange of freedom for security.

Discussion Questions

> **1–7.** In what ways do you think hiring permanent employees gives a company greater control of the production process?
>
> **1–8.** What kinds of freedom do you think permanent employees exchange for security?

When we see the word *factory,* we tend to think of the huge factories of the 20th century. Actually, early factories were still small businesses. Management accounting did not develop because of the size or complexity of the organization. Rather, it developed because the accounting systems then in existence did not provide business people with enough information to determine the cost of a manufactured product.

Discussion Question

> **1–9.** Why do you think the emergence of the factory (even a small one) made it more difficult to determine the cost of a manufactured product?

The Industrial Revolution

Industrial Revolution
The 19th century transition of the United States from an agricultural-based economy to a manufacturing-based economy.

The **Industrial Revolution** was the 19th-century transition of the United States from an agricultural-based economy to a manufacturing-based economy. From 1825 to 1925 businesses greatly increased their investment in property, plant, and equipment and began to rely more on machines instead of human labor to produce products. As companies grew in size and complexity, owners found it impossible to be in all places at all times. They were forced to create hierarchical levels of management for their organizations. These managers sought needed information to control costs and production processes. Over time, businesses developed methods to measure the conversion of raw materials into units of finished product. These methods were the foundation for present-day management accounting. Their focus was on the effectiveness and efficiency of various internal processes, rather than on the overall profitability of the company.

Scientific Management

scientific management A management philosophy based on the notion that factories were run by machines—some mechanical and some human. Scientific management experts believed they could improve production efficiency by establishing standards of performance for workers.

The scientific management movement began near the end of the 19th century and had a tremendous influence on business management and management accounting. **Scientific management** was a philosophy based on the notion that factories were run by machines—some mechanical and some human. You may think it insensitive to treat employees as nothing more than machines plugged into the production process. Nonetheless, scientific management took this view. Experts in this area believed they could improve production efficiency by establishing standards of performance for workers. In a tool-manufacturing company, for instance, experts conducted time-and-motion studies to set a standard for the time workers should take to convert a given amount of resources into a finished product, such as a hammer.

These standards of performance were quickly adapted to accounting for the purpose of determining how much it *should* cost to manufacture a product. The experts, often engineers, determined how much material, labor, and other resources a business needed to manufacture a single unit of product. This information served as a yardstick to measure whether resources were used efficiently or squandered during the production process. Such standards were the beginning of what is referred to as *standard costing,* one of the most important developments in management accounting. We will discuss standard costing in greater detail in Chapter 9.

Discussion Questions

Assume a company manufactures tables. Scientific management studies show that each tabletop requires 4 square feet of wood, and it takes a worker 45 minutes to convert the wood into a tabletop.

1–10. If the wood costs the company $2 per square foot and the company's workers are paid $10 per hour, how much does each tabletop cost to produce?

1–11. What other costs should be considered in the calculation of the cost to produce the tabletop? Explain.

Diversification

During the first two decades of the 20th century, companies began to diversify. Before this time, virtually all companies undertook only one activity, for example, railroad companies were strictly in the railroad business and steel companies were strictly in the steel business. The primary investment decision for these single-activity companies was whether to expand. The emergence of diversified, multi-activity companies changed the nature of decision making.

Discussion Question

1-12. Why do you think companies began to diversify in the early years of the 20th century?

Owners of diversified companies could not directly manage all the various business operations. Instead, they relied on others to manage operations that they could not personally oversee; and they obtained additional management accounting information from the various parts of the business so they could plan, control, and evaluate performance. Company accountants tailored reports to meet the needs of managers at each level of the organization. Lower-level managers, such as production supervisors, received reports that focused on production efficiencies. Higher-level managers received reports that focused on product profits.

Emergence of Management Accounting

Institute of Management Accountants (IMA) A professional association of management accountants.

In 1919, the formation of the **Institute of Management Accountants (IMA)** signified that management accounting was a recognized branch of the accounting profession separate and distinct from financial accounting. Among other purposes, the IMA provided the same sort of professional status for management accountants as the American Institute of Certified Public Accountants (AICPA) did for financial accountants.

The growth of publicly held corporations, the stock market crash, and the Great Depression led to the establishment of Generally Accepted Accounting Principles (GAAP) and the Securities and Exchange Commission (SEC). The new rules and regulations governed financial reporting to external parties and required that corporations file audited financial statements with the SEC that were prepared in accordance with GAAP. The rules and regulations led to the design of accounting systems that could provide financial information and reports to outsiders. These financial accounting systems, however, failed to consider the need for information that managers could use to make decisions about the internal processes of their companies. At the time, most accounting records were manual systems.

Consider also the legal environment existing in the 1930s after the creation of the SEC. If a company failed to have an accounting system designed to produce financial accounting information for external parties in accordance with GAAP, there would be serious legal consequences. If a company's accounting system did not produce management accounting information, however, there were no legal consequences. Given this situation, it is not surprising that at that time financial accounting requirements drove the creation and use of accounting information.

Discussion Question

1-13. What possible problems do you think arise when a company's single accounting system is designed to produce financial accounting information? Explain.

During the 20th century, focus remained on external financial information. With the rise of computer technology, and in particular the advent of the personal computer, coupled with database management systems, accountants began to have virtually unlimited ability to obtain nearly instant management accounting data.

Coupled with fierce global competition, the need for new management accounting techniques arose to fit new leaner management practices including just-in-time (JIT) inventory systems, activity-based managment (ABM), activity-based costing (ABC), design for manufacturing (DFM), process value added (PVA), and the balanced score card.

As we move into the 21st century, businesses face many challenges. Global competition is one we have discussed already. Another is a basic consideration of what kind of economy is going to exist in the United States in the future. Many business analysts believe that we are moving away from the traditional manufacturing-based economy toward a service-based economy. If so, management accounting techniques must adapt to such a change. The majority of firms today still employ traditional management accounting techniques and practices, and they likely will for many years. Some companies, however, have embraced new techniques as they develop. We discuss both traditional and new management accounting techniques throughout the following chapters.

CONSUMERS OF MANAGEMENT ACCOUNTING INFORMATION

To make effective decisions, business managers must understand the firm's management accounting system, know whether the information is reliable, and recognize that no system will provide perfect information. Decision making by its very nature is forward-looking, and the future always contains an element of uncertainty. Managers should look for ways to reduce the amount of that uncertainty.

Every decision results in an outcome, and even good decisions can lead to bad outcomes. For example, say that you are about to get in the checkout line at the grocery store. You evaluate the lines leading to open cash registers and, after counting the number of people in line and eyeballing the amount of groceries each customer is about to buy, you select what appears to be the shortest line. Your decision is sound and based on the information available. Well, just as the person ahead of you is about to pay, shopping disaster strikes. That customer does not have an acceptable check guarantee card. You must now wait for the manager to arrive and resolve the problem (a process that seems to take as long as college registration) before the cashier can help you. Quickly you look to see whether you can jump to another line, but it is too late: The other lines are now too long, and you must wait it out. Did you make a poor decision? No, you made the best decision you could with the available information. Your good decision simply led to a poor outcome.

Regardless of your career, at some point you will probably use accounting information to make a decision. If you are studying marketing, you may start as an assistant who helps prepare and implement marketing programs. As you advance in the firm, you may manage a staff of people who handle marketing programs, so you will need the accounting tools to make well-informed decisions. When you are responsible for the well-being of a company, department, division, or management team, you will face decisions that depend on your using management accounting information. The following chapters will teach you to be a careful consumer of accounting information.

SUMMARY

Management accounting is the process of identifying, measuring, and communicating financial information used by managers to plan, evaluate, and control their organization.

Financial accounting, which is intended for use by external parties, is subject to Generally Accepted Accounting Principles (GAAP). No such rules apply to management accounting, which is intended for use by internal parties. The general-purpose financial statements produced by financial accounting focus on past results. Reports produced by management accounting are much more detailed and focus on the future of the organization.

Although accounting and accounting records have existed since the dawn of civilization, the need for accounting information for use by management did not exist prior to the early 19th century. The emergence of permanent employees, the Industrial Revolution, scientific management, and the diversification by businesses all contributed to significant development of management accounting techniques between 1825 and 1925.

American companies face significant competitive challenges as we move toward the 21st century, and the role of management accounting information in helping these companies will be critical.

REVIEW THE FACTS

A. What are the differences among management accounting, managerial accounting, and cost accounting?
B. What is the purpose of management accounting?
C. What are the primary differences between financial accounting and management accounting?
D. Financial accounting information must be prepared in conformity with GAAP. Why are there no such rules for management accounting?
E. List four significant changes in business that led to the development of management accounting.
F. What is the IMA and what is its purpose?
G. Explain the difference between a good decision and a good outcome.
H. Why is an understanding of management accounting an important ingredient of success in your career?

APPLY WHAT YOU HAVE LEARNED

LO 1: Contrast Management Accounting and Financial Accounting

1–14. Following are certain characteristics of either financial accounting information or management accounting information.

1. _____ Must conform to GAAP.
2. _____ Tends to be quite detailed.
3. _____ Generally limited to presenting historical information.
4. _____ Need not conform to a formal set of rules and standards.
5. _____ Information prepared primarily for external users.
6. _____ Tends to include only a limited amount of detail.

7. _____ Information prepared on a quarterly or yearly basis.
8. _____ Information prepared on a monthly, weekly, or daily basis.
9. _____ Information often includes future projections.
10. _____ Information prepared for use by internal parties.

REQUIRED:
Designate each of the characteristics as pertaining to (a) financial accounting information or (b) management accounting information.

LO 1: Describe Management Accounting

1–15. Is management accounting important for not-for-profit organizations as well as for-profit organizations? Explain.

LO 1: Describe Management Accounting

1–16. If you were the manager of a Blockbuster Entertainment Store, what accounting information would you desire to help you do your job better?

LO 3: Changes in Management Accounting

1–17. Explain why there has been a renewed emphasis on the development of management accounting in the United States in the last two decades.

LO 1: Contrast Management Accounting and Financial Accounting

1–18. Following are examples of users of financial accounting information and users of management accounting information.

1. _____ Sales supervisor
2. _____ Salespersons
3. _____ Wall Street analyst
4. _____ Suppliers
5. _____ Current shareholders
6. _____ Potential shareholders
7. _____ Personnel manager
8. _____ Maintenance supervisor
9. _____ Maintenance worker
10. _____ Loan officer at a company's bank

REQUIRED:
Designate each of the users of accounting information as either (a) external party or (b) internal party.

Chapter 2

Classifying Costs

*S*uppose for a moment that your boss has asked you to organize a consumer catalog of all the toys in the world. You need to classify the toys in several ways so users of your catalog will be able to find information easily. After thinking about your task for a while, you start a list of toy classifications—toys organized by age or gender of user, by price, or by design. Your initial list of categories may look like the following:

Classification

By Age of User:
Toys for infants
Toys for toddlers ages one to three
Toys for children ages three to five
Toys for children ages five to nine
Toys for children ages 10 and older

By Gender of User:
Toys designed for girls
Toys designed for boys
Toys for all children

By Price:
Toys under $10
Toys for $10 to $50
Toys for $51 to $99
Toys over $100

By Design:
Electronic toys vs. nonelectronic toys
Toys with wheels vs. toys without wheels
Breakable vs. unbreakable toys

Your boss now wants you to pick only one or two categories, to make your job easier. You scan your list to see which classifications will be most useful. You realize that the catalog must have each classification to be as useful as possible, because purchasers may need different information for different decisions.

For instance, if purchasers are choosing toys to donate to the annual toy drive for needy children, they may want to focus on price so they can donate several toys. In this case, the price classification would be most helpful. Further, those same purchasers may want to use the gender classification to find toys for all children because they would not know in advance whether the child receiving the toy is a girl or a boy.

If buyers are shopping for a birthday gift intended for a two-year-old relative, they would use the age classification to find appropriate toys. They might also want to use the price category to help them decide how much to spend. As these examples show, even in making just one decision, more than one classification may provide useful information.

Like our hypothetical toy purchasers, managers must have information to make effective planning and controlling decisions. Cost information is one of the key components of financial decision making; but what exactly is a cost? In accounting, a cost is' how much we have to give up to get something. Put more formally, a **cost** is the resources forfeited to receive some goods or services. Note that cost is different from price. Price is what we charge; cost is what we pay.

cost The resources forfeited to receive some goods or services.

Business managers classify costs in many different ways because, just like the vast array of toys, there are many types of costs. Each classification can provide managers with useful information. In this chapter, we explore several different cost classifications that managers use to make decisions. ∎

LEARNING OBJECTIVES

After completing your work on this chapter, you should be able to do the following:

1. Classify costs by cost objects, and distinguish between direct and indirect costs.
2. Distinguish between product costs and period costs, and contrast their accounting treatment.
3. Explain the differences between product cost for a merchandiser and for a manufacturer.
4. Describe the components of the costs included in each of the three types of inventory in a manufacturing operation.
5. Calculate cost of goods manufactured and cost of goods sold.
6. Describe the components of the cost of services provided by a service firm.

MAJOR COST CLASSIFICATIONS

Businesses incur many different costs as they operate and there are many useful ways to classify these costs. As managers make each internal business decision, they must determine what cost classifications will help them most. We will first identify important cost terms and investigate several cost classifications.

Exhibit 2–1
Common Cost Object Designations

Cost Object	Examples
• Activity	• Repairing equipment, testing manufactured products for quality
• Product	• Paper towels, personal computers, automobiles (These can be either purchased or manufactured products.)
• Service	• Performing surgery, accounting work, legal work
• Project	• Constructing a bridge, designing a house
• Geographic region	• A state, a city, a county
• Department	• Marketing department, accounting department

Assigning Costs to Cost Objects

cost object Any activity or item for which a separate cost measurement is wanted.

One of the most useful classifications of cost is by cost object. A **cost object** is any activity or item for which we want a separate cost measurement. Think of any noun associated with business and you have a potential cost object. Exhibit 2–1 lists some cost objects commonly used by companies.

We identify a cost object to determine the cost of that particular object. Such classification can provide useful information. For example, a manufacturer may need information about the cost of the products it manufactures. In this case, the individual products are the cost objects. All costs associated with a particular product are grouped to determine the full cost of that product. Managers may also want to determine the cost associated with a group of products, such as a fleet of delivery trucks. When we assign costs to cost objects, we classify costs as direct or indirect.

direct cost A cost that can be easily traced to an individual cost object.

indirect cost A cost that supports more than one cost object.

common cost Another name for *indirect cost.*

A cost that is easily traced to individual cost objects is a **direct cost.** Many times, however, a cost may benefit more than one cost object, so tracing that cost to individual cost objects becomes difficult or even impossible. A cost that supports more than one cost object is an **indirect cost.** An indirect cost may also be called a **common cost,** because it is common to more than one cost object.

To illustrate the difference between direct and indirect costs, consider 12 Sears stores in Alabama. Each store has a manager who is responsible for the day-to-day operation of that store. Sears also has a general manager who is responsible for the operation of all stores in the state. If we define each of the 12 stores as cost objects, the salary of each store manager would be considered a direct cost to his or her store. The salary of the general manager is not incurred to support any one of the 12 stores. Rather, it supports all 12 stores. Therefore, the general manager's salary would be considered an indirect cost of each cost object (the individual stores).

Discussion Questions

Assume that instead of defining each individual Sears store as a cost object, we define the entire Sears operation in Alabama as a cost object.

2-1. In this case, would the salaries of the 12 store managers be considered direct or indirect costs? Explain your reasoning.

2-2. Would the salary of the general manager be considered a direct or an indirect cost? Explain your reasoning.

2-3. Why do you think managers at various levels in a company would find it useful to classify costs as direct or indirect?

Product Cost

product cost The cost of the various products a company sells.

When you see inventory on store shelves, you know the store did not get the inventory for free. Rather, each unit of product had some cost. The cost of the various products that a company sells is called **product cost.** More specifically, product costs are the costs associated with making the products available and ready to sell. For a bookstore, such as Barnes & Noble or WaldenBooks, product cost is the cost of the books purchased for resale, the freight to get the books to the store (also known as freight-in), and other costs involved in getting the books ready to sell.

inventoriable cost Another name for *product cost.*

Product costs are also known as **inventoriable costs**—product costs become part of a company's inventory until the goods associated with the costs are sold. Because product held for sale is considered an asset, its cost is shown on the balance sheet (inventory) until the product is actually sold. When the goods are sold, the product cost is converted from an asset on the balance sheet to an expense (cost of goods sold) on the income statement.

For example, when Payless Shoe Source buys shoes to sell, the cost of the shoes is a product cost and is added to inventory on the balance sheet. The cost remains in inventory on the balance sheet until the shoes are sold. When the shoes are sold, the reality of the reduced inventory caused by the sale is reflected in the company's accounting records by reducing inventory on the balance sheet and increasing cost of goods sold on the income statement.

Period Cost

period cost All costs incurred by a company that are not considered product cost. Includes selling and administrative cost.

Period costs are all the costs that a company incurs which are not considered product costs. They include selling and administrative expenses, but not any costs associated with acquiring product or getting it ready to sell.

selling cost The cost of locating customers, attracting customers, convincing customers to buy, and the cost of necessary paperwork to document and record sales.

Selling Cost Selling cost includes the cost of locating customers, attracting them, convincing them to buy, and the cost of necessary paperwork to document and record sales. Examples of selling cost include salaries paid to members of the sales force, sales commissions, and advertising.

Two selling costs are less obvious: the cost of delivering product to customers (also known as freight-out) and the cost of storing merchandise inventory. The reason delivery cost is considered a selling cost is that companies probably would not provide delivery unless it helped sell more product. If customers would buy with or without free delivery, the seller would probably not offer it.

Do not confuse freight-out (period cost) with freight-in (product cost). The key to keeping the two straight is to think about when they are incurred. Freight-in is a cost incurred before the product is ready to sell and is therefore considered a product cost. Freight-out is incurred after the product is ready for sale and is therefore classified as a period cost.

The cost of storing merchandise inventory is also classified as a selling cost, because merchandise on hand enhances its sales potential. Businesses cannot easily sell what they do not have. For example, if you went to your local music shop to buy a compact disc and the salesperson told you, "We don't keep that CD in stock, but we'll be glad to order it for you," you would probably walk out and find another store that carries a better-stocked inventory of compact discs rather than wait. Because both delivery and merchandise inventory enhance sales, these items are considered selling costs.

administrative cost All costs incurred by a company that are not product costs or selling costs. Includes the cost of accounting, finance, employee relations, and executive functions.

Administrative Cost Administrative cost includes all costs that are not product or selling cost. These costs are typically associated with support functions—areas that offer support to the product and selling areas, such as accounting, finance, human resources, and executive functions.

Generally, period costs are shown as operating expenses (selling and administrative expenses) on the income statement. Most period costs—administrators' salaries, for example—are presented as expenses when the expenditure is made. When long-lived assets that will be used for selling or administrative functions are purchased, a slightly different treatment is necessary. At the time they are purchased, the cost of long-lived assets is shown on the balance sheet. As time passes, the depreciation expense associated with these assets becomes part of selling and administrative expense.

Discussion Questions

Assume that you are using a felt-tip highlighter to mark this book as you read it. Assume further that you purchased the marker at the college bookstore.

2–4. What costs associated with the marker do you think the bookstore would consider to be product costs? Explain your reasoning for each cost you included.

2–5. What costs associated with operating the bookstore do you think would be considered period costs (selling and administrative)? Explain your reasoning for each cost you included.

Comparing Product and Period Costs

The distinction between product cost and period cost is based on whether the cost in question benefits the process of getting products ready for sale (product cost), or the selling and administrative functions (period cost). Let us look at some examples to make sure you understand the distinction. The cost of a factory security guard is a product cost because it benefits the plant. Conversely, the cost of a security guard in the sales office is a selling expense, which is a period cost. Note that the classification depends on the company function that benefits from the cost.

What about the salary of the vice president of manufacturing? Even though vice president of manufacturing may sound like an administrative position, the cost of it benefits the manufacturing function, so it is a product cost. Further, all costs associated with that position, including the depreciation on the vice president's desk, the cost of his or her support personnel, travel costs, and all other costs associated with this position, would be classified as a product cost. Likewise, the vice president of marketing would be an example of selling expense, which is a period cost. The depreciation on a company sales representative's car would be a selling expense, because it benefits the sales area of the company.

Next, we examine how manufacturing, merchandising, and service firms identify their product costs.

PRODUCT COST IDENTIFICATION FOR MERCHANDISING FIRMS

Merchandising firms, whether wholesale or retail, purchase products ready to sell, add a markup, and resell the goods. They generate profits by selling merchandise for a price that is higher than their cost. Wholesalers generally buy products from manufacturers (or other wholesalers) and sell them to retailers. Retailers buy from manufacturers or the wholesalers and sell their products to the final consumers.

In this section we explore how a merchandising company identifies product costs and how those product costs flow through the balance sheet and income statement.

For a merchandising firm, product cost includes the cost of the merchandise itself, freight costs to obtain the merchandise, and any other costs incurred to get the product ready to sell. Because merchandisers buy goods for resale, often the cost of getting products ready to sell is minor or nonexistent. Product cost does not include any cost incurred after the product is in place and ready to sell.

Product cost is often the most significant of all costs for a merchandiser. It is not uncommon for merchandising companies to have cost of goods sold as high as 80 percent of the selling price of the product sold, indicating of course that they have a gross profit as low as 20 percent. Besides increasing sales, managers are always interested in reducing expenses, which is impossible without an understanding of what items are included in product cost. Efforts to reduce total cost of goods sold may focus on any component of that expense, that is, any component of product cost.

The Flow of Product Cost—Merchandising Company

If you were responsible for the profitability of a product or group of products, not only would you want to know total product cost, but you would also want to know and understand the various components of each product's cost. With this understanding, you could analyze reports detailing these products' cost components and work to isolate costs that could be reduced or eliminated. The diagram in Exhibit 2–2 illustrates the flow of costs in a merchandising operation.

Exhibit 2–2
Flow of Product Costs—
Merchandising
Company

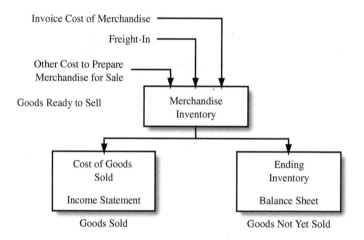

Exhibit 2–2 indicates that as goods are purchased, their cost is classified as merchandise inventory. In fact, all product costs are originally shown like those in Exhibit 2–2, as an asset on the balance sheet. Typically, a merchandising firm has only one inventory classification, which is usually referred to as *merchandise inventory* or, simply, *inventory*. As the units of product are sold, their cost is converted to an expense and shown on the income statement as the cost of goods sold.

Cost of Goods Sold

Exhibit 2–3 is a cost of goods sold schedule for Jason's Supply Company. As the exhibit shows, we add purchases to the inventory on hand at the beginning of the period to arrive at the goods available for sale. Generally, one of two things can

Exhibit 2–3
Cost of Goods Sold
Schedule

> **JASON'S SUPPLY COMPANY**
> **Cost of Goods Sold Schedule**
> **For the Year Ending December 31, 2007**
>
> | | | |
> |---|---|---:|
> | | Beginning Inventory at January 1, 2007 | $ 23,000 |
> | + | Purchases during 2007 | 300,000 |
> | = | Goods Available for Sale in 2007 | $323,000 |
> | − | Ending Inventory at December 31, 2007 | (30,000) |
> | = | Cost of Goods Sold for 2007 | $293,000 |

happen to the goods available for sale: They are either sold or remain on hand at the end of the period and are reflected as ending inventory. Thus, when ending inventory is subtracted from the goods available for sale, we can determine the cost associated with the products that have been sold—the cost of goods sold.

The January 1, 2007, beginning inventory amount shown in Exhibit 2–3 is actually the ending inventory from Jason's balance sheet at December 31, 2006, and the ending inventory amount shown is from Jason's balance sheet at December 31, 2007. The cost of goods sold amount is included as an expense item on the company's income statement for the year ending December 31, 2007.

Discussion Question

2-6. Accounting for the flow of product cost for a merchandiser seems to be a lot of bother. If all merchandise inventory will eventually be sold anyway, why not just record it as an expense (cost of goods sold) on the income statement when it is purchased?

Any company that sells tangible, physical product must sell its product for more than the product costs or it will eventually go bankrupt. This may seem very obvious, and in fact, good business managers are well aware of this necessity. Understanding the need is one thing; making sure it happens is another. Competitive pressures exist in most industries that cause companies to sell their products for less than desired. Managers of these businesses must have a solid understanding of the relationship between the selling price of their products and the cost of those products, or they may actually sell product for less than it costs.

It's like the two guys who bought watermelons for $1 each and were selling them for $0.90 each. Business was certainly brisk because they were underselling all their competition. Finally, one guy turned to the other and said, "Harry, we need to get a bigger truck." Well, a bigger truck would not help. They could never sell enough watermelons to be profitable because they were selling each melon for less than it cost. Without a thorough understanding of the relationship between the cost of a product and the selling price of that product, managers cannot hope to make prudent business decisions.

Virtually all the products that consumers purchase have undergone some manufacturing process. In this section we explore how a manufacturing company identifies product costs and how those product costs flow through the balance sheet and income statement. As in merchandising firms, product cost for a manufacturer includes all costs associated with acquiring the product and getting it ready to sell. For manufacturers, however, getting the product ready to sell is usually an extensive process requiring the use of factory facilities such as production machinery and factory workers.

For a manufacturer, units of product are normally considered cost objects and their cost encompasses three distinct elements. We will introduce them briefly here and then discuss each of them in more detail a bit later. As we present each of the elements, think back to our discussion earlier in the chapter about cost objects and direct versus indirect costs.

direct materials cost The cost of all raw materials that can be traced directly to a unit of manufactured product.

1. **Direct materials cost.** Direct materials cost is the cost of all raw materials that can be traced directly to a single unit of manufactured product, or the cost incurred for only one cost object. Note that direct materials cost is not the cost of all materials used in the manufacture of the product. In most manufacturing operations some materials costs are incurred for multiple cost objects. These costs are indirect materials cost, which we consider a part of manufacturing overhead.

direct labor cost The cost of all production labor that can be traced directly to a unit of manufactured product.

2. **Direct labor cost.** Direct labor cost is the cost of all production labor that can be traced directly to a unit of manufactured product. Note that direct labor cost is not the cost of all labor incurred in the manufacture of product. In most manufacturing operations some labor costs are incurred for multiple cost objects. That type of cost is indirect labor cost, which we consider a part of manufacturing overhead, discussed next.

manufacturing overhead cost All costs associated with the operation of the manufacturing facility besides direct materials cost and direct labor cost. It is composed entirely of indirect manufacturing cost incurred to support multiple cost objects.

3. **Manufacturing overhead cost.** Manufacturing overhead is all the costs associated with the operation of the manufacturing facility other than direct materials cost and direct labor cost. It is composed entirely of indirect manufacturing cost—that is, manufacturing cost incurred to support multiple cost objects. Among others, manufacturing overhead includes indirect materials and indirect labor as discussed in items 1 and 2.

Inventory Classifications

As with merchandising firms, product costs for a manufacturer are inventoriable costs. However, manufacturing companies have not just one, but three types of inventory: raw materials, work in process, and finished goods. Note that these three types of inventory are not the same as the three elements of manufactured product we just introduced. Rather, these inventory classifications specify where manufactured product is at any given time in the production process.

As we discuss the three inventory classifications used by manufacturers, consider the following thoughts. First, our discussion in this chapter is intended to serve only as a broad introduction to the flow of product cost through a manufacturing company. The following chapter deals with specific methods used to accumulate product cost for a manufacturer. Second, there is a difference between reality and the measurement of reality. Reality is physical units of product moving through the production process, separate from our attempt to measure that reality.

raw materials inventory Materials that have been purchased but have not yet entered the production process.

material stores Another name for *raw materials inventory.*

Raw materials inventory, sometimes called **material stores,** consists of materials that have been purchased but have not yet entered the production process. Included in raw materials inventory are those that will eventually be accounted for as either direct or indirect materials. For example, Steelcase, Inc. manufactures metal desks, filing cabinets, and other metal office furniture. Raw materials inventory for Steelcase would consist of the sheet metal, screws, paint, and glue it has on hand with which to make metal office furniture. It would not include any of the material in the office furniture the company has begun to manufacture but has not yet finished, nor would it include the material in the office furniture that has been completed. Until raw materials actually enter the production process, the cost associated with those materials is classified as raw materials inventory on the balance sheet.

work-in-process inventory
Products that have entered the production process but have not yet been completed.

Work-in-process inventory consists of products that have entered the production process but have not yet been completed—those units currently on the production line or in the production process. In our Steelcase example, work-in-process inventory at any given time would consist of the desks, filing cabinets, and other metal office furniture that have been started but are not yet finished. The reality is partially completed desks, filing cabinets, and other metal office furniture. The measurement of reality counts the costs associated with these partially completed units of product and classifies them as work-in-process inventory on the balance sheet. These costs include the cost of the materials associated with these units, the labor cost incurred so far in the production process, and some amount of manufacturing overhead applied to each of the partially completed units of product.

Work-in-process inventory does not include the cost of raw materials that have not yet entered the production process, nor does it include the cost associated with products that have been completed.

finished goods inventory
Products that have been completed and are ready to sell.

As you might imagine, **finished goods inventory** consists of products that have been completed and are ready to sell. With respect to Steelcase, finished goods inventory would be the pieces of metal office furniture completed but not yet sold. Remember, these are real units of finished product: They are reality. They have completed the production process and are sitting in a warehouse somewhere waiting to be sold. The measurement of that reality is a classification of inventory on the balance sheet called finished goods inventory. Included in that amount are all the materials, labor, and manufacturing overhead costs accumulated for those units completed, but not yet sold.

Discussion Question

2-7. Why do you think managers of a manufacturing firm would find it beneficial to separate the amount and cost of inventory items into raw materials, work in process, and finished goods?

If managers in manufacturing businesses are to make prudent production decisions, they must have relevant information. The decisions they must make include how much and what type of materials they need to purchase, how many production workers they need, what skill level these workers must possess, and whether production capacity is sufficient to produce the product required. The information that managers need to help them make these and many other production decisions includes the amount and cost of raw materials on hand, the composition of the labor force, the capacity and cost of production facilities, and the amount and cost of both work-in-process and finished goods inventory.

Although marketing and sales personnel provide relevant information managers need to make those decisions, accountants provide vital information concerning the cost of raw materials, work in process, and finished goods. All three classifications of inventory have one or more of the product cost elements introduced earlier: direct material, direct labor, and manufacturing overhead. We will now discuss each of those elements in more detail.

Direct Material

Direct material is the raw material that becomes part of the final product and can be easily traced to the individual units produced. Obviously, direct materials cost is the cost of these raw materials. Examples of direct materials used in the manufacture of automobiles are sheet metal, plastic, and window glass. At Steelcase, Inc., direct materials would include the sheet metal used to manufacture the desks, filing cabinets, and other metal office furniture.

Often, the final product of one company is purchased by another to be used as part of its raw material in the manufacturing process. For example, direct materials used in the manufacture of Cessna aircraft include aluminum, wheels, tires, cables, and engines. The tires that Cessna uses as raw materials in the manufacture of its aircraft are the finished product of one of the company's suppliers, Goodyear Tire and Rubber Company.

Discussion Questions

2–8. In addition to the tires supplied by Goodyear, what other finished products do you think Cessna uses in its production of small aircraft? What companies might produce these products?

2–9. Name three additional pairs of manufacturing companies that have a supplier-buyer relationship—that is, the finished product of one company becomes the raw material of another company.

When materials are purchased for use in the manufacture of products, their cost at first is added to raw materials inventory. Once the material has entered the production process (reality), its cost is removed from raw materials inventory and added to work-in-process inventory (measurement of reality). Thus, in our Steelcase example, as sheet metal is purchased, its cost is added to raw materials. Once the metal has been used to make a desk or other piece of office furniture, its cost is removed from raw materials inventory and becomes part of work-in-process inventory.

Direct Labor

Direct labor hours are defined as the time spent by production workers as they transform raw materials into units of finished products. Direct labor costs are the salaries and wages paid to these workers, which can be easily traced to the products the workers produce.

Think about some article of clothing, say a pair of pants, you are wearing at this moment. Certainly there is material in the pants. But how did the pants become pants? Well, you may not know all the steps, but you do know that somewhere, someone sat at a sewing machine and stitched the cut material into a pair of pants. The money paid to that person, whether in Taiwan, Korea, or New Jersey, is considered direct labor, because her or his efforts (and therefore cost) can easily be traced to that single cost object (the pair of pants).

The accounting treatment of direct labor cost may surprise you. In prior chapters, employees' wages were classified as wage expense, salaries expense, or some similar expense. However, direct labor needed to get products ready to sell is a product cost that enhances the value of direct material. Because product costs are inventoriable costs, direct labor cost is added to the value of work-in-process inventory, along with direct material. Why? Because the work of production-line personnel increases the value of material as it is fabricated, assembled, painted, or processed. As a result, the cost of production-line labor should increase the value of inventory, shown as an asset on the balance sheet and ultimately as cost of goods sold on the income statement. In our Steelcase example, then, wages paid to workers who actually make the desks, filing cabinets, and other metal office furniture would be considered direct labor and added to work-in-process inventory.

Thus far we have explored two elements of product costs for a manufacturing firm: direct material and direct labor. Next, we consider the third and last element of manufacturers' product costs—manufacturing overhead.

Manufacturing Overhead

manufacturing overhead
All activities involved in the manufacture of products besides direct materials or direct labor.

overhead In a manufacturing company, another name for manufacturing overhead cost; in a service type business, the indirect service cost.

indirect materials
Materials consumed in support of multiple cost objects.

Manufacturing overhead is defined as all activities involved in the manufacture of products besides direct materials or direct labor. Manufacturing overhead cost is the cost of these indirect manufacturing activities, also called *indirect manufacturing cost*. To be considered part of the manufacturing overhead, the cost must be associated with the manufacturing facility, not some other aspect of the company such as selling or administrative functions. Manufacturing overhead includes three groups of costs: indirect materials, indirect labor, and other indirect manufacturing costs.

Indirect Material **Indirect materials** are those consumed in a manufacturing facility in support of multiple cost objects. There are two types of indirect material costs in manufacturing. The first is the cost of raw materials so insignificant that the added benefit of physically tracing these materials to individual products is not worth the effort. Examples include glue, rivets, solder, small nails, and caulking. In fact, businesses could physically trace all material cost to their products, but in the case of indirect materials, the effort required to trace the cost outweighs the benefit of the additional information. The second type of indirect material is factory supplies. These are materials used in the manufacturing facility but not incorporated into the product. Examples include paper towels, janitorial supplies, and lubricants for production machinery. The cost of all indirect materials, whether the materials actually become part of manufactured product, is added to the cost of the product as part of manufacturing overhead.

indirect labor The labor incurred in support of multiple cost objects.

Indirect Labor **Indirect labor** is labor incurred in a manufacturing facility in support of multiple cost objects. As was the case with indirect material costs, there are two types of indirect labor in manufacturing. The first is the cost associated with factory workers who are neither on the production line nor directly involved in the manufacturing process. Examples include the cost of materials handlers, production supervisors, plant security personnel, plant janitorial personnel, factory secretarial and clerical personnel, and the vice president of manufacturing. Although the effort of these workers is important to the production process, their labor costs are not easily traceable to products. They are therefore classified as indirect labor.

The second type of indirect labor is the cost of wages paid to direct labor employees when they are doing something other than working on the product they produce. These activities might include setting up equipment for production runs or sweeping up at the end of a shift. The idea is that direct labor should include only the cost of direct labor personnel when they are actually working on the product. The cost of all indirect labor is added to the cost of the product as part of manufacturing overhead.

Some manufacturers in the United States now consider *all* labor as indirect labor. In some types of operations, the direct labor element of a manufactured product is as low as four percent of the total manufacturing cost. If managers believe labor cost is insignificant, they may choose not to separate it into direct and indirect labor cost and may instead classify all labor costs as indirect.

Other Overhead Costs In addition to indirect material and indirect labor, manufacturing overhead includes other costs associated with the production facility. Examples include depreciation on the factory building, rent paid for production equipment, factory insurance, property taxes for the factory, and telephone service for the factory. All the costs in this category are associated with the operation of the production facility.

We have seen that manufacturing overhead is the sum of all indirect material, indirect labor, and other overhead costs. Manufacturing overhead costs are necessary costs to produce products and enhance the value of the goods being manufactured. Accordingly, as products are being manufactured, manufacturing overhead costs are added to work-in-process inventory.

Discussion Question

2-10. The textbook you are reading was published (manufactured) by Pearson Custom. What costs of manufacturing this book do you think Pearson Custom would include as

   a. direct materials?

   b. direct labor?

   c. manufacturing overhead?

The Flow of Product Cost—Manufacturing Company

In a manufacturing environment, just as in merchandising operations, managers must understand the flow of product costs to successfully control and plan for them. Product cost information is also an essential element of the information needed when making pricing and sales decisions. How could a business price a product if none of its managers knew how much the product cost to produce? Having the information is not enough, though. Managers must also understand the components of product cost and the way these costs will affect the company's assets as reported on the balance sheet and the profits as on the income statement. Exhibit 2–4 shows the flow of product costs through a manufacturing operation.

Exhibit 2–4
The Flow of Product
Costs—Manufacturing
Company

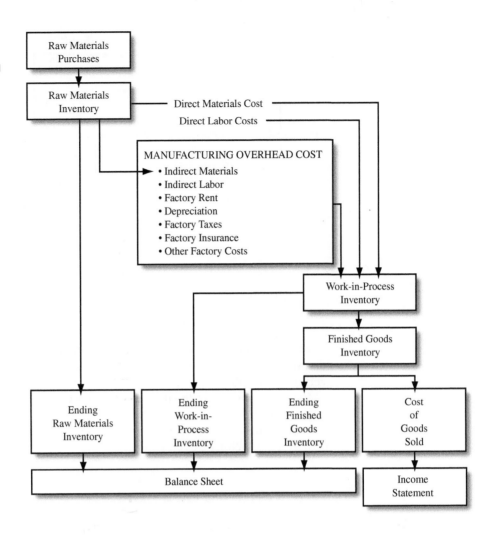

Exhibit 2–4 looks more complicated than it really is. In fact, this exhibit summarizes our entire discussion of product cost identification for a manufacturer. Let us take some time to walk through the diagram.

As raw materials are purchased, they become part of raw materials inventory (a).

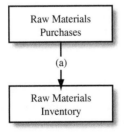

When materials actually enter the production process, their cost is classified as either direct materials (b) or indirect materials (c) depending on the type of material. The cost of any raw materials still on hand at the end of the production period is classified as ending raw materials inventory on the balance sheet at the end of the period (d).

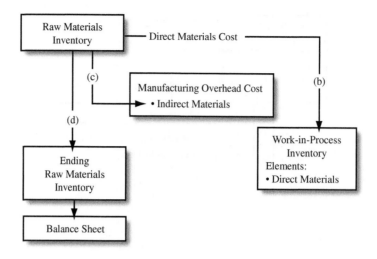

Note that the cost of direct materials is added to work-in-process inventory at this point, whereas the cost of indirect materials is classified as manufacturing overhead. We will return to manufacturing overhead in a moment.

We now have one of the three elements of product cost in work-in-process inventory (direct materials). The next element added is labor. Note that direct labor (e) is added directly to work-in-process inventory, whereas indirect labor (f) is classified as manufacturing overhead.

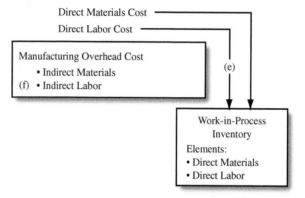

We now have two of the three elements of product cost in work-in-process inventory (direct materials and direct labor). The last element added is manufacturing overhead. In addition to indirect materials and indirect labor (which we classified as manufacturing overhead earlier), all other indirect manufacturing costs are classified as manufacturing overhead (g). The ones we have provided in Exhibit 2–4 are representative only. In reality, the list is almost endless.

Once the manufacturing overhead items and amounts have been accumulated, the cost of manufacturing overhead is added to work in process (h).

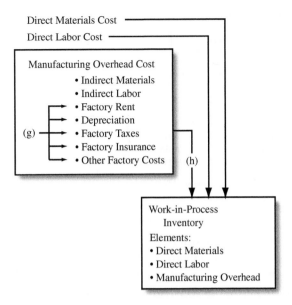

Work-in-process inventory consists of the direct material, direct labor, and manufacturing overhead cost associated with goods that are currently in production. As units are completed, the cost associated with these units is transferred from work-in-process inventory to finished goods inventory (i). The cost of product still in production at the end of the production period is classified as ending work-in-process inventory on the balance sheet at the end of the period (j).

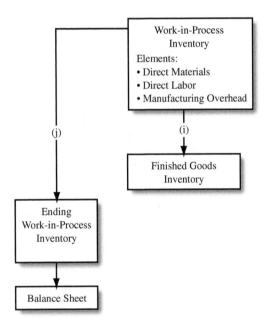

Once finished units of product (and their cost) have been transferred to finished goods inventory, usually only one of two things will happen to the actual units: Either they will be sold by the end of the accounting period or they will not be sold. If they are sold, we transfer the cost associated with them to cost of goods sold (k). We classify the cost of finished product still on hand at the end of the accounting period as ending finished goods inventory on the balance sheet at the end of the period (l).

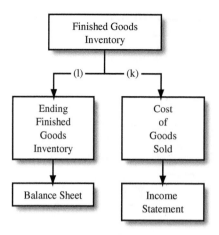

For most manufacturers, inventory is a sizeable asset requiring considerable financial resources. A walk through a manufacturing facility would make you aware of the significance of inventory, because you would be able to see stacks of it sitting there. Raw materials, work in process, and finished goods are all important assets of a manufacturer. Proper measurement of these assets is crucial if managers are to make good decisions about inventory management. For this reason, business people should understand the component costs of each type of inventory.

Cost of Goods Manufactured

We have seen that a manufacturer's product cost consists of direct material, direct labor, and manufacturing overhead. These three product classifications are summarized on the cost of goods manufactured schedule. You will find a typical presentation of this schedule for Lowell Manufacturing, Inc. in Exhibit 2–5.

Exhibit 2–5
Cost of Goods
Manufactured Schedule

LOWELL MANUFACTURING, INC.
Cost of Goods Manufactured Schedule
For the Year Ending December 31, 2007

Direct Materials:		
Beginning Direct Material Inventory	$ 13,000	
+ Purchases during 2007	400,000	
= Materials Available during 2007	$413,000	
− Ending Direct Material Inventory	(20,000)	
= Direct Materials Used during 2007		$ 393,000
Direct Labor during 2007		220,000
Manufacturing Overhead Cost:		
Indirect Materials	$ 5,000	
Indirect Labor	20,000	
Factory Rent	144,000	
Depreciation of Equipment	250,000	
Repairs and Maintenance on Equipment	40,000	
Utilities	39,000	
Property Taxes	15,000	
Total Manufacturing Overhead Cost during 2007		513,000
Manufacturing Cost for Current Period		$1,126,000
+ Beginning Work-in-Process Inventory (1/1/07)		41,000
= Cost of Goods Available to be Finished in 2007		$1,167,000
− Ending Work-in-Process Inventory (12/31/07)		(65,000)
= Cost of Goods Manufactured during 2007		$1,102,000

Although this schedule looks quite involved, it consists of four relatively simple parts.

1. Direct Materials Section. This section is similar in format to the cost of goods sold section of the income statement. In both cases, we deal with costs stored in inventory to determine the cost of the inventory that has been used.

LOWELL MANUFACTURING, INC.
Cost of Goods Manufactured Schedule
Direct Materials Section
For the Year Ending December 31, 2007

Direct Materials:		
Beginning Direct Material Inventory	$ 13,000	
+ Purchases during 2007	400,000	
= Materials Available during 2007	$413,000	
− Ending Direct Material Inventory	(20,000)	
= Direct Materials Used during 2007		$393,000

2. Direct Labor Section. We see that the direct labor section of Lowell Manufacturing's cost of goods manufactured schedule consists of only one line, which is a common way to present this information. Remember, direct labor represents the cost of employees directly involved in the production process.

LOWELL MANUFACTURING, INC.
Cost of Goods Manufactured Schedule
Direct Labor Section
For the Year Ending December 31, 2007

Direct Labor during 2007	$220,000

3. The Manufacturing Overhead Section. This section lists manufacturing overhead costs by functional description. Depending on the level of detail desired, this section can be as short as one line, which depicts total manufacturing overhead. Lowell's cost of goods manufactured schedule provides several lines detailing the various components of manufacturing overhead.

LOWELL MANUFACTURING, INC.
Cost of Goods Manufactured Schedule
Manufacturing Overhead Section
For the Year Ending December 31, 2007

Manufacturing Overhead Cost:		
Indirect Materials	$ 5,000	
Indirect Labor	20,000	
Factory Rent	144,000	
Depreciation of Equipment	250,000	
Repairs and Maintenance on Equipment	40,000	
Utilities	39,000	
Property Taxes	15,000	
Total Manufacturing Overhead Cost during 2007		$513,000

4. Cost Summary and Work-in-Process Section. The last section of the cost of goods manufactured schedule summarizes the current period's product cost and incorporates the beginning and ending work-in-process inventory balances. Note that as in a cost of goods sold schedule, beginning inventory is added and ending inventory is subtracted to arrive at inventory used.

LOWELL MANUFACTURING, INC.
Cost of Goods Manufactured Schedule
Cost Summary and Work-in-Process Section
For the Year Ending December 31, 2007

	Manufacturing Cost for Current Period	$1,126,000
+	Beginning Work-in-Process Inventory (1/1/07)	41,000
=	Cost of Goods Available to be Finished during 2007	$1,167,000
−	Ending Work-in-Process Inventory (12/31/07)	(65,000)
=	Cost of Goods Manufactured during 2007	$1,102,000

Using the information from the cost of goods manufactured schedule, we can prepare a cost of goods sold schedule, such as the one for Lowell Manufacturing, Inc. shown in Exhibit 2–6.

Exhibit 2–6
Cost of Goods Sold
Schedule

LOWELL MANUFACTURING, INC.
Cost of Goods Sold Schedule
For the Year Ending December 31, 2007

	Beginning Finished Goods Inventory	$ 70,000
+	Cost of Goods Manufactured during 2007	1,102,000
=	Goods Available for Sale in 2007	$1,172,000
−	Ending Finished Goods Inventory	(28,000)
=	Cost of Goods Sold for 2007	$1,144,000

PRODUCT COST IDENTIFICATION FOR SERVICE FIRMS

In contrast to both merchandisers and manufacturers, service type businesses such as law firms, health care providers, airlines, and accounting firms do not sell tangible, physical products. Many service firms are huge. For example, Hilton Hotels Corporation is a diversified service company in the hospitality industry. The company reported revenues from hotel and casino services of over $4.4 billion for 2005.

Service companies offer their customers a product just as real as those sold by merchandisers and manufacturers, but service products lack physical substance. Determining the cost of its product is as important for a service company as it is for merchandisers and manufacturers, but the procedures differ because service type businesses have no inventory.

We can accumulate cost for almost any facet of a service company's operation. To illustrate, consider the Marston Medical Clinic. The three doctors at the clinic

(Dr. Helen Marston and two of her medical school classmates) perform routine physical exams, examinations in response to specific patient symptoms, immunizations, and minor surgery. Major surgery is performed by the doctors at a local hospital. Any one of these services could be designated as a cost object, and cost could be accumulated for a particular service provided to an individual patient. Likewise, we can accumulate costs for a particular category of procedure, for a department or a particular area of the medical practice, or for each of the three doctors or the five nurses.

The three broad cost classifications included in the cost of services provided are materials, labor, and indirect service cost (sometimes called overhead). The cost classifications for a service firm look almost exactly like the classifications used in costing manufactured products, with some important differences.

Materials

The materials used in performing services are normally incidental supplies. The cost of these materials is relatively insignificant compared to the direct materials used in the production of manufactured products. In the case of Marston Medical Clinic, materials would include items such as tongue depressors, the needles and serum used for immunizations, bandages, and so forth.

Some service companies separate material significant enough to trace to individual cost objects from insignificant material simply treated as indirect overhead cost. In many cases, however, the materials used in performing a service are actually more like the indirect materials used by a manufacturer. Whereas a manufacturer such as Steelcase might consider glue and screws to be indirect materials, a legal firm would probably consider legal pads, computer discs, and pens as indirect materials, and all costs of materials are treated as indirect (overhead) cost.

Labor

Generally, service businesses are labor intensive, meaning that the largest component of product cost for service organizations is often labor cost. It includes costs of those people who perform part or all the service. In the case of Marston Medical Clinic, labor cost would certainly include the salaries of the three doctors and the five nurses. It would not, however, include the amount paid to the receptionist or bookkeeper. Even though their work is important, these employees do not perform the health care services provided by the clinic. The labor cost of the receptionist and bookkeeper, then, would be considered a period cost.

Overhead or Indirect Service Costs

The overhead costs in a service business are similar to those for a manufacturer. They are costs that are associated specifically with performing the services provided but that cannot easily be traced to one specific cost object. In the case of the Marston Clinic, rent on the clinic building is an indirect cost of providing health care—the building is necessary to provide patient services. However, its cost is hard to trace to one cost object, so it is considered an overhead cost.

Discussion Question

2-11. Airline companies, such as United Airlines, often define the routes they fly as cost objects. Given that definition, consider a specific route from New York to Los Angeles and describe the costs you believe United Airlines would include as

   a. materials
   b. labor
   c. overhead

The Flow of Service Cost—Service Company

Just as managers in manufacturing and merchandising operations must understand the flow of costs associated with products they sell, managers of service type businesses must understand the flow of service costs if they are to control and plan for them. Also, service cost information is an essential element of the information needed when making pricing and sales decisions. Having the information is not enough though. Managers must also understand how these costs will affect the company's assets reported on the balance sheet and profits on the income statement. The flow of costs through a typical service firm is shown in Exhibit 2–7.

Exhibit 2-7
The Flow of Service
Costs—Service
Company

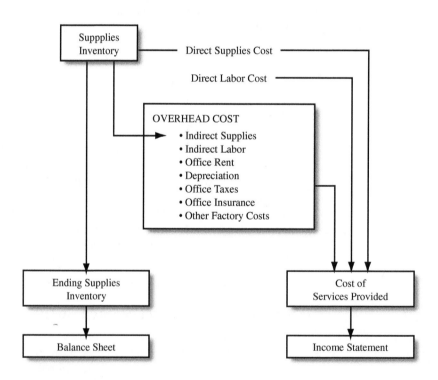

Cost of Services

As Exhibit 2–7 indicates, cost of services has three parts: direct labor, overhead, and supplies. With this in mind, we can easily create a schedule computing the cost of service products. As an example, the schedule in Exhibit 2–8 shows the computation of cost of medical services for Marston Medical Clinic.

Exhibit 2–8
Cost of Services
Schedule

MARSTON MEDICAL CLINIC		
Cost of Services Schedule		
For the Year Ending December 31, 2007		
Direct Labor Cost		$ 940,000
Overhead Cost:		
Indirect Supplies	$12,000	
Office Rent	24,000	
Depreciation	18,000	
Office Taxes	2,000	
Office Insurance	8,000	
Other Indirect Costs	6,000	
Total Overhead Cost		70,000
Direct Supplies Cost		$ 20,000
Cost of Services Provided		$1,030,000

Exhibit 2–8 shows that the cost of services for Marston Medical Clinic was $1,030,000 for the year ended December 31, 2007. The total cost included the three components of service product cost: direct labor, overhead, and direct supplies.

We have examined how service firms identify product costs and how those costs flow through the firm. We now turn briefly to hybrid firms, which produce both goods and services.

HYBRID FIRMS

hybrid firms   Companies that generate revenue from both providing services and selling products.

Some companies, called **hybrid firms,** generate revenue from both providing services and selling products. For example, although the majority of Blockbuster Entertainment's revenue comes from its videotape rental service, the company also generates significant revenue from videotape product sales. In accounting for an operation that combines service and products, companies such as Blockbuster must incorporate techniques used by both service and merchandising firms. A single company, such as General Motors, might actually be a manufacturer (making cars and trucks), a merchandiser (selling floor mats and other accessories to GM dealers), and a service type business (offering GMAC Financing).

MERCHANDISING, MANUFACTURING, AND SERVICE— A COMPARISON

Now that we have explored how merchandising, manufacturing, and service businesses identify their product costs and how those costs flow through each type of operation, we can see how merchandisers, manufacturers, and service businesses present product costs and period costs on their income statements. We begin with a merchandising operation, then we look at a manufacturer and a service business.

JASON'S SUPPLY COMPANY
Cost of Goods Sold Schedule
For the Year Ending December 31, 2007

Beginning Inventory at January 1, 2007	$ 23,000
+ Purchases during 2007	300,000
= Goods Available for Sale in 2007	$323,000
− Ending Inventory at December 31, 2007	(30,000)
= Cost of Goods Sold for 2007	$293,000

JASON'S SUPPLY COMPANY
Income Statement
For the Year Ending December 31, 2007

Sales		$673,000
Cost of Goods Sold		293,000
Gross Profit		$380,000
Operating Expenses:		
Selling Expense	$120,000	
Administrative Expense	80,000	
Total Operating Expenses		200,000
Operating Income		$180,000

Exhibit 2–9 illustrates how a merchandiser reports its product costs and period costs on an income statement. This exhibit shows the 2007 income statement for Jason's Supply Company and includes the cost of goods sold schedule we developed for Jason earlier in the chapter (presented as Exhibit 2–3).

As Exhibit 2–9 indicates, the amount of product cost recognized as expense (cost of goods sold) on Jason's 2007 income statement ($293,000) is calculated in the cost of goods sold schedule. The period cost recognized is the total of the operating expenses ($200,000).

Exhibit 2–10 illustrates how a manufacturer reports its product costs and period costs on an income statement. This exhibit shows the 2007 income statement for Lowell Manufacturing, Inc. and includes the cost of goods manufactured schedule (presented as Exhibit 2–5) and cost of goods sold schedule (presented as Exhibit 2–6) we developed for Lowell earlier in the chapter.

As Exhibit 2–10 indicates, the amount of product cost recognized as expense (cost of goods sold) on Lowell's 2007 income statement ($1,144,000) is calculated in the cost of goods manufactured schedule and the cost of goods sold schedule. The period cost recognized is the total of the operating expenses ($430,000).

Exhibit 2–11 illustrates how a service type company reports its cost of services and period costs on an income statement. This exhibit shows the 2007 income statement for Marston Medical Clinic and includes the cost of services schedule we developed for Marston earlier in the chapter (presented as Exhibit 2–8).

As Exhibit 2–11 indicates, the amount of services cost recognized as expense (cost of services) on Marston's 2007 income statement ($1,030,000) is calculated in the cost of services schedule. The period cost recognized is the total of the operating expenses ($175,000).

Whether the costs are related to products purchased for sale, products manufactured for sale, or services provided, cost information is an important input in the

LOWELL MANUFACTURING, INC.
Cost of Goods Manufactured Schedule
For the Year Ending December 31, 2007

Direct Materials:		
Beginning Direct Material Inventory	$ 13,000	
+ Purchases during 2007	400,000	
= Materials Available during 2007	$413,000	
− Ending Direct Material Inventory	(20,000)	
= Direct Materials Used during 2007		$393,000
+ Direct Labor during 2007		220,000
+ Manufacturing Overhead Cost:		
Indirect Materials	$ 5,000	
Indirect Labor	20,000	
Factory Rent	144,000	
Depreciation of Equipment	250,000	
Repairs and Maintenance on Equipment	40,000	
Utilities	39,000	
Property Taxes	15,000	
Total Manufacturing Overhead Cost during 2007		513,000
= Manufacturing Cost for Current Period		$1,126,000
+ Beginning Work-in-Process Inventory (1/1/07)		41,000
= Cost of Goods Available to be Finished		$1,167,000
− Ending Work-in-Process Inventory (12/31/07)		(65,000)
= Cost of Goods Manufactured during 2007		$1,102,000

Cost of Goods Sold Schedule
For the Year Ending December 31, 2007

Beginning Finished Goods Inventory	$ 70,000
+ Cost of Goods Manufactured during 2007	1,102,000
= Goods Available for Sale in 2007	$1,172,000
− Ending Finished Goods Inventory	(28,000)
= Cost of Goods Sold for 2007	$1,144,000

Income Statement
For the Year Ending December 31, 2007

Sales		$1,884,000
Cost of Goods Sold		1,144,000
Gross Profit		$ 740,000
Operating Expenses:		
Selling Expense	$250,000	
Administrative Expense	180,000	
Total Operating Expenses		430,000
Operating Income		$ 310,000

decision-making process. Remember that management accounting information helps internal decision makers plan and control the firm's future. In the chapters that follow, you will see how the cost classifications and cost flows you learned about in this chapter will help you understand and apply management accounting decision-making techniques.

Exhibit 2-11
Cost of Services and
Period Costs on the
Income Statement—
Service Type Company

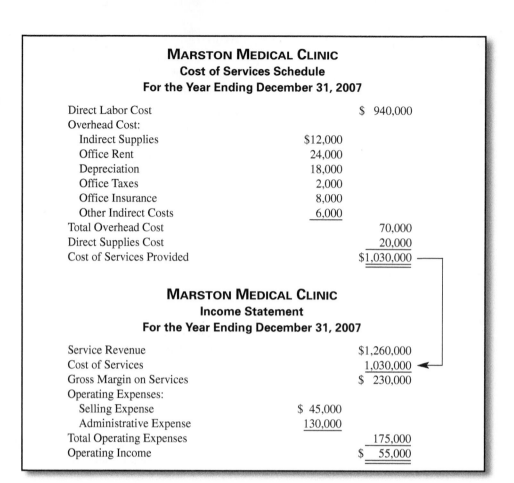

MARSTON MEDICAL CLINIC
Cost of Services Schedule
For the Year Ending December 31, 2007

Direct Labor Cost		$ 940,000
Overhead Cost:		
Indirect Supplies	$12,000	
Office Rent	24,000	
Depreciation	18,000	
Office Taxes	2,000	
Office Insurance	8,000	
Other Indirect Costs	6,000	
Total Overhead Cost		70,000
Direct Supplies Cost		20,000
Cost of Services Provided		$1,030,000

MARSTON MEDICAL CLINIC
Income Statement
For the Year Ending December 31, 2007

Service Revenue		$1,260,000
Cost of Services		1,030,000
Gross Margin on Services		$ 230,000
Operating Expenses:		
Selling Expense	$ 45,000	
Administrative Expense	130,000	
Total Operating Expenses		175,000
Operating Income		$ 55,000

SUMMARY

Businesses incur many different costs as they operate in the modern business world. These costs can be classified in many different ways and managers must determine what cost classifications will be most helpful if they are to make effective planning and control decisions.

Costs can be accumulated by cost object, which is any activity or item for which we desire a separate cost measurement. Some of the costs associated with a cost object can be traced directly to that cost object. These are called direct costs. Other costs incurred to support multiple cost objects are known as indirect costs.

The classification of costs as either product cost or period cost is very important because it determines how costs are reported on a company's income statement. Product cost is the sum of all costs required to make the products available and ready to sell and is reported on the income statement as cost of goods sold. Period costs are all costs a company incurs that are not classified as product cost. Period costs are divided into selling and administrative costs and are reported on the income statement as expenses.

There are significant differences in the way product cost is determined for merchandising companies and for manufacturing companies. For a merchandiser, product cost includes the cost of the merchandise itself and freight costs to obtain the merchandise. For a manufacturer, product cost includes the direct materials, direct labor, and manufacturing overhead required to produce finished units of product.

Manufacturing companies have additional cost classification challenges because they have three distinct types of inventory: raw materials that have been purchased but have not yet entered the production process, work-in-process units that have begun the production process but are not yet complete, and units that have been completed and are ready for sale.

Cost of services performed for a service type business is similar in many ways to product cost for a manufacturer. It includes the cost of materials, labor, and overhead required to perform services.

APPENDIX

This appendix is intended to provide a basic overview of how costs are accumulated in the accounting records of a manufacturer. To keep the example simple, we assume that the factory makes only one product and manufacturing overhead is attributed directly to work in process. The technical aspects of the application of manufacturing overhead to production will be covered in the next chapter.

After completing your work in this appendix, you should be able to record the following types of entries:

1. The purchase of raw material
2. The three main components of manufacturing cost
   a. Direct material
   b. Direct labor
   c. Manufacturing overhead
3. The transfer of the cost of completed units from work in process to finished goods
4. The sale of completed units

The following accounts will be used for the entries in this appendix:

1. Cash
2. Accounts receivable
3. Raw materials inventory
4. Work-in-process inventory
5. Finished goods inventory
6. Accounts payable
7. Sales
8. Cost of goods sold

Recall that debits increase assets, expenses, and losses, while credits increase liabilities, equity, revenues, and gains. The dollar amount of the debits must equal that of the credits in each journal entry.

1. $90,000 of raw material was purchased on account on January 2, 2007:

2007
Jan. 2	Raw material inventory	90,000	
	Accounts payable		90,000
	To record the purchase of raw material.		

2. a. $70,000 of direct material was transferred to production on January 3, 2007:

2007
Jan. 3	Work-in-process inventory	70,000	
	Raw material inventory		70,000
	To record the transfer of direct material to production.		

2. b. $80,000 of direct labor cost was incurred during January 2007.

2007
Jan. 31	Work-in-process inventory	80,000	
	Cash		80,000
	To record wages paid for direct labor in January.		

2. c. Paid for various factory overhead items totaling $110,000 during January 2007. To keep the example simple, manufacturing overhead is attributed directly to production. As you will see in the next chapter, manufacturing overhead is generally allocated to production which necessitates the use of more complicated accounting procedures.

2007			
Jan. 31	Work-in-process inventory	110,000	
	Cash		110,000
	To record manufacturing overhead for January.		

After the above entries have been posted, the balance in the work-in-process account is $260,000 as shown in the t-account below.

Work-in-Process

70,000	
80,000	
110,000	
260,000	

3. At January 31, a physical count of the goods in production revealed that $230,000 or all but $30,000 of the goods were completed and transferred to finished goods inventory. The amount transferred from work-in-process to finished must equal the cost of goods manufactured.

2007			
Jan. 31	Finished goods inventory	230,000	
	Work-in-process inventory		230,000
	To transfer completed goods from production to finished goods.		

After the $230,000 is transferred to finished goods, the work-in-process account and finished goods have balances of $30,000 and $260,000, respectively, as shown below.

Work-in-Process

70,000	230,000
80,000	———
110,000	
260,000	230,000
30,000	

Finished Goods

230,000	

4. Goods that cost $210,000 to manufacture were sold on account for $300,000. This transaction is recorded in two parts. First the sale on account is recorded:

2007			
Jan. 31	Accounts receivable	300,000	
	Sales		300,000

Next the reduction in finished goods inventory and increase in cost of goods sold is recorded:

2007			
Jan. 31	Cost of goods sold	210,000	
	Finished goods		210,000

The following t-accounts depict balances after recording the $300,000 sale.

Work-in-Process

70,000	230,000
80,000	
110,000	
260,000	230,000
30,000	

Finished Goods

230,000	210,000
20,000	

Accounts Receivable

300,000	

Sales

	300,000

Cost of Goods Sold

210,000	

Exhibit 2–A1
Basic Flow of Costs Through Manufacturing Accounts

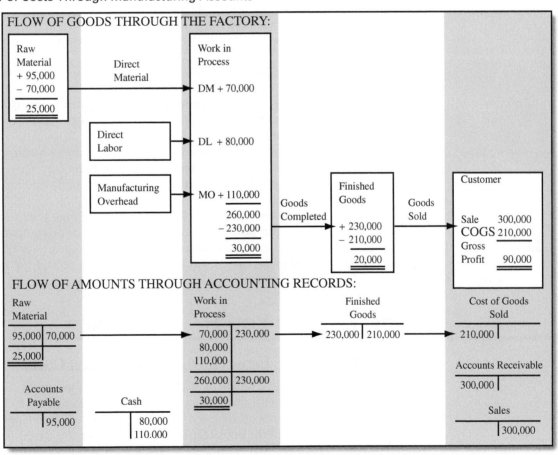

APPENDIX SUMMARY

Recording basic manufacturing entries involves eight accounts: cash, accounts receivable, accounts payable, raw material, work in process, finished goods, cost of goods sold, and sales. The basic flow through the accounts is depicted in Exhibit 2–A1. The purchase of raw material is recorded with a debit to raw material. Work in process is debited to record the transfer of direct material to production and the incurrence of direct labor and manufacturing overhead costs. When goods are completed, work in process is credited and finished goods is debited for the amount of the cost of the goods manufactured. When the finished goods are sold, separate entries are made to reflect the sale and to reflect the decrease in inventory and increase in cost of goods sold.

REVIEW THE FACTS

A. What is a cost object?

B. What is the difference between a direct cost and an indirect cost?

C. What is product cost?

D. What is period cost?

E. Why is the cost of delivering merchandise to customers included in selling expense?

F. Why is the cost of storing inventory that is ready to sell included in selling expense?

G. What classification includes costs that are neither product costs nor costs directly associated with selling activities?

H. Why are product costs called inventoriable costs?

I. Describe the difference between the accounting treatment for product costs and period costs.

J. Describe the flow of inventory costs for a merchandising operation as goods are bought and then sold.

K. What are the inventory classifications for a manufacturing type firm?

L. What are the three main cost components included in product cost for a manufacturing type firm?

M. What is the difference between direct material and indirect material?

N. What is the difference between direct labor and indirect labor?

O. In which product cost classification would you most likely find indirect material and indirect labor?

P. With respect to the cost of goods sold section of an income statement, what is the similarity between purchases for a merchandising type company and cost of goods manufactured for a manufacturing type company?

Q. What is included in the cost of services provided for a service type firm?

APPLY WHAT YOU HAVE LEARNED

LO 1: Distinguish between Direct and Indirect Costs

2–12. Brittany operates a small chain of five children's shoe stores called Baby Feet. She employs a store manager and two sales clerks for each store. In addition, she rents office space which houses her office, the personnel department, and the bookkeeping department for the chain.

Brittany has collected the following information regarding the stores and has asked you to determine which costs are direct and which are indirect costs.

REQUIRED:
For each of the following items, indicate which would describe a direct cost (D) for the store at the corner of Elm Street and Main and which would describe an indirect cost (I) for an individual store.

_____ 1. Rent for the office space
_____ 2. Rent for the store
_____ 3. Brittany's salary
_____ 4. The store manager's salary
_____ 5. The company personnel manager's salary
_____ 6. Bookkeeper's salary
_____ 7. Maintenance cost for the store
_____ 8. Depreciation on sales equipment
_____ 9. Depreciation on bookkeeping computer
_____ 10. Sales clerks' salaries
_____ 11. Cost of shoes
_____ 12. Advertising cost for the chain

LO 1: Distinguish between Direct and Indirect Costs

2–13. Sue Lee is the president of Baby Care. The company operates a chain of four child care centers in southern Florida. In addition to the four Baby Care locations, the company rents office space which is used by the company's bookkeeper and Sue Lee.

REQUIRED:
a. List four costs that would be considered direct costs of one of the four child care centers.
b. List four costs that would be considered indirect costs of one of the four child care centers.

LO 1: Distinguish between Direct and Indirect Costs

2–14. Blue Water Travel operates a chain of travel agent offices in the eastern United States. Blue Water Travel's home office is in New York. There are six sales offices and a district office located in Florida.

REQUIRED:
If the cost object is one of the sales offices in Florida, indicate which of the following would describe a direct cost (D) and which would describe an indirect cost (I).

1. _____ Rent for the Florida district office building
2. _____ Rent for the home office building in New York
3. _____ Rent for the sales office
4. _____ The company president's salary
5. _____ The salary of the vice president in charge of the Florida division
6. _____ The salary of a sales office manager
7. _____ The salary of a sales associate

LO 2:   Types of Cost for a Manufacturer

2–15. Following are several representative costs incurred in a typical manufacturing company. For each of the costs, indicate in the space provided whether the cost is a direct material (DM), direct labor (DL), manufacturing overhead (MO), selling (S), or administrative (A) cost.

1. _____ Material incorporated into products
2. _____ Sales supplies
3. _____ Supplies used in the factory
4. _____ Wages of plant security guard
5. _____ Wages of security guard for the sales office
6. _____ Depreciation on a file cabinet used in the factory
7. _____ Depreciation on a file cabinet used in the general accounting office
8. _____ President's salary
9. _____ President's secretary's salary
10. _____ Manufacturing vice president's salary
11. _____ Salary of the manufacturing vice president's secretary
12. _____ Wages paid to production-line workers
13. _____ Factory rent
14. _____ Accounting office rent
15. _____ Depreciation on a copy machine used in the sales department
16. _____ Depreciation on a copy machine used to copy work orders in the factory
17. _____ Salary of plant supervisor

LO 2:   Types of Cost for a Manufacturer

2–16. Following are several representative costs incurred in a typical manufacturing company. For each of the costs, indicate in the space provided whether the cost is a product cost (PR) or a period cost (PE).
1. _____ Material incorporated into products
2. _____ Sales supplies
3. _____ Supplies used in the factory
4. _____ Wages of plant security guard
5. _____ Wages of security guard for the sales office
6. _____ Depreciation on a file cabinet used in the factory
7. _____ Depreciation on a file cabinet used in the general accounting office
8. _____ President's salary
9. _____ President's secretary's salary
10. _____ Manufacturing vice president's salary
11. _____ Salary of the manufacturing vice president's secretary
12. _____ Wages paid to production-line workers
13. _____ Factory rent
14. _____ Accounting office rent
15. _____ Depreciation on a copy machine used in the sales department
16. _____ Depreciation on a copy machine used to copy work orders in the factory
17. _____ Salary of plant supervisor

LO 5:   Calculate Costs for a Manufacturer, No Inventories

2–17. The following data pertain to the Anderson Table Manufacturing Company for January 2007. The company made 1,000 tables during January, and there are no beginning or ending inventories.

DM Wood used in production	$25,000
DM Cleaning supplies used in the factory	300
DM Machine lubricants used in the factory	100
Factory rent	2,000
Rent on the sales office	3,000
Sales salaries	20,000
DL Production-line labor cost	50,000
DL Plant security guard cost	1,200
DL Plant supervision	2,500
DL Office supervision	3,000
Depreciation on production equipment	4,000
Depreciation on office equipment	1,000

REQUIRED:

a. What is the cost of direct material used in production during January 2007?
b. What is the cost of direct labor for January 2007?
c. What is the cost of manufacturing overhead for January 2007?
d. What is the total cost of tables manufactured in January 2007?
e. What is the cost of each table manufactured in January 2007?
f. Do you think the cost per table is valuable information for Carole Anderson, the company's owner? How might she use this information?

LO 5: Calculate Ending Inventory

2–18. Steiferman Window Company makes aluminum window units. At the beginning of November, the company's direct material inventory included 900 square feet of window glass. During November Steiferman purchased another 12,000 square feet of glass. Each completed window unit requires 9 square feet of glass. During November, 9,900 square feet of glass was transferred to the production line.

REQUIRED:

How many square feet of glass remain in the ending direct material inventory?

LO 4: Analyzing Inventory

2–19. Van Kirk Manufacturing Company has been in business for many years. Dottie Van Kirk, the company president, is concerned that the cost of raw material is skyrocketing. The production foreman assured Van Kirk that the use of direct material actually dropped in 2008.

Van Kirk has engaged your services to provide insight into what she thinks may be a sizable problem. Not only does it seem that the cost of direct material is increasing, but it also seems that her production foreman is being less than honest with her.

The following information is available:

VAN KIRK MANUFACTURING COMPANY
Direct Materials Schedule
For the Year Ending December 31, 2007

Beginning Direct Material Inventory	$ 25,000
Purchases during 2007	435,000
Materials Available during 2007	$460,000
Ending Direct Material Inventory	(30,000)
Direct Materials Used during 2007	430,000

VAN KIRK MANUFACTURING COMPANY
Direct Materials Schedule
For the Year Ending December 31, 2008

Beginning Direct Material Inventory	$ 30,000
Purchases during 2008	501,000
Materials Available during 2008	$531,000
Ending Direct Material Inventory	(103,000)
Direct Materials Used during 2008	428,000

REQUIRED:

Examine the information presented and write a brief report to Dottie Van Kirk detailing your findings relative to her concerns.

LO 3: Analyze Costs of a Merchandiser

2–20. Ralph Brito opened Brito Auto Sales several years ago. Since then, the company has grown and sales have steadily increased. In the last year, however, income has declined despite successful efforts to increase sales. In addition, the company is forced to borrow more and more money from the bank to finance the operation.

The following information is available:

BRITO AUTO SALES
Income Statement
For the Year Ending December 31, 2007

Sales		$758,000
Cost of Goods Sold		
Beginning Inventory	$ 66,000	
+ Cost of Goods Purchased	639,000	
= Goods Available for Sale	$705,000	
− Ending Inventory	85,000	
= Cost of Goods Sold		620,000
Gross Profit		138,000
Operating Expense:		
Selling Expense	$ 55,000	
Administrative Expense	60,000	(115,000)
Operating Income		$ 23,000

BRITO AUTO SALES
Income Statement
For the Year Ending December 31, 2008

Sales		$890,000
Cost of Goods Sold		
Beginning Inventory	$ 85,000	
+ Cost of Goods Purchased	799,000	
= Goods Available for Sale	$884,000	
− Ending Inventory	123,000	
= Cost of Goods Sold		761,000
Gross Profit		129,000
Operating Expense:		
Selling Expense	$ 66,000	
Administrative Expense	60,000	(126,000)
Operating Income		$ 3,000

REQUIRED:

Assume that you are hired by Mr. Brito as a consultant. Review the Brito income statement and write a report to Mr. Brito that addresses his concerns.

LO 4: Calculate Ending Direct Material Inventory for a Manufacturer

2–21. Matheis Designs, Inc. manufactures swimming suits. At the beginning of October 2007, the company had $1,450 worth of cloth on hand which was included in its direct material inventory. During October, Matheis purchased cloth costing $12,360 and used material costing $12,750 in production.

REQUIRED:

What is the cost of the ending direct material inventory of cloth for Matheis Designs, Inc.?

LO 4: Calculate Direct Material Used

2–22. The following information relates to the Penny Manufacturing Company.

Beginning direct material inventory	$ 540,000
Ending direct material inventory	$ 480,000
Direct material purchased	$4,680,000

REQUIRED:

a. Compute the cost of direct material used in production.
b. Appendix: Prepare a journal entry to record the use of direct material in production.

LO 4: Calculate Direct Material Used

2–23. The following information relates to the Montoya Manufacturing Company.

Beginning direct material inventory	$ 40,000
Ending direct material inventory	$ 48,000
Direct material purchased	$437,000

REQUIRED:

a. Compute the cost of direct material used in production.
b. Appendix: Prepare a journal entry to record the use of direct material used in production.

LO 4: Calculate the Cost of Supplies Used

2–24. The following information relates to Pons Maintenance Service.

Maintenance supplies at January 1, 2007	$ 4,210
Maintenance supplies at December 31, 2007	$ 3,840
Maintenance supplies purchased during 2007	$27,530

REQUIRED:

What was the cost of maintenance supplies consumed by Pons Maintenance Service during 2007?

LO 6:   Calculate Cost of Materials Used by a Service Company

2–25. On January 1, 2007, Bowden Auto Repair had $3,560 worth of auto parts on hand. During the year, Bowden purchased auto parts costing $286,000. At the end of 2007, the company had parts on hand amounting to $4,260.

REQUIRED:

What was the cost of the auto parts used by Bowden Auto Repair during 2007.

LO 3:   Calculate the Cost of Goods Sold for a Merchandiser

2–26. On January 1, 2007, the cost of merchandise on hand at Margaret's Fashions was $56,530. Purchases during the month amounted to $488,668 and the cost of merchandise on hand at the end of January was $52,849.

REQUIRED:

Determine January's cost of goods sold for Margaret's Fashions.

LO 5:   Inventory and Production Costs for a Manufacturer

2–27. The following data pertain to the Hudik Manufacturing Company for the year ended December 31, 2007. The company made 115,000 light fixtures during 2007. There are no beginning or ending inventories.

Metal used in production	$750,000
Wire used in production	40,000
Factory supplies	5,200
Depreciation on the factory	48,000
Depreciation on the sales office	3,000
Sales salaries	90,000
Assembly-line labor cost	960,000
Factory security guard cost	8,200
Factory supervision	62,500
General accounting cost	43,000
Depreciation on production equipment	454,850
Depreciation on office equipment	9,200

REQUIRED:

a. What is the cost of direct material used during 2007?
b. What is the cost of direct labor during 2007?
c. What is the cost of manufacturing overhead during 2007?
d. What is the total product cost for 2007 production?
e. What is the cost per light fixture for 2007?

LO 5:   Inventory and Production Costs Including Cost of Goods Manufactured and Cost of Goods Sold, No Inventories

2–28. The following data pertain to the Epstein Manufacturing Company for the year ended December 31, 2007. The company made 60,000 SW20 switching units during 2007.

Beginning direct material inventory	$ 42,000
Ending direct material inventory	48,000
Beginning work-in-process inventory	84,000
Ending work-in-process inventory	93,000

Beginning finished goods inventory	124,000
Ending finished goods inventory	133,000
Direct material purchased	850,000
Indirect material used in production	4,000
Factory supplies	6,200
Depreciation on the factory	60,000
Depreciation on the sales office	4,000
Depreciation on the administrative office	3,000
Sales salaries	120,000
Assembly-line labor cost	820,000
Factory security guard cost	12,000
Factory supervision	82,600
Depreciation on production equipment	560,000
Depreciation on office equipment	22,200

REQUIRED:

a. What is the cost of direct material used during 2007?

b. What is the cost of direct labor during 2007?

c. What is the cost of manufacturing overhead for 2007?

d. What is total manufacturing cost incurred during 2007?

e. What is the cost of goods manufactured for 2007?

f. What is the cost of goods sold for 2007?

LO 5: Inventory and Production Costs Including Cost of Goods Manufactured and Cost of Goods Sold

2–29. The following data pertain to the Oliver Manufacturing Company for the year ended December 31, 2008.

Beginning finished goods inventory	$ 255,000
Ending finished goods inventory	270,000
Beginning direct material inventory	82,000
Ending direct material inventory	98,000
Beginning work-in-process inventory	164,000
Ending work-in-process inventory	184,000
Direct material purchased	1,740,000
Indirect material used in production	3,000
Factory supplies	12,500
Depreciation on the factory	134,000
Depreciation on the sales office	14,000
Depreciation on the administrative office	9,000
Sales salaries	350,000
Assembly-line labor cost	2,120,000
Factory security guard cost	22,000
Factory supervision	183,500
Depreciation on production equipment	1,340,000
Depreciation on office equipment	52,200

REQUIRED:

a. What is the cost of direct material used during 2008?

b. What is the cost of direct labor during 2008?

c. What is the cost of manufacturing overhead for 2008?

d. What is total manufacturing cost incurred during 2008?

e. What is the cost of goods manufactured for 2008?

f. What is the cost of goods sold for 2008?

LO 5: Inventory and Production Costs Including Cost of Goods Manufactured and Cost of Goods Sold

2–30. The following data pertain to the Price Manufacturing Company for the year ended December 31, 2008.

Beginning direct material inventory	$ 2,000
Ending direct material inventory	3,000
Beginning work-in-process inventory	4,000
Ending work-in-process inventory	5,000
Beginning finished goods inventory	9,500
Ending finished goods inventory	8,000
Direct material purchased	22,000
Factory supplies	12,500
Depreciation on the factory	34,000
Assembly-line labor cost	120,000
Depreciation on production equipment	42,000
Other indirect factory costs	12,000

REQUIRED:

a. What is the cost of direct material used during 2008?
b. What is the cost of direct labor during 2008?
c. What is the cost of manufacturing overhead for 2008?
d. What is total manufacturing cost incurred during 2008?
e. What is the cost of goods manufactured for 2008?
f. What is the cost of goods sold for 2008?

LO 5: Inventory and Production Costs Including Cost of Goods Manufactured and Cost of Goods Sold

2–31. The following data pertain to the Schafer Manufacturing Company for the year ended December 31, 2008.

Beginning direct material inventory	$ 22,000
Ending direct material inventory	28,000
Beginning finished goods inventory	30,000
Ending finished goods inventory	28,000
Beginning work-in-process inventory	16,000
Ending work-in-process inventory	15,000
Direct material purchased	280,000
Production worker labor cost	290,000
Depreciation on production equipment	80,000
Factory rent	24,000
Other indirect factory costs	36,000

REQUIRED:

a. What is the cost of direct material used during 2008?
b. What is the cost of direct labor during 2008?
c. What is the cost of manufacturing overhead for 2008?
d. What is total manufacturing cost incurred during 2008?
e. What is the cost of goods manufactured for 2008?
f. What is the cost of goods sold for 2008?

LO 5: Preparation of Cost of Goods Manufactured and Cost of Goods Sold Schedules

2–32. The following data pertain to the Adler Manufacturing Company for the year ended December 31, 2008.

Beginning direct material inventory	$ 12,000
Ending direct material inventory	13,000
Beginning work-in-process inventory	24,000
Ending work-in-process inventory	25,000
Beginning finished goods inventory	29,500
Ending finished goods inventory	28,000
Direct material purchased	122,000
Factory utilities	2,500
Rent on the factory	64,000
Assembly worker labor cost	86,000
Depreciation on production equipment	92,000
Other indirect factory costs	22,000

REQUIRED:
a. Prepare a cost of goods manufactured schedule for 2008.
b. Prepare a cost of goods sold schedule for 2008.

LO 5: Preparation of Cost of Goods Manufactured and Cost of Goods Sold Schedules

2–33. The following data pertain to the Clifford Manufacturing Company for the year ended December 31, 2008.

Beginning direct material inventory	$ 2,300
Ending direct material inventory	3,400
Beginning work-in-process inventory	5,500
Ending work-in-process inventory	4,100
Beginning finished goods inventory	6,500
Ending finished goods inventory	5,100
Direct material purchased	12,300
Factory supplies used	500
Depreciation on the factory	22,000
Assembly-line labor cost	48,600
Depreciation on production equipment	12,000
Other indirect factory costs	4,700

REQUIRED:
a. Prepare a cost of goods manufactured schedule for 2008.
b. Prepare a cost of goods sold schedule for 2008.

LO 5: Preparation of Cost of Goods Manufactured Schedule, Cost of Goods Sold Schedule, and Multistep Income Statement

2–34. The following data pertain to the Lowell Manufacturing Company for the year ended December 31, 2008.

Sales	$1,267,000
Beginning direct material inventory	40,000

Ending direct material inventory	50,000
Beginning work-in-process inventory	70,000
Ending work-in-process inventory	60,000
Beginning finished goods inventory	90,000
Ending finished goods inventory	80,000
Direct material purchased	350,000
Indirect material used in production	24,000
Factory supplies used	6,000
Depreciation on the factory	90,000
Depreciation on the sales office	24,000
Depreciation on the administrative office	36,000
Sales salaries	110,000
Assembly-line labor cost	220,000
Factory security guard cost	22,000
Factory supervision	42,000
Depreciation on production equipment	160,000
Depreciation on office equipment	16,000

REQUIRED:
a. Prepare a cost of goods manufactured schedule for 2008.
b. Prepare a cost of goods sold schedule for 2008.
c. Prepare a multistep income statement for 2008.

LO 5:   Preparation of Cost of Goods Manufactured Schedule, Cost of Goods Sold Schedule, and Multistep Income Statement

2–35. The following data pertain to the Quintana Manufacturing Company for the year ended December 31, 2008.

Sales	$1,302,000
Beginning finished goods inventory	93,000
Ending finished goods inventory	86,000
Beginning direct material inventory	45,000
Ending direct material inventory	56,000
Beginning work-in-process inventory	72,000
Ending work-in-process inventory	77,000
Direct material purchased	370,000
Indirect material used in production	34,000
Depreciation on production equipment	145,000
Depreciation on office equipment	19,000
Factory supplies used	8,000
Depreciation on the factory	96,000
Depreciation on the sales office	34,000
Depreciation on the administrative office	30,000
Sales salaries	122,000
Assembly-line labor cost	240,000
Factory security guard cost	32,000
Factory supervision	48,000

REQUIRED:
a. Prepare a cost of goods manufactured schedule for 2008.
b. Prepare a cost of goods sold schedule for 2008.
c. Prepare a multistep income statement for 2008.

LO 5: Preparation of Cost of Goods Manufactured Schedule, Cost of Goods Sold Schedule, and Multistep Income Statement

2–36. The following data pertain to the Rodriguez Manufacturing Company for the year ended December 31, 2008.

Sales	$1,124,000
Beginning direct material inventory	55,000
Ending direct material inventory	56,000
Beginning finished goods inventory	83,000
Ending finished goods inventory	96,000
Beginning work-in-process inventory	62,000
Ending work-in-process inventory	67,000
Direct material purchased	290,000
Direct labor cost	220,000
Manufacturing overhead	286,000
Selling expense	122,000
Administrative expense	140,000

REQUIRED:

a. Prepare a cost of goods manufactured schedule for 2008.
b. Prepare a cost of goods sold schedule for 2008.
c. Prepare a multistep income statement for 2008.

LO 5: Preparation of Cost of Goods Manufactured Schedule, Cost of Goods Sold Schedule, and Multistep Income Statement

2–37. The following data pertain to the Avener Manufacturing Company for the year ended December 31, 2008.

Sales	$333,000
Beginning direct material inventory	5,000
Ending direct material inventory	4,000
Beginning work-in-process inventory	6,000
Ending work-in-process inventory	7,000
Beginning finished goods inventory	8,000
Ending finished goods inventory	10,000
Direct material purchased	56,000
Direct labor cost	96,000
Manufacturing overhead	86,000
Selling expense	46,000
Administrative expense	34,000

REQUIRED:

a. Prepare a cost of goods manufactured schedule for 2008.
b. Prepare a cost of goods sold schedule for 2008.
c. Prepare a multistep income statement for 2008.

LO 5: Preparation of Cost of Goods Manufactured Schedule

2–38. The following information is for Megan Hat Manufacturing Company.

Inventory information:

	January 1, 2008	December 31, 2008
Raw materials inventory	$ 9,000	$11,000
Work-in-process inventory	22,000	18,000
Finished goods inventory	42,000	38,000

Other information:

Direct materials purchases	$120,000
Direct labor cost	250,000
Manufacturing overhead	140,000

REQUIRED:

a. What is the cost of direct material used in production?
b. Prepare a cost of goods manufactured schedule in good form.
c. Prepare a cost of goods sold schedule.
d. Appendix: Prepare journal entries to record the following:
  1. The purchase of direct material
  2. The use of direct material in production
  3. Direct labor cost
  4. Manufacturing overhead cost (Use "various accounts" for the credit side of the entry.)
  5. The cost of goods manufactured
  6. The sale of finished goods assuming the sale price was $600,000

LO 5: Preparation of Cost of Goods Manufactured Schedule

2–39. The following information is for Friedman Shelving Manufacturing Company.

Inventory information:

	January 1, 2008	December 31, 2008
Raw materials inventory	$22,000	$24,000
Work-in-process inventory	42,000	43,000
Finished goods inventory	82,000	78,000

Other information:

Direct materials purchases	$280,000
Direct labor cost	540,000
Manufacturing overhead	240,000

REQUIRED:

a. What is the cost of direct material used in production?
b. Prepare a cost of goods manufactured schedule in good form.
c. Prepare a cost of goods sold schedule.
d. Appendix: Prepare journal entries to record the following:
  1. The purchase of direct material
  2. The use of direct material in production
  3. Direct labor cost
  4. Manufacturing overhead cost (Use "various accounts" for the credit side of the entry.)
  5. The cost of goods manufactured
  6. The sale of finished goods assuming the sale price was $1,400,000

LO 5: Preparation of Cost of Goods Manufactured Schedule

2–40. The following information is for Tatum Manufacturing Company.

Inventory information:

	January 1, 2008	December 31, 2008
Raw materials inventory	$2,000	$4,000
Work-in-process inventory	4,000	3,000
Finished goods inventory	8,000	6,000

Other information:

Direct materials purchases	$ 8,000
Direct labor cost	12,000
Manufacturing overhead	9,000

REQUIRED:
a. Prepare a cost of goods manufactured schedule in good form.
b. Appendix: Prepare journal entries to record the following:
   1. The purchase of direct material
   2. The use of direct material in production
   3. Direct labor cost
   4. Manufacturing overhead cost (Use "various accounts" for the credit side of the entry.)
   5. The cost of goods manufactured
   6. The sale of finished goods assuming the sale price was $40,000

LO 5: Preparation of Cost of Goods Manufactured Schedule

2–41. The following information is for Munter Manufacturing Company.

Inventory information:

	January 1, 2008	December 31, 2008
Raw materials inventory	$6,000	$5,000
Work-in-process inventory	3,000	4,000
Finished goods inventory	7,000	9,000

Other information:

Direct materials purchases	$ 9,000
Direct labor cost	10,000
Manufacturing overhead	11,000

REQUIRED:
a. Prepare a cost of goods manufactured schedule in good form.
b. Appendix: Prepare journal entries to record the following:
   1. The purchase of direct material
   2. The use of direct material in production
   3. Direct labor cost
   4. Manufacturing overhead cost (Use "various accounts" for the credit side of the entry.)
   5. The cost of goods manufactured
   6. The sale of finished goods assuming the sale price was $39,000

LO 5: Preparation of Cost of Goods Manufactured Schedule and Multistep Income Statement

2–42. The following information is for Collins Manufacturing Company.

Inventory information:

	January 1, 2008	December 31, 2008
Raw materials inventory	$16,000	$14,000
Work-in-process inventory	23,000	25,000
Finished goods inventory	33,000	36,000

Other information:

Sales	$760,000
Direct materials purchases	159,000
Direct labor cost	110,000

Manufacturing overhead	221,000
Selling expense	62,000
Administrative expense	47,000

REQUIRED:

a. Prepare a cost of goods manufactured schedule in good form.

b. Prepare a multistep income statement in good form.

LO 5: Preparation of Cost of Goods Manufactured Schedule and Multistep Income Statement

2–43. The following information is for Richard Manufacturing Company.

Inventory information:

	January 1, 2008	December 31, 2008
Raw materials inventory	$14,000	$16,000
Work-in-process inventory	25,000	28,000
Finished goods inventory	32,000	36,000

Other information:

Sales	$790,000
Direct materials purchases	162,000
Direct labor cost	140,000
Manufacturing overhead	234,000
Selling expense	72,000
Administrative expense	57,000

REQUIRED:

a. Prepare a cost of goods manufactured schedule in good form.

b. Prepare a multistep income statement in good form.

LO 3: Preparation of a Multistep Income Statement for a Merchandiser

2–44. Bonnie's Pet Cage Company has the following information for 2008:

Sales	$300,000
Cost of goods manufactured	200,000
Selling expense	30,000
Administrative expense	25,000
Beginning finished goods inventory	21,000
Ending finished goods inventory	28,000

REQUIRED:

Prepare a multistep income statement for Bonnie's Pet Cage Company.

LO 3: Preparation of a Multistep Income Statement for a Manufacturer

2–45. Albert's Manufacturing Company has the following information for 2008:

Beginning finished goods inventory	$ 41,000
Ending finished goods inventory	58,000
Sales	600,000
Cost of goods manufactured	400,000
Selling expense	90,000
Administrative expense	60,000

REQUIRED:
Prepare a multistep income statement for Albert's Manufacturing Company for 2008.

LO 5: Preparation of cost of a Multistep Income Statement for a Merchandiser

2-46. Phillips Merchandising Company has the following information for 2008:

Sales	$400,000
Cost of merchandise purchased	300,000
Selling expense	30,000
Administrative expense	20,000
Beginning finished goods inventory	40,000
Ending finished goods inventory	50,000

REQUIRED:
Prepare a multistep income statement for Phillips Merchandising Company for 2008.

LO 5: Preparation of Cost of a Multistep Income Statement for a Merchandiser

2-47. Robinson Merchandising Company has the following information for 2008:

Beginning finished goods inventory	$ 60,000
Ending finished goods inventory	50,000
Sales	840,000
Cost of merchandise purchased	630,000
Selling expense	90,000
Administrative expense	40,000

REQUIRED:
Prepare a multistep income statement for Robinson Merchandising Company for 2008.

LO 6: Determine the Cost of Services Provided and Preparation of a Single-Step Income Statement for a Service Company

2-48. Butterfield's Bookkeeping Service began operations on January 1, 2008. The following information is taken from its accounting records as of December 31, 2008.

Bookkeeping service revenue	$80,000
Bookkeeping salaries	42,000
Bookkeeping office rent	12,000
Depreciation on bookkeeping equipment	2,000
Bookkeeping supplies used	700
Advertising	800

REQUIRED:
a. What is the cost of services provided?
b. Prepare a single-step income statement for Butterfield's Bookkeeping Service.

LO 6:   Determine the Cost of Services Provided and Preparation of a Single-Step Income Statement for a Service Company

2–49. Tony's Film Delivery Service began operations on January 1, 2008. The following information is taken from its accounting records as of December 31, 2008.

Delivery revenue	$40,000
Driver wages	22,000
Depreciation on truck	4,000
Fuel cost	2,700
Advertising	800
Bookkeeping cost	240

REQUIRED:

a. What is the cost of services provided?

b. Prepare a single-step income statement for Tony's Film Delivery Service.

LO 3:   Preparation of a Multistep Income Statement for a Merchandiser

2–50. Cam's Swimsuit Shop provided the following information for 2008.

Merchandise inventory, January 1, 2008	$ 16,000
Merchandise inventory, December 31, 2008	19,000
Sales	190,000
Advertising	1,200
Store rent	2,400
Purchases of merchandise	82,000
Sales salaries	22,000
Store utilities	3,600
Sales supplies used during 2008	1,000
Sales supplies on hand, December 31, 2008	500
Office rent	800
Administrative salaries	18,000

REQUIRED:

Prepare a multistep income statement for Cam's Swimsuit Shop for 2008.

LO 3:   Preparation of a Multistep Income Statement for a Merchandiser

2–51. Keller Auto Parts provided the following information for 2008.

Merchandise inventory, January 1, 2008	$ 19,000
Merchandise inventory, December 31, 2008	21,000
Sales	280,000
Advertising	2,200
Depreciation on the store	18,000
Purchases of merchandise	182,000
Sales salaries	21,000
Store utilities	1,200
Depreciation on office building	4,000
Administrative salaries	15,000
Office utilities	600

REQUIRED:

Prepare a multistep income statement for Keller Auto Parts for 2008.

LO 6: Preparation of a Single-Step Income Statement for a Service Company

2–52. Dan's Security Service provided the following information for 2008.

Security revenue	$480,000
Advertising	12,000
Depreciation on the home office building	12,000
Security guard wages	362,000
Administrative salaries	21,000
Sales salaries	24,000
Utilities	1,200

REQUIRED:
Prepare a single-step income statement for Dan's Security Service for 2008.

LO 3: Preparation of a Multistep Income Statement for a Merchandiser

2–53. Diane's Flower Shop provided the following information for 2008.

Merchandise inventory, January 1, 2008	$ 1,000
Merchandise inventory, December 31, 2008	1,200
Sales	42,400
Advertising	3,200
Store rent	1,200
Purchases of merchandise	18,000
Sales salaries	21,000
Utilities	1,300
Sales supplies used during 2008	9,000
Sales supplies on hand, December 31, 2008	300

REQUIRED:
Prepare a multistep income statement for Diane's Flower Shop for 2008.

LO 2, 3, & 4: Understanding Cost of Goods Sold

2–54. The management of Diversified Incorporated is concerned that few of its employees understand cost of goods sold. The company president has decided that a series of presentations will be made focusing on cost of goods sold.

Assume that the company has formed two teams, Team A and Team B. You and several of your classmates have been assigned to Team B.

Team A is given the responsibility of preparing a presentation detailing the cost of goods sold pertaining to a subsidiary that operates a chain of hardware stores. Team B, your team, has been given the responsibility of preparing a presentation detailing the cost of goods sold of a subsidiary that manufactures electronic calculators.

In short order, Team A has completed its assignment and is ready to make its presentation. Your team, however, is still working. Company executives question why Team A is so far ahead of your team's progress.

REQUIRED:
Working as a group, develop a response to the concerns relating to your teams slow progress. Explain why Team A could complete their assignment so quickly, and why your team will have to work longer.

LO 6: Understanding Service Company Costs

2–55. Assume that you are the manager of an accounting practice. You are concerned about billing your clients so that the company covers all costs and makes a reasonable profit.

REQUIRED:
a. What information might you desire to help develop a method of billing clients?
b. How would you use the information to ensure that costs are covered and profits result?

LO 1, 2, & 4: Understanding Inventory Cost Classifications

2–56. The inventory of a manufacturer is typically grouped into one of three classifications—raw material inventory, work-in-process inventory, and finished goods inventory.

REQUIRED:
Discuss why it provides more useful information to use three classifications of inventory rather than one for a manufacturer.

LO 1, 2, & 4: Understanding Inventory Costs

2–57. Assume that you work for the Acme Wire Manufacturing Company. Some employees in the company are unsure of which costs should be included in inventories and which costs should not. There is also some confusion regarding the logic of including some items while excluding others.

   You have been assigned to a group that is responsible for making a presentation on which of Acme's costs would properly be classified as inventory costs and which would not.

REQUIRED:
Prepare a presentation describing the type of items that would be included in inventories and those that would not. Comment on the logic of including some cost items in inventory while excluding others.

LO 1, 2, & 3: General Inventory and Cost Analysis

2–58. One year ago, Herb Smith quit his job at Adcox Medical where he earned $28,000 a year as a health care technician to start the Super CD Store. He invested almost his entire life's savings in the venture and is now concerned. He notes that, when his money was in the bank, he earned about 4% interest. Now, when he compares his company profits to the amount invested in the store, the profits seem lower than what he could have earned if he had simply left the money in the bank. The following information is available for the company's first year of business:

Annual sales	$600,000
Cost of goods sold	450,000
Selling expense	90,000
Administrative expense	50,000
Inventory	300,000
Other assets	30,000
Total liabilities	50,000

The administrative expense includes $30,000 received by Herb in the form of salary. Herb's friend Bill has suggested that a simple $5,000 computer might help with company record keeping and ordering inventory. Herb has indicated that he does not mind the added work or ordering the merchandise without a computer. In fact, when it comes to ordering product, he seems quite proud of the job he is doing as he almost always has the CDs his customers want.

Herb has engaged your services as a consultant to determine whether his feelings are correct about the low earnings of the company and to suggest some possibilities to improve the situation. Also, Herb would like some input regarding the computer.

REQUIRED:
Prepare a report for Herb addressing each of his concerns.

LO 1, 2, & 3: General Inventory and Cost Analysis

2–59. Alberto Manufacturing Company has been in business for many years. Toward the end of 2007, management began to notice that the company had to rely more and more on borrowing to support the cash flow needs of the operation. Although sales increased in 2008, profits declined and the cash flow problem worsened. The company president is very concerned that the cash shortfall is caused by mismanagement of the daily operation of the factory. Managers argue that the company's operations are quite satisfactory. They cite that expenses have increased only slightly as sales have risen, and that production levels have been dictated by customer demand.

The president has hired your team of consultants to review the situation and comment on the possible problems that exist. The following information is available for 2007 and 2008.

ALBERTO MANUFACTURING COMPANY
Schedule of Cost of Goods Manufactured
For the Year Ending December 31, 2007

Direct Materials:		
Beginning Direct Material Inventory	$ 15,000	
Purchases during 2007	420,000	
Materials Available during 2007	$435,000	
Ending Direct Material Inventory	(45,000)	
Direct Materials Used during 2007		$ 390,000
Direct Labor during 2007		225,000
Total Manufacturing Overhead Cost during 2007		415,000
Manufacturing Cost for Current Period		$1,030,000
Beginning Work-in-Process Inventory 1/1/07		40,000
Cost of Goods Available to be Finished		$1,070,000
Ending Work-in-Process Inventory 12/31/07		(82,000)
Cost of Goods Manufactured during 2007		$ 988,000

ALBERTO MANUFACTURING COMPANY
Income Statement
For the Year Ending December 31, 2007

Sales		$1,758,000
Cost of Goods Sold		
Beginning Finished Goods Inventory	$ 65,000	
+ Cost of Goods Manufactured	988,000	
= Goods Available for Sale in 2007	$1,053,000	
− Ending Finished Goods Inventory	(75,000)	
= Cost of Goods Sold for 2007		978,000
Gross Profit		780,000

Operating Expense:		
Selling Expense	$ 355,000	
Administrative Expense	190,000	(545,000)
Operating Income		$ 235,000

ALBERTO MANUFACTURING COMPANY
Schedule of Cost of Goods Manufactured
For the Year Ending December 31, 2008

Direct Materials:		
Beginning Direct Material Inventory	$ 45,000	
Purchases during 2008	457,000	
Materials Available during 2008	$502,000	
Ending Direct Material Inventory	(73,000)	
Direct Materials Used during 2008		$ 429,000
Direct Labor during 2008		263,000
Total Manufacturing Overhead Cost during 2008		450,000
Manufacturing Cost for Current Period		$1,142,000
Beginning Work-in-Process Inventory 1/1/08		82,000
Cost of Goods Available to be Finished		$1,224,000
Ending Work-in-Process Inventory 12/31/08		(154,000)
Cost of Goods Manufactured during 2008		$1,070,000

ALBERTO MANUFACTURING COMPANY
Income Statement
For the Year Ending December 31, 2008

Sales		$1,772,000
Cost of Goods Sold		
Beginning Finished Goods Inventory	$ 75,000	
+ Cost of Goods Manufactured during 2008	1,070,000	
= Goods Available for Sale in 2008	$1,143,000	
− Ending Finished Goods Inventory	(93,000)	
= Cost of Goods Sold for 2008		$1,052,000
Gross Profit		720,000
Operating Expense:		
Selling Expense	$ 365,000	
Administrative Expense	228,000	(593,000)
Operating Income		$ 127,000

REQUIRED:

Your team should review the provided information and comment on problems that exist. It may help to segment the statements into sections and assign group members to a particular area. For example, a group member might be assigned to review the purchase and use of direct material, another member might be assigned the direct labor and manufacturing overhead areas, and so forth. Each group member should comment on his or her assigned area as it pertains to cash flow and income.

Chapter 4

Cost Behavior

*L*aura Jorgensen is the newly elected social chairperson of her mountain climbing club. Her first duty is to plan the club's big kickoff party for the upcoming year. Of course funds are limited, so she must plan well and estimate costs carefully.

Laura's first step in estimating the total cost of the party is to identify the individual costs involved. As she begins the planning process, she identifies two major costs:

1. Entertainment—A live band is a must.
2. Food and drinks—Large amounts are essential.

When Laura checks the records of last year's social chairperson, she discovers he spent $3,650 on these two items for last year's party ($525 for entertainment and $3,125 for food and drinks). Assuming the prices for entertainment and food and drinks have remained the same, the club should be able to have this year's party for $3,650. In fact, Laura has money to spare because the spending limit for this year's event is $5,500.

But wait. . . . The mountain climbing club has grown, so about 175 guests are expected to attend this year's party, compared to 125 last year. Laura must estimate the party's cost for 175 guests, not 125. How should she begin?

To determine the total expected cost of the party, Laura needs to know which costs are and which costs are not affected by the number of guests attending. Let us examine Laura's two major costs for the party:

1. Entertainment: Will the band charge more if more guests attend? No.
2. Food and drinks: Will the caterer charge more if the number of guests increases? Yes.

How should Laura determine the cost of this year's party when the number of people attending is 175 rather than 125? Clearly, she knows her cost for the item that is unaffected by the activity level (the band), but what about the cost that is affected by a change in activity level (food and drinks)? This chapter will demonstrate how to determine these amounts.

As managers plan for business success, they must know which costs will vary with changes in business activity and which will remain constant. That is, managers must determine cost behavior. **Cost behavior** is the reaction of costs to changes in levels of business activity. ■

cost behavior The reaction of costs to changes in levels of business activity.

LEARNING OBJECTIVES

After completing your work on this chapter, you should be able to do the following:

1. Describe the differences between fixed costs and variable costs.
2. Classify costs by cost behavior.
3. Explain the concept of relevant range and its effect on cost behavior information.
4. Describe the characteristics of a mixed cost and the four basic approaches to separating a mixed cost into its fixed and variable components.
5. Determine the fixed and variable components of a mixed cost using scatter graphs, the high-low method, and the results of regression analysis.

COMMON COST BEHAVIOR PATTERNS

Costs may react in various ways to changes in activity levels, creating many different cost behavior patterns. In this chapter we describe and compare the two most common patterns: fixed and variable.

Fixed Costs

fixed cost A cost that remains constant in total regardless of the level of activity.

Fixed costs are costs that remain constant *in total* regardless of the level of activity. In our chapter-opening example, the entertainment cost is a fixed cost. As the number of guests increases, this cost does not change. The band will cost $525 for the night, regardless of how many guests attend the club's party.

Suppose Laura is interested in determining the fixed cost *per guest.* Would the fixed cost amount change per guest as the number of guests changes? Let us take a look.

	125 Guests	175 Guests
Total fixed cost	$525	$525
Cost per guest	$525 ÷ 125 = $4.20	$525 ÷ 175 = $3.00

As you can see, the fixed cost *per unit* (in this case, the entertainment cost per guest) changes as the activity level changes. A fixed cost, then, is a cost that remains constant in total, but changes per unit as the activity level changes. Fixed cost per unit decreases as activity increases.

Discussion Question

4–1. Consider the costs involved in operating a fast-food restaurant such as McDonald's. What are three examples of fixed costs?

Variable Costs

variable cost A cost that changes in total proportionately with changes in the level of activity.

Variable costs are costs that change *in total* proportionately with changes in the level of activity. As activity increases, total variable cost also increases. In our party example, the variable cost is the catering cost of $25 per guest. We know this because the total cost for food and drinks last year was $3,125 for 125 guests, and $3,125 / 125 = $25. For each additional guest added to the party, the total cost for food and drinks will increase by $25.

If 175 guests attend, the total catering cost is as follows:

$$175 \text{ guests} \times \$25 = \$4,375$$

Variable cost per unit stays the same as activity changes. In our example, the catering cost per guest remains constant. Variable cost is a cost that increases in total, but remains constant per unit as activity increases.

Discussion Question

4–2. Consider the costs involved in operating a fast-food restaurant such as McDonald's. What are three examples of variable costs and the activity or activities that cause them to change?

Comparison of Cost Behaviors

Cost and activity can be plotted on a graph to yield a visual representation of cost behavior. When doing so, the activity is plotted on the horizontal axis (called the x-axis). The type of cost is plotted on the vertical axis (called the y-axis). You may recall from past math classes that x is the independent variable, and y is the dependent variable, which means that the item depicted on the x-axis (activity) affects the item shown on the y-axis (cost).

A graphical representation of a fixed cost is as follows:

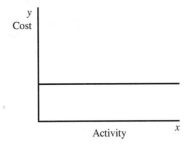

Examples of activities and fixed costs are shown in Exhibit 4–1. Notice that each example in Exhibit 4–1 suggests a cost that remains constant even if the level of the activity changes.

Exhibit 4–1
Examples of Fixed
Costs

Activity	Fixed Cost
Production	Rent on the factory building
Production	Depreciation on production equipment
Sales	Salary of vice president of sales
Delivery	Vehicle insurance

From our party example, we can graph the cost of the band as an example of a fixed cost, as shown in Exhibit 4–2.

Exhibit 4–2
Graph of Fixed Cost
Behavior Pattern of
Entertainment at the
Climbing Club Party

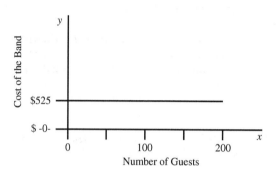

The horizontal line on the graph in Exhibit 4–2 shows that the fixed cost of entertainment stays constant no matter how the number of guests changes.

A graphical representation of variable cost is as follows:

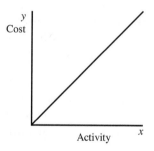

Examples of activities and variable costs are shown in Exhibit 4–3. Notice that for each example in Exhibit 4–3, a change in the level of the activity results in a change in the total cost.

The cost of catering is a variable cost and can be graphically depicted as shown in Exhibit 4–4. The upward sloping line in Exhibit 4–4 shows us that as the number of guests increases from 125 to 175, the catering cost increases proportionately.

Exhibit 4–3
Examples of Variable
Costs

Activity	Variable Cost
Production	Direct material
Production	Direct labor
Sales	Sales commissions
Delivery	Gasoline

Exhibit 4–4
Graph of Variable Cost
Behavior Pattern for
Catering Cost at the
Climbing Club Party

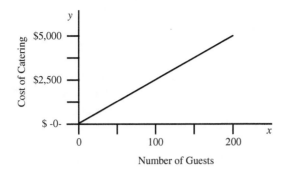

Discussion Question

4-3. Identify four additional costs of hosting the mountain climbing club party and describe the cost behavior of each if the number of guests changes.

In this section, we defined and compared the two most common types of cost behavior. Next, we see how to estimate the total cost of an activity.

Determining Total Cost

Once managers classify costs according to cost behavior, they can determine the total cost of an activity. The formula for finding total cost is as follows:

TOTAL COST = FIXED COST + VARIABLE COST

Recall from our example that we have $525 of fixed cost for the band, and $4,375 of variable cost for the food and drinks (based on 175 guests). Using this information, Laura can calculate the total cost of the party as $4,900, as follows:

$4,900 = $525 + $4,375

The total cost of the party is shown on the graph in Exhibit 4–5.

The graph in Exhibit 4–5 shows both the horizontal line depicting the fixed cost of the band and the upward sloping line representing the fixed cost plus the variable

Exhibit 4–5
Graph of Total Climbing
Party Cost

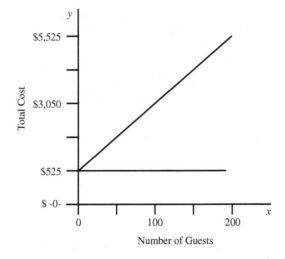

cost of the food and drinks. Exhibit 4–5, then, is actually a combination of the graphs in Exhibits 4–2 and 4–4. These graphs are consistent with the statement that total cost is equal to fixed cost plus variable cost.

Since the budget for the event was $5,500, and Laura plans to spend only $4,900, she must have planned well, right? Not necessarily. Keep in mind that the numbers only tell part of the story. As a decision maker, Laura must not be lulled into thinking that she has made the most effective spending choices just because she failed to spend every budgeted dollar. Is it wise to spend nearly $5,000 on one event? Could some costs be reduced? To make strong decisions, managers must consider all issues—not just whether the budget has been met. In this chapter, we examine cost behaviors to equip you with a cost estimation tool. Remember, however, that when making decisions the numbers tell part, not all, of a story.

Discussion Question

4-4. The total cost of $4,900 covers the cost of 175 guests. Based on the cost behavior information available, what is the largest possible number of guests that could attend the party within the $5,500 budget?

RELEVANT RANGE

Are there any situations when a cost behavior might change? Let us reexamine the cost of entertainment in the party example to answer this question. We assumed the cost of the band would remain fixed if the number of guests attending the party increased; however, if the number of guests increased well outside normal expectations to 500 or 1,000, the guests could not be entertained with a single band. At least two bands would be needed. Once the number of guests exceeds a certain range, the entertainment cost does not remain fixed at $525.

relevant range The range of activity within which cost behavior assumptions are valid.

The range of activity within which cost behavior assumptions are valid is the **relevant range.** In the party example, the relevant range might be up to 250 guests. If more than 250 guests attend, another band will be needed. For a business, relevant range is usually considered to be the normal range of activity for the company.

Activity that is outside the relevant range can affect costs in a business setting. For example, in Exhibit 4–1, we described rent for a factory building as a fixed cost relative to production. This fixed cost behavior holds true only within the relevant range. On the one hand, if production dropped to two units there would be no point in having a factory. Work could be contracted to an outside party. Conversely, if the factory building provided just enough space to produce 1,000 units per month, and production requirements increased to 1,500 units per month, a second factory would be needed. If the activity level were higher than the relevant range, factory rent would no longer be fixed at the original cost level.

Variable costs also have a relevant range. To illustrate, we return to the catering costs for the party example. The caterer charged the club $25 per guest for food and drinks for a party with 125 to 175 guests. Would the caterer offer the same service for $25 per guest if the event were a private evening with only six people attending? Probably not. The caterer's fee is based on a relatively large number of guests. Conversely, the caterer might be willing to provide food and drinks for a cost of less than $25 per guest if the crowd were significantly larger. For example, the caterer might offer a $25 per guest charge for groups of 50 to 200, and a $20 per guest charge for groups of more than 200. In such a case, the relevant range of the variable cost behavior would be from 50 to 200 guests.

In business settings, similar types of quantity discounts exist. For example, if IBM were to purchase just enough electrical wire to manufacture one computer, it would likely pay a higher price for the wire than if it were buying enough to make 1,000 computers. Buying enough electrical wire to make 1,000 computers allows IBM to get quantity discounts that would be unavailable otherwise. At the other extreme, if IBM were to make such a large number of computers that it outstripped its normal source for wire and had to resort to secondary, more expensive suppliers, the cost for electrical wire per computer could actually increase as production increased.

With these examples in mind, how can fixed cost be described as a cost that remains constant in total, and variable cost be described as cost that remains constant per unit regardless of activity? For most decision situations, the fixed and variable cost information provided to managers assumes activity will be within the relevant range, that is, the normal operating range for the company. The relevant range can be depicted graphically as shown in Exhibit 4–6.

Exhibit 4–6
Relevant Ranges of Fixed and Variable Costs

FIXED COST

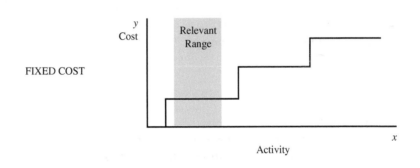

VARIABLE COST

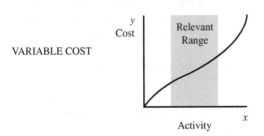

As shown in Exhibit 4–6, the fixed cost remains constant in total and the variable cost is constant per unit within the relevant range.

Decision makers usually assume activity levels will be within a company's relevant range. Activity levels may exceed or fall below the relevant range, such as when growth in production activity is significant. However, unless some evidence suggests the contrary, you should assume in our text discussion that the activity levels will be within the relevant range.

MIXED COSTS

The costs we have looked at thus far have been either completely fixed (the cost of entertainment at the party) or completely variable (the cost of food and drinks at the party). Some costs, however, are actually a combination of fixed and variable

mixed cost An individual cost that has both a fixed cost and a variable cost component. It also describes a company's total cost structure.

cost, and are known as mixed costs. A **mixed cost** is an individual cost that has elements of both fixed and variable costs.

For decision-making purposes, it is useful to identify the fixed and variable components of a mixed cost. For example, consider the cost of electricity consumed in a manufacturing facility. When production lines are completely shut down on weekends, production is zero. Even without any production, however, the facility will still require minimal electricity to operate water heaters, refrigerators, and security lighting. This minimum cost of keeping the factory ready for use is the fixed portion of electricity cost. When production begins and production machinery cranks up, much more electric power is used. This incremental cost, which is driven by the actual use of the manufacturing facility, is the variable portion of electricity cost. Exhibit 4–7 shows a graph of a mixed cost.

Exhibit 4–7
Graph of a Mixed Cost

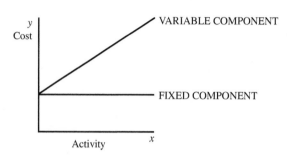

Exhibit 4–7 shows that even when the activity level is at zero (the intercept of the x-axis and the y-axis), cost is incurred. This cost is the fixed element of the mixed cost. As activity increases, the cost rises from that initial point. This cost is the variable component of the mixed cost.

You may have observed that the graph in Exhibit 4–7 is quite similar to that in Exhibit 4–5 depicting the total cost of the climbing club party. This similarity occurs because total cost (which is composed of its fixed costs and its variable costs) could be described as one giant mixed cost.

Discussion Questions

4-5. Consider the costs involved in operating a fast-food restaurant such as McDonald's. What are three examples of activities that would have mixed costs?

Assume you are the sales manager for the Hinds Wholesale Supply Company, and you are trying to estimate the cost of operating the fleet of delivery vehicles for the coming year. The only information you have is that $110,000 was spent last year to operate the fleet.

4-6. Would it help you to know which delivery vehicle costs are fixed and which are variable? Why?

4-7. What other information would you need to gather before being able to estimate next year's costs?

4-8. Why would the sales manager at Hinds Wholesale Supply Company be concerned about the cost of delivery vehicles?

IDENTIFYING THE FIXED AND VARIABLE ELEMENTS OF A MIXED COST

We often know that a cost has behavioral characteristics of both fixed and variable costs, but we have no information to tell us how much of the cost is unaffected by the level of activity (fixed) and how much of it will increase as activity increases (variable). Mixed cost information is much more useful for cost control, planning, and decision-making purposes if the manager can determine which part of the mixed cost is fixed and which is variable. In this section we will discuss four methods commonly used to identify the fixed and variable elements of a mixed cost: the engineering approach, scatter graphing, the high-low method, and regression analysis.

The Engineering Approach

engineering approach
A method used to separate a mixed cost into its fixed and variable components using experts who are familiar with the technical aspects of the activity and associated cost.

The **engineering approach** relies on engineers or other professionals who are familiar with the technical aspect of the activity and the associated cost to analyze the situation and determine which costs are fixed and which are variable. This approach may employ time-and-motion studies or other aspects of scientific management.

For example, experts in the field of aviation and aircraft operations could analyze the cost of operating a corporate aircraft to determine which portion of the operating cost increases as aircraft usage increases and which portion of the cost remains constant. Based on the experts' industry experience and evaluations, they would then separate the fixed and variable components of this mixed cost.

Analysts would be likely to use flying time as the activity level base because hours of use will affect costs. They would then classify the cost of insurance and of renting hangar space in which to store the plane as fixed costs. Why? The insurance and rental costs are unaffected by the number of hours the plane may be flown. The cost of the airplane's battery will likely be classified as a fixed cost because the deterioration of this item and the need for replacement are affected more by the passing of time and very little by the number of flight hours.

Aviation experts would probably classify fuel costs and expected maintenance and repair costs as variable costs, as both depend on usage. For example, experts may estimate that a plane's engines require an overhaul every 2,000 hours of flight time.

Discussion Questions

Again assume you are a sales manager for the Hinds Wholesale Supply Company trying to estimate the cost of operating the fleet of delivery vehicles for the coming year.

4-9. Would you engage the services of an automotive expert to help separate costs into fixed and variable? Why or why not?

4-10. List four costs you (or the automotive expert) would identify as part of the cost of operating the fleet of delivery trucks. Classify each by its cost behavior and the activity to which it relates.

4-11. If an expert determined that the fixed cost of operating each vehicle is $3,000 per year and the variable cost is $0.10 per mile, what would be the expected cost of operating the fleet? (Assume there are eight trucks, and they are driven an average of 25,000 miles each.)

The engineering approach to separating mixed cost relies on an expert's experience and judgment to classify costs as fixed or variable. It is often used when the company has no past experience concerning a cost's reaction to activity. In contrast, the other three methods we examine use historical data and mathematical computations to approximate the fixed and variable components of mixed cost.

Scatter Graphing

scatter graphing A method used to separate a mixed cost into its fixed and variable components by plotting historical activity and cost data to see how a cost relates to various levels of activity.

Scatter graphing plots historical activity and cost data on a graph to see how a cost relates to various levels of activity. The analyst places a straight line through the *visual center* of the points plotted on the graph, so roughly half the dots are above the line and half are below the line, as shown in Exhibit 4–8.

With some simple calculations, an analyst can now approximate the fixed and variable elements of the cost being analyzed.

Exhibit 4–8
A Scatter Graph

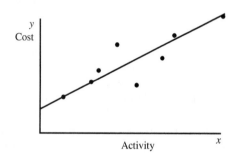

To demonstrate how scatter graphing is used, imagine you are again the sales manager for the Hinds Wholesale Supply Company with the task of estimating the expected delivery vehicle maintenance cost for 2007. Your first step is to obtain relevant historical cost data. At your request, the accounting department provides you with the following maintenance cost information about the company's delivery vehicles for 2006:

Truck Number	Maintenance Cost
202	$2,000
204	1,600
205	2,200
301	2,400
422	2,600
460	2,200
520	2,000

You now ask yourself a couple of questions. First, is vehicle maintenance cost a fixed cost? Clearly it is not a fixed cost, because the cost is not the same for all trucks. Second, is this cost a variable cost? Well, if it is a variable cost, it varies based on some activity. After careful consideration, you determine that activity might be either (1) the number of miles driven or (2) the number of packages delivered. On request, the accounting department provides you with the following expanded data for 2006:

Truck Number	Maintenance Cost	Miles Driven	Packages Delivered
202	$2,000	15,000	1,200
204	1,600	11,000	1,000
205	2,200	24,000	1,500
301	2,400	30,000	1,500
422	2,600	31,000	500
460	2,200	26,000	1,000
520	2,000	20,000	2,000

Remember, if a cost is truly variable, it changes proportionately as activity changes. Let us consider miles driven first and see whether there is a proportional change in total vehicle maintenance cost as activity changes. Compare trucks 202 and 301. The miles driven for truck 301 are exactly twice as many as for truck 202. If vehicle maintenance cost is variable based on miles driven, then the cost for truck 301 should be twice the cost for truck 202, but it is not.

Now we look at packages delivered as the activity. Compare truck 204 with truck 422. Truck 204 delivered twice as many packages as truck 422. If vehicle maintenance cost is variable based on the number of packages delivered, the cost for truck 204 should be exactly twice the cost for truck 422. Again, it is not.

If a cost is neither fixed nor variable, then it is mixed, meaning it has both a fixed element and a variable element. This is the case with Hinds' delivery vehicle maintenance cost. Therefore, you must find a way to estimate the amount of fixed and variable costs associated with the maintenance cost if you are to reasonably predict the vehicle maintenance cost for 2007.

You have decided to use the scatter graph method to determine the fixed and variable elements of the vehicle maintenance cost. The first step is to plot the information for each observation (in this case, each delivery vehicle) on a graph. Remember, the vertical axis on a graph is the y-axis (total cost), and the horizontal axis is the x-axis (activity). Recall also that the independent variable, shown as the x-axis, is not affected by a change in y. However, the dependent variable value, shown on the y-axis, depends on the numerical value of the x variable. The assumption is that a change in x will lead to a change in y.

If a truck driver travels 1,000 miles, for example, Hinds must spend money on gasoline. In our case, driving is the independent (x) variable and the company's gasoline cost is the dependent (y) variable. Driving affects the company's gasoline cost; however, the reverse does not hold true. The mere purchase of gasoline, which increases the dependent (y) variable, will not cause a change in the number of miles driven.

For mixed cost calculations, the y variable is the cost affected by the activity and it is the cost you are trying to estimate. The x variable represents the activity you believe will affect the cost behavior. Do not fall into the trap of thinking that the dependent variable (y) will be measured in dollars and the independent variable (x) will not. It is possible to predict a cost such as sales commissions, expressed in dollars, based on an activity such as sales, also expressed in dollars.

Recall the Hinds Wholesale Supply Company example. The data provided by the company's accounting department show two possible activity-cost pairs. The first pair is the number of miles driven and vehicle maintenance cost. The second pair is the number of packages delivered and vehicle maintenance cost.

We begin by graphing maintenance cost and miles driven. When we plot the data on a graph, we plot each observation as a pair of values. The maintenance cost for a particular vehicle, the dependent variable, is plotted using the index on the y-axis. The miles driven for the same vehicle, the independent variable, are plotted using the index on the x-axis. The position on the graph occupied by the plotted pair of numbers is called a *coordinate*. As the graph in Exhibit 4–9 indicates, each observation is represented by a dot.

Exhibit 4–9
Partial Scatter Graph for Hinds Company Vehicle Maintenance Cost and Miles Driven

DATA:

Truck Number	Maintenance Cost	Miles Driven
202	$2,000	15,000
204	1,600	11,000
205	2,200	24,000
301	2,400	30,000
422	2,600	31,000
460	2,200	26,000
520	2,000	20,000

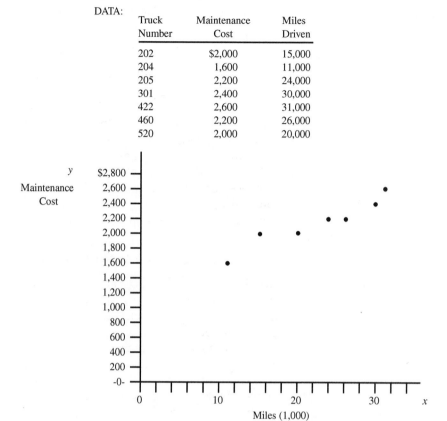

The next step is to place a straight line through the visual center of the plotted coordinates, which we have done in Exhibit 4–10.

In Exhibit 4–10 it is easy to place the straight line through the points on the graph because they seem to line up in a nearly straight line on their own. This straight line

Exhibit 4–10
Completed Scatter Graph for Vehicle Maintenance Cost and Miles Driven

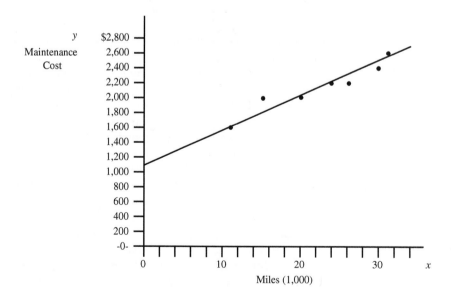

effect occurs when the relationship of the two variables is relatively constant, or linear. The graph in Exhibit 4–10 suggests a relatively constant relationship between the miles driven (x) and maintenance cost (y). The straight line represents the behavior of maintenance cost as it relates to the number of miles driven.

Now that we have a completed scatter graph for Hinds's vehicle maintenance cost, we can employ some simple calculations to approximate the fixed and variable portion of that cost. As you recall from earlier in the chapter:

Total Cost = Fixed Cost + Variable Cost

For total mixed costs we can modify the equation slightly as follows:

Total Mixed Cost = Fixed Cost Element + Variable Cost Element

When using the scatter graph method, we identify the fixed element of the maintenance cost first. Note that in Exhibit 4–10 the straight line that indicates the relationship of miles driven and maintenance cost intercepts the y-axis at $1,100. At this point, the x variable (miles) is zero, which suggests that when activity is zero, maintenance cost will still be $1,100. That $1,100 represents fixed cost. In the scatter graph method, fixed cost is determined simply by noting where the straight line intercepts the y-axis. Thus, in our example we now know the following information:

Total Mixed Cost = $1,100 + Variable Cost Element

Next, we find the variable cost per mile using simple mathematics. First we choose two points along the scatter graph line to determine the effect of the x variable on the y variable. Note: We select two points on the *scatter graph line*, not two points as plotted to represent our original data. Any two positions on the line are fine, but it is better to select points that are somewhat separated. That way, the error caused by our visual estimation in reading the graph will be small relative to the numerical difference between the two points selected.

As one coordinate for our variable cost per unit calculations, we select the point at which activity is zero and cost is $1,100. We then choose as our second point the coordinate at which the activity level is 34,000 miles and cost is $2,700. As the graph in Exhibit 4–11 indicates, we determined that coordinate by choosing a position on the line and following the lines to the x-axis and the y-axis. The locations on these axes indicate the cost and activity level represented by that position on the line.

Exhibit 4–11
Scatter Graph with
Activity Points Selected

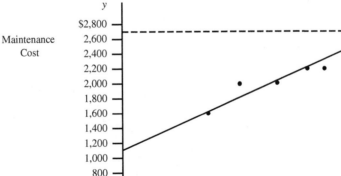

The next step is to determine the mathematical difference between the two coordinates.

Miles	Cost
34,000	$2,700
(-0-)	(1,100)
34,000	$1,600

We can see from our calculations that the maintenance cost at 34,000 miles is $1,600 higher than it is for zero miles. What do you think caused the $1,600 difference? We assume it is the change in the activity level that causes changes in the cost. That is, it cost an additional $1,600 in maintenance cost to drive the 34,000 extra miles.

Now we can calculate the average amount of maintenance cost per mile caused by the additional activity. We do this by dividing the 34,000 mileage difference into the $1,600 increased maintenance cost:

$$\$1,600 \div 34,000 = \$0.047059, \text{ or about 4.7 cents per mile}$$

The calculations show that each additional mile of driving causes maintenance cost to rise by $0.047. If we add this information to the fixed cost information determined earlier, we can create a cost formula for vehicle maintenance cost:

$$\text{Vehicle Maintenance Cost} = \$1,100 + (\$0.047 \text{ per mile driven})$$

We have now used scatter graphing to separate maintenance cost into its fixed and variable components. With this information, we can project maintenance cost at any level of activity. To do this, we add the fixed cost to the activity multiplied by the cost per unit of activity. For example, the estimated maintenance cost for a single delivery truck that is to be driven 28,000 miles is $2,416, calculated as follows:

$$\$1,100 + (\$0.047 \times 28,000) = \$2,416$$

Discussion Questions

4-12. Based on the information obtained from the scatter graph, what would be the maintenance cost of operating one delivery truck if we expected the truck to be driven 25,000 miles next year?

4-13. Based on the information obtained from the scatter graph, what would be the maintenance cost of operating a fleet of delivery trucks? (Assume there are eight trucks, and they are driven an average of 25,000 miles each.)

Now we turn to the information the accounting department provided about the number of packages delivered. Then we use the scatter graphing method to plot maintenance cost as the dependent (y) variable and packages delivered as the independent (x) variable. Exhibit 4–12 shows a partial scatter graph of the maintenance cost and packages delivered.

We draw a straight line through the points depicted by the observations, as in Exhibit 4–13.

Note in Exhibit 4–13 that placing a straight line through the points on this graph is considerably more challenging than in the previous scatter graph. This is because a straight line could take any one of several paths through the points on the graph. Each of the lines seems to depict the relationship between maintenance cost and packages delivered, but none does a very good job. The reason for the difficulty is

Exhibit 4–12
Partial Scatter Graph
for Vehicle
Maintenance Cost and
Packages Delivered

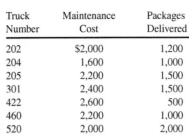

DATA:

Truck Number	Maintenance Cost	Packages Delivered
202	$2,000	1,200
204	1,600	1,000
205	2,200	1,500
301	2,400	1,500
422	2,600	500
460	2,200	1,000
520	2,000	2,000

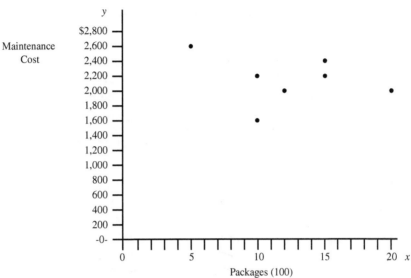

Exhibit 4–13
Completed Scatter
Graph for Vehicle
Maintenance Cost and
Packages Delivered

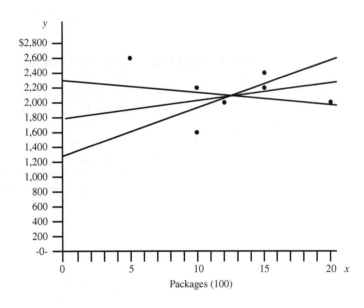

that the relationship between the variables is not linear. The question is, how do we use this method if the data do not have a clear linear relationship? The answer is, we don't. Before we employ the scatter graph method, we must be sure the activity we have chosen has a relatively linear relationship with the cost in question. If we plot points on a graph and the coordinates resemble a random pattern with little linearity, the data do not indicate a constant relationship between the activity and the cost. In the case of a random pattern, any conclusions drawn from the data will be useless for predicting future cost, and may cause trouble if used. Once we see that random pattern, then, we should not use the packages delivered data to estimate the fixed and variable elements of vehicle maintenance cost.

Even if a scatter graph appears to represent a linear relationship between an activity and a cost, we must be cautious to not imply relationships that do not exist. For instance, if we tried to determine cost behavior of vehicle maintenance cost by relating it to an activity such as the number of direct labor hours worked, we might possibly get mathematically reasonable results. However, common sense tells us that no relationship exists between direct labor hours and vehicle maintenance cost, so the results would be meaningless. A random guess would provide as good or better information. The activity and cost should have a clear, common sense relationship.

The High-Low Method

high-low method A method used to separate a mixed cost into its fixed and variable components using the mathematical differences between the highest and lowest levels of activity and cost.

Like the scatter graph approach, the **high-low method** uses historical data and mathematical computations to approximate the fixed and variable components of mixed cost. To illustrate the steps required by the high-low method, we review the following vehicle maintenance cost and activity data gathered for the Hinds Wholesale Supply Company:

Truck Number	Maintenance Cost	Miles Driven	
202	$2,000	15,000	
204	1,600	11,000	Low
205	2,200	24,000	
301	2,400	30,000	
422	2,600	31,000	High
460	2,200	26,000	
520	2,000	20,000	

The high-low method focuses on the mathematical differences between the highest and lowest activity observations. If we examine the data list, we see that the highest observation is 31,000 miles with a maintenance cost of $2,600. The lowest observation is 11,000 miles with a maintenance cost of $1,600.

Remember, our purpose is to find the amount of the fixed and variable elements of a mixed cost. With the high-low method, we focus on determining the variable component of the cost first. The calculations to determine variable cost per unit are similar to those used in scatter graphing. By comparing the differences in activity and cost between the highest observation and the lowest observation, we can calculate a per unit cost that describes the relationship shown by these differences as follows:

	Miles	Cost
High	31,000	$2,600
Low	(11,000)	(1,600)
Difference	20,000	$1,000

Notice the mileage difference of 20,000 miles is accompanied by a cost difference of $1,000. So, to drive the extra 20,000 miles, the company spent $1,000 more in maintenance cost. We assume that the $1,000 increase in maintenance cost was caused exclusively by the increase in the number of miles from 11,000 to 31,000 miles. The cost per mile, then, is simply the $1,000 increased cost divided by the 20,000 additional miles as shown here:

$$\$1,000 \div 20,000 = \$0.05, \text{ or 5 cents per mile}$$

Before we calculate the fixed cost element, recall that total mixed cost is total fixed cost plus total variable cost (Total Mixed Cost = Fixed Cost Element +

Variable Cost Element). The variable cost element can be calculated by multiplying the variable cost per unit by the activity. In this case we multiply the variable cost per mile by the number of miles. With what we have determined thus far, we can begin to construct a cost formula for vehicle maintenance cost as follows:

Total Mixed Cost = Fixed Cost Element + ($0.05 per mile driven)

For each of our observations (high and low), we know the total mixed cost and variable cost element. Therefore, we can easily determine the fixed cost element with simple calculations. Let us determine the fixed cost element associated with the high observation used in our example.

Total Mixed Cost = Fixed Cost Element + ($0.05 per mile driven)
$2,600 = ? + ($0.05 × 31,000)
$2,600 = ? + $1,550

To solve the equation, the fixed cost element must be $2,600–$1,550, or $1,050, shown as follows:

Total Mixed Cost = Fixed Cost Element + ($0.05 per mile driven)
$2,600 = $1,050 + $1,550

We now know both the variable cost per mile and the total fixed cost of operating one of the delivery vehicles. To check our math, we can do the same calculation for the low observation, as follows:

Total Mixed Cost = Fixed Cost Element + ($0.05 per mile driven)
$1,600 = ? + ($0.05 × 11,000)
$1,600 = ? + $550

For the low observation, to solve the equation, fixed cost must be $1,600–$550, or $1,050, as we see next.

Total Mixed Cost = Fixed Cost Element + ($0.05 per mile driven)
$1,600 = $1,050 + $550

The high-low method yields a fixed cost for maintenance of $1,050, and a variable cost of 5 cents per mile. As with scatter graphing, to estimate the mixed cost at a particular level of activity, we add the fixed cost to the activity multiplied by the cost per unit of activity. For example, the estimated maintenance cost for a single delivery truck that is to be driven 28,000 miles is $2,450, calculated as follows:

$1,050 + ($0.05 × 28,000) = $2,450

Discussion Questions

4-14. Using the high-low method and the data from our example, what would be the maintenance cost for operating one of the delivery trucks if we expected the truck to be driven 25,000 miles next year?

4-15. Using the high-low method and the information from our Hinds Company example, what would be the maintenance cost for operating the fleet of eight trucks, if each is to be driven 25,000 miles on average?

When we compare the scatter graph method with the high-low method, we find that the fixed and variable cost results are somewhat different. If you were going to present your cost estimates to the vice president of marketing, which method would you use? Which provides the most dependable information? The scatter graph method is based on visual estimation whereas the high-low method is based on hard mathematics with no visual estimation. Does that make the high-low method better? No, because the high-low method considers only two observations. What if these two observations are not representative of the data in general? Then the cost behavior conclusions will be flawed and possibly misleading.

Another drawback to the high-low method is that users cannot assess whether the data items have a linear relationship, which is necessary to find meaningful results. Because the scatter graph method considers all observations and indicates whether the data items have a linear relationship, practitioners regard it as superior to the high-low method, despite the fact that it is more time consuming to use and it is based on visual estimation.

Regression Analysis

regression analysis A mathematical model that uses all the items in the data set to compute a least squares regression line that equals the total cost formula.

Regression analysis is a mathematical model that uses all the items in the data set to compute a least squares regression line that equals the total cost formula. Regression analysis derives a statistically accurate total cost formula provided that the historical accounting information is a reliable predictor of future costs. If there has been a major change in the amounts of a particular expense, we use historical data only from the time since the change in the cost occurred. We are not going to learn the regression mathematics in this section because generic computer worksheet programs can calculate the regression data. Instead, we will use the computer output to determine the total cost formulas. The regression analysis provides the equation:

$$\gamma = \alpha + bX \quad \text{where}$$
$$\gamma = \text{total costs}$$
$$\alpha = \text{fixed costs}$$
$$b = \text{unit variable cost}$$
$$X = \text{the activity level.}$$

This formula corresponds to **TC = FC + (UVC × V)**. Many advanced business calculators and any computer worksheet program can provide these statistics.

Exhibit 4–14 contains abbreviated regression output from an Excel® spreadsheet for the data used to determine the cost behavior pattern of the truck maintenance. We entered the data into columns labeled to identify the information. By selecting Data Analysis and then Regression in the Tools menu, you can generate the regression output data. First, identify the "input X range" by highlighting the data under miles driven. Second, identify the "input Y range" by highlighting the data under maintenance costs. Finally, select the "output range" by selecting a cell for the program to write the "summary output."

Using the Summary Output for maintenance cost, we can write the total cost formula generated by the computer program. The intercept is the fixed cost and the X variable is the unit variable costs.

We can convert the output into an equation as follows:

Total Cost   TC = $1.228.26 + ($0.04 × miles driven)

When you compare this formula to that produced by the high low method on page M-78, the formula is different. Applying the newly computed formula to the estimated miles of 28,000, we find the total estimated cost to be:

TC = $1.228.26 + ($0.040778 × miles driven)
TC = $1.228.26 + $1,141.78
TC = $2,370.04

Comparing the results from the regression information of $2,370.04, to the results from the high-low method of $2,416, you can see that the high-low method results

Exhibit 4–14
Excel® Regression
Analysis Data Output

Truck Number	Miles Driven	Maintenance Costs
202	15,000	$2,000
204	11,000	1,600
205	24,000	2,200
301	30,000	2,400
422	31,000	2,600
460	26,000	2,200
520	20,000	2,000

SUMMARY OUTPUT—Maintenance Costs
Regression Statistics

Observations	7

Coefficients

Intercept	1228.257	⬅	Fixed Cost
X Variable 1	0.040778	⬅	Unit Variable Cost

are within $46 of the regression results. Regression analysis will always provide more accuracy, and it is a more robust estimate because it considers all the data points instead of just two data points. Both methods, however, provide useful information for management.

No matter which of the methods a company uses to separate mixed costs into fixed and variable elements, the outcome of the mixed cost analysis is useful information for controlling costs, setting prices, and assessing profitability. Indeed, a variety of internal users of accounting information, from marketing managers to production managers, will want access to such cost behavior information.

Whether large or small, simple or complex, managers of all companies must understand cost behavior. Production managers at companies as diverse as Caterpillar Tractor and Campbell Soup Company need this information to plan and control their operations. Marketing managers at companies as different as General Motors and Gerber Baby Foods must know how costs react to activity if they are to do their jobs properly.

Once a determination has been made as to a cost's behavior, an appropriate notation can be made in the accounting records to designate it as fixed, variable, or mixed. Then, the accounting system can produce reports sorted by cost behavior. Internal reports providing cost behavior information are valuable in a variety of decision-making settings. We will explore several of these settings in more detail in the next chapter.

SUMMARY

If managers are to plan and control their operations effectively, they must understand cost behavior. Cost behavior is the reaction of costs to changes in levels of business activity.

The most common cost behavior patterns are fixed cost, variable cost, and mixed cost. A fixed cost is a cost that remains constant in total regardless of the level of activity within the relevant range. A variable cost is a cost that changes in total proportionately with changes in the level of activity within the relevant range. The relevant range is the range of activity within which fixed and variable cost assumptions are valid. A mixed cost is a cost that has both a fixed cost element and a variable cost element.

Over the years, several methods have been developed to separate a mixed cost into its fixed and variable components. The most commonly used methods are the engineering approach, scatter graphing, the high-low method, and regression analysis.

The engineering approach to separating a mixed cost into its fixed and variable components uses experts who are familiar with the technical aspects of the activity and associated cost. Scatter graphing separates a mixed cost into its fixed and variable components by plotting historical activity and cost data to see how a cost relates to various levels of activity. The high-low method uses the mathematical differences between the highest and lowest levels of activity and cost. Regression analysis uses complex mathematical formulas, but the results are more mathematically precise than those of the scatter graph or high-low method.

Regardless of the method that managers choose to separate mixed costs into fixed and variable elements, the analysis provides useful information for a myriad of business decisions.

REVIEW THE FACTS

A. What is cost behavior?
B. For fixed costs, what happens to total cost as activity increases?
C. For fixed costs, what happens to the cost per unit as activity increases?
D. For variable cost, what happens to total cost as activity increases?
E. For variable cost, what happens to the cost per unit as activity increases?
F. With respect to cost behavior, what is the relevant range?
G. Does the relevant range pertain to fixed costs, variable costs, or both fixed and variable costs?
H. What are the two elements of a mixed cost?
I. What are the four methods of separating a mixed cost into its two cost components?
J. Compare the high-low method to the scatter graph method. Which provides the more dependable information?
K. What is the major limitation of the high-low method?
L. What is another name for regression analysis?
M. If you desired the reliability of the regression analysis method but did not want to suffer through the difficulty of doing the mathematics manually, what would you do?

APPLY WHAT YOU HAVE LEARNED

LO 2: Classifying Cost by Cost Behavior

4–16. Indicate whether the following costs are more likely to be fixed (F), variable (V), or mixed (M) with respect to the number of units produced.

1. _____ Direct material
2. _____ Direct labor
3. _____ Cost of plant security guard
4. _____ Straight line depreciation on production equipment
5. _____ Maintenance on production equipment
6. _____ Maintenance on factory building
7. _____ Cost of cleaning supplies used in the factory
8. _____ Rent on the factory building
9. _____ Salary for the two factory supervisors
10. _____ Vice president of manufacturing's salary
11. _____ Cost of electricity used in the factory
12. _____ Cost of production machine lubricants

LO 2:   Classifying Cost by Cost Behavior

4–17. Assume that you are trying to analyze the costs associated with driving your car. Indicate whether the following costs are more likely to be fixed (F), variable (V), or mixed (M) with respect to the number of miles driven.

1. _____ Cost of the car
2. _____ Insurance cost
3. _____ Maintenance cost
4. _____ Cost of gasoline
5. _____ The cost of a college parking permit
6. _____ AAA membership

LO 2:   Classifying Cost by Cost Behavior

4–18. Assume that you are planning a large party. As you are trying to figure out how much the party will cost, you decide to separate the costs according to cost behavior. Indicate whether the following costs are more likely to be fixed (F), variable (V), or mixed (M) with respect to the number of guests attending the party.

1. _____ Rent for the party hall
2. _____ Cost of the band
3. _____ Cost of cold drinks
4. _____ Cost of food
5. _____ Cost of party decorations
6. _____ Cost of renting tables and chairs

LO 2:   Classifying Cost by Cost Behavior

4–19. Assume that you have been assigned to analyze the costs associated with operating the law firm of Moore & Moore and Company. The law firm just moved into a new, large office building that it purchased last year. Indicate whether the following costs are more likely to be fixed (F), variable (V), or mixed (M) with respect to the number of attorneys working for the firm.

1. _____ Cost of the new office building
2. _____ Basic telephone service
3. _____ Cost of attorney salaries
4. _____ Cost of the receptionist's wages

LO 2:   Classifying Cost by Cost Behavior

4–20. Assume that you have been assigned to analyze the costs of a retail merchandiser, Auto Parts City. Indicate whether the following costs are more likely fixed (F), variable (V), or mixed (M) with respect to the dollar amount of sales.

1. _____ Cost of store rent
2. _____ Basic telephone service
3. _____ Cost of salaries for the two salespeople
4. _____ Cost of advertising
5. _____ Cost of store displays
6. _____ Cost of electricity
7. _____ Cost of merchandise sold

LO 4: Evaluating a Mixed Cost Situation

4–21. Assume that you work for Wilma Manufacturing Company and have been asked to review the cost of delivery truck maintenance. The company president, Wilma Hudik, is dissatisfied with the accounting department's reluctance to calculate the fixed and variable cost of truck maintenance as it pertains to the number of units produced in the factory.

The accounting department prepared the following scatter graph:

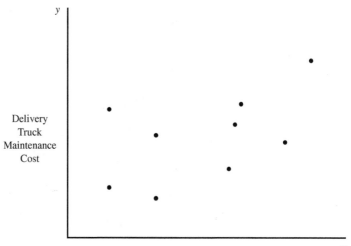

Number of Units Produced in the Factory

The accounting department personnel seem unable to use the graph to determine fixed and variable cost. The company president knows that regression analysis will provide mathematically accurate amounts for the fixed and variable truck maintenance cost, but no one in the accounting department seems to know how to do it.

REQUIRED:

Prepare a short memo to the president that details the feasibility of using the scatter graph and regression analysis to determine the fixed and variable components of delivery truck maintenance relative to the amount of factory production. In addition, your memo should recommend an alternative approach that could be used to evaluate the cost and cost behavior of truck maintenance.

LO 5: Use of a Scatter Graph for Separating Mixed Cost

4–22. Consider the following scatter graphs:

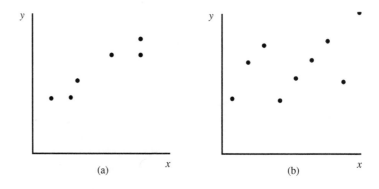

REQUIRED:
Which of the scatter graphs (a or b) do you think would be more appropriate for determining the fixed and variable portions of a mixed cost? Explain your reasoning.

LO 5: Separating Mixed Cost Using the High-Low Method

4–23. The following information pertains to Jacobs Incorporated:

2006	Information:	
	Sales	$2,300,000
	Selling expense	347,000
2007	Information:	
	Sales	$2,860,000
	Selling expense	369,400

REQUIRED:
Using the high-low method, determine the following:
a. The variable cost element for selling expense
b. The fixed selling expense
c. The selling expense that can be expected if sales are $2,500,000

LO 5: Separating Mixed Cost Using the High-Low Method

4–24. The following information pertains to the Robin Rappaport Company:

2006	Information:	
	Units packaged	14,500
	Packaging cost	$32,567
2007	Information:	
	Units packaged	15,300
	Packaging cost	$33,191

REQUIRED:
Using the high-low method, determine the following:
a. The variable cost element for packaging cost
b. The fixed packaging cost
c. The packaging cost that can be expected if 15,000 units are packaged

LO 5: Separating Mixed Cost Using the High-Low Method

4–25. The inspection department at the Rose Spiegel Company inspects every third unit produced. The following information is available for the inspection department:

2006	Information:	
	Number of inspections	41,950
	Inspection cost	$77,273
2007	Information:	
	Number of inspections	48,600
	Inspection cost	$83,790

REQUIRED:
Using the high-low method, determine the following:
a. The variable cost element for inspection cost
b. The fixed inspection cost
c. The inspection cost that can be expected if 45,000 units are inspected

LO 5: Separating Mixed Cost Using the High-Low Method

4–26. The plant manager has asked you to analyze the cost of electricity used in the manufacturing facility. Information for 2006 and 2007 follows:

	2006	2007
Machine hours	100,000	120,000
Cost of electricity	$188,000	$221,600

REQUIRED:
a. Determine the variable rate for electricity per machine hour.
b. Determine the total fixed cost of electricity.
c. Determine the estimated cost of electricity for next year if machine hours are expected to be 115,000.

LO 5: Separating Mixed Cost Using the High-Low Method

4–27. The office manager has asked you to analyze the cost of service and supplies for the office copy machines. Information for 2006 and 2007 follows:

	2006	2007
Number of copies produced	52,550	77,800
Cost of service and supplies	$1,961.57	$2,592.82

REQUIRED:
a. Determine the variable cost per copy.
b. Determine the total fixed cost for service and supplies for the copy machines.
c. Determine the estimated cost of service and supplies for next year if 75,000 copies are made.

LO 5: Separating Mixed Cost Using the High-Low Method

4–28. The production manager has asked you to analyze the cost of materials handling. Information for 2006 and 2007 follows:

	2006	2007
Number of parts handled	154,300	185,400
Materials handling cost	$9,244.77	$10,675.37

REQUIRED:
a. Determine the variable cost per part handled.
b. Determine the total fixed cost for materials handling.
c. Determine the estimated cost of materials handling if 160,000 parts are handled next year.

LO 5: Separating Mixed Cost Using the High-Low Method

4–29. The sales manager has asked you to estimate the shipping cost that can be expected for next year. Following is information for 2006 and 2007:

	2006	2007
Sales in units	15,000	18,000
Shipping cost	$30,000	$35,400

REQUIRED:
Estimate next year's shipping cost assuming sales of 16,500 units.

LO 5: Separating Mixed Cost Using the High-Low Method

4–30. The transportation manager has asked you to estimate the operating cost that can be expected for the company jet for next year. Following is information for 2006 and 2007:

	2006	2007
Flight time in hours	1,250	1,875
Aircraft operating cost	$1,563,750	$2,148,125

REQUIRED:
Estimate the cost of operating the company jet for next year assuming that flight time will be 1,500 hours.

LO 5: Separating Mixed Costs Using the High-Low Method

4–31. Charlie Nibarger is the owner of Nibarger Fishing Guide Service. He is trying to estimate the cost of operating his fishing service next year. He expects to have 220 charters during 2007. The following information is available:

	2005	2006
Number of charters	150	230
Operating cost	$15,250	$22,000

REQUIRED:
a. Determine the estimated operating cost for 2007.
b. Assume that Charlie needs to make $50,000 before tax to support his family. What must he charge for each charter to meet his needs?
c. What constraints might prevent him from charging the amount determined in (b)?
d. How should Charlie determine his price?

LO 5: Separating Mixed Cost Using the High-Low Method

4–32. The following information pertains to Pioneer Manufacturing for 2006:

	Number of Purchase Orders Issued	Cost of Operating the Purchasing Department
Fourth quarter of 2005	2,500	$130,000
First quarter of 2006	1,000	80,000
Second quarter of 2006	1,500	110,000
Third quarter of 2006	2,000	115,000
Fourth quarter of 2006	3,000	140,000

REQUIRED:
Using the high-low method, determine the following:
a. The variable cost per purchase order
b. The fixed cost of operating the purchasing department for one quarter
c. The estimated cost of operating the purchasing department in 2007 assuming that 7,000 purchase orders will be issued. (Hint: Remember that the fixed cost for one year is four times the amount of fixed cost for one quarter.)

LO 5: Separating Mixed Cost Using the Scatter Graph Method

4–33. Refer to the information from problem 4–32.

REQUIRED:
Using the scatter graph method, determine the following:
a. The variable cost per purchase order
b. The fixed cost of operating the purchasing department for one quarter
c. The estimated cost of operating the purchasing department in 2007 assuming that 7,000 purchase orders will be issued. (Hint: Remember that the fixed cost for one year is four times the amount of fixed cost for one quarter.)

LO 5: Separating Mixed Costs Using Regression Analysis Data

4–34. Refer to the information from problem 4–32.
A regression anlysis on this information yields the following output:

Regression Statistics
Observations 5

	Coefficients
Intercept	59000.0000000000001
X Variable 1	28

REQUIRED:
Using the regression output, determine the following:
a. The regression equation.
b. The variable cost per purchase order.
c. The fixed cost of operating the purchasing department for one quarter.
d. The estimated cost of operating the purchasing department next year assuming that 8,000 purchase orders will be issued. (Hint: Remember that the fixed cost for one year is four times the amount of fixed cost for one quarter).

LO 5: Separating Mixed Cost Using the High-Low Method

4–35. The following information pertains to Tessy Soda Company:

	Number of Sales Invoices Processed	Cost of Operating the Invoicing Department
Fourth quarter of 2007	10,500	$50,574.65
First quarter of 2008	11,000	52,711.12
Second quarter of 2008	15,000	58,231.51
Third quarter of 2008	12,000	59,439.73
Fourth quarter of 2008	9,000	46,299.73

REQUIRED:
Using the high-low method, determine the following:
a. The variable cost per invoice processed
b. The fixed cost of operating the invoicing department for one quarter
c. The estimated cost of operating the invoicing department in 2009 assuming that 45,000 invoices will be processed. (Hint: Remember that the fixed cost for one year is four times the amount of fixed cost for one quarter.)

LO 5: Separating Mixed Costs Using Regression Analysis Data

4–36. Refer to the information from problem 4–35.
A regression anlysis on this information yields the following output:

Regression Statistics
Observations 5

	Coefficients
Intercept	29962.2443750000001
X Variable 1	2.04253074999999999

REQUIRED:
Using the regression output, determine the following:
a. The regression equation.
b. The variable cost per invoice order.
c. The fixed cost of operating the invoicing department for one quarter.
d. The estimated cost of operating the invoicing department next year assuming that 52,000 invoices will be issued. (Hint: Remember that the fixed cost for one year is four times the amount of fixed cost for one quarter).

LO 5: Separating Mixed Cost Using the High-Low Method

4–37. The following information pertains to Jim Willis & Associates:

	Number of Computers Repaired	Cost of Operating the Repair Department
Fourth quarter of 2007	125	$26,100.91
First quarter of 2008	130	26,529.16
Second quarter of 2008	110	25,400.65
Third quarter of 2008	105	25,212.91
Fourth quarter of 2008	115	25,799.88

REQUIRED:
Using the high-low method, determine the following:
a. The variable cost per computer repair
b. The fixed cost of operating the repair department for one quarter
c. The estimated cost of operating the repair department in 2009 assuming that 450 invoices will be processed. (Hint: Remember that the fixed cost for one year is four times the amount of fixed cost for one quarter.)

LO 5: Separating Mixed Costs Using Regression Analysis Data

4–38. Refer to the information from problem 4–37.
A regression analysis on this information yields the following output:

Regression Statistics
Observations 5

	Coefficients
Intercept	19898.2674418604652
X Variable 1	50.513953488372092

REQUIRED:
Using the regression analysis output, determine the following:
a. The regression equation.
b. The variable cost per computer repair.
c. The fixed cost of operating the repair department for one quarter.
d. The estimated cost of operating the repair department next year assuming that 450 invoices will be processed. (Hint: Remember that the fixed cost for one year is four times the amount of fixed cost for one quarter).

LO 5: Separating Mixed Cost Using the High-Low Method

4–39. The following information is taken from Calzone Manufacturing Company:

	Number of Calzones Produced	Total Production Cost
January	9,800	$17,100
February	7,000	15,000
March	8,000	16,000
April	7,500	15,500
May	10,100	17,200
June	9,000	17,000
July	10,500	19,000
August	11,600	20,000
September	10,600	18,200
October	8,500	16,800
November	12,100	20,500
December	11,000	18,000

REQUIRED:

Using the high-low method, determine the following:
  a. The variable production cost per unit
  b. The total fixed production cost
  c. The expected production cost to produce 12,000 calzones

LO 5: Separating Mixed Cost Using the Scatter Graph Method

4–40. Refer to the information in problem 4–39.

REQUIRED:

Using the scatter graph method, determine the following:
  a. The variable production cost per unit
  b. The total fixed production cost
  c. The expected production cost to produce 12,000 calzones

LO 5: Separating Mixed Costs Using Regression Analysis Data

4–41. Refer to the information from problem 4–39.
A regression analysis on the data yields the following:

Regression Statistics	
Observations	12
	Coefficients
Intercept	8017.47542738051652
X Variable 1	0.986087250401329323

REQUIRED:

Using the regression analysis output, determine the following:
  a. The regression equation.
  b. The variable cost per calzone.
  c. The fixed cost of operating the manufacturing plant for one year.
  d. The estimated cost of operating the manufacturing plant next year assuming that 10,800 calzones will be made.

LO 5: Separating Mixed Cost Using the High-Low Method

4–42. Ace Computer Training offers short computer courses. The number of course sessions offered depends on student demand. The following information pertains to 2007:

	Number of Sessions	Cost
First quarter	30	$ 75,000
Second quarter	35	78,000
Third quarter	15	42,000
Fourth quarter	20	48,000
Total	100	$243,000

REQUIRED:
Using the high-low method, determine the following:
a. The variable cost per session
b. The total fixed cost of operating the company
c. The expected cost for a quarter if 25 sessions are offered

LO 5: Separating Mixed Cost Using the Scatter Graph Method

4–43. Refer to the information in problem 4–42.

REQUIRED:
Using the scatter graph method, determine the following:
a. The variable cost per session
b. The total fixed cost of operating the company
c. The expected cost for a quarter if 25 sessions are offered

LO 5: Separating Mixed Cost Using the High-Low Method

4–44. The following information is taken from Montana Avionics Testing Service:

	Number of Tests Performed	Total Cost of Testing
January	61,000	$1,420,000
February	55,000	1,340,000
March	50,000	1,290,000
April	72,000	1,430,000
May	78,000	1,440,000
June	81,000	1,540,000
July	90,000	1,590,000
August	108,000	1,610,000
September	111,000	1,700,000
October	128,000	1,720,000
November	140,000	1,860,000
December	132,000	1,810,000

REQUIRED:
Using the high-low method, determine the following:
a. The variable cost per test
b. The total fixed cost of operating the testing facility
c. The expected cost for a month if 125,000 tests are performed

LO 5: Separating Mixed Cost Using the Scatter Graph Method

4–45. Refer to the information in problem 4–44.

REQUIRED:
Using the scatter graph method, determine the following:
a. The variable cost per test
b. The total fixed cost of operating the testing facility
c. The expected cost for a month if 125,000 tests are performed

LO 5: Separating Mixed Costs Using Regression Analysis Data

4–46. Refer to the information from problem 4–45.
A regression analysis on the data yields the following:

Regression Statistics

Observations	12
	Coefficients
Intercept	1026101.26979150337
X Variable 1	5.81987772378115692

REQUIRED:
Using the regression analysis output, determine the following:
a. The regression equation.
b. The variable cost per test.
c. The fixed cost of operating for one month.
d. The estimated cost of operating for one month assuming that 125,000 tests are performed.

LO 5: Separating Mixed Cost Using the High-Low Method

4–47. The following information is for the Valdez Supply Company:

	2007	2008
Sales	$1,000,000	$1,150,000
COSTS:		
Cost of goods sold	$ 800,000	$ 920,000
Sales commissions	15,000	17,250
Store rent	3,000	3,000
Depreciation	20,000	20,000
Maintenance cost	3,800	4,100
Office salaries	34,000	35,500

REQUIRED:
Assuming sales is the activity base, use the high-low method to determine the variable cost element and the fixed cost component of each of the costs just listed.

LO 5: Separating Mixed Cost Using the High-Low Method

4–48. The following information is for the General Production Company:

	2007	2008
Units produced	257,000	326,000
COSTS:		
Direct material	$ 611,660	$ 775,880
Direct labor	1,662,790	2,109,220
Manufacturing overhead	1,781,820	1,868,760

REQUIRED:
Assuming units produced is the activity base, use the high-low method to determine the variable cost element and fixed cost component of each of the costs just listed.

LO 5:   Separating Mixed Cost Using the High-Low Method

4–49. The following information is for the Maupin Gift Shop:

	2007	2008
Sales	$100,000	$150,000
COSTS:		
Cost of goods sold	$ 75,000	$112,500
Sales commissions	5,000	7,500
Store rent	1,000	1,000
Depreciation	500	500
Maintenance cost	200	250
Office salaries	5,000	6,000

REQUIRED:
a. Assuming sales is the activity base, use the high-low method to determine the variable cost element and the fixed cost component of each of the costs just listed.
b. Why is it useful to know the information requested in requirement a?

LO 4:   Components of Mixed Cost

4–50. Consider the following mathematical formula:

$$Y = a + bX$$

REQUIRED:
Match the variables to the correct descriptions. Some variables have two correct matches.

1. Y _____   a. Independent variable
                        b. Variable cost per unit
2. a _____   c. Dependent variable
                        d. Total fixed cost
3. b _____   e. Activity
                        f. Total cost
4. X _____

LO 4:   Describing the Methods of Separating Mixed Cost

4–51. Besides the engineering approach, this chapter discussed three methods of separating a mixed cost into its variable and fixed components.

REQUIRED:
Write a brief memo outlining the relative advantages and disadvantages of the high-low method, the scatter graph method, and regression analysis in estimating the variable and fixed portions of a mixed cost.

LO 4:   Describing the Methods of Separating Mixed Cost

4–52. Mr. Robinson, the director of Medical Diagnostics Clinic, is preparing a presentation to the clinic's board of directors about the fee charged for thallium stress tests. Part of the presentation will include information about the variable cost element and fixed costs associated with the tests. The accounting department has provided the director with a report which details the monthly costs associated with the thallium stress tests and the number of tests performed each month. Mr. Robinson is contemplating whether to use the scatter graph method, the high-low method, or regression analysis to separate the cost into its variable cost element and fixed cost. The director has asked your help in choosing an appropriate method.

REQUIRED:
Prepare a short report to Mr. Robinson providing insight into the strengths and weaknesses of the scatter graph method, the high-low method, and regression analysis. Your report should conclude with support for a final recommendation of one of the methods of separating mixed cost.

LO 1, 2, 4, and 5:   Analyzing a Situation Using Cost Behavior

4–53. Accents Furniture Company has been in business for two years. When the business began, Accents established a delivery department with a small fleet of trucks. The delivery department was designed to be able to handle the substantial future growth of the company. As expected, sales for the first two years of business were low and activity in the delivery department was minimal.

In an effort to control costs, Accents Furniture Company's store manager is considering a proposal from a delivery company to deliver the furniture sold by Accents for a flat fee of $30 per delivery.

The following information is available regarding the cost of operating Accents's delivery department during its first two years of business.

	2006	2007
Number of deliveries	600	700
Cost of operating the delivery department	$25,480	$26,480

Sales and the number of deliveries are expected to increase greatly in the coming years. For example, sales next year will require an estimated 1,250 deliveries, while in 2009, it is expected that 1,775 deliveries will be required.

Due to the high growth rate, the store manager is concerned that the delivery cost will grow out of hand unless the proposal is accepted. He states that the cost per delivery was about $42.47 ($25,480/600) in 2006 and $37.83 ($26,480/700) in 2007. Even at the lower cost of $37.83, it seems the company can save about $7.83 ($30.00–$37.83) per delivery. For 2009, the store manager believes the proposal can save the company about $13,898.25 (1,775 $\times$ $7.83).

REQUIRED:
Assume that you have been assigned to a group which has been formed to analyze the delivery cost of Accents Furniture Company. Your group should prepare a report and presentation that indicates the advantage or disadvantage of accepting the proposed delivery contract. Your report and presentation should not only include calculations to support your recommended course of action, but should also address the nonmonetary considerations of contracting with an outside source for delivery services.

LO 1, 2, 3, and 4: Addressing a Situation Using Cost Behavior Concepts

4–54. Mr. Reed is considering starting his own business. He has worked for a large corporation all his life and desires a change of pace. He is most interested in retail merchandising, but does not know what products his new business should sell. Mr. Reed is unsure about how to proceed with this major change in his life and has hired a consulting firm to help.

Assume that you have been assigned to the consulting group that will advise Mr. Reed.

REQUIRED:

Your group is to prepare a report that recommends a particular product line for Mr. Reed's new retail merchandising business. In addition, your report should recommend ways for Mr. Reed to gather information about the various costs associated with the merchandising business you have recommended. Finally, your report should explain how costs are classified as variable, fixed, and mixed costs, and why such classification by cost behavior is important.

LO 1, 2, and 4: Analyzing a Situation Using Cost Behavior

4–55. The Bowl-O-Mat operates a small chain of bowling alleys in southern Florida. Bowl-O-Mat's president, Al Palmer, is considering adding a supervised playground facility to each of the bowling alley properties. The playgrounds would require that a small addition be built onto each of the bowling alley buildings. Each playground would include a swing, a slide, climbing bars, and some other small-scale playground equipment. Each child would be charged an admission fee to use the facility. It is expected that parents will stay at the bowling alleys longer while their children are occupied in the playground area.

Mr. Palmer is interested in obtaining cost information relative to the proposed playground project. He understands that the more hours each playground area is open for business, the higher the cost of operating the playground will be. Beyond that, he knows nothing of cost behavior patterns.

REQUIRED:

Prepare a memorandum to Mr. Palmer that describes the following:
  a. The various variable, fixed, and mixed costs that are likely to be associated with the new playground facilities
  b. The concept of fixed costs, variable costs, and mixed costs
  c. Why an understanding of the methods available for estimating cost behavior patterns will help him to better plan and control his operations

Chapter 5

Business Decisions Using Cost Behavior

*C*laudia June is the owner of Upstart T-Shirt Shop, one of many souvenir shops located on Highway A1A in Daytona Beach, Florida. Upstart sold 3,000 T-shirts during 2007 (the company's first year of operation), and Claudia's accountant prepared the following multistep income statement for the year.

UPSTART T-SHIRT SHOP
Income Statement
For the Year Ended December 31, 2007

Sales		$36,000
Cost of Goods Sold		21,600
Gross Profit		$14,400
Operating Expense:		
Selling Expense	$9,500	
Administrative Expense	7,900	(17,400)
Operating Loss		$(3,000)

Frankly, Claudia was quite pleased with the results for 2007 because she did not expect the store to be profitable in its first year. As Claudia planned for 2008, she figured she needed to increase sales by only 625 T-shirts to break even for the year. Her reasoning was based on the fact that each T-shirt cost $7.20 and sold for $12, resulting in $4.80 gross profit on each T-shirt ($12.00 − $7.20 = $4.80). If the shop sold 3,625 T-shirts, it would earn a gross profit of $17,400 (3,625 × $4.80), which would be exactly enough to cover the selling and administrative expenses of $17,400. If Claudia met her sales goal, the store would break even in only its second year of operation.

As luck would have it, Upstart T-Shirt Shop sold exactly 3,625 T-shirts during the year ended December 31, 2008. Each T-shirt sold for exactly $12 and cost the company exactly

$7.20. Confident that the shop had broken even for the year, Claudia excitedly opened the envelope from her accountant and found the following multistep income statement for 2008.

UPSTART T-SHIRT SHOP
Income Statement
For the Year Ended December 31, 2008

Sales		$43,500
Cost of Goods Sold		26,100
Gross Profit		$17,400
Operating Expense:		
Selling Expense	$10,438	
Administrative Expense	8,897	(19,335)
Operating Loss		$(1,935)

Claudia was disappointed and discouraged when she saw an operating loss of $1,935 for the year. She rechecked the arithmetic and her assumptions about what it would take to break even for 2008 and could not understand why the store had an operating loss.

Claudia may not understand what happened, but after having studied Chapter 4 and its discussion of cost behavior, you should understand the problem. Claudia failed to consider that some costs are affected by changes in activity level and others are not. In this chapter, we explore cost-volume-profit analysis and see how business people use an understanding of this analytical technique to predict financial performance effectively. ■

LEARNING OBJECTIVES

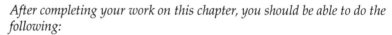

After completing your work on this chapter, you should be able to do the following:

1. Describe the differences between a functional income statement and a contribution income statement.
2. Determine per unit amounts for sales, variable cost, and the contribution margin.
3. Determine the contribution margin ratio and explain its importance as a management tool.
4. Prepare and analyze a contribution income statement for a merchandising firm.
5. Describe cost-volume-profit (CVP) analysis and explain its importance as a management tool.
6. Use CVP analysis to determine the amount of sales required to break even or to earn a targeted profit.
7. Use CVP to perform sensitivity analysis.

THE CONTRIBUTION INCOME STATEMENT

functional income statement An income statement that classifies cost by function (product cost and period cost).

contribution income statement An income statement that classifies cost by behavior (fixed cost and variable cost).

As discussed in Chapter 4, separating costs by means of cost behavior provides managers insight about forecasting cost at different levels of business activity. This valuable cost behavior information, however, is not presented in either the multi-step or the single-step income statement used for financial reporting. The traditional income statement prepared for external parties separates costs (expenses) as either product costs or period costs.

An income statement that separates product and period costs is called a **functional income statement.** Management accountants have developed a special income statement format for internal use that categorizes costs by behavior (fixed cost and variable cost) rather than by function (product cost and period cost). An income statement that classifies costs by behavior is a **contribution income statement.** Now, do not be alarmed, as this new format is no more complicated than the income statements you studied in earlier chapters. The main difference between the two is that the contribution income statements list variable costs first, followed by fixed costs. Note that the contribution income statement cannot be used for financial accounting information prepared for external decision makers; it is only used for internal decision-making purposes.

Purpose of the Contribution Income Statement

Let us return to the Upstart T-Shirt Shop example to see how a contribution income statement could have helped Claudia better predict the future profitability of her merchandising company. The two income statements presented for Upstart (2007 and 2008) were functional income statements. Upstart's 2007 functional income statement is reproduced as Exhibit 5–1.

Exhibit 5–1
Upstart's 2007 Functional Income Statement

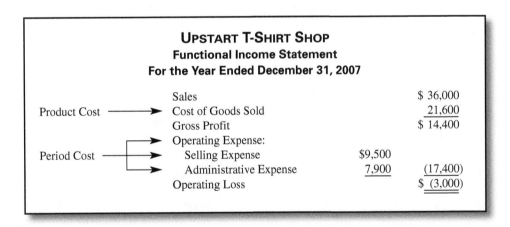

UPSTART T-SHIRT SHOP
Functional Income Statement
For the Year Ended December 31, 2007

	Sales		$ 36,000
Product Cost →	Cost of Goods Sold		21,600
	Gross Profit		$ 14,400
	Operating Expense:		
Period Cost →	Selling Expense	$9,500	
	Administrative Expense	7,900	(17,400)
	Operating Loss		$ (3,000)

We see that the cost information in Exhibit 5–1 is separated into product cost (cost of goods sold) and period cost (selling expenses and administrative expenses). Next we will examine how Claudia can convert her functional income statement into a contribution income statement.

First, Claudia needs additional information about the cost behavior of the expenses in Upstart's 2007 functional income statement. On request, Claudia's accountant provides the following information:

Cost of goods sold	All variable
Selling expense	$5,700 fixed, $3,800 variable
Administrative expense	$6,300 fixed, $1,600 variable

Discussion Question

5-1. With the cost behavior information just presented, can you help Claudia determine how much her profit will change if she sells 5,000 shirts in 2009? (Remember to look at the 2008 income statement shown at the beginning of the chapter.)

Now that she has Upstart's cost behavior information, Claudia can prepare a contribution income statement for 2007. The contribution income statement lists sales first, as does the functional income statement, with variable costs listed next. These costs are subtracted from sales to arrive at the contribution margin. **Contribution margin** is defined as the amount remaining after all variable costs have been deducted from sales revenue. The contribution margin is an important piece of information for managers, because it tells them how much of their company's original sales dollars remain after deduction of variable costs. This remaining portion of the sales dollars contributes to fixed costs and, once fixed costs have been covered, to profit.

Upstart's 2007 contribution income statement (through the contribution margin) is presented as Exhibit 5–2.

contribution margin The amount remaining after all variable costs have been deducted from sales revenue.

Exhibit 5–2
Upstart's Partial 2007 Contribution Income Statement

UPSTART T-SHIRT SHOP **Partial Contribution Income Statement** **For the Year Ended December 31, 2007**		
Sales		$36,000
Variable Cost:		
Cost of Goods Sold	$21,600	
Variable Selling Expense	3,800	
Variable Administrative Expense	1,600	
Total Variable Cost		(27,000)
Contribution Margin (Sales Less Total Variable Cost)		$ 9,000

Discussion Questions

5-2. Why is the gross margin found on the functional income statement different from the contribution margin found on the contribution income statement?

5-3. Why is the operating loss shown on Upstart's 2007 contribution income statement exactly the same as the operating loss shown on the company's 2007 functional income statement?

Finally, fixed costs are listed and subtracted from the contribution margin to arrive at operating income, as shown in Exhibit 5–3.

Like a functional income statement, the contribution income statement can be detailed or condensed depending on the needs of the information users. It can also

Exhibit 5–3
Upstart's Completed
2007 Contribution
Income Statement

UPSTART T-SHIRT SHOP
Contribution Income Statement
For the Year Ended December 31, 2007

Sales		$36,000
Variable Cost:		
Cost of Goods Sold	$21,600	
Variable Selling Expense	3,800	
Variable Administrative Expense	1,600	
Total Variable Cost		(27,000)
Contribution Margin (Sales Less Total Variable Cost)		$ 9,000
Fixed Cost:		
Fixed Selling Expense	$ 5,700	
Fixed Administrative Expense	6,300	
Total Fixed Cost		(12,000)
Operating Loss		$ (3,000)

Exhibit 5–4
Upstart's Condensed
2007 Contribution
Income Statement

UPSTART T-SHIRT SHOP
Contribution Income Statement
For the Year Ended December 31, 2007

	Total	Per Unit	Sales (%)
Sales in Units	3,000	1	
Sales	$36,000	$12.00	100
Variable Cost	(27,000)	(9.00)	(75)
Contribution Margin	$9,000	$ 3.00	25
Fixed Cost	(12,000)		
Operating Loss	$ (3,000)		

be prepared showing the per unit costs and percentage of sales calculations. A condensed version of Upstart's 2007 contribution income statement, including per unit and percentage of sales figures, is presented as Exhibit 5–4.

Throughout the rest of the chapter we will use a condensed version of the contribution income statement.

Looking at the per unit column in Exhibit 5–4, we note that the contribution margin per unit is $3. We calculate this by dividing the total contribution margin of $9,000 by the number of units sold—in this case 3,000 ($9,000 / 3,000 = $3). The $3 per unit contribution margin means that for every T-shirt sold, the sale generates $3 to contribute toward fixed costs. Then, once fixed costs have been covered, $3 per T-shirt sold contributes to profit. That is, if Upstart sells one more shirt for $12, then the $12 selling price less the $9 variable cost leaves $3. The contribution margin contributes toward fixed cost first, then to profits.

Note in the percentage column of Exhibit 5–4 that the contribution margin is 25 percent of sales. When the contribution margin is expressed as a percentage of sales, it is called the **contribution margin ratio.**

contribution margin ratio
The contribution margin expressed as a percentage of sales.

The contribution margin ratio is calculated by dividing the total contribution margin by total sales, or by dividing the per unit contribution margin by per unit selling price, as follows:

$$\frac{\text{Total Contribution Margin}}{\text{Total Sales}} = \text{Contribution Margin Ratio}$$

or

$$\frac{\text{Per Unit Contribution Margin}}{\text{Per Unit Selling Price}} = \text{Contribution Margin Ratio}$$

In the case of Upstart T-Shirt Shop, the calculations are as follows:

$$\frac{\$9,000}{\$36,000} = 25\%$$

or

$$\frac{\$3}{\$12} = 25\%$$

The contribution margin ratio is the same whether it is computed using total figures or per unit figures, because the contribution margin is based on sales minus only variable costs. Thus, the variable costs and contribution margin change in direct proportion to sales. This proportional relationship holds true whether we are using per unit amounts or amounts in total.

In our example, the 25 percent contribution margin ratio means 25 percent (or 25 cents) of each sales dollar is available to contribute toward fixed cost and profit.

Discussion Question

5-4. If Upstart's sales increase by $20,000, and the contribution margin ratio is 25%, by how much will profits increase?

The contribution income statement allows managers to see clearly the amounts of fixed and variable costs incurred by the company. Understanding which costs are variable and which are fixed is essential if managers are to reasonably predict future costs. More importantly, a solid understanding of the contribution income statement approach and the concept of the contribution margin and contribution margin ratio is the backbone of another important decision-making tool: cost-volume-profit analysis.

COST-VOLUME-PROFIT ANALYSIS

cost-volume-profit (CVP) analysis The analysis of the relationship between cost and volume and the effect of these relationships on profit.

Cost-volume-profit (CVP) analysis examines the relationships between cost and volume (the levels of sales), and the effect of those relationships on profit. In this section, we explore how managers can use CVP concepts to predict sales levels at which a firm will break even or attain target profits. CVP analysis is a useful tool for managers, business owners, and potential business owners for determining the profit potential of a new company or the profit impact of changes in selling price, cost, or volume on current businesses.

Thousands of businesses are started every day. Unfortunately, most of them fail a short time later, and the people who start these businesses suffer significant financial and emotional hardship. Such hardships might be avoided if new business owners used CVP analysis to evaluate the potential profit of their business ventures. With CVP analysis, a new business owner can discover potential disaster before starting the business, thereby preserving savings that could be used more productively elsewhere.

Breakeven

We begin our coverage of CVP analysis with a discussion of breakeven. **Breakeven** occurs when a company generates neither a profit nor a loss. The sales volume required to achieve breakeven is called the **break-even point.** Because most businesses exist to earn a profit, why would managers be interested in calculating a break-even point? In at least two situations this kind of information is valuable. First, the break-even point will show a company how far product sales can decline before the company will incur a loss. This information could provide the encouragement to continue in business, or may provide an early warning of impending business failure. Second, owners and managers may use break-even analysis when starting a business, just as Claudia did with the Upstart T-Shirt Shop. Recall that Upstart experienced a $3,000 operating loss in its first year of operation, but Claudia expected the loss because she understood most businesses are not profitable in their first year. Her break-even prediction for Upstart's second year, however, failed to allow for certain cost increases as sales increased. With our understanding of cost behavior and the contribution income statement, we can predict the level of sales that Upstart will need to break even for the year.

Let us look again at the 2007 contribution income statement for Upstart T-Shirt Shop, reproduced in Exhibit 5–5.

breakeven   Occurs when a company generates neither a profit nor a loss.

break-even point   The sales required to achieve breakeven. This can be expressed either in sales dollars or in the number of units sold.

Exhibit 5–5
Upstart's Condensed 2007 Contribution Income Statement

UPSTART T-SHIRT SHOP
Contribution Income Statement
For the Year Ended December 31, 2007

	Total	Per Unit	Sales (%)
Sales in Units	3,000	1	
Sales	$36,000	$12.00	100
Variable Cost	(27,000)	(9.00)	(75)
Contribution Margin	$9,000	$ 3.00	25
Fixed Cost	(12,000)		
Operating Loss	$ (3,000)		

Managers who use CVP analysis must apply simple formulas to obtain useful information. Understanding and applying these formulas during this course should be relatively simple, but remembering them when you are actually working as a manager may be difficult. To make these formulas easier to remember, we will relate them to the most basic math used in an income statement, beginning with sales minus cost equals profit. Next, recall that cost can be broken down into variable and fixed cost. We use this information to derive a basic CVP equation, as shown in Exhibit 5–6.

The basic equation for CVP analysis in Exhibit 5–6 requires that the costs be identified as fixed or variable, and that any mixed cost be separated into its fixed and variable components. In the examples that follow, we assume costs have been properly classified as fixed or variable.

Exhibit 5-6
Basic CVP Equation

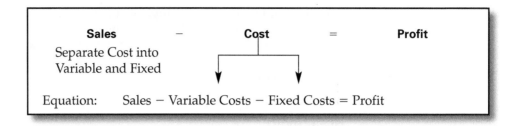

Managers can calculate the break-even point based either on units or on sales dollars. We will demonstrate the process in units first, and then in sales dollars.

Break-Even Point in Units To illustrate how to find the break-even point in units, we examine the Upstart T-Shirt Shop example. As shown in Exhibit 5–5, the selling price per T-shirt is $12, the variable cost is $9 per shirt, the contribution margin is $3 per T-shirt, and fixed costs total $12,000 per year. With this information, we can determine the number of T-shirts Upstart must sell to achieve a break-even point by dividing the contribution margin per unit into the total fixed cost, as shown in the following CVP formula:

CVP Formula 1—Break-Even Point in Units

$$\frac{\text{Total Fixed Cost}}{\text{Contribution Margin Per Unit}} = \text{Break-Even Point in Units}$$

Using the information from Upstart, we calculate the following:

$$\frac{\$12,000}{\$3} = 4,000 \text{ T-shirts}$$

By using this simple formula (and our knowledge of the cost behavior patterns associated with Upstart T-Shirt Shop), we see that if Upstart had sold exactly 4,000 T-shirts in 2008, the company would have broken even for the year. We can prove this fact if we use the equation from Exhibit 5–6 and the information from Upstart as follows:

Sales		Variable Costs		Fixed Costs		Profit
Sales	–	Variable Costs	–	Fixed Costs	=	Profit
(4,000 × $12)	–	(4,000 × $9)	–.	$12,000	=	Profit
$48,000	–	$36,000	–	$12,000	=	$ 0

We can also prove it by preparing a contribution income statement based on the results of our calculation, as shown in Exhibit 5–7.

Break-Even Point in Sales Dollars Because business performance is measured in total dollar sales and in the number of units of product sold, managers also

Exhibit 5-7
Upstart's Condensed 2008 Contribution Income Statement

UPSTART T-SHIRT SHOP
Projected Contribution Income Statement
For the Year Ended December 31, 2008

	Total	Per Unit	Sales (%)
Sales in Units	4,000	1	
Sales	$ 48,000	$12.00	100
Variable Cost	(36,000)	(9.00)	(75)
Contribution Margin	$ 12,000	$ 3.00	25
Fixed Cost	(12,000)		
Operating Income	$ -0-		

find it useful to have breakeven presented in both sales dollars and unit sales. To demonstrate the calculation of the break-even point in sales dollars, we once again use the information provided by Upstart T-Shirt Shop's contribution income statement in Exhibit 5–5.

When calculating the break-even point in sales dollars, we divide the contribution margin ratio into total fixed cost, as shown in the second of the CVP formulas.

CVP Formula 2—Break-Even Point in Sales Dollars

$$\frac{\text{Total Fixed Cost}}{\text{Contribution Margin Ratio}} = \text{Break-Even Point in Sales Dollars}$$

Using the information from Upstart's contribution income statement, we know that total fixed cost is $12,000 and the contribution margin ratio is 25 percent. The break-even point calculation is

$$\frac{\$12,000}{25\%} = \$48,000 \text{ Sales Dollars}$$

A quick review of the contribution income statement in Exhibit 5–7 shows that our calculation of $48,000 sales at the break-even point is correct.

We have examined the calculation of a break-even point in required units and in sales dollars. As stated earlier, however, companies are not in business to break even. Rather, they are usually interested in earning profits. In the next section, we discuss how the break-even calculations are modified to predict a company's profitability.

Predicting Profits Using CVP Analysis

Claudia June now knows that her T-shirt business must sell 4,000 T-shirts to break even, assuming of course that the T-shirt selling price and the variable and fixed costs remain unchanged. Claudia can also use CVP analysis to predict Upstart's profit for any given level of sales above the break-even point. Assume, for example, that Upstart expects to sell 7,500 shirts in 2009. Claudia can quickly predict the expected profit at that sales level by preparing a contribution income statement, such as that in Exhibit 5–8.

Exhibit 5–8
Upstart's Condensed 2009 Projected Contribution Income Statement

UPSTART T-SHIRT SHOP
Projected Contribution Income Statement
For the Year Ended December 31, 2009

	Total	Per Unit	Sales (%)
Sales in Units	7,500	1	
Sales	$ 90,000	$12.00	100
Variable Cost	(67,500)	(9.00)	(75)
Contribution Margin	$ 22,500	$ 3.00	25
Fixed Cost	(12,000)		
Operating Income	$ 10,500		

If we did not want to take the time required to construct an actual contribution income statement, we could calculate the same operating income using the following basic CVP equation shown in Exhibit 5–6.

Sales	−	Variable Costs	−	Fixed Costs	=	Profit
(7,500 × $12)	−	(7,500 × $9)	−	$12,000	=	Profit
$90,000	−	$67,500	−	$12,000	=	$10,500

The sales figure in this calculation is the number of T-shirts multiplied by the selling price per unit (7,500 × $12 = $90,000). Variable cost is the number of T-shirts sold multiplied by the variable cost per unit (7,500 × $9 = $67,500). The fixed cost of $12,000 remains the same in total. With these three figures in place, simple arithmetic gave us the expected profit of $10,500 if 7,500 T-shirts are sold.

Projecting Sales Needed to Meet Target Profits Using CVP Analysis

Using CVP analysis to project profits at a given level of sales is only one application of this technique. Next we explore how to use CVP analysis when price and cost information are known, and a manager wants to determine the sales required to meet a specific target profit objective. As with the break-even point, we can apply CVP analysis to determine the sales needed to meet target profits in either units or sales dollars.

Projecting Required Sales in Units Assume Claudia targets $27,000 as Upstart's profit for 2009. By making a simple addition to the formula we used to calculate the break-even point, Claudia can determine how many T-shirts Upstart must sell to earn that target profit. The modified formula is as follows:

CVP Formula 3—Unit Sales Required to Achieve Target Profits

$$\frac{\left(\text{Total Fixed Cost} + \text{Target Profit}\right)}{\text{Contribution Margin Per Unit}} = \text{Required Unit Sales}$$

Recall that the contribution margin is the amount available to contribute to covering fixed cost and profits. When considering the break-even point, we calculated the number of units required to cover the fixed cost. In our present discussion, we are looking for the number of units required not only to cover the fixed cost, but also to achieve a specific target profit. As shown in CVP formula 3, we simply add the target profit to the total fixed cost and then divide the sum by the contribution margin per unit. This equation will tell us how many units must be sold to cover all the fixed cost and to attain the target profit. Using the information from Upstart, the calculation is as follows:

$$\frac{\left(\$12,000 + \$27,000\right)}{\$3} = \text{Required Unit Sales}$$

or

$$\frac{\$39,000}{3} = 13,000 \text{ T-Shirts}$$

We see that with a fixed cost of $12,000 and a contribution margin per unit of $3, Upstart will need to sell 13,000 T-shirts to earn $27,000 profit.

Discussion Question

5-5. How would you prove to Claudia that 13,000 T-shirts must be sold to earn a $27,000 profit?

Projecting Required Sales in Dollars To demonstrate the calculation of the sales dollars required to attain target profits, we once again use the information provided by Upstart T-Shirt Shop's contribution income statement in Exhibit 5–5.

We use the contribution margin ratio as the denominator in the CVP formula, instead of the unit contribution margin, as follows:

CVP Formula 4—Sales Dollars Required to Achieve Target Profits

$$\frac{(\text{Total Fixed Cost} + \text{Target Profit})}{\text{Contribution Margin Ratio}} = \text{Required Sales Dollars}$$

With the information from Upstart, the calculation is as follows:

$$\frac{(\$12{,}000 + \$27{,}000)}{25\%} = \text{Required Sales Dollars}$$

or

$$\frac{\$39{,}000}{25\%} = \$156{,}000 \text{ in Sales}$$

Discussion Question

5-6. How would you prove to Claudia that sales must total $156,000 to earn a $27,000 profit?

In this section we introduced you to four cost-volume-profit formulas, as summarized in Exhibit 5–9.

Exhibit 5–9
Cost-Volume-Profit
Formulas

Formula	Calculation	Purpose
CVP Formula 1	$\dfrac{\text{Total Fixed Cost}}{\text{Contribution Margin Per Unit}}$	To determine the break-even point in units
CVP Formula 2	$\dfrac{\text{Total Fixed Cost}}{\text{Contribution Margin Ratio}}$	To determine the break-even point in sales dollars
CVP Formula 3	$\dfrac{(\text{Total Fixed Cost} + \text{Target Profit})}{\text{Contribution Margin Per Unit}}$	To determine the unit sales required to achieve a target profit
CVP Formula 4	$\dfrac{(\text{Total Fixed Cost} + \text{Target Profit})}{\text{Contribution Margin Ratio}}$	To determine the sales dollars required to achieve a target profit

These formulas are used daily by managers of manufacturing, merchandising, and service type companies as they attempt to predict the future performance of their firms. Regardless of the career you choose, if it involves business you will see these formulas again and will be using them much sooner than you might think.

Cost-Volume-Profit Graph

In addition to the calculations we have been studying, CVP analysis can also be depicted graphically. The graph used to present CVP analysis is similar to those used

Exhibit 5–10
CVP Graph—Upstart
T-Shirt Shop

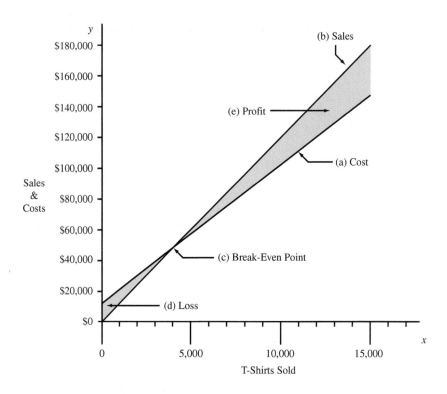

in the discussion of cost behavior in Chapter 4. A CVP graph for Upstart T-Shirt Shop is presented as Exhibit 5–10.

The main difference between the graph in Exhibit 5–10 and those in Chapter 4 is the graph in Exhibit 5–10 shows sales in addition to variable and fixed costs. The cost line (a) on the graph is exactly like those in Chapter 4. Note that this line intercepts the y-axis at $12,000, the total fixed cost for Upstart T-Shirt Shop. Thus, Upstart incurs $12,000 fixed cost even if the company sells no T-shirts. The cost line slopes upward at $9 for each T-shirt sold (variable cost).

Now consider the sales line (b) on the graph. If Upstart sells no T-shirts, there would obviously be no sales dollars, which explains why the sales line intercepts the y-axis at zero. The line slopes upward at $12 for every T-shirt sold. The point at which the cost line and the sales line cross (c) is Upstart's break-even point, which we know from our calculations in this chapter to be 4,000 T-shirts, or $48,000 in sales revenue. The loss area (d) on the graph and the profit area (e) represent a loss and profit, respectively, for Upstart. Thus, if Upstart sells fewer than 4,000 T-shirts, the company will experience a loss. If it sells more than 4,000 T-shirts, the company will earn a profit.

Discussion Question

5-7. Using the CVP graph in Exhibit 5–10, can you plot the level of sales (in units and dollars) where Upstart will earn a profit of

    a. $10,500?

    b. $27,000?

The CVP graph is a useful management tool. Although it should not take the place of the calculations we have demonstrated thus far in this chapter, it has a distinct advantage over the calculations in that it allows managers to view the entire cost-volume-profit picture. Claudia June can, for example, assess Upstart's profit potential at any level of business within the relevant range of activity.

Discussion Question

5-8. If Claudia is faced with competition from a new T-shirt shop in town, and is forced to lower her selling price to $11 per T-shirt, how much profit can she expect in 2008? (Assume that Claudia expects to sell 13,000 shirts and the cost information stays the same.)

To demonstrate the basics of CVP analysis, we have assumed that the selling price per unit, variable costs per unit, and total fixed cost all remained unchanged. Businesses, however, experience daily pressures that can cause each of these items to change. CVP analysis can adapt to any such change.

Now that we have covered the basics, we are ready to put CVP to perhaps its greatest use: sensitivity analysis.

Sensitivity Analysis—What If?

sensitivity analysis A technique used to determine the effect on cost-volume-profit when changes are made in the selling price, cost structure (variable and/or fixed), and volume used in the CVP calculations. Also called "what if" analysis.

Sensitivity analysis is a technique used to determine the effect on CVP when changes are made in the selling price, cost structure (variable and/or fixed), and volume used in the calculations. Sensitivity analysis is also called "what if?" analysis. Managers are often looking for answers to the following types of questions, in terms of the effect on projected profits: "What if we raised (or lowered) the selling price per unit?" "What if variable cost per unit increased (or decreased)?" and "What if fixed cost increased (or decreased)?" Sensitivity analysis can provide those answers.

One other item to note before we proceed with the discussion of sensitivity analysis is that we will be using only CVP formula 3 and CVP formula 4. Although sensitivity analysis can certainly be used to assess the effect of changes in selling price, variable cost, and fixed cost on breakeven, all our examples will include target profits.

To demonstrate how sensitivity analysis is used, we return to Claudia June and the Upstart T-Shirt Shop. Assume 2009 has now ended. Upstart's contribution income statement for the year is presented as Exhibit 5–11.

Exhibit 5-11
Upstart's Condensed 2009 Contribution Income Statement

UPSTART T-SHIRT SHOP
Contribution Income Statement
For the Year Ended December 31, 2009

	Total	Per Unit	Sales (%)
Sales in Units	11,286	1	
Sales	$135,432	$12.00	100
Variable Cost	(101,574)	(9.00)	(75)
Contribution Margin	$ 33,858	$ 3.00	25
Fixed Cost	(12,000)		
Operating Income	$ 21,858		

Claudia is quite pleased with the $21,858 profit Upstart earned in 2009 and is aiming for a target profit of $27,000 in 2010 (the same target profit as 2009). The problem is that a new T-shirt shop just opened three doors from Upstart. Claudia feels she must lower her selling price to $11 due to competitive pressure and wants to know how many T-shirts Upstart must now sell to attain the $27,000 target profit. Claudia can use CVP analysis to determine the required sales level to achieve a targeted profit even if she changes her selling price.

Change in Selling Price

If the selling price changes but variable cost does not, the number of units required to attain a target profit is determined using CVP formula 3 and a recalculated contribution margin based on the new selling price. In the case of Upstart T-Shirt Shop, the new contribution margin is $2 (new selling price of $11 − variable cost of $9). We now apply this contribution margin to the formula. (Remember, the fixed cost is unchanged.)

$$\frac{\left(\$12{,}000 + \$27{,}000\right)}{\$2} = \text{Required Unit Sales}$$

or

$$\frac{\$39{,}000}{\$2} = 19{,}500 \text{ T-shirts}$$

Our calculations show that with a lower selling price, as reflected in the revised contribution margin per unit, Upstart must sell 19,500 T-shirts to attain the target profit of $27,000.

Discussion Question

5-9. How would you prove to Claudia that 19,500 T-shirts must be sold to earn a $27,000 profit if she reduces the selling price per T-shirt from $12 to $11?

We can also calculate the sales dollars required to attain the target profit of $27,000. To do this, we first calculate a new contribution margin ratio and then use CVP formula 4 to determine the sales dollars needed to earn the target profit. The new contribution margin ratio is 18.182 percent (rounded), which is calculated by dividing the new selling price ($11) into the new contribution margin ($2). We now apply this new information to CVP formula 4.

$$\frac{\left(\$12{,}000 + \$27{,}000\right)}{18.182\% \text{ (rounded)}} = \text{Required Sales Dollars}$$

or

$$\frac{\$39{,}000}{18.182\% \text{ (rounded)}} = \$214{,}500 \text{ Sales Dollars (rounded)}$$

By applying the revised contribution margin ratio to CVP formula 4, we see that Upstart will need $214,498 in sales to achieve the target profit of $27,000.

Discussion Questions

5-10. How would you prove to Claudia that sales must total $214,498 to earn a $27,000 profit if she reduces the selling price per T-shirt from $12 to $11?

5-11. Why must we calculate a new contribution margin ratio when the per unit selling price changes?

5-12. Under what other circumstances must we calculate a new contribution margin ratio?

If Claudia reduces her selling price to $11, then Upstart must sell 19,500 T-shirts in 2010 to earn the target profit of $27,000. Claudia believes it would be impossible to sell that many shirts, so she begins to consider alternative ways to earn a $27,000 profit in a competitive environment.

Notice that Claudia was able to determine by CVP analysis that her business may be in trouble. The analysis itself, however, does nothing whatever to solve the problem—that is up to Claudia. Management accounting can provide the informational tools to help managers and business owners spot problems, but it is ultimately up to the manager or owner to make the decisions and solve the problems.

Discussion Question

5-13. If Claudia must lower her selling price to $11 per shirt to be competitive, and it would be impossible to sell 19,500 T-shirts, what are some of the alternatives she might consider to attain the $27,000 profit?

Change in Variable Cost and Fixed Cost

Alternatives to changing the selling price include changing variable cost or fixed cost. Because Claudia believes the selling price per T-shirt must be $11, either the variable cost per unit or the total fixed cost must be reduced. We start with an analysis of possible changes in variable cost.

First, we must analyze how Upstart determined its original variable cost. We determine per unit variable cost by dividing the total variable cost by the number of units sold. Recall from the earlier discussion and Exhibit 5–4 that Upstart sold 3,000 T-shirts during 2007, and total variable cost was $27,000. Therefore, the variable cost per unit was calculated as $9 ($27,000 variable cost / 3,000 units sold).

To analyze how a change in variable cost will affect the variable cost per unit of $9, we must look at the three components of per unit variable cost: the cost of each T-shirt, the variable selling expenses, and the variable administrative expenses. We need to know what portion of the $9 variable unit cost relates to each component. We can determine these portions by dividing the 3,000 units sold into each of the three cost components. We use 3,000 because that number of units caused these costs to be incurred. We find the cost of each variable cost component in the contribution income statement presented in Exhibit 5–3. The cost and per unit calculation for each component are presented in Exhibit 5–12.

Claudia does not believe any change can be made in either the variable selling expenses or the variable administrative expenses. Any possible reduction in variable cost, then, must be in the cost of the T-shirts. Our calculations in Exhibit 5–12 show that the per unit cost of each T-shirt is $7.20.

Exhibit 5–12
Analysis of Upstart's
Variable Cost
Components

	Total Cost	Units Sold		Unit Cost
Cost of Goods Sold (T-shirts)	$21,600 ÷	3,000	=	$7.20
Variable Selling Expenses	3,800 ÷	3,000	=	1.27
Variable Administrative Expenses	1,600 ÷	3,000	=	.53
Variable Cost	$27,000 Total			$9.00 Per Unit

Assume Claudia has contacted her shirt supplier which has agreed to lower its price from $7.20 to $6 per T-shirt. This reduction of $1.20 ($7.20 − $6.00 = $1.20) will reduce Upstart's variable cost from $9 per shirt to $7.80 per shirt ($9.00 − $1.20 = $7.80). The new contribution margin is $3.20 ($11 selling price − $7.80 variable cost = $3.20), and the new contribution margin ratio is 29.091 percent ($3.20 contribution margin / $11 selling price = 0.29091 or 29.091 percent rounded).

Now consider a change in Upstart's fixed cost. Recall that Upstart's total fixed cost is $12,000. Assume that Claudia has agreed to provide fellow businesswoman Susan Williams with space in her shop to sell bathing suits to Claudia's customers. Susan has agreed to pay Claudia $250 per month as rent on the space she will use. The $250 per month works out to be $3,000 per year ($250 per month × 12 months = $3,000). Thus, Upstart's total fixed cost decreases from $12,000 to $9,000.

With these proposed changes in Upstart T-Shirt Shop's variable cost and fixed cost, we can now do sensitivity analysis. Let us see what effect these changes would have on Claudia's company. To do this, again, we will use CVP formulas 3 and 4. We simply need to plug the new cost structures (variable and fixed) into the formulas as follows:

CVP Formula 3—Unit Sales Required to Achieve Target Profits

$$\frac{\left(\text{Total Fixed Cost} + \text{Target Profit}\right)}{\text{Contribution Margin Per Unit}} = \text{Required Unit Sales}$$

$$\frac{\left(\$9,000 + \$27,000\right)}{\$3.20} = 11,250 \text{ T-shirts}$$

By using CVP formula 3 (and Upstart's new variable and fixed cost structure), we found that if Upstart sells 11,250 T-shirts in 2010, the company will earn a profit of $27,000.

To calculate the sales dollars required to attain Upstart's target profit of $27,000, we use the company's new contribution ratio and CVP formula 4:

CVP Formula 4—Sales Dollars Required to Achieve Target Profits

$$\frac{\left(\text{Total Fixed Cost} + \text{Target Profit}\right)}{\text{Contribution Margin Ratio}} = \text{Required Sales Dollars}$$

$$\frac{\left(\$9,000 + \$27,000\right)}{29.091\% \text{ (rounded)}} = \$123,750 \text{ in Sales (rounded)}$$

With the changes in cost structure Claudia has negotiated, she will be able to earn $27,000 profit in 2010 even if her sales drop from 11,286 T-shirts (the 2009 sales level) to 11,250 T-shirts.

Discussion Questions

5-14. How would you prove to Claudia that sales must total $123,750 (11,250 T-shirts) to earn a $27,000 profit if she reduces the cost per T-shirt from $7.20 to $6 and reduces total fixed cost from $12,000 to $9,000?

5-15. If Claudia is more successful than anticipated in 2000 and sells 13,000 T-shirts by reducing her selling price to $11, and she also implements the variable and fixed cost changes described earlier, what will be Upstart's profits for 2010?

5-16. What complications do you foresee in using CVP analysis if Claudia begins selling a deluxe line of T-shirts that cost $11.50 each and sell for $17?

Multiple Products and CVP

In reality, most companies sell more than one product. Companies that sell multiple products often have information about total variable cost and total sales for a given income statement period, but have no one variable cost and selling price that can be easily determined and used for CVP.

When a company sells multiple products, managers may still use CVP analysis, but they must apply CVP formula 2 for break-even analysis and CVP formula 4 to determine the required level of sales to attain target profits. CVP formulas 1 and 3 are useless in a multiproduct situation if the various products sold have different unit contribution margins.

To demonstrate how managers use CVP analysis in a multiproduct situation when per unit information is unavailable, let us consider the example of Margaret's Frame Factory.

Margaret's Frame Factory makes and sells picture frames of various size and quality. Exhibit 5–13 presents Margaret's condensed contribution income statement for 2007.

There is a per unit variable cost and selling price for each of the frame models Margaret's manufactures and sells, but they are not included in Exhibit 5–13. All we have are the totals. The $185,000 contribution margin comes from the sale of several different products, each with its own contribution margin. The 37 percent contribution margin ratio, then, is an average contribution margin ratio based on the sales mix of these different products. Even with this limited information, however, we can use CVP analysis to both calculate a break-even point and predict target profits.

Exhibit 5–13
Margaret's Condensed 2007 Contribution Income Statement

MARGARET'S FRAME FACTORY
Contribution Income Statement
For the Year Ended December 31, 2007

	Total	% of Sales
Sales	$ 500,000	100%
Variable Cost	(315,000)	(63%)
Contribution Margin	$ 185,000	37%
Fixed Cost	(143,000)	
Operating Income	$ 42,000	

Break-Even Point in a Multiproduct Situation

To calculate the break-even point in a multiproduct situation, we use CVP formula 2.

CVP Formula 2—Break-Even Point in Sales Dollars

$$\frac{\text{Total Fixed Cost}}{\text{Contribution Margin Ratio}} = \text{Break-Even in Sales Dollars}$$

Using the information from Margaret's, the calculation is as follows:

$$\frac{\$143,000}{37\%} = \$386,486 \text{ Sales Dollars (rounded)}$$

We know that Margaret's is well above the break-even point because the company earned a profit of $42,000 in 2007. The break-even calculation is still valuable to company management because it reveals how far sales could decline before the company would experience a loss. In this example, sales could decline by $113,514 ($500,000 2007 sales − $386,486 break-even point = $113,514 decline) before Margaret's would experience a loss.

Projecting Required Sales in a Multiproduct Situation

Assume that Margaret's is interested in increasing profits to $80,000 in 2008. Based on the information contained in the 2007 contribution income statement presented in Exhibit 5–13, what would be the required sales to earn this target profit of $80,000? To find out, we use CVP formula 4:

CVP Formula 4—Sales Dollars Required to Achieve Target Profits

$$\frac{\left(\text{Total Fixed Cost} + \text{Target Profit}\right)}{\text{Contribution Margin Ratio}} = \text{Required Sales Dollars}$$

Using the information from Margaret's Frame Factory's contribution income statement, we know that total fixed cost is $143,000, the target profit is $80,000, and the contribution margin ratio is 37 percent. The calculation of the required sales dollars is as follows:

$$\frac{\$143,000 + \$80,000}{37\%} = \$602,703 \text{ in Sales (rounded)}$$

Our calculations indicate that Margaret's Frame Factory will need $602,703 in sales to attain a target profit of $80,000.

Discussion Question

5-17. How would you prove to Margaret's that sales must total $602,703 to earn an $80,000 profit?

We have demonstrated how CVP analysis can provide useful information about how changes in selling price, variable cost, and fixed cost affect a company's break-even point. Managers can also use CVP analysis to see what sales (in either units or dollars) the company needs to attain target profits.

CVP analysis is highly adaptable. It works equally well when managers are trying to determine profit potential, whether of a small segment of a large business or of an entire company. Before a company expands an existing business market or makes the decision to enter new markets, management should invest some time in gathering revenue and cost data, separating the cost-by-cost behavior, developing a contribution income statement, and applying these simple CVP procedures.

CVP Assumptions

CVP analysis is a great "what if?" management tool because it is used by managers to estimate a company's profit performance under a variety of different scenarios. It is, however, an estimation technique only, and the following assumptions are made when this type of analysis is used.

1. All costs can be classified as either fixed or variable. Implicit in this assumption is that a mixed cost can be separated into its fixed and variable components.
2. Fixed costs remain fixed throughout the relevant range of activity.
3. Variable cost per unit remains the same throughout the relevant range of activity.
4. Selling price per unit remains the same throughout the relevant range of activity.
5. The average contribution margin ratio in a multiproduct company remains the same throughout the range of activity.

These assumptions rarely, if ever, match reality. Market pressures, inflation, and a myriad of other factors cause revenue and cost structures to change in ways that place limitations on CVP analysis. Notwithstanding these limitations, however, CVP helps managers make more realistic estimates of future profit potential. It is a technique used every day by managers of large and small companies worldwide as they attempt to better manage their businesses.

SUMMARY

The functional income statement, which separates the costs shown into product cost and period cost, is limited in its usefulness to managers as they attempt to plan and control their operations. It does not take into account that some costs change as volume changes, and some do not. The contribution income statement is more useful to managers as a planning tool because it separates the costs presented into fixed costs and variable costs rather than into product costs and period costs.

An integral part of the contribution income statement is the contribution margin, which is the amount remaining after all variable costs have been deducted from sales revenue. When the contribution margin is presented as a percentage of sales, it is called the contribution margin ratio. Both the contribution margin and the contribution margin ratio are used in cost-volume-profit analysis.

Cost-volume-profit (CVP) analysis is the analysis of the relationships between cost and volume, and the effect of those relationships on profit. The first application of CVP analysis is the calculation of breakeven, which is the sales level resulting in neither a profit nor a loss. Breakeven can be calculated either in sales dollars or in the number of units of product that must be sold.

Cost-volume-profit analysis can also be used to calculate the sales level required to achieve a target profit. As was the case with breakeven, the sales level required to achieve a target profit can be calculated in both sales dollars and the number of units of product that must be sold.

Cost-volume-profit analysis can also be used to perform sensitivity analysis, which is a technique used to determine the effect on CVP when changes are made in the selling price, cost structure (variable and/or fixed), and volume used in the calculations.

Although CVP analysis is easier to perform in a single-product situation, it can also be used to calculate breakeven and sales required to achieve target profits in a multiple product situation.

REVIEW THE FACTS

A. What is the difference between a contribution income statement and a functional income statement?
B. What is the contribution margin?
C. What does the contribution margin "contribute toward"?
D. How does total contribution margin differ from contribution margin per unit?
E. What is the contribution margin ratio and how does it differ from the contribution margin?
F. What is cost-volume-profit (CVP) analysis?
G. What does the term *break-even point* mean?
H. In what ways does the calculation of the break-even point in units differ from the calculation of the break-even point in sales dollars?
I. How would you calculate the required sales in units to attain a target profit?
J. How would you calculate the required sales in dollars to attain a target profit?
K. What does the term *sensitivity analysis* mean in the context of CVP analysis?
L. What does the term *average contribution margin ratio* mean for a company that sells multiple products?
M. Which two of the four CVP formulas are used to calculate breakeven and sales required to attain target profits for a multiproduct company?
N. Why are two of the CVP formulas useless in a multiproduct situation when contribution margins for individual products are unknown?

APPLY WHAT YOU HAVE LEARNED

LO 4: Prepare a Contribution Income Statement

5–18. Fresh Baked Cookie Company sells cookies in a large shopping mall. The following multistep income statement was prepared for the year ending December 31, 2007.

FRESH BAKED COOKIE COMPANY
Income Statement
For the Year Ended December 31, 2007

Sales		$36,000
Cost of Goods Sold		4,000
Gross Profit		$32,000
Operating Expense:		
Selling Expense	$18,000	
Administrative Expense	10,000	28,000
Operating Income		$ 4,000

Cost of goods sold is a variable cost. Variable selling expense is $3,600 and fixed selling expense is $14,400; administrative expense is $500 variable and $9,500 fixed.

REQUIRED:

Prepare a contribution income statement for the Fresh Baked Cookie Company.

LO 4:   Prepare a Contribution Income Statement

5–19. The following multistep income statement was prepared for Stieferman's Bait Shop for the year ending December 31, 2007.

STIEFERMAN'S BAIT SHOP
Income Statement
For the Year Ended December 31, 2007

Sales		$98,000
Cost of Goods Sold		22,000
Gross Profit		$76,000
Operating Expense:		
Selling Expense	$27,000	
Administrative Expense	36,000	63,000
Operating Income		$13,000

Cost of goods sold is a variable cost. Variable selling expense is $8,100 and fixed selling expense is $18,900; administrative expense is $3,600 variable and $32,400 fixed.

REQUIRED:

Prepare a contribution income statement for Stieferman's Bait Shop.

LO 4:   Prepare a Contribution Income Statement

5–20. Quality Fishing Gear Company sells high-quality fiberglass fishing rods to retailers. The following multistep income statement was prepared for the year ending December 31, 2007.

QUALITY FISHING GEAR COMPANY
Income Statement
For the Year Ended December 31, 2007

Sales		$540,000
Cost of Goods Sold		360,000
Gross Profit		$180,000
Operating Expense:		
Selling Expense	$88,000	
Administrative Expense	72,000	160,000
Operating Income		$ 20,000

Cost of goods sold is a variable cost. Variable selling expense is $57,200 and fixed selling expense is $30,800; administrative expense is $18,000 variable and $54,000 fixed.

REQUIRED:

Prepare a contribution income statement for Quality Fishing Gear Company.

LO 4 & 6:   Prepare a Contribution Income Statement and Compute Breakeven

5–21. Shannon Davis is considering opening a greeting card shop in a local mall. Shannon contacted the mall manager and determined that the store rent will be $550 per month. In addition, he called the telephone company and based on the information from the telephone company representative, he estimates that the cost of telephone service will be about $95 per month. Based upon the size of the store, Shannon believes that cost of electricity will average about $200 per month. Shannon will be able to buy the greeting cards for $.50 each and plans to sell them for $2.00 each. Salaries are expected to be $1,200 per month regardless of the number of cards sold. Shannon estimates that other miscellaneous fixed costs will total $150 per month and miscellaneous variable cost will be $.10 per card. Shannon anticipates that he will be able to sell about 3,000 greeting cards per month. If Shannon opens the store, his first month of business will be November of 2007.

REQUIRED:
a. Prepare a projected contribution income statement for November 2007.
b. How many cards must be sold per hour to breakeven if the store is open from 10:00 a.m. to 9:00 p.m. each day, 6 days per week?
c. Compute the breakeven sales volume and sales dollars for the card shop.
d. How many cards must he sell to earn $40,000 per year? Is this feasible?

LO 4 & 6: Prepare a Contribution Income Statement and Compute Breakeven

5–22. Jon's Pretzel Stand is located in the Rose Bowl stadium and sells pretzels during sporting events. The following information is available:

- Selling price per pretzel $2.00
- Cost of each pretzel $0.25
- Cost of renting the pretzel stand is $12,000 per year.
- Instead of an hourly wage, Jon pays college students $0.20 per pretzel sold to run the pretzel stand.

REQUIRED:
a. Prepare a contribution income statement for 2007 assuming that 8,000 pretzels are sold.
b. Should Jon continue to operate the stand at the volume of 8,000 units? What are his opportunity costs?
c. Determine three different ways that Jon might increase his profits?

LO 4 & 6: Prepare a Contribution Income Statement and Compute Breakeven

5–23. The following information is available for Janet's Snow Cone Stand:

- Selling price per snow cone $2.00
- Cost of each snow cone $0.30
- Cost of renting the stand at a local flea market is $2,400 per year.
- Instead of an hourly wage, Jan pays college students $0.40 per snow cone sold.

REQUIRED:
a. Prepare a contribution income statement for 2007 assuming that 6,000 snow cones are sold.
b. Should Janet continue to operate the stand at the volume of 6,000 units? What are her opportunity costs?
c. Determine three different ways that Janet might increase her profits?

LO 4:   Prepare a Condensed Contribution Income Statement

5–24. The following is the contribution income statement for The Bevens Company:

THE BEVENS COMPANY
Contribution Income Statement
For the Year Ended December 31, 2008

Sales		$800,000
Variable Cost:		
Cost of Goods Sold	$420,000	
Variable Selling Expense	75,000	
Variable Administrative Expense	33,000	
Total Variable Cost		528,000
Contribution Margin		$272,000
Fixed Cost:		
Fixed Selling Expense	$128,000	
Fixed Administrative Expense	53,000	
Total Fixed Cost		181,000
Operating Income		$ 91,000

REQUIRED:
Based on the contribution income statement for The Bevens Company, prepare a condensed contribution income statement.

LO 1:   Prepare a Multistep Income Statement

5–25. Refer to the information presented in problem 5–24.

REQUIRED:
Prepare a multi-step income statement for the Bevens Company.

LO 4:   Prepare a Condensed Contribution Income Statement

5–26. Following is the contribution income statement for The Heidi Company:

THE HEIDI COMPANY
Contribution Income Statement
For the Year Ended December 31, 2008

Sales		$4,800,000
Variable Cost:		
Cost of Goods Sold	$2,320,000	
Variable Selling Expense	265,000	
Variable Administrative Expense	484,000	
Total Variable Cost		3,069,000
Contribution Margin		$1,731,000
Fixed Cost:		
Fixed Selling Expense	$ 648,000	
Fixed Administrative Expense	973,000	
Total Fixed Cost		1,621,000
Operating Income		$ 110,000

REQUIRED:
Based on The Heidi Company's contribution income statement, prepare a condensed contribution income statement.

LO 1:   Prepare a Multistep Income Statement

5–27. Refer to the information presented in problem 5–26.

REQUIRED:

Prepare a multi-step income statement for The Heidi Company.

LO 4:   Prepare a Condensed Contribution Income Statement

5–28. The following is the contribution income statement for Carl's Athletic Shop:

CARL'S ATHLETIC SHOP
Contribution Income Statement
For the Year Ended December 31, 2008

Sales		$422,000
Variable Cost:		
Cost of Goods Sold	$205,000	
Variable Selling Expense	55,000	
Variable Administrative Expense	22,000	
Total Variable Cost		282,000
Contribution Margin		$140,000
Fixed Cost:		
Fixed Selling Expense	$ 75,000	
Fixed Administrative Expense	34,000	
Total Fixed Cost		109,000
Operating Income		$ 31,000

REQUIRED:

Based on this contribution income statement, prepare a condensed contribution income statement for Carl's Athletic Shop.

LO 1:   Prepare a Multistep Income Statement

5–29. Refer to the information presented in problem 5–28.

REQUIRED:

Prepare a multi-step income statement for Carl's Athletic Shop.

LO 4:   Prepare a Contribution Income Statement

5–30. Paradise Manufacturing makes weight-lifting equipment. During 2007, the following costs were incurred:

	Amount	Percent Fixed	Percent Variable
Direct material	$680,000	–	100
Direct labor	420,000	–	100
Variable manufacturing overhead	130,000	–	100
Fixed manufacturing overhead	900,000	100	–
Selling cost	300,000	20	80
Administrative cost	220,000	10	90

Sales for 2007 totaled $2,780,000 and there were no beginning or ending inventories.

REQUIRED:

Prepare a contribution income statement for the year ended December 31, 2008.

LO 4:   Prepare a Contribution Income Statement

5–31. The following information is available for Nicole's Toy Manufacturing Company for 2007:

	Amount	Percent Fixed	Percent Variable
Direct material	$440,000	-	100
Direct labor	90,000	-	100
Variable manufacturing overhead	70,000	-	100
Fixed manufacturing overhead	800,000	100	-
Selling cost	950,000	45	55
Administrative cost	570,000	85	15

Sales for 2007 totaled $3,164,000 and there were no beginning or ending inventories.

REQUIRED:
Prepare a contribution income statement for the year ended December 31, 2007.

LO 4:   Prepare a Contribution Income Statement

5–32. The following information is available for Rick's Watch Company for 2007:

	Amount	Percent Fixed	Percent Variable
Direct material	$534,000	-	100
Direct labor	129,000	-	100
Variable manufacturing overhead	397,000	-	100
Fixed manufacturing overhead	998,000	100	-
Selling cost	196,000	33	67
Administrative cost	243,000	78	22

Sales for 2007 totaled $2,745,000 and there were no beginning or ending inventories.

REQUIRED:
Prepare a contribution income statement for the year ended December 31, 2007.

LO 4:   Prepare a Contribution Income Statement

5–33. Alumacraft Manufacturing makes aluminum serving carts for use in commercial jetliners. During 2008, the following costs were incurred:

	Amount	Percent Fixed	Percent Variable
Direct material	$2,600,000	-	100
Direct labor	1,820,000	-	100
Variable manufacturing overhead	540,000	-	100
Fixed manufacturing overhead	1,900,000	100	-
Selling cost	380,000	15	85
Administrative cost	230,000	5	95

Sales for 2008 totaled $7,900,000 and there were no beginning or ending inventories.

REQUIRED:
Prepare a contribution income statement for the year ended December 31, 2008.

LO 6: Determine Breakeven and Sales Required to Earn Target Profit Using Per Unit Amounts

5–34. The following information is available for Medical Testing Corporation:

Amount charged for each test performed	$ 90
Annual fixed cost	200,000
Variable cost per test	25

REQUIRED:
a. Calculate how many tests Medical Testing must perform each year to break even.
b. Calculate how many tests Medical Testing must perform each year to earn a profit of $25,000.
c. Calculate how many test per hour must be performed to breakeven.
d. Assuming that each test takes 15 minutes, what is the potential annual income of this business with one employee working eight hours a day, 50 weeks per year?
e. What is the source of potential customers and how would you promote the business?

LO 6: Determine Breakeven and Sales Required to Earn Target Profit Using Per Unit Amounts

5–35. The following information is available for Dottie's Donut Shop.

Amount charged per dozen doughnuts	$ 0.99
Annual fixed cost	385,000.00
Variable cost per dozen doughnuts	0.22

REQUIRED:
a. Calculate how many dozen doughnuts Dottie must sell each year to break even.
b. Calculate how many dozen doughnuts Dottie must sell each year to earn a profit of $35,000.

LO 6: Determine Breakeven and Sales Required to Earn Target Profit Using Per Unit Amounts

5–36. Jim is considering starting a small company to paint driveways. The following information is available.

Amount charged per square yard painted	$ 5
Annual fixed cost	3,000
Variable cost per square yard painted	2

REQUIRED:
a. Calculate how many square yards of driveway Jim must paint each year to break even.
b. Calculate how many square yards of driveway Jim must paint each year to earn a profit of $5,000.

LO 6: Determine Breakeven and Sales Required to Earn Target Profit Using Per Unit Amounts

5–37. Carbonnel Calendar Company is considering adding a new calendar design to their line. The following information is available.

Selling price	$ 3.97
Additional annual fixed cost	4,558.00
Variable cost per calendar	3.11

REQUIRED:

a. Calculate how many calendars must be sold each year to break even.

b. Calculate how many calendars must be sold each year to earn a profit of $2,580.

LO 3 & 6: Use Ratios to Determine Breakeven and Sales Required to Earn Target Profit

5–38. Melissa Valdez is planning to expand her clothing business by opening another store. In planning for the new store, Melissa believes that selling prices and costs of the various merchandise sold will be similar to that of the existing store. In fact, she thinks that variable and fixed costs for the new store will be similar to that of the existing store, except that rent for the new store will be $300 per month more than the rent paid for the existing store.

The following information is available for the existing store for the year ended December 31, 2007:

Sales	$200,000
Variable cost	130,000
Fixed cost	48,000

REQUIRED:

a. Determine the sales required for the new store to break even.

b. Determine the sales required for the new store to earn a profit of $20,000 per year. (Hint: Keep in mind that the $300 increase in rent is a monthly amount and the fixed cost of $48,000 is an annual amount.)

LO 3 & 6: Use Ratios to Determine Breakeven and Sales Required to Earn Target Profit

5–39. Emergency Medical, Inc. is considering opening a new emergency care facility. The fees charged and costs of the new facility will be similar to that of the existing facility. The only exception is that the annual fixed cost for the new facility is expected to be $75,000 more than that of the existing facility.

The following information is available for Emergency Medical's existing facility for 2007:

Revenue	$1,250,000
Variable cost	600,000
Fixed cost	420,000

REQUIRED:

a. Determine the revenues required for the new emergency care facility to break even.

b. Determine the revenues required for the new emergency care facility to earn a profit of $120,000 per year.

LO 3 & 6: Use Ratios to Determine Breakeven and Sales Required to Earn Target Profit

5–40. Wendt Industries is considering opening a second school supply store. The annual fixed cost of the new store is expected to be $225,000 per year. The following information is available for Wendt's first school supply store for 2007.

Revenue	$3,650,000
Variable cost	1,387,000

REQUIRED:

a. Based on this information, what is the required revenue for the second store to break even?

b. Based on this information, what is the required revenue for the second store to earn a profit of $125,000?

LO 2, 4, & 6: Use Per Unit Amounts to Determine Breakeven and Sales Required to Earn Target Profit and Prepare a Contribution Income Statement

5–41. Richard Davenport owns a clothing store and is considering renting a soda vending machine for his store. He can rent the soda machine for $125 per month. Richard would supply the soda for the machine which he can buy for $3 per twelve pack. Richard plans to charge $0.75 per can.

REQUIRED:

a. List the fixed costs for renting and stocking the soda machine.
b. List the variable costs for renting and stocking the soda machine.
c. Calculate the contribution margin per can of soda.
d. (1) Calculate how many cans of soda Richard must sell each month to break even.
　　(2) Prepare a contribution income statement that proves the answer you just calculated.
e. (1) Calculate how many cans of soda Richard must sell each month to earn a profit of $50.
　　(2) Prepare a contribution income statement that proves your answer to the previous requirement.

LO 2, 4, & 6: Use Per Unit Amounts to Determine Breakeven and Sales Required to Earn Target Profit and Prepare a Contribution Income Statement

5–42. Erich Traebeecke owns the Kenpo Karate School in Miami. He is considering renting a candy vending machine for his school lobby. He can rent the candy machine for $90 per month. Erich would supply the candy bars for the machine. He can buy a box of six candy bars for $1 per box. Erich plans to sell each candy bar for $0.50.

REQUIRED:

a. List the fixed costs of renting and stocking the candy machine.
b. List the variable costs of renting and stocking the candy machine.

c. Calculate the contribution margin per candy bar.

d. **(1)** Calculate how many candy bars must be sold each month to break even.

   (2) Prepare a contribution income statement that proves the answer you just calculated.

e. **(1)** Calculate how many candy bars must be sold each month to earn a profit of $180.

   (2) Prepare a contribution income statement that proves your answer to the previous requirement.

LO 2, 4, and 6: Use Per Unit Amounts to Determine Breakeven and Sales Required to Earn Target Profit and Prepare a Contribution Income Statement

5–43. Monica Llobet owns Monica's School of Dance. She is considering installing a cappuccino machine in the school's dance studio. Monica can rent the cappuccino machine for $48.88 per month. Coffee and supplies would cost about $.40 per cup of cappuccino. Monica plans to sell each cup of cappuccino for $3.

REQUIRED:

a. List the fixed costs of renting and stocking the cappuccino machine.

b. List the variable costs of renting and stocking the cappuccino machine.

c. Calculate the contribution margin per cup of cappuccino.

d. **(1)** Calculate how many cups of cappuccino must be sold each month to break even.

   (2) Prepare a contribution income statement that proves the answer you just calculated.

e. **(1)** Calculate how many cups of cappuccino must be sold each month to earn a profit of $200. (Round your answer to the nearest unit.)

   (2) Prepare a contribution income statement that proves your answer to the previous requirement.

LO 2 & 6: Use Per Unit Amounts to Determine Breakeven and Sales Required to Earn Target Profit

5–44. Alberto Pons is interested in selling pin-on buttons at school pep rallies. The button machine will cost $200, and the material to produce each button costs $0.15. In exchange for the right to sell the buttons, Alberto has agreed to donate $300 per year and $0.20 per button to the school's booster club. Alberto plans to sell the buttons for $2 each and to operate the service for four years. By then it will be time to graduate, and the button machine will be worn out.

REQUIRED:

a. Assuming the button machine will be able to produce buttons for four years, calculate the cost per year for the button machine.

b. Calculate the total fixed cost per year for Alberto's button business.

c. Calculate the variable cost per button.

d. Calculate the annual break-even point
   (1) in units.
   (2) in dollars.

e. Calculate how many buttons must be sold to earn an annual profit of $1,200.

f. Calculate the sales in dollars required to earn an annual profit of $1,200.

LO 2 & 6: Use Per Unit Amounts to Determine Breakeven and Sales Required to Earn Target Profit

5–45. Betty Lopez is interested in setting up a stand to sell mylar helium balloons at a local roller rink. The stand would cost $250, and the material for each balloon would cost $0.75. In exchange for the right to sell the balloons, Betty has agreed to pay $500 per year and $0.50 per balloon to the roller rink's owner. Betty plans to sell the balloons $3 each. Betty thinks the stand will last four years.

REQUIRED:

a. Assuming the balloon stand has an estimated useful life of four years, with no salvage value, calculate the cost per year for the balloon stand.
b. Calculate the total fixed cost per year for Betty's balloon business.
c. Calculate the variable cost per balloon.
d. Calculate the annual break-even point
   (1) in units.
   (2) in dollars.
e. Calculate how many balloons must be sold to earn an annual profit of $2,000.
f. Calculate the sales in dollars required to earn an annual profit of $2,000.

LO 2 & 6: Use Per Unit Amounts to Determine Breakeven and Sales Required to Earn Target Profit

5–46. Bill Smith is interested in selling ice cream bars at school events. The vendor stand will cost $800, and the ice cream bars cost $0.65. In exchange for the right to sell the ice cream bars, Bill has agreed to donate $600 per year and $0.25 per ice cream bar to the school's booster club. Bill plans to sell the ice cream bars for $2.00 each. Bill intends to sell the ice cream bars and run the stand for four years. By then it will be time to graduate, and the vendor stand will be worn out.

REQUIRED:

a. Assuming the vendor stand can be used for four years, calculate the cost per year for the vendor stand.
b. Calculate the total fixed cost per year for Bill's ice cream business.
c. Calculate the variable cost per ice cream bar.
d. Calculate the annual break-even point.
   (1) in units.
   (2) in dollars.
e. Calculate how many ice cream bars must be sold to earn an annual profit of $3,000.
f. Calculate the sales in dollars required to earn an annual profit of $3,000.
g. Calculate Bill's profit if sales were $8,000 for this year.

LO 3 & 6: Determine the Contribution Margin Ratio and Determine Breakeven and Sales Required to Earn Target Profit

5–47. Amanda is considering opening a gift shop. She has collected the following information:

Monthly rent	$2,800
Monthly sales salaries	1,200

In addition to the sales salaries, Amanda intends to pay sales commissions of 5% of sales to her sales staff. The cost of the merchandise sold is expected to be 40% of sales.

REQUIRED:

a. Determine the following:
   (1) Amanda's break-even point in monthly sales dollars
   (2) The monthly sales dollars required to earn a profit of $2,000 per month
   (3) Amanda's break-even point if she is able to reduce rent by $200
b. Assume that Amanda has negotiated a 10% discount on all merchandise purchases. The new cost of merchandise will not change the selling price of product. Determine the following:
   (1) The new contribution margin ratio
   (2) The new break-even point in monthly sales dollars
   (3) The new sales volume needed to earn a profit of $2,000 per month.

LO 3 & 6: Determine the Contribution Margin Ratio and Determine Breakeven and Sales Required to Earn Target Profit

5–48. Nicole is considering opening a bookstore. She has collected the following information:

Monthly rent	$3,286
Monthly sales salaries	4,200

In addition to the sales salaries, Nicole intends to pay sales commissions of 10% of sales to her sales staff. The cost of the merchandise sold is expected to be 30% of sales.

REQUIRED:

a. Determine the following:
   (1) Nicole's break-even point in monthly sales dollars
   (2) The monthly sales dollars required to earn a profit of $1,500 per month
   (3) Nicole's break-even point if she is able to reduce rent by $300
b. Assume that Nicole has negotiated a 5% discount on all merchandise purchases. The new cost of merchandise will not change the selling price of product. Determine the following:
   (1) The new contribution margin ratio
   (2) The new break-even point in monthly sales dollars
   (3) The new sales volume needed to earn a profit of $1,500 per month.

LO 2 & 6: Use Per Unit Amounts to Determine Breakeven and Sales Required to Earn Target Profit

5–49. Clarice is considering buying a DVD rental business. If she finances the entire purchase price, the payments will be $2,900 per month. Store rent would be $2,000 per month and cost of sales clerks, replacement DVDs, and other expenses would be $1,200 per month. Clarice plans to rent the DVDs for $2 each.

REQUIRED:

a. Calculate the variable cost (if any) per tape rental.
b. Calculate the total fixed cost per month.
c. Determine how many tapes Clarice must rent each month to break even.
d. Determine how many tapes Clarice must rent each month to earn a profit of $2,000 per month.

LO 3 & 6: Determine the Contribution Margin Ratio and Determine Breakeven and Sales Required to Earn Target Profit

5–50. Margaret Pitman is considering opening a gift shop. She has collected the following information:

Monthly rent	$1,800
Monthly sales salaries	1,200

The cost of the merchandise sold is expected to be 55% of sales.

REQUIRED:
a. What is the annual rent cost?
b. What is the annual sales salaries cost?
c. What is the contribution margin ratio?
d. What is the break-even point in dollars?
e. Determine the amount of sales needed to earn a profit of $24,000 for the year.

LO 3 & 6: Determine the Contribution Margin Ratio and Determine Breakeven and Sales Required to Earn Target Profit

5–51. Sara Foster is considering opening a frame shop. She has collected the following information:

Monthly rent	$ 600
Monthly sales salaries	1,100

The cost of the merchandise sold is expected to be 45% of sales.

REQUIRED:
a. What is the annual rent cost?
b. What is the annual sales salaries cost?
c. What is the contribution margin ratio?
d. What is the break-even point in dollars?
e. Determine the amount of sales needed to earn a profit of $18,000 for the year.

LO 3 & 6: Determine the Contribution Margin Ratio and Determine Breakeven and Sales Required to Earn Target Profit

5–52. Sonja Deavers is considering opening a beauty supply store. She has collected the following information:

Monthly rent	$3,400
Monthly sales salaries	2,800

The cost of the merchandise sold is expected to be 68% of sales.

REQUIRED:
a. What is the annual rent cost?
b. What is the annual sales salaries cost?
c. What is the contribution margin ratio?
d. What is the break-even point in dollars?
e. Determine the amount of sales needed to earn a profit of $36,000 for the year.

LO 3 & 6:   Determine the Contribution Margin Ratio and Determine Breakeven and Sales Required to Earn Target Profit

5–53. Lola Jolldashi is considering opening a music store. She has collected the following information:

Monthly rent	$1,400
Monthly sales salaries	1,700

The cost of the merchandise sold is expected to be 52% of sales.

REQUIRED:
a. What is the annual rent cost?
b. What is the annual sales salaries cost?
c. What is the contribution margin ratio?
d. What is the break-even point in dollars?
e. Determine the amount of sales needed to earn a profit of $40,000 for the year.

LO 2, 3, 4, & 5:   Analyze a Situation Using CVP

5–54. Quality Instrument Company manufactures various industrial thermometers. Last year the company sold 600 model QI-22 thermometers for $129 each. Managers are concerned that the profits from the QI-22 were only $7,740 last year. Fixed costs for this product are $50,000 per year. In an effort to increase profits, the company raised the price of the QI-22 to $148. Based on annual sales of 600 units, managers are confident that profits from the QI-22 will be increased to $19,140 next year.

The sales manager is concerned about the price increase. He believes the company should move a little slower in making the pricing decision and has suggested that a group be formed to explore the ramifications of such a pricing move.

REQUIRED:
Assume that you have been assigned to the group who will evaluate the proposed price change. The group is to create a report discussing the various ramifications of the price increase including its effect on projected sales and profits. Your report should make recommendations that are supported by calculations similar to those found in this chapter.

LO 2, 3, 4, & 5:   Analyze a Situation Using CVP

5–55. Reuben Steinman's Sliding Glass Door Company manufactured and sold 1,000 model SD4896 doors for $88 each. Managers are concerned that the profits from the SD4896 doors were only $8,000 last year. In an effort to increase profits, the company raised the price of the SD4896 to $106. Based on annual sales of 1,000 units, managers are confident that profits from the SD4896 will increase to $26,000 next year. Fixed costs of $40,000 are allocated to the SD4896 based on the number of units produced.

The sales manager is concerned about the price increase. He believes the company should move a little slower in making the pricing decision and has suggested that a group be formed to explore the ramifications of such a pricing move.

REQUIRED:

Assume that you have been assigned to the group who will evaluate the proposed price change. The group is to create a report discussing the various ramifications of the price increase including its effect on projected sales and profits. Your report should make recommendations that are supported by calculations similar to those found in this chapter.

LO 2, 3, 4, & 5: Analyze a Situation Using CVP

5–56. Carol Juriet is considering the purchase of a hot dog vending cart to sell hot dogs in a busy parking lot. The city of Daytona Beach requires that the cart be licensed at a cost of $500 per year.

REQUIRED:

a. (1) How would Carol determine the cost to rent a small space in the parking lot to operate the hot dog cart?
 (2) How much do you think the monthly rent would be?
 (3) How much do you think the hourly wage would be for an employee to operate the stand?
 (4) How many hours per day do you think the stand should be open?
 (5) Based on your answers to 3 and 4, what would you estimate monthly wage cost to be for the hot dog stand?
 (6) How much do you think Carol should charge for each hot dog?
b. Answer the following questions using your answers to question 1.
 (1) What is the variable cost per hot dog?
 (2) What is the monthly fixed cost for operating the hot dog stand?
 (3) What is the contribution margin per hot dog?
 (4) What is the contribution ratio?
 (5) What is the variable cost ratio?
 (6) a) How many hot dogs must Carol sell each month to break even?
 b) Prepare a contribution income statement which proves your answer.
 (7) a) How many hot dogs must Carol sell each month to earn a profit of $300?
 b) Prepare a contribution income statement that proves your answer.

Chapter 6

Making Decisions Using Relevant Information

F inancial accounting information provided to external decision makers must be relevant to be useful. Not surprisingly, management accounting information provided to internal decision makers must also possess the characteristic of relevance. It is critically important that managers make their decisions based on relevant information and that they disregard all irrelevant information. To be relevant, the information must be pertinent to the decision at hand. In accounting, **relevant costing** is the process of determining which dollar inflows and outflows pertain to a particular management decision.

Determining which costs are relevant is not always an easy job. For instance, consider an actual example about a couple that went to Disney World with their three-year-old daughter, Jessica. The family stayed at a Disney hotel to be close to the Disney attractions, and to take advantage of the hotel's staff of baby-sitters. The baby-sitting service required payment of a 4-hour minimum at $11 per hour, or $44. Users must cancel 3 hours in advance to avoid the $44 minimum fee. Jessica's parents planned to take her to the Magic Kingdom early in the day and then leave her with a sitter in the late afternoon while they visited EPCOT on their own.

Jessica and her parents went to Disney's Magic Kingdom as they had planned and were having a wonderful time. As the day progressed, Jessica enjoyed the amusement park so much that Jessica's parents were having second thoughts about leaving her with the sitter. They had to make a decision: Should they take Jessica to EPCOT or leave her with the sitter as planned?

relevant costing The process of determining which dollar inflows and outflows pertain to a particular management decision.

Because the family's admission tickets permitted them to enter all the Disney parks, the main issue was the minimum $44 charge for the sitter, because it was too late to cancel. As Jessica's parents discussed the pros and cons of each alternative, they realized the $44 charge would have to be paid whether they took Jessica to EPCOT or not. The baby-sitter's fee, therefore, was an irrelevant cost in this decision, because Jessica's parents would have to pay the baby-sitting fee no matter which alternative they chose. Once Jessica's parents determined that the fee was irrelevant, they dismissed the sitter and Jessica was off to EPCOT with them.

In business, the issue of what is relevant often confuses even the most seasoned business executive. To make the best possible decisions, decision makers must learn to consider only relevant information. ■

LEARNING OBJECTIVES

After completing your work on this chapter, you should be able to do the following:

1. Identify the characteristics of a relevant cost.
2. Explain why sunk costs and costs that do not differ between alternatives are irrelevant costs.
3. Describe the qualitative factors that should be considered when making a business decision.
4. Use accounting information and determine the relevant cost of various decisions.
5. Explain the effects of fixed costs and opportunity costs on outsourcing decisions.

RELEVANT COSTS

You may wonder why an entire chapter of this text is devoted to determining which costs are relevant. Isn't it understood that decision makers should disregard superfluous information and concentrate on the facts that relate to the decision at hand? Yes, but with so many cost considerations to muddy the water, determining what information is relevant is not always as easy as it might seem.

relevant cost A dollar inflow or outflow that pertains to a particular management decision in that it has a bearing on which decision alternative is preferable.

A **relevant cost** is a cost that is pertinent to a particular decision in that it has a bearing on which decision alternative is preferable. A relevant cost possesses two important characteristics: (1) The cost must be a future cost, and (2) the cost must differ between decision alternatives.

sunk cost A past cost that cannot be changed by current or future actions.

A relevant cost must be a future cost because current decisions can have no effect on past expenditures. Expenditures that have already occurred are called **sunk costs** and they cannot be changed by current or future actions. Because sunk costs are unaffected by current decisions, they are irrelevant and should not be considered when evaluating current decision alternatives. For example, if your firm was deciding whether to replace an old printing press with a new, labor-saving model, the cost of the old press would be irrelevant. Why? The firm already bought the old press. The purchase of the new printing press would not lessen or change the amount paid for the old press. Whether the company purchases the new press or not, the cost of the old press is a sunk cost: Nothing we can do now can change it. Sunk costs include both amounts paid in the past and past commitments to pay. That is, once there is a binding commitment to pay cash or otherwise transfer resources, the cost associated with that commitment is a sunk cost.

A relevant cost must differ between decision alternatives. If a cost remains the same regardless of the alternative we choose, it is irrelevant. Again, focus on the decision to buy a new printing press or to keep the old one. If the new printing press will use the same quantity and type of ink as the old one, the cost of ink is irrelevant no matter how large the dollar figure.

Discussion Questions

6-1. Refer back to the decision faced by Jessica's parents in Disney World. Which criteria of relevance did the $44 baby-sitting cost fail to meet? Explain your reasoning.

6-2. Have you ever made a decision and later found that you mistakenly let irrelevant factors sway your choice? Explain.

The term *relevant cost* is something of a misnomer. Perhaps a better description of this topic would be *relevant factors*. The reason for this is that the term relevant cost is used to describe not only changes in cost, but also changes in revenue. These cost and revenue changes often result in inflows of resources rather than outflows.

quantitative factors
Factors that can be measured by numbers.

qualitative factors Factors that cannot be measured by numbers—they must be described in words.

Quantitative factors are those that can be represented by numbers. Almost all accounting information is quantitative, including relevant cost. However, managers often consider additional factors that cannot be quantified. **Qualitative factors** are factors that cannot be measured numerically—they must be described in words. Examples include customer satisfaction, product quality, employee morale, and customer perceptions.

In addition to their financial impact, business decisions affect a multitude of nonfinancial areas. For example, closing an outdated factory may reduce production cost, but it will also adversely impact employee moral. The employees that remain after the plant closing may believe that the company's loyalty is to profits, not their well-being. Lower employee moral is likely to lead to less productivity. Qualitative factors should also be considered in smaller, routine decisions. For example, a furniture store manager considering a proposal to switch from company owned and operated delivery trucks to a delivery service should consider her lack of control if the delivery service is used. Even though it may be less expensive to use a delivery service, the furniture store's manager may not want to lose the ability to select the most responsible truck drivers and to schedule deliveries exactly as desired. When making a decision, managers should evaluate all relevant quantitative and qualitative factors.

Discussion Questions

Assume you are planning a trip from Los Angeles to Texas to visit some friends. You have a job, but your boss will let you take off as many days as you wish for the trip. Your car is unreliable, so you compare two alternatives—take a bus or take an airplane.

6-3. What are the relevant quantitative factors you should consider in making your decision?

6-4. What are the relevant qualitative factors you should consider in making your decision?

Decision makers must question the relevance of accounting information. As discussed in Chapter 1, managers and engineers no longer specify accounting information requirements. Instead, accountants provide information to managers based on accepted accounting techniques, so its relevance to management decision makers has diminished. Although some businesses have taken steps to make management accounting information more relevant to internal decision makers, managers should be able to determine for themselves what is relevant so they can make sound, well-informed decisions (see Exhibit 6–1).

Exhibit 6–1
Determining
Relevant Cost

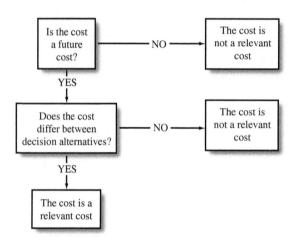

Throughout the remainder of this chapter, we will explore several common business situations to demonstrate how to determine relevant cost and its importance to good decision making. For each example, we will gather all costs associated with the decision. Next, we will determine the relevant cost of each decision alternative. Finally, we will compare the relevant costs of the alternative and determine the preferred alternative. The first example we will explore is an equipment replacement decision.

EQUIPMENT REPLACEMENT

To apply the concepts of relevant costing, we examine a proposed equipment replacement project. Our example highlights the treatment of depreciation, sunk costs, and costs that do not differ between alternatives.

Bill Smith & Partners, a local law firm, purchased and installed a sophisticated computer system two weeks ago at a cost of $35,500. Bill's brother, John, stops by the law office to say hello. While there, he notices the new system. He remarks that it is too bad the system is not the latest and quickest because, if it were, the data input time could be cut in half. John suggests that Bill consider updating. Bill responds, "I can't buy a new system. I just bought this one two weeks ago." John advises Bill to take a closer look before deciding.

Gather All Costs Associated with the Decision

Bill turns to you for advice. He explains that the recently installed computer system cost $35,500 to purchase, has an estimated useful life of five years, with a residual value of $500. He notes that the firm plans to use straight-line depreciation, so it will recognize $7,000 depreciation per year. The cost of operating the recently installed system, which we will call the "old" system, includes two operators at $18,000 per year, and a maintenance contract at $1,000 per year. The maintenance agreement, however, can be canceled at any time. After calling around, Bill informs you that he can sell the old system now, but he will get only $10,000 for it (everyone wants the new model). The new model would cost $76,000 and also has an estimated useful life of five years with a $1,000 residual value. Using the straight-line method, annual depreciation would be $15,000. Because data entry is twice as fast, the new computer system would require only one operator at $18,000 per year. The maintenance contract on the new machine would cost $1,000 per year and would be cancelable at any time.

A summary of the cost of each system is shown in Exhibit 6–2. These costs are generally classified as start-up costs, operating costs, and shutdown costs.

Exhibit 6–2
Computer System
Replacement
Cost Summary

	Old System	Replacement System
Start-up costs:		
Cost of system	$ 35,500	$76,000
Operating costs:		
Annual depreciation	$ 7,000	$15,000
Total depreciation	35,000	75,000
Annual labor cost	36,000	18,000
Total labor cost	180,000	90,000
Annual maintenance cost	1,000	1,000
Total maintenance cost	5,000	5,000
Shutdown costs:		
Residual value of system	$ 500	$ 1,000
Current sale price of old system	10,000	

To help Bill make a wise decision about the new computer system, you must first look at each cost and determine whether it is relevant. To make an informed decision, a manager must consider the total cost of each alternative, including all the costs incurred over the life of the alternative. For our computer replacement decision, the annual costs associated with each system are multiplied by the number of years the system will be used (five) to determine the total cost of the system over its lifetime.

Determine the Relevant Cost of Each Alternative

Next we determine the relevant cost of each decision alternative. As you consider each cost, try to determine whether it is relevant to the equipment replacement decision. Ask yourself the following two questions: (1) Is the cost a future cost? and (2) Does the cost differ between alternatives? We will examine the cost associated with the old computer system first.

Relevant Cost of the Old Computer System   The $35,500 cost of the old system is not relevant because it is a sunk cost. Bill's decision to purchase or not to purchase the new computer system cannot change the past expenditure for the old one.

Although it may appear that depreciation is a future cost, it is nothing more than an allocation of an asset's original cost. The cost of an asset purchased in the past is a sunk cost, and, therefore, depreciation simply allocates this sunk cost. If depreciation expense relates to an asset purchased in the past, it is irrelevant. In this situation, the depreciation for the old computer system is not relevant because the depreciation is an allocation of the purchase price, which is a sunk cost.

The total cost of $180,000 to pay for two operators is relevant, because it is a future cost and it differs between alternatives. The old system requires two operators, each costing $18,000 per year. Over the five-year expected life of the old system, that totals $180,000 (2 operators × $18,000 × 5 years).

The $5,000 total cost of the maintenance contract for the old system is irrelevant, because it does not differ between decision alternatives. The cost of the maintenance contract for the old system is the same as that for the new one. Therefore, although this is a future cost, it is irrelevant because it does not differ between alternatives.

The $500 residual value of the old system is relevant because it is a future cost and it differs between alternatives. If Bill stays with the old computer system, he will be able to sell it at the end of its useful life for $500. If, however, he buys the new one, he will sell the old one now for $10,000, and therefore he will be unable to sell it for its residual value in five years.

The $10,000 that Bill could get if he sells the old system now is a future cost that differs between alternatives, and therefore it is relevant. If Bill buys the new computer system, he can sell the old one for $10,000, but if he does not buy the new system, he will need the old one so he would not sell it.

Relevant Costs of the Replacement System

Next, we will analyze the start-up, operating, and shutdown costs of the replacement computer system. The only start-up cost for the replacement system is the $76,000 to purchase and install it. This cost is relevant because it is a future cost and it differs between alternatives.

The $75,000 in total depreciation on the new computer system is an allocation of the replacement system's cost. Because we have already considered the cost of the new computer system, we avoid double-counting by excluding its depreciation expense from our analysis of relevant costs.

The $90,000 ($18,000 × 5 years) total labor cost for the replacement system's one operator is relevant because it is a future cost that differs between alternatives. The labor cost for the old system is $180,000, whereas the labor cost for the replacement system is $90,000.

The total cost of the maintenance contract on the replacement system is $5,000. As it happens, the maintenance cost of the old system is also $5,000. In this situation, although maintenance cost is a future cost, it is irrelevant because it does not differ between alternatives.

The $1,000 residual value for the new computer system is relevant because it is a future cost that differs between alternatives. If Bill replaces his current system with a new one, then he can sell the new system for $1,000 at the end of its useful life (in the future). If he does not buy the new one, he obviously cannot sell it.

Compare the Relevant Costs and Select an Alternative

Now that you have determined which costs are relevant, you compare them to see which alternative is best for Bill's firm. It is important to differentiate between inflows and outflows. In Exhibit 6–3 we use parentheses to identify outflows.

As this analysis shows, Bill would save $24,500 over the next five years by buying the new computer system. So he should buy the new system to save money,

Exhibit 6–3
Relevant Cost
Comparison for Bill
Smith & Partners

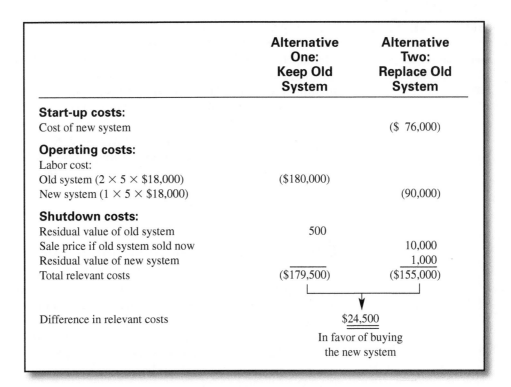

	Alternative One: Keep Old System	Alternative Two: Replace Old System
Start-up costs:		
Cost of new system		($ 76,000)
Operating costs:		
Labor cost:		
Old system (2 × 5 × $18,000)	($180,000)	
New system (1 × 5 × $18,000)		(90,000)
Shutdown costs:		
Residual value of old system	500	
Sale price if old system sold now		10,000
Residual value of new system		1,000
Total relevant costs	($179,500)	($155,000)
Difference in relevant costs		$24,500
		In favor of buying the new system

right? From a purely monetary point of view, he should. However, can he? The replacement system is not cheap. Often business decision makers determine the best alternative, only to learn the business does not have enough available cash to take advantage of a course of action that would save money in the long run. Considering only relevant costs in decision making will lead to better business decisions, but it will not necessarily enable a company to take advantage of what can be learned in the process.

Discussion Questions

6-5. Assuming all purchases and sales of computer systems are cash transactions, how much cash would Bill need to buy the new system?

6-6. Now that we know the relevant cost associated with the computer replacement, what qualitative factors should Bill consider before he makes his final decision?

Interest—The Time Value of Money

New equipment purchase decisions generally have long-term effects. Because of the long life of the equipment, the associated cash inflows and outflows will occur for many years. Therefore, decision makers should consider the interest-earning potential of the cash flows associated with equipment acquisitions. The interest earning potential of cash is sometimes called the **time value of money.** Chapter 7 covers special techniques developed to incorporate the effect of interest and the timing of cash flows.

time value of money The interest earning potential of cash.

SPECIAL ORDERS

special order An order that is outside a company's normal scope of business activity.

Manufacturing businesses must often consider whether to accept a **special order**—an order that is outside its normal scope of business activity. As we will see, proper treatment of fixed cost is critical in making sound special order decisions.

Assume that your company, Alumafloat, makes small aluminum boats. Alumafloat has been in operation for almost 10 years and sells boats to marine supply stores in southern Florida. One day, a Sears Roebuck and Company representative approaches you with an interesting proposition. Sears is interested in purchasing 1,000 of your boats for $125 each. The largest order your company has received to date was for 100 boats, so obviously, this huge order requires special consideration.

Gather All Costs Associated with the Decision

The $125 offer from Sears is considerably less than Alumafloat's normal selling price of $160 per boat. In fact, the boats cost $130 each to produce, so the company would lose $5 per boat if it accepts Sears's $125 offer.

As you discuss the order with the representative from Sears, you tell her that you would be willing to sell the boats to Sears at a discounted price of $140 each because of the large quantity of boats they need. Sears refuses your offer. The store will only pay $125 per boat, and the representative expects you to accept or reject the order within five days.

You gather all the information necessary to make a wise decision. First, you meet with your company's cost accountant, who confirms that your cost per unit is $130. You also request a report detailing production cost so you can see how the cost per unit figure was calculated. Using expected total sales (**excluding** the special order from Sears) and production costs for the year, the cost accountant prepares the report shown in Exhibit 6–4.

Exhibit 6–4
Per Unit Cost Report for Alumafloat

Expected sales (5,500 units at $160 each)		$880,000
Less: Cost of goods sold (see detail below)		(715,000)
Expected gross margin		$165,000

Detailed calculation for cost of goods sold:

	Per Unit	Total
Number of units	1	5,500
Direct material costs	$ 50	$275,000
Direct labor costs	55	302,500
Variable production costs	10	55,000
Fixed production costs	15	82,500
Total cost of goods sold	$130	$715,000

We must determine the potential effect on Alumafloat's revenues and expenses of accepting the order. Which costs shown in Exhibit 6–4 would be affected by the decision to accept the special order from Sears? To determine which costs are relevant, we will again ask the following two questions: (1) Is the cost a future cost? and (2) Does the cost differ between alternatives?

Determine the Relevant Cost of Each Alternative

Next you must determine which costs are relevant. In this situation, the alternatives are to accept the order or reject it. Generally speaking, because no cost is associated with rejecting the order, our analysis focuses on the alternative to accept.

If the order is accepted, sales will increase by $125,000 (1,000 boats × $125 per boat). The increase in sales due to the special order is relevant, because it is something that will happen in the future and it differs between alternatives.

All variable costs are relevant because they are future costs that differ between alternatives. If the special order is accepted, variable costs will be incurred to produce the 1,000 boats. In this example, variable cost includes direct material, direct labor, and variable production costs.

Depending on the decision situation, fixed cost may or may not be relevant. Often fixed production costs are not relevant costs because total fixed cost for the company will be unaffected by the increase in production volume. This fact holds true unless specific fixed cost increases occur due to the special order, or the order is so substantial that production would exceed the relevant range if the company accepts the order. As the report in Exhibit 6–4 indicates, the company expects total fixed costs to be $82,500. Assume in our example that the decision to accept or reject the special order from Sears would not affect total fixed cost. Therefore, in this case, fixed cost does not differ between alternatives and is irrelevant to the special order decision.

Compare the Relevant Costs and Select an Alternative

Armed with information about relevant cost, you can make an informed decision about the Sears order. Exhibit 6–5 presents a schedule of relevant costs for this special order. The schedule excludes fixed costs because they are irrelevant.

Exhibit 6–5
Relevant Costs for
Special Order of
1,000 Boats

	Per Unit	Total
Sales from special order	$125	$125,000
Direct material costs	(50)	(50,000)
Direct labor costs	(55)	(55,000)
Variable production costs	(10)	(10,000)
Total relevant production costs	(115)	(115,000)
Total increase in income	$ 10	$ 10,000

Alumafloat's income would increase by $10,000 if it accepted the special order. The reasoning in the Alumafloat example may seem logical, but companies often reject special orders that would increase profits, because managers do not understand the concept of relevant cost as it pertains to fixed cost. To avoid making poor decisions, managers must carefully consider how a special order will affect fixed cost.

An accountant for a Fortune 500 manufacturing company once remarked, "I can't believe that the product sales manager is selling below cost. He is disregarding fixed cost as he sets prices to move old stock." In fact, the manager may have made a good decision about the price of the product, depending on whether the fixed costs are relevant to the pricing decision. As a manager, you should know that routinely prepared accounting information cannot be relevant to every decision. Accounting information must be tailored, sometimes by the information user, to provide information that is relevant to the decision at hand.

Discussion Questions

6-7. What would happen if you treated every order as a special order and routinely disregarded fixed cost considerations from your pricing decisions?

6-8. Assume that the production manager at Alumafloat reminds you that four years ago sales skyrocketed for a while. Demand was so great that production increased to the limit of the company's capacity. Alumafloat produced 6,950 boats in a 12-month period. What implications does this information have on your decision to accept the special order from Sears?

6-9. What qualitative factors should you consider regarding accepting an order to sell Sears the boats for less than the price you charge your regular customers? For example, what would your regular customers think if they found that Sears was selling the same style boat they buy from you?

OUTSOURCING: THE MAKE OR BUY DECISION

outsourcing Buying services, products, or components of products instead of producing them.

Often companies purchase subcomponents used to manufacture their products instead of making them in their in-house manufacturing facilities. Buying services, products, or components of products from outside vendors instead of producing them is called **outsourcing.** Decision makers considering a make or buy decision must pay close attention to fixed costs and opportunity costs.

Assume you are a product manager at Microbake, a plant that manufactures microwave ovens. A vendor has approached you about supplying the timer assemblies for your ovens for $12 each. Currently, Microbake makes the timers in its own subassembly department. The subassembly department makes many of the small component parts for the various products manufactured at the plant. When you review the cost sheets for the timers, you discover that the company uses 80,000 timers each year and they cost $14 each to produce in-house.

Gather All Costs Associated with the Decision

You call a meeting with Microbake's cost accounting department to discuss the situation and confirm that the $14 in-house manufacturing cost is correct. Even when pressed, the cost accountants are confident their cost figures are carefully prepared and accurate. In fact, they are surprised the company can buy the timers from the outside vendor for only $12 each. At your request, the cost accounting department prepares the cost breakdown for the timers shown in Exhibit 6-6.

Exhibit 6-6
Cost of Producing Oven Timers In-House

Number of timers produced each year		80,000
	Per Unit	**Total**
Direct material	$ 5	$ 400,000
Direct labor	4	320,000
Variable manufacturing overhead	1	80,000
Fixed manufacturing overhead	4	320,000
Total	$14	$1,120,000

Exhibit 6–7
Selecting Relevant
Costs of Producing
Oven Timers

	Future?	Differs?	Relevant?
Direct material:	yes	yes	yes
Direct labor:	yes	yes	yes
Variable manufacturing overhead:	yes	yes	yes
Fixed manufacturing overhead:	yes	**no**	**no**

Determine the Relevant Cost of Each Alternative

Once again we assess whether each cost is relevant by asking the following questions: (1) Is the cost a future cost? and (2) Does the cost differ between alternatives? The answers follow in Exhibit 6–7.

By definition, *fixed* manufacturing overhead remains constant in total regardless of the level of activity (in this case "activity" is the number of units produced). The fixed cost presented by the cost accountants is an allocation of the total fixed overhead cost of the whole factory, or possibly of the subassembly department. If the company stops making the timers, the subassembly department will not go away and neither will its fixed cost, because the company needs the subassembly department to produce other components. Unless fixed cost changes based on management's decision to buy the timers, it is irrelevant.

Compare the Relevant Costs and Select an Alternative

We compare the relevant costs of the make or buy decision in Exhibit 6–8.

Exhibit 6–8
Relevant Cost of Make
or Buy Decision for
Oven Timers

	Make	Buy
Cost to purchase		$960,000
Direct material	$400,000	
Direct labor	320,000	
Variable manufacturing overhead	80,000	
Total relevant cost	$800,000	$960,000
Difference in relevant costs		$160,000

In favor of making the
oven timers in-house

As Exhibit 6–8 indicates, once we have screened out the irrelevant fixed costs it becomes apparent that Microbake can save $160,000 per year by making the timers rather than buying them. Based on this relevant cost comparison, you decide to not purchase the timer assemblies from the outside vendor.

In a final effort to get the sale, the vendor contacts several people at Microbake informing them that you are squandering your company's money. The vendor points out to other Microbake managers that its price is $2 per unit less than your in-house production cost as determined by Microbake's highly trained cost accountants. Other managers are pressing to accept the outside vendor's proposal.

To settle the issue, you call a meeting of the managers and present your relevant cost findings. Several managers comment that your information disregards fixed manufacturing overhead. You explain that the fixed manufacturing overhead is irrelevant. The other managers argue that fixed manufacturing overhead is a very real part of business cost and that it should be included in your presentation. As it happens, this presents little problem. Including fixed manufacturing overhead, although irrelevant, may highlight how fixed costs are affected (or in this case, unaffected) by changes in production. You must demonstrate, however, that if the units are manufactured in-house, fixed manufacturing overhead cost will happen; and that if the units are purchased from the outside vendor, the fixed manufacturing overhead will still occur. The relevant cost comparison can include the irrelevant fixed cost as shown in Exhibit 6–9.

Exhibit 6–9
Relevant Cost of Make or Buy Decision for Oven Timers with Fixed Costs Shown

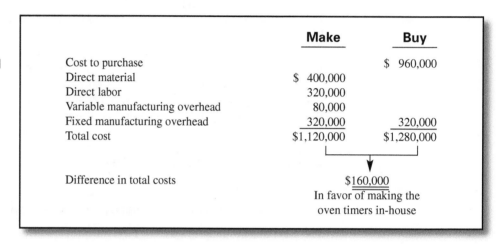

	Make	Buy
Cost to purchase		$ 960,000
Direct material	$ 400,000	
Direct labor	320,000	
Variable manufacturing overhead	80,000	
Fixed manufacturing overhead	320,000	320,000
Total cost	$1,120,000	$1,280,000

Difference in total costs $160,000
In favor of making the oven timers in-house

As Exhibit 6–9 shows, because fixed manufacturing overhead is the same for the two alternatives, the outcome of the comparison is the same as that in Exhibit 6–8. Microbake can save $160,000 by making the timers instead of buying them.

Discussion Question

6-10. What will happen to the cost of producing other Microbake products if your decision is overturned and the company outsources the timer assemblies?

Special Relevant Cost Considerations for Fixed Costs

In some situations, fixed costs are affected by the alternative selected. For example, suppose Microbake could eliminate an entire 8-hour production shift if it no longer made the timers. Eliminating that shift thus eliminates one line supervisor whose annual salary is $45,000 per year and reduces other fixed costs by $150,000. Therefore, fixed manufacturing overhead would decrease by 195,000 ($45,000 + $150,000). Exhibit 6–10 shows the relevant cost of the make or buy decision when the alternative to buy the timers enables the company to eliminate a production shift.

Exhibit 6-10
Relevant Cost of the Make or Buy Decision for Oven Timers with Relevant Fixed Costs

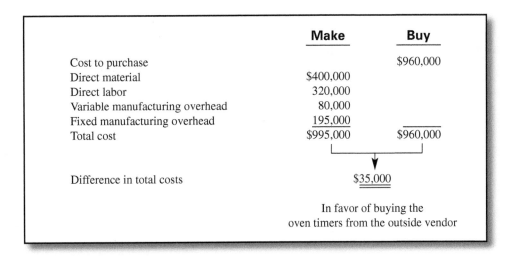

	Make	Buy
Cost to purchase		$960,000
Direct material	$400,000	
Direct labor	320,000	
Variable manufacturing overhead	80,000	
Fixed manufacturing overhead	195,000	
Total cost	$995,000	$960,000
Difference in total costs		$35,000

In favor of buying the
oven timers from the outside vendor

Exhibit 6–10 shows that the savings in fixed manufacturing overhead alters the cost comparison such that Microbake should opt to buy the timers. If the $195,000 reduction in fixed costs were realized, Microbake would save $35,000 by purchasing the timer assemblies from the vendor instead of making them.

Discussion Question

6-11. What qualitative factors should managers at Microbake consider with respect to their outsourcing decision?

Considering Opportunity Costs

opportunity cost The benefit foregone (given up) because one alternative is chosen over another.

Recall that an **opportunity cost** is the value of what is foregone (given up) because one alternative is chosen over another. For example, the opportunity cost of attending college rather than working full time is what you could have earned by working instead of going to college.

If Microbake buys the timer assemblies from an outside vendor, it may have an alternate use for the production capacity or assets used to make the timers—it may have an opportunity to enhance its earnings through an alternate use of the facilities. Assume that Microbake can use the production capacity freed up by purchasing the timers to make electronic alarm clocks. Assume further that the electronic alarm clocks would provide an annual contribution margin of $200,000 with no significant changes to fixed cost. If Microbake continues to make the timer assemblies, it would forego the opportunity to earn the $200,000. The foregone $200,000 contribution margin on the electronic alarm clocks is an opportunity cost.

Because opportunity cost is the cost of *not* doing something, it is not reflected in the accounting records of a business and is not reported in the company's external financial statements or internal management reports. This does not mean an opportunity cost is not real—remember, reality and the measurement of reality are not the same thing. Opportunity cost is an economic reality. Although it is not generally part of financial accounting measures, opportunity cost is a relevant consideration in business decisions.

Returning to the Microbake timer example, the relevant costs of making or buying the 80,000 timers, including the $200,000 opportunity, is presented in Exhibit 6–11.

Exhibit 6-11
Relevant Cost of Make
or Buy Decision for
Oven Timers with
Opportunity Cost

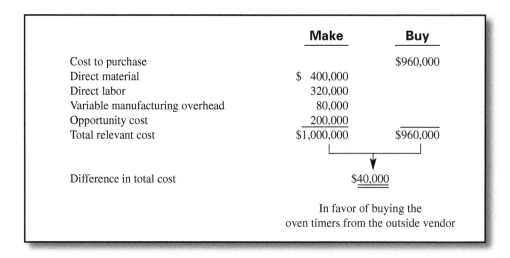

	Make	Buy
Cost to purchase		$960,000
Direct material	$ 400,000	
Direct labor	320,000	
Variable manufacturing overhead	80,000	
Opportunity cost	200,000	
Total relevant cost	$1,000,000	$960,000
Difference in total cost	$40,000	

In favor of buying the
oven timers from the outside vendor

Exhibit 6–11 suggests that if the $200,000 contribution margin from the production of alarm clocks could be realized, Microbake should buy the timer assemblies from the outside vendor. The production capacity no longer needed to produce the timers could then be used to produce the alarm clocks, resulting in a $40,000 difference in the relevant cost in favor of buying the timers.

Microbake's outsourcing problem is an example of a very real business dilemma. Managers cannot rely solely on the cost information from accountants. They themselves must have enough accounting knowledge to determine the relevant cost of each decision alternative.

A few years ago, an accounting instructor overheard some graduate students talking among themselves during a make or buy lecture. The students were engineers at a manufacturing plant that made sophisticated health care products. After some time, the instructor's curiosity prompted him to ask the students what they were discussing. They explained how their company had been outsourcing more and more components, and profits were declining. The problem had snowballed and production costs on the remaining in-house components seemed to rise as more components were outsourced. It seemed that outsiders found it progressively easier to sell components to the company for less than the in-house production cost. During the lecture, the students figured out that their company was treating fixed costs improperly in make or buy decisions. Oddly enough, the students had questioned company cost accountants, only to be told the product cost information provided was correct. Indeed, the product cost information probably was correct; however, was it all relevant? Probably not. As an economic decision maker, you need to be able to evaluate accounting information for yourself.

Although we have explored relevant cost using only three examples, you should understand that relevant cost concepts apply to almost every business decision. Relevant costing is even helpful with personal decisions such as whether to attend summer school at a local university or enroll in a student exchange program and study abroad. Business situations and life in general provide an array of quantitative and qualitative considerations for every decision alternative. As a decision maker, you must be able to seek out the relevant considerations and disregard the irrelevant ones.

SUMMARY

All management decision making entails choosing between or among alternatives. If managers are to have any chance of making the best decision in a given situation, they must attempt to consider only relevant information.

A relevant cost is a cost that makes a difference in a given decision situation. What is relevant in one situation may not be relevant in another. Relevant costs are also always future costs, because past costs cannot be changed by any current or future actions. Further, a future cost must differ between or among the alternatives to be considered relevant. Opportunity costs are often relevant and should be considered by managers making decisions. An opportunity cost is the value of benefits foregone because one alternative is chosen over another.

In addition to the quantitative information managers must consider in making decisions, qualitative information such as customer satisfaction, product quality, and employee morale must also be considered. Oftentimes the qualitative considerations should outweigh purely quantitative considerations.

There are many applications of relevant costing in management decision making. Careful application of relevant costing techniques can help managers to make appropriate decisions in various business situations.

REVIEW THE FACTS

A. What is relevant costing?
B. What is a relevant cost?
C. What two important characteristics do all relevant costs possess?
D. What is a sunk cost?
E. Describe the difference between qualitative and quantitative factors.
F. When trying to determine whether a cost is relevant, what are the two questions the decision maker should ask?
G. Why is the depreciation for existing assets considered irrelevant for equipment replacement decisions?
H. What is the time value of money?
I. Why is the time value of money important for decisions involving the purchase of long-lived assets?
J. What would cause a fixed cost to be relevant for a special order decision?
K. What is outsourcing?
L. Define opportunity cost.
M. The concepts of relevant costing apply to what types of decisions?

APPLY WHAT YOU HAVE LEARNED

LO 1: Determine Which Costs Are Relevant

6–12. The production manager at Ace Manufacturing is contemplating whether he should upgrade some old production equipment. He is considering the following factors:

1. _____ The cost of the old equipment
2. _____ The cost of the new equipment
3. _____ Depreciation on the old equipment
4. _____ Depreciation on the new equipment
5. _____ Trade-in value of the old equipment
6. _____ Salvage value of the old equipment
7. _____ Salvage value of the new equipment

REQUIRED:

For each item listed, indicate whether it is relevant (R) or irrelevant (I).

LO 3: Quantitative and Qualitative Considerations

6–13. Tom Robinson is thinking about buying a portable computer. He has a computer at home, but the portable computer would allow him to work during his frequent business trips. Tom is trying to convince his boss that the computer would save the company some money. Tom hopes that his company will pay at least part of the computer's purchase price and the monthly fee for internet service.

Tom has asked a group of friends to help him think of all the advantages of buying the computer. Assume you are part of the group.

GROUP REQUIREMENTS:

a. Prepare an informal schedule of the costs associated with the computer purchase.
b. List as many quantitative benefits as you can that the company will gain if Tom buys the portable computer.
c. List as many quantitative benefits as you can that Tom will gain if he buys the portable computer.
d. List as many qualitative benefits as you can that the company will gain if Tom buys the portable computer.
e. List as many qualitative benefits as you can that Tom will gain if he buys the portable computer.
f. How much of the computer's cost do you think Tom should pay? How much should Tom's employer pay?

LO 3 & 4: Determine Relevant Cost Schedule and Qualitative Factors

6–14. Tina Alberts is thinking about trading her car for a new one. Her present car is only three years old, completely paid for, but out of warranty. The car's original cost was $22,000. Lately, the car has been somewhat undependable and the repair bills have been quite high. In the last three months, Tina paid over $1,200 for repairs. Tina intends to use her trade-in as the down payment and then finance the balance. She is looking at a new Nissan which she can get for about $23,000, less her trade.

Tina has asked a group of close friends to help her think of all the relevant advantages and disadvantages of getting the new car. Assume you are part of this group.

GROUP REQUIREMENTS:

  a. Prepare an informal schedule listing the relevant quantitative factors that Tina should consider. Do not limit your answer to the items found in the problem. Include all the factors you can think of. When possible, try to include estimated dollar amounts in your schedule.
  b. Prepare an informal schedule listing the relevant qualitative factors that Tina should consider.
  c. From a quantitative point of view, do you think Tina should buy the new car?
  d. Considering both quantitative and qualitative factors, do you think Tina should buy the new car?

LO 1: Determine Which Costs Are Relevant

6–15. Jean Parks is a salesperson for Quality Food Products, Inc. She is considering a 250-mile trip to visit a potential customer, ByLots. Following are factors she is pondering.

  1. _____ The cost of traveling the 250 miles to ByLots
  2. _____ The time she will spend on the road
  3. _____ The time she will spend visiting with ByLots's executives
  4. _____ The amount of time already devoted to ByLots
  5. _____ The revenue potential from ByLots
  6. _____ The cost of her last visit to ByLots
  7. _____ The probability that her visit will result in new sales
  8. _____ The cost of lunch for herself if she visits ByLots
  9. _____ The cost of the lunch she would buy for ByLots's executives

REQUIRED:
For each item listed, indicate whether it is relevant (R) or irrelevant (I).

LO 3: Determine Quantitative and Qualitative Factors

6–16. Managers at Ace Manufacturing are considering upgrading some production equipment. They are considering the following factors:

  1. _____ Maintenance cost
  2. _____ Changes in product quality ı
  3. _____ Salvage value of the old equipment
  4. _____ Cost of new equipment
  5. _____ Difficulty of training employees to use new equipment
  6. _____ Salvage value of the new equipment
  7. _____ The ill feelings due to the possible reduction in the labor force

REQUIRED:
For each item listed, indicate whether it is quantitative (A) or qualitative (B).

LO 1, 2, 3, & 5: List All Costs, Indicate Relevant Costs, Indicate Qualitative Factors

6–17. Assume that you are deciding whether to live in a campus dormitory room or an off-campus apartment.

REQUIRED:
  a. List all the costs that come to mind as you think about this decision.
  b. Review your list and indicate which costs are relevant and which are irrelevant to the decision.

c. What are some qualitative factors that you should consider when making this decision?

LO 1, 2, 3, & 5:   List Costs, Indicate Relevant Costs, Indicate Qualitative Factors

6–18. Assume that you are deciding what to do next summer. You are considering two alternatives: Go to summer school, or tour Europe.

REQUIRED:
a. List all the costs that come to mind as you think about this decision.
b. Review your list and indicate which costs are relevant and which are irrelevant to your decision.
c. What are some qualitative factors that you should consider when making this decision?

LO 1, 2, 3, & 5:   List Costs, Indicate Relevant Costs, Indicate Qualitative Factors

6–19. Robert Epstein's car is seven years old. The car is no longer under warranty and requires frequent repairs. Robert is trying to decide whether to buy a new car. He has asked you what you think about his idea.

REQUIRED:
a. List all the costs that come to mind as you think about his decision.
b. Review your list and indicate which costs are relevant and which are irrelevant to the decision.
c. What are some qualitative factors that he should consider when making this decision?

LO 4:   Determine Relevant Cost for Equipment Replacement

6–20. The managers at Enid Manufacturing Company are considering replacing the industrial mixer used in the company's factory.

Information about the old mixer:

Cost	$28,000
Estimated useful life	10 years
Estimated salvage value	$0
Current age	5 years
Estimated current fair value	$8,000
Annual operating cost	$15,000

Information about the new mixer:

Cost	$34,000
Estimated useful life	5 years
Estimated salvage value	$0
Annual operating cost	$12,000

REQUIRED:
Prepare a relevant cost schedule showing the benefit of keeping the old mixer or buying the new one.

LO 4:   Determine Relevant Cost for Equipment Replacement

6–21. The managers at Walker Manufacturing Company are considering replacing the industrial lathe used in the company's factory.

Information about the old lathe:

Cost	$57,000
Estimated useful life	8 years
Estimated salvage value	$0
Current age	2 years
Estimated current fair value	$32,000
Annual operating cost	$32,000

Information about the new lathe:

Cost	$61,000
Estimated useful life	6 years
Estimated salvage value	$0
Annual operating cost	$24,000

REQUIRED:

Prepare a relevant cost schedule showing the benefit of keeping the old lathe or buying the new one.

LO 4: Determine Relevant Cost for Equipment Replacement

6–22. Kyle Hobbs, president of Hobbs Boat Hauling, is considering replacing the company's industrial lift used to haul boats. The new lift would allow the company to lift larger boats out of the water.

Information about the old lift:

Cost	$94,000
Estimated useful life	12 years
Estimated salvage value	$10,000
Current age	4 years
Estimated current fair value	$48,000
Annual contribution margin	$50,000

Information about the new lift:

Cost	$128,000
Estimated useful life	8 years
Estimated salvage value	$ 25,000
Annual contribution margin	$ 65,000

REQUIRED:

Prepare a relevant cost schedule showing the benefit of keeping the old lift or buying the new one.

LO 4: Determine Relevant Cost for Equipment Replacement

6–23. The managers at Oliver Manufacturing are considering replacing a printing press with a new, high-speed model.

Information about the old printing press:

Cost	$255,000
Estimated useful life	10 years
Estimated salvage value	$ 25,000
Annual depreciation	$ 23,000
Current age	3 years
Accumulated depreciation to date	$184,000
Estimated current fair value	$150,000
Annual contribution margin	$110,000

Information about the new printing press:

Cost	$535,000
Estimated useful life	7 years
Estimated salvage value	$ 45,000
Annual depreciation	$ 70,000
Annual contribution margin	$150,000

REQUIRED:

Prepare a relevant cost schedule showing the benefit of keeping the old printing press or buying the new one.

LO 4: Determine Relevant Cost for New Business Segment

6–24. Pipkin Photo operates a small camera store in Edmond, Oklahoma. The store has two departments, camera sales and photo finishing. Rent, utilities, and other operating expenses are allocated to the departments based on the square footage occupied by the department. Currently, the camera sales department occupies 3,000 square feet and the photo finishing department occupies 2,000 square feet.

Pipkin Photo president, Peggy Pipkin, is thinking about buying a computer system to produce poster prints. The poster print system would occupy 200 square feet of the store's floor space.

Budgeted monthly information for the store:

Store rent	$ 5,000
Salaries and wages	10,500
Utilities	750
Other operating expenses	3,000
Sales	125,000
Cost of goods sold	95,000

Information about the poster print system:

Cost of the poster system	$25,700
Estimated useful life	5 years
Estimated salvage value	$ 500
Floor space required	200 square feet
Monthly cost of electricity used by poster system	$ 50
Budgeted monthly amounts:	
Poster sales revenue	$ 1,200
Poster supplies	200
Wages for poster operation	250
Store rent	200
Utilities	32
Other operating expenses	120

Peggy believes the company should not buy the poster system because it will show a loss every month. Because she is not sure, she has contacted a small consulting group to seek advice. Assume you are part of the consulting group.

REQUIRED:

a. Would the poster system show a loss every month as Peggy suggests? Prepare a schedule to substantiate your answer.

b. Would the company's overall monthly profits increase or decrease as a result of buying the poster system? Prepare a schedule to substantiate your answer.

c. Prepare a relevant cost schedule showing the advantage or disadvantage of buying the poster system.

LO 4: Determine Relevant Cost for New Business Segment

6–25. The Largo Gift Hut operates a small souvenir shop in Key Largo. The shop has two departments, retail sales and mail order. Rent, utilities, and other operating expenses are allocated to the departments based on the square footage occupied by the department. Currently, the retail sales department occupies 5,000 square feet and the mail order department occupies 1,000 square feet.

Largo's president, Virginia Gurney, is thinking about buying a silk screen machine to make souvenir T-shirts. The silk screen machine would occupy 500 square feet of the souvenir shop's floor space.

Budgeted monthly information for the store:

Store rent	$ 5,100
Salaries and wages	8,500
Utilities	1,000
Other operating expenses	3,000
Sales	80,000
Cost of goods sold	57,000

Information about the silk screen machine:

Cost of the silk screen machine	$9,640
Estimated useful life	5 years
Estimated salvage value	$ 400
Floor space required	500 square feet
Monthly cost of electricity used by silk screen machine	$ 20
Budgeted monthly amounts:	
T-shirt sales revenue	$1,700
Cost of T-shirts	450
Cost of T-shirt supplies	100
Wages for the T-shirt operation	250
Store rent	425
Utilities	85
Other operating expenses	250

Gurney believes she should not buy the silk screen machine because it will show a loss every month. Because she is not sure, she has contacted a small consulting group to seek advice. Assume you are part of the consulting group.

REQUIRED:

a. Would the silk screen machine show a loss every month as Gurney suggests? Prepare a schedule to substantiate your answer.

b. Would the company's overall monthly profits increase or decrease as a result of buying the silk screen machine? Prepare a schedule to substantiate your answer.

c. Prepare a relevant cost schedule showing the advantage or disadvantage of buying the silk screen machine.

LO 4: Determine Relevant Cost for Equipment Replacement

6–26. Frank's Marine Service purchased a forklift five years ago for $16,000. When it was purchased the forklift had an estimated useful life of 10 years and a salvage value of $4,000. The forklift can be sold now for $6,000. The operating cost for the forklift is $4,500 per year.

Frank is thinking about buying a newer forklift for $17,000. The newer model would have an estimated useful life of five years and a salvage value of $7,000. The operating cost for the newer forklift would be $3,000 per year.

REQUIRED:

a. What are the relevant costs associated with the decision to replace the forklift?

b. Prepare a relevant cost schedule showing the advantage or disadvantage of buying the forklift.

LO 4:   Determine Relevant Cost for Equipment Replacement

6–27. Al Hart of Hart Engineering is considering whether to purchase a new copy machine. He purchased the old machine two years ago for $8,500. When purchased, the old machine had an estimated useful life of eight years and a salvage value of $500. The operating cost of the old machine is $3,000 per year. The old machine can be sold today for $2,000. A new machine can be bought today for $10,000 and would have an estimated useful life of six years with a salvage value of $1,000. The operating cost of the new copy machine is expected to be $1,500 per year.

REQUIRED:

a. Prepare a schedule showing all the costs associated with the current copy machine.

b. Prepare a schedule showing all the costs associated with the new copy machine.

c. Prepare a schedule showing the relevant cost of the copy machine replacement decision and the favored alternative.

d. Discuss the qualitative factors that Hart should consider.

e. Would you buy the newer copy machine?

LO 4:   Determine Relevant Cost for Equipment Replacement

6–28. Mike Shirley is considering whether to replace one of his delivery trucks. He purchased the current delivery truck four years ago for $24,000, and it came with a three-year, 75,000-mile warranty. When purchased, the current truck had an estimated useful life of five years and a salvage value of $2,000. Shirley uses the straight-line method for depreciation. The new truck would be identical to the current truck, except it would be new and would have the new truck warranty. The operating cost for the current truck is $4,000 for fuel, $23,200 for the driver's salary, and maintenance cost is about $5,000 per year. If Shirley keeps the old truck, it will last another five years, but would require the $5,000 in maintenance each year. The current truck can be sold now for $4,000, or it can be sold in five years for $1,000. The new truck would cost $25,500, has an estimated useful life of five years, and can be sold at the end of the five years for $4,000. At the end of the warranty period, the new truck will require maintenance of $5,000 per year.

REQUIRED:

a. Prepare a schedule showing all the costs associated with the current truck.

b. Prepare a schedule showing all the costs associated with the new truck.

c. Prepare a schedule showing the relevant cost of the truck replacement decision and the favored alternative.

d. Discuss the qualitative factors that Shirley should consider.

e. If the old truck had an estimated useful life of five years when it was purchased, and it has already been used for four years, discuss the ramifications of using the truck for another five years.

f. Would you buy the new truck? Why or why not?

LO 4: Determine Relevant Cost for Equipment Replacement

6–29. Tim Bridges is considering whether to replace a piece of production equipment with a new model. The new machine would cost $170,000, have an eight-year life, and have no salvage value. The variable cost of operating the machine would be $180,000 per year. The present machine was purchased one year ago, and could be used for the next eight years. When it was purchased, the present machine had an estimated useful life of nine years and a salvage value of zero. The present machine can be sold now for $28,000, but will have no salvage value in eight years. The variable cost of operating the present machine is $200,000 per year.

REQUIRED:

a. Prepare a schedule showing the costs associated with the present machine.

b. Prepare a schedule showing the costs associated with the new machine.

c. Prepare a schedule showing the relevant cost of the equipment replacement decision and the favored alternative.

d. Discuss the qualitative factors that Bridges should consider.

LO 3 & 4: Determine the Relevant Cost of Buying a House and List Qualitative Factors

6–30. John Camey is in the process of buying a house. He is interested in two houses. One house is two miles from his work, the other is on the outskirts of town, 34 miles from work. Surprisingly, the two houses are nearly identical, except the closer house is much more expensive. The house that is two miles from John's work is $177,000, whereas the other house is only $159,000. Maintenance, taxes, insurance, and other costs would be the same for both houses.

　　John goes to work 250 days each year. John has just traded his old car for a new one. Each time his car reaches 80,000 miles, John trades it for a new model. Generally, he expects to pay about $25,000 when he trades for a new car. His cars usually get about 20 miles per gallon of regular, $2.00-per-gallon gasoline. Maintenance on his car runs about $0.05 per mile on average. Other than driving to and from work, John drives about 15,000 miles each year.

　　Regardless of which house John buys, he expects to be transferred to another area of the country in five years. John is about to buy the less expensive house when he asks your advice.

REQUIRED:

a. Which house should John buy?

b. How much will John save if he follows your advice? (Disregard the time value of money.)

c. What qualitative factors should John consider?

LO 4: Relevant Cost of a Make or Buy Decision

6–31. Microline is considering buying computer cabinets from an outside vendor. Currently, Microline makes the cabinets in its own manufacturing facility. Microline can buy the cabinets for $15 each. The company uses 15,000 cabinets each year. Information about Microline's cost to manufacture the 15,000 cabinets follows:

	Per Unit	Total
Direct material	$ 4	$ 60,000
Direct labor	6	90,000
Variable overhead	7	105,000
Fixed overhead	5	75,000
Total	$22	$330,000

Fixed cost for Microline would not change if the company stopped making the cabinets.

REQUIRED:
Prepare a relevant cost schedule that indicates whether Microline should buy the cabinets or continue to make them.

LO 4: Relevant Cost of a Make or Buy Decision

6–32. Gem Products is considering buying the casters it uses in the manufacture of office chairs from an outside vendor. Currently, Gem Products makes the casters in its own manufacturing facility. Gem Products can buy the casters for $1.15 each. The company uses 450,000 casters each year.

Information about Gem Products' cost to manufacture the 450,000 casters follows:

	Per Unit	Total
Direct material	$ .50	$225,000
Direct labor	.10	45,000
Variable overhead	.40	180,000
Fixed overhead	.25	112,500
Total	$1.25	$562,500

Fixed cost for Gem Products would not change if the company stopped making the casters.

REQUIRED:
Prepare a relevant cost schedule that indicates whether Gem Products should buy the casters or continue to make them.

LO 4: Relevant Cost of a Make or Buy Decision

6–33. RJ Manufacturing is considering buying the mounting brackets it uses to make its fire extinguishers from an outside supplier. Currently, RJ Manufacturing makes the brackets in its own manufacturing facility. RJ Manufacturing can buy the brackets for $0.75 each. The company uses 700,000 brackets each year.

Information about RJ Manufacturing's cost to manufacture the 700,000 brackets follows:

	Per Unit	Total
Direct material	$.30	$210,000
Direct labor	.10	70,000
Variable overhead	.40	280,000
Fixed overhead	.14	98,000
Total	$.94	$658,000

Fixed cost for RJ Manufacturing would not change if the company stopped making the brackets.

REQUIRED:
Prepare a relevant cost schedule that indicates whether RJ Manufacturing should buy the brackets or continue to make them.

LO 4: Relevant Cost of an Outsourcing Decision

6–34. Jumbo Chinese Restaurant operates a small laundry facility to launder the uniforms, tablecloths, and other linens used by its restaurant chain. Jumbo's laundry operation occupies space in an industrial area close to the company's home office and its largest restaurant. Jumbo is considering using a laundry service to perform the laundering needed by the company.

Jumbo's $180,000 administrative expense is allocated based on the number of employees. Jumbo employs 90 people.

Information about the laundry facilities follows:

Direct cost information:	
Wages for two employees	$38,000
Cost of equipment	$ 7,500
Original estimated useful life of equipment	5 years
Estimated remaining useful life of equipment	1 year
Building rent per year	$ 3,000
Utilities	$ 2,000
Miscellaneous cost	$ 1,500
Indirect cost information:	
Administrative expense	$ 4,000

An outside laundry service has offered to provide Jumbo's laundering services for $50,000 per year. The fee is guaranteed for one year. If the offer is accepted, Jumbo will scrap the laundry equipment and close down its laundry operation completely.

REQUIRED:
The president of Jumbo has asked you to prepare a report that details the qualitative and quantitative factors that should be considered in making the decision about whether to close the laundry operation. Your report should discuss the relevant qualitative and quantitative factors for each alternative and include a relevant cost schedule. Your report should conclude with a well-supported recommended course of action.

LO 4: Relevant Cost of an Outsourcing Decision

6–35. Fast Track Delivery Service operates a small auto repair facility to service its fleet of 35 delivery vehicles. Fast Track's repair facility occupies space in an industrial area close to the company's home office. Fast Track is considering using a local repair shop to service its vehicles. Fast Track's $120,000 administrative expense is allocated based on the number of employees. Fast Track employs 50 people.

Information about the repair facility follows:

Direct cost information:	
Wages for three employees	$64,000
Cost of equipment used	$33,500
Original estimated useful life of equipment	12 years
Estimated remaining useful life of equipment	9 years
Building rent per year	$ 6,000
Utilities	$ 2,000
Cost of automobile parts	$30,000
Miscellaneous cost	$ 1,500
Indirect cost information:	
Administrative expense	$ 7,200

A dependable automotive service center has offered to provide maintenance contracts of each vehicle for $3,000 per vehicle. If Fast Track accepts the offer it would close the maintenance facility. The company estimates that it can sell the maintenance equipment for $10,000.

REQUIRED:

The president of Fast Track has asked you to prepare a report that details the qualitative and quantitative factors that should be considered in making the decision about whether to close the maintenance facility. Your report should discuss the relevant qualitative and quantitative factors for each alternative and include a relevant cost schedule. Your report should conclude with a well-supported recommendation.

LO 3 & 4: Relevant Cost and Qualitative Factors of a Special Order Decision

6–36. Abraham Manufacturing produces 22,000 rubber engine mounts each year for use in its electric cart manufacturing plant. Abraham's engine mounts have an excellent reputation for strength and durability. At a production level of 22,000, the cost per unit is as follows:

Direct material	$ .53
Direct labor	1.45
Variable overhead	.92
Fixed overhead	1.27
Total	$4.17

A competitor, Jenkins Cart Company, is interested in purchasing 14,000 rubber engine mounts from Abraham. Jenkins has offered to pay $4.17 each for the engine mounts. Abraham Manufacturing has the capacity and can easily manufacture the engine mounts for Jenkins.

Several managers at Abraham are concerned that there would be no financial benefit whatsoever for Abraham if the engine mounts are sold at cost.

REQUIRED:

a. Prepare a schedule that details the advantage or disadvantage of selling the 14,000 engine mounts to Jenkins.

b. Discuss the qualitative aspects of selling the parts to Jenkins.

LO 3 & 4: Relevant Cost and Qualitative Factors of a Special Order Decision

6–37. Kelly Gas Grill Company produces 200,000 RV22 propane gas regulator and valve assemblies each year for use in its gas grill factory. Kelly's gas grills are known for quality and have a reputation of lasting a lifetime.

At 200,000 units per year, the cost per unit is as follows:

Direct material	$ 3.02
Direct labor	2.44
Variable overhead	1.20
Fixed overhead	5.60
Total	$12.26

A competitor, Econo Grill, is interested in purchasing 80,000 RV22 assemblies from Kelly. Econo Grill has offered to pay $12.30 per unit. Kelly has the capacity and can easily manufacture the parts for Econo Grill.

Several managers at Kelly are concerned that there would be almost no financial benefit if the RV22 assemblies are sold for $12.30 each.

REQUIRED:

a. Prepare a schedule that details the advantage or disadvantage of selling the 80,000 RV22 assemblies to Econo Grill.

b. Discuss the qualitative aspects of selling the parts to Econo Grill.

LO 3 & 4: Relevant Cost and Qualitative Factors of a Special Order Decision

6–38. Eiroa Marine Cable Company produces 400,000 feet of SS316 cable each year. At 400,000 feet per year, the cost per foot is as follows:

Direct material	$.32
Direct labor	.14
Variable overhead	.08
Fixed overhead	.73
Total	$1.27

A competitor, Garcia Marine, is interested in purchasing 175,000 feet of SS316 cable from Eiroa. Garcia has offered to pay $0.92 per foot for the cable. Eiroa has the capacity and can easily manufacture the cable for Garcia Marine.

Frank Eiroa, president of Eiroa Marine Cable, is concerned that there is no financial benefit for the company if it sells the cable for only $0.92 per foot.

REQUIRED:

a. Prepare a schedule that details the advantage or disadvantage of selling the 175,000 feet of cable to Garcia Marine.

b. Discuss the qualitative aspects of selling the cable to Garcia.

LO 3 & 4: Relevant Cost and Qualitative Factors of a Special Order Decision

6–39. Gator Corporation manufactures camping equipment. One of the Gator's most popular product is its T1012 tent which the company sells for $28 each. Gator sells about 9,000 T1012 tents each year through its mail-order business. Another camping equipment company, TreeClimb Corporation has approached Gator about purchasing 2,000 T1012 tents. The tents would be the same as the T1012 except they would bear the TreeClimb brand. TreeClimb is willing to pay $20 per tent. Although Gator has plenty of plant capacity to produce the additional 2,000 tents, the company's manufacturing cost is $23 per unit, or $3 more per tent than TreeClimb is willing to pay.

The following per unit information pertains to Gator's cost to produce 9,000 T1012 tents.

Direct material	$ 9
Direct labor	4
Variable manufacturing overhead	2
Fixed manufacturing overhead	5
Total	$20

REQUIRED:

a. By what amount would Gator's operating income increase or decrease if the company accepts the special order?

b. Discuss the qualitative aspects of this special order decision.

LO 3 & 4: Relevant Cost and Qualitative Factors of a Special Order Decision

6–40. Refer to problem 6–39. Assume that Gator Corporation would have to purchase an additional sewing machine to accept the special order from TreeClimb. The cost of the new sewing machine is $2,500.

REQUIRED:

a. By what amount would Gator's operating income increase or decrease if the company accepts the special order under these circumstances?

b. Discuss the qualitative aspects of this special order decision.

LO 4: Relevant Cost of a Special Order Decision

6–41. Hi-Cast Corporation manufactures fishing rods. Part of Hi-Cast's sales success comes from a patented material, tuflex, used to make the fishing rods. Tuflex allows the fishing rods to be very flexible, yet nearly unbreakable. Hi-Cast sells about 150,000 fishing rods annually to wholesalers for $18 each. A major department store chain, Sale-Mart, is interested in purchasing 30,000 fishing rods that would bear the Sale-Mart's brand name. Sale-Mart is willing to pay only $9 per fishing rod, considerably less than Hi-Cast's normal selling price. Although Hi-Cast has plenty of plant capacity available to make the additional 30,000 fishing rods, the company's manufacturing cost is $11 per fishing rod, or

$2 more per rod than Sale-Mart is willing to pay. Sale-Mart has indicated that the 30,000 fishing rods do not have to be as flexible and tough as the regular Hi-Cast rods.

The following per unit information pertains to Hi-Cast's cost to produce 150,000 fishing rods.

Direct material:	
Tuflex	$4
Other material	1
Direct labor	3
Variable manufacturing overhead	1
Fixed manufacturing overhead	2
Total	$11

If fiberglass is used in place of tuflex, the direct material cost can be reduced by $2 per rod.

REQUIRED:

By what amount would Hi-Cast's operating income increase or decrease if the company accepts the special order?

LO 3 & 4: Relevant Cost and Qualitative Factors of an Outsourcing Decision

6–42. Ace Equipment Company makes high-pressure pumps. Ace makes 10,000 V1 valve assembles per year for use in production. The manufacturing facilities used to make the V1 valves are also used to produce a variety of other subassemblies and products. Accordingly, no special production equipment is needed to make the V1 valves.

The production cost for V1 valve assembles is as follows:

Direct material	$ 55,000
Direct labor	140,000
Variable manufacturing overhead	70,000
Fixed manufacturing overhead	210,000
Total	$475,000

Sure Flow Valve Company has offered to supply the V1 valve assemblies to Ace for $32 each.

REQUIRED:

a. Prepare a schedule that shows whether Ace should buy the valves from Sure Flow or continue to make them.
b. Discuss the qualitative factors that Ace should consider in this make or buy decision.

LO 3 & 4: Relevant Cost and Qualitative Factors of an Outsourcing Decision

6–43. Refer to problem 6–42. Assume Ace could use the manufacturing facilities which are no longer needed to make the V1 valves to produce a new line of small pumps. The small pumps would provide a contribution margin of $60,000.

REQUIRED:

a. Prepare a schedule that shows whether Ace should buy the valves from Sure Flow or continue to make them.
b. Discuss the qualitative factors that Ace should consider in this make or buy decision.

LO 3 & 4: Relevant Cost and Qualitative Factors of an Outsourcing Decision

6–44. General Manufacturing Company makes residential aluminum windows. A company has offered to supply General with the window crank assembly it needs for $3.50 each. General uses 50,000 crank assemblies each year. The machinery used to make the window cranks is used to produce a variety of other subassemblies and products.

The production cost for the window crank assemblies is as follows:

Direct material	$ 70,000
Direct labor	40,000
Variable manufacturing overhead	55,000
Fixed manufacturing overhead	35,000
Total	$200,000

REQUIRED:

a. Prepare a schedule that shows the relevant cost and the preferred alternative of this make or buy decision.

b. Discuss the qualitative factors that General should consider when deciding whether to buy the window cranks from the outside supplier.

LO 3 & 4: Relevant Cost and Qualitative Factors of an Outsourcing Decision

6–45. Hutchens Electric produces electric fans. Hutchens manufactures 19,000 small electric fan motors each year. Delta Motor Company has offered to supply Hutchens with the small electric motors for $12.50 each. The facilities that Hutchens uses to make the small motors is used to make larger motors and other components.

Hutchens's production cost for the small electric fan motors is as follows:

Direct material	$132,000
Direct labor	26,500
Variable manufacturing overhead	43,500
Fixed manufacturing overhead	77,500
Total	$279,500

REQUIRED:

a. Prepare a schedule that shows whether Hutchens Electric should buy the electric fans or continue to make them.

b. Discuss the qualitative factors that Hutchens should consider when making this make or buy decision.

LO 3 & 4: Relevant Cost and Qualitative Factors of an Outsourcing Decision

6–46. Refer to problem 6–45. Assume that Hutchens Electric can use the facilities freed up by purchasing the electric motors from Delta Motor Company to produce a new model fan that would have a contribution margin of $95,000.

REQUIRED:

a. Prepare a relevant cost schedule that shows whether Hutchens Electric should buy the electric fans or continue to make them.

b. Discuss the qualitative factors that Hutchens should consider when making this make or buy decision.

LO 3 & 4: Relevant Cost and Qualitative Factors of an Outsourcing Decision

6–47. Nunez Inc. requires 12,000 units of part X45 per year. At the current level of production, the cost per unit is as follows:

Direct material	$ 3
Direct labor	1
Variable overhead	2
Fixed overhead	4
Total	$10

JLW Inc. has offered to sell Nunez 12,000 units of X45 for $8 each. If Nunez is no longer required to produce the X45s, a supervisor can be eliminated. The supervisor's salary of $24,000 is part of fixed overhead cost. Other fixed overhead costs would remain the same.

REQUIRED:
a. Prepare a schedule that details the advantage or disadvantage of buying the 12,000 units of X45 from JLW Inc.
b. Discuss the qualitative aspects of purchasing the parts from JLW Inc.

LO 3 & 4: Relevant Cost and Qualitative Factors of an Outsourcing Decision

6–48. Cox Inc. requires 3,000 spindles per year. At the current level of production, the cost per unit is as follows:

Direct material	$ 38
Direct labor	12
Variable overhead	14
Fixed overhead	44
Total	$108

AMW Inc. has offered to sell Cox the 3,000 spindles for $100 each. If Cox is no longer required to produce the spindles, a supervisor can be eliminated. The supervisor's salary of $36,000 is part of fixed overhead cost. Other fixed overhead costs would remain the same.

REQUIRED:
a. Prepare a schedule that details the advantage or disadvantage of buying the 300 spindles from AMW Inc.
b. Discuss the qualitative aspects of purchasing the parts from AMW Inc.

LO 3 & 4: Relevant Cost and Qualitative Factors of an Outsourcing Decision

6–49. Adcox Inc. requires 4,000 switch assemblies per year. At the current level of production, the cost per unit is as follows:

Direct material	$ 3
Direct labor	3
Variable overhead	2
Fixed overhead	2
Total	$10

Camron Inc. has offered to sell Adcox Inc. the 4,000 switch assemblies for $9 each. If Adcox is no longer required to produce the switch assemblies, part of the building can be leased to another company for $10,000 per year. Other fixed overhead costs would remain the same.

REQUIRED:

a. Prepare a schedule that details the advantage or disadvantage of buying the 4,000 switch assemblies from Camron Inc.

b. Discuss the qualitative aspects of purchasing the parts from Camron Inc.

LO 1, 2, & 4: Prepare a Report for an Equipment Replacement Decision

6–50. The Sakura Company operates a chain of Japanese restaurants. Restaurant managers are paid bonuses based on the financial profits of their restaurants.

Last year, the manager of the South Austin Sakura Restaurant installed a new oven that cost $5,000. At the time, the oven had an estimated useful life of five years with no salvage value. Annual repair and maintenance on the oven is $900, and the cost of electricity used by the oven is $3,400 per year. The old oven can be sold now for $1,500.

A salesperson is trying to convince the store manager to replace the oven purchased last year with a new, energy-efficient model. The salesperson says the new oven will increase company profits. The new oven can be purchased for $6,000, and has an estimated useful life of four years with a salvage value of $1,000. The annual repair and maintenance would be the same as the old oven, or $900 per year, but the annual cost of electricity used by the oven would drop to $1,800.

The manager is not convinced by the salesperson. "If I buy this new oven, my financial income will drop and I'll never get my bonus. The loss in the first year will make me look like a fool!"

REQUIRED:

a. Prepare a report showing the relevant cost of keeping the old oven versus buying the new one.

b. Based on your report, what do you think of the restaurant manager's comments?

Chapter 7

The Capital Budget: Evaluating Capital Expenditures

*S*uppose for a moment that you are contemplating two very different kinds of purchases: a DVD and a new automobile. You would probably devote different amounts of time and effort to each purchase. You probably would not spend time reviewing your long-term goals and annual budget for the DVD purchase. Nor would you be likely to create a list of costs and benefits to decide which DVD to buy. If you were in the market for a new car, however, you might spend considerable time deciding whether you needed a new car, and if you did, which car to buy. The purchase of an expensive item that will be used for a long time, such as a car, warrants careful planning. Such planning is needed because once you have bought the expensive item, it is usually costly to change your mind—in our example, you would have to sell or trade the new car, probably at a substantial discount.

What is true in your personal financial decisions is also true in business. Unlike personal expenditures made for comfort or convenience, business expenditures are made to further the goals of the business. In fact, most business expenditures are made to increase a company's profits. For this reason, business expenditures are really investments, by which the company hopes to earn both a return *of* the investment and a return *on* the investment.

Business expenditures for acquiring expensive assets that will be used for more than one year are called **capital investments**. Because of the cost and extended useful life of these assets, companies devote tremendous time and energy to evaluating potential capital investments. For example, according to

capital investments Business expenditures in acquiring expensive assets that will be used for more than one year.

capital projects Another name for *capital investments*.

capital budgeting The planning and decision process for making investments in capital projects.

information in its annual report, Family Dollar Stores, Inc. invested more than $229 million in capital expenditures during 2005. Certainly, this magnitude of investment required serious analysis on the part of this company before it committed to the various projects represented by those dollars.

Generally, capital investments, also known as **capital projects,** are investments in property, plant, and equipment. Examples include investments in computer equipment, production equipment, another factory, a new wing of a hospital, or a new campus dormitory. **Capital budgeting** is the planning and decision process for making investments in capital projects. Although we focus on business firms in our discussion, all types of organizations can use capital budgeting techniques: for-profit, not-for-profit, and social organizations.

In this chapter, we explain how firms make capital budgeting decisions. Capital budgeting, however, is only part of a much more involved planning process, which we also discuss in this chapter.

Two of the evaluation techniques used to evaluate potential capital projects rely heavily on a knowledge of the time value of money. For this reason, we have included an appendix to the chapter that details the time value of money. ■

LEARNING OBJECTIVES

After completing your work on this chapter, you should be able to do the following:

1. Describe the overall business planning process and where the capital budget fits in that process.
2. Explain in your own words the process of capital budgeting.
3. Discuss the four shared characteristics of all capital projects.
4. Describe the cost of capital and the concept of scarce resources.
5. Determine the information relevant to the capital budgeting decision.
6. Evaluate potential capital investments using three capital budgeting decision models: net present value, internal rate of return, and payback period method.
7. Determine present and future values using present value tables and future value tables (chapter appendix).

THE BUSINESS PLANNING PROCESS

Managers use accounting information for two main types of business decisions, planning and control. In this section, we give an overview of how organizations plan for the future. We discuss the *why*, the *what*, the *how*, and the *who* of business planning. Though management accounting information is used in all steps in the planning process, it is especially important to the *what, how,* and *who* decisions.

Company Goals: The Why

People form an organization to accomplish a purpose or purposes—the organization's goals. These goals define why the organization exists. Setting goals, then, is the *why* of the business.

organizational goals The core beliefs and values of the company. They outline why the organization exists and are a combination of financial and nonfinancial goals.

Organizational goals constitute the core beliefs and values of the company, so those goals should not be subject to short-term economic pressures. Examples of some organizational goals might be to earn profits, to save lives, or to improve communication among employees. Most companies' goals are stated in general terms that are not easily quantified, which means that although progress toward fulfillment can be measured, it is not really possible to determine when the goals have been attained. For instance, a firm with the goal of earning profits usually does not specify exactly how much profit it must earn to meet its goal.

The goals of a business organization are usually a combination of nonfinancial and financial aspirations. Whether nonfinancial or financial, however, almost all goals have either a direct or indirect effect on the company's financial well-being. Does this sound strange? The next section explains why almost all goals can affect the financial health of a business.

Nonfinancial Goals

Typically, nonfinancial goals do not mention money. Rather, they refer to activities that may or may not result in profits. A hospital's nonfinancial goals, for instance, might be to provide the best health care possible to its patients; to recruit and employ highly qualified workers; to provide a safe, pleasant environment for its employees and patients; and to create an atmosphere of caring for both the physical and the emotional concerns of its patients.

Discussion Questions

7-1. Consider the hospital's nonfinancial goals. What financial effect will occur if the hospital *does* work toward those goals?

7-2. What financial effect will result if the hospital *does not* work toward those goals?

7-3. Review the hospital's nonfinancial goals. How would you determine when those goals have been reached?

Note that the nonfinancial goals for the hospital are stated in very general language. More than specific results, these goals represent standards of conduct and performance toward which the hospital should always be striving. They are stated in such a way that it is very difficult, if not impossible, to determine when the goals have been attained.

Financial Goals

For most business organizations, the primary financial goal is to earn a profit. What this really means, of course, is that the goal is to earn a return *on* investment for the business owner or owners. This goal may be worded as "achieving superior financial performance," "earning a reasonable return for the stockholders," "maximizing shareholder value," or similar language. As was the case with the nonfinancial goals, it is difficult to determine when these financial goals have been attained.

Goal Awareness

mission statement A summary of the main goals of the organization.

Once goals have been set, the company should communicate them to every person in the organization. This communication maximizes the likelihood that a business will achieve its goals. Many companies use a **mission statement**—a summary of the main goals of the organization—to communicate the firm's goals to all employees. Exhibit 7–1 is a sample mission statement from Johnson & Johnson. This mission statement is representative of those of many large companies.

The goals in the Johnson & Johnson mission statement address the concerns of all parties who have a stake in how the company conducts its business. For instance, Johnson & Johnson's stakeholders include health care providers, consumers, suppliers, employees, the community, and stockholders. Johnson & Johnson's mission statement communicates the firm's goals and presents the image of a responsible, ethical business.

Exhibit 7–1
Johnson & Johnson Mission Statement. Copyright © Johnson & Johnson, Inc.

Our Credo

We believe our first responsibility is to the doctors, nurses and patients, to mothers and fathers and all others who use our products and services. In meeting their needs everything we do must be of high quality. We must constantly strive to reduce our costs in order to maintain reasonable prices. Customers' orders must be serviced promptly and accurately. Our suppliers and distributors must have an opportunity to make a fair profit.

We are responsible to our employees, the men and women who work with us throughout the world. Everyone must be considered as an individual. We must respect their dignity and recognize their merit. They must have a sense of security in their jobs. Compensation must be fair and adequate, and working conditions clean, orderly and safe. We must be mindful of ways to help our employees fulfill their family responsibilities. Employees must feel free to make suggestions and complaints. There must be equal opportunity for employment, development and advancement for those qualified. We must provide competent management, and their actions must be just and ethical.

We are responsible to the communities in which we live and work and to the world community as well. We must be good citizens—support good works and charities and bear our fair share of taxes. We must encourage civic improvements and better health and education. We must maintain in good order the property we are privileged to use, protecting the environment and natural resources.

Our final responsibility is to our stockholders. Business must make a sound profit. We must experiment with new ideas. Research must be carried on, innovative programs developed and mistakes paid for. New equipment must be purchased, new facilities provided and new products launched. Reserves must be created to provide for adverse times. When we operate according to these principles, the stockholders should realize a fair return.

Johnson & Johnson

Merely stating lofty goals in a mission statement is not enough to reach the goals. Businesses must act consistently with their goals to ensure progress. Consider the following two examples. In 1982 Johnson & Johnson demonstrated the company's commitment to its goals after two fatalities occurred in the Chicago area when someone injected cyanide into six bottles of Tylenol. Once aware of these events, Johnson & Johnson immediately responded by recalling all Tylenol bottles. The company also instituted a nationwide advertising campaign advising consumers *not* to use Tylenol and provided full disclosure about the situation. In short, the company responded in a manner consistent with its goals.

Compare Johnson & Johnson's actions to Ford Motor Company's response to faulty ignition systems in some of its cars. These faulty ignition systems caught fire without warning and created a dangerous and potentially fatal situation. Ford's response was to wait for the federal government to tell the company which cars it had to recall. Legal? Certainly. A smart way to conduct business? In the short run, it cost Ford less than a total recall of the affected vehicles. In the long run, however, the company may not be conducting its business in a way consistent with its stated goal of total quality.

strategic plan A long-range plan that sets forth the actions a company will take to attain its organizational goals.

Once a business has set its goals, the firm must then create a **strategic plan**—a long-range plan that sets forth the actions the firm will take to attain its goals. In the following section, we explore briefly how firms develop strategic plans.

Strategic Plan: The What

The steps outlined in the strategic plan, sometimes referred to as a long-range budget, are the *what* of doing business. The actions specified in the strategic plan describe what actions a business must take to implement its goals. To be effective, then, strategic plans should support—not conflict with—the company's goals.

Companies make long-range plans so they are well positioned to reach their goals and benefit as the future unfolds. For example, it can take Dow Chemical Company five years or longer to build a production facility, so Dow managers must anticipate product demand accurately in advance, in order to build a plant of the appropriate size in time to produce enough to meet consumer demand.

A company's strategic plan tends to have objectives that are quantifiable, and a time frame for attainment of the objectives. A company might specify, for instance, that it plans to replace its four least-efficient production facilities over the next five years, reduce customer complaints by 20 percent over the next three years, or increase market share for its newest product by 25 percent within 10 years. As you can readily see, a firm can determine exactly when it has met all these objectives.

After an organization has developed a strategic plan that specifies the actions it will take to reach its goals, the company then decides how to allocate its monetary resources to implement its strategies, and who will be responsible for the day-to-day activities of the business. This step in the planning process is the preparation of budgets.

Preparation of the Capital Budget: The How

capital budget The budget that outlines how a company intends to allocate its scarce resources over a five-year, 10-year, or even longer time period.

The capital budget is the *how* of the planning process. The **capital budget** is the budget that outlines how a firm intends to allocate its scarce resources over a five-year, 10-year, or even longer time period.

The capital budget lays out plans for the acquisition and replacement of long-lived expensive assets such as land, buildings, machinery, and equipment. During the capital budgeting process, companies decide whether and what items should be purchased, how much should be spent, and how much profit can be generated from the items. In sum, capital budgeting decisions should further the strategic plan and goals of the business.

Operating Budget: The Who

operating budget The budget that plans a company's routine day-to-day business activities for one to five years.

Companies not only must budget for long-term activities, they also must plan and budget for day-to-day business activities. The budget that pertains to routine company operations for one to five years in the future is called the **operating budget.** The operating budget establishes who is responsible for the day-to-day operation of the organization, so we refer to it as the *who* of the planning process. The operating budget will be our focus in Chapter 8.

An important thing to understand about the planning process is the interrelationship among goals, strategic plan, capital budget, and operating budget. Exhibit 7–2 demonstrates that interrelationship.

Exhibit 7–2
Interrelationship among the Planning Elements

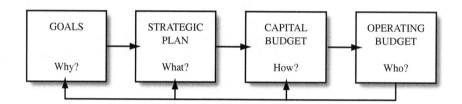

The overall function of management accounting is to provide a substantial portion of the information that company management needs not only to achieve the *what*, the *how*, and the *who*, but also to ensure that these functions are achieved within the context of the *why*.

THE CAPITAL BUDGET: WHAT IS IT?

capital assets Long-lived expensive items such as land, buildings, machinery, and equipment.

The capital budget plans for the acquisition and replacement of long-lived expensive items such as land, buildings, machinery, and equipment. These long-lived items are called **capital assets.** The capital budget focuses on the long-term operations of the company to determine how an organization intends to allocate its scarce resources over the next five, 10, or even 20 years. Thus, we refer to this part of the planning process as the *how* of being in business and doing business.

During the capital budgeting process, companies decide whether items should be purchased, how much should be spent, and how much profit the items promise to generate. No decisions made in the capital budgeting process, however, should conflict with the company's strategic plan or organizational goals.

Capitalizing Assets

Capital budgeting deals with decisions regarding investments that will benefit the company for many years, so most companies do not use capital budgeting techniques for small purchases or those that provide benefits for only the current year.

When an expenditure is made, the cost of the item purchased will be reflected either as an expense on the company's income statement for the year of purchase, or as an increase in the company's assets on its balance sheet. Theoretically, the distinction lies in whether the item purchased will provide economic value to the company beyond the year of purchase. If a purchased item is expected to provide economic benefits beyond the year in which it was purchased, it should be capitalized, which means that its cost has been recorded as an increase in long-term assets and will be depreciated (converted from asset to expense) over the item's estimated useful life. Conversely, if a purchased item is not expected to provide economic benefit to the company beyond the year of purchase, its cost should be reflected as an expense on the income statement for that year.

To illustrate, the cost of a delivery truck should be reflected as an increase in assets because the truck will likely be used for several years. In contrast, the cost of last month's lawn service does not provide any future value and therefore should be reflected as an expense immediately.

Judgment plays an important role in determining whether a purchased item should be capitalized or expensed. For example, how should the cost of a $3 wastebasket with an estimated useful life of three years be recorded? Because the wastebasket will be used for several years, the item should theoretically be capitalized—its cost should be added to long-term assets and depreciated over the wastebasket's estimated useful life.

From a practical standpoint, it is senseless to expend the additional accounting effort to capitalize and then depreciate the wastebasket. Why? Because, whether the wastebasket is capitalized and depreciated over its estimated useful life or expensed immediately, the effect on a company's financial statements would be so minimal that no economic decision maker will be influenced by the alternative selected. Thus, the cost of the wastebasket is immaterial, so due to the modifying convention of materiality discussed in financial accounting, the wastebasket is expensed when purchased.

Capitalization Amount

Generally, companies set a cost threshold that helps determine the appropriate accounting treatment for capitalizing long-lived items. For example, a company might say that any long-lived item costing less than $3,000 will be expensed when purchased, while those costing $3,000 or more will be capitalized. There are no hard and fast rules for setting the capitalization threshold, but most businesses choose an amount between $500 and $5,000 as their capitalization amount.

Characteristics of Capital Projects

Capital budgeting deals with planning for purchases of items that will be capitalized, meaning they will be classified as assets when purchased and then depreciated over their estimated useful lives. While the capitalization amount and the evaluation process for capital projects vary from company to company, all capital projects share certain characteristics. The four main shared characteristics include

1. *Long lives.* Capital projects are expected to benefit the company for at least two years. Usually the kinds of purchases we are discussing in this chapter benefit the company longer than two years, perhaps five, 10, or an even greater number of years.

2. *High cost.* Technically, the purchase of any long-lived item for which the cost exceeds a company's capitalization amount is considered a capital project. As stated earlier, this may be as low as $500 for some firms. As a practical matter, however, the capital budgeting techniques we consider in this chapter are used to evaluate high-cost projects. A good example is the cost of a new distribution facility built by Family Dollar Stores. Such a facility may cost $100 million or more. Another example is the decision by Wal-Mart or Sears to open a new store in a particular location. Many millions of dollars are involved in opening a store for these companies.

3. *Quickly sunk costs*. Costs that cannot be recovered are called sunk costs. A capital project usually requires a firm to incur substantial cost in the early stages of the project. As new information about market size, technology, and so on becomes available, the company's management may decide the project should be abandoned. Unfortunately, much of the cost already incurred may not be able to be recouped. For example, consider the case of a manufacturer that begins construction on a new factory with an estimated cost of $500 million. After spending $200 million on construction, the company decides the new factory is not needed because the product it planned to manufacture in the facility has become obsolete. The company cannot sell the partially completed factory and has no other use for it. The $200 million is a sunk cost because it cannot be recovered.

4. *High degree of risk*. Capital projects have a high degree of business risk because they involve the future, which always entails uncertainty. Because of the long lives, high costs, and sunk costs of capital projects, companies must try to estimate the returns from those projects in future years. These characteristics increase the likelihood of erroneous estimates. The uncertainty of the future coupled with the high initial investment make capital projects quite risky.

Discussion Question

Consider these questions: "Will I be paid?" "How much will I be paid?" and "When will I be paid?"

7–4. Why do you think these questions were extremely difficult for Microsoft to answer as the company considers the development of any potential capital project?

THE COST OF CAPITAL AND THE CONCEPT OF SCARCE RESOURCES

cost of capital The cost of obtaining financing from all available financing sources.

cost of capital rate Another name for *cost of capital*.

required rate of return Another name for *cost of capital*.

hurdle rate Another name for *cost of capital*.

When you put money into a savings account, you expect to earn interest. This interest is the return on your investment. Like most people, you would like the return to be as high as possible. If you were going to deposit $5,000 in a savings account, you would probably shop for a secure bank, with a return as high as or higher than that of competing banks.

Businesses shop for capital projects the same way you would shop for a bank in which to deposit your $5,000. If it appears that a capital project will be profitable, how does a company determine whether it will be profitable enough to warrant investing its money? A proposed project should promise a return that is equal to or exceeds the firm's cost of capital.

In evaluating potential capital projects, a company must determine a benchmark rate of return to help select which capital project or projects it will undertake. The benchmark return rate for selecting projects is usually the company's **cost of capital,** which is the cost of obtaining financing from all available financing sources. Cost of capital is also referred to as the **cost of capital rate,** the **required rate of return,** or the **hurdle rate.** For the sake of consistency, we use cost of capital throughout all our discussions in this chapter.

As you may recall from financial accounting, companies can obtain financing from two sources, borrowing from creditors (debt financing) and investments by owners (equity financing). When a company invests in a capital project, the money must come from one or both of these sources. Both creditors and owners require a return on the funding they provide to the company, and the company must seek investments that provide a return at least equal to the cost of obtaining funding from debt and equity sources. If a company borrows funds at an interest rate of 9 percent, then the expected return on a capital project must be at least 9 percent. Similarly, if a company's owners provide the financing and expect a return of 20 percent on their investment, then the expected return from a capital project should be at least 20 percent to be acceptable.

Blended Cost of Capital

The funding for a company's capital projects usually comes from a combination of debt and equity financing. The combined cost of debt and equity financing is called the **blended cost of capital.** The rate for the blended cost of capital represents the combined rate of the cost of both debt and equity financing.

blended cost of capital
The combined cost of debt financing and equity financing.

cost of debt capital The interest a company pays to its creditors.

cost of equity capital
What equity investors give up when they invest in one company rather than another.

The **cost of debt capital** is the interest a company pays to its creditors. The interest rate, say 8 percent, is agreed upon when a company borrows from either the bank or the bond market. The amount of interest a company pays is easy to determine because it is reported on the company's income statement as interest expense.

The cost of a company's equity financing is more challenging to determine than the cost of its debt financing, because the **cost of equity capital** is what equity investors relinquish when they invest in one company rather than another. To illustrate, assume Elizabeth Sauer has $5,000 to invest and she is considering the purchase of either Boardman Company stock or Emry Company stock. The question is, what does Elizabeth give up if she invests her $5,000 in Boardman? She relinquishes what she would have earned had she invested in Emry. That is, she lost the opportunity to earn whatever she would have earned had she purchased Emry's stock rather than Boardman's.

The amount an equity investor earns is a combination of dividends received and the appreciation in the market value of the stock the investor owns. In Elizabeth's case, the amount earned if she buys the Boardman Company stock is a combination of the dividends she receives from Boardman, plus any increase in the market value of the Boardman stock she owns.

Discussion Question

Assume Elizabeth buys the Boardman stock and consistently earns an 8% return on her investment (dividends plus appreciation of the Boardman stock).

7–5. If Elizabeth could earn a 17% return on an investment in Emry Company stock (or some other company), what would you advise her to do? Explain your reasoning.

It's all well and good for us to discuss this topic from the investor's point of view (in this case Elizabeth Sauer), but what has this to do with the cost of equity capital for Boardman Company? Well, if Boardman wants to keep Elizabeth as a stockholder, it must return to her an amount at least as great as she could earn by investing her money somewhere else. If Elizabeth can earn 17 percent from an investment in Emry, Boardman must give her that kind of return or she may sell her Boardman stock and invest in Emry (or some other company). Boardman, then, would use 17 percent as the cost of the equity capital it received from Elizabeth, because that is what she could earn elsewhere. In other words, that is what she gave up by investing in Boardman.

In a real-world situation, Boardman Company would not know about the alternatives being considered by Elizabeth Sauer and her $5,000. Therefore, the company cannot determine the specific percentage return Elizabeth must earn to keep her happy. What Boardman must do is try to determine what percentage return equity investors can generally expect on their investments and use that percentage as the cost of equity capital.

Unlike debt financing costs (interest expense), the cost of equity financing is not reported in financial statements in its entirety. Firms do report profit distributions to stockholders in the form of dividends, but the larger part of the cost of equity capital is the appreciation in the market value of stockholders' ownership interest. This market value is not reported on financial statements.

To determine the full cost of equity capital, we must examine how stocks appreciate in value. We assume first that rational investors would desire a return on an investment in an individual company at least equal to the return they could receive from investing in other, similar publicly traded companies.

If all companies whose stocks are traded on recognized stock markets (NYSE, AMEX, NASDAQ, and so on) were separated based on the percentage return they provide their stockholders, the breakdown would appear as shown in Exhibit 7–3.

Exhibit 7–3
Returns Provided by the Stock Market

| HIGH RETURN COMPANIES |
25% of Firms
MEDIUM RETURN COMPANIES
50% of Firms
LOW RETURN COMPANIES
25% of Firms

The high return companies in Exhibit 7–3 represent one-fourth of all the companies whose stock is publicly traded. The medium return companies comprise one-half of the companies, and the low return companies represent one-fourth of the total.

Discussion Question

7-6. If you owned stock in a publicly traded company, in which group of companies in Exhibit 7–3 would you want your company to be?

Most equity investors desire to own stock in high return companies because they naturally want their investment to earn the highest possible return. Many high return companies in the stock market yield as high as 17 percent to 20 percent annually to their stockholders in the form of dividends and appreciation in stock value.

Discussion Questions

Assume you own stock in a publicly traded company and you consistently earn an 8% return on your investment (dividends plus appreciation of the company's stock).

7-7. If you are certain you could earn a 20% return on an investment in some other company's stock, what would you do? Explain your reasoning.

7-8. Because a publicly traded company receives money only when its stock is originally issued, why do you think it would care about the stock's market value in the stock market?

It is important to note here that the issue is not whether investors can, in fact, earn a 20 percent return by selling their stock in one company and investing in another. They only need to *think* they can earn the higher return.

If enough of a company's stockholders begin selling their stock, the market price of the stock will drop—the economic law of supply and demand at work. As the stock price drops, more stockholders may decide to sell their stock before the price drops even lower. This, of course, makes the stock price drop further.

Discussion Question

7-9. What would you think about a company whose stock was selling for $50 a share in January and $12 a share in December?

Stock analysts, customers, suppliers, and many other parties have a tendency to gauge a company's health by the market value of its stock. For this reason, companies have a vested interest in making sure the market value of their stock does not begin a downward spiral.

Because the investors in the stock market think they can earn a 17 to 20 percent return by investing in the top performing companies, a company must return 17 to 20 percent annual return to its stockholders to be considered one of the high performing companies. Publicly traded companies usually consider their cost of equity financing to be as high as 20 percent. This percentage is commonly used to compute the company's blended cost of capital.

To illustrate the calculation of the blended cost of capital, we consider the case of Adler Enterprises, which has $2,000,000 in assets. A total of $1,200,000 (60 percent) of these assets were obtained using debt financing with an interest rate of 7.5 percent. The remaining $800,000 (40 percent) was financed through equity capital and the company uses a 20 percent cost of equity financing. We find the blended cost of capital for Adler Enterprises using the following calculation.

Method of Financing	Proportion of Financing Provided		Cost of Financing		Weighted Cost of Financing
Debt	60%	×	7.5%	=	4.5%
Equity	40%	×	20.0%	=	8.0%
			Blended Cost of Capital		12.5%

We see that Adler's weighted cost of debt financing is the proportion of debt financing (60 percent) multiplied by the cost of that financing (7.5 percent). The company's weighted cost of equity financing is the proportion of equity financing (40 percent) times the cost of the equity financing (20 percent). Its blended cost of capital is the sum of the weighted cost of each type of financing—12.5 percent.

Firms use their blended cost of capital as a benchmark rate of return to evaluate capital projects. For example, suppose Adler Enterprises is considering a capital project that requires an investment of $200,000. If Adler decides to undertake this project, it must obtain $200,000 to fund it. Recall that Adler's blended cost of capital is 12.5 percent. Unless the expected rate of return on the project is 12.5 percent or higher, Adler's management will probably reject the project. Otherwise, it would cost more to fund the project than the project could earn.

Discussion Questions

7-10. When you consider that companies are generally in business to earn a profit, why might it be acceptable to select a capital project that promises a return that is just equal to the blended cost of capital?

7-11. Under what circumstances do you think a company might accept one capital project over another even though the project selected promises a lower return?

7-12. Do you think there would ever be a situation when a company should proceed with a capital project even though the project promises a return lower than the cost of capital? Explain your reasoning.

7-13. What do you think might cause a company to reject a proposed capital project even though it promises a return significantly higher than the cost of capital?

Scarce Resources

I'm so broke that if they was selling steamboats for a dime apiece, I could run up and down the bank saying 'ain't that cheap'.

—Roy Clark

In our personal lives, what we buy is usually not limited by how much we want, but rather by how much money we have available to spend. Well, what is true for individuals is also true for businesses. The number and size of capital projects a company undertakes is not limited by a lack of viable alternative projects. What limits companies is that they simply do not have access to enough money to take advantage of all the opportunities available to them. This limitation on the amount available to spend is commonly called **scarce resources.** Even huge multinational companies must select only investments they consider most favorable from a virtually unlimited pool of possible investment opportunities, because firms do not have access to enough money to invest in every good project that comes along. Managers must carefully evaluate the alternative capital projects available to their companies so they can select the projects that promise the highest return (as long as the projects are consistent with the company's goals and strategies).

scarce resources A term describing the limited amount of money a company has to invest in capital projects.

EVALUATING POTENTIAL CAPITAL PROJECTS

Because capital projects are usually long lived, costly, and high risk, managers must carefully evaluate capital expenditure decisions, especially in light of their financial limitations. The evaluation process generally includes the following four steps.

1. Identifying possible capital projects
2. Determining the relevant cash flows for alternative projects
3. Selecting a method of evaluating the alternatives
4. Evaluating the alternatives and selecting the capital project or projects to be funded

Let us investigate each of these steps from the manager's point of view.

Identifying Possible Capital Projects

Businesses usually make capital expenditures to maximize profits by either increasing revenue, reducing costs, or a combination of the two. A project that satisfies the company's desire to maximize profits will be identified as a potential capital expenditure.

Firms often generate revenue increases by investing in projects that increase capacity or draw more customers. For a hotel chain, an increase in available rooms might increase revenue. For a restaurant, revenue might be enhanced by investing in cooking equipment that prepares food more rapidly. For a hospital, the ability to provide additional services or an increased number of beds might be the key to added revenue.

To reduce operating costs a manufacturer might upgrade production equipment so less direct labor or less electricity is required. An airline catering company could invest in more energy-efficient ovens to reduce food preparation cost. Reducing cost has exactly the same effect as increasing revenue. As Benjamin Franklin said, "A penny saved is a penny earned." If you think about it, this really makes sense. If a company saves $1 by reducing costs by $1, the cost reduction has the same impact on profits as increasing selling price to increase revenue by $1.

Although the majority of potential capital projects are intended to either increase revenue or reduce costs, in certain instances a company must make a capital expenditure that will result in neither. These projects are usually concerned with safety or environmental issues and may come as a result of governmental regulation requirements; or, a company may simply determine such an expenditure is necessary given its goal of worker safety or good corporate citizenship.

In any event, capital projects that are deemed necessary but do not promise either to increase revenue or reduce costs are usually not evaluated using the same criteria as those projects that do promise increased profits. In this chapter, we restrict ourselves to the evaluation of potential capital projects that promise to either increase revenue or reduce costs.

As the need for increasing revenue or reducing costs presents itself, all alternative courses of action should be explored. Brainstorming sessions and input from multiple sources both within and outside a firm can help generate ideas for alternative options.

Determining Relevant Cash Flows for Alternative Projects

Throughout our discussion of capital budgeting, we have discussed capital projects that promise to increase a company's profits by either increasing revenue or reducing costs (expenses). Recall, however, that under accrual accounting, revenue is not the same as cash inflow and expense is not the same as cash outflow in the short run. Recall also that in the long run, revenue and expenses measured using accrual accounting *are* the same as cash inflow and cash outflow.

net cash flows Cash inflow less cash outflow.

Because capital projects usually are long lived, most business managers believe it is appropriate to analyze an alternative using cash inflow and cash outflow over the life of the project. They do this by determining the **net cash flow** of a project—the project's expected cash inflows minus its cash outflows for a specific time period. For example, if a manager estimates that investing in a new production machine will yield $40,000 in cash inflows during the useful life of the machine but will require spending $30,000 for the same period, the net cash flow would be $10,000 ($40,000 − $30,000).

relevant net cash flows
Future net cash flows that differ between or among the alternatives being considered.

Only relevant net cash flows should be considered in a capital budgeting decision. **Relevant net cash flows** are future cash flows that differ between or among alternatives. Thus, a relevant cash flow must be one that will occur in the future, not one that has already occurred, and it must be affected by the investment decision. Past cash flows, or cash flows that will not change as a result of the investment decision, are irrelevant and should not be considered in the decision process. This concept should seem familiar because it follows the same reasoning as our discussion of relevant costs, the subject of Chapter 6.

Once a company obtains and assesses the relevant cash flows for each alternative project, the next step is to choose a method to measure the value of each project.

Selecting a Method of Evaluating the Alternatives

Over time, many capital budgeting decision methods have been developed to evaluate potential capital projects. In this chapter, we present three methods:

- Net present value
- Internal rate of return
- Payback period method

Each of these methods offers a different way to measure a project's value, and sometimes the different methods render conflicting rankings. In such a case, managers should be aware of the strengths and weaknesses of each capital budgeting method. In the next section we discuss each of the four methods and the advantages and disadvantages of each.

Selecting Capital Budgeting Projects

To select a capital budgeting project, firms decide first whether to accept or reject a project using one or more capital budgeting techniques to measure the project's value. If the project does not generate an acceptable rate of return, it will probably be rejected. Furthermore, any proposed capital project that is inconsistent with a company's goals and strategic plan should be rejected, even if the promised return on that project is higher than some other potential project.

Once a project has been accepted as viable, the project can then be ranked with other acceptable projects based on expected performance.

CAPITAL BUDGETING DECISION METHODS

In this section, we explain three capital budgeting methods: net present value, internal rate of return, and payback period method. The first two methods, which are discounted cash flow methods, are used more frequently in business because they include the concept of the time value of money.

time value of money The increase in the value of cash over time due to investment income.

A dollar received at some point in the future does not have the same value as a dollar received today. The reason for the difference in value is that if cash is available now, it can be invested now and earn a return as time passes. This increase in the value of cash over time due to investment income is referred to as the **time value of money.** The concept of the time value of money is used to determine either the future value of money invested today or the present value of money to be received at some point in the future.

In the following discussion of net present value and internal rate of return, we assume you have a working knowledge of the time value of money, discussed in detail in the appendix to this chapter. Refer to it now if you need to refresh your understanding.

discounting cash flows Determining the present value of cash to be received in the future.

Capital projects deal with cash flows that begin in the present and extend into the future, sometimes for many years. Therefore, the evaluation of these kinds of projects uses the concept of present value. Determining the present value of cash to be received in future periods is called **discounting cash flows.**

Discounted Cash Flow Methods

Business managers use two discounted cash flow methods to evaluate potential capital projects: net present value and internal rate of return.

net present value (NPV) The present value of all cash inflows associated with a proposed capital project minus the present value of all cash outflows associated with the proposed capital project.

Net Present Value The **net present value (NPV)** of a proposed capital project is the present value of cash inflows minus the present value of cash outflows associated with a capital budgeting project. Note that the net present value is different from the present value. The former is the difference between the present value of a capital project's net cash flows. The latter is the amount a future payment or series of payments is in today's dollars evaluated at the appropriate discount rate. The net present value method is used to determine whether a proposed capital project's return is higher or lower than the blended cost of capital.

A company calculates the NPV of a capital project by discounting the net cash flows for all years of the project using the company's blended cost of capital as the discount rate. A positive net present value indicates that the expected return on a proposed project is higher than the company's cost of capital. A negative net present value indicates that the expected return on a proposed project is lower than the company's cost of capital. A net present value of zero shows that the expected return on a project is exactly equal to the company's cost of capital.

To illustrate the net present value calculations, assume the Juan Rodriguez Company is considering a computer hardware upgrade that would require an investment of $100,000. Assume further that the enhanced speed of the computer is expected to save $31,000 annually in operator salaries. Remember, this reduction of cash outflow is a cash inflow in net present value analysis. The computer has an estimated useful life of five years with no residual value.

The cash flows associated with the computer upgrade are shown in Exhibit 7–4.

Exhibit 7–4
Expected Cash Flows for Juan Rodriguez Company Computer Upgrade

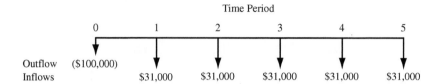

Notice in Exhibit 7–4 that the initial cash outlay of $100,000 occurs at "time 0." When working with present values, time 0 is considered today, or the present. Unless otherwise specified, we assume all other cash flows for this project will occur at the end of each period.[1]

Juan Rodriguez Company has a 14 percent blended cost of capital, so we use 14 percent as the discount rate to evaluate whether the company should accept the computer upgrade project; that is, we use a 14 percent discount rate to calculate the present value of the project's cash outflows and cash inflows. In this case, the project's $100,000 cash outflow occurs today (time 0), so that amount is already stated in present value terms.

Next, we must find the present value of the project's cash inflows, which occur at the end of each of the next five years. Because the stream of $31,000 positive cash flows constitutes an annuity, we use the *Present Value of an Annuity of $1 Table*, found in the chapter appendix in Exhibit A7–10, to find the present value factor of a five-year annuity, with a discount rate of 14 percent. We have reproduced a portion of the table as Exhibit 7–5. As you can see from the highlighted portion in this exhibit, the factor for five years with a discount rate of 14 percent is 3.433.

Exhibit 7–5

Present Value of Annuity of $1

Period	4%	5%	6%	7%	8%	10%	12%	14%	16%
1	.962	0.952	0.943	.935	0.926	0.909	0.893	0.877	0.862
2	1.886	1.859	1.833	1.808	1.783	1.736	1.690	1.647	1.605
3	2.775	2.723	2.673	2.624	2.577	2.487	2.402	2.322	2.246
4	3.630	3.546	3.465	3.387	3.312	3.170	3.037	2.914	2.798
5	4.452	4.629	4.212	4.100	3.993	3.791	3.605	3.433	3.274
6	5.242	5.076	4.917	4.767	4.623	4.355	4.111	3.889	3.685
7	6.002	5.786	5.582	5.389	5.206	4.868	4.564	4.288	4.039

---

[1]We also ignore depreciation in our analysis because depreciation is a noncash expense under accrual accounting and the NPV method focuses on cash flow rather than accrual operating income.

We multiply $31,000, the amount of the annuity, by the 3.433 present value factor and find that the present value of the annuity is $106,423 ($31,000 × 3.433 = $106,423). Finally, we find the net present value of the project by subtracting the present value of cash outflows from the present value of cash inflows. In our example, the net present value calculations are presented in Exhibit 7–6.

Exhibit 7-6
Net Present
Value Calculations

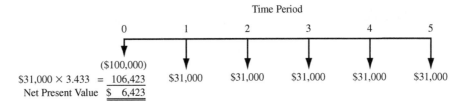

NPV = PV of project's expected returns - initial cash outlay

NPV = $106,423 - $100,000

NPV = $6,423

As Exhibit 7–6 shows, the positive net present value of $6,423 indicates that the project's expected return exceeds Juan Rodriguez Company's 14 percent blended cost of capital.

A word of caution here. A net present value of $6,423 does not mean that the project's return is only $6,423. Rather, it means that the project's return *exceeds* the company's 14 percent cost of capital by $6,423.

Discussion Questions

7-14. How would you explain the difference between present value and net present value?

7-15. Should a business accept or reject a project with an NPV of zero? Explain your reasoning.

The Juan Rodriguez Company example was relatively easy to calculate because the project's expected cash flows were the same each year (an annuity). When the expected cash flows are uneven, we find the present value of each year's cash flow and then add those amounts. To demonstrate, assume that the Juan Rodriguez Company's computer upgrade has expected annual returns of $31,000, but in year 3 the computer system will require $12,000 in maintenance fees (a cash outflow), and at the end of year 5, the system can be sold for $6,000 (a cash inflow). A time line depicting these additional cash flows is shown in Exhibit 7–7.

Exhibit 7-7
Uneven Expected Cash
Flows for Juan
Rodriguez Company
Computer Upgrade

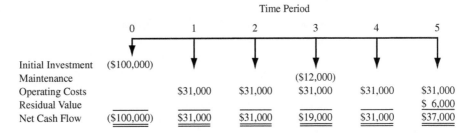

Each of the amounts for the five years shown in Exhibit 7–7 can be discounted to present value using the *Present Value of $1 Table,* found in the chapter appendix in Exhibit A7–5, a portion of which is reproduced as Exhibit 7–8.

Exhibit 7–8

Present Value of $1

Period	4%	5%	6%	7%	8%	10%	12%	14%	16%
1	0.962	0.952	0.943	0.935	0.926	0.909	0.893	0.877	0.862
2	0.925	0.907	0.890	0.873	0.857	0.826	0.797	0.769	0.743
3	0.889	0.864	0.840	0.816	0.794	0.751	0.712	0.675	0.641
4	0.855	0.823	0.792	0.763	0.735	0.683	0.636	0.592	0.552
5	0.882	0.784	0.747	0.713	0.681	0.621	0.567	0.519	0.476
6	0.790	0.746	0.705	0.666	0.630	0.564	0.507	0.456	0.410
7	0.760	0.711	0.665	0.623	0.583	0.513	0.452	0.400	0.354

The calculation of the present values, using the highlighted factors in the 14 percent discount rate column, are shown in Exhibit 7–9.

Exhibit 7–9
Net Present Value
Calculations with
Uneven Cash Flows

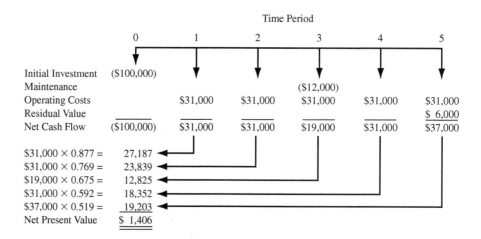

As Exhibit 7–9 demonstrates, the positive $1,406 net present value indicates that the computer upgrade exceeds the 14 percent blended cost of capital for the Juan Rodriguez Company. This positive NPV indicates that the project is acceptable for the company.

Although the net present value method indicates whether a proposed capital project is acceptable, it does have limitations as a ranking method to compare competing projects. A direct comparison of the net present values of various projects may lead to poor decisions regarding project selection, because NPV is measured in dollars rather than percentages. For example, assume that management intends to select one of two projects, Project A and Project B. Calculations indicate that the NPV of Project A is $5,000, whereas the NPV of Project B is $6,000.

Although choosing the project with the higher NPV seems wise, this is not always a good choice because NPV analysis does not consider the relative investments required by the projects. In our example, for instance, say the present value of Project A's cash inflows was $105,000 and the present value of its cash outflows was $100,000. Then suppose that the present value of Project B's cash inflows was

$206,000 and the present value of its cash outflows was $200,000. We see that Project A requires an investment of $100,000, whereas Project B requires double that investment amount. In firms with scarce funds, the relatively small increase in the NPV from $5,000 to $6,000 may not justify selecting a project that requires double the amount of investment. How then can the net present value method be used when ranking various projects? The problem of selecting among projects is solved by using a profitability index.

profitability index   A method used to rank acceptable proposed capital projects.

Profitability Index   The **profitability index** is an index of the values of alternative but acceptable capital budgeting projects, whose index values are calculated by dividing the present value of the project's cash inflows by the present value of its cash outflows. To illustrate, we return to our example. We know that both Projects A and B have positive NPVs and are acceptable projects. Suppose, however, we want to rank the projects in order of preference.

We find that the profitability index for Project A is 1.05 ($105,000/$100,000 = 1.05). The profitability index for Project B is 1.03 ($206,000/$200,000 = 1.03). We would rank Project A higher than Project B because Project A's index value is 1.05 compared to Project B's lower index value of 1.03. We see, then, how the profitability index is a tool that allows firms to rank competing projects.

Although the NPV method indicates whether a project's return is lower or higher than the required rate of return, it does not show the project's expected percentage return. Many managers find it helpful to know the expected rate of return of projects when making capital budgeting decisions. The internal rate of return method, discussed in the following section, is a capital budgeting method that provides this information.

internal rate of return (IRR)   The calculated expected percentage return promised by a proposed capital project.

real rate of return   Another name for *internal rate of return.*

time-adjusted rate of return   Another name for *internal rate of return.*

Internal Rate of Return   The **internal rate of return (IRR)** of a proposed capital project is the calculated expected percentage return promised by the project. Just like the net present value method, the internal rate of return method considers all cash flows for a proposed project and adjusts for the time value of money. However, the IRR results are expressed as a percentage, not a dollar amount. This method, also known as the **real rate of return,** or the **time-adjusted rate of return,** determines the discount rate that makes the present value of a project's cash inflows and the present value of a project's outflows exactly the same.

To calculate a project's IRR, we use the same present value tables we use to calculate net present value, but we interpret them differently. In this application, we consult the tables to determine a discount rate (a percentage), rather than present value amounts (expressed in dollars).

As an example, assume that Project C requires an initial investment of $300,000 and will provide cash inflows of $56,232 per year for eight years. Because this project is an annuity, to determine the IRR we use the *Present Value of an Annuity of $1 Table* found in the chapter appendix in Exhibit A7–10, a portion of which is reproduced as Exhibit 7–10.

First we calculate the present value factor for the project as follows:

$$\frac{\text{Initial Investment}}{\text{Expected Annual Return}} = \text{Present Value Factor}$$

In the case of Project C, the present value factor is

$$\frac{\$300,000 \text{ Initial Investment}}{\$56,232 \text{ Expected Annual Return}} = 5.335 \text{ Present Value Factor}$$

Now that we know the present value factor, we can find Project C's internal rate of return by moving down the time period column on the table in Exhibit 7–10 to eight periods, as that is the life of the project. Next we follow across the row corresponding to eight periods until we find a factor that is close to the one we calculated (5.335). As we follow across the row for eight periods, we find a factor that is not just close but matches exactly. The factor of 5.335 is in the 10 percent column, which indicates the internal rate of return for Project C is 10 percent. Thus, the actual rate of return promised by Project C is 10 percent.

Exhibit 7–10
Partial Present Value of an Annuity of $1 Table

Present Value of Annuity of $1

Period	4%	5%	6%	7%	8%	10%	12%
1	0.962	0.952	0.943	.935	0.926	0.909	0.893
2	1.886	1.859	1.833	1.808	1.783	1.736	1.690
3	2.775	2.723	2.673	2.624	2.577	2.487	2.402
4	3.630	3.546	3.465	3.387	3.312	3.170	3.037
5	4.452	4.629	4.212	4.100	3.993	3.791	3.605
6	5.242	5.076	4.917	4.767	4.623	4.355	4.111
7	6.002	5.786	5.582	5.389	5.206	4.868	4.564
8	6.733	6.463	6.210	5.971	5.747	5.335	4.968
9	7.435	7.108	6.802	6.515	6.247	5.759	5.328
10	8.111	7.722	7.360	7.024	6.710	6.145	5.650
11	8.760	8.306	7.877	7.499	7.139	6.495	5.938
12	9.382	8.863	8.384	7.943	7.536	6.814	6.194

Once determined, the internal rate of return is compared to the cost of capital to gauge the project's acceptability. An internal rate of return that exceeds the firm's cost of capital indicates an acceptable project. For example, if the company's cost of capital is nine percent, Project C's 10 percent internal rate of return shows that the firm would find the project acceptable.

In the example for Project C, we contrived the dollar amounts so that the factor we calculated exactly equaled one of the factors in the present value table. In a real-life situation, the calculated factor will usually fall between two factors on the present value table. For example, assume Project D would require an investment of $330,000 and would generate estimated annual returns of $64,900 for eight years. The present value factor for this project is 5.085, determined as follows:

$$\frac{\$330,000 \text{ Initial Investment}}{\$64,900 \text{ Annual Returns}} = 5.085 \text{ Present Value Factor}$$

Returning to the table in Exhibit 7–10 and following across the year 8 row, we find that our calculated 5.085 factor is between the factors 5.335 (the 10 percent column) and 4.968 (the 12 percent column), but is much closer to 4.968. Therefore, the project's return would fall between 10 and 12 percent, but would be much closer to 12 percent. We then estimate that the internal rate of return for Project D is slightly less than 12 percent.

Comparing Projects Using the IRR Method Managers can use the internal rate of return method to rank projects. For example, the internal rate of return of Project C (10 percent), can be compared to the approximate internal rate of return of Project D (almost 12 percent). Assuming both projects were acceptable, Project D would be ranked higher than Project C because it promises a higher IRR.

Comparing the NPV and IRR Methods   Both the net present value method and the internal rate of return method are well-respected techniques used to determine the acceptability of a proposed capital project for two reasons. First, they are based on cash flows, not accounting income. Second, both methods consider the time value of money.

The net present value method is used to determine whether the promised return from a proposed capital project meets the minimum acceptable return requirements (cost of capital). A drawback of this method is that the calculated net present value is stated in dollars rather than percentages. Thus, comparison between projects is difficult. The profitability index overcomes this difficulty.

The internal rate of return method is used to calculate a proposed capital project's actual expected rate of return. Because this method is calculated using percentages rather than dollars, it can be used as a direct comparison of various proposed projects.

Nondiscounted Cash Flow Methods

The net present value and internal rate of return methods are generally considered the most reliable techniques available because they utilize the time value of money in their evaluation of potential capital projects. Other methods that ignore the time value of money exist, however, and are used to some degree by many companies. We now discuss the payback period method.

payback period method
A capital budgeting technique that measures the length of time a capital project must generate positive cash flows that equal the original investment in the project.

Payback Period Method   As its name implies, the **payback period method** is a capital budgeting technique that measures the length of time a capital project must generate positive net cash flows that equal, or "pay back," the original investment in the project. For instance, assume that a project's estimated initial outlay is $40,000. Assume further that the project is expected to generate a net cash inflow of $12,500 per year. When net cash inflows are equal from one year to the next, we determine the payback period by dividing the required initial investment by the annual cash inflows. In our example, we find that the payback period is 3.2 years. The calculations follow:

$$\frac{\text{Required Initial Investment}}{\text{Annual Net Cash Inflow}} = \text{Payback Period in Years}$$

$$\frac{\$40,000}{\$12,500} = 3.2 \text{ Years}$$

If a project has uneven cash flows, we can determine the payback period by adding the cash inflows year by year until the total equals the required initial investment. For example, suppose a project requires an initial investment of $50,000 and is expected to generate the following net cash inflows:

2001	$12,000
2002	$15,000
2003	$18,000
2004	$15,000
2005	$12,000

We find the payback period by totaling the net cash inflows until we reach $50,000 as shown in Exhibit 7–11.

Exhibit 7–11
Payback Period with
Uneven Cash Flows

Year	Cash Received in Prior Years		Cash Received in Current Year		Accumulated Cash Received
1	0	+	$12,000	=	$12,000
2	$12,000	+	$15,000	=	$27,000
3	$27,000	+	$18,000	=	$45,000
4	$45,000	+	$15,000	=	$60,000
5	$60,000	+	$12,000	=	$72,000

As Exhibit 7–11 shows, the initial investment will be "paid back" after the third year, but before the end of the fourth year. At the end of the third year, it is anticipated that $45,000, or all but $5,000 of the initial $50,000 investment will be recouped. The remaining $5,000 will be received during the fourth year as part of the $15,000 net cash inflows anticipated for that year. It will take about 1/3 ($5,000/$15,000) of the fourth year to collect the final $5,000 to make up the $50,000 needed to payback the initial investment. Therefore the payback period is 3 1/3 years.

The payback period method highlights the liquidity of an investment and can be used as a screening device to reject projects with unreasonably low cash flow expectations. This method is simple to use, is easily understood, and offers some limited insight into a project's liquidity.

The payback period method is not often used to make final capital investment decisions because it does not consider three crucial elements: (1) the expected returns of a project after the payback period, (2) how the returns will compare to the firm's cost of capital, or (3) the time value of money.

Because the payback method ignores the firm's cost of capital, total cash flow, and time value of money concerns, managers do not normally accept or reject a project based solely on the payback period method. If used at all, the payback period method is usually a screening device only to eliminate potential projects from further evaluation. Companies often establish a maximum payback period for potential projects. If a proposed capital project promises a payback of longer than the established maximum period, that project would be eliminated from further consideration. For example, assume a company has established a maximum payback period of three years. Using this standard, the project presented in Exhibit 7–11 would be rejected because its payback period is longer than three years.

FACTORS LEADING TO POOR CAPITAL PROJECT SELECTION

The process of determining which capital projects to select is serious business for any company. We mentioned earlier in the chapter that Family Dollar Stores reported investment in capital projects of over $229 million in 2005. If managers do not treat capital budgeting with the seriousness it deserves, they run the risk of making poor decisions as to the capital projects selected. At the very least, selecting the wrong capital projects is enormously costly. At worst, investing in the wrong projects can lead to financial ruin for any company, regardless of its size or past performance. The two main factors leading to poor capital project selection are natural optimism on the part of managers and the tendency of some managers to turn the capital project evaluation process into a game.

Natural Optimism

Human beings are essentially optimistic. As managers they estimate both the cash inflows and outflows associated with a proposed project they are sponsoring with an overly optimistic outlook. This means they will likely overstate the estimated cash inflows and understate the estimated cash outflows. At the very minimum, this natural optimism limits the effectiveness of any of the evaluation techniques we have discussed in this chapter, because all of them use inflow and outflow estimates as the basis of evaluation.

There is nothing wrong with thinking positively. Optimism is, in fact, a desirable trait. Managers must understand, however, that such optimism can cloud their judgment as they assess potential capital projects. Good managers attempt to be as realistic as possible as they prepare proposals for the evaluation of potential capital projects.

Capital Budgeting Games

The managers who propose potential capital projects understand that there is usually not enough money available to fund all projects, even if they all promise a return greater than the cost of capital. A manager who proposes a capital project is, in fact, competing with other managers' projects for a limited number of capital investment dollars. For this reason, the capital project evaluation process is sometimes treated like some sort of game with little consideration of the potentially disastrous consequences. Some managers manipulate the estimates of cash inflow and cash outflow to get "pet" projects approved, often at the expense of other, more deserving projects. Do not confuse this idea with the natural optimism we discussed a moment ago. The manipulation we are talking about here is an additional factor that can lead to selecting the wrong capital projects.

For example, consider the Electronics Division of Monolith Enterprises. This division has established a limit of $3 million for capital projects in 2002. Mary and Fred are the only two managers within the division who have potential capital projects to propose to division upper management. Both the potential projects will require an initial investment of $2 million, so only one of them is going to be approved.

Mary is in her office late one night putting the finishing touches on her proposal. She is reviewing the cash inflow and cash outflow estimates she has made for her project. As she goes over the estimates one last time, she is feeling a little guilty because she knows she has purposely overstated the inflows and understated the outflows to make her project look more favorable. She is convinced, however, that if she is totally realistic in her estimates, her project will stand no chance of being approved. Why? Because she knows Fred is in his office down the hall putting the finishing touches on his proposal, and she is sure he has manipulated the inflow and outflow estimates on his project to make it look better. To have any chance of approval, then, Mary must "play the game." The sad part of this situation is that Fred is down the hall in his office thinking exactly the same thing about Mary. He is certain she has manipulated her estimates, so he must also, or his project has no chance of being approved. Now we introduce one more person to our scenario—Bill, the division controller. Bill is the person who will evaluate the proposed projects submitted by Mary and Fred and will decide which of the two projects will be funded. He knows that both Mary and Fred have manipulated their estimates, so when he receives them, he compensates by arbitrarily revising their proposals or by using a higher cost of capital percentage in the NPV and IRR evaluations.

Does this seem to you to be an intelligent way to run a business? No, but this kind of game is played every day in many companies by otherwise bright and honest managers.

Discussion Question

Assume you have been hired as a consultant by Monolith Enterprises to help the company improve its capital project evaluation process.

7-16. What suggestions would you make to help Monolith eliminate the kind of "game" being played by Mary, Fred, and Bill?

How does a company make its capital project evaluation process more cooperative and less competitive? This question is difficult, if not impossible, to answer. What we do know, however, is that the global nature of business in the 21st century will not allow these kinds of budget games to continue. U.S. companies are competing with companies from all over the world, and the kind of behavior we have been discussing does not seem to exist in many of these businesses. If U.S. firms are to compete in this worldwide market, they must eliminate dysfunctional business practices. The stakes are simply too high for managers of these companies to continue this approach to capital budgeting.

In a very short time, you will occupy the positions held by Mary, Fred, or Bill. Not at Monolith, of course, because it is a fictitious company. The company that employs you, however, may approach capital budgeting the same way Monolith does. If so, you must do all you can to help the company find a better, more constructive capital budgeting process.

SUMMARY

There are four elements in the overall planning process for any organization. These elements include the establishing of goals, the formulation of a strategic plan, the preparation of the capital budget, and the preparation of the operating budget.

The capital budgeting process has been described as the *how* of being in business and doing business, which means that the capital budget outlines how a company will allocate its scarce resources over the next 5, 10, or even 20 years.

All capital projects have at least four shared characteristics. Such projects are usually long lived, carry with them high costs, have costs associated with the project that usually become sunk almost immediately, and usually involve a high degree of risk.

In the long run, the capital projects a company undertakes must cover at least the cost of the company's capital. The cost of capital is the cost of obtaining financing from both debt and equity sources. The combination of the cost of debt financing and equity financing is referred to as the blended cost of capital. If the capital project being considered does not at least cover the cost of capital, it makes no sense, from a purely financial standpoint, to undertake it.

Over time, several methods have been developed to evaluate potential capital projects. Among these are the net present value method, the internal rate of return method, and the payback period method. Each of these three methods has certain advantages and disadvantages relative to the other methods. The NPV and IRR methods are generally considered to be superior to the payback method because they incorporate the time value of money in their approach to evaluating potential capital projects.

APPENDIX: THE TIME VALUE OF MONEY

The Time Value of Money—The Concept of Interest

> *Interest is an interesting thing—*
> *Those who understand it, get it.*
> *Those who don't, pay it.*
>
> —Anonymous

A dollar received at some point in the future does not have the same value as a dollar received today. If you were asked why this is so, you might think the change in value is due to inflation. Even if inflation did not exist, a dollar received in the future would not have the same value as a dollar received today. The reason for the difference in value is that if cash is available now, it can be invested now and earn a return as time passes. This increase in the value of cash over time, due to investment income, is referred to as the time value of money. The concept of the time value of money is used to determine either the future value of money invested today or the present value of money to be received at some point in the future.

LEARNING OBJECTIVES

After completing your work in the appendix to this chapter, you should be able to do the following:

1. Explain the concept of simple interest and compound interest.
2. Determine the future value of a single amount invested today using a future value table.
3. Determine the present value of a single amount to be received at some point in the future using a present value table.
4. Describe the concept of an annuity.
5. Determine the future value of an annuity using a future value table.
6. Determine the present value of an annuity using a present value table.

Future Value

future value The value of a payment, or series of payments, at some future point in time calculated at some interest rate.

Future value is the value of a payment, or series of payments, at some future point in time calculated at some interest rate. For example, if you were to invest $2,000 at an annual interest rate of 10 percent, your investment would grow to $2,200 in one year. How? The amount of the increase is calculated by multiplying the principal—the original investment—by the interest rate. In our case the principal is $2,000, the interest rate is 10 percent, so the total return on your investment is $200. The $200 is added to the $2,000 investment for a total of $2,200. So far, so good. But suppose you left the investment untouched for three years. What would be its total value at the end of the three years? The answer depends on whether the interest is calculated as simple interest or compound interest.

simple interest Interest calculated on the original principal amount invested only

Simple interest is interest calculated only on the original principal. A calculation of interest earned at 10 percent per year for three years on a $2,000 principal using simple interest is presented in Exhibit A7–1.

Exhibit A7–1
Simple Interest
Calculation

	Year 1	Year 2	Year 3
Principal	$2,000	$2,000	$2,000
Times the interest rate	× 10%	× 10%	× 10%
Equals interest earned	$ 200	$ 200	$ 200

Note in Exhibit A7–1 that interest for each of the three years is calculated only on the original investment of $2,000. At the end of three years you would receive your $2,000 (return of your principal) and $600 interest (return on your investment).

compound interest Interest calculated on the original principal amount invested plus all previously earned interest.

Compound interest is interest calculated on the investment principal *plus* all previously earned interest. Continuing with our example, a principal of $2,000 that earns a compounded rate of 10 percent interest per year for three years is shown in Exhibit A7–2.

Note in Exhibit A7–2 that interest for each of the three years is calculated not only on the original investment of $2,000, but also on the interest earned in previous years. At the end of three years you would receive your $2,000 back (return of principal) and $662 interest (return on your investment). The difference of $62 between the interest earned using compound interest ($662) and the interest earned using simple interest ($600) is interest earned on your previously earned interest.

The power of compounding is tremendous. To demonstrate, let us extend our example of the $2,000 investment. Suppose Dick Gustufson invests $2,000 at 10 percent annual interest when he is 18 years old and leaves it untouched until he is 38 years old. Using the simple interest calculation, Dick's investment will earn interest of $4,000 ($2,000 × 10% × 20 years). If, however, the interest over that same 20 years is compounded, the total interest earned would be $11,454. The $7,454 difference in interest earned is due entirely to interest earning interest on previously earned interest.

We could calculate the amount of compound interest on Dick's investment by extending the three-year example presented in Exhibit A7–2 for another 17 years. This, however, would be cumbersome, time consuming, and tiresome. Fortunately, future value tables greatly simplify the calculation of compound interest.

Future value tables are previously calculated values of $1 at various rates of interest and time periods. The tables are used to determine either the future value of a single payment or the future value of an annuity—that is, a stream of equal payments made at equal intervals.

Exhibit A7–2
Compound Interest
Calculations

	Year 1	Year 2	Year 3
Principal + Previously earned interest	$2,000	$2,200*	$2,420**
Times the interest rate	× 10%	× 10%	× 10%
Equals interest earned	$ 200	$ 220	$ 242

* Principal ($2,000) plus the interest earned in year 1 ($200) becomes the amount earning interest in year 2.

** Principal ($2,000) plus the interest earned in year 1 ($200) and the interest earned in year 2 ($220) becomes the amount earning interest in year 3.

The *Future Value of $1 Table* (Exhibit A7–3) is used to determine the future value of a single amount deposited today. With this information, we can quickly determine the future value of Dick Gustufson's $2,000 investment at a 10 percent interest rate compounded annually.

As we see in Exhibit A7–3, by moving across the interest rate column headings to the 10 percent column, and then down the time period row to the 20 time periods row, we find a number on the table at the point where the row and column intersect, at a value of 6.727. This number is called a future value factor. Because we are using the *Future Value of $1 Table*, the 6.727 factor tells us that the value of a single dollar 20 years into the future is $6.727, or about $6.73. That is to say that if $1 is invested today at 10 percent, it will be worth $6.73 in 20 years.

But Dick invested $2,000, not $1. To determine the future value of $2,000, we multiply $2,000 by the factor of 6.727 to determine that $2,000 invested today at 10 percent will be worth $13,454 after 20 years ($2,000 × 6.727 = $13,454). If you subtract his initial investment of $2,000, the amount of interest he will earn is $11,454.

A *Future Value of an Annuity of $1 Table*, presented as Exhibit A7–4, is used to determine the future value of a stream of cash flows when the stream of cash flows constitutes an annuity. An **annuity** is a stream of cash flows where the dollar amount of each payment and the time interval between each payment are uniform.

annuity A stream of equal periodic cash flows.

To see how the table in Exhibit A7–4 is used, assume Susan Pate intends to deposit $2,000 in an account at the end of each year for four years at a compound interest rate of 12 percent per year. Using the *Future Value of an Annuity of $1 Table* we determine that the factor for 4 years at 12 percent is 4.779. Accordingly, if Susan deposits $2,000 at the end of each year for four years at 12 percent, the account balance will be approximately $9,558 ($2,000 × 4.779).

Exhibit A7–3
Future Value of $1 Table

Future Value of $1

Period	4%	5%	6%	7%	8%	9%	10%	12%	14%	16%
1	1.040	1.050	1.060	1.070	1.080	1.090	1.100	1.120	1.140	1.160
2	1.082	1.103	1.124	1.145	1.166	1.188	1.210	1.254	1.300	1.346
3	1.125	1.158	1.191	1.225	1.260	1.295	1.331	1.405	1.482	1.561
4	1.170	1.216	1.262	1.311	1.360	1.412	1.464	1.574	1.689	1.811
5	1.217	1.276	1.338	1.403	1.469	1.539	1.611	1.762	1.925	2.100
6	1.265	1.340	1.419	1.501	1.587	1.677	1.772	1.974	2.195	2.436
7	1.316	1.407	1.501	1.606	1.714	1.828	1.949	2.211	2.502	2.826
8	1.369	1.477	1.594	1.718	1.851	1.993	2.144	2.476	2.853	3.278
9	1.423	1.551	1.689	1.838	1.999	2.172	2.358	2.773	3.252	3.803
10	1.480	1.629	1.791	1.967	2.159	2.367	2.594	3.106	3.707	4.411
11	1.539	1.710	1.898	2.105	2.332	2.580	2.853	3.479	4.226	5.117
12	1.601	1.796	2.012	2.252	2.518	2.813	3.138	3.896	4.818	5.936
13	1.665	1.886	2.113	2.410	2.720	3.066	3.452	4.363	5.492	6.886
14	1.732	1.980	2.261	2.579	2.937	3.342	3.797	4.887	6.261	7.988
15	1.801	2.079	2.397	2.759	3.172	3.642	4.177	5.474	7.138	9.266
16	1.873	2.183	2.540	2.952	3.426	3.970	4.595	6.130	8.137	10.748
17	1.948	2.292	2.693	3.159	3.700	4.328	5.054	6.866	9.276	12.468
18	2.026	2.407	2.854	3.380	3.996	4.717	5.560	7.690	10.575	14.463
19	2.107	2.527	3.026	3.617	4.316	5.142	6.116	8.613	12.056	16.777
20	2.191	2.653	3.207	3.870	4.661	5.604	6.727	9.646	13.743	19.461

Exhibit A7–4
Future Value of an Annuity of $1 Table

Future Value of Annuity of $1

Period	4%	5%	6%	7%	8%	9%	10%	12%	14%	16%
1	1.000	1.000	1.000	1.000	1.000	1.000	1.000	1.000	1.000	1.000
2	2.040	2.050	2.060	2.070	2.080	2.090	2.100	2.120	2.140	2.160
3	3.122	3.153	3.184	3.215	3.246	3.278	3.310	3.374	3.440	3.506
4	4.246	4.310	4.375	4.440	4.506	4.573	4.641	4.779	4.921	5.006
5	5.416	5.526	5.637	5.751	5.867	5.985	6.105	6.353	6.610	6.877
6	6.633	6.802	6.975	7.153	7.336	7.523	7.716	8.115	8.536	8.977
7	7.898	8.142	8.394	8.654	8.923	9.200	9.487	10.089	10.730	11.414
8	9.214	9.549	9.897	10.260	10.637	11.028	11.436	12.300	13.233	14.240
9	10.583	11.027	11.491	11.978	12.488	13.021	13.579	14.776	16.085	17.519
10	12.006	12.578	13.181	13.816	14.487	15.193	15.937	17.549	19.337	21.321
11	13.486	14.207	14.972	15.784	16.645	17.560	18.531	20.665	23.045	25.733
12	15.026	15.917	16.870	17.888	18.977	20.141	21.384	24.133	27.271	30.850
13	16.627	17.713	18.882	20.141	21.495	22.953	24.523	28.029	32.089	36.786
14	18.292	19.599	21.015	22.550	24.215	26.019	27.975	32.393	37.581	43.672
15	20.024	21.579	23.276	25.129	27.152	29.361	31.772	37.280	43.842	51.660
16	21.825	23.657	25.673	27.888	30.324	33.003	35.950	42.753	50.980	60.925
17	23.698	25.840	28.213	30.840	33.750	36.974	40.545	48.884	59.118	71.673
18	25.645	28.132	30.906	33.999	37.450	41.301	45.599	55.750	68.394	84.141
19	27.671	30.539	33.760	37.379	41.446	46.018	51.159	63.440	78.969	98.603
20	29.778	33.066	36.786	40.995	45.762	51.160	57.275	72.052	91.025	115.380

Present Value (Discounting)

The basic premise of the present value of money is that it is more valuable to receive cash today (so it can be invested to receive interest) than to receive the cash later. The question is, just *how* valuable is it to receive cash sooner rather than later?

If we know the expected rate of return, it is possible to actually calculate the value of receiving cash sooner rather than later. For example, if you are offered the option of receiving $1,000 today or $1,000 one year from now, how much more valuable is it to receive the $1,000 today? If the $1,000 received today can be invested in a savings account earning six percent interest, then it will grow by $60 during the year. At the end of one year, it will be worth $1,060 and you would be $60 richer than if you had opted to receive the $1,000 one year from now. The $60 growth in value over time exemplifies the time value of money. Clearly, if money is available and invested, it grows as time passes.

If cash can be invested at six percent, $1,000 received today is equivalent to receiving $1,060 one year from now. The amount a future cash flow or stream of cash flows is worth today evaluated at the appropriate interest rate is the cash flow's **present value.** Determining the present value of an amount of cash to be received in the future is called *discounting*.

present value   The amount future cash flows are worth today based on an appropriate interest rate.

Present value tables greatly simplify the calculation of discounting to find the present value of a single amount or an annuity. Present value tables are previously calculated values of $1 at various interest rates and time periods. The tables are used to determine either the present value of a single amount or the present value of an annuity.

A *Present Value of $1 Table,* presented as Exhibit A7–5, is used to determine the present value of a single amount to be received at some point in the future.

To see how we use the *Present Value of $1 Table,* suppose you visited your rich Aunt Hattie and helped her wash her dog. Your aunt was so touched by your kindness, she offers to give you a gift of $1,000. You are excited and hold out your hand for the money, but she informs you that she is not going to give you the money now. Rather she intends to give you the money one year from now. Her only request is that you tell her how much to deposit in a six percent savings account today so that the account will equal $1,000 one year from now.

In this case, you know that the future value of the amount is $1,000 one year from now. The amount your Aunt Hattie wants to know is the present value, the amount that must be deposited today at six percent so that the account will be worth $1,000 in one year. To find out how much Aunt Hattie must deposit, we use the *Present Value of $1 Table* in Exhibit A7–5. We quickly scan the table to find the point of intersection between the six percent interest rate column and the number of time periods row which is 1. The point of intersection, the present value factor, is 0.943. This factor indicates that the present value of one dollar discounted at six percent is $0.943, or about 94 cents. Thus, if $0.943 is invested today at six percent, it will be worth $1 one year from now.

But Aunt Hattie is going to give you $1,000, not $1. To determine the present value of $1,000, we simply multiply $1,000 by the factor of 0.943 to determine that $943 invested today at six percent will be worth $1,000 in one year, as shown by the time line presentation in Exhibit A7–6.

Exhibit A7–5
Present Value of $1 Table

Present Value of $1

Period	4%	5%	6%	7%	8%	10%	12%	14%	16%
1	0.962	0.952	0.943	0.935	0.926	0.909	0.893	0.877	0.862
2	0.925	0.907	0.890	0.873	0.857	0.826	0.797	0.769	0.743
3	0.889	0.864	0.840	0.816	0.794	0.751	0.712	0.675	0.641
4	0.855	0.823	0.792	0.763	0.735	0.683	0.636	0.592	0.552
5	0.882	0.784	0.747	0.713	0.681	0.621	0.567	0.519	0.476
6	0.790	0.746	0.705	0.666	0.630	0.564	0.507	0.456	0.410
7	0.760	0.711	0.665	0.623	0.583	0.513	0.452	0.400	0.354
8	0.731	0.677	0.627	0.582	0.540	0.467	0.404	0.351	0.305
9	0.703	0.645	0.592	0.544	0.500	0.424	0.361	0.308	0.263
10	0.676	0.614	0.558	0.508	0.463	0.386	0.322	0.270	0.227
11	0.650	0.585	0.527	0.475	0.429	0.350	0.287	0.237	0.195
12	0.625	0.557	0.497	0.444	0.397	0.319	0.257	0.208	0.168
13	0.601	0.530	0.469	0.415	0.368	0.290	0.229	0.182	0.145
14	0.557	0.505	0.442	0.388	0.340	0.263	0.205	0.160	0.125
15	0.555	0.481	0.417	0.362	0.315	0.239	0.183	0.140	0.108
16	0.534	0.458	0.394	0.339	0.292	0.218	0.163	0.123	0.093
17	0.513	0.436	0.371	0.317	0.270	0.198	0.146	0.108	0.080
18	0.494	0.416	0.350	0.296	0.250	0.180	0.130	0.095	0.069
19	0.475	0.396	0.331	0.277	0.232	0.164	0.116	0.083	0.060
20	0.456	0.377	0.312	0.258	0.215	0.149	0.104	0.073	0.051

Exhibit A7–6
Time Line Presentation
of Present Value of $1

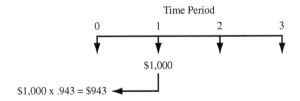

Exhibit A7–6 shows that to earn $1,000 a year from now, given an expected rate of interest of six percent per year, Aunt Hattie must deposit $943. So, the present value of $1,000 to be received one year from now at six percent is $943. The $943 will grow in value as it accumulates interest. This growth is the time value of money. You immediately inform your aunt Hattie that she must deposit $943 today at six percent to have the $1,000 gift ready for you one year from now.

Aunt Hattie is so happy with your quick response that she offers you an additional $1,000 gift. The second $1,000 gift, however, will be given two years from now, which means you will receive the first $1,000 gift at the end of year 1, and the second $1,000 gift at the end of year 2. You are thrilled, but again, your Aunt Hattie requests that you tell her exactly how much she must deposit today at six percent to have the additional $1,000 in two years. We use the *Present Value of $1 Table* in Exhibit A7–5 to find that the present value factor for a time period of two and an interest rate of six percent is 0.890. Accordingly, the present value of $1,000 to be received two years from now is $890 ($1,000 × 0.890). You quickly inform your aunt that she must deposit a total of $1,833 ($943 + $890) today to pay both the $1,000 at the end of year 1, and the $1,000 at the end of year 2. The time line and calculations are shown in Exhibit A7–7.

Exhibit A7–7
Time Line Presentation

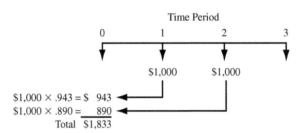

Now suppose your Aunt Hattie planned to give you a gift of $1,000 per year for the next three years. We could rely on the *Present Value of $1 Table* and add the totals for each year as shown in Exhibit A7–8.

Exhibit A7–8
Time Line Presentation

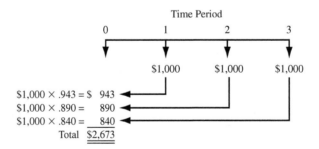

We can simplify the calculations, however, by multiplying the $1,000 by the sum of the three present value factors, which is 2.673. Accordingly, instead of multiplying $1,000 by 0.943, then $1,000 by 0.890, then $1,000 by 0.840, and summing the total, we simply multiply the $1,000 by the sum of the factors as shown in Exhibit A7–9.

Exhibit A7–9
Time Line Presentation

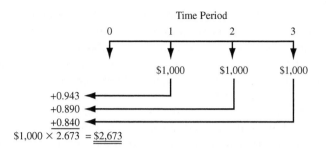

Because the stream of cash flows in our example is an annuity—three equal payments made at regular intervals of one year—we can use the *Present Value of an Annuity of $1 Table*, presented as Exhibit A7–10.

By examining the table in Exhibit A7–10, we find that the present value factor of an annuity for three periods at six percent is 2.673. Notice that the 2.673 equals the sum of the individual present value of $1 factors for each of the three years in Exhibit A7–9. Next, we multiply the $1,000 by the 2.673 factor to find that the present value of Aunt Hattie's $1,000, three-year annuity paid yearly is $2,673.

As you use the future value and present value tables provided in this book, note that the number of interest rates and time periods is limited. Although these smaller tables are useful for learning the basics, in business practice future value and present value tables include a much larger number of interest rates and time periods. If needed, comprehensive tables are available at bookstores and office supply stores.

Exhibit A7–10
Present Value of an Annuity of $1 Table

Present Value of Annuity of $1

Period	4%	5%	6%	7%	8%	10%	12%	14%	16%
1	0.962	0.952	0.943	0.935	0.926	0.909	0.893	0.877	0.862
2	1.886	1.859	1.833	1.808	1.783	1.736	1.690	1.647	1.605
3	2.775	2.723	2.673	2.624	2.577	2.487	2.402	2.322	2.246
4	3.630	3.546	3.465	3.387	3.312	3.170	3.037	2.914	2.798
5	4.452	4.629	4.212	4.100	3.993	3.791	3.605	3.433	3.274
6	5.242	5.076	4.917	4.767	4.623	4.355	4.111	3.889	3.685
7	6.002	5.786	5.582	5.389	5.206	4.868	4.564	4.288	4.039
8	6.733	6.463	6.210	5.971	5.747	5.335	4.968	4.639	4.344
9	7.435	7.108	6.802	6.515	6.247	5.759	5.328	4.946	4.607
10	8.111	7.722	7.360	7.024	6.710	6.145	5.650	5.216	4.833
11	8.760	8.306	7.877	7.499	7.139	6.495	5.938	5.453	5.029
12	9.382	8.863	8.384	7.943	7.536	6.814	6.194	5.660	5.179
13	9.986	9.394	8.853	8.358	7.904	7.103	6.424	5.842	5.342
14	10.563	9.899	9.295	8.745	8.244	7.367	6.628	6.002	5.468
15	11.118	10.380	9.712	9.108	8.559	7.606	6.811	6.142	5.575
16	11.652	10.838	10.106	9.447	8.851	7.824	6.974	6.265	5.669
17	12.166	11.274	10.477	9.763	9.122	8.022	7.120	6.373	5.749
18	12.659	11.690	10.828	10.059	9.372	8.201	7.250	6.467	5.818
19	13.134	12.085	11.158	10.336	9.604	8.365	7.366	6.550	5.877
20	13.590	12.462	11.470	10.594	9.818	8.514	7.469	6.623	5.929

As an alternative to using future and present value tables, we can compute future value and present value using nothing more than a somewhat sophisticated business handheld calculator. (It must be a business calculator. Engineering and scientific calculators generally do not have present value and future value functions.) In the business world, most managers rely on calculators and computers to calculate future and present values.

Most computers can also be used to solve present value and future value problems. Many software packages now include modules that can handle simple and advanced calculations dealing with the time value of money.

A working knowledge of present and future value concepts will be extremely important to you not only in your college course work but also in your professional career. Whether the task is the evaluation of potential capital projects, as in this chapter, or any of its many other applications, you will find these concepts invaluable throughout your life.

REVIEW THE FACTS

A. What constitutes a firm's goals?
B. What is a mission statement and how does it relate to a company's goals?
C. What is a strategic plan and how does it relate to a company's goals?
D. What is the purpose of a capital budget and how does it relate to the strategic plan and a company's goals?
E. What is the purpose of an operating budget and how does it relate to the capital budget, the strategic plan, and a company's goals?
F. What are capital investments?
G. What is the difference between a capital investment and a capital project?
H. What is the focus of the capital budget?
I. What does it mean when the cost of a purchased item is capitalized?
J. What does it mean when the cost of a purchased item is expensed?
K. What are the four shared characteristics of virtually all capital projects?
L. What are some other terms used to describe the cost of capital?
M. Describe what is meant by the net present value of an investment.
N. With respect to net present value calculations, what is the advantage of calculating the profitability index?
O. What is determined by the internal rate of return?
P. What is determined by the payback method?
Q. What are two factors that can lead to poor capital project selection?
R. What is the basic difference between simple interest and compound interest? (Appendix)
S. What is an annuity? (Appendix)

APPLY WHAT YOU HAVE LEARNED

LO 1:   Match Elements of Planning to Characteristics

7–17. Following are the elements of the planning process as discussed in this chapter, with some characteristics pertaining to those elements.

a. Goals
b. Strategic plan
c. Capital budget
d. Operating budget

1. _____ Pertains to day-to-day activities
2. _____ Pertains to the allocation of scarce resources
3. _____ Consists of both financial and nonfinancial considerations
4. _____ Stated in terms that are not easily quantified
5. _____ Stated in terms that are easily quantified
6. _____ Constitutes the *who* of business planning
7. _____ Constitutes the *why* of business planning
8. _____ Constitutes the *how* of business planning
9. _____ Constitutes the *what* of business planning
10. _____ Relates to long-lived, expensive assets

REQUIRED:
Match each element of the planning process with the appropriate characteristics. Each letter may be used more than once.

LO 4: Discuss and Calculate the Cost of Capital

7–18. The Marcus Company is in the process of determining a return rate to use for its cost of capital.

Upon review of the financial statements it was determined that the total interest bearing debt is $1,400,000 and total stockholders equity is $1,000,000. In addition, it was determined that the cost of debt financing is 8%, and the cost of equity financing is 18%.

REQUIRED:
a. What proportion of the Marcus Company's total financing comes from debt?
b. What proportion of the Marcus Company's total financing comes from equity?
c. Calculate the Marcus Company's blended cost of capital rate.

LO 4: Discuss and Calculate the Cost of Capital

7–19. The Byrne Company is in the process of determining a return rate to use for its cost of capital.

Upon review of the financial statements it was determined that the total interest bearing debt is $4,800,000 and total stockholders' equity is $14,400,000. In addition, it was determined that the cost of debt financing is 7%, and the cost of equity financing is 22%.

REQUIRED:
a. What proportion of The Byrne Company's total financing comes from debt?
b. What proportion of The Byrne Company's total financing comes from equity?
c. Calculate The Byrne Company's blended cost of capital rate.

LO 4: Discuss and Calculate the Cost of Capital

7–20. The Cunningham Company is in the process of determining a return rate to use for its cost of capital.

Upon review of the financial statements it was determined that the total interest bearing debt is $800,000 and total stockholders' equity is $1,700,000. In addition, it was determined that the cost of debt financing is 9%, and the cost of equity financing is 20%.

REQUIRED:

a. What proportion of The Cunningham Company's total financing comes from debt?

b. What proportion of The Cunningham Company's total financing comes from equity?

c. Calculate The Cunningham Company's blended cost of capital rate.

LO 2: Determine the Sequence of Evaluating Capital Expenditures

7–21. Following in random order are the five steps for evaluating a capital expenditure.

    a. _____ Identify alternative capital projects.

    b. _____ Identify the need for a capital expenditure.

    c. _____ Select a method for evaluating the alternatives.

    d. _____ Evaluate the alternatives and select the project or projects to be funded.

    e. _____ Determine relevant cash inflow and cash outflow information.

REQUIRED:

In the space provided, indicate a logical sequence of the steps for evaluating a capital expenditure.

LO 6 & 7: Determine Net Present Value, No Residual Value

7–22. Florence Kundrat owns Discount Fashions. She is contemplating the purchase of a soda machine which would be used to sell soft drinks to customers for $0.75 each. The following estimates are available:

Initial outlay	$3,500
Annual cash inflow	$1,000
Cost of capital	10%
Estimated life of the soda machine	5 years
Estimated residual value of the soda machine	$ -0-

REQUIRED:

Determine the net present value of the soda machine purchase.

LO 6 & 7: Determine Net Present Value, No Residual Value

7–23. Brianna Garcia is contemplating the purchase of an ice cream vending machine which would be used to sell ice cream to customers for $2 each. The following estimates are available.

Initial outlay	$4,000
Annual cash inflow	$1,200
Cost of capital	12%
Estimated life of the ice cream machine	5 years
Estimated residual value of the ice cream machine	$ -0-

REQUIRED:

Determine the net present value of the ice cream machine purchase.

LO 6 & 7: Determine Net Present Value, No Residual Value

7–24. Javier Cruz is contemplating the purchase of a machine which will automate the production of baseball bats in his factory. The following estimates are available.

Initial outlay	$97,000
Annual reduction in manufacturing labor cost	$22,500
Cost of capital	14%
Estimated life of the baseball bat machine	8 years
Estimated residual value of the bat machine	$ -0-

REQUIRED:
Determine the net present value of the baseball bat machine purchase.

LO 6 & 7:   Determine Net Present Value, No Residual Value

7–25. Dahlia Garcia is contemplating the purchase of a machine which will automate the production of hosiery in her factory. The following estimates are available.

Initial outlay	$112,000
Annual reduction in manufacturing labor cost	$ 22,500
Cost of capital	12%
Estimated life of the hosiery machine	8 years
Estimated residual value of the hosiery machine	$ -0-

REQUIRED:
Determine the net present value of the hosiery machine purchase.

LO 6 & 7:   Determine Net Present Value and Profitability Index, Various Rates, No Residual Value

7–26. Michael Diaz Sporting Goods is considering the purchase of a machine that is used to cut material to make baseball gloves. The cost of the machine is $265,000. The machine has an estimated useful life of eight years, with no residual value. Currently, the company leases a similar machine for $50,000 per year. If the new machine is purchased, the company's cost of labor would be reduced by $12,000 per year.

REQUIRED:
a. Determine the net present value of the machine under each of the following assumptions.
   1. The cost of capital is 12%
   2. The cost of capital is 14%
   3. The cost of capital is 16%
b. Determine the profitability index under each of the following assumptions.
   1. The cost of capital is 12%
   2. The cost of capital is 14%
   3. The cost of capital is 16%

LO 6 & 7:   Determine Net Present Value and Profitability Index, Various Rates, No Residual Value

7–27. Carlos Urriola Manufacturing is considering the purchase of a computer-controlled manufacturing machine that is used in its factory. The cost of the machine $3,600,000. The machine has an estimated useful life of 10 years, with no residual value. If the new machine is purchased, the company's cost of labor would be reduced by $650,000 per year.

REQUIRED:

a. Determine the net present value of the machine under each of the following assumptions.
    1. The cost of capital is 10%
    2. The cost of capital is 12%
    3. The cost of capital is 14%

b. Determine the profitability index under each of the following assumptions.
    1. The cost of capital is 10%
    2. The cost of capital is 12%
    3. The cost of capital is 14%

LO 6 & 7:   Determine Net Present Value, No Residual Value

7–28. Frank Eiroa is considering the purchase of an engine lift for use in his marine repair business. He has determined that a used lift is available for $5,500. The engine lift has an estimated useful life of eight years and a residual value of zero. Currently, Frank rents engine lifts as needed. If the lift is purchased, annual rental payment of $1,400 would be saved. The cost of capital is 16%.

REQUIRED:
Calculate the net present value of the engine lift purchase.

LO 6 & 7:   Determine Net Present Value, No Residual Value

7–29. Alfredo Lomando is considering the purchase of an industrial glass-cutting machine for use in his business. He has determined that a used glass cutter is available for $25,800. The cutter has an estimated useful life of 10 years and a residual value of zero. Currently, Alfredo rents an industrial cutter for $4,400 annually. The cost of capital is 14%.

REQUIRED:
Calculate the net present value of the industrial glass cutter.

LO 6 & 7:   Determine Net Present Value, with Residual Value

7–30. The owner of Wynn Sports Cards is contemplating the purchase of a machine which will automate the production of baseball cards in her factory. The following estimates are available.

Initial outlay	$35,000
Annual reduction in manufacturing labor cost	$ 8,500
Cost of capital	14%
Estimated life of the card machine	5 years
Estimated residual value of the card machine	$ 2,000

REQUIRED:
Determine the net present value of the baseball card machine purchase.

LO 6 & 7:   Determine Net Present Value, with Residual Value

7–31. Kevin Petty owns Discount Auto Parts. He is contemplating the purchase of a brake lathe that could be used to refurbish brake parts for customers. The following estimates are available.

Initial outlay	$6,500
Annual cash inflow	$1,500
Cost of capital	16%
Estimated life of the brake lathe	6 years
Estimated residual value of the brake lathe	$1,000

REQUIRED:

Determine the net present value of the brake lathe purchase.

LO 6 & 7:   Determine Net Present Value, with Residual Value

7–32. Paola Grillon owns Grillon Skin Care Products. She is contemplating the purchase of an industrial mixer that would be used to mix cosmetics in her factory. The following estimates are available.

Initial outlay	$78,500
Annual cash inflow	$19,500
Cost of capital	16%
Estimated life of the mixer	7 years
Estimated residual value of the mixer	$ 4,000

REQUIRED:

Determine the net present value of the industrial mixer purchase.

LO 6 & 7:   Determine Net Present Value, with Residual Value

7–33. Elianne Vinas owns Vinas Shoe Company. She is contemplating the purchase of a cutting machine that would be used to make shoes in her factory. The following estimates are available.

Initial outlay	$58,000
Annual cash inflow from reduced labor cost	$11,500
Cost of capital	12%
Estimated life of the cutter	8 years
Estimated residual value of the cutter	$ 2,000

REQUIRED:

Determine the net present value of the cutting machine purchase.

LO 6 & 7:   Determine Net Present Value and Profitability Index, Various Rates, with Residual Value

7–34. George Gonzalez Construction Company is considering the purchase of a new road grader. The cost of the road grader is $68,000. The road grader has an estimated useful life of seven years and an estimated residual value of $5,000. Currently, the company rents road graders as needed. If the road grader is purchased, annual rental payments of $17,000 would be saved.

REQUIRED:

a. Determine the net present value of the grader purchase under each of the following assumptions.
   1. The cost of capital is 12%
   2. The cost of capital is 14%
   3. The cost of capital is 16%
b. Determine the profitability index under each of the following assumptions.
   1. The cost of capital is 12%
   2. The cost of capital is 14%
   3. The cost of capital is 16%

LO 6 & 7:   Determine Net Present Value and Profitability Index, Various Rates, with Residual Value

7–35. Wesley Parks Pencil Company is considering the purchase of a new machine to make pencils. The cost of the machine is $248,000. The pencil machine has an estimated useful life of 10 years and an estimated residual value of $25,000. Currently, the company leases a similar machine for $45,000 per year.

REQUIRED:

a. Determine the net present value of the pencil machine purchase under each of the following assumptions.
  1. The cost of capital is 10%
  2. The cost of capital is 12%
  3. The cost of capital is 14%
b. Determine the profitability index under each of the following assumptions.
  1. The cost of capital is 10%
  2. The cost of capital is 12%
  3. The cost of capital is 14%

LO 6 & 7: Determine Net Present Value and Profitability Index, Various Rates, with Residual Value

7–36. Sylvia Heain's Catering Service is considering the purchase of new energy-efficient cooking equipment. The cost of the new equipment is $78,000. The equipment has a estimated useful life of eight years and an estimated residual value of $5,000. Currently, the company leases similar cooking equipment for $10,000 per year. If the new cooking equipment is purchased, the company's cost of electricity would be reduced by $8,000 per year.

REQUIRED:

a. Determine the net present value of the cooking equipment under each of the following assumptions.
  1. The cost of capital is 12%
  2. The cost of capital is 14%
  3. The cost of capital is 16%
b. Determine the profitability index under each of the following assumptions.
  1. The cost of capital is 12%
  2. The cost of capital is 14%
  3. The cost of capital is 16%

LO 6 & 7: Determine Internal Rate of Return, Various Rates, No Residual Value

7–37. Penny Williams is contemplating the purchase of a new computer system for her company, Williams Manufacturing. She has made the following estimates.

Initial outlay	$18,023.88
Annual cash savings	$ 5,000.00
Estimated life of the computer	5 years
Estimated residual value of the computer	$ -0-

REQUIRED:

a. Determine the internal rate of return for the computer purchase.
b. Indicate whether the computer purchase should be accepted under each of the following assumptions.
  1. The cost of capital is 9%
  2. The cost of capital is 11%
  3. The cost of capital is 13%
  4. The cost of capital is 15%

LO 6 & 7: Determine Internal Rate of Return, Various Rates, No Residual Value

7–38. Valdez Moving and Storage is contemplating the purchase of a new delivery truck. The following estimates are available.

Initial outlay	$ 51,590
Annual cash flow from the new truck	$14,000.00
Estimated life of the truck	6 years
Estimated residual value of the truck	$ -0-

REQUIRED:

a. Determine the internal rate of return for the truck purchase.
b. Indicate whether the truck purchase should be accepted under each of the following assumptions.
1. The cost of capital is 14%
2. The cost of capital is 16%
3. The cost of capital is 18%

LO 6 & 7: Determine Internal Rate of Return for Three Projects, Select Project, No Residual Value

7–39. Hank Larsen & Company is in the process of replacing its existing computer system. The following three proposals are being considered.

	System A	System B	System C
Initial outlay	$18,023.88	$22,744.72	$24,031.57
Annual cash savings	$ 5,000.00	$ 6,000.00	$ 7,000.00
Estimated useful life	5 years	5 years	5 years

The estimated residual value of all computer systems under consideration is zero.

REQUIRED:

a. Determine the internal rate of return for each of the proposed computer systems.
b. Which computer system would you recommend? Explain your reasoning.

LO 6 & 7: Determine Internal Rate of Return for Three Projects, Select Project, No Residual Value

7–40. Pomeroy Equipment Company is in the process of selecting some new manufacturing equipment. The following three proposals are being considered.

	Equipment A	Equipment B	Equipment C
Initial outlay	$14,902.92	$18,555.46	$26,674.63
Annual cash savings	$ 3,000.00	$ 4,000.00	$ 5,000.00
Estimated useful life	8 years	8 years	8 years

The estimated residual value of all equipment under consideration is zero.

REQUIRED:

a. Determine the internal rate of return for each of the proposed pieces of equipment.
b. Which piece of equipment would you recommend? Explain your reasoning.

LO 6 & 7:   Determine Net Present Value, Profitability Index, and Internal Rate of Return, Various Rates, No Residual Value

7–41. Sheets Manufacturing Company is considering the purchase of a factory that makes valves. These valves would be used by Sheets to manufacture water pumps. The purchase would require an initial outlay of $1,564,800. The factory would have an estimated life of 10 years and no residual value. Currently, the company buys 500,000 valves per year at a cost of $1.50 each. If the factory were purchased, the valves could be manufactured for $0.90 each.

REQUIRED:

a. Determine the net present value of the proposed project and whether it should be accepted under each of the following assumptions.
  1. The cost of capital is 12%
  2. The cost of capital is 14%
  3. The cost of capital is 16%

b. Determine the profitability index under each of the following assumptions.
  1. The cost of capital is 12%
  2. The cost of capital is 14%
  3. The cost of capital is 16%

c. Determine the internal rate of return of the proposed project and indicate whether it should be accepted under each of the following assumptions.
  1. The cost of capital is 12%
  2. The cost of capital is 14%
  3. The cost of capital is 16%

LO 6:   Determine Payback Period, Even Cash Flows

7–42. Andrew Griffith owns Discount Hardware. He is contemplating the purchase of a copy machine which would be used to make copies to sell to customers for five cents each. The following estimates are available.

Initial outlay	$4,500
Annual cash inflow	$1,800

REQUIRED:
Determine the payback period for the copy machine purchase.

LO 6:   Determine Payback Period, Even Cash Flows

7–43. Mary Teal owns Magic Makers Manufacturing. She is contemplating the purchase of a machine that would be used to manufacture various products that would be sold to magic shops. The following estimates are available.

Initial outlay	$23,539.20
Annual cash inflow	$ 7,356.00

REQUIRED:
Determine the payback period for the machine purchase.

LO 6:   Determine Payback Period, Even Cash Flows

7–44. Jaime Elliott is contemplating the purchase of a machine that would be used in her business. The following estimates are available.

| Initial outlay | $5,826.50 |
| Annual cash inflow | $1,355.00 |

REQUIRED:
Determine the payback period for the machine purchase.

LO 6: Determine Payback Period, Even Cash Flows

7–45. Dan Haskin is contemplating the purchase of a machine that would be used in his business. The following estimates are available.

| Initial outlay | $323,400.00 |
| Annual cash inflow | $ 33,000.00 |

REQUIRED:
Determine the payback period for the machine purchase.

LO 6: Determine Payback Period, Uneven Cash Flows

7–46. Allen Arnold is considering the purchase of a fuel truck that he would use to sell gasoline at motor sport racing events in Puerto Rico. He has determined that a used truck is available for $11,000. He believes that the cash inflows would grow each year as he is able to sign fuel supply contracts at more and more events. He has made the following cash inflow estimates.

First year	$3,000
Second year	$4,500
Third and subsequent years	$5,000

REQUIRED:
Determine the payback period for the purchase of the fuel truck.

LO 6: Determine Payback Period, Uneven Cash Flows

7–47. Wede Brownell is considering opening a ceramic studio. She has determined that it would require an investment of $14,000 to open the store. She believes that the cash inflows would grow each year as more and more people learn of the store. She has made the following cash inflow estimates.

First year	$2,000
Second year	$4,000
Third and subsequent years	$5,000

REQUIRED:
Determine the payback period for the ceramic studio.

LO 6: Determine Payback Period, Uneven Cash Flows

7–48. Joan Stone is considering adding a new style of gym shorts to her product line. She has determined that it would require an investment of $22,000 to add the new style shorts. She believes that the cash inflows would grow each year as the new style becomes more popular. She has made the following cash inflow estimates.

First year	$ 4,000
Second year	$ 6,000
Third and subsequent years	$10,000

REQUIRED:
Determine the payback period for the new style of gym shorts.

LO 6:   Determine Accounting Rate of Return

7–49. JPH Construction Company is contemplating the purchase of scaffolding at the cost of $32,000. Currently, the company rents similar scaffolding for use at each of its construction sites. The scaffolding has an estimated useful life of five years and an estimated residual value of $2,000. By purchasing the scaffolding, JPH could save rental fees of $11,760 per year.

REQUIRED:
Determine the accounting rate of return for JPH's investment in the scaffolding.

LO 6:   Determine Accounting Rate of Return

7–50. Parrish and Parrish & Associates is contemplating the purchase of equipment that would cost $196,600. Currently, the company rents similar equipment for $45,076 per year. The proposed new equipment has an estimated useful life of eight years and an estimated residual value of $9,000.

REQUIRED:
Determine the accounting rate of return for the Parrish and Parrish & Associates investment in the new equipment.

LO 6:   Determine Accounting Rate of Return

7–51. Hora & Company is contemplating the purchase of a machine that would cost $142,790. The machine would provide an annual contribution margin of $47,262.55 each year. The proposed new machine has an estimated useful life of five years and an estimated residual value of $10,000.

REQUIRED:
Determine the accounting rate of return for Hora & Company's investment in the new machine.

LO 5, 6, & 7:   Determine Relevant Information, Net Present Value, Screen Project, with Residual Value

7–52. Frank's Marine Service purchased a forklift five years ago for $16,000. When it was purchased, the forklift had an estimated useful life of 10 years and a salvage value of $4,000. The forklift can be sold now for $6,000. The operating cost for the forklift is $4,500 per year.

   Frank is thinking about buying a newer forklift for $17,000. The newer forklift would have an estimated useful life of five years and a salvage value of $7,000. The operating cost for the newer forklift would be 3,000 per year.

   The company's cost of capital is 10%.

REQUIRED:
a. Prepare a relevant cost schedule showing the benefits of buying the new forklift. (For this requirement, ignore the time value of money.)
b. How much must the company invest today to replace the old forklift?

c. If the company replaces the old forklift, what is the increase in the company's annual contribution margin?

d. If the company sells the old forklift now to make room for the new one, it will not receive the $4,000 salvage value at the end of its useful life. Instead, the company will receive the $7,000 salvage value from the new forklift. With this in mind, if the company buys the forklift, what is the change in the salvage value the company is to receive at the end of the five-year life of the equipment?

e. Calculate the net present value of replacing the old forklift.

f. Do you think the company should replace the old forklift?

LO 5, 6, & 7: Determine Relevant Information, Net Present Value, Screen Project, with Residual Value

7–53. Randy Ice of Ice Engineering is considering the purchase of a new copy machine. He purchased the old machine two years ago for $8,500. When it was purchased the old machine had an estimated useful life of eight years and a salvage value of $500. The operating cost of the old machine is $3,000 per year. The old machine can be sold today for $2,000. A new machine can be bought today for $10,000 and would have an estimated useful life of six years with a salvage value of $1,000. The operating cost of the new copy machine is expected to be $1,500 per year.

The company's cost of capital is 8%.

REQUIRED:

a. Prepare a relevant cost schedule showing the benefit of buying the new copy machine. (For this requirement, ignore the time value of money.)

b. How much must the company invest today to replace the old copy machine?

c. If the company replaces the old copy machine, what is the increase in the company's annual contribution margin?

d. If the company sells the old copy machine now to make room for the new one, it will not receive the $500 salvage value at the end of its useful life. Instead, the company will receive the $1,000 salvage value from the new copy machine. With this in mind, if the company buys the copy machine, what is the change in the salvage value the company is to receive at the end of the six-year life of the equipment?

e. Calculate the net present value of replacing the old copy machine.

f. Do you think the company should replace the old copy machine?

LO 5, 6, & 7: Determine Relevant Information, Net Present Value, Screen Project, No Residual Value

7–54. The managers at Denson Manufacturing Company are considering replacing an industrial mixer used in the company's factory. The company's cost of capital is 10%.

Information about the old mixer:

Cost	$28,000
Estimated useful life	10 years
Estimated salvage value	$ 0
Current age	5 years
Estimated current fair value	$ 8,000
Annual operating cost	$18,000

Information about the new mixer:

Cost	$34,000
Estimated useful life	5 years
Estimated salvage value	$ 0
Annual operating cost	$12,000

REQUIRED:

a. Prepare a relevant cost schedule showing the benefit of buying the new mixer.

b. How much must the company invest today to replace the industrial mixer?

c. If the new mixer is purchased, how much would be saved in operating costs each year?

d. How much would the company receive at the end of the five-year useful life of the new mixer?

e. Calculate the net present value of replacing the old mixer.

f. Do you think the company should replace the old mixer?

LO 5, 6, & 7: Determine Relevant Information, Net Present Value, Screen Project, No Residual Value

7–55. The managers at Calvert Manufacturing Company are considering replacing the industrial lathe used in the company's factory. The company's cost of capital is 12%.

Information about the old lathe:

Cost	$57,000
Estimated useful life	8 years
Estimated salvage value	$ 0
Current age	2 years
Estimated current fair value	$32,000
Annual operating cost	$32,000

Information about the new lathe:

Cost	$61,000
Estimated useful life	6 years
Estimated salvage value	$ 0
Annual operating cost	$24,000

REQUIRED:

a. Prepare a relevant cost schedule showing the benefit of buying the new lathe. (For this requirement, ignore the time value of money.)

b. How much must the company invest today to replace the old lathe?

c. If the company replaces the old lathe, how much will be saved in operating costs each year?

d. Calculate the net present value of replacing the old lathe.

e. Do you think the company should replace the old lathe?

LO 5, 6, & 7: Determine Relevant Information, Net Present Value, Screen Project, with Residual Value

7–56. Lisa Miller, president of Miller Boat Hauling, is considering replacing the company's industrial lift used to haul boats. The new lift would allow the company to lift larger boats out of the water. The company's cost of capital is 14%.

Information about the old lift:

Cost	$94,000
Estimated useful life	12 years
Estimated salvage value	$10,000
Current age	4 years
Estimated current fair value	$48,000
Annual contribution margin	$50,000

Information about the new lift:

Cost	$128,000
Estimated useful life	8 years
Estimated salvage value	$ 25,000
Annual contribution margin	$ 65,000

REQUIRED:

a. Prepare a relevant cost schedule showing the benefit of buying the new lift. (For this requirement, ignore the time value of money.)

b. How much must the company invest today to replace the old lift?

c. If the company replaces the old lift, what is the increase in the company's annual contribution margin?

d. If the company sells the old lift now to make room for the new one, it will not receive the $10,000 salvage value at the end of its useful life. Instead, the company will receive the $25,000 salvage value from the new lift. With this in mind, if the company buys the new lift, what is the change in the salvage value the company is to receive at the end of the eight-year life of the equipment?

e. Calculate the net present value of replacing the old lift.

f. Do you think the company should replace the old lift?

LO 5, 6, & 7: Determine Relevant Information, Net Present Value, Screen Project, with Residual Value

7–57. The managers at Cary Manufacturing are considering replacing a printing press with a new, high-speed model. The company's cost of capital is 12%.

Information about the old printing press:

Cost	$255,000
Estimated useful life	10 years
Estimated salvage value	$ 25,000
Annual depreciation	$ 23,000
Current age	3 years
Accumulated depreciation to date	$184,000
Estimated current fair value	$150,000
Annual contribution margin	$110,000

Information about the new printing press:

Cost	$535,000
Estimated useful life	7 years
Estimated salvage value	$ 45,000
Annual depreciation	$ 70,000
Annual contribution margin	$150,000

REQUIRED:

a. Prepare a relevant cost schedule showing the benefit of buying the new printing press. (For this requirement, ignore the time value of money.)

b. How much must the company invest today to replace the old printing press?

c. If the company replaces the old printing press, what is the increase in the company's annual contribution margin?

d. If the company sells the old printing press now to make room for the new one, it will not receive the $25,000 salvage value at the end of its useful life. Instead, the company will receive the $45,000 salvage value from the new printing press. With this in mind, if the company buys the printing press, what is the change in the salvage value the company is to receive at the end of the seven-year life of the equipment?

e. Calculate the net present value of replacing the old printing press.

f. Do you think the company should replace the old printing press?

APPENDIX

LO 7: Calculate Simple, Compound Interest, Full Years

7–58. Greg Gluck Marine borrowed $5,000 from National Bank on January 1, 2000.

REQUIRED:

a. Assuming 9% simple interest is charged, calculate interest for 2000, 2001, and 2002.

b. Assuming 9% compound interest is charged, calculate interest for 2000, 2001, and 2002.

LO 7: Calculate Simple, Compound Interest, Full Years

7–59. Gary borrowed $8,000 from Orlando National Bank on January 1, 2000.

REQUIRED:

a. Assuming 8% simple interest is charged, calculate interest for 2000, 2001, and 2002.

b. Assuming 8% compound interest is charged, calculate interest for 2000, 2001, and 2002.

LO 7: Calculate Simple, Compound Interest, Full Years

7–60. Cam borrowed $2,000 from First National Bank on January 1, 2000.

REQUIRED:

a. Assuming 6% simple interest is charged, calculate interest for 2000, 2001, and 2002.

b. Assuming 6% compound interest is charged, calculate interest for 2000, 2001, and 2002.

LO 7: Calculate Future Value, Single Cash Flow, Various Rates and Maturities

7–61. Susan Jones made the following investments on January 1, 2000:

1. $ 2,000 at 10% for 5 years
2. $12,000 at 4% for 8 years
3. $ 9,000 at 14% for 15 years

Assume the interest on each investment is compounded annually.

REQUIRED:
Calculate the future value of each of the investments listed above at their maturity.

LO 7:   Calculate Future Value, Single Cash Flow, Various Rates and Maturities

7–62. Ivan Zhang made the following investments on January 1, 2000:
  1. $3,000 at 8% for 6 years
  2. $4,000 at 6% for 8 years
  3. $5,000 at 10% for 5 years
  Assume the interest on each investment is compounded annually.

REQUIRED:
Calculate the future value of each of the investments listed above at their maturity.

LO 7:   Calculate Future Value, Single Cash Flow, Various Rates and Maturities

7–63. Orlando Gonzalez made the following investments on January 1, 2000:
  1. $1,000 at 14% for 3 years
  2. $2,000 at 10% for 5 years
  3. $4,000 at 8% for 8 years
  Assume the interest on each investment is compounded annually.

REQUIRED:
Calculate the future value of each of the investments listed above at their maturity.

LO 7:   Calculate Future Value, Yearly Cash Flows, Various Rates and Maturities

7–64. Consider the following investments:
  1. $2,000 at the end of each of the next five years at 10% interest compounded annually.
  2. $12,000 at the end of each of the next eight years at 4% interest compounded annually.
  3. $9,000 at the end of each of the next 15 years at 14% interest compounded annually.

REQUIRED:
Calculate the future value of each of the investments listed above at their maturity.

LO 7:   Calculate Future Value, Yearly Cash Flows, Various Rates and Maturities

7–65. Consider the following investments.
  1. $12,000 at the end of each of the next three years at 12% interest compounded annually.
  2. $16,000 at the end of each of the next five years at 10% interest compounded annually.
  3. $20,000 at the end of each of the next 10 years at 8% interest compounded annually.

REQUIRED:
Calculate the future value of each of the investments listed above at their maturity.

LO 7: Calculate Future Value, Yearly Cash Flows, Various Rates and Maturities

7–66. Consider the following investments.
1. $1,000 at the end of each of the next five years at 6% interest compounded annually.
2. $1,000 at the end of each of the next five years at 8% interest compounded annually.
3. $1,000 at the end of each of the next five years at 10% interest compounded annually.

REQUIRED:
Calculate the future value of each of the investments listed above at their maturity.

LO 7: Calculate Present Value, Single Cash Flow, Single Rate

7–67. Jim Johnson is planning to buy a new car when he graduates from college in three years. He would like to invest a single amount now, in order to have the $24,000 he estimates the car will cost.

REQUIRED:
Calculate the amount Jim must invest today, to have enough to buy the new car assuming his investment will earn 4% compounded annually for the three-year investment.

LO 7: Calculate Present Value, Single Cash Flow, Single Rate

7–68. Lowell Pitman needs to have $50,000 at the end of five years. Lowell would like to invest a single amount now, to have the $50,000 in five years.

REQUIRED:
Calculate the amount Lowell must invest today, to have the amount of money he needs assuming his investment will earn 8% compounded annually for the five-year investment.

LO 7: Calculate Present Value, Single Cash Flow, Single Rate

7–69. Lauren Elsea is planning to buy a house when she graduates from college. She would like to have $20,000 for the down payment. Lauren would like to invest a single amount now, to have the $20,000 at the end of three years.

REQUIRED:
Calculate the amount Lauren must invest today, to have the amount of money she needs assuming her investment will earn 6% compounded annually for the three-year investment.

LO 7: Calculate Present Value, Yearly Cash Flows, Single Rate

7–70. Linda Chrisco is planning to send her son, Edward, to college. While he is in college, Linda intends to give him $3,000 at the end of each year.

REQUIRED:

How much must Linda invest today so she will have enough to give Edward $3,000 at the end of each of the next four years assuming the investment will earn 6% interest.

LO 7: Calculate Present Value, Yearly Cash Flows, Single Rate

7–71. Alex Malpin is planning to spend the next three years doing research in China. An Asian studies research institute has agreed to pay Alex $20,000 at the end of each of the three years he is in China.

REQUIRED:

How much must be invested today to have enough to pay Alex $20,000 at the end of each of the next three years assuming the investment will earn 10% interest.

LO 7: Calculate Present Value, Yearly Cash Flows, Single Rate

7–72. Photo Factory is planning to purchase some photo processing equipment from Ace Equipment Company. The equipment will provide cash flow of $15,000 at the end of each of the next eight years.

REQUIRED:

How much should Photo Factory pay for the equipment assuming it will provide $15,000 at the end of each of the next eight years and Ace has promised that it will earn a return of exactly 14%?

Chapter 8

The Operating Budget

*I*magine for a moment that midway through your accounting class you and three of your classmates decide to go to Europe. You stand up, excuse yourself from class, and the four of you head for the airport. At the airport you discover that the next flight to Europe departs in four hours and there are only three seats available. You buy three tickets, send one friend back to class, and begin the long wait until boarding. After what seems like an eternity, you board the flight and are on your way.

When you arrive in Paris, your friends ask, "Well, we're here. What now?" You respond, "I don't know, this is a spontaneous thing. We have the freedom to do whatever we want." Your friends have many questions: "Where will we stay? Did you bring any money? Who has a French/English dictionary? Are the clothes we are wearing adequate for the weather in Paris? By the way, what *is* the weather in Paris? Now that we're here, how long will we stay? What will we do? Is there anything other than the Eiffel Tower here? Why did we go to Paris and not some other place? How will we get back home?"

What's wrong with this Paris trip? The obvious answer is a complete lack of planning. Thoughtful planning increases the possibility of success in almost anything we might do, whether business related or not.

Careful planning is in fact a key element of business success. Without such planning, business activities founder and a company almost certainly loses direction. In Chapter 7 we described planning as the *why,* the *what,* the *how,* and the *who* of being in business. Recall that the *why* is the process of setting company goals. The *what* is the development of a strategic plan to implement those goals in the long term. These two planning elements were discussed in some detail in Chapter 7. The *how* is the process of capital budgeting to allocate scarce resources and was the major topic of Chapter 7.

operating budget A budget for a specific period, usually one to five years, that establishes who is responsible for the day-to-day operation of a business during that time.

master operating budget Another name for *operating budget.*

master budget Another name for *operating budget.*

The *who* is the final step—the preparation of the operating budget. The **operating budget** is a budget for a specific time, usually one to five years, that establishes who is responsible for the day-to-day operation of the business during that time. This budget is also sometimes called the **master operating budget** or simply the **master budget.** For the sake of consistency, we will use the term *operating budget* throughout our discussions of this topic.

The operating budget will be an important part of your business life, regardless of your occupation or the type of company for which you choose to work. Whether the organization is profit or not for profit, and whether it is a service, merchandising, or manufacturing firm, budgeting has become increasingly more important in charting the success of today's organizations. Gone are the days when companies could succeed on simple luck and optimism. Gone, too, are the days when a select group of top managers prepared operating budgets with little input from others in the organization. Many companies today involve all managers and employees in the budgeting process. Fortune 500 companies such as General Electric, Target, Family Dollar Stores, and others have recognized that better budgeting is achieved when they involve those who actually work in the area or function for which the budget is being prepared. As you read the pages that follow, we hope you remember that budgets will be an important ingredient in your personal business success, and that you will very likely be involved in the budgeting process much earlier in your career than you expect.

The chapter is divided into two main parts. Part One contains an overview of the operating budget, its purpose, and where it fits into the overall management process. Part Two contains a detailed presentation of how the operating budget is actually prepared and how it should and should not be used by managers. ■

LEARNING OBJECTIVES

After completing your work on this chapter, you should be able to do the following:

1. Describe some of the benefits of the operating budget.
2. Describe the three budgeted financial statements contained in the operating budget and the other budgets that support the budgeted financial statements.
3. Compare and contrast various approaches to the preparation and use of the operating budget.
4. Describe the role of the sales forecast in the budgeting process.
5. Prepare the budgets included in the operating budget.
6. Describe the appropriate use of the operating budget in the overall management process.

The Operating Budget: What Is It?

What exactly *is* an operating budget? We know it is the plan for a company's operating activities for some period of time, but what is in that plan? The operating budget includes a set of estimated financial statements.

Recall that the three main financial statements are the balance sheet, the income statement, and the statement of cash flows. Businesses prepare these statements at the end of a given time period to show the effects of past transactions and events. An operating budget contains those same three financial statements, except they are estimates—or forecasts—of future transactions and events. The forecasted financial statements in the operating budget are sometimes called pro forma financial statements. *Pro forma* is a Latin phrase meaning "provided in advance."

The only difference between the financial statements businesses use to show the effects of past events and transactions, and the ones you will explore in this chapter, is that the budgeted financial statements are used to predict future events.

BENEFITS OF BUDGETING

A well-prepared operating budget can create many benefits for the company. In this section, we will explore four of them. First, budgeting serves as a guide. Second, it helps organizations allocate resources. Third, it encourages communication and coordination. Fourth, it sets performance standards, or *benchmarks*.

Serves as a Guide

The operating budget should serve as a guide for a company to follow during the budgeted period. Notice that we used the term *guide*. A business is dynamic and change occurs rapidly at times. A business must remain flexible and open to opportunities—therefore, management should adjust its budget when desirable or necessary.

To illustrate, suppose the budget for Pam's Flower Shop forecasted sales revenue of $310,000 for the first three months of 2008. Business was better than expected and the flower shop had sales of $310,000 by the end of February. Should Pam close the flower shop until April 1 because she attained her budgeted sales figure for the quarter? Of course not. Or suppose Pam has the opportunity to purchase 20 dozen roses just before Valentine's Day at a bargain basement price. She can probably sell all of them for a large profit, but she did not budget for this special purchase. Should Pam bypass this opportunity because the special purchase is not in the budget? As long as the company has the money to buy the roses she should take advantage of this opportunity.

In many organizations, especially governmental and not-for-profit organizations, management views the budget as static or unchangeable. In some organizations meeting the budget becomes the primary business objective. An unwillingness to adjust a budget based on new information is often detrimental to the company because management misses opportunities and makes poor decisions.

Assists in Resource Allocation

All organizations have scarce resources. No company can afford to do everything it desires, or even everything it needs to do within a given time period. A budget can help management decide where to allocate its limited resources.

The budgeting process may uncover potential bottlenecks and allow managers to address these issues in advance as the budget is being prepared rather than as problems occur during the year. Consider the manufacturing environment presented for Montrose Manufacturing Company in Exhibit 8–1.

Exhibit 8–1
Example of Production Bottleneck at Montrose Manufacturing

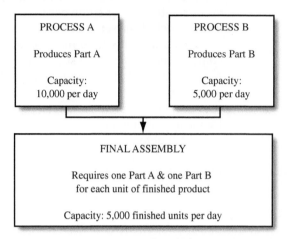

Each unit of finished product Montrose manufactures requires one Part A and one Part B. The maximum number of finished units of product the company can produce per day is 5,000 because Process B can produce only 5,000 parts per day. Montrose could increase the capacity of Process A and the company *still* could produce only 5,000 finished units per day because of the restriction caused by Process B. Process B is the bottleneck in the production process.

Suppose Montrose Manufacturing Company moved production machinery from Process A to Process B. This change reduces the capacity of Process A by 2,500 units per day, but increases the capacity of Process B by 2,500 units per day as reflected in Exhibit 8–2.

Exhibit 8–2
Elimination of Production Bottleneck at Montrose Manufacturing

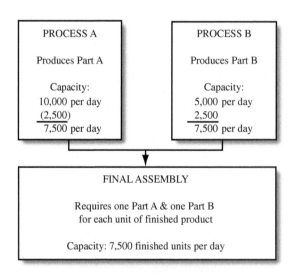

With this simple action, Montrose increased its capacity for finished units by 50 percent (from 5,000 units to 7,500 units) without adding additional machinery costs to its operation.

The issue of resource allocation is also important for a merchandising business. For example, February may be so busy for Pam's Flower Shop that she will need extra workers. If Pam knows this in advance, she will have time to hire the needed workers at the least cost so she can offer quality service and sell more flowers. In contrast, if Pam did not plan for the February rush, she would find herself understaffed and unable to provide quality, timely service. Budgeting helps Pam make good decisions about how to allocate her resources.

Fosters Communication and Coordination

As managers from different functional areas in an organization work together to prepare the budget, they gain a better understanding of the entire business. When managers from all areas learn of difficulties facing others and spot duplication of effort, the firm can then solve problems and coordinate efforts more effectively. Our previous example of Montrose Manufacturing Company and its production bottleneck points out the possibilities of increased communication and coordination through the budgeting process. In working to solve this production problem, the managers of Process A, Process B, and Final Assembly had the opportunity to view the production process from a broader perspective of the company's overall production process rather than continuing to focus only on this part of the process. They were forced to communicate with one another and to better coordinate their efforts.

Establishes Performance Standards

As managers prepare budgets for their companies, they must estimate performance levels they both want and can attain. If a company's actual sales, for example, are less than its budgeted sales for a period, the sales manager should review the deficit and determine why the variance occurred.

Performance standards introduce accountability into all levels of an organization and become the benchmarks against which firms can compare the actual results. Differences between the actual results and the budget can be explored and improvements made. The improvements may focus on performance, the budgeting process, or both.

Discussion Question

8-1. In what other ways do you think a company might benefit from preparing an operating budget?

Now let's turn our attention to different approaches to budgeting.

Different Approaches to Budgeting

Not all companies or industries use the same approach to the budget process. The approach depends on the needs of the business and its managerial philosophy. Because its is so highly influenced by the managerial style of its top leaders and its accounting system software, the budgeting process is unique to each business entity. We will investigate seven of the most common budgeting approaches: perpetual, incremental, zero-based, top-down, bottom-up, imposed, and participative.

Perpetual Budgeting

perpetual budgeting A budgeting approach management uses so that as one month ends, another month's budget is added to the end of the budget so that, at any time, the budget projects twelve months into the future. Also called **rolling budgeting.**

Some companies continually update their operating budgets. When management uses **perpetual budgeting,** or rolling budgeting, as one month ends, another month's budget is added to the end of the budget so that, at any given time, the budget projects twelve months into the future.

The main advantage of perpetual budgeting is that it spreads the workload for budget preparation evenly over the year, allowing employees to incorporate budgeting into their normal monthly work schedule. Another advantage is that the budget always extends 12 months into the future, instead of decreasing from twelve months to one month at the end of each budget cycle.

One disadvantage of perpetual budgeting may be that the budget preparation process becomes so routine that employees lose the creativity required to look for better ways to operate. Another disadvantage is that many managers feel overburdened with daily responsibilities. Adding the responsibility of preparing a perpetual budget to a heavy workload can lead to ineffective budgeting.

Incremental Budgeting

incremental budgeting The process of using the prior year's budget or the company's actual results to build the new operating budget.

Incremental budgeting is the process of using the prior year's budget or the company's actual results to build the new operating budget. If, for example, a company's 2007 budget included $100,000 for maintenance and repairs on the equipment in its plant, $100,000 becomes the starting point for this item in preparing the 2008 budget. The only question to be answered is whether the company needs to include more or less than $100,000 for repairs and maintenance in 2008. This budgeting approach is used by governmental entities such as the federal government and by many companies. One way to implement the new budget is to mandate a 10 percent decrease or five percent increase in last year's budget. Therefore, the new budget amount totals $90,000 (a 10 percent decrease) or $105,000 (a five percent increase)—regardless of the amount needed for 2008.

The trouble with the incremental budgeting approach is that if the prior year's budget included unnecessary costs, or items that did not optimize performance, this waste may be simply rolled over into the next year's budget. Some managers feel obligated to spend the current budget, whether or not the expense is necessary, because if the manager does not spend the current budget, he fears superiors will reduce next year's budget. This is the "use it or lose it" philosophy. The advantage to this approach is its simplicity. Some practitioners and many experts believe the disadvantages greatly outweigh the advantages.

Discussion Question

8-2. Why would a manager feel obligated to spend the full amount of a budgeted expense, regardless of its necessity?

Zero-Based Budgeting

zero-based budgeting An approach to budgeting where managers start from scratch, or zero, when preparing a new budget, and they must justify each item on the budget every year as though it were a brand new budget item.

An alternative to the incremental budgeting approach is zero-based budgeting. Managers using **zero-based budgeting** start from scratch, or zero, when preparing a new budget, and they must justify each item on the budget every year as though it were a brand new budget item. Zero-based budgeting requires more effort than incremental budgeting, but many organizations believe the results are worth that time and effort because managers are forced to re-examine the items included in the budget and justify their continuation.

Top-Down and Bottom-Up Budgeting

Budget information for a firm can flow either from the upper-level managers down to managers and employees at lower levels, or the other way around. For obvious reasons, the former approach is known as top-down and the latter approach is known as bottom-up. Each of these two approaches has distinct advantages and disadvantages.

Top-Down Budgeting

top-down budgeting An approach to budgeting in which the top executives prepare the budget, and lower-level managers and employees work to meet that budget.

In **top-down budgeting** the top executives prepare the budget, and lower-level managers and employees work to meet that budget. The top-down approach has several advantages. The company's top executives know the most about the firm's overall operations, strategic planning, and goals, so they will prepare the budget with company goals in mind. The top-down budgeting approach involves fewer people, so it causes fewer disruptions, takes less time, and is more efficient than the bottom-up approach. The top-down approach to budgeting, however, also has two disadvantages. First, lower level managers and employees are less accepting of budgets when they have no part in setting them. Second, top managers may know the goals and strategic plans for the enterprise, but they do not always have the working knowledge of daily activities needed to prepare the detailed budgets for all company activities.

A typical publicly-traded company in the United States uses some element of top-down budgeting. Why? The firm's top management has a responsibility to maximize returns for stockholders in the form of increased market prices of the stock even more than dividends. Company profits have the greatest influence on the selling price of a company's stock. So, to ensure maximum stock appreciation, the top executives must manage the company to perform at its peak profitability. In top-down budgeting, the target profit figures become the starting and ending points of the budgeting process.

imposed budget A budget for which upper management sets budget amounts for all operating activities with little possibility of negotiation.

Traditionally, most firms that used top-down budgeting also used an imposed budgeting process. An **imposed budget** is one for which upper management sets amounts for all operating activities with little possibility of negotiation. No matter how unreasonable the budget numbers are, top management expects all other managers to abide by them. This type of budgeting process can do more harm than good because different groups in the organization may be working at cross purposes. Today, however, not all top-down budgets are imposed budgets.

Bottom-Up Budgeting

bottom-up budgeting An approach to budgeting for which lower level managers and employees prepare the initial budget.

In **bottom-up budgeting,** lower level managers and employees prepare the initial budget. For example, members of the sales force prepare the sales schedule for their own sales territories. The sales manager then reviews these sales schedules, makes any necessary changes, and combines them to form the overall company sales schedule. Likewise, employees in the production facility prepare schedules for production, including schedules for direct material, direct labor, and manufacturing overhead. All the budget data flows upward from each segment of the company to the accounting or budget department where budget specialists compile the data into usable information.

Bottom-up budgeting has three main advantages. First, the budget may be more realistic than if it were prepared by top managers. If lower-level managers and employees take the process seriously, they are likely to create an operating budget based on accurate, realistic information. Second, lower-level managers and employees are more likely to work toward budgeted performance standards because they helped to set those standards. Third, as employees prepare the budget, they envision the company's goals, consider how various activities may affect the future, and assess their own participation. In short, they begin to think long-term.

Bottom-up budgeting, however, has two disadvantages. First, employees at every level must make time to prepare, review, revise, and approve the budget. Employees may perceive this as an unwanted interruption in their daily activities. Second, some employees may be tempted to prepare a budget that underestimates performance and overestimates costs so that the department will easily outperform the budget.

Participative and Imposed Budgeting

participative budget A budget approach in which managers and employees at many levels of the company are engaged in setting performance standards and preparing the budget.

empower To give employees the authority to make decisions concerning their job responsibilities, including decisions about items in the operating budget.

Bottom-up budgeting is always a participative budgeting process. A **participative budget** approach is one in which managers and employees at many levels of the company are engaged in setting performance standards and preparing the budget. Although a bottom-up budget process will always be participative, a top-down budget can be either imposed or participative. In recent years, top executives discovered they could empower employees by allowing them more participation in the budgeting process. To **empower** employees means to give them the authority to make decisions concerning their job responsibilities, including decisions about items in the operating budget. A company committed to both top-down budgeting and empowered employees must combine the top-down and bottom-up approaches to budgeting. Rather than having all budget information flow from the top down, upper managers provide profit targets to lower-level managers. The lower-level managers prepare the operating budget for their functional areas, using the profit targets provided by upper management.

Discussion Questions

8-3. What positive results do you think come from more employee empowerment

    a. for the firm as a whole? Explain your reasoning.
    b. for managers and employees? Explain your reasoning.

8-4. What negative results do you think come from more employee empowerment

    a. for the firm as a whole? Explain your reasoning.
    b. for managers and employees? Explain your reasoning.

When the lower-level managers cannot meet the profit requirements of top managers, we see the real distinction between participative and imposed budget approaches. If the profit requirement is negotiable, the process is participative. When the profit requirement is non-negotiable, the process is imposed. The key to making a top-down budget a participative budget is upper management's ability and willingness to negotiate and compromise.

Discussion Questions

8-5. If you were the chief executive officer of your company, would you prefer a top-down or bottom-up budgeting process? Why?

8-6. If you were in middle management, would you prefer a top-down or bottom-up budgeting process? Why?

8-7. If you were the company CEO, do you think it would be wise for you to spend time tending to the details of the various budgets, given all your other responsibilities?

The overall approach a company takes to preparing its operating budget may actually be a combination of several of the approaches we have discussed here. For example, one company may have a top-down, participative, zero-based budgeting approach. Another company may be committed to an incremental, participative, bottom up, perpetual budgeting philosophy. The object is not to select a particular approach from a laundry list. Rather, managers must approach the preparation of the operating budget in a way that makes sense in their circumstances.

BUILDING THE OPERATIONS BUDGET

Far more complex than the simple budget of cash inflows and outflows we prepare personally, the business operating budget is a set of forecasted financial statements that includes the balance sheet, income statement, and statement of cash flows. This is true regardless of whether the business preparing the budget is a manufacturer, a merchandiser, or a service company. The budget, however, includes several supporting schedules which provide the necessary information to complete the budgeted financial statements.

The Sales Forecast

sales forecast   The prediction of sales for the budget period.

The **sales forecast** is the prediction of sales for the budget period. It is the cornerstone of the budgeting process because all other budgets depend upon the amount of forecasted sales. Sales become the basis for the cost of goods sold, the amount of purchases or production required, the amounts of the selling and administrative expenses, and ultimately net income. If the sales forecast is unrealistic, so will the budget be unrealistic.

Even with the most careful predictions, however, many factors can influence the accuracy of the sales forecast as a year or more progresses. It is critical for managers to scan the external environment during strategic planning to help protect the firm against four factors that most influence sales: the general economy, industry conditions, competitors actions, and technological developments. Changes in any of these factors can affect the accuracy of the sales forecast. For that reason, managers should disseminate economic, industrial, and technological information throughout the sales organization.

Polaroid is a perfect example of a company losing its market due to technology and competitive pressures. Polaroid pictures were the only type that could be developed instantly from the 1950s to 1975. Its technology was unique and used by both consumers for personal pictures and photographers to check lighting and to get a preview. Around 1975 Kodak decided to challenge Polaroid and created its own instant picture camera and film. The challenge cost Kodak a great amount of money, and Polaroid once again was the king of instant pictures. Consumers, however, were not happy about using a Polaroid for all pictures because they were difficult and expensive to reproduce. You got an instant picture, but you only got one copy. Polaroid continued to slide in sales. Digital cameras rang the death knell of the company in the 1990s. Technological advances in computerization allowed all consumers to see pictures instantly and reproduce them at will. Possibly Polaroid should have spent its resources on solving the shortcomings of its products instead of protecting its niche of instant pictures.

In the past few years, many states have reduced their budgets because state revenue has fallen short of predictions. State agencies find it impossible to stop their activities mid-year. Common schools, state universities, welfare agencies and others have struggled to maintain minimal service levels as they put a number of employees on indefinite leave. States, like businesses, depend upon revenue streams to fuel their budgets. Some states can trace their budget woes back to a slow-down of economic activity in the late 1990s. For many others, the abrupt change can be traced back to political events in 2001. Sales tax, income tax, and transportation tax revenues experienced dramatic decreases during the last quarter of that year. Could anyone have predicted this disruption? Only a very few people in the world knew what might happen.

As you can see, the sales force must listen to its customers, stay abreast of technological advances, and pay close attention to industrial, economic, and political information to hope to estimate reasonably accurate sales forecasts.

Sales Budget

sales budget A budget which details the expected sales revenue from a company's primary operating activities during the budget period.

The Sales Budget drives the budgeting process because all expenses are related to the level of sales. The **Sales Budget** details the expected sales revenue from a company's primary operating activities during the budget period. For manufacturing and merchandising firms, like Ford and Sears, the Sales Budget details the number of units of each product the firm expects to sell at their anticipated sales price. The Sales Budget for a service firm, like H & R Block, details the dollar amount of services the firm expects to render. Because sales revenue is an income statement item, we use the information provided by the Sales Budget to construct the Budgeted Income Statement.

Production or Purchases Budget

production budget A budget which plans for the cost and number of units that must be manufactured to meet the sales forecast and the desired quantity of ending finished goods inventory.

purchases budget A budget which plans for the cost and number of units that must be purchased to meet the sales forecast and the desired quantity of ending finished goods inventory.

For manufacturers, the **Production Budget** plans for the cost and number of units that must be manufactured to meet the sales forecast and the desired quantity of ending finished goods inventory. While merchandisers, like JCPenney, call this budget the **Purchases Budget,** the two are functionally equivalent. The Production Budget and the Purchases Budget are the pro forma cost of goods manufactured schedule and the pro forma cost of purchases schedule we discussed in Chapter 6. A Production Budget includes schedules for materials, labor, and manufacturing overhead. An operating budget for a service business does not include a Production Budget or Purchases Budget because a service company does not sell products.

A manufacturer or merchandiser intends to sell some of the product scheduled to be produced or purchased during the budget period and to retain the balance in inventory. The projected ending inventory is classified as an asset, so some of the information provided by the Production Budget or Purchases Budget is used to construct the Budgeted Balance Sheet. The product projected to be sold during the period covered by the budget is classified as an expense item and will be shown on the Budgeted Income Statement as cost of goods sold. The cost of goods sold information needed to construct the budgeted income statement comes from the Cost of Goods Sold Budget.

Cost of Goods Sold or Cost of Services Budget

cost of goods sold budget A budget which calculates the total cost of all the product a company estimates it will sell during the budget period. Also called a **cost of services budget** for a service business.

A **Cost of Goods Sold Budget** calculates the total cost of all the product a company estimates it will sell during the budget period. This budget differs from the Production or Purchases Budget because the Cost of Good Sold Budget includes only the cost of goods anticipated to be sold during the budget period and the other two may be more or less depending upon whether management plans to increase or decrease the amount of inventory on hand. For a service type business, this budget is called the **Cost of Services Budget.**

Selling and Administrative Expense Budget

selling and administrative expense budget A budget that calculates all costs other than the cost of product or services required to support a company's forecasted sales.

After managers prepare the sales forecast and estimate the product or service cost, they can estimate all other costs needed to support that level of sales. A **Selling and Administrative Expense Budget** calculates all costs, other than the cost of product or services, required to support a company's forecasted sales. The kinds of items included in this budget are exactly the same as the ones included in the income statements, and what we described as period costs in Chapter 4, including such items as advertising, sales salaries, rent, utilities.

Cash Budget

cash budget A budget which shows whether the expected amount of cash generated by operating activities will be sufficient to pay anticipated expenses during the budget period.

A **Cash Budget** shows whether the expected amount of cash generated by operating activities will be sufficient to pay anticipated expenses during the budget period. It also reveals whether a company should expect a need for short-term external financing during the budget period. Be careful not to confuse the Cash Budget with the Budgeted Statement of Cash Flows that we will discuss a little later. The Budgeted Statement of Cash Flows is more comprehensive than a simple Cash Budget.

Budgeted Financial Statements

budgeted income statement A pro forma income statement which shows the expected net income for the budget period.

A **Budgeted Income Statement** shows the expected net income for the budget period. It subtracts all estimated product or service cost and period cost from estimated sales revenue. This budget is prepared using information from the Sales Budget, the Cost of Goods Sold (or Cost of Services) Budget, and the Selling and Administrative Expense Budget.

budgeted balance sheet A presentation of estimated assets, liabilities, and owners' equity at the end of the budget period.

A **Budgeted Balance Sheet** is a presentation of estimated assets, liabilities, and owners' equity at the end of the budget period. It is created exactly the way a balance sheet based on actual historical results is prepared. At the start of the budget period, a company has a balance sheet that presents its assets, liabilities, and owners' equity. Most of the company's asset, liability, and equity items will be changed by the forecasted results of the Budgeted Income Statement, the Production or Purchases Budget, and the Cash Budget. For a service type company, there is no Production or Purchases Budget, so the Budgeted Balance Sheet is prepared using information from the actual balance sheet at the beginning of the budget period, the Budgeted Income Statement, and the Cash Budget. The result is an estimated balance sheet at the end of the budget period.

budgeted cash flow statement A statement of a company's expected sources and uses of cash during the budget period.

A **Budgeted Cash Flow Statement** is a statement of a company's expected sources and uses of cash during the budget period. Manufacturers, merchandisers, and service companies create the Budgeted Statement of Cash Flows in a manner similar to the way they create the Budgeted Balance Sheet. At the start of the period being budgeted, they report their cash balance. Based on the estimated results of the Budgeted Income Statement and other business activities that either generate or use cash, they estimate the cash balance at the end of the budget period. The purpose of the Budgeted Statement of Cash Flows is to explain how that change in cash is to happen.

Interrelationship Among the Budgets

The budgets we presented are closely interrelated. Exhibit 8–3 shows the extent of this interrelationship. Arrows indicate the flow of information among the different budgets. Notice that the flow is not linear from the Sales Forecast forward. Rather, once information feeds to the Financial Statements, information flows back and forth among the individual statements for their completion.

Exhibit 8–3
Interrelationship
Among the Budgets

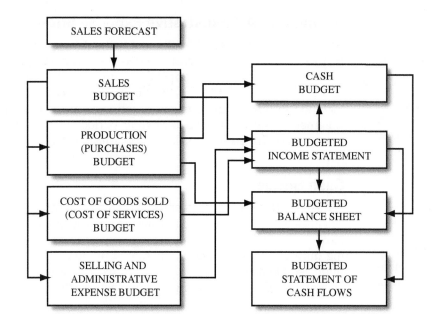

Discussion Questions

8-8. From what you have learned so far about the operating budget, which of the budgets do you think will be affected by the amounts in the sales forecast? Explain how each is affected.

8-9. A change in which of the budgets will affect the least number of other budgets? Explain your reasoning.

A change in any one of the various budgets contained in the operating budget will cause a ripple effect throughout all the others. Because these budgets are so closely tied together, the preparation of the operating budget in most organizations is time consuming and complicated. Depending on the size of the company, it may take several months to prepare the operating budget. For example, a manufacturer like Lazy-Boy or merchandiser like Gap, Inc. prepares a Sales Budget for each product the company sells. If the company sells eighty products, it must prepare eighty Sales Budgets. If the company sells 10,000 products, it must prepare 10,000 sales budgets. Some large companies have budget departments that work year around on budgets. Let's see how they do it.

PART TWO: PREPARING AND USING THE OPERATING BUDGET

Preparing a Master Operating Budget

Marcy's Surf Shop is a retail store that sells only one product (surfboards) and deals in only one product model. The company's fiscal year ends June 30. At Marcy's request, we will prepare the operating budget for the first quarter of the fiscal year ending June 30, 2008. Thus, we will be budgeting for the quarter ending September 30, 2007.

We start with Marcy's budgeted income statement and the budgets that provide information used to construct that budgeted financial statement. We will then prepare the budgeted balance sheet along with all other budgets required to prepare the budgeted balance sheet. Finally, we will prepare the budgeted statement of cash flows.

Because we focus on a merchandising company rather than a manufacturer, we will work with a purchases budget rather than a production budget.

Budgeted Income Statement

To prepare the budgeted income statement, we need information about sales, cost of goods sold, and selling and administrative expenses for the period covered by the budget. Therefore, we must prepare a budget for each of those items before we can construct the budgeted income statement.

Sales Budget   The first information we need to build the budgeted income statement is the sales budget. Our first task is to request that Marcy's marketing and sales personnel provide a sales forecast. Before Marcy's Surf Shop can forecast its sales realistically, sales management and the sales personnel must first consider the factors that influence market conditions. After much discussion, Marcy's staff decided to research the following items:

- Current customer spending patterns
- The ability to attract new customers through market promotions
- The introduction of any new products
- The discontinuation of any products
- The competition
- Price changes
- The general economy
- Technological changes

The sales department's recent customer satisfaction survey shows, for example, that 60 percent of all current customers plan to buy another product in the next quarter and that price is the number one consideration in surfboard purchases. Any increase in price is therefore likely to have a negative impact on repeat business. The market research done by the company indicates that thanks to planned market promotions, Marcy's can expect a 20 percent growth in first-time customer purchases.

Once the sales team considers all its research, it develops a forecast of unit sales for each month in the quarter. The sales team forecasts sales for Marcy's Surf Shop of 30 units in July, 50 units in August, and 40 units in September, shown as Exhibit 8–4.

Exhibit 8–4
Sales Forecast for
Marcy's Surf Shop

MARCY'S SURF SHOP
Sales Forecast
For the Quarter Ended September 30, 2007

	July	August	September	Total
Forecasted Sales in Units	30	50	40	120

Based on this forecast, we can prepare Marcy's sales budget for the quarter, as shown in Exhibit 8–5.

We simply used the sales forecast of unit sales and the projected selling price of $200 per surfboard to develop the sales budget.

A real sales budget for an actual company is no more complicated than this one. Of course, in our example, Marcy's sells only one product. Remember from our earlier discussion that if Marcy's sold 80 different products, the company would need to prepare 80 of these sales budgets. If Marcy's sold 80 different products in 80 different locations, the company would need to prepare 6,400 of these sales budgets (80 products × 80 locations).

Exhibit 8–5
Sales Budget for
Marcy's Surf Shop

MARCY'S SURF SHOP
Sales Budget
For the Quarter Ended September 30, 2007

	July	August	September	Total
Forecasted Unit Sales	30	50	40	120
× Forecasted Sales Price	$ 200	$ 200	$ 200	$ 200
= Budgeted Sales Dollars	$6,000	$10,000	$8,000	$24,000

Discussion Question

8–10. What factors should Marcy's management consider when setting the $200 budgeted selling price for its surfboards?

Cost of Goods Sold Budget Once we know how many units Marcy's Surf Shop plans to sell, and the cost per unit, we can prepare a cost of goods sold budget. As its name implies, this budget is used to determine how much cost of goods sold should be based on forecasted sales. Preparing the cost of goods sold budget consists of multiplying forecasted unit sales by the cost per unit. The cost of goods sold budget for Marcy's Surf Shop is presented in Exhibit 8–6.

Exhibit 8–6
Cost of Goods Sold
Budget for Marcy's
Surf Shop

MARCY'S SURF SHOP
Cost of Goods Sold Budget
For the Quarter Ended September 30, 2007

	July	August	September	Total
Forecasted Unit Sales	30	50	40	120
× Forecasted Unit Cost	$ 120	$ 120	$ 120	$ 120
= Budgeted COGS	$3,600	$6,000	$4,800	$14,400

Exhibit 8–6 shows that Marcy's forecasted cost of goods sold for the quarter is $14,400 ($3,600 + $6,000 + $4,800 = $14,400). The cost of goods sold budget provides the forecasted product cost information that is used to prepare the budgeted income statement. This product cost information helps Marcy's management determine whether the company will be profitable based on its budget, or whether changes should be planned now to ensure profits in the budget period.

Discussion Questions

Compare the sales budget in Exhibit 8–5 with the cost of goods sold budget in Exhibit 8–6.

8–11. What are the similarities?
8–12. What are the differences?

Realistically, Marcy's will need to purchase more units of product than just the ones it expects to sell in July, August, and September. Thus, in addition to the budgets required to prepare the budgeted income statement, Marcy's will need to prepare a purchases budget. For our demonstration purposes, however, we will wait until after we have prepared the budgeted income statement to present the purchases budget. The only additional budget we need to prepare before we can prepare the budgeted income statement is the selling and administrative expense budget.

Selling and Administrative Expense Budget   The various expenses associated with the selling and administrative functions are estimated and used to prepare this budget. Selling and administrative expenses include salaries, advertising, rent, utilities, etc. The selling and administrative expense budget for Marcy's Surf Shop is presented in Exhibit 8–7.

Exhibit 8–7
Selling and
Administrative
Expense Budget for
Marcy's Surf Shop

MARCY'S SURF SHOP
Selling and Administrative Expense Budget
For the Quarter Ended September 30, 2007

	July	August	September	Total
Salaries and Wages	$1,600	$2,000	$1,800	$5,400
Rent	200	200	200	600
Depreciation	100	100	104	304
Others	800	1,000	900	2,700
Total	$2,700	$3,300	$3,004	$9,004

The types of items and the amounts included in the selling and administrative expense budget vary from company to company. As we said earlier, the items included in this budget are determined by what is required to support the level of sales in the sales budget.

Discussion Questions

8–13. If you were preparing a selling and administrative expense budget, what are some of the things you would consider as you mapped out strategies to increase sales?

8–14. Besides those included in Exhibit 8–7, what are some other administrative costs you think would normally be included in a selling and administrative expense budget?

8–15. What do you think might explain the increase in anticipated depreciation expense in September from $100 to $104?

Building the Budgeted Income Statement

To prepare the budgeted income statement, we use information from the sales, cost of goods sold, and selling and administrative expense budgets. The budgeted income statement depicts the amount of profit or loss a business can expect from its budgeted operating activities. First, we take the total forecasted sales revenue from the sales budget and subtract the forecasted cost of goods sold from the cost of goods sold budget. The result is a forecasted gross profit. We then subtract the to-tal selling and administrative expense which we get from the selling and adminis-trative expense budget. The result is the company's budgeted net income for the period covered by the budget. The budgeted income statement for Marcy's Surf Shop is presented in Exhibit 8–8.

Exhibit 8–8
Budgeted Income
Statement for
Marcy's Surf Shop

MARCY'S SURF SHOP				
Budgeted Income Statement				
For the Quarter Ended September 30, 2007				
	July	August	September	Total
Sales	$6,000	$10,000	$8,000	$24,000
− Cost of Goods Sold	3,600	6,000	4,800	14,400
= Gross Profit	2,400	4,000	3,200	9,600
− Selling and Admin. Expense	(2,700)	(3,300)	(3,004)	(9,004)
= Net Income	$(300)	$ 700	$ 196	$ 596

We see from Exhibit 8–8 that Marcy's Surf Shop is projecting a $300 net loss for July. In August Marcy's is projecting a net income of $700 and in September $196. The total net income for the quarter is $596.

After the budgeted income statement has been prepared, Marcy's manage-ment team may want to change its plans so that it meets its profit goals more ef-fectively. For instance, management may look at the budgeted income statement in Exhibit 8–10 and find the $300 loss in July unacceptable. If so, it would review all the information used to build the budgeted income statement and either adjust its expectations or adjust the assumptions used to prepare the budget.

Whatever the outcome of this evaluation, Marcy's Surf Shop has a better chance of planning for a successful future if management takes the budgeting process seri-ously. If budgets are used properly, managers will have an opportunity to see trou-ble spots in advance and make the adjustments in the operations.

Budgeted Balance Sheet

Now that we have prepared the budgeted income statement, we have much of the information we need to prepare the budgeted balance sheet. First, however, we must prepare two more budgets: the purchases budget and the cash budget.

Purchases Budget

The cost of goods sold budget we prepared accounts only for the units projected to be sold during the period covered by the budget. A company like Marcy's must be-gin and end each period with a certain amount of merchandise on hand. These in-ventory requirements create the need for the purchases budget. Marcy's purchases budget for the three months ended September 30, 2007, is presented as Exhibit 8–9.

As you can see by looking at Exhibit 8–9, the purchases budget, even for a small company like Marcy's Surf Shop, can seem rather complicated. A line-by-line analysis of this budget, however, reveals that much of the information it contains is already known, and the new information is basically straightforward.

(a) *Forecasted Unit Sales.* These numbers come directly from the sales forecast presented in Exhibit 8–4 and were used to construct the sales budget in Exhibit 8–5 and the cost of goods sold budget in Exhibit 8–6.

Exhibit 8–9
Purchases Budget for
Marcy's Surf Shop

MARCY'S SURF SHOP
Purchases Budget
For the Quarter Ended September 30, 2007

	July	August	September	Total	
Forecasted Unit Sales	30	50	40	120	(a)
+ Desired Ending Inventory*	20	16	24	24	(b)
= Total Units Needed	50	66	64	144	(c)
− Beginning Inventory	(8)	(20)	(16)	(8)	(d)
= Units to Be Purchased	42	46	48	136	(e)
× Cost Per Unit	$ 120	$ 120	$ 120	$ 120	(f)
= Cost of Purchases	$5,040	$ 5,520	$5,760	$16,320	(g)

*40% of the next month's sales requirements

(b) *Desired Ending Inventory.* These numbers represent the number of units of product the company believes it needs on hand at the end of a given period to support sales in the early days of the next period. As the asterisk note in Exhibit 8–9 explains, Marcy's has decided it should have inventory of product on hand at the end of any given month equal to 40 percent of the next month's sales requirements. At the end of July, for example, Marcy's desires an ending inventory of 20 units, which is 40 percent of August's sales of 50 units (50 × 40% = 20 units).

Managers consider at least two factors when determining the amount of desired ending inventory. First, how long does it usually take to get product from the company's suppliers? The purchasing department can supply this information. Second, how many units of product will it sell in the early days of each month? This information comes from historical sales records and discussions with sales personnel.

The desired ending inventory amounts for July, August, and September will be important to us when we construct the budgeted balance sheet, but we will defer our discussion of how they are used until we actually prepare that budget.

(c) *Total Units Needed.* Add (a) and (b).

(d) *Beginning Inventory.* Because the purpose of the purchases budget is to determine how many units of inventory must be purchased during each month included in the budget period, any inventory forecasted to be on hand at the beginning of each month must be subtracted from the total units needed to determine how many units must be purchased during the month.

The beginning inventory for any period is the ending inventory for the previous period. You will note in the purchases budget in Exhibit 8–9 that the beginning inventory for August (20 units) is the same as the desired ending inventory for July, and the beginning inventory for September (16 units) is the same as the desired ending inventory for August. You should also note that the beginning inventory in the total column (eight units) is the same as the beginning inventory for July, because the total column is for the entire quarter and the quarter begins in July.

Discussion Question

8–16. Can you tell by looking at the purchases budget in Exhibit 8–9 how many surfboards Marcy's has forecasted it will sell in October? Explain your reasoning.

Discussion Question

8-17. The purchases budget in Exhibit 8–9 indicates that Marcy's desires ending inventory equal to 40% of the next month's sales requirements. Because sales in July are expected to be 30 surfboards, the beginning inventory in July (which is the ending inventory for June) should be 12 units (30 × 40%). Why do you think the beginning inventory in July is only eight surfboards?

(e) *Units to Be Purchased.* This number is (c) minus (d) and tells us the number of surfboards that must be purchased in each of the three months of the budget period and the total for the quarter.

(f) *Cost Per Unit.* The cost per unit is the same as the cost per unit for the cost of goods sold budget presented in Exhibit 8–6.

(g) *Cost of Purchases.* This number is (e) multiplied by (f) and tells us what the purchase of surfboards will cost Marcy's in each of the three months of the budget period and the total for the quarter.

Cash Budget

When a company uses accrual accounting, revenue is recognized when earned rather than when the cash associated with that revenue is collected, and expenses are recognized when the benefit is received rather than when the cash associated with the expenses is paid. Meaning of course, that while the budgeted income statement (including the sales budget, cost of goods sold budget, and the selling and administrative expense budget) provides information about Marcy's projected earnings activities for the budget period, it does not provide direct information about what is projected to happen during that period in terms of cash. Also, unless Marcy's pays cash for its purchase of surfboards, the purchases budget suffers from the same limitation.

Before we can prepare the budgeted balance sheet, we must determine the effect on cash of the budgets we have prepared so far. We do that by preparing a cash budget, which is composed of a cash receipts schedule and a cash payments schedule.

cash receipts schedule
Details the amount of cash a company expects to collect during the budget period.

Cash Receipts Schedule The **cash receipts schedule** details the amount of cash a company expects to collect during the budget period from the sales of its product. Before we can prepare Marcy's cash receipts schedule, we must make certain estimates about the composition of the company's sales (cash or credit) and the pattern of collecting the accounts receivable created by the credit sales. We estimate that 25 percent of Marcy's sales are for cash and the remaining 75 percent are on account (credit sales). Of the sales on account, we estimate that 30 percent are collected in the month of the sale, 60 percent in the month following the sale, and 10 percent in the second month following the sale. Because of the lag between the time a credit sale is made and the time cash is collected, some of the cash for credit sales made in May and June will not have been collected by the end of June, which means that those amounts will be collected during the three months included in our budget period. Therefore, we need to know May credit sales were $4,500, and June credit sales were $6,000.

Using the credit sales figures from May and June, and our assumptions about when cash is collected, we can prepare Marcy's cash receipts schedule for the three months ended September 30, 2007 as shown in Exhibit 8–10.

Exhibit 8-10
Cash Receipts Schedule for Marcy's Surf Shop

MARCY'S SURF SHOP
Cash Receipts Schedule
For the Quarter Ended September 30, 2007

	Jul	Aug	Sep	Total	
Credit Sales Collected:					
From Accounts Receivable at 6/30/07:					
May Credit Sales ($4,500)					
Collected in July (10%)	$ 450			$ 450	
June Credit Sales ($6,000)					(a)
Collected in July (60%)	3,600			3,600	
Collected in August (10%)		$ 600		600	
From New Credit Sales:					
July Credit Sales ($4,500)					
Collected in July (30%)	1,350			1,350	
Collected in August (60%)		2,700		2,700	
Collected in September (10%)			$ 450	450	
August Credit Sales ($7,500)					(b)
Collected in August (30%)		2,250		2,250	
Collected in September (60%)			4,500	4,500	
September Credit Sales ($6,000)					
Collected in September (30%)			1,800	1,800	
Budgeted Receipts from Credit Sales	$5,400	$5,550	$6,750	$17,700	(c)
Cash Sales:					
July Cash Sales	1,500			1,500	
August Cash Sales		2,500		2,500	(d)
September Cash Sales			2,000	2,000	
Budgeted Cash Receipts	$6,900	$8,050	$8,750	$23,700	(e)

Although the cash receipts schedule presented in Exhibit 8–10 seems quite complex, it is more straightforward than it first appears. It is broken into two major parts. The first presents the amount of cash collected from credit sales during the period covered by the schedule (a through c) and the second part presents the amount of cash collected from cash sales during the budget period (d).

Let us take a few minutes to examine this schedule and see where the numbers came from and what they mean.

(a) *From Accounts Receivable at 6/30/07.* The accounts receivable balance at 6/30/07 is composed of receivables arising from sales in May and June. May's credit sales were $4,500. Based on our collection assumption, 30 percent of that amount was collected in May and 60 percent in June. If 90 percent had been collected by the end of June, the remaining $450 ($4,500 × 10%) had not and was included in the balance of accounts receivable at 6/30/07. Since July is the second month following the credit sales in May, the $450 balance is shown as a collection in July ($4,500 × 10%).

Credit sales in June totaled $6,000. Only $1,800 of that amount was collected in June ($6,000 × 30%). If 30 percent had been collected by the end of June, $4,200 ($6,000 × 70%) had not and was included in the balance of accounts receivable at 6/30/07. Since July is the month following the credit sales in June, $3,600 is shown as a collection in July ($6,000 × 60%); and because August is the second month following the credit sales in June, the remaining $600 balance is shown as a collection in August ($6,000 × 10%).

(b) *From New Sales.* Recall from the sales budget in Exhibit 8–5 that budgeted sales for the three months covered by our budget example were $6,000 in July, $10,000 in August, and $8,000 in September. One of the assumptions we made as we began our discussion of the cash receipts schedule was that 75 percent of Marcy's sales were credit sales. Therefore, the amounts we are dealing with in this section of the schedule are $4,500 for July ($6,000 × 75%), $7,500 for August ($10,000 × 75%), and $6,000 for September ($8,000 × 75%).

The collection pattern for each of the three months is the same: 30 percent of credit sales are collected in the month of sale, 60 percent in the month following the sale, and 10 percent in the second month following the sale. So for July's credit sales, for example, the schedule shows $1,350 will be collected in July ($4,500 × 30%), $2,700 will be collected in August ($4,500 × 60%), and $450 ($4,500 × 10%) in September. The amounts projected to be collected for August and September credit sales are calculated exactly the same way.

(c) *Budgeted Receipts from Credit Sales.* Add (a) and (b). It presents the total amount of cash Marcy's expects to collect during the period covered by the schedule from credit sales.

(d) *Cash Sales.* If 75 percent of the sales made in a given month are credit sales, then 25 percent will be cash sales. Therefore, in July the cash sales will be $1,500 ($6,000 × 25%); August is $2,500 ($10,000 × 25%); and September $2,000 ($8,000 × 25%).

(e) *Budgeted Cash Receipts.* This figure is simply the sum of (c) and (d). As the description indicates, it presents the total amount of cash Marcy's plans to collect from the accounts receivable balance at 6/30/02, the credit sales it will have during the period covered by the schedule, and the cash sales made during the period.

cash payments schedule
Details the amount of cash a company expects to pay out during the budget period.

Cash Payments Schedule   The **cash payments schedule** details the amount of cash a company expects to pay out during the budget period. We assume that payment for the purchase of surfboards is made in the month following the purchase. Because of the lag time between the time a purchase is made and the time cash is paid, the purchases made in June will not have been paid by the end of June, which means that this amount will be paid in July, one of the months included in our budget period. Therefore, we need to know that purchases of merchandise in June totaled $5,200. All cash selling and administrative expenses are paid in the month incurred.

Using these assumptions about when cash is paid and the purchases figure from June, we can prepare Marcy's cash payments schedule for the three months ended September 30, 2007, as shown in Exhibit 8–11.

As you can see from Exhibit 8–11, the cash payments schedule is not nearly as complex as either the purchases budget or the cash receipts schedule. There are a couple of tricky parts, however, so let us examine the items included.

(a) *Purchases.* These are payments for the purchase of surfboards made in the month following purchase. The projected payment of $5,200 in July, then, is for purchases made in June, the payment of $5,040 in August will be for

Exhibit 8–11
Cash Payments Schedule for Marcy's Surf Shop

MARCY'S SURF SHOP
Cash Payments Schedule
For the Quarter Ended September 30, 2007

	July	August	September	Total	
Purchases	$5,200	$5,040	$5,520	$15,760	(a)
Selling and Admin. Expense:					
Salaries and Wages	1,600	2,000	1,800	5,400	
Rent	200	200	200	600	(b)
Other Selling and Admin. Expense	800	1,000	900	2,700	
Purchase of Display Case		240		240	(c)
Budgeted Cash Payments	$7,800	$8,480	$8,420	$24,700	(d)

July purchases, and the $5,520 payment in September will be for August purchases.

Discussion Question

8-18. In our assumptions about cash payments, we said that June purchases of merchandise totaled $5,200 so it is easy to see where the July payment originated. Where do you suppose the payment amounts ($5,040 and $5,520) originated for August and September?

(b) *Selling and Administrative Expense.* These are payments for the support costs Marcy's anticipates for each month of the budget period. The amounts come directly from the selling and administrative expense budget in Exhibit 8–7.

Discussion Question

8-19. Look back at the selling and administrative expense budget in Exhibit 8–7. All the expense items included in that budget are included in the cash payments schedule *except* depreciation. Why do you think depreciation expense was included in the selling and administrative expense budget but excluded from the cash payments schedule?

(c) *Purchase of Display Case.* Evidently, Marcy's is planning to purchase a new display case for the showroom during the month of August. This purchase will be addition to Marcy's property, plant, and equipment and will be important to us when we prepare the budgeted balance sheet and the budgeted statement of cash flows. Incidently, the planned purchase of this display case is what caused depreciation expense in Exhibit 8–7 to increase by $4 in September.

(d) *Budgeted Cash Payments.* Add (a), (b), and (c). As the description indicates, it presents the total amount of cash Marcy's plans to pay out during the period covered by the schedule.

Building the Cash Budget

Now that we have prepared the cash receipts schedule and the cash payments schedule, we can prepare Marcy's cash budget for the quarter ended September 30, 2007. As was the case with the schedules, we must make some assumptions for the cash budget. First, we estimate that Marcy's Surf Shop will have a cash balance of $2,170 on June 30, 2007. Second, Marcy's desires to maintain a cash balance of at least $1,900 at all times. If cash falls below $1,900, the company will borrow from a local bank. Finally, we ignore the interest Marcy's would be required to pay on any borrowings from the bank.

Using the assumption about Marcy's desired minimum cash balance, and the information from the cash receipts schedule and the cash payments schedule, we can prepare the company's cash budget for the quarter ending September 30, 2007, as shown in Exhibit 8–12.

Although the cash budget is fairly straighforward, let's review the source of the numbers.

(a) *Beginning Cash Balance.* July's beginning cash balance will be June's ending cash balance of $2,170. The same pattern holds true for the other months presented. The beginning balance in the total column ($2,170) is the same as the beginning balance for July. Likewise, the ending balance in the total column ($1,900) is the same as the ending balance for September, because the total column represents the entire quarter.

(b) *Cash Receipts.* Cash receipts amounts come directly from the cash receipts schedule shown in Exhibit 8-10.

(c) *Cash Available.* Add (a) and (b).

(d) *Cash Payments.* Cash payments amounts come directly from the cash payments schedule shown in Exhibit 8-11.

(e) *Balance before Borrowing.* Subtract (d) from (c).

(f) *Borrowing/(Repayment).* Marcy's wants to maintain a cash balance of at least $1,900. If the balance before borrowing drops too low, Marcy's will borrow enough money from the bank to bring the balance up to the desired ending cash balance of $1,900. As you can see, July's balance before borrowing is expected to be only $1,270. Therefore, Marcy's can anticipate the need to borrow $630 to bring the balance up to $1,900. So, if the balance before borrowing is less than the desired ending cash balance, as it will be in July and again in August, the amount that must be borrowed to bring the cash balance to the desired amount can be

Exhibit 8–12
Cash Budget for
Marcy's Surf Shop

MARCY'S SURF SHOP
Cash Budget
For the Quarter Ended September 30, 2007

		July	August	September	Total	
	Beginning Cash Balance	$2,170	$ 1,900	$ 1,900	$ 2,170	(a)
+	Cash Receipts	6,900	8,050	8,750	23,700	(b)
=	Cash Available	$9,070	$ 9,950	$10,650	$25,870	(c)
−	Cash Payments	(7,800)	(8,480)	(8,420)	(24,700)	(d)
=	Balance before Borrowing	$1,270	$ 1,470	$ 2,230	$ 1,170	(e)
+/−	Borrowing/(Repayment)	630	$ 430	$ (330)	$ 730	(f)
=	Ending Cash Balance	$1,900	$ 1,900	$ 1,900	$ 1,900	(g)

easily calculated. If, on the other hand, the expected balance before borrowing is greater than $1,900, as is the case in September, any amount in excess of the desired ending cash balance will be used to repay the loan ($330 in this instance).

(g) *Ending Cash Balance.* If line (f) is positive, add (e) to (f). If line (f) is negative, subtract (f) from line (e).

Building the Budgeted Balance Sheet

You already know how to construct a balance sheet from a worksheet taken from the general ledger. Budgeted amounts, however, are not recorded in the general ledger.

Although some of the amounts needed to prepare the budgeted balance sheet come directly from the budgets already prepared, many amounts are not specifically included in any of those budgets. For example, we have not prepared a budget or schedule that shows the ending balances for accounts receivable, inventory, property, plant, and equipment, accumulated depreciation, accounts payable, notes payable, common stock, additional paid-in capital, or retained earnings. For each of these items, we will present a brief discussion and a schedule to show how to calculate the amounts that should appear on the budgeted balance sheet.

You will find as you examine each of these items that the budgeted ending balance is calculated by taking the beginning balance and adding or subtracting the changes that are expected to occur during the budget period. So, for each of these items, the beginning balance is our starting point. As discussed, the *beginning* balance of any balance sheet item is the prior month's *ending* balance. Therefore, all we need is the balance sheet for June 30 to determine the beginning balance for July. The balance sheet of June 30, 2007, for Marcy's Surf Shop is shown in Exhibit 8–13.

Exhibit 8–13
Balance Sheet as of June 30, 2002, for Marcy's Surf Shop

MARCY'S SURF SHOP
Balance Sheet
June 30, 2007

Assets	
Current Assets	
Cash	$ 2,170
Accounts Receivable	4,650
Inventory	960
Total Current Assets	$ 7,780
Property, Plant, and Equipment	
Equipment	6,000
Less Accumulated Depreciation	(1,200)
Equipment, Net	$ 4,800
Total Assets	$12,580
Liabilities	
Current Liabilities	
Accounts Payable	$ 5,200
Total Liabilities	$ 5,200
Owner's Equity	
Paid-in Capital	
Common Stock	$ 1,000
Additional Paid-in Capital	5,475
Total Paid-in Capital	$ 6,475
Retained Earnings	$ 905
Total Equity	$ 7,380
Total Liabilities and Equity	$12,580

Using the June 30, 2007, balance sheet in Exhibit 8–13 and information from the other budgets we have prepared so far, we can prepare a budgeted balance sheet for each of the three months included in our budget period, as shown in Exhibit 8–14.

The balance sheets presented in Exhibit 8–14 are much like the other balance sheets you have seen throughout your studies. The essential difference is not the format, but rather, the time frame. These are projected balance sheets whereas the others have presented past results. There is no total column for this budget, because the balance sheet is a financial snapshot of a business taken at the end of a period. Therefore, in a very real sense, the snapshot taken at the end of September is the total column.

Let's take a closer look at each of the items on the budgeted balance sheet.

(a) *Cash.* This amount is taken directly from the ending cash balance line of the cash budget shown in Exhibit 8–12. The amount shown as the ending cash balance of $1,900 in the July column of the cash budget is shown as cash in the July column of the budgeted balance sheet.

(b) *Accounts Receivable.* To determine the ending accounts receivable balance for each month shown in Exhibit 8–14 take the beginning accounts receivable balance, add budgeted credit sales for that month, and subtract budgeted collections for that month.

	Jul	Aug	Sep
Beginning Balance	$4,650	$3,750	$5,700
+ Credit sales	4,500	7,500	6,000
− Collections	(5,400)	(5,550)	(6,750)
Ending Balance	$3,750	$5,700	$4,950

Exhibit 8–14
Budgeted Balance
Sheets for Marcy's
Surf Shop

MARCY'S SURF SHOP
Budgeted Balance Sheet
For the Quarter Ended September 30, 2007

	July	August	September	
Assets				
Current Assets				
Cash	$ 1,900	$ 1,900	$ 1,900	(a)
Accounts Receivable, Net	3,750	5,700	4,950	(b)
Inventory	2,400	1,920	2,880	(c)
Total Current Assets	$ 8,050	$ 9,520	$ 9,730	
Property, Plant, and Equipment				
Equipment	$ 6,000	$ 6,240	$ 6,240	(d)
Less Accumulated Depreciation	(1,300)	(1,400)	(1,504)	(e)
Equipment, Net	$ 4,700	$ 4,840	$ 4,736	
Total Assets	$12,750	$14,360	$14,466	
Liabilities				
Current Liabilities				
Accounts Payable	$ 5,040	$ 5,520	$ 5,760	(f)
Bank Loan Payable	630	1,060	730	(g)
Total Liabilities	$ 5,670	$ 6,580	$ 6,490	
Owner's Equity				
Paid-in Capital				
Common Stock	$ 1,000	$ 1,000	$ 1,000	
Additional Paid-in Capital	5,475	5,475	5,475	(h)
Total Paid-in Capital	$ 6,475	$ 6,475	$ 6,475	
Retained Earnings	$ 605	$ 1,305	$ 1,501	(i)
Total Equity	$ 7,080	$ 7,780	$ 7,976	
Total Liabilities and Equity	$12,750	$14,360	$14,466	

The beginning accounts receivable balance of $4,650 for July is taken from the June 30, 2007, balance sheet shown in Exhibit 8–13. The cash receipts budget shows the projected credit sales and the total expected to be collected from credit sales. For July, the cash receipts budget shows credit sales of $4,500 and a total of $5,400 collected from credit sales. After adding the credit sales of $4,500 to the beginning balance of $4,650, we subtract the collections of $5,400 to arrive at the ending accounts receivable balance of $3,750. This amount is shown on the budgeted balance sheet for July. The ending accounts receivable amounts for other months are calculated the same way.

(c) *Inventory.* To determine the ending inventory balance for each month shown in Exhibit 8–14, we simply take the beginning inventory balance, add purchases made during the month, and subtract that month's cost of goods sold.

	Jul	Aug	Sep
Beginning Balance	$ 960	$2,400	$1,920
+ Purchases	5,040	5,520	5,760
− Cost of goods sold	(3,600)	(6,000)	(4,800)
Ending Balance	$2,400	$1,920	$2,880

The beginning inventory balance for July of $960 is taken from the June 30, 2002, balance sheet shown in Exhibit 8–13. By looking at the purchases budget in Exhibit 8–9 and the cost of goods sold budget in Exhibit 8–6, we find that expected purchases for July are $5,040 and cost of goods sold are expected be $3,600. After adding the purchases of $5,040 to the beginning balance of $960, we subtract the cost of goods sold of $3,600 to arrive at the ending inventory balance of $2,400. This amount is shown on the budgeted balance sheet for July. The ending inventory amounts for other months are calculated the same way.

(d) *Equipment.* To determine the ending balance in the equipment, we adjust the beginning balance by adding the cost of equipment purchased and subtracting the cost of any equipment sold. In our example, the only change in equipment is the $240 for the showcase the company is planning to buy in August. We add $240 to the $6,000 beginning balance to arrive at the budgeted ending balance of $6,240.

(e) *Accumulated Depreciation.* To determine the ending balance for accumulated depreciation, we adjust the beginning balance by adding the depreciation for the period and subtracting the accumulated depreciation associated with any assets that have been sold or scrapped. In our example, the company does not expect to sell or otherwise dispose of any equipment, so the only changes to accumulated depreciation are increases relating to the budgeted monthly depreciation. You might notice that the amount added to accumulated depreciation in September is slightly higher than that for July and August. This is so because of the added depreciation for the showcase the company expects to buy in August.

(f) *Accounts Payable.* To determine the ending accounts payable balance for each month shown in Exhibit 8–14, we simply take the beginning accounts payable balance, add budgeted purchases for that month, and subtract budgeted payments for that month.

	Jul	Aug	Sep
Beginning Balance	$5,200	$5,040	$5,520
+ Purchases	5,040	5,520	5,760
− Payments	(5,200)	(5,040)	(5,520)
Ending Balance	$5,040	$5,520	$5,760

The beginning accounts payable balance for July of $5,200 is taken from the June 30, 2007, balance sheet shown in Exhibit 8–13. By looking at the purchases budget in Exhibit 8–9 and the cash payments budget in Exhibit 8–11, we find that expected purchases for July are $5,040 and cash payments are expected be $5,200. After adding the purchases of $5,040 to the beginning balance of $5,200, we subtract the cash payments of $5,200 to arrive at the ending accounts payable balance of $5,040. This amount is shown on the budgeted balance sheet for July. The ending accounts payable amounts for other months are calculated the same way.

(g) *Bank Loan Payable.* To determine the ending notes payable balance for each month shown in Exhibit 8–14, we simply take the beginning notes payable balance, add the budgeted borrowing for that month, and subtract budgeted payments for that month.

	Jul	Aug	Sep
Beginning Balance	$ -0-	$ 630	$1,060
+ Borrowing	630	430	-0-
− Repayments	-0-	-0-	(330)
Ending Balance	$630	$1,060	$ 730

The beginning notes payable balance for July would normally come from the June 30, 2007, balance sheet shown in Exhibit 8–13; however, in this example the beginning balance for notes payable on June 30, 2007, is zero, so notes payable does not appear. By looking at the cash budget in Exhibit 8–12, we find that borrowing of $630 is expected in July, borrowing of $430 is expected in August, and a repayment of $330 is expected in September.

(h) *Common Stock and Additional Paid-in Capital.* In this example, no common stock or additional paid in capital transactions are expected during the budget period. Therefore, the beginning July balance for these items found on the June 30, 2007, balance sheet in Exhibit 8–13 remains unchanged during the budget period.

(i) *Retained Earnings.* To determine the ending retained earnings balance, we add the income for the period or, if the company has a loss, subtract the loss and deduct dividends, if they exist, from the beginning retained earnings balance.

	Jul	Aug	Sep
Beginning Balance	$ 905	$ 605	$1,305
+ Income/Loss	(300)	700	196
− Dividends	-0-	-0-	-0-
Ending Balance	$ 605	$1,305	$1,501

In our example, the $905 beginning balance of retained earnings is found on the June 30, 2007, balance sheet shown in Exhibit 8–13. To find the ending retained earnings that should appear on the budgeted balance sheet for July, we deduct the budgeted loss for that month of $300 from the beginning retained earnings balance of $905. That amount becomes the beginning balance in August. To determine the August ending balance of retained earnings we add August's budgeted net income. September's ending balance would be calculated the same way. There are no dividends in our example so the dividend amount is zero for each month presented.

Budgeted Statement of Cash Flows

Now that we have prepared all the other budgets, we can prepare the budgeted statement of cash flows (SCF). This statement must be the final budget prepared because, as you recall from your earlier study of this financial statement, it is a form of financial statement analysis. An SCF prepared on historical results analyzes the income statement and the balance sheet to explain what caused cash to change from the beginning of a period to the end of the period. The budgeted statement of cash flows does exactly the same thing, except that it analyzes the budgeted income statement and the budgeted balance sheet to explain what will cause the projected change in cash from the start to the end of the budget period.

A budgeted statement of cash flows for Marcy's Surf Shop is presented as Exhibit 8–15.

Exhibit 8–15
Budgeted Statement of Cash Flows for Marcy's Surf Shop

MARCY'S SURF SHOP
Budgeted Statement of Cash Flows
For the Quarter Ended September 30, 2007

	July	August	September	Total
Cash Flows from				
Operating Activities:				
Net Income	($ 300)	$ 700	$ 196	$ 596
Add: Depreciation	100	100	104	304
Changes in CA & CL:				
Accounts Receivable	900	(1,950)	750	(300)
Inventory	(1,440)	480	(960)	(1,920)
Accounts Payable	(160)	480	240	560
Net Cash Flow from Op Act	($ 900)	($ 190)	330	($ 760)
Cash Flow From				
Investing Activities:				
Cash Paid for Showcase	—	(240)	—	(240)
Net Cash Flow from Inv Act		(240)		(240)
Cash Flow From				
Financing Activities:				
Borrowing	$ 630	$ 430		$1,060
Loan Payments			($ 330)	(330)
Net Cash Flow from Fin Act	$ 630	$ 430	($ 330)	$ 730
Increase/(Decrease) in Cash	($ 270)	$ -0-	$ 0	($ 270)
Budgeted Beginning Cash Balance	2,170	1,900	1,900	2,170
Budgeted Ending Cash Balance	$1,900	$1,900	$1,900	$1,900

We will not do a line-by-line analysis of the presentation in Exhibit 8–15 because we have explained all the items elsewhere in this chapter as we have constructed the other budgets. It is worthwhile, however, for us to discuss what this budget reveals in overall terms.

In the normal course of business, a company can obtain cash from only three sources: borrowing, owner contributions, and profitable operations. Ultimately, the only source of cash for any company, including Marcy's Surf Shop, is the profitable operation of the business. If a company does not generate enough cash from operations to run the business, it must seek outside financing (borrowing and owner contributions).

The budgeted statement of cash flows in Exhibit 8–15 reveals that for the three months covered by the budget Marcy's does not anticipate generating enough cash through operations to run the business and must borrow the money. Marcy may not like what she sees when she looks at this budget. If she finds the prospects unacceptable, she may want to continue the budgeting process and make adjustments in how she plans to operate her business.

CONNECTING THE BUDGET TO THE STRATEGIC PLAN

One of the most important budgeting functions is for top management to ensure that each budget aligns with the goals and objectives of the strategic plan. At least annually, the board of directors and officers of a firm should review the strategic plan to see how well the company has followed the plan, how well the company achieved its goals, and what changes might be necessary in the plan. The strategic plan and the master budget control the allocation of resources. They must, therefore, be in conformity with one another. They are, however, living and dynamic documents. They can function together to make sure that the board of directors sets achievable goals and remains accountable for their attainment. Investors require such behavior, and they express their approval or disapproval by their willingness to buy the company's stock at any given price.

ANALYZING BUDGET VARIANCES

We have seen that the operating budget can serve as a guide for managers to follow, assist managers in allocating the firm's scarce resources, and foster communication and coordination among managers from different functional areas within the company. It can also establish performance standards, or benchmarks, against which the company can compare the actual results. This fourth application, however, presents some serious challenges to managers.

Most of the challenges arise because managers consider the budget to be an authority to spend, or their bonuses or promotions are based on their ability to beat the budget, or they prepare inflated budgets to guarantee that they can come in under budget. This behavior does not improve the firm's operations in the long run. Using the budget for these purposes encourages managers to make bad decisions and discourages them from making good decisions.

The Budget Performance Report

budget performance report
A report that compares the actual amounts against the budgeted amounts for a budget category.

budget variance The difference between the actual and budgeted amounts for a budget category.

Most firms require managers to prepare or review a **budget performance report,** a report that compares the actual amounts against the budgeted amounts for a budget category. The difference between the actual and budgeted amounts for a budget category is known as a **budget variance.** A typical budget performance report has four columns as shown in Exhibit 8–16. As you can see from Exhibit 8–16, the report is not complicated. For each area of responsibility, it gives the budgeted amount, the actual amount, and the difference. A positive variance means the actual exceeded the budget and a negative amount indicates that the actual was less than the budgeted amount.

Exhibit 8–16
Budget Performance Report

(a) Description	(b) Budget	(c) Actual	(d) Variance
Salaries and Wages	$25,000	$23,000	$2,000 F
Office Rent	10,000	10,000	-0-
Office Supplies	1,000	1,200	200 U

When we discuss revenues, positive variances are favorable because they indicate sales in excess of the budget and negative variances are unfavorable because they represent underachievement. The opposite is true for expenses. Negative variances are favorable because they indicate cost savings, and positive variances are unfavorable because they represent cost overruns.

The budget performance report can provide data, but its information value is limited without further investigation. What caused the variance? Was the variance a factor of price or of quantity? The following are the possible causes of variances:

1. The number of units of product remained the same but the price increased or decreased. The sales forecast was accurate, but due to competitive forces, management lowered or raised the price of the product.
2. The price remained the same, but due to uncontrollable forces, such as the weather or the economy, the number of units sold varied from the budgeted amounts. Say, for example, that Hawaii experienced a long rainy season by a short, unseasonably cool summer. A retailer dependent upon tourists for sales might experience a costly decrease in sales. Weather conditions cannot be predicted with a high degree of accuracy.

When we look at costs, the same types of questions are important. Did the quantity of units of an expense increase or did the price per unit of the expense increase? Quantity increases may indicate waste and quantity decreases may indicate frugal use. Price per unit increases sometimes can be controlled by switching suppliers, but frequently they are caused by imbalances in the economy.

Should managers investigate all variances, favorable or unfavorable, regardless of amounts? Some firms only look at variances over a certain amounts. The better management understands the company's revenues and expenses and learns from the budgeting process, the less likely it will be caught short of information. When favorable budget variances mean that management will automatically reduce next year's budget, some managers seek to keep the actual amounts as close as possible to the budget amounts, somehow believing they will be losing something if the next budget is reduced. Instead of being rewarded for savings, they believe they are being punished. When an expense decreases, it no longer requires funding at the previous level. The manager loses nothing. When the manager wishes to use that saved amount for another purpose, he or she should request a new budget item. A firm that has a clear strategic plan, mission, values, and goals can achieve better overall performance when the budget process is an extension of its corporate strategy, instead of a territorial fight.

Regardless of the care taken with the budget process, variances will occur. Because of the interrelationships among the budgets, if the sales forecast is inaccurate, the operating budget will be inaccurate. The sales forecast will always be inaccurate because it is always an estimate. Therefore, the operating budget will always be inaccurate so there will always be variances. Inaccuracy is not bad—but variances should always be investigated. The focus of this analysis, however, should be on how to improve the budgeting process rather than to eliminate the inevitable variances that have occurred.

SUMMARY

The operating budget is an integral part of the overall planning process for any company. Besides serving as a guide for the business throughout the period covered by the budget, the operating budget can assist management in the allocation of resources, foster communication and coordination among various segments of the company, and establish performance standards.

The operating budget is a set of estimated financial statements. These are the budgeted income statement, the budgeted balance sheet, and the budgeted statement of cash flows. Besides the budgeted financial statements, the operating budget includes several other budgets prepared to support the budgeted financial statements. These are the sales budget, the production (or purchases) budget, the cost of goods sold (or cost of services) budget, the selling and administrative expense budget, and the cash budget (including the cash receipts schedule and the cash payments schedule).

There are several different approaches to the preparation of the operating budget. Perpetual, incremental, zero-based, top-down, bottom-up, imposed, and participative approaches to budgeting are just some that have developed over time. Each approach has certain advantages and certain disadvantages relative to the other approaches.

All the budgets included in the operating budget are dependent on the sales forecast. Indeed, the accuracy of the entire budget is dependent on the accuracy of the forecast. Many factors, including the state of the general economy, the condition of the company's industry, the actions of competitors, and technological developments all influence a company's ability to forecast its sales reasonably.

Management should analyze variances to improve the budgeting process.

REVIEW THE FACTS

A. What is the operating budget?
B. What is the master budget?
C. Which financial statements are part of the operating budget?
D. What is the difference between the financial statements included in the operating budget and other financial statements you have learned about in this course?
E. List the main benefits of budgeting.
F. What is the basic difference between the production budget and the purchases budget?
G. What are two advantages of perpetual budgeting?
H. What is a disadvantage of perpetual budgeting?
I. What is incremental budgeting?
J. What problem is associated with incremental budgeting?
K. What is zero-based budgeting?
L. Describe the differences between top-down and bottom-up budgeting.
M. Describe the differences between an imposed budget and a participative budget.
N. Why is the sales forecast often called the cornerstone of budgeting?
O. Why is the sales forecast often called the keystone of budgeting?
P. List three factors that should be considered when preparing the sales forecast.
Q. Why does the number of units budgeted to be purchased differ from the number of units budgeted to be sold?
R. When preparing the purchases budget, what two factors should be considered when determining the budgeted ending inventory?

S. What is presented on the cash receipts schedule?

T. For a particular budget period, why doesn't the budgeted cash collections from customers equal budgeted sales?

U. What is the basic difference between a budgeted balance sheet and an historical balance sheet?

V. In the normal course of business, what are the three sources from which a company can obtain cash?

APPLY WHAT YOU HAVE LEARNED

LO 3 & 4:   Determine Order of Operating Budget Preparation

8–20. During the budgeting process, not all budgets are prepared at the same time. Following are several operating budgets.

1. _____ Cash budget
2. _____ Budgeted financial statements
3. _____ Purchases budget
4. _____ Sales budget
5. _____ Administrative expense budget
6. _____ Selling expense budget

REQUIRED:
Indicate a logical sequence for the preparation of the master budget.

LO 3:   Indicate Advantages and Disadvantages of Top-Down, Bottom-Up Approaches

8–21. The master budget can be prepared using either the top-down or bottom-up approach. Following in random order are several advantages and disadvantages of each approach.

Top-down Bottom-up	Advantage Disadvantage	
1. _____	_____	Budgeting process forces managers at various levels to think about future activities.
2. _____	_____	Top manager is more knowledgeable.
3. _____	_____	Employees at various levels must take time from their schedules to work on the budget.
4. _____	_____	Employees will be more eager to work toward goals they helped set.
5. _____	_____	Employees feel more like part of the company team.
6. _____	_____	Top manager is more aware of company goals.
7. _____	_____	Employees may try to pad the budget.
8. _____	_____	Employees are less accepting of budgeted goals if they had no part in setting them.
9. _____	_____	Top manager lacks detailed knowledge required to prepare budgets.

REQUIRED:
For each of these items, indicate whether it is associated with top-down (T) or bottom-up (B), and whether it is an advantage (A) or disadvantage (D).

LO 3: Indicate Budgeting Approaches

8–22. Following are approaches to budgeting, with a partial definition of those items in scrambled order.

    a. Perpetual budgeting   **d.** Top-down budgeting
    b. Incremental budgeting   **e.** Bottom-up budgeting
    c. Zero-based budgeting

1. _____ Lower-level managers and employees initially prepare the budget.

2. _____ Each item on the budget must be justified each year.

3. _____ The budget is updated every month.

4. _____ Lower-level managers generally do not participate in budget preparation.

5. _____ Uses the prior year's budget to build the new budget.

REQUIRED:

For each partial definition, identify the budgeting approach to which it refers.

LO 5: Prepare a Sales Budget

8–23. For 2007, David's Computer Game Company expects to sell 6,000 games in the first quarter, 7,000 games in the second quarter, 9,000 games in the third quarter, and 12,000 games in the fourth quarter. Each game sells for $11.

REQUIRED:

Prepare the 2007 sales budget for David's Computer Game Company.

LO 5: Prepare a Sales Budget

8–24. For 2007, Paul Elsea's Barber Supply Company expects to sell 100 hair dryers in the first quarter, 90 hair dryers in the second quarter, 130 hair dryers in the third quarter, and 150 hair dryers in the fourth quarter. Each hair dryer sells for $67.

REQUIRED:

Prepare the 2007 sales budget for hair dryers for Paul Elsea's Barber Supply Company.

LO 5: Prepare a Sales Budget

8–25. For 2007, Taub Yo Yo Company expects to sell 20,000 units in January, 25,000 units in February, and 30,000 units in March. Each unit sells for $1.20.

REQUIRED:

Prepare the sales budget for Taub Yo Yo Company for the first quarter of 2007.

LO 5: Prepare a Sales Budget

8–26. The Golden Bird Cage Company intends to sell 11,500 bird cages during 2007. The budgeted selling price per cage is $88. The following sales forecast is available:

	Units
First quarter	2,500
Second quarter	2,100
Third quarter	3,800
Fourth quarter	3,100

REQUIRED:

Prepare the 2007 sales budget for Golden Bird Cage Company.

LO 5: Prepare a Sales Budget

8–27. Easy-Glide Strollers intends to sell 73,000 baby strollers in the first quarter of 2007. The budgeted selling price per stroller is $59. The following sales forecast is available:

	Units
January	22,500
February	22,500
March	28,000

REQUIRED:

Prepare the sales budget for Easy-Glide Strollers for the first quarter of 2007.

LO 5: Prepare a Purchases Budget

8–28. Florence Marie's Hat Shop plans to sell the following quantity of hats during the first four months of 2007.

	Units
January	200
February	250
March	300
April	320

Florence pays $6 for each hat which she sells for $15.

At the beginning of January, Florence plans to have 40 hats on hand, and hopes to maintain an ending inventory equal to 20% of next month's sales.

REQUIRED:

Prepare a purchases budget for the first quarter of 2007 for Florence Marie's Hat Shop. Remember, the first quarter is January, February, and March. April sales are only provided to help compute the ending inventory for March.

LO 5: Prepare a Sales Budget and Cost of Goods Sold Budget

8–29. Refer to the information in problem 8–28.

REQUIRED:

a. Prepare a sales budget for the first quarter of 2007 for Florence Marie's Hat Shop.
b. Prepare a cost of goods sold budget for the first quarter of 2007 for Florence Marie's Hat Shop.

LO 5: Prepare a Purchases Budget

8–30. Anahi's Art Supplies plans to sell the following quantity of model AB222 airbrush during the first four months of 2007.

	Units
January	400
February	26
March	22
April	20

Anahi's pays $44 for each airbrush and sells them for $65.

At the beginning of January, Anahi's Art Supplies plans to have six airbrushes on hand, and hopes to maintain an ending inventory equal to 15% of next month's sales.

REQUIRED:

Prepare a purchases budget for the first quarter of 2007 for Anahi's Art Supplies. Remember, the first quarter is January, February, and March. April sales are only provided to help compute the ending inventory for March.

LO 5: Prepare a Sales Budget and Cost of Goods Sold Budget

8–31. Refer to the information in problem 8–30.

REQUIRED:

a. Prepare a sales budget for the first quarter of 2007 for Anahi's Art Supplies.
b. Prepare a cost of goods sold budget for the first quarter of 2007 for Anahi's Art Supplies.

LO 5: Prepare a Sales Budget, Cost of Goods Sold Budget, and Purchases Budget

8–32. Diaz Lumber plans to sell the following quantity of BC Grade 1/2-inch plywood during the first four months of 2007.

January	220 sheets
February	250 sheets
March	200 sheets
April	300 sheets

Diaz pays $7 for each sheet of plywood and sells them for $12.

At the beginning of January, Diaz plans to have 66 sheets of plywood on hand, and hopes to maintain an ending inventory equal to 30% of next month's sales.

REQUIRED:

a. Prepare a sales budget for the first quarter of 2007 for Diaz Lumber.
b. Prepare a cost of goods sold budget for the first quarter of 2007 for Diaz Lumber.
c. Prepare a purchases budget for the first quarter of 2007 for Diaz Lumber.

LO 5: Prepare a Budgeted Income Statement Using Information Provided in Other Budgets

8–33. Smith Manufacturing has prepared the following budgeted information for January 2007.

SMITH MANUFACTURING
Sales Budget
For January 31, 2007

Budgeted Sales in Units	3,300
× Budgeted Sales Price	$ 200
= Budgeted Sales Dollars	$660,000

SMITH MANUFACTURING
Cost of Goods Sold Budget
For January 31, 2007

Budgeted Sales in Units	3,300
× Budgeted Cost Per Unit	$ 110
= Budgeted COGS	$363,000

SMITH MANUFACTURING
Selling and Administrative Expense Budget
For January 31, 2007

Salaries and Wages	$101,500
Rent	64,000
Depreciation	53,200
Other	2,300
Budgeted S & A Expense	$221,000

REQUIRED:

Prepare a budgeted income statement for January 2007 for Smith Manufacturing.

LO 5: Prepare a Budgeted Income Statement Using Information Provided in Other Budgets

8–34. Gomez Sales Company has prepared the following budgeted information for March 2007.

GOMEZ SALES COMPANY
Sales Budget
For March 31, 2007

Budgeted Sales in Units	110,000
× Budgeted Sales Price	$ 4.95
= Budgeted Sales Dollars	$544,500

GOMEZ SALES COMPANY
Cost of Goods Sold Budget
For March 31, 2007

Budgeted Sales in Units	110,000
× Budgeted Cost Per Unit	$ 3.35
= Budgeted COGS	$368,500

GOMEZ SALES COMPANY
Selling and Administrative Expense Budget
For March 31, 2007

Sales Salaries	$ 51,500
Sales Commission	11,000
Other Salaries and Wages	35,000
Store Rent	24,000
Other Expenses	10,500
Budgeted S & A Expense	132,000

REQUIRED:

Prepare a budgeted income statement for March 2007 for Gomez Sales Company.

LO 5: Prepare a Budgeted Income Statement Using Information Provided in Other Budgets

8–35. Copas Company has prepared the following budgeted information for December 2007.

COPAS COMPANY
Sales Budget
For December 31, 2007

	Budgeted Sales in Units	10,000
×	Budgeted Sales Price	$ 1,200
=	Budgeted Sales Dollars	$120,000

COPAS COMPANY
Cost of Goods Sold Budget
For December 31, 2007

	Budgeted Sales in Units	10,000
×	Budgeted Cost Per Unit	$ 800
=	Budgeted COGS	$80,000

COPAS COMPANY
Selling and Administrative Expense Budget
For December 31, 2007

Sales Salaries	$18,500
Sales Commission	3,000
Store Rent	9,000
Other Expenses	1,500
Budgeted S & A Expense	32,000

REQUIRED:

Prepare a budgeted income statement for December 2007 for Copas Company.

LO 5: Prepare a Budgeted Income Statement

8–36. For the first quarter of 2008, Philip's Sales Corporation has budgeted sales of $390,000 and budgeted cost of goods sold of $280,000. In addition, the budget for the first quarter of 2008 includes wages and salaries of $42,000, rent of $9,000, utilities of $2,000, maintenance of $1,000, and other expenses of $3,000.

REQUIRED:

Prepare a budgeted income statement for the first quarter of 2008 for Philip's Sales Corporation.

LO 5: Prepare a Budgeted Income Statement

8–37. For January 2007, Edwardo Manufacturing has budgeted sales of $1,200,000 and budgeted cost of goods sold of $980,000. In addition, the budget for January 2007 includes sales salaries of $98,000, administrative salaries of $54,000, rent of $24,000, utilities of $8,000, and other expenses of $9,000.

REQUIRED:

Prepare a budgeted income statement for January 2007 for Edwardo Manufacturing.

LO 5: Prepare a Budgeted Income Statement

8–38. For the year 2007, Martin Sales Corporation has budgeted sales of $3,500,000 and budgeted cost of goods sold of $2,800,000. In addition, the budget for 2007 includes sales salaries of $220,000, administrative salaries of $130,000, depreciation of $180,000, utilities of $38,000, and other expenses of $22,000.

REQUIRED:
Prepare a budgeted income statement for 2007 for Martin Sales Corporation.

LO 5: Prepare a Budgeted Income Statement for One Quarter

8–39. The following budgets were prepared for Gary's Jean Store.

GARY'S JEAN STORE
Sales Budget
For the Quarter Ended June 30, 2008

	Apr	May	Jun	Total
Budgeted Sales in Units	300	350	400	1,050
× Budgeted Sales Price	$ 27	$ 27	$ 27	$ 27
= Budgeted Sales Dollars	$8,100	$9,450	$10,800	$28,350

GARY'S JEAN STORE
Cost of Goods Sold Budget
For the Quarter Ended June 30, 2008

	Apr	May	Jun	Total
Budgeted Sales in Units	300	350	400	1,050
× Budgeted Cost Per Unit	$ 14	$ 14	$ 14	$ 14
= Budgeted Cost of Goods Sold	$4,200	$4,900	$5,600	$14,700

GARY'S JEAN STORE
Selling and Administrative Expense Budget
For the Quarter Ended June 30, 2008

	Apr	May	Jun	Total
Salaries and Wages	$1,800	$2,200	$1,900	$ 5,900
Rent	500	500	500	1,500
Depreciation	100	100	100	300
Other	600	900	800	2,300
Budgeted Sales Dollars	$3,000	$3,700	$3,300	$10,000

REQUIRED:
Prepare a budgeted income statement for the second quarter of 2008 for Gary's Jean Store.

LO 5: Prepare a Budgeted Income Statement for One Quarter

8–40. Franco's Cart Company manufactures small carts that are designed to be pulled behind a small tractor or riding lawn mower. The following budgets were prepared for Franco's Cart Company.

FRANCO'S CART COMPANY
Sales Budget
For the Quarter Ended March 31, 2008

	Jan	Feb	Mar	Total
Budgeted Sales in Units	1,300	1,450	1,700	4,450
× Budgeted Sales Price	$ 186	$ 186	$ 186	$ 186
= Budgeted Sales Dollars	$241,800	$269,700	$316,200	$827,700

FRANCO'S CART COMPANY
Cost of Goods Sold Budget
For the Quarter Ended March 31, 2008

	Jan	Feb	Mar	Total
Budgeted Sales in Units	1,300	1,450	1,700	4,450
× Budgeted Cost Per Unit	$ 154	$ 154	$ 154	$ 154
= Budgeted COGS	$200,200	$223,300	$261,800	$685,300

FRANCO'S CART COMPANY
Selling and Administrative Expense Budget
For the Quarter Ended March 31, 2008

	Jan	Feb	Mar	Total
Salaries and Wages	$21,950	$22,200	$23,600	$67,750
Rent	4,000	4,500	4,500	13,000
Depreciation	3,200	3,200	3,200	9,600
Other	2,300	2,500	2,800	7,600
Budgeted S & A Expense	$31,450	$32,400	$34,100	$97,950

REQUIRED:

Prepare a budgeted income statement for the first quarter of 2008 for Franco's Cart Company.

LO 5: Prepare a Budgeted Income Statement for One Quarter

8–41. The following budgets were prepared for Byrne Manufacturing.

BYRNE MANUFACTURING
Sales Budget
For the Quarter Ended September 30, 2007

	Jul	Aug	Sep	Total
Budgeted Unit Sales	900	1,100	1,300	3,300
× Budgeted Sales Price	$ 225	$ 225	$ 225	$ 225
= Budgeted Sales Dollars	$202,500	$247,500	$292,500	$742,500

BYRNE MANUFACTURING
Cost of Goods Sold Budget
For the Quarter Ended September 30, 2007

	Jul	Aug	Sep	Total
Budgeted Unit Sales	900	1,100	1,300	3,300
× Budgeted Cost Per Unit	$ 204	$ 204	$ 204	$ 204
= Budgeted COGS	$183,600	$224,400	$265,200	$673,200

BYRNE MANUFACTURING
Selling and Administrative Expense Budget
For the Quarter Ended September 30, 2007

	Jul	Aug	Sep	Total
Salaries and Wages	$ 4,800	$ 5,200	$ 5,800	$15,800
Rent	2,400	2,400	2,400	7,200
Depreciation	1,150	1,150	1,150	3,450
Other	1,800	2,000	2,200	6,000
Budgeted S & A Expense	$10,150	$10,750	$11,550	$32,450

REQUIRED:
Prepare a budgeted income statement for the third quarter of 2007 for Byrne Manufacturing.

LO 5: Prepare a Cash Receipts Schedule for One Quarter

8–42. The Deacon Company is preparing a cash receipts schedule for the first quarter of 2008. Sales for November and December of 2007 are expected to be $180,000 and $200,000, respectively. Budgeted sales for the first quarter of 2008 are presented here.

THE DEACON COMPANY
Sales Budget
For the Quarter Ended March 31, 2008

	Jan	Feb	Mar	Total
Budgeted Sales	$220,000	$240,000	$260,000	$720,000

Twenty percent of sales are for cash, the remaining 80% are on account. Ten percent of the sales on account are collected in the month of the sale, 60% in the month following the sale, and the remaining 30% in the second month following the sale. There are no uncollectible accounts receivable.

REQUIRED:
Prepare a cash receipts schedule for the first quarter of 2008.

LO 5: Prepare a Cash Receipts Schedule for One Quarter

8–43. The V & A Velez Company is preparing a cash receipts schedule for the first quarter of 2008. Sales for November and December of 2007 are expected to be $300,000 and $310,000, respectively. Budgeted sales for the first quarter of 2008 are presented here.

THE V & A VELEZ COMPANY
Sales Budget
For the Quarter Ended March 31, 2008

	Jan	Feb	Mar	Total
Budgeted Sales	$220,000	$290,000	$340,000	$850,000

Ten percent of sales are for cash, the remaining 90% are on account. Twenty percent of the sales on account are collected in the month of the sale, 70% in the month following the sale, and the remaining 10% in the second month following the sale. There are no uncollectible accounts receivable.

REQUIRED:
Prepare a cash receipts schedule for the first quarter of 2008.

LO 5:   Prepare a Cash Receipts Schedule for One Quarter

8–44. The Arauz Company is preparing a cash receipts schedule for the first quarter of 2007. Sales for November and December of 2006 are expected to be $30,000 and $50,000, respectively. Budgeted sales for the first quarter of 2007 are presented here.

THE ARAUZ COMPANY
Sales Budget
For the Quarter Ended March 31, 2007

	Jan	Feb	Mar	Total
Budgeted Sales	$20,000	$25,000	$40,000	$85,000

Fifteen percent of sales are for cash, the remaining 85% are on account. Twenty percent of the sales on account are collected in the month of the sale, 50% in the month following the sale, and the remaining 30% in the second month following the sale. There are no uncollectible accounts receivable.

REQUIRED:
Prepare a cash receipts schedule for the first quarter of 2007.

LO 5:   Prepare a Cash Receipts Schedule for One Quarter

8–45. The Phillips Company is preparing a cash receipts schedule for the first quarter of 2007. Sales for November and December of 2006 are expected to be $33,000 and $55,000, respectively. Budgeted sales for the first quarter of 2007 are presented here.

THE PHILLIPS COMPANY
Sales Budget
For the Quarter Ended March 31, 2007

	Jan	Feb	Mar	Total
Budgeted Sales	$20,000	$30,000	$45,000	$95,000

Fifteen percent of sales are for cash, the remaining 85% are on account. Twenty percent of the sales on account are collected in the month of the sale, 50% in the month following the sale, 30% in the second month following the sale. There are no uncollectible accounts receivable.

REQUIRED:
Prepare a cash receipts schedule for the first quarter of 2007.

LO 5:   Prepare a Cash Receipts Schedule for One Quarter

8–46. The Aimin Company is preparing a cash receipts schedule for the first quarter of 2007. Sales for November and December of 2006 are expected to be $40,000 and $80,000, respectively. Budgeted sales for the first quarter of 2007 are presented here.

THE AIMIN COMPANY
Sales Budget
For the Quarter Ended March 31, 2007

	Jan	Feb	Mar	Total
Budgeted Sales	$30,000	$40,000	$50,000	$120,000

Ten percent of sales are for cash, the remaining 90% are on account. Fifteen percent of the sales on account are collected in the month of the sale, 60% in the month following the sale, 25% in the second month following the sale. There are no uncollectible accounts receivable.

REQUIRED:
Prepare a cash receipts schedule for the first quarter of 2007.

LO 5: Prepare a Cash Receipts Schedule for One Quarter

8-47. The Gabriel Diaz Company is preparing a cash receipts schedule for the first quarter of 2008. Sales on account for November and December of 2007 are expected to be $500,000 and $750,000, respectively. Budgeted sales for the first quarter of 2008 are presented here.

THE GABRIEL DIAZ COMPANY
Sales Budget
For the Quarter Ended March 31, 2008

	Jan	Feb	Mar	Total
Budgeted Cash Sales	$ 40,000	$ 45,000	$ 55,000	$ 140,000
Budgeted Sales on Account	$400,000	$450,000	$550,000	$1,400,000
Total Sales	$440,000	$495,000	$605,000	$1,540,000

Expected collection pattern for sales on account:
  15% in the month of sale
  60% in the month following the sale
  25% in the second month following the sale
  0% uncollectible

REQUIRED:
Prepare a cash receipts schedule for the first quarter of 2008.

LO 5: Prepare a Cash Receipts Schedule for One Quarter

8-48. The Lila Steinman Company is preparing a cash receipts schedule for the first quarter of 2007. Sales on account for November and December of 2006 are expected to be $200,000 and $400,000, respectively. Budgeted sales for the first quarter of 2007 are presented here.

The Lila Steinman Company
Sales Budget
For the Quarter Ended March 31, 2007

	Jan	Feb	Mar	Total
Budgeted Cash Sales	$ 20,000	$ 25,000	$ 27,000	$ 72,000
Budgeted Sales on Account	$180,000	$210,000	$250,000	$640,000
Total Sales	$200,000	$235,000	$277,000	$712,000

Expected collection pattern for sales on account:
  10% in the month of sale
  70% in the month following the sale
  20% in the second month following the sale
  0% uncollectible

REQUIRED:
Prepare a cash receipts schedule for the first quarter of 2007.

LO 5: Prepare a Cash Receipts Schedule for One Quarter

8–49. The Lowensohn Company is preparing a cash receipts schedule for the first quarter of 2008. Sales on account for November and December of 2007 are expected to be $320,000 and $550,000, respectively. Budgeted sales for the first quarter of 2008 are presented here.

THE LOWENSOHN COMPANY
Sales Budget
For the Quarter Ended March 31, 2008

	Jan	Feb	Mar	Total
Budgeted Cash Sales	$120,000	$150,000	$125,000	$395,000
Budgeted Sales on Account	$180,000	$225,000	$190,000	$595,000
Total Sales	$300,000	$375,000	$315,000	$990,000

Expected collection pattern for sales on account:
  30% in the month of sale
  50% in the month following the sale
  20% in the second month following the sale
  0% uncollectible

REQUIRED:
Prepare a cash receipts schedule for the first quarter of 2008.

LO 5: Prepare a Cash Receipts Schedule for One Quarter

8–50. The S.R. Jackson Company is preparing a cash receipts schedule for the second quarter of 2008. Sales on account for February and March of 2008 are expected to be $50,000 and $60,000, respectively. Budgeted sales for the second quarter of 2008 are presented here.

THE S.R. JACKSON COMPANY
Sales Budget
For the Quarter Ended June 30, 2008

	Apr	May	Jun	Total
Budgeted Cash Sales	$15,000	$20,000	$25,000	$ 60,000
Budgeted Sales on Account	$30,000	$40,000	$50,000	$120,000
Total Sales	$45,000	$60,000	$75,000	$180,000

Expected collection pattern for sales on account:
25% in the month of sale
50% in the month following the sale
25% in the second month following the sale
0% uncollectible

REQUIRED:

Prepare a cash receipts schedule for the second quarter of 2008.

LO 5: Prepare a Cash Receipts Schedule for One Quarter

8–51. The Hodson Company is preparing a cash receipts schedule for the third quarter of 2008. Sales on account for May and June of 2008 are expected to be $100,000 and $120,000, respectively. Budgeted sales for the third quarter of 2008 are presented here.

THE HODSON COMPANY
Sales Budget
For the Quarter Ended September 30, 2008

	Jul	Aug	Sep	Total
Budgeted Cash Sales	$ 8,000	$ 9,000	$ 11,000	$ 28,000
Budgeted Sales on				
Account	$80,000	$90,000	$110,000	$280,000
Total Sales	$88,000	$99,000	$121,000	$308,000

Expected collection pattern for sales on account:
- 10% in the month of sale
- 60% in the month following the sale
- 30% in the second month following the sale
- 0% uncollectible

REQUIRED:

Prepare a cash receipts schedule for the third quarter of 2008.

LO 5: Prepare a Cash Receipts Schedule for One Quarter

8–52. The A.R. Oddo Company is preparing a cash receipts schedule for the fourth quarter of 2008. Sales on account for August and September of 2008 are expected to be $200,000 and $220,000, respectively. Budgeted sales for the fourth quarter of 2008 are presented here.

THE A.R. ODDO COMPANY
Sales Budget
For the Quarter Ended December 31, 2008

	Oct	Nov	Dec	Total
Budgeted Cash Sales	$ 42,000	$ 46,000	$ 60,000	$148,000
Budgeted Sales on				
Account	$210,000	$230,000	$300,000	$740,000
Total Sales	$252,000	$276,000	$360,000	$888,000

Expected collection pattern for sales on account:
- 20% in the month of sale
- 70% in the month following the sale
- 10% in the second month following the sale
- 0% uncollectible

REQUIRED:

Prepare a cash receipts schedule for the fourth quarter of 2008.

LO 5 Prepare a Cash Receipts Schedule for One Quarter

8–53. The law firm of Hendricks & Hendricks is preparing a cash receipts schedule for the first quarter of 2008. Service revenue for November and

December of 2007 are expected to be $90,000 and $50,000, respectively. All billings are on account. There are no "cash sales." Budgeted service revenue for the first quarter of 2008 is presented here.

HENDRICKS & HENDRICKS
Service Revenue Budget
For the Quarter Ended March 31, 2008

	Jan	Feb	Mar	Total
Budgeted Service Revenue	$40,000	$50,000	$65,000	$155,000

Expected collection pattern:
  30% in the month of sale
  60% in the month following the sale
  10% in the second month following the sale
  0% uncollectible

REQUIRED:
Prepare a cash receipts schedule for the first quarter of 2008.

LO 5: Prepare a Cash Receipts Schedule for One Quarter

8–54. The medical practice of Healit & Quick is preparing a cash receipts schedule for the first quarter of 2008. Service revenue for November and December of 2007 are expected to be $120,000 and $110,000, respectively. All billings are on account. There are no "cash sales." Budgeted service revenue for the first quarter of 2008 is presented here.

HEALIT & QUICK
Service Revenue Budget
For the Quarter Ended March 31, 2008

	Jan	Feb	Mar	Total
Budgeted Service Revenue	$120,000	$130,000	$140,000	$155,000

Expected collection pattern:
  20% in the month of sale
  60% in the month following the sale
  20% in the second month following the sale
  0% uncollectible

REQUIRED:
Prepare a cash receipts schedule for the first quarter of 2008.

LO 5: Prepare a Cash Payments Schedule for One Quarter

8–55. Marcy Steinmann and Company has prepared the following budgets for the first quarter of 2007.

MARCY STEINMANN AND COMPANY
Selling and Administrative Expense Budget
For the Quarter Ended March 31, 2007

	Jan	Feb	Mar	Total
Salaries and Wages	$1,700	$2,200	$1,900	$ 5,800
Rent	300	300	300	900
Depreciation	200	200	200	600
Other	900	1,200	1,000	3,100
Total	$3,100	$3,900	$3,400	$10,400

MARCY STEINMANN AND COMPANY
Purchases Budget
For the Quarter Ended March 31, 2007

		Jan	Feb	Mar	Total
	Forecasted Unit Sales	50	60	70	180
+	Desired Ending Inventory	12	14	16	16
=	Total Units Needed	62	74	86	196
−	Beginning Inventory	(10)	(12)	(14)	(10)
=	Units to Be Purchased	52	62	72	186
×	Cost Per Unit	$ 220	$ 220	$ 220	$ 220
=	Cost of Purchases	$11,440	$13,640	$15,840	$40,920

Selling and administrative expenses are paid in the month incurred and purchases are paid in the month following the purchase. Purchases for December 1999 are $10,500. No equipment purchases or additional expenditures are made during the quarter.

REQUIRED:
Prepare a cash payment schedule for the first quarter of 2007.

LO 5: Prepare a Cash Payments Schedule for One Quarter

8–56. Jackson Sales Company has prepared the following budgets for the second quarter of 2007.

JACKSON SALES COMPANY
Selling and Administrative Expense Budget
For the Quarter Ended June 30, 2007

	Apr	May	Jun	Total
Salaries	$1,000	$1,200	$1,300	$3,500
Rent	200	200	200	600
Utilities	120	180	220	520
Depreciation	80	80	80	240
Other	500	600	650	1,750
Total	$1,900	$2,260	$2,450	$6,610

JACKSON SALES COMPANY
Purchases Budget
For the Quarter Ended June 30, 2007

		Apr	May	Jun	Total
	Forecasted Unit Sales	70	80	90	240
+	Desired Ending Inventory	16	18	19	19
=	Total Units Needed	86	98	109	259
−	Beginning Inventory	(15)	(16)	(18)	(15)
=	Units to Be Purchased	71	82	91	244
×	Cost Per Unit	$ 100	$ 100	$ 100	$ 100
=	Cost of Purchases	$ 7,100	$ 8,200	$ 9,100	$24,400

Selling and administrative expenses are paid in the month incurred and purchases are paid in the month following the purchase. Purchases for March 2007 are $6,800. No equipment purchases or additional expenditures are made during the quarter.

REQUIRED:
Prepare a cash payment schedule for the second quarter of 2007.

LO 5:   Prepare a Cash Payments Schedule for One Month

8–57. The following budgeted information is available for the Top Coat Clothing Company for January 2008.

Salaries	$120,000
Rent	9,000
Utilities	1,200
Depreciation	3,200
Others Expenses	1,500
Purchases	380,000

Selling and administrative expenses are paid in the month incurred and purchases are paid in the month following the purchase. Purchases for December 2007 are $350,000. No equipment purchases or additional expenditures are made during the month.

REQUIRED:
Prepare a cash payment schedule for January 2008.

LO 5:   Prepare a Cash Payments Schedule for One Month

8–58. The following budgeted information is available for Jack's Feed Store in June 2008.

Salaries	$12,000
Rent	600
Electricity	140
Depreciation	800
Others Expenses	700
Purchases	80,000

Selling and administrative expenses are paid in the month incurred and purchases are paid in the month following the purchase. Purchases for May 2008 are $75,000. No equipment purchases or additional expenditures are made during the month.

REQUIRED:
Prepare a cash payment schedule for June 2008.

LO 5:   Prepare a Cash Budget for One Quarter

8–59. The following information is available for the Art Kriner Company for the first quarter of 2007.

	Jan	Feb	Mar
Budgeted Receipts from Credit Sales	$5,000	$5,500	$5,800
Budgeted Cash Sales	1,200	1,250	1.300
Budgeted Cash Payments	6,300	7,185	6,520

Beginning cash balance for January 2007 is expected to be $1,500. The company intends to maintain a cash balance of at least $1,000. The company has made arrangements to borrow from a local bank if necessary.

REQUIRED:
Prepare a cash budget for the first quarter of 2007.

LO 5: Prepare a Cash Budget for One Quarter

8–60. The following information is available for the Dixon Company for the second quarter of 2007.

	Apr	May	Jun
Budgeted Receipts from Credit Sales	$500,000	$520,000	$550,000
Budgeted Cash Sales	100,000	105,000	112,000
Budgeted Cash Payments	670,000	615,000	627,000

Beginning cash balance for April 2007 is expected to be $90,000. The company intends to maintain a cash balance of at least $50,000. The company has made arrangements to borrow from a local bank if necessary.

REQUIRED:
Prepare a cash budget for the second quarter of 2007.

LO 5: Prepare a Cash Budget for One Quarter

8–61. The following information is available for the Ortega Company for the first quarter of 2007.

	Jan	Feb	Mar
Budgeted Receipts from Credit Sales	$100,000	$110,000	$115,000
Budgeted Cash Sales	80,000	95,000	98,000
Budgeted Cash Payments	178,000	215,000	206,000

Beginning cash balance for January 2007 is expected to be $20,000. The company intends to maintain a cash balance of at least $15,000. The company has made arrangements to borrow from a local bank if necessary.

REQUIRED:
Prepare a cash budget for the first quarter of 2007.

LO 5: Prepare a Cash Budget for One Month

8–62. The following information is available for November 2007.

Budgeted Receipts from Credit Sales	$25,100
Budgeted Cash Sales	5,900
Budgeted Cash Payments	32,600

Beginning cash balance for November is expected to be $5,800. The company intends to maintain a cash balance of at least $5,000. The company has made arrangements to borrow from a local bank if necessary.

REQUIRED:
Prepare a cash budget for November 2007.

LO 5: Prepare a Cash Budget for One Month

8–63. The following information is available for October 2007.

Budgeted Receipts from Credit Sales	$300,000
Budgeted Cash Sales	80,000
Budgeted Cash Payments	410,000

Beginning cash balance for October is expected to be $60,000. The company intends to maintain a cash balance of at least $50,000. The company has made arrangements to borrow from a local bank if necessary.

REQUIRED:
Prepare a cash budget for October 2007.

LO 5: Prepare a Cash Budget for One Month

8–64. The following information is available for July 2008.

Budgeted Receipts from Credit Sales	$500,000
Budgeted Cash Sales	40,000
Budgeted Cash Payments	577,000

Beginning cash balance for July is expected to be $95,000. The company intends to maintain a cash balance of at least $75,000. The company has made arrangements to borrow from a local bank if necessary.

REQUIRED:
Prepare a cash budget for July 2008.

LO 5: Prepare a Budgeted Balance Sheet and Budgeted Statement of Cash Flows for Three Months

8–65. The following information is available for the Perlmuter Printing Supply Company.

PERLMUTER PRINTING SUPPLY COMPANY
Sales Budget
For the Quarter Ended September 30, 2007

	July	August	September
Budgeted Sales Dollars	$90,000	$80,000	$70,000

PERLMUTER PRINTING SUPPLY COMPANY
Cost of Goods Sold Budget
For the Quarter Ended September 30, 2007

	July	August	September
Budgeted COGS	$54,000	$48,000	$42,000

PERLMUTER PRINTING SUPPLY COMPANY
Selling and Administrative Expense Budget
For the Quarter Ended September 30, 2007

	July	August	September
Salaries and Wages	$12,600	$12,000	$11,800
Rent	1,000	1,000	1,000
Depreciation	1,800	1,800	1,800
Other	3,800	3,000	2,900
Total	$19,200	$17,800	$17,500

PERLMUTER PRINTING SUPPLY COMPANY
Budgeted Income Statement
For the Quarter Ended September 30, 2007

	July	August	September
Sales	$90,000	$80,000	$70,000
Cost of Goods Sold	54,000	48,000	42,000
Gross Profit	36,000	32,000	28,000
Selling and Admin. Expense	19,200	17,800	17,500
Net Income	$16,800	$14,200	$10,500

PERLMUTER PRINTING SUPPLY COMPANY
Purchases Budget
For the Quarter Ended September 30, 2007

	July	August	September
Cost of Purchases	$52,000	$46,000	$41,000

PERLMUTER PRINTING SUPPLY COMPANY
Cash Receipts Schedule
For the Quarter Ended September 30, 2007

	July	August	September
Budgeted Receipts from Credit Sales	$78,000	$76,000	$68,000
Budgeted Cash Sales	9,000	8,000	7,000
Total Cash Receipts	$87,000	$84,000	$75,000

PERLMUTER PRINTING SUPPLY COMPANY
Cash Payments Schedule
For the Quarter Ended September 30, 2007

	July	August	September
Purchases	$56,000	$52,000	$46,000
Selling and Admin. Expense:			
Salaries and Wages	$12,600	$12,000	$11,800
Rent	1,000	1,000	1,000
Other	3,800	3,000	2,900
Budgeted Cash Payments	$73,400	$68,000	$61,700

PERLMUTER PRINTING SUPPLY COMPANY
Cash Budget
For the Quarter Ended September 30, 2007

		July	August	September
	Beginning Cash Balance	$ 18,500	$ 32,100	$ 48,100
+	Cash Receipts	87,000	84,000	75,000
=	Cash Available	$105,500	$116,100	$123,100
−	Cash Payments	(73,400)	(68,000)	(61,700)
=	Balance before Borrowing	$ 32,100	$ 48,100	$ 61,400
+/−	Borrowing/(Repayment)	-0-	$ -0-	$ -0-
=	Ending Cash Balance	$ 32,100	$ 48,100	$ 61,400

PERLMUTER PRINTING SUPPLY COMPANY
Balance Sheet
June 30, 2007

Assets	
Current Assets	
Cash	$ 18,500
Accounts Receivable	20,000
Inventory	16,000
Total Current Assets	$ 54,500
Property, Plant, and Equipment	
Equipment	108,000
Less Accumulated Depreciation	(43,200)
Equipment, Net	$ 64,800
Total Assets	$119,300
Liabilities	
Current Liabilities	
Accounts Payable	$ 56,000
Total Liabilities	$ 56,000
Owner's Equity	
Paid-in Capital	
Common Stock	$ 1,000
Additional Paid-in Capital	10,000
Total Paid-in Capital	$ 11,000
Retained Earnings	$ 52,300
Total Equity	$ 63,300
Total Liabilities and Equity	$119,300

REQUIRED:
a. Prepare budgeted balance sheets for July, August, and September of 2007.
b. Prepare budgeted statements of cash flows for July, August, and September of 2007.

LO 5: Determine Missing Budget Information

8–66. Following is a partial performance report.

Description	Budget	Actual	Variance
Wages	$5,000	$ 5,200	$?
Store Rent	6,000	?	200 F
Utilities Expense	?	1,200	50 U

REQUIRED:
Provide the missing information.

LO 5: Determine Budget Variances

8–67. Following is a partial performance report.

Description	Budget	Actual	Variance
Sales	$25,000	$22,000	$?
Cost of Goods Sold	20,000	17,600	?
Gross Profit	5,000	4,400	?

REQUIRED:
Calculate the variances for this information and indicate whether they are favorable (F) or unfavorable (U).

LO 5: Determine Budget Variances

8–68. Following is a partial performance report.

Description	Budget	Actual	Variance
Rent Revenue	$15,000	$14,000	$?
Interest Expense	15,000	14,000	?

REQUIRED:
Calculate the variances for this information and indicate whether they are favorable (F) or unfavorable (U).

LO 6: Discuss Variances

8–69. Robin Wince owns a small chain of frame shops. All the frames and other merchandise the company sells is purchased by the company's central purchasing department. A partial performance report showing the direct costs for one of Robin's stores appears as follows:.

	Budget	Actual	Variance
Sales	$200,000	$200,000	$ 0
Cost of Goods Sold	120,000	110,000	10,000 F
Selling and Admin. Expense	40,000	50,000	10,000 U
Income	$ 40,000	$ 40,000	$ 0

REQUIRED:
Robin is concerned even though the variance in income is zero. Because the total variance is zero, the store manager believes that there is no problem. Do you agree with the manager? Why?

LO 6: Prepare a Memo Regarding Variances

8–70. Matt Lehti owns the Zap Record Shop. He is in the process of examining the following performance report.

	Budget	Actual	Variance
Sales	$100,000	$120,000	$20,000 F
Cost of Goods Sold	60,000	72,000	12,000U
Selling and Admin. Expense	10,000	9,000	1,000 F
Income	$ 30,000	$ 39,000	$ 9,000 F

Matt is very pleased that the company had favorable variances for sales and income. However, he finds the sizable unfavorable variance for cost of goods sold very disturbing. He is preparing himself for a serious discussion with the purchasing agent who is responsible for purchasing the merchandise sold.

REQUIRED:
Assume that Matt Lehti has asked you for assistance in preparing for the meeting with the purchasing agent. Prepare a memo to Matt that provides him with any information you think would be helpful.

Index: Financial and Management Accounting

L

Labor, **F-6**. *See also* Employees
    costs of, **M-22**, **M-24–26**
    in service firms, **F-33**
Last-in, first-out (LIFO), **F-306–7**
    in a periodic inventory system, **F-312–13**, **F-314**
    in a perpetual inventory system, **F-316–17**, **F-319**
    product cost and, **F-310**
    U.S. tax laws and, **F-308**
Least squares regression line. *See* Regression analysis
Legal ownership. *See* Title
Liabilities
    analysis of. *See* Ratio analysis
    current. *See* Current liabilities
    debits/credits and, **F-218**
    deferred revenues and, **F-183**
    limiting. in stock transaction, **F-76**
    long-term, **F-362**, **F-393**, **F-444**
    recording on balance sheet, **F-69**
LIFO. *See* Last-in, first-out (LIFO)
Limited liability company (LLC), **F-12**
Limited liability partnership (LLP), **F-12**
Limited partnership, **F-12**
Linear regression analysis. *See* Regression analysis
Liquidation, **F-79**
Liquidity, **F-361**
    assets and, **F-361**
    liabilities and, **F-362**
    measuring, **F-439–42**
LLC. *See* Limited liability company (LLC)
LLP. *See* Limited liability partnership (LLP)
Loans, **F-101**, **F-102**
Long-lived assets. *See* Assets, long-lived
Long-term assets, **F-360–61**, **F-362**, **F-393**
Long-term creditors, **F-429**
Long-term financing, **F-100**, **F-106–7**
Long-term liabilities, **F-362**, **F-393**, **F-444**
Losses, **F-271**. *See also* Expenses
    calculating, **F-272**, **F-274–75**
    net, **F-131**, **F-132**
    recording, **F-284**
    SCF and, **F-404**
    taxes and, **F-367**
    true meaning of (application), **F-275–80**

M

MACRS. *See* Modified Accelerated Cost Recovery System
    (MACRS)
Management, objectives of, **F-430**
Management accounting, **F-17**, **M-5**
    activities in, **F-22**
    challenges and trends in, **M-12**
    consumers of, **M-12**
    evolution of, **M-8–12**
    financial *vs.*, **M-5–7**, **M-11**
    purpose of, **M-111**

Management advisory services. *See* Consulting services
Managerial accounting. *See* Management accounting
Managers. *See* Internal decision makers
Manufacturing-based economy, **M-12**
Manufacturing companies, **F-13**. *See also* Hybrid
    companies; Merchandising companies
    CVP analysis by, **M-107**
    direct *vs.* indirect costs, **M-17**
    general economic conditions for, **F-431**
    Industrial Revolution and, **M-9**
    operating budget for. *See* Operating budget
    operating cycle for, **F-360**
    overhead. *See* Overhead
    product cost identification in, **M-22–31**, **M-37**, **M-39–41**
    resource allocation by, **M-216**
    scientific management in, **M-10**
    special orders, **M-138–39**
    tracking inventory costs, **F-302**
Market economy, **F-6**
Market interest rate. *See* Effective interest rate
Market price. *See* Selling price
Market value, **F-272**
Master budget. *See* Operating budget
Master operating budget. *See* Operating budget
Matching maturities, **F-107**
Matching principle, **F-180–81**
    applied to inventory, **F-300**
    depreciation and, **F-262**, **F-264**
Materiality, **F-50**
Materials
    direct, **M-22**, **M-24**, **M-27**, **M-28**
    indirect, **M-25**, **M-27**
    for service firms, **M-33**
Material stores. *See* Raw materials inventory
Maturity value. *See* Face value (of a bond)
Measurement. *See* Economic measurement
Merchandise inventory, **F-300**
    classifications of, **M-20**, **M-22–24**
    cost flow assumptions
        inventory cost effects, **F-319–24**
        under periodic system, **F-310–14**
        under perpetual system, **F-314–19**
        specific identification, **F-309–10**
    purchasing issues, **F-325–26**
    recording, **F-327–34**
    SCF and, **F-404**
    selling cost and, **M-18**
    tracking costs of, **F-300–301**
Merchandising companies, **F-14**. *See also* Hybrid
    companies; Manufacturing companies
    CVP analysis by, **M-107**
    general economic conditions for, **F-431**
    operating budget for. *See* Operating budget
    operating cycle for, **F-360**
    product cost identification for, **M-19–21**, **M-36**
    resource allocation by, **M-216–17**
    types of, **M-19–20**
Mergent Industry Review, **F-434**
Midwest Stock Exchange, **F-81**

Real accounts. *See* Permanent accounts
Reality *vs.* measurement of reality
   in economic measurement, **F**-170–74, **F**-180, **F**-187
   on income statement, **F**-171–72
   in inventory analysis, **F**-305–8, **F**-321, **M**-23, **M**-24
   net profit (net income), **F**-171–72
   opportunity costs, **M**-143
Realization, **F**-174
Real rate of return. *See* Internal rate of return (IRR)
Reasoned decision making, **F**-39, **F**-40–41
Receivable, **F**-178
Receivables turnover ratio, **F**-441–42, **F**-445, **F**-448
Recognition, **F**-173
   expenses, **F**-173, **F**-174, **F**-179–80
   matching principle, **F**-180–81
   revenue, **F**-173, **F**-174, **F**-179–80
Reconciliation, of bank statements, **F**-215, **F**-228, **F**-230–31
Reconciliation schedule, **F**-399
Recording
   assets/equity/liability on balance sheet, **F**-69
   income tax expenditures, **F**-376–77
   interest on financial statement, **F**-185
   long-lived assets and depreciation, **F**-282–85
   for periodic inventory system, **F**-327–29
   for perpetual inventory system, **F**-331–33
Recurring items, **F**-364–66
Regression analysis, **M**-80–81
Relevance, **F**-50–51
Relevant cost, **M**-132, **M**-134. *See also* Relevant costing
Relevant costing, **M**-131
   analyzing alternatives, **M**-135–37, **M**-139, **M**-141
   equipment replacement, **M**-134–37
   gathering information, **M**-134, **M**-138, **M**-140
   outsourcing, **M**-140–44
Relevant net cash flow, **M**-176
Relevant range, **M**-68–69, **M**-115
Reliability, **F**-50, **F**-51
Reporting
   gains and losses
      on balance sheet, **F**-273, **F**-274–75, **F**-276
      on income statement, **F**-271–75, **F**-276
   operating income, **F**-271
Representational faithfulness of accounting information, **F**-51
Required rate of return. *See* Cost of capital
Residual value, **F**-181–82
   depreciable base and, **F**-262–63
   relevant costing and, **M**-135, **M**-136
Resource allocation, **M**-215–17. *See also* Scarce resources
Retail merchandiser (retailer), **F**-14, **M**-19–20. *See also* Merchandising companies
Retained earnings, **F**-76, **F**-144
   on budgeted balance sheet, **M**-238
   dividend payments and, **F**-143
   owner's equity and, **F**-140
   statement of, **F**-144–45
Return of investment, **F**-47
Return on assets ratio, **F**-436, **F**-445, **F**-447
Return on equity before tax ratio, **F**-438–39, **F**-445, **F**-447
Return on equity ratio, **F**-438, **F**-445, **F**-447

Return on investment, **F**-47
   distributions to owners, **F**-141, **F**-142–43
   interest as, **M**-170
Revenue, **F**-130. *See also* Gains
   accrued, **F**-183
   debits/credits and, **F**-218
   deferred, **F**-183
   listing in income statement, **F**-132–33
   owner's equity and, **F**-137
   recognition of, **F**-173, **F**-174, **F**-178–79
   sales, **F**-134
Risk/reward trade-off, **F**-38, **F**-115–16, **M**-170
Rolling budgeting. *See* Perpetual budgeting
Routine decisions, **F**-38, **F**-40
Rules ethics, **F**-43–44

S

Sales
   budgeting for, **M**-222, **M**-223, **M**-225–26, **M**-232
   forecasting, **M**-221–22, **M**-225, **M**-227–28
   producing revenue, **F**-134, **F**-184. *See also* Revenue
   projecting with CVP analysis, **M**-106–7, **M**-110, **M**-112, **M**-114
Sales journal, **F**-212
Salvage value. *See* Residual value
Sarbanes-Oxley Act of 2002, **F**-19
Savings and loan associations (S&Ls), **F**-101
Scarce resources, **M**-174–75. *See also* Resource allocation
Scatter graphing, **M**-72–80
SCF. *See* Statement of cash flows (SCF)
Scientific management, **M**-10
Scrap value. *See* Residual value
SEC. *See* Securities and Exchange Commission (SEC)
Secondary bond market, **F**-111–12
Secondary stock market, **F**-81
Secretary, corporate. *See* Corporate secretary
Securities Act of 1933, **F**-17
Securities and Exchange Commission (SEC)
   authority of, **F**-17
   documents required by, **F**-110, **F**-373
   NAICS and, **F**-446
   oversight by, **F**-18–19, **F**-82, **F**-107, **M**-11
   state commissions compared to, **F**-81
Securities Exchange Act of 1934, **F**-17
Selling and administrative expense budget, **M**-223, **M**-227
Selling cost, **M**-18
Selling price
   of bonds, **F**-108, **F**-111, **F**-112
   changes in, **M**-110–11
   sensitivity analysis and, **F**-109–10
Sensitivity analysis, **M**-109–10, **M**-112
Separate entity assumption, **F**-11
Service-based economy, **M**-12
Service companies, **F**-14. *See also* Hybrid companies; Manufacturing companies; Merchandising companies
   CVP analysis by, **F**-107

T

T-account, **F**-219
Tangible property, **F**-262
Tariffs, **F**-15
Taxation (tax planning), **F**-21, **F**-366–67
Technological change, **F**-433
Technological obsolescence, **F**-271
Temporary accounts, **F**-216–17
Thrifts, **F**-101
Time-adjusted rate of return. *See* Internal rate of return (IRR)
Timeliness of accounting information, **F**-50, **M**-7
Times interest earned ratio. *See* Coverage ratio
Time value of money, **M**-137, **M**-177, **M**-187
   future value, **M**-187–89
   payback period and, **M**-184
   present value, **M**-190–94
Title, **F**-178, **F**-326
Top-down budgeting, **M**-219, **M**-220
Total asset turnover ratio, **F**-435, **F**-437, **F**-447, **F**-449
Total cost, **M**-67–68, **M**-75, **M**-80–81
Tracking inventory costs, **F**-300–302
Trade agreements, **F**-15
Trade creditors, **F**-429
Trading securities, **F**-392, **F**-440
Transactions
   analyzing, **F**-211–12, **F**-221–23
   inventory, **F**-303. *See also* under Cost flow assumptions
   journalizing, **F**-212–13, **F**-221–23
   posting to general ledger, **F**-213–14, **F**-223, **F**-224–27
Translation of currency, **F**-15
Treasurer, **F**-75, **M**-7–8
Treasury stock, **F**-75–76, **F**-393
Trend analysis, **F**-428
Trends
   in companies, **F**-448–50
   in management accounting, **M**-12
Trial balance (worksheet), **F**-214
   post-closing, **F**-217, **F**-237–38
   preparing, **F**-214, **F**-227–28, **F**-229

U

Uncertainty, **F**-38
Underwriters. *See* Investment bankers
Unit costs. *See* Costs, per unit
United States–Canada Free Trade Pact of 1989, **F**-15
Universal Product Codes (UPCs), **F**-304

V

Value Line Industry, **F**-434
Variable costs, **M**-65
   changes in, **M**-111–12
   contribution margin and, **M**-100
   CVP analysis of. *See* Cost-volume-profit (CVP) analysis
   examples of, **M**-66
   mixed costs analysis of, **M**-70–81
   relevant costing and, **M**-139
   relevant range of, **M**-68–69, **M**-115
   total cost equation, **M**-67, **M**-75, **M**-78–79
Variances, in budgets, **M**-240–41
Verifiability of accounting information, **F**-51
Virtues ethics, **F**-43
Volume-profit analysis. *See* Cost-volume-profit (CVP) analysis

W

Wall Street Journal, **F**-432
What-if analysis, **M**-115. *See also* Sensitivity analysis
Wholesale merchandiser (wholesaler), **F**-14, **M**-19–20. *See also* Merchandising companies
Withdrawals. *See* Drawings
Working capital, **F**-390
Work in-process inventory, **F**-302, **M**-23, **M**-28–29
Worksheet. *See* Trial balance (worksheet)

Y

Yield rate. *See* Effective interest rate

Z

Zero-based budgeting, **M**-218
Zero-sum game, **F**-7